Conceptual Models and Outcomes of Advancing Knowledge Management:

New Technologies

Murray E. Jennex
San Diego State University, USA

T0309492

Managing Director:	Lindsay Johnston
Senior Editorial Director:	Heather Probst
Book Production Manager:	Sean Woznicki
Development Manager:	Joel Gamon
Development Editor:	Mike Killian
Acquisitions Editor:	Erika Gallagher
Typesetters:	Lisandro Gonzalez
Print Coordinator:	Jamie Snavely
Cover Design:	Nick Newcomer

Published in the United States of America by
Information Science Reference (an imprint of IGI Global)
701 E. Chocolate Avenue
Hershey PA 17033
Tel: 717-533-8845
Fax: 717-533-8661
E-mail: cust@igi-global.com
Web site: http://www.igi-global.com

Library of Congress Cataloging-in-Publication Data

Conceptual models and outcomes of advancing knowledge management: new technologies / Murray E. Jennex, editor.
  p. cm.
 Includes bibliographical references and index.
  ISBN 978-1-4666-0035-5 (hardcover) -- ISBN 978-1-4666-0036-2 (ebook) -- ISBN 978-1-4666-0037-9 (print & perpetual access) 1. Knowledge management. 2. Organizational learning--Management. 3. Information technology--Management.
I. Jennex, Murray E., 1956-
  HD30.2.C653 2012
  658.4'038--dc23
                            2011044134

British Cataloguing in Publication Data
A Cataloguing in Publication record for this book is available from the British Library.

All work contributed to this book is new, previously-unpublished material. The views expressed in this book are those of the authors, but not necessarily of the publisher.

Table of Contents

Detailed Table of Contents

Chapter 1

Yang Lin, McGill University, Canada
Kimiz Dalkir, McGill University, Canada

This paper reviews past research on KM to identify key factors affecting Chinese KM implementation. It begins with a chronological overview of 76 KM related publications, followed by two separate discussions of socio-cultural and non-socio-cultural factors affecting KM implementation within the Chinese community. A preliminary typology of these factors is proposed. In addition to individual factors that have direct impact on how people behave in the process of KM implementation, specific factors that strongly influence Chinese KM implementation are: (1) relationship networks and collectivist thinking, (2) competitiveness and knowledge hoarding, (3) management involvement and support, and (4) organizational culture that encourages knowledge sharing and learning and that minimizes knowledge hoarding. Several directions for future research are also presented.

Chapter 2

Lena Aggestam, University of Skövde, Sweden
Per Backlund, University of Skövde, Sweden
Anne Persson, University of Skövde, Sweden

Knowledge forms an important asset in modern organizations. In order to gain and sustain competitive advantage knowledge has to be managed. One aspect of this is to use Electronic Knowledge Repositories (EKR) to enhance knowledge sharing, reuse and learning. The success of an EKR is dependent on the quality of its content. For knowledge to be stored in an EKR, it has to be captured. One crucial part of the capture process is to evaluate whether the identified knowledge should be incorporated in the EKR or not. Therefore, to increase quality in an EKR, the evaluation stage of the capture process must be successfully carried out. Based on an interpretive field study and an extensive literature review, this paper identifies and characterizes Critical Success Factors (CSF) in the evaluation stage and presents guidance aiming to support implementation of the evaluation stage with the purpose to increase the quality of an EKR. In particular, the guidance supports the decision whether identified knowledge should be stored or not and it highlights the importance of performing evaluation addressing correctness, relevance, protection and redundancy. The characterization of the capture process contributes mainly to KM theory, and the guidance to KM practice.

Chapter 3

Amine Nehari Talet, King Fahd University of Petroleum & Minerals, Saudi Arabia
Samer Alhawari, Applied Science Private University, Jordan
Haroun Alryalat, The Arab Academy for Banking and Financial Sciences, Amman-Jordan

Organizations have increasingly recognized the importance of managing customer relationships, and Knowledge Management (KM) from the perspective of a process approaches assure positive impact on customer retention. Many organizations are turning to Customer Relationship Management (CRM) to better serve customers and facilitate closer relationships. This paper investigates how Knowledge Process for customers is used in practice by Jordanian companies to achieve Customer Knowledge Retention. The current practice is based on the data collected from 156, randomly drawn and reported from a survey of CRM applications and evaluation of CRM analytical functions provided by three software business solution companies working in the CRM area, and four companies that used the CRM system. Based on data collected from the companies, results from the analysis indicated that the knowledge process for customers had a positive effect on customer knowledge retention. The paper also verified the hypotheses of the effect of knowledge processes for customers on customer retention. The findings shed light on the potential relationship between the knowledge processes for customers and customer retention. It also provides guidance for the Information Technology (IT) industry as to how an analytical knowledge process for customers should be taken into account in developing countries to support to achieve customer knowledge retention due to cultural, social and educational differences.

Chapter 4

Chalard Chantarasombat, Mahasarakham University, Thailand
Boonchom Srisa-ard, Mahasarakham University, Thailand
Matthew H. S. Kuofie, University of Central Michigan, USA
Murray E. Jennex, San Diego State University, USA

Many look at knowledge management as an organizational initiative. However, can KM also be used to assist low technology situations such as rural villages? This paper describes the application of KM to the creation of a self-reliant community in Thailand. Changing demographics are threatening the ability of rural villages to sustain their viability as traditional methods of passing knowledge from one generation to the next are circumvented by the movement of the young to more urbanized areas of Thailand. KM is seen as a way of changing the traditional knowledge transfer process to something that assists those who remain in the villages. The KM approach investigated consisted of five stages: 1) Preparation, 2) Create motivation, awareness, promote participation, 3) Develop the KM plan, 4) Implement the KM plan, and 5) Evaluation. The approach was assessed and found to be successful by using eight organizations over an 8-month period.

Chapter 5

Donald P. Ballou, State University of New York, USA

Salvatore Belardo, State University of New York, USA

Harold L. Pazer, State University of New York, USA

When the systems analysis phase produces faulty requirements, it can often be traced to the failure of the requirements determination team and the client to communicate effectively. This failure is frequently a consequence of inadequate knowledge of the client's domain possessed by the development team. This paper presents concepts and procedures designed to facilitate communication between requirements determination teams and clients across a full set of IS projects with potentially differing priorities. A systematic framework for staffing requirements determination teams is provided. The importance and interdependence of two types of knowledge, explicit and tacit, to the success of the requirements determination phase is extensively explored. A metric for explicit knowledge coupled with a model that captures the impact of various levels of tacit knowledge upon the acquisition rate of explicit knowledge serve as key inputs to our Project Staffing Model. The appropriately weighted area under an explicit knowledge curve captures the totality of explicit knowledge. Summing such values, weighted to reflect project importance, provides a mechanism for evaluating alternative staffing assignments. An illustrative case highlights implementation issues and suggests procedures when uncertainty exists concerning key inputs. A research agenda is recommended for the estimation of factors required by the analysis.

Chapter 6

Hannu Kivijärvi, Aalto University School of Economics, Finland

Kalle Piirainen, Lappeenranta University of Technology, Finland

Markku Tuominen, Lappeenranta University of Technology, Finland

This paper aims to provide a conceptual basis for creating semi-virtual communities that facilitate knowledge creation and sharing that seeks to promote organizational innovativeness. In addition, based on the theoretical discussion, the paper proposes a concrete context that supports and stimulates the conversion of personal knowledge into new innovations and organizational decisions. As a methodological means, scenario driven innovation process is employed as a way to enhance creativity and knowledge convergence within an organization. The authors discuss that in its deepest sense knowledge is the capability to make decisions. Scenarios aim to increase that capability, and are thus a piece of organizational knowledge. The practical implementations of the contexts and the experiences with these implementations are evaluated by two real case studies in real life contexts.

Chapter 7

Pankaj Kamthan, Concordia University, Canada

An understanding of knowledge artifacts such as patterns is a necessary prerequisite for any subsequent action. In this article, as an initial step for formulating a theoretical basis for patterns, a conceptual model of primitive viewpoints is proposed and, by exploring one of the viewpoints, a conceptual model for stakeholders of a pattern is presented. This is followed by the description of a conceptual model of a process, namely P3, for the production of patterns. The workflows of P3 highlight, as appropriate, the interface of patterns to humans and/or machines. The implications of the Semantic Web and the Social Web towards P3 are briefly discussed.

Chapter 8

Jörg Rech, Semantic Technologies, Germany
Christian Bogner, Technical University of Kaiserslautern, Germany

In many agile software engineering organizations there is not enough time to follow knowledge management processes, to retrieve knowledge in complex processes, or to systematically elicit knowledge. This chapter gives an overview about the human-centered design of semantically-enabled knowledge management systems based on Wikis used in agile software engineering environments. The methodology – developed in the RISE (Reuse in Software Engineering) project – enables and supports the design of human-centered knowledge sharing platforms, such as Wikis. Furthermore, the paper specifies requirements one should keep in mind when building human-centered systems to support knowledge management. A two-phase qualitative analysis showed that the knowledge management system acts as a flexible and customizable view on the information needed during working-time which strongly relieves software engineers from time-consuming retrieval activities. Furthermore, the observations gave some hints about how the software system supports the collection of vital working experiences and how it could be subsequently formed and refined.

Chapter 9

Subramanian Sivaramakrishnan, University of Manitoba, Canada
Marjorie Delbaere, University of Saskatchewan, Canada
David Zhang, University of Saskatchewan, Canada
Edward Bruning, University of Manitoba, Canada

In this paper, the authors examine critical success factors and outcomes of market knowledge management, which is the management of knowledge pertaining to a firm's customers, competitors, and suppliers. Using data collected from 307 managers in 105 businesses across Canada, the authors show that a firm's extent of information technology adoption, its analytical capabilities, and market orientation are critical success factors for the firm's market knowledge management. An important outcome of market knowledge management is the organization's financial performance, mediated by customer satisfaction and customer loyalty. Results of this study indicate that superior business performance depends not only on the effective management of knowledge, but also on what type of knowledge is managed. Finally, implications of results and avenues for future research are discussed.

Chapter 10

Trevor A. Smith, University of the West Indies, Jamaica
Annette M. Mills, University of Canterbury, New Zealand
Paul Dion, Susquehanna University, USA

The effective management of knowledge resources is a key imperative for firms that want to leverage their knowledge assets for competitive advantage and improved performance. However, most firms do not attain the required performance levels even when programs are in place for managing knowledge resources. Research suggests this shortcoming can be addressed by linking knowledge management to business strategy. This study examines a model that links business strategy to knowledge management capabilities and organizational effectiveness. Using data collected from 189 managers, the results suggest that business strategy is a key driver of knowledge capabilities, and that both business strategy and knowledge capabilities impact organizational effectiveness. Additionally, the authors' findings indicate that knowledge infrastructure capability is a key imperative for effective knowledge process capability. Managerial implications, limitations and opportunities for future research are also discussed.

Chapter 11

Due to corporate portal playing a major role on organizational knowledge management (KM), this study was conducted to assess the impact of supporting KM processes through a corporate portal on business processes and employees at an academic institution. This paper specifically assesses the impact of knowledge acquisition, knowledge conversion, knowledge application and knowledge protection on business processes' effectiveness, efficiency and innovation, and employees' learning, adaptability, and job satisfaction. Findings suggest that the ending KM process, knowledge application, produces the highest impact on business processes and employees. First, supporting knowledge application through a corporate portal was positively associated with business processes' effectiveness and innovation and employees' learning, adaptability, and job satisfaction. Second, supporting knowledge conversion was positively associated with business processes' effectiveness and employees' learning, whereas supporting knowledge protection was positively associated with business processes' effectiveness and efficiency but negatively associated with employees' learning. Finally, supporting knowledge acquisition was positively associated with only business processes' innovation.

Chapter 12

Information and communication technologies have invaded the field of training, though their performances have been judged by companies to be insufficient. Among the origins of this state of affairs, the author considers that the lack of knowledge of what happens in a "real use situation" plays an important role. Indeed, understanding what is involved in learners-system interactions is fundamental to improve the system appropriation and its efficient usage. This appropriation is a dual necessity for learners as they must take over the offered possibilities of interactions and acquire the necessary knowledge. As appropriation is made through offered interactions, the author considers computer interactions traces as potential appropriation facilitators. This conceptual article presents bibliographical research concerning the use of computer interactions traces and proposes a classification of 'tracing systems'. Additionally, the links between these works and the process of appropriation in an instrumented training situation is provided, while the author also presents an experimental study conducted on the role of traces of interactions in a collaborative mediated task by using a numerical environment.

   Ravi S. Sharma, Nanyang Technological University, Singapore
   Ganesh Chandrasekar, Nanyang Technological University, Singapore
   Bharathkumar Vaitheeswaran, Nanyang Technological University, Singapore

In this article, the authors investigate the diverse dimensions of a knowledge society. First, the relevant literature on post industrial societies is reviewed to identify the key constituents of successful growth and development. The authors then propose a 10-dimension framework within political, economic, social and technological parameters that describe the state of evolution of a given knowledge society. Knowledge assessment scores, human development indices, technology readiness scores and competitiveness scores are selected as composite indicators of knowledge societies. Proxy indicators are assigned for the dimensions, and secondary data was gathered from reputed international sources. Partial Pearson Correlation Analysis was done between the proxy indicators and the composite scales to determine the direction and strength of relationships. Hygiene factors and competitive factors of a knowledge society are distilled from the empirical results and recommendations are suggested to address some areas of concern when pursuing policies for knowledge based development.

   Wen Bing Su, Nanjing University, China
   Xin Li, Nanjing University, China
   Chee W. Chow, San Diego State University, USA

This study explores the extent and impediments of knowledge sharing in Chinese firms because they are becoming dominant entities in the global economy, yet limited research exists on this important aspect of their operations. Survey data are obtained from experienced managers of 164 Chinese firms from a wide range of industries, sizes, and ownership types. The responses indicate that knowledge sharing is not open and complete in Chinese firms. Similar to findings from developed economies in the West, a large number of factors impede knowledge sharing in Chinese firms. These range from Chinese cultural values—which had been identified as being important by prior China-based studies—to attributes of the firm (e.g., incentive system, communication channels, organizational culture), as well as those of knowledge holders and potential recipients (e.g., judgment ability, organizational commitment). Implications of these findings for practice and research are discussed.

   Seung Won Yoon, Western Illinois University, USA
   Alexandre Ardichvili, University of Minnesota, USA

Current Knowledge Management (KM) design approaches recognize the importance of integrating codification, personalization, and collaboration strategies. Incorporating various database systems, search functions, managerial support, performance appraisal, personalized widgets, and case summaries into seamless functions are exemplary efforts. However, KM is rarely integrated with organizational learning and development systems. In this article, the authors use concepts from the situated learning literature, Vygotskian cultural-historical theory of cognition, and a holistic learning and performance architecture to signify the integration of KM and organizational learning systems.

Increasing interest exists in understanding the factors that explain knowledge transfer capacity (KTC) at the societal level. In this paper, the authors posit that national culture may explain the differences among countries in their knowledge transfer capacities. The authors adopt House and colleagues' (2004) national culture taxonomy as the theoretical framework to derive and test eighteen hypotheses relating national culture values and practices to societal KTC. KTC correlates positively with gender egalitarianism values, uncertainty avoidance practices, and future orientation practices. KTC also correlates negatively with uncertainty avoidance values, future orientation values, institutional collectivism values, in-group collectivism values, humane orientation practices, in-group collectivism values and practices, and power distance practices. Further analysis using gross domestic product (GDP) as a control variable revealed that only humane orientation practices influence KTC. The research findings are discussed, research limitations are identified, and implications are drawn.

Chapter 17

The voluntary service not-for-profit sector (VSNFP), also called the charitable sector, is a neglected setting for knowledge management research. It is also an area with distinctive characteristics that preclude direct importation of knowledge management approaches developed for the for-profit sector. In this paper, the authors adapt a model for examining knowledge management research issues to the charitable sector and examine what is known about knowledge management in this important sector of society. Research and practitioner suggestions are provided.

Preface

THE SEARCH FOR KNOWLEDGE MANAGEMENT SUCCESS

How do we know when a knowledge management (KM) project or initiative is successful? Jennex, Smolnik, and Croasdell (2007, 2009) explored KM success and proposed that KM success is getting the right knowledge to the right people at the right time and is measured in four dimensions: impact on business processes, impact on knowledge management strategy, leadership/management support, and knowledge content. This chapter continues the previous studies by reporting on a further study that used a proposed set of measures and a survey to see if these measures were observed in a specific knowledge management project or initiative. The results of these studies are a definition of KM success and a set of measures that shows KM practitioners and researcher where to look for KM success.

Knowledge is a new currency used by an organization's knowledge workers to achieve goals or produce an economic benefit. Knowledge systems and knowledge management (KM) initiatives support knowledge workers in the performance of their jobs. An organizations ability to access its corporate knowledge stores (organizational memory) and to make that knowledge actionable (organizational learning) potentially improves its competitive stature/position in global business environments (Davenport, DeLong, and Beers, 1998). Organizational strategy is necessary, but not sufficient, for implementing knowledge-based initiatives that will support and enable knowledge workers while also enhancing organizational performance, effectiveness, and competitive position (Jennex and Olfman, 2002, 2006). Knowledge systems should consider success factors, effectiveness metrics, and key performance indicators to assess the systems' success and usefulness.

Given the prevalence of knowledge work and knowledge workers in global business environments, it becomes increasingly important to assess knowledge management systems and initiatives (Jennex and Olfman, 2002). Earlier work by Jennex, Smolnik, and Croasdell (2007, 2009) sought to define knowledge management success along with appropriate measures for assessing and measuring KM success. This work resulted in the definition:

"KM success is a multidimensional concept. It is defined by capturing the right knowledge, getting the right knowledge to the right user, and using this knowledge to improve organizational and/or individual performance. KM success is measured by means of the dimensions: impact on business processes, impact on KM strategy, leadership/management support, and knowledge content."

This chapter presents research that validates the above success dimensions and examines metrics for assessing these dimensions. The research hypothesis is that KM projects/initiatives that are perceived to be successful will use more measures of success from each of the above dimensions. The converse is also expected; those KM projects/initiatives perceived to be less successful or not successful will use significantly fewer measures that may not be from all of the above dimensions.

The contribution of this research is a validated knowledge management success model and a set of metrics that should be used by organizations for determining the success of their knowledge management projects and initiatives.

BACKGROUND

Knowledge is information combined with experience, context, interpretation, and reflection (Davenport, DeLong, and Beers, 1998). Knowledge management (KM) has been defined as the process of selectively applying knowledge from previous experiences of decision-making to current and future decision-making activities with the express purpose of improving organizational effectiveness (Jennex and Olfman, 2006). The goals for KM are to identify critical organizational knowledge assets, acquire those assets in an accessible repository, establish mechanisms for sharing the assets among organizational workers, apply the appropriate knowledge to specific decision domains, determine the effectiveness of knowledge application, and adjust knowledge artifacts to improve their effectiveness (Jennex and Olfman, 2006). Knowledge management systems (KMS) are IT-based systems designed to manage organizational knowledge by supporting and enhancing the creation, storage, retrieval, transfer, and application of knowledge (Alavi and Leidner, 2001). KMS support KM through the creation and enhancement of network based corporate memories and support for project teams.

Measuring the success of KM initiatives provides a basis for company valuations, stimulates management focus on what's important, justifies investments in KM activities, and helps managers understand how KMS should be designed and implemented (Jennex and Olfman, 2006; Turban and Aronson, 2001). However, metrics for assessing KM success are not well understood or agreed on (Jennex and Olfman, 2005). Defining and demonstrating effective KM success metrics helps establish constructs and variables, and assists those who manage and perform knowledge work to understand how KM initiative should be designed and implemented. Such metrics identify critical success factors (CSFs) for designing and integrating knowledge into organizational processes (Alazami and Zairi, 2003; Conley and Zheng, 2009; Wong, 2005). They also help establish key performance indicators (KPIs) for assessing the outcomes associated with knowledge-based projects (Marr, Schiuma, and Neely, 2004).

LITERATURE REVIEW

The relative success of an organization can be explored in many ways. Historically, organizations have gauged success using some measure of financial performance such as profit, cash flow, or Return on Invest (ROI). However, financial reports are insufficient, because they do not necessarily reflect process performance, and project outcomes are more micro-levels in an organization. Assessing success is also seen as an organization's ability to identify and track progress against business objectives, to identify opportunities for improvement, and to create benchmarks against internal and external standards (see, for example, (Palte, Hertlein, Smolnik, and Riempp, 2011)). Measurement plays a key role in quality and productivity improvement activities. Assessing performance and relative success within the organization is also an important step in developing a strategic business plan.

From a knowledge perspective, success can be considered via an organization's ability to effectively utilize knowledge assets to affect performance and improve overall efficiency and effectiveness (Bose, 2004; Jennex, Smolnik, and Croasdell, 2007). Davenport et al. identify four objectives for knowledge-based projects: create knowledge repositories, improve knowledge access, enhance knowledge environments, and manage knowledge as an asset (Davenport, DeLong, and Beers, 1998). An organization's ability to identify and leverage knowledge assets can support overall organizational success (O'Dell and Grayson, 1998). The benefits of successful KM include greater collaboration among workers, operational efficiencies, better decision making, and reduced risk (Jennex and Olfman, 2002). Project performance can be improved by using KM as a tool to capture and disseminate knowledge, thereby facilitating learning among team members and enabling action (Jennex and Weiss, 2002).

Establishing a KM strategy is essential for achieving KM success (Jennex and Olfman, 2002). Developing strategies leads to improved processes and procedures, better application of knowledge across functional areas, and greater overall effectiveness. The lack of strategy leads to failure in realizing the benefits of knowledge assets with the organization.

The following sections discuss dimensions of KM success, critical success factors in designing and implementing KMS, and key performance indicators to assess outcomes associated with the effectiveness and success of knowledge initiatives in organizations.

Dimensions of KM Success

KM projects are successful when there is a growth in resources attached to the project, a growth in knowledge content, a likelihood that a project would survive without the support of a particular individual or two, and some evidence of financial return (Davenport, DeLong, and Beers, 1998). Some common types of success in KM projects involve operational improvements for a particular process or function. Factors that lead to success for KM related projects include flexible knowledge structures, knowledge-friendly culture, clear purpose and language, and multiple channels for knowledge transfer (Davenport, DeLong, and Beers, 1998).

Jennex et al. modified DeLone and McLean's IS Success Model to reflect dimensions of success for knowledge systems (Jennex, Olfman, Panthawi, and Park, 1998). Their model uses knowledge quality, information quality, and service quality as functional drivers for the use and impact of knowledge-based systems. Knowledge quality refers to the usefulness of knowledge artifacts in terms of their correctness and inclusion of contextual meaning. System quality refers to how well KMSs perform with regard to knowledge creation, storage, retrieval, and application. Service quality is a measurement of support for the systems in use. Performance impact is judged by the ability of these constructs to affect use of the systems and overall user satisfaction. Knowledge benefits are derived from the quality of the knowledge in the system and service dimensions associated with the system. Benefits are also a result of increased use and user satisfaction.

KM Critical Success Factors

Critical success factors (CSFs) are areas in which satisfactory results ensure successful competitive performance. They are the minimum key factors that an organization must have or do in order to achieve some goal (Alazami and Zairi, 2003). CSFs represent managerial areas that must be given special attention in order to achieve high performance.

Jennex and Oflman summarized CSFs as they related to knowledge systems (Jennex and Olfman, 2005). These factors include a strong technical infrastructure, automated and transparent knowledge capture mechanisms, an integrated enterprise wide system, management support, appropriate maintenance resources, appropriate training, a strong KM strategy, security mechanisms, models for knowledge intensive business processes, and incentives to use organizational knowledge systems. While these factors identify what is needed for successful KM, they do not establish measures for the success.

KM Key Performance Indicators

KM performance can be examined in terms of processes and outcomes. Process measures reflect improvements in process efficiencies, integration of decision artifacts in knowledge intensive business processes, and positive outcomes. In particular, process outcomes can be assessed in terms of productivity, satisfaction, and increases in knowledge sharing (Jennex, Smolnik, and Croasdell, 2009).

Key performance indicators (KPIs) are financial and non-financial metrics used to quantify objectives and reflect strategic performance. KPIs are often used to apply "value" to difficult to measure activities (Stanfield and Mullen, 2008). KPIs can used in KM to assess such things as: 1) the overall KM effort in the organization; 2) the success of KM activities such as knowledge sharing and the number of knowledge assets created; and 3) the effectiveness of KMS and KM tools for finding, accessing, and using KM artifacts (Stanfield and Mullen, 2008; Orth, Smolnik, and Jennex, 2009).

In order to be useful to the organization, KPIs must be aligned with corporate strategy and objectives (Scope Consulting, 2010). This is consistent with recommendations made by Jennex and Olfman in their analysis of CSFs for effective KM efforts (2005). KPIs should be both predictive (i.e., measure value as an indicator of business performance) and actionable. Monitoring KPIs should trigger action and positive change (Scope Consulting, 2010).

PRIOR RESEARCH ACTIVITY

The original inspiration for this research endeavor was the question of what determines when KM is successful. KM and KMS success are issues needing to be explored as identified during the KM Foundations workshop held at the Hawaii International Conference on System Sciences (HICSS-39) in January 2006. This workshop focused on trying to reach consensus definitions on basic issues in KM. KM success was discussed, and while a definition could not be agreed upon, consensus was reached that it was important for the credibility of the KM discipline that it be able to define KM success. This was a one-day workshop attended by approximately 35 KM researchers and chaired by two of the contributors of this book. Additionally, from the perspective of KM academics and practitioners, identifying the factors, constructs, and variables that define KM success is crucial to understanding how these initiatives and systems should be designed and implemented.

Motivated by the workshop's results, a first survey was applied to look at how KM practitioners, researchers, KM students, and others interested in KM view what constitutes KM success (Jennex, Smolnik, and Croasdell, 2007). A series of perspectives on KM success, which were derived by analyzing responses by workshop attendees on how they defined KM success, were discussed. These perspectives were then turned into the survey that was used to gather opinions on what defined KM success. A second survey was subsequently used to refine these findings into a preliminary KM success definition.

Eventually, building on the two surveys' data as well as on the analysis of the respondents' comments, a refined KM success definition, as well as a list of KM success dimensions and measures, were found (Jennex, Smolnik, and Croasdell, 2009). The base definition of KM success is as follows:

"KM success is a multidimensional concept. It is defined by capturing the right knowledge, getting the right knowledge to the right user, and using this knowledge to improve organizational and/or individual performance. KM success is measured by means of the dimensions: impact on business processes, impact on strategy, leadership, and knowledge content."

METHODOLOGY

The basic methodology is the use of a Likert-based survey to assess perceptions of success and observed results. The basic research model is shown in Figure 1. This figure illustrates the approach of having respondents use perceptions of a specific KM project/initiative to respond to items operationalizing the previously discussed dimensions of KM success.

Survey Generation

The survey was initially generated using the previously cited literature to generate a list of items representative of each dimension. Additional questions related to the primary function of the respondent (KM practitioner, KM manager, KM user, academic, KM researcher, and KM student), the experience level of the respondent (0-2 years, 3-5 years, 6-10 years, or over 10 years), and if the KM project/initiative being referred to was successful or not (7-point Likert scale).

The measures used to operationalize the dimensions were validated via an expert panel. Fifteen experts were given the items and asked to identify the dimension each belonged to and if more items were needed. Results of the expert panel were used to adjust the wording and placement of the items, and to clarify what each dimension meant. The final measures were:

Figure 1. Research model

Impact on Business Processes:
1. My last KM project improved the efficiency of the supported processes
2. My last KM project reduced costs for the supported business process
3. My last KM project had a positive return on investment for the supported processes
4. My last KM project improved the effectiveness of the supported processes.
5. My last KM project improved decision making in the supported processes
6. My last KM project improved resource allocation in the supported process

Impact on KM Strategy:
1. My last KM project resulted in changes to my organization's KM goals
2. My last KM project resulted in the creation or modification of knowledge related key performance indicators
3. My last KM project resulted in changes to the way my organization assessed knowledge use in the organization
4. My last KM project resulted in changes in my organization's incentives for using and sharing knowledge
5. My last KM projected resulted in my organization increasing its awareness/mapping of knowledge sources and users
6. My last KM projected resulted in increased resources for our KM systems and repositories
7. My last KM project resulted in the creation of new or additional knowledge capture processes

Leadership/Management Support:
1. My last KM project resulted in increased verbal/political support for KM by top management
2. My last KM project resulted in increased financial support for KM by top management
3. My last KM project resulted in increased awareness of KM by top management
4. My last KM project resulted in increased use/reliance on KM by top management

Knowledge Content:
1. My last KM project resulted in increased knowledge content in our repositories
2. My last KM project improved knowledge content quality of our repositories
3. My last KM project resulted in my increased use or intention to use of knowledge content
4. My last KM project resulted in others increased use or intention to use of knowledge content
5. My last KM project resulted in my increased identification of needed knowledge content and knowledge content sources
6. My last KM project resulted in others increased identification of needed knowledge content and knowledge content sources
7. My last KM project resulted in my increased demand and/or searching for knowledge content
8. My last KM project resulted in others increased demand and/or searching for knowledge content

Survey Distribution and Collection

Survey Monkey was used to post the survey and collect responses. Requests to respond to the survey (with the survey link) were posted on AISWorld list server, three KM practitioner list servers, and through individual invitations sent to KM researchers and practitioners known by the authors. Surveys were collected over a two month period with two reminders posted to the above list servers (responses were still being collected at the time of submission in an attempt to get a larger response base). A total of

144 surveys were collected, of which, 88 were usable. The large number of rejected surveys is based on many potential respondents starting the survey but realizing that they were not familiar with a specific KM project/initiative and that general opinions were not being requested. This was determined based on comments included in the responses and through list server postings to the authors.

Responses were not discarded if they were not complete. Responses that were substantially complete were used. No values were input for missing data as it is not known why the respondents did not complete the survey, although it is assumed it is because they did not know about that item.

Data Analysis

The 88 responses were divided into two analysis groups. Those respondents who responded agree (6) or strongly agree (7) that their last KM project/initiative was considered successful (57 responses) were placed in the successful group, while all other respondents (31 responses) were placed in the unsuccessful group. Respondents who responded slightly agree (5) to the success of their last KM project/initiative were placed in the unsuccessful group to help make the groups more equal in number and because it was felt that those who responded slightly agree may be biased against reporting their project/initiative as a failure.

The focus of this preface is to validate dimensions and to see if there are behaviors that are done more so by successful projects/initiatives than by those that are not. For this reason, a factor analysis on the item responses was not performed but is left as future research (a further reason was the desire to collect more response before this analysis is performed). Dimensions were analyzed using three methods: method 1 used the highest score for the associated items; method 2 used the average of the scores for the associated items; and method 3 used the total number of associated items met with an item score of 6 or 7 being needed to consider the item met. Scores were further analyzed to determine if the dimension was met for each response. Methods 1 and 2 determined the dimension was met if the score was greater than 5. Method 3 considered the dimension met if at least half of the items scores were greater than 5. Finally, responses were analyzed by determining how many dimensions were met and how many total items were met. Means for each of these were generated for each group and t-tests were used to determine if the differences between groups were significant. A final analysis that was done was the splitting of the success group into *agree* (41 responses) and *strongly agree* (16 responses) and t-tested to determine if the differences between these two groups were significant.

Responses that had missing data were analyzed as they were with no attempt made to interpolate data. This means that the generated means only include the values actually responded. This means that n is not always the total number of responses in the group.

RESULTS

The results were mostly as expected: the more successful the KM project/initiative the more the KM project/initiative measured items in more dimensions. This suggests that the model of KM success (Jennex, Smolnik, and Croasdell, 2009) is correct and that KM project/initiative managers should use multiple measures in each of the four dimensions in order to measure success. Specific results follow.

Table 1. Respondent position %(#)

Position	Overall n=89	Successful Project n=57	Unsuccessful Project n=32
KM Practitioner	20.2% (18)	24.6% (14)	12.5% (4)
KM Manager	29.2% (26)	31.6% (18)	25.0% (8)
Academic	21.3% (19)	12.3% (7)	37.5% (12)
KM Researcher	20.2% (18)	22.8% (13)	15.6% (5)
KM Student	9.0% (8)	8.8% (5)	9.4% (3)

Table 2. Respondent experience %(#)

Experience (years)	Overall n=89	Successful Project n=57	Unsuccessful Project n=32
0-2	13.5% (12)	14.0% (8)	12.5% (4)
3-5	22.5% (20)	21.1% (12)	25.0% (8)
6-10	21.3% (19)	21.1% (12)	21.9% (7)
>10	42.7% (38)	43.9% (25)	40.6% (13)

Respondent Demographics

Two demographics were gathered, respondent position and experience level. These demographics are summarized in Tables 1 and 2.

The tables show that there is nearly a 50-50 split between practitioners and researchers/academics/students. Additionally, the majority of respondents are experienced and only a few have 2 or fewer years of experience. It is interesting to note that practitioners were more apt to report on a successful KM project/initiative while the academic focused respondents were more apt to report on unsuccessful KM projects/initiatives.

Dimension Results

This section is focused on the analysis of the survey results with respect to validating the four dimensions of the research model. This was accomplished using three methods as previously discussed. The following tables provide the results for the dimensions:

The dimensions were analyzed by determining the number of dimensions that were "met." A dimension was determined to be met if the high or average value was greater than 5.0 or if the number of items met was greater than or equal to half of the total items for the dimension. Table 6 summarizes the dimensions that were met and the total number of items met. Note that items that were not answered were not considered met.

Table 3. Highest value method (mean/(std. dev)/(n))

Dimension	Success Group	NonSuccess Group
Impact on Business Processes	6.4 0.7285 (57)	5.6 (1.3137) (32)
Impact on KM Strategy	6.2 (0.9502) (57)	5.8 (0.8980) (31)
Leadership/ Management Support	6.0 (1.0516) (57)	5.4 (1.3336) (31)
Knowledge Content	6.3 (0.8536) (53)	5.8 (1.0816) (29)

Table 4. Average value method (mean/(std. dev)/(n))

Dimension	Success Group	NonSuccess Group
Impact on Business Processes	5.7 (0.7047) (57)	4.7 (1.0573) (32)
Impact on KM Strategy	5.0 (0.1150) (57)	4.5 (0.8914) (31)
Leadership/ Management Support	5.2 (1.1978) (57)	4.4 (1.3052) (31)
Knowledge Content	5.4 (0.9768) (53)	4.7 (1.1217) (29)

Table 5. Item count value method (mean/(std. dev) /(n))

Dimension	Success Group	NonSuccess Group
Impact on Business Processes	4.0 (1.6743) (57)	2.1 (1.6412) (32)
Impact on KM Strategy	3.3 (2.3433) (57)	2.0 (1.8439) (31)
Leadership/ Management Support	1.9 (1.4914) (57)	1.3 (1.3757) (31)
Knowledge Content	4.6 (2.6129) (53)	2.6 (2.2294) (29)

Table 6. Dimensions and items met (mean/(std. dev))

Method	Success Group n=57	Nonsuccess Group n=32
High Value	3.4 (0.9909)	2.7 (1.3102)
Average Value	2.6 (1.3595)	1.3 (1.2854)
Item Count	2.5 (1.3379)	1.4 (1.3664)
Total Items (25 possible)	13.4 (6.71091)	7.7 (5.0902)

Table 7. T-Test comparison between groups: (Success vs nonsuccess)

High Value	$t_{51}=2.61$	$p < 0.01$
Average Value	$t_{64}=4.26$	$p < 0.01$
Item Count	$t_{60}=3.46$	$p < 0.01$
Total Items (25 possible)	$t_{79}=4.57$	$p < 0.01$

Group Comparisons

Significance tests using a 1-sided t-test assuming unequal variance were used to determine if the differences listed in Table 6 between the two groups were significant. Table 7 lists the results of these tests, and it should be noted that all differences were considered significant at 0.01.

DISCUSSION

The results were as expected in that more successful KM projects/initiatives used more measures of success in more dimensions than non-successful KM projects/initiatives. What this really means is that organizations who are successful with KM projects/ initiatives are more aware of the impacts that KM has on their organization and thus implement more measures to ensure those impacts are observed and met. The implications are many. The first is that an organization needs to fully understand the impact knowledge use has on their organization. What is meant here is that knowledge is not simply a commodity that is used to make a process better. It is also something that spurs innovation and competitiveness, and successful use of knowledge leads to more and varied use, more desire to identify, capture, and make available key knowledge, more awareness of the value of knowledge, and the acquisition of a knowledge inventory that can be applied to current and future activities. This is exactly what was expected when Jennex, Smolnik, and Croasdell proposed their definition of KM success:

"KM success is a multidimensional concept. It is defined by capturing the right knowledge, getting the right knowledge to the right user, and using this knowledge to improve organizational and/or individual performance. KM success is measured by means of the dimensions: impact on business processes, impact on KM strategy, leadership/management support, and knowledge content" (Jennex, Smolnik, and Croasdell, 2007, 2009).

However, the above results are not sufficient to validate the four dimensions listed in the above dimension since it appears that successful KM projects/ initiatives may only use around three of the dimensions. Also, the results are not sufficient to validate the items used to represent the dimensions as it also appears that successful KM projects/initiatives may only use 7 to 21 of the items surveyed. One explanation is that since the items are each representative of the dimensions, organizations only need to use a few, or perhaps only one measure in each dimension, to measure adequately and achieve success. This would indicate that the high value measure of dimension success is the one that should be used to assess the data.

Another explanation is that the criteria for "meeting" a dimension are too high. The high and average score had to be greater than 5 for the dimension to be met, while for the item count method, half or more of the items had to have a score of greater than 5 for the dimension to be met.

Lowering the criteria for determining if a dimension is met to items scores greater than 4 is justified as any score over 4 reflects a degree of agreement; the criteria of meeting half or more of the items for a dimension to be met is admittedly arbitrary. However, it is not chosen to do so. It is felt that success should be obvious and readily observable. This is the basis for using scores over 5 (*slightly agree*). Additionally, the items were taken from the literature and all have been used by KM projects/ initiatives. It is believed that all items could and perhaps should be observed by successful KM projects/ initiatives.

To confirm these basic beliefs on KM success, the data was further analyzed grouping on the actual scores on agreement of KM success, i.e. the group who responded 7, the group who responded 6, the group responding 5, the group responding 4, and, due to the very low number of unsuccessful KM project/initiative responses, the group responding 1, 2, or 3. This analysis provides a fascinating insight.

The first comparison was done between the 6 and 7 groups. This was done as it was perceived that "best practices" could be derived from the 7 group. The results are shown in Table 8:

All differences between the groups were significant. Additionally, the 7 group reflects the expected findings in that all three methods reflect more than three dimensions being met, and it shows a large number of items being met. This is the expected results of the study and led to the conclusion that the KM success model (Jennex, Smolnik, and Croasdell, 2007, 2009) is valid, and the items used to operationalize the dimensions are acceptable.

Data tables for the other analyses are not provided due to page limitations. However, only two significant differences were found: between the 6 – 5 groups on the average score for dimensions met and for the total items met. This lack of significance is likely due to the small number of responses with respect to KM projects/initiatives perceived to be unsuccessful. Further research will attempt to collect sufficient

Table 8. Group 7 vs 6 dimensions and items met, (mean/(std. dev))

Method	7 Group n=16	6 Group n=41	t-test data
High Value	3.8 (0.5439)	3.2 (1.0701)	t_{51}=2.9787 p<0,01
Average Value	3.5 (1.0328)	2.3 (1.3233)	t_{35}=3.7243 p<0,01
Item Count	3.4 (0.8851)	2.3 (1.3398)	t_{41}=2.9997 p<0,01
Total Items (25 possible)	17.4 (6.1207)	11.9 (6.3332)	t_{28}=3.0513 p<0,01

Figure 2. #Dimensions met vs success (7 most successful, 4 not successful, 4 dimensions max)

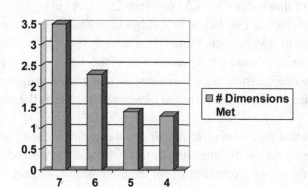

Figure 3. #Items met vs success (7 most successful, 4 not successful, 25 items max)

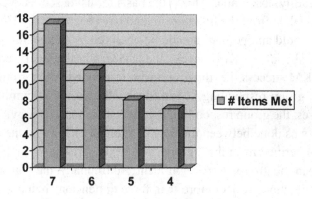

responses from perceived unsuccessful KM projects/ initiatives to make this analysis meaningful. No significant differences were found between the other group pairings, as these groups all reflect mild to no success, and thus, the items and dimensions are not expected to be observed.

A final point of discussion is to visualize what the findings mean. Figure 2 and figure 3 visualize the results using the average value for dimensions met and total items met (as these were the significant differences between groups 7, 6, and 5).

These figures show the findings of this study: the more successful a KM project/initiative is perceived to be, the more dimensions from the KM success definition (Jennex, Smolnik, and Croasdell, 2007, 2009) are met, and the more item measures from this study are met. This is a significant finding with implications for practice. First, though, why these findings occurred must be discussed.

Why more dimensions and more items for successful KM projects? This study postulates that KM does not exist in an organizational vacuum. KM cannot be bolted onto an organization nor can it be done independent of the organization. Knowledge use and value only occurs within context of the users and the organization. To be successful with KM, organizations need to fully understand what knowledge is needed, who needs it, how it is used, and why it is used. Successful KM projects/initiatives understand this and so look for knowledge use and value in a large variety of ways. Knowledge use, and thus, KM, must impact the processes that they support. Improved processes impact leadership/management, whose purpose is to guide the organization to perform at its best. Improved knowledge use drives the KM organization to modify their KM strategy to reflect that which is working. Finally, like any resource, the organization strives to accumulate useful knowledge. The KM success definition recognizes that KM success is in getting the right knowledge to the right people at the right time. The dimensions recognize that being successful with KM will be reflected in these definitions as discussed above.

Understanding the impact of successful KM leads to the implication of this study: KM project managers/initiative leaders need to do thorough business cases and analyses up front so that they fully understand the impacts their KM projects/initiatives will have on the organization. This study helps by providing 25 measures that should be looked at for these business cases and analyses and as potential measures of success. In all cases, this study should drive KM project managers/initiative leaders to consider using many measures in multiple dimensions. This should be done regardless of the scope of the project/initiative, as this study believes that these dimensions and item measures apply regardless of the scope of the project or initiative.

CONCLUSION

The conclusion of this study is that the KM success definition, including its four dimensions of impact on business processes, impact on KM strategy, leadership/management support, and knowledge content, are a valid definition and measure of KM success. The second conclusion is that the set of 25 items representing the success dimensions are a good set for use by organizations as success measures. They are where organizations, practitioners, and researchers should be looking for KM success. The third conclusion is that organizations implementing KM projects/initiatives should use multiple measures in all four dimensions to ensure all benefits of the project/initiative are recognized and measured.

These are considered to be highly generalizable conclusions due to the respondents' demographics. Half are practitioners, and only 9% reported themselves as KM students. This is not to imply that a KM student is not a valid respondent; many KM practitioners return to school to further their academic training, and in many cases, these are the responders to KM surveys. What makes this set of responders especially valid is their experience. Sixty-four percent of responders have over 6 years of KM experience, and 42.7% have over 10 years. Couple this with only 13.5% reporting their experience level at 0-2 years, and this respondent pool has a very high level of experience. It is expected that these respondents possess a great deal of insight and should provide accurate responses with respect to the project they are responding.

Limitations

The major limitation of the study is the low number of responses reflecting KM projects/initiatives that are perceived to be unsuccessful. While this limitation is significant for obtaining the full picture of KM success, it is not considered a threat to the validity of the current findings due to the significant differences observed between projects perceived to have various degrees of success. This limitation is being mitigated by continuing data collection.

A second limitation is the use of perceived success as a control for classifying perceptions on the items measuring success. This is an acceptable risk as it is difficult for respondents to obtain hard measures of success, if such measures even exist.

Areas for Future Research

The main area for future research is to conduct a factor analysis and test the model to fully validate that the survey items used are a fully validated set of success measures. Also, the set of 25 measures used in the survey is not considered to be an exhaustive list, nor is considered to be set. It is expected that the set of measures will be an evolving set as research and practice evolve. Future research should continue to look at this set of success measures and evolve it as necessary.

Another area for future research is to tie these measures into the proposed model for measuring KM value proposed by Fischer, Hertlein, Smolnik, and Jennex (2011). This should be done using the integrative KM model using key performance indicators (KPIs) and KM critical success factors (CSFs) as proposed by Orth, Smolnik, and Jennex (2009).

Murray E. Jennex
San Diego State University, USA

REFERENCES

Alavi, M., & Leidner, D. E. (2001). Review: Knowledge management and knowledge management systems: Conceptual foundations and research issues. *Management Information Systems Quarterly, 25*(1), 107–136. doi:10.2307/3250961

Alazami, M., & Zairi, M. (2003). Knowledge management critical success factors. *Total Quality Management, 14*(2), 199–204. doi:10.1080/1478336032000051386

Bhatti, W. A., Zaheer, A., & Ur Rehman, K. (2011). The effect of knowledge management practices on organizational performance: A conceptual study. *African Journal of Business Management, 5*(7), 2847–2853.

Bose, R. (2004). Industrial knowledge management metrics. *Management & Data Systems, 104*(6), 457–468. doi:10.1108/02635570410543771

Conley, C. A., & Zheng, W. (2009). Factors critical to knowledge management success. *Advances in Developing Human Resources, 11*(3), 334–348. doi:10.1177/1523422309338159

Davenport, T. H., DeLong, D. W., & Beers, M. C. (1998). Successful knowledge management projects. *Sloan Management Review*, (Winter): 43–57.

Fischer, N., Hertlein, M., Smolnik, S., & Jennex, M. E. (2011). Measuring value of knowledge-based initiatives – Evaluation of existing models and development of a new measurement framework. *Proceedings of the 44th Hawaii International Conference on System Sciences*, IEEE Computer Society, Lihui.

Jennex, M. E., & Olfman, L. (2002). Organizational memory/knowledge effects on productivity: A longitudinal study. *Proceedings of the 35th Hawaii International Conference on System Sciences*, IEEE Computer Society, Waikoloa.

Jennex, M. E., & Olfman, L. (2005). Assessing knowledge management success. *International Journal of Knowledge Management, 1*(2), 33–49. doi:10.4018/jkm.2005040104

Jennex, M. E., & Olfman, L. (2006). A model of knowledge management success. *International Journal of Knowledge Management, 2*(3), 51–68. doi:10.4018/jkm.2006070104

Jennex, M. E., Olfman, L., Panthawi, P., & Park, Y. (1998). An organizational memory Information Systems success model: An extension of DeLone and McLean's I/S success model. *Proceedings of the 31st Annual Hawaii International Conference on System Sciences,* IEEE Computer Society Kohala, HI.

Jennex, M. E., Smolnik, S., & Croasdell, D. T. (2007). Towards defining knowledge management success. *Proceedings of the 40th Hawaii International Conference on System Sciences,* IEEE Computer Society, Waikoloa, HI.

Jennex, M. E., Smolnik, S., & Croasdell, D. T. (2009). Towards a consensus knowledge management success definition. *VINE: The Journal of Information and Knowledge Management Systems, 39*(2), 174–188.

Jennex, M. E., & Weiss, J. (2002). A study of knowledge benefits gained from projects: The electric utility industry Y2K project experience . In White, D. (Ed.), *Knowledge mapping and management.* Hershey, PA: Idea Group Publishing.

Marr, B., Schiuma, G., & Neely, A. (2004). Intellectual capital – Defining key performance indicators for organizational knowledge assets. *Business Process Management Journal, 10*(5), 551–569. doi:10.1108/14637150410559225

O'Dell, C., & Grayson, C. J. (1998). *If only we knew what we know: The transfer of internal knowledge and best practice.* New York, NY: The Free Press.

Orth, A., Smolnik, S., & Jennex, M. E. (2009). *The relevance of integration for knowledge management success: Conceptual and empirical findings.* 42nd Hawaii International Conference on System Sciences, HICSS42, IEEE Computer Society, January.

Palte, R., Hertlein, M., Smolnik, S., & Riempp, G. (2011). The effects of a KM strategy on KM performance in professional services firms. *International Journal of Knowledge Management, 7*(1), 16–34. doi:10.4018/jkm.2011010102

Scope Consulting. (2010). *Performance management: KPI identification.* Retrieved June 16, 2011, from http://www.slideshare.net/ Alastairs1/introduction-to-kpis? src=related_normal&rel=273406

Stanfield, K., & Mullen, J. (2008). *Knowledge connections.* Retrieved June 16, 2011, from http://www.slideshare.net/jampesmullan/ key-performance-indicators-and-knowledge-management

Turban, E., & Aronson, J. E. (2001). *Decision support systems and intelligent systems* (6th ed.). Prentice.

Wong, M. E. (2005). Critical success factors for implementing knowledge management in small and medium enterprises. *Industrial Management & Data Systems, 105*(3), 261–279. doi:10.1108/02635570510590101

Chapter 1
Factors Affecting KM Implementation in the Chinese Community

Yang Lin
McGill University, Canada

Kimiz Dalkir
McGill University, Canada

ABSTRACT

This paper reviews past research on KM to identify key factors affecting Chinese KM implementation. It begins with a chronological overview of 76 KM related publications, followed by two separate discussions of socio-cultural and non-socio-cultural factors affecting KM implementation within the Chinese community. A preliminary typology of these factors is proposed. In addition to individual factors that have direct impact on how people behave in the process of KM implementation, specific factors that strongly influence Chinese KM implementation are: (1) relationship networks and collectivist thinking, (2) competitiveness and knowledge hoarding, (3) management involvement and support, and (4) organizational culture that encourages knowledge sharing and learning and that minimizes knowledge hoarding. Several directions for future research are also presented.

1. INTRODUCTION

In business, Knowledge Management (KM) is often defined as a series of activities undertaken by organizations to identify, acquire, retain, transfer, and create knowledge-based assets with the aim of sustaining core competency and innovation capabilities. More business managers are realizing that a firm's core competency mainly stems from the knowledge possessed by its knowledge workers and that one necessary approach to sustaining such competency is to integrate KM into business strategies. The business world has therefore turned to research communities to help them pursue better KM solutions and implementation within different contexts.

Research to date has shown that the theoretical underpinnings of KM are rooted in two premises.

DOI: 10.4018/978-1-4666-0035-5.ch001

First, the heterogeneous knowledge-based assets essentially determine a firm's core competency and superior performance (Reed & Defillipi, 1990; Kogut & Zander, 1992; Nonaka, 1994; Grant, 1996; Kusunoki et al., 1998; Galunic & Rodan, 1998; Rodan & Galunic, 2004). Second, with concrete theoretical frameworks and sophisticated methodologies, skills, and techniques, KM is able to assist a firm to efficiently and effectively manage such assets (Wiig, 1995, 1997; Stewart, 1997; Sveiby, 1997; Nonaka & Takeuchi, 1995; Murray, 2002; Standfield, 2002) and thus succeed in the 21st century knowledge age (Drucker, 1995; Earl & Scott, 1999; Saint-Onge, 1999; Liebowitz, 2000).

While KM has been applied and developed in the Western world for nearly two decades, it has not received much attention from the Chinese community until the late 1990s. Peng et al. (2007) indicated that this might be due to lack of access to Chinese KM practitioners. China is now home to twenty-five per cent of the world's population. As a rapidly developing country, it has been gaining increased importance in global economic and political system over the past fifty years. It is estimated that by 2020 China' economy may surpass Japan's and become the second largest in the world (Asian Economic News, 2005).

This paper reviews past research on KM to identify key factors affecting Chinese KM implementation and discusses critical implications for future research. Three specific types of KM practices are addressed: (1) knowledge sharing and transfer, (2) knowledge acquisition and dissemination, and (3) knowledge creation. A chronological overview of KM research related to the Chinese community is presented, followed by discussions of socio-cultural and non-socio-cultural factors affecting KM implementation within the Chinese community. A preliminary typology of factors for Chinese KM implementation is then proposed.

2. A CHRONOLOGICAL OVERVIEW OF KM RESEARCH RELATED TO THE CHINESE COMMUNITY

When KM started gaining attention from the Western community, China was experiencing dramatic changes. The "Open Door" policy, announced in 1978 by Deng Xiaoping, was an alarming signal indicating that soon China's original centrally planned economics were going to be replaced by market economics. As a result, Chinese business managers who used to wait for direct orders from the government were suddenly thrown into the unfamiliar territory of market competition and autonomy. In order to survive, they must discard their old mental models and be ready to learn new knowledge and skills about how to judge, analyze and lead in this completely novel situation. Unsurprisingly, business leaders turned to Western management theory, distilled from Western market economics, as a model to emulate.

In the 1990s the Chinese academic world went through intensive debates about why, what, and how to transfer Western management knowledge to China. Most Chinese managers and employees were brought up in an environment in which people placed a greater value on collectivism rather than individualism, and focused more on means, long-term relationships and implicit exchanges than on ends and the intended outcomes (Hall, 1976; Mead, 1994; Berrell et al., 2001). In addition, compared to the people living in Western countries, Chinese people with quite different historical, cultural, and political backgrounds always remain cautious about the reliability and validity of Western theories and generally believe that truth must be situated within contexts. Therefore, transferring management knowledge from the West to China cannot be a simple direct attempt, because it is based on invalid assumptions about the nature of knowledge and involves implicit knowledge and experiences transfer between different social contexts (Warner, 1993; Hofstede, 1994; Newell, 1999).

Figure 1. Numbers of annual KM publications related to the Chinese community

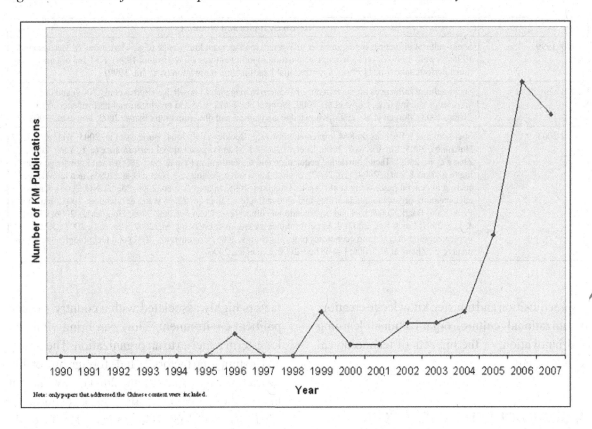

It is difficult to determine exactly when KM was first introduced to China; however, some researchers believe the concept was not properly explained to the country until the late 1990s (Voelpel & Han, 2005; Lin & Kwok, 2006). In fact, before the late 1990s there were very few KM publications related to the Chinese community (see Figure 1). Related research topics (see Table 1) involved the relationship between KM and organizational performance (Luo, 1999), organizational learning and innovation (Jin, 1999), and socio-cultural influences on the transfer of Western management in general (e.g., Martinsons & Martinsons, 1996; Branine, 1996; Newell, 1999) or on knowledge acquisition in joint ventures (Si & Bruton, 1999). Possible reasons might be that at that moment many scholars and practitioners did spend substantial efforts on KM but needed time to process and publish their thoughts, or

that they did not have much time and eagerness to investigate particularly KM but concentrated on the management knowledge transfer from the West to China in general.

KM received slightly increased attention in China between the late 1990s and the early 2000s. Researchers continued to focus on socio-cultural effects on KM implementation or the relationship between KM and organizational performance, with only two papers focusing on how to acquire and disseminate knowledge (see Lau et al., 2002; Tsang, 2002). After the mid 2000s, KM research developed at an accelerating rate. Not only did the number of annual publications increase significantly, but the range of related research topics also became broader to produce a notable body of literature on the influence of socio-cultural factors on KM practice. Scholars subsequently studied other related aspects such as tacit knowl-

Table 1. A summary of research topics related to KM and the Chinese community

Year	Research Topics and Examples
1990–1999	Socio-cultural influences on the transfer of Western management knowledge (e.g., Martinsons & Martinsons, 1996; Newell, 1999) or on knowledge acquisition in joint ventures (Si & Bruton, 1999); KM and organizational performance (Luo, 1999); Organizational Learning and innovation (e.g., Jin, 1999).
2000–2003	Socio-cultural influences on the transfer of Western management knowledge (Berrel et al., 2001) and on knowledge sharing (e.g., Chow et al., 2000; Wong et al., 2002); KM and organizational performance (Yan & Zhang, 2003; Morgan et al., 2003); Knowledge acquisition and dissemination (Tsang, 2002; Lau et al., 2002).
After 2003	Socio-cultural influences on KM implementation (e.g. Buckley et al, 2004; Burrows et al. 2005; Weir & Hutchings, 2005; Lin & Kwok, 2006; Li et al. 2007); KM and organizational performance (e.g., Yang, 2005; Zhang et al., 2006); Tacit knowledge acquisition and dissemination (Yin & Bao, 2006); Tacit knowledge sharing (e.g., Bao & Zhao, 2004; Lin, 2007), explicit knowledge sharing (e.g., Geng et al., 2005), and knowledge sharing in general (e.g., Wang et al., 2004; Hutchings, 2005; Inkpen & Pien, 2006; Mei & Nie, 2007); Knowledge creation, organizational learning, and innovation (e.g., Ju et al., 2006; Wang & Nicholas, 2005; Inkpen & Pien, 2006; Baark, 2007); KM and organizational culture (e.g., Chan & Chau, 2005; Hong et al., 2006; Chang & Lee, 2007; Lai & Lee, 2007); KM performance measurement (Chen et al., 2007; Han & Ji, 2007); KM implementation in emerging economics (e.g., Hutchings, 2005; Bruton et al., 2007) and technological development (e.g., Zhang et al., 2006; Lin & Lee, 2006; Lee et al., 2006).

edge acquisition and transfer, knowledge creation, organizational culture, organizational learning and innovation, or the impacts of technological development.

3. SOCIO-CULTURAL FACTORS AFFECTING KM IMPLEMENTATION IN THE CHINESE COMMUNITY

A number of socio-cultural factors that shape peoples' thinking and action must also be considered since an organization's knowledge is mainly "possessed" by its knowledge workers who are socially connected and situated within contexts. Papers published between 1999 and 2007 which examined, either explicitly or implicitly, socio-cultural influences on KM implementation within the Chinese community were identified and classified by author(s) along four key dimensions: key factors, practice focus, and major findings or key arguments (see Table 2).

Socio-cultural factors affecting KM implementation in the Chinese community can be broadly classified into two groups: (1) policy and institutional factors and (2) national cultural factors. Policy and institutional factors are macro

factors highly associated with a country's social political environment. They can bring vital and long-term benefits to an organization. The policy and institutional factors include foreign ownership restrictions (Buckley et al., 2004), government interventions (Wong et al., 2002), institutional gaps (Lau et al., 2002; Hutchings, 2005; Fu et al., 2006; Li & Scullion, 2006), and China's transition economics (Hutchings, 2005). Most are considered barriers to Chinese KM development, and some researchers suggest that China's government should be fully aware of its role and be ready to adjust its policies to encourage KM practices (Wong et al., 2002; Buckley et al., 2004).

Schein (1985) defines culture as the often unstated beliefs, values, and assumptions shared by the people of a national community. Culture may play a more complex and decisive role than policy and institutional factors in Chinese KM implementation (Hutchings & Michailova, 2004; Hutchings, 2005; Fu et al., 2006). The national cultural factors identified in this study can be organized into five groups: collectivism such as in-group vs. out-group and collective interests (Berrel et al., 2001; Chow et al., 2000; Burrows et al., 2005; Voelpel & Han, 2005; Ardichvili et al., 2006; Michailova & Hutchings, 2006; Zhang

Table 2. Socio-cultural factors affecting KM implementation

Study	Key factors	Practice focus	Major findings or key arguments
Chow et al., 2000	National cultural factors: Collectivism: Collective interests In-group vs. Out-group Confucianism	Knowledge sharing	Collective interest conflicts give rise to variations of willingness towards knowledge sharing between American and Chinese employees. Because China is a high collectivism-oriented country, Chinese employees are more open to share knowledge within groups, compared to American counterparts.
Berrel et al., 2001	National cultural factors: Collectivism: Collective interests	Knowledge transfer	The transfer of Western management knowledge to China may be problematic due to the dynamic learning environment the mixture of both Chinese and Western culture creates.
Wong et al., 2002	Policy and institutional factors: Policy constraints: Government interventions	Knowledge transfer	The transfer of strategic management knowledge from the parent companies to their joint ventures is limited due to strong interventions of China's government such as giving them limited access to China's market in their operations.
Lau et al., 2002	Policy and institutional factors: Institutional support National cultural factors: Social capital (guanxi)	Knowledge acquisition and dissemination	Institutional support and social capital affects knowledge acquisition and dissemination in Chinese high-tech firms. Social capital influences knowledge commercialization as well.
Buckley et al., 2004	Policy and institutional factors: Policy constraints: Foreign ownership restrictions	Knowledge transfer	China's foreign ownership restrictions cause goal conflicts between international joint ventures and their partners, thus impeding the speed of knowledge-transfer process.
Hutchings & Michailova, 2004	National cultural factors: Guanxi (relationship networks) Collectivism: In-group vs. Out-group	Knowledge sharing	Strong in-group commitment and healthy guanxi should still be crucial for building the trust in the process of knowledge sharing in the Chinese community.
Voelpel & Han, 2005	National cultural factors: Collectivism In-group vs. Out-group Confucianism Face saving Guanxi	Knowledge sharing	Facing saving and group distinction become two cultural barriers to Chinese employees' knowledge-sharing behaviour. Guanxi (personal information networks) could significantly enhance knowledge sharing.
Burrows et al., 2005	National cultural factors: Collectivism In-group vs. Out-group Confucianism Seniority Hierarchy Knowledge hoarding	KM implementation in general	Cultural barriers such as over-respecting seniority, in-group commitment, social attitudes of knowledge hoarding, and high social hierarchical concern must be overcome in order to successfully manage the knowledge in the Chinese context.
Hutchings, 2005	Policy and institutional factors: Transition economics: Institution National cultural factors: Guanxi	Knowledge sharing	Institutional impact on knowledge sharing in the Chinese community are increasing, but where institutions may be absent or poorly developed, the influence of traditional cultural factors such as guanxi built on trust may still surpass that of China's institutional development in facilitating knowledge sharing.
Weir & Hutchings, 2005	National cultural factors: Guanxi	Knowledge sharing	KM sharing in the Chinese community cannot be accomplished without taking cultural context into account, and traditional cultural factors such as guanxi play vital roles in the process of knowledge sharing.
Ardichvili et al., 2006	National cultural factors: Confucianism: Modesty Authority or seniority Hierarchy Collectivism: In-group vs. Out-group Face saving Competitiveness	Knowledge sharing	Modesty and high competitiveness can seriously impede knowledge sharing in China. There is strong in-group knowledge-sharing commitment among Chinese managers. Confucianism is gradually losing its influences on knowledge sharing in China. Face saving is not a significant factor affecting knowledge sharing.

continued on following page

Table 2. Continued

Study	Key factors	Practice focus	Major findings or key arguments
Ramasamy et al., 2006	National cultural factors: Guanxi	Knowledge transfer	Guanxi was operationalized in terms of three individual factors: trust, relationship commitment, and communication. Trust and communication are significantly related to knowledge transfer, while relationship commitment is not.
Lin & Kwok, 2006	National cultural factors: Competitiveness Knowledge hoarding	Knowledge implementation in general	High competitiveness reduced the willingness of HP employees to share knowledge, as they were worried about being replaced. Cultural constraints such as knowledge hoarding still exist and became major obstacles to KM implementation in HP China.
Fu et al., 2006	National cultural factors: Guanxi Policy and institutional factors: Institution: Immature legal systems	KM implementation in general	Given that China's current legal system for business operations is not yet mature, Chinese business leaders should be fully aware of the dynamics of guanxi, and cultivate or use proper guanxi during the course of KM implementation.
Assimako-poulos & Yan, 2006	National cultural factors: Guanxi Renqing (favor)	KM implementation in general	Major sources for Chinese software engineers to acquire, share and create knowledge include technological books, online information sources, team colleagues, and internet software technology forums. Cultural factors such as guanxi and renqing were not significant factors in knowledge acquisition.
Michailova & Hutchings, 2006	National cultural factors: Collectivism: In-group vs. Out-group Universalism vs. Particularism	Knowledge sharing	Collectivism and special social relations in China would lead to strong knowledge sharing among in-group members.
Zhang et al., 2006	National cultural factors: Collectivism: In-group vs. Out-group	Knowledge sharing	Both Chinese and American undergraduate students prefer to share personal knowledge with in-group members than with out-group members.
Barrk, 2007	National cultural factors: Traditional historical legacies: The pursuit of balance between innovation and social stability Symbiotic relationship between power and knowledge	Knowledge creation	China's traditional historical legacies including the pursuit of balance between innovation and social stability and symbiotic relationship between power and knowledge are still deeply shaping China's current institutional development of innovation and knowledge creation, thus maintaining their significant impact on China's social development.
Yao et al., 2007	National cultural factors: Collectivism Knowledge hoarding Competitiveness Confucianism	Knowledge sharing	Chinese cultural factors, particularly high competitiveness and knowledge hoarding, still function as critical barriers to knowledge sharing in the Chinese context.
Li & Scullion, 2006	Policy and institutional factors: Institutional gaps National cultural factors: Cultural distance	Knowledge creation	Chinese knowledge holders have substantial physical and institutional gaps and may be human barriers for effective knowledge building. A multi-layered knowledge platform and a "pull and push" system (an institutionalized KM system) could break such barriers and facilitate knowledge building.
Li et al., 2007	National cultural factors: Collectivism Face-saving Confucianism Hierarchy Competitiveness	Knowledge sharing	Traditional cultural factors such as collective thinking, face-saving, and hierarchical concern may not significantly affect knowledge sharing through online communities of practice. However, high competitiveness could still explain why Chinese employees hoard knowledge. Both national and organizational culture can shape how employees, especially younger ones, think and behave in a knowledge-sharing process.
Li et al., 2007	National cultural factors: Social control Transition economy	Tacit knowledge acquisition	Firms with greater incentives to acquire tacit knowledge from partners perceive social and formal control as equally important. The uncertainties brought by China's current transition economy, social control could promote radical innovation.

et al., 2006; Li et al., 2007), knowledge hoarding (Lin & Kwok, 2006; Burrows et al., 2005; Yao et al., 2007), competitiveness (Lin & Kwok, 2006; Li et al., 2007; Yao et al., 2007; Ardichvili et al., 2006), guanxi, also called relationship networks, (Hutchings & Michailova, 2004; Weir & Hutchings, 2005; Ramasamy et al., 2006; Fu et al., 2006), and Confucianism such as modesty, authority or seniority, and hierarchy (Chow et al., 2000; Ardichvili et al., 2006; Li et al., 2007; Burrows et al., 2005).

Collective thinking still deeply shapes Chinese attitudes towards knowledge sharing, which causes significant in-group sharing, as opposed to out-group sharing (Chow et al., 2000; Michailova & Hutchings, 2006; Voelpel & Han, 2005; Ardichvili et al., 2006; Zhang et al., 2006). Guanxi built upon long-term credibility was found to be positively related to knowledge sharing (Hutchings & Michailova, 2004; Hutchings, 2005; Yao et al., 2007; Ramasamy et al., 2006; Fu et al., 2006). Guanxi also influenced knowledge acquisition and dissemination in Chinese high-tech firms (Lau et al., 2002) as well as in local Chinese manufacturing firms (Wu et al., 2007). Hierarchical concern and face-saving, two cultural legacies existing in the Chinese community for over hundreds of years, however, may not significantly affect knowledge sharing in the Chinese community (Chow et al., 2000; Zhang et al., 2006; Li et al., 2007; Ardichvili et al., 2006). This could be partially due to the fact that China is currently undergoing a transition from a relationship-based to a rule-based social structure (Peng, 2003) and certain traditional cultural elements are gradually losing their power in shaping people's decision making. Furthermore, knowledge hoarding has been regarded as one of the key cultural barriers to KM implementation within the Chinese context (Hutchings & Michailova, 2004; Lin & Kwok, 2006; Zhang et al., 2006; Yao et al., 2007; Ramasamy et al., 2006). High competitiveness mainly caused by China's current social environment can seriously damage Chinese people's knowledge-sharing

willingness, and thus may become a major reason for their knowledge hoarding (Ardichvili et al., 2006; Lin & Kwok, 2006; Yao et al., 2007; Li et al., 2007). Other socio-cultural factors found possibly related to their knowledge hoarding include guanxi, modesty, and social hierarchy (Burrows et al., 2005; Hutchings & Michailova, 2004; Yao et al., 2007; Ramasamy et al., 2006). Some of these factors were have also been reported to affect knowledge sharing in Russian and Arabian contexts (Weir & Hutchings, 2005; Michailova & Hutchings, 2006).

Li et al. (2007) pointed out that firms with strong incentives for tacit knowledge acquisition would perceive social and formal control as being equally important. Li et al. (2007) further explained that social control focused on using social norms and values to influence individual behaviour, while formal control concentrated on using organizational rules and policies to achieve goals. Similarly, Li and Scullion (2006) purported that knowledge holders with substantial physical and institutional gaps might behave as human barriers for effective knowledge building and therefore, a "pull and push" system may contribute to knowledge creation in the Chinese business settings. Zhang et al. (2005), Hutchings (2005), Chang and Li (2007), and Peng et al. (2007) challenged the traditional notion that efficient knowledge sharing cannot be forced and that it ultimately depends on individuals' willingness to identify the knowledge they possess and share the knowledge when required (Nonaka, 1994; Kim & Mauborgne, 1997; Buckman 1999; Chan & Chau, 2005)

4. NON-SOCIO-CULTURAL FACTORS AFFECTING CHINESE KM IMPLEMENTATION

A number of non-sociocultural factors affecting Chinese KM implementation were also identified, in addition to socio-cultural factors that pertain to an organization's external environment. Non-socio-cultural factor are mainly derived from the inter-organizational interactions, organizational characteristics, and from organizational management and individual members. Table 3 presents articles published between 1999 and 2007 which examined non-socio-cultural effects on KM implementation in the Chinese community.

Non-socio-cultural factors affecting KM implementation in the Chinese community can be divided into two groups: organizational and individual factors. Organizational factors can be further divided into two sub-groups: inter-organizational and intra-organizational factors. Inter-organizational factors focus on the interactions between firms (e.g., multinational corporations and their joint ventures) on KM practices, including firm-level relationship (Bao & Zhao, 2004; Wang & Nicholas, 2005; Li et al., 2007; Miesing et al., 2007; Wu et al., 2007), intent to transfer and learn (Wang et al., 2004; Wang & Nicholas, 2005), capacity to transfer and learn (Bao & Zhao, 2004; Wang et al., 2004; Wang & Nicholas, 2005; Wu et al., 2007), method to transfer and learn (Bao & Zhao, 2004; Yin & Bao, 2006), collaboration (Yin & Bao, 2006; Chen et al., 2007), and shared vision (Li et al., 2007). Intra-organizational factors concentrate on the influences of an organization's characteristics and its management in the process of KM implementation, including organizational culture (Chan & Chau, 2005; Zhang et al., 2005; Xing, 2006; Lin & Lee, 2006; Yeh et al., 2006; Yao et al., 2007; Chang & Lee, 2007; Lai & Lee, 2007; Chang & Li, 2007), management involvement (Tsang, 2002; Yeh et al., 2006; Chan & Chau, 2005), IT infrastructure (Zhang et al., 2005; Lin & Lee, 2006; Yeh et al., 2006; Chang & Li, 2007), organizational policy and strategy such as reward system and formalized KM strategy (Zhang et al., 2005; Yao et al., 2007; Chang & Li, 2007; Li et al., 2007), and team-level constellation, shared awareness, shared understanding and aligned action (Fong et al., 2007). Management involvement here refers to the overall con-

tribution of an organization's management in facilitating KM practices.

Individual factors differ from the other three groups of factors in that they are concerned with the influence of Chinese organizational members' psychological and cognitive characteristics on KM implementation. Ultimately, KM is applied by people. Factors such as value and perception directly affect how people think and act and should therefore be closely related to KM implementation status. Individual factors include value (Newell, 1999), perception (Lin & Lee, 2006), worldview (Miesing et al., 2007), mental model (Newell, 1999), willingness (Chan & Chau, 2005; Ding et al., 2007), self-motivation (Yin & Bao, 2006), self-efficacy (Lee et al., 2006), self-fulfillment (Lee et al., 2006), organizational commitment (Lin, 2007), interpersonal trust (Lin, 2007; Ding et al., 2007), attitude, personality, ability, and social interaction (Ding et al., 2007).

"Firm-level relationship" and "interpersonal trust" are similar to "guanxi" in the Chinese context. "Intent to transfer and learn" is parallel to "willingness" but on different levels: the former affects KM implementation on an inter-organizational level, while the latter on an individual level. "Capacity to transfer and learn" is close to the concept of "absorptive capacity", but more comprehensive than it. Absorptive capacity commonly refers to "a dynamic capability of a firm pertaining to knowledge creation and utilization" (Zahra & George, 2002, p.185), so in theory it does not cover a firm's ability to transfer knowledge. Furthermore, all inter-organizational factors are dynamic, relative, and logically interrelated. For example, the better the relationship between a knowledge-holding and knowledge-receiving firm, the higher the intent for both firms to transfer and learn in a collaborative learning process, and thus the relatively greater the chance the method to be used for facilitating the transferring and learning processes will be effective. In addition, a firm's capacity to transfer and learn will vary, depending on the type, form, and content

Table 3. Non-socio-cultural factors affecting KM implementation

Study	Key factors	Practice focus	Major findings or Key arguments
Newell (1999)	Individual factors: Value Mental model	Knowledge sharing	Transferring Western management knowledge especially tacit management knowledge to China cannot be a linear attempt because the knowledge receivers and knowledge producers do not share similar mental models and socio-cultural contexts.
Tsang (2002)	Organizational factors: Intra-organizational factors: Management involvement Overseeing effort	Knowledge acquisition	Overseeing effort and management involvement are critical factors for foreign parent companies to acquire knowledge from their international joint ventures.
Bao and Zhao (2004)	Organizational factors: Inter-organizational factors: Transaction-specific organization of absorptive capacity, relationship, method, context, and incentive.	Knowledge transfer	Transaction-specific method, context, relationship, and organization of absorptive capacity are positively related to the performance of tacit knowledge absorption, while transaction-specific incentive fails to confirm this positive relationship at the significance level of 0.05. Strictly owner-based hierarchical control hinders the performance of tacit knowledge transfer.
Wang et al. (2004)	Organizational factors: Inter-organizational factors: Willingness and capacity to transfer Capacity and intent to learn	Knowledge transfer	Both the parent company's capacity and willingness to transfer knowledge and the subsidiary company's capacity and intent to learn knowledge substantially affect the results of knowledge transfer from MNC parent to Chinese subsidiary
Wang and Nicholas (2005)	Organizational factors: Inter-organizational factors: Learning intent and ability Trust Collective learning	Knowledge sharing Knowledge creation	Local Chinese managers' learning intent and ability significantly affect knowledge sharing and creation between Hong Kong parent companies and their local contractual joint ventures (CJVs). Process-based trust also plays an important role in the collective learning process between CJVs Hong Kong and Chinese managers.
Chan and Chau, (2005)	Organizational factors: Intra-organizational factors: Organizational culture Upper management support Individual factors: Willingness	KM implementation in general	A KM plan must be realistic and fully supported by upper management. It needs to be implemented under a human-oriented organizational culture, so that employees' willingness to acquire, share, and create knowledge will be stimulated and nurtured, instead of being reinforced.
Zhang et al., (2005)	Organizational factors: Intra-organizational factors: Management involvement Organizational structure Organizational culture Information infrastructure Organizational policy and strategy: Motivation system	Knowledge sharing	The success of knowledge sharing requires a systematic strategic-planning process. An organization's management involvement and characteristics such as organizational policy, structure and culture should all contribute to the sharing process.
Xing, 2006	Organizational factors: Intra-organizational factors: Organizational culture	Knowledge creation	To motivate employees to create knowledge in the Chinese business environment, a company should set up an individual-oriented context, create more opportunities for its employees, and emphasize the role of the mechanism as a whole.
Yin and Bao, 2006	Individual factors: Individual embeddedness Individual motivation Organizational factors: Inter-organizational factors: Recipient collaborativeness Recipient readiness Method comprehensiveness	Tacit knowledge acquisition	The individual embeddedness of foreign expatriates in the joint venture significantly affects tacit knowledge acquisition in local Chinese firms, while recipient collaborativeness, recipient readiness, and method comprehensiveness also play critical roles in the knowledge-acquisition process.

continued on following page

Table 3. Continued

Study	Key factors	Practice focus	Major findings or Key arguments
Lin and Lee, 2006	Organizational factors: Intra-organizational factors: Organizational climate IT support Individual factors: Perceived relative advantage Perceived compatibility Perceived complexity	Knowledge sharing	Chinese decision makers who believe that knowledge sharing is positively related to organizational goals would have strong willingness to facilitate it. Organizational climate significantly affects the perceptions of Chinese decision makers (particularly, perceived relative advantage, compatibility and complexity) regarding knowledge sharing, and thus greatly influences their intention of encouraging knowledge sharing. IT support is not a significant factor facilitating such intention.
Inkpen and Pien, 2006	Organizational factors: Inter-organizational factors: Competitive learning	Knowledge transfer	Competitive learning during the process of knowledge transfer between China and Singapore's alliances could both facilitate and impede the results of the knowledge transfer.
Lee et al., 2006	Individual factors: Self-efficacy Self-fulfillment	Knowledge sharing	Self-fulfillment is the major reason for Chinese customers to share their knowledge on web-based discussion boards, while lack of knowledge self-efficacy appears to be the major obstacle for them to hoard their knowledge.
Yeh et al., 2006	Organizational factors: Intra-organizational factors: Top management support Organizational culture Information technology	KM implementation in general	Top management support, organizational culture, and information technology are crucial KM enablers in China. A dedicated people-oriented KM implementation unit should also be necessary.
Chang and Lee, 2007	Organizational factors: Intra-organizational factors: Organizational culture	KM implementation in general	Organizational culture significantly influences KM implementation within the Chinese context.
Li et al., 2007	Organizational factors: Inter-organizational factors: Shared interaction Trust Shared vision Intra-organizational factors: Location	Knowledge transfer	Subsidiaries located in Finland more actively transfer knowledge than those located in China. There are insignificant yet positive effects of trust and shared vision on knowledge transfer in Chinese subsidiaries than those in Finnish ones.
Miesing et al., 2007	Organizational factors: Inter-organizational factors: Relationship bonds Absorptive capacity Individual factors: Worldviews	KM implementation in general	It is proposed that flexible worldviews, relationship bonds and absorptive capacity were key enablers for knowledge creation, knowledge sharing, and knowledge use within the trans-national context.
Yao et al., 2007	Organizational factors: Intra-organizational factors: Organizational culture High pressure of workload Organizational strategy and policy: Reward system Formal KM strategy Management support	Knowledge sharing	Management support, organizational culture, and an effective formalized KM strategy are necessary for facilitating knowledge sharing in the Chinese enterprises. Lack of time due to high pressure of workload and lack of incentive or rewards become two major organizational barriers for knowledge sharing in the Community as well.
Lai and Lee, 2007	Organizational factors: Intra-organizational factors: Organizational culture	KM implementation in general	Organizational culture was conceptualized in terms of task-goal-accomplished smooth-running and entrepreneurial culture. Entrepreneurial culture has a significant positive effect on knowledge activities, while both task-goal-accomplished and smooth-running cultures have significant negative effects.
Lin, 2007	Individual factors: Organizational commitment Trust	Tacit knowledge sharing	An individual's organizational commitment and trust in co-workers significantly mediate his behaviour of tacit knowledge-sharing.

continued on following page

Table 3. Continued

Study	Key factors	Practice focus	Major findings or Key arguments
Fong et al., 2007	Organizational factors: Intra-organizational factors: Team constellation Shared awareness Shared understanding Aligned action	Knowledge creation	On a team level, "managing team constellation, creating shared awareness, developing shared understanding, and producing aligned action" among team members are important in the process of knowledge creation.
Chang and Li, 2007	Organizational factors: Intra-organizational factors: KM infrastructure (e.g., IT support) Organizational strategy and policy: Formalized KM framework Organizational culture	KM implementation in general	A well-developed KM infrastructure, a thoughtful KM implementation framework, and a healthy organizational culture bridging people with people are essential to facilitate KM implementation. "One key success for implementing KM to an organization is to link it with organizational rules and regulations because they represent the administrative power under which employees must comply" (p.492).
Chen et al., 2007	Organizational factors: Inter-organizational factors: Collaboration	KM implementation in general	To facilitate KM implementation on an inter-firm level, project-level collaboration and firm level linkage should be taken into account.
Ding et al., 2007	Individual factors: Interpersonal trust Willingness Working attitude Working ability Personality Social interaction	Knowledge sharing	On a team level, a team member's working attitude, working ability, personality, and social interaction will affect their interpersonal trust and willingness to share knowledge. Interpersonal trust may also have a mediating effect on willingness to share knowledge.
Li et al., 2007	Organizational factors: Intra-organizational factors: Organizational strategy and policy Formal control	Tacit knowledge acquisition	Firms with greater incentives to acquire tacit knowledge from alliances perceive social and formal control to be equally important. Under the uncertainties brought by China's current transition economy, formal control could be beneficial to incremental innovation.
Wu et al., 2007	Organizational factors: Inter-organizational factors: Absorptive capacity Network embeddedness	Knowledge acquisition	A local Chinese manufacturing firm's absorptive capacity significantly affects its knowledge acquisition in the global manufacturing networks, and its network embeddedness also has a moderating effect on it.

of the knowledge to be transferred and learned, on the intent of both the knowledge-holding and knowledge-receiving firm to transfer and learn, and on the extent to which both firms share long-term vision and goals.

On an intra-organizational level, our analysis of the identified publications supports the notion that upper management support and organizational culture are two critical determinants of the ultimate success of KM (Thong et al., 1996; Nadler & Nadler, 1996; Davenport & Prusak, 1998; Dess & Picken, 2000; Goh, 1998; Murrary, 2002; Holsapple & Joshi, 2002; Chan & Chau, 2005; Liebowitz & Beckman, 1998). When na-

tional cultural factors function as barriers to KM applications, management possesses the ability to help foster a proper environment in their organizations to alleviate such cultural drawbacks (Chang and Li,2007; Li and Scullion,2006; Li et al.,2007; Zhang et al.,2005; Peng et al.,2007; and Hutchings, 2005). In addition, because KM are organizational activities, management should be responsible for planning, implementing, and evaluating these activities (Hedlund, 1994; Hiebeler, 1996; Holsapple & Joshi, 2002), and be prepared to adjust current organizational context as needed and have more direct impacts on employees' daily KM practices (Hiebeler, 1996; Davenport, De

Long, & Beers, 1998; Earl & Scott, 1999; Saint-Onge, 1999; Bukowitz & Williams, 1999; Horibe, 1999; Kouloupoulos & Frappaolo, 1999; Liebowitz, 2000; Zhang et al., 2005). The task of changing an organization's culture is a difficult one (Bate, 1994; Nadler & Tushman, 1997; Carnall, 1997), and one that cannot be accomplished without top management support. The analysis of KM success factors will form the topic of a future publication.

On an individual level, because culture may virtually affect all aspects of the ways in which people interact with each other, some identified individual factors such as worldview and mental model developed through a long (mostly life-time) process of cultural inculcation should be more or less associated with certain socio-cultural factors (e.g., Confucianism), and cannot be easily altered. For example, good guanxi (relationship networks) can help to build up positive interpersonal relationships and enhance the extent of trust and communication quality, thus contributing to successful knowledge sharing (Hutchings & Michailova, 2004; Ramasamy et al., 2006; Fu et al., 2006; Li et al., 2007). Some such as willingness, organizational commitment, and interpersonal trust, however, are intertwined with organiza-

tional culture and management involvement, and can be nurtured or changed over time through organizational means such as reward systems and formalized KM strategies. For example, a healthy organizational culture is one that nurtures willingness and trustworthy relationships among employees, whereas a highly competitive organizational environment is one in which employees are afraid of being replaced which can result in extensive knowledge-hoarding attitudes.

5. A PRELIMINARY TYPOLOGY OF FACTORS FOR CHINESE KM IMPLEMENTATION

Based on our review of the identified publications, a preliminary typology of factors for Chinese KM implementation is proposed in Table 4. This typology offers a framework for organizing all of the identified factors affecting Chinese KM implementation.

In summary, factors affecting Chinese KM implementation can be broadly organized into two groups: socio-cultural and non-socio-cultural factors. Socio-cultural factors can be further

Table 4. A preliminary typology of factors for Chinese KM implementation

Socio-cultural factors	Non-socio-cultural factors	
Policy and institutional factors	*Organizational factors*	
Foreign ownership restrictions Government interventions Institutional gaps China's transition economics	Intra-organizational	Inter-organizational
	Organizational culture **Management involvement** IT infrastructure Organizational policy and strategy Team-level constellation, shared awareness, shared understanding and aligned action	Firm-level relationship Intent to transfer and learn Method to transfer and learn Capacity to transfer and learn Collaboration Shared vision
National cultural factors	***Individual factors***	
Collectivism **Knowledge hoarding** **Guanxi (relationship networks)** **Competitiveness** Confucianism (authority/seniority, modesty, seniority)	Value Self-fulfillment Mental model Interpersonal trust Self-efficacy Willingness Self-motivation Perception Organizational commitment Worldview	

divided into policy and institutional factors and national cultural factors. Non-socio-cultural factors can be divided into organizational and individual factors. Depending on whether KM implementation occurs between or within organizations, organizational factors can be sub-divided into two streams: intra-organizational and inter-organizational factors.

Other specific factors found to strongly influence Chinese KM implementation are: (1) relationship networks and collectivist thinking, (2) competitiveness and knowledge hoarding, (3) management involvement and support, (4) organizational culture that encourages knowledge sharing and learning and that minimizes knowledge hoarding. This is a preliminary typology and more work needs to be done on KM implementation both in the Chinese community and in other countries in order to better identify which factors are the most influential. A larger set of publications to draw from would allow us to make more rigorous assessments of the significance of these factors and may also lead to the identification of additional critical factors.

6. DISCUSSION AND FUTURE RESEARCH

Chronological analysis of KM publications produced a trend analysis of KM awareness that began around 2003 and evolved into rapidly accelerating research and implementation publications shortly thereafter. The impetus for KM's emergence is far from a one-time occurrence and its evolution continues to integrate a variety of fields to devise valid methods to manage social and organizational knowledge.

Analysis of the content of KM publications in China identified a number of socio-cultural and non-sociocultural factors that affected KM implementation in the Chinese context. Knowledge hoarding was identified as one of the key cultural barriers affecting KM implementation.

Thus, there is a strong possibility that many KM strategies to be implemented in Chinese firms will be first undertaken in an environment in which the majority of employees harbour a strong resistance to knowledge sharing and transfer. If, as Nonaka (1994) maintains, knowledge sharing eventually depends on employees' willingness to identify and share the knowledge, then there is no guarantee at least in the Chinese context that Chinese employees will share their knowledge no matter how successful management can be in developing an organizational culture that is conducive to cooperation. It is possible, for example, that not all employees are able to visualize both organizational and individual benefits by sharing their own knowledge with other colleagues. The approach of institutionalizing KM practices could be used to moderate the negative effects of potential knowledge-hoarding attitudes among Chinese employees and initiate knowledge-sharing actions. Once institutionalized, knowledge sharing becomes a "formal requirement". Employees with positive intent to share knowledge receive official rewards and continue their sharing behaviours; those reluctant to share knowledge will be formally informed to collaborate as required. This can be another area for future exploration.

A typology of factors affecting KM implementation in the Chinese community was then developed based on key Chinese KM publication findings. We believe it is one of the first attempts to classify factors affecting KM implementation in a particular country setting, in this case, China. Such a classification scheme may also be applied in other countries or cultural settings as a review scheme to better analyze past research findings with respect to KM implementation, and hopefully guide future research.

Further research is also needed on the influence of management and leadership on Chinese KM implementation. Studies show that leadership could affect subordinates' learning behaviour and organizational sustainability (Beckhard & Pritchard, 1992; Bandura, 1996) and that many traditional leadership styles would be no longer suitable for the development of new learning organizations (Marquardt, 1996; Lundberg, 1996). Many authors (e.g., Bukowitz & Williams, 1999; Earl & Scott, 1999; Horibe, 1999; Koulopoulos & Frappaolo, 1999; Liebowitz, 2000; Saint-Onge, 1999) contend that nowadays knowledge leadership with its role in promoting a positive cultural orientation toward knowledge sharing and acquisition is an essential element for organizations to perform competitively (Davenport et al., 1998; Brown & Duguid, 2000). Finally, our own future work will be on identifying KM success factors.

REFERENCES

Allee, V. (1997). *The knowledge evolution: Expanding organizational intelligence.* Boston: Butterworth-Heinemann.

Ardichvili, A., Maurer, M., Li, W., Wentling, T., & Stuedemann, R. (2006). Cultural influences on knowledge sharing through online communities of practice. *Journal of Knowledge Management, 10*(1), 94–107. doi:10.1108/13673270610650139

Argyris, C., & Schön, D. (1978). *Organizational learning: A theory of action perspective.* Reading, MA: Addison Wesley.

Asian Economic News. (2005). Chinese economy to surpass Japan by 2020: World bank. Retrieved February 11, 2009, from http://findarticles.com/p/articles/mi_m0WDP/is_/ ai_n15801767

Assimakopoulos, D., & Yan, J. (2006). Sources of knowledge acquisition for Chinese software engineers. *R & D Management, 36*(1), 97–106. doi:10.1111/j.1467-9310.2005.00418.x

Baark, E. (2007). Knowledge and innovation in China: Historical legacies and emerging institutions. *Asia Pacific Business Review, 13*(3), 337–356. doi:10.1080/13602380701291917

Bandura, A. (1996). *Social foundations of thought and action: a social cognitive theory.* Englewood Cliffs, NJ: Prentice-Hall.

Bao, Y., & Zhao, S. (2004). MICRO contracting for tacit knowledge – a study of contractual arrangements in international technology transfer. *Problems and Perspectives in Management, 2,* 279–303.

Barsky, N., & Marchant, G. (2000). The most valuable resource: measuring and managing intellectual capital. *Strategic Finance Magazine, 81*(8), 58–62.

Bass, B. (1985). *Leadership and performance beyond expectations.* New York: The Free Press.

Bassi, L., & Van Buren, M. (1999). Valuing investments in intellectual capital. *International Journal of Technology Management, 18*(5), 414–432. doi:10.1504/IJTM.1999.002779

Bate, P. (1994). *Strategic for culture change.* Oxford, UK: Butterworth-Heinemann.

Becker, S., & Whisler, T. (1967). The innovative organization: A selective review of current theory and research. *The Journal of Business, 40,* 462–469. doi:10.1086/295011

Beckhard, R., & Pritchard, P. (1992). *Changing the essence: the art of creating and leading fundamental change in organizations.* San Francisco: Jossey-Bass.

Berrell, M., Wrathall, J., & Wright, P. (2001). A model for Chinese management education: Adapting the case study method to transfer management knowledge. *Cross Cultural Management, 8*(1), 28–44. doi:10.1108/13527600110797182

Bierly, P., & Chakrabarti, A. (1999). Generic knowledge strategies in the U.S. pharmaceutical industry. In M. H. Zack (Ed.), *Knowledge and strategy.* Boston: Butterworth-Heinemann.

Birkinshaw, J., & Hood, N. (1998). Multinational subsidiary evolution: Capability and charter change in foreign-owned subsidiary companies. *Academy of Management Review, 23*(4), 773–795. doi:10.2307/259062

Birkinshaw, J., Hood, N., & Jonsson, S. (1998). Building firm-specific advantages in multinational corporations: the role of subsidiary initiative. *Strategic Management Journal, 19*(3), 221–242. doi:10.1002/(SICI)1097-0266(199803)19:3<221::AID-SMJ948>3.0.CO;2-P

Branine, M. (1996). Observations on training and management development in the People's Republic of China. *Management Development in China, 25*(1), 25–39.

Brown, J. S., & Duguid, P. (1991). Organizational learning and communities of practice: Toward a unified view of working, learning, and innovation. *Organization Science, 2*(1), 40–57. doi:10.1287/orsc.2.1.40

Brown, J. S., & Duguid, P. (2000). *The social life of information*. Boston: Harvard Business School Press.

Bruton, G. D., Dess, G. G., & Janney, J. J. (2007). Knowledge management in technology-focused firms in emerging economics: Caveats on capabilities, networks, and real options. *Asia Pacific Journal of Management, 24*(2), 115–130. doi:10.1007/s10490-006-9023-2

Buckley, P. J., Clegg, J., & Tan, H. (2004). Knowledge transfer to China: Policy lesions from foreign affiliates. *Transnational Corporations, 13*(1), 31–72.

Buckman, R. (1999). Collaborative knowledge. *Human Resource Planning, 22*(1), 22–23.

Bukowitz, W., & Petrash, G. (1997). Visualizing, measuring and managing knowledge. *Research Technology Management, 40*(4), 24–31.

Bukowitz, W. R., & Williams, R. L. (1999). *The knowledge management field book*. Upper Saddle River, NJ: Prentice-Hall.

Burrows, G. R., Drummond, D. L., & Martinsons, M. G. (2005). To understand KM in China. *Communications of the ACM, 48*(4), 73–76. doi:10.1145/1053291.1053322

Cai, J., Gao, J., Wang, H. Y., & Bai, C. L. (2006). Factorings effecting core competency of knowledge organization in China. [Science and Technology]. *Journal of Tsinghua University, 46*(s1), 970–974.

Carnall, C. (1997). *Strategic change*. Boston: Butterworth-Heinmann.

Carroll, J. (1967). A note on departmental autonomy conflict. *Administrative Science Quarterly, 14*, 507–522.

Chan, I., & Chau, P. Y. K. (2005). Why knowledge management fails – lessons from a case study. In M. Jennex (Ed.), *Case studies in knowledge management*. Hershey, PA: Idea Group Publishing.

Chang, S.-C., & Lee, M.-S. (2007). The effects of organizational culture and knowledge management mechanisms on organizational innovation: an empirical study in Taiwan. *Business Review (Federal Reserve Bank of Philadelphia), 7*(1), 295–301.

Chang, W.-C., & Li, S.-T. (2007). Fostering knowledge management deployment in R&D workspaces: a five-stage approach. *R & D Management, 37*(5), 479–493. doi:10.1111/j.1467-9310.2007.00484.x

Chen, J., Tong, L., & Ngai, E. W. T. (2007). Inter-organizational knowledge management in complex products and systems: challenges and an exploratory framework. *Journal of Technology Management in China, 2*(2), 134–144. doi:10.1108/17468770710756077

Chen, S. C., Yang, C. C., Lin, W. T., Yeh, T. M., & Lin, Y. S. (2007). Construction of key model for knowledge management system using AHP-QFD for semiconductor industry in Taiwan. *Journal of Manufacturing Technology Management, 18*(5), 576–598. doi:10.1108/17410380710752671

Child, J., & Tse, D. (2001). China's transition and its implications for international business. *Journal of International Business Studies, 32,* 5–21. doi:10.1057/palgrave.jibs.8490935

Choo, C. W. (2006). *The knowing organization: how organizations use information to construct meaning, create knowledge, and make decisions.* New York: Oxford University Press.

Chow, C. W., Deng, F. J., & Ho, J. L. (2000). The openness of knowledge sharing within organizations: a comparative study of the United States and the People's Republic of China. *Journal of Management Accounting Research, 12,* 65–95. doi:10.2308/jmar.2000.12.1.65

Contractor, F., & Lorange, P. (1988). *Cooperative strategies in international business.* Lexington, MA: Lexington Books.

Davenport, T. H. (1998). Enterprise systems. *Harvard Business Review,* (July-August): 121.

Davenport, T. H., De Long, D. W., & Beers, M. C. (1998). Successful knowledge management projects. *Sloan Management Review, 39*(2), 10–18.

Davenport, T. H., Jarvenpaa, S. L., & Beers, M. C. (1996). Improving knowledge work processes. *Sloan Management Review, 39*(2), 43–57.

Davenport, T. H., & Prusak, L. (1998). *Working knowledge: how organizations know what they know.* Cambridge, MA: Harvard Business School Press.

De Long, D. (1997). *Building the knowledge-based organization: How culture drives knowledge behavior. Working paper for the center for business innovation.* London: Ernst & Young LLP.

Dess, G., & Picken, J. (2000). Changing roles, leadership in the 21st century. *Organizational Dynamics, 28*(3), 18–34. doi:10.1016/S0090-2616(00)88447-8

Ding, Z., Ng, F., & Cai, Q. (2007). Personal constructs affecting interpersonal trust and willingness to share knowledge between architects in project design teams. *Construction Management and Economics, 25,* 937–950. doi:10.1080/01446190701468828

Drucker, P. F. (1995). *Managing in time of great change.* New York: Truman Talley Books.

Dyer, J. H., & Singh, H. (1998). The relational view: Cooperative strategy and sources of interorganizational competitive advantage. *Academy of Management Review, 23,* 660–679. doi:10.2307/259056

Earl, M. J., & Scott, I. A. (1999). What is a chief knowledge officer? *Sloan Management Review, 40*(2), 29–38.

Fong, P. S.-W., Hills, M. J., & Hayles, C. S. (2007). Dynamic knowledge creation through value management teams. *Journal of Management Engineering, 23*(1), 40–49. doi:10.1061/(ASCE)0742-597X(2007)23:1(40)

Fu, P. P., Tsui, A. S., & Dess, G. G. (2006). The dynamics of Guanxi in Chinese high-tech firms: Implications for knowledge management and decision making. *Management International Review, 46*(3), 277–305. doi:10.1007/s11575-006-0048-z

Galunic, D. C., & Rodan, S. A. (1998). Resource recombinations in the firm: Knowledge structures and the potential for Schumpeterian innovation. *Strategic Management Journal, 19*(12), 1193–1201. doi:10.1002/(SICI)1097-0266(1998120)19:12<1193::AID-SMJ5>3.0.CO;2-F

Geng, Q., Townley, C., Huang, K., & Zhang, J. (2005). Comparative knowledge management: a pilot study of Chinese and American universities. *Journal of the American Society for Information Science and Technology, 56*(10), 1031–1044. doi:10.1002/asi.20194

Getzels, J. W., & Guba, E. G. (1957). Social behavior and the administrative process. *The School Review, 65*, 423–444. doi:10.1086/442411

Ghoshal, S., & Bartlett, C. (1990). The multinational corporation as an interorganizational network. *Academy of Management Review, 15*(4), 603–625. doi:10.2307/258684

Goh, S. (1998). Towards a learning organization: The strategic building blocks. *Advanced Management Journal, 63*(2), 15–18.

Grant, R. M. (1996). Toward a knowledge-based theory of the firm. *Strategic Management Journal, 17*, 109–122. doi:10.1002/(SICI)1097-0266(199602)17:2<109::AID-SMJ796>3.0.CO;2-P

Guthrie, D. (1998). The declining significance of guanxi in China's economic transition. *The China Quarterly, 3*, 254–282. doi:10.1017/S0305741000002034

Hagedoorn, J. (1993). Understanding the rationale of strategic technology partnering: Interorganizational modes of cooperation and sectoral differences. *Strategic Management Journal, 14*, 371–385. doi:10.1002/smj.4250140505

Hall, E. T. (1976). *Beyond culture*. NY: Anchor Press.

Han, W., & Ji, S. (2006). Empirical study on the effect of knowledge creation at the individual and group levels. [Science and Technology]. *Journal of Tsinghua University, 46*(s1), 942–948.

Harrigan, K. R. (1988). Strategic alliances and partner asymmetries. *Management International Review, 28*, 53–72.

Hendriks, P. (1999). Why share knowledge? The influence of ICT on the motivation for knowledge sharing. *Knowledge and Process Management, 6*(2), 91–100. doi:10.1002/(SICI)1099-1441(199906)6:2<91::AID-KPM54>3.0.CO;2-M

Hofstede, G. (1994). *Cultures and organizations: Software of the mind-intercultural cooperation and its importance for survival*. London: Harper-Collins.

Holsapple, C., & Joshi, K. D. (2000). An investigation of factors that influence the management of knowledge in organizations. *The Journal of Strategic Information Systems, 9*, 235–261. doi:10.1016/S0963-8687(00)00046-9

Holsapple, C. W., & Joshi, K. D. (2002). Knowledge management: A threefold framework. *The Information Society, 18*, 47–64. doi:10.1080/01972240252818225

Hong, J. F. L., Easterby-Smith, M., & Snell, R. S. (2006). Transferring organizational learning systems to Japanese subsidiaries in China. *Journal of Management Studies, 43*(5), 1027–1058. doi:10.1111/j.1467-6486.2006.00628.x

Horibe, F. (1999). *Managing knowledge workers: New skills and attitudes to unlock the intellectual capital in your organization*. New York: John Wiley.

Hutchings, K. (2005). Examining the impacts of institutional change on knowledge sharing and management learning in the PRC. *Thunderbird International Business Review, 47*(4), 447–468. doi:10.1002/tie.20062

Hutchings, K., & Michailova, S. (2004). Facilitating knowledge sharing in Russian and Chinese subsidiaries: The role of personal networks and group membership. *Journal of Knowledge Management, 8*(2), 84–94. doi:10.1108/13673270410529136

Inkpen, A. C., & Pien, W. (2006). An examination of collaboration and knowledge transfer: China-Singapore Suzhou industrial park. *Journal of Management Studies*, *43*(4), 779–811. doi:10.1111/j.1467-6486.2006.00611.x

Jin, Z. (1999). Organizational innovation and virtual institutes. *Journal of Knowledge Management*, *3*(1), 75–83. doi:10.1108/13673279910259420

Ju, T. L., Li, C.-Y., & Lee, T.-S. (2006). A contingency model for knowledge management capability and innovation. *Industrial Management & Data Systems*, *106*(6), 855–877. doi:10.1108/02635570610671524

Kao, H., Kao, P. H., & Mazzuchi, T. A. (2006). Taiwanese executive practice knowledge management in mainland China and Southeast Asia (Malaysia). *The Journal of Information and Knowledge Management Systems*, *36*(3), 341–352.

Kim, C. W., & Mauborgne, R. (1997). Fair process: managing in the knowledge economy. *Harvard Business Review*, (July-August): 65–75.

Kogut, B. (1988). Joint ventures: Theoretical and empirical perspectives. *Strategic Management Journal*, *9*, 319–332. doi:10.1002/smj.4250090403

Kogut, B., & Zander, U. (1992). Knowledge of the firm, combinative capabilities and the replication of technology. *Organization Science*, *3*(3), 383–397. doi:10.1287/orsc.3.3.383

Koulopoulos, T. M., & Frappaolo, C. (1999). *Smart things to know about knowledge management*. New York: John Wiley.

Kusunoki, K., Nonaka, I., & Nagata, A. (1998). Organizational capabilities in product development of Japanese firms: A conceptual framework and empirical findings. *Organization Science*, *9*(6), 699–718. doi:10.1287/orsc.9.6.699

Lai, I. L. A. (2005). Knowledge management for Chinese medicines: A conceptual model. *Information Management & Computer Security*, *13*(3), 244–255. doi:10.1108/09685220510602059

Lai, M.-F., & Lee, G.-G. (2007). Relationships of organizational culture toward knowledge activities. *Business Process Management Journal*, *13*(2), 306–322. doi:10.1108/14637150710740518

Lau, C.-M., Lu, Y., Makino, S., Chen, X., & Yeh, R.-S. (2002). Knowledge management of high-tech firms. In A. S. Tsui & C. M. Lau (Eds.), *Management of enterprises in People's Republic of China* (pp. 183-210). Boston: Kluwer Academic Publishers.

Lee, M. K. O., Cheung, C. M. K., Lim, K. H., & Sia, C. L. (2006). Understanding customer knowledge sharing in web-based discussion boards: An exploratory study. *Internet Research*, *16*(3), 289–303. doi:10.1108/10662240610673709

Levinson, N. S., & Asahi, M. (1995). Cross-national alliances and interorganizational learning. *Organizational Dynamics*, *24*, 50–63. doi:10.1016/0090-2616(95)90071-3

Levitt, B., & March, J. G. (1988). Organizational learning. *Annual Review of Sociology*, *14*, 319–340. doi:10.1146/annurev.so.14.080188.001535

Li, J. (2003). U.S. and Chinese cultural beliefs about learning. *Journal of Education & Psychology*, *95*(2), 258–267. doi:10.1037/0022-0663.95.2.258

Li, L., Barner-Rasmussen, W., & Björkman, I. (2007). What difference does the location make? A social capital perspective on transfer of knowledge from multinational corporation subsidiaries located in China and Finland. *Asia Pacific Business Review*, *13*(2), 233–249. doi:10.1080/13602380601133185

Li, S., & Scullion, H. (2006). Bridging the distance: Managing cross-border knowledge holders. *Asia Pacific Journal of Management, 23*, 71–92. doi:10.1007/s10490-006-6116-x

Li, W., Ardichvili, A., Maurer, M., Wentling, T., & Stuedemann, R. (2007). Impact of Chinese culture values on knowledge sharing through online communities of practice. *International Journal of Knowledge Management, 3*(3), 46–59.

Li, Y., Liu, Y., Li, M. F., & Wu, H. B. (2007). Transformational offshore outsourcing: empirical evidence from alliances in China. *Journal of Operations Management.* doi:.doi:10.1016/j.jom.2007.02.011

Liebowitz, J. (2000). *Building organizational intelligence: A knowledge management primer.* Boca Raton, FL: CRC Press.

Liebowitz, J., & Beckman, T. (1998). *Knowledge organizations: What every manager should know.* Boca Raton, FL: St. Luice Press.

Lien, B. Y. H., Hung, R. Y., & McLean, G. N. (2007). Organizational learning as an organization development intervention in six high-technology firms in Taiwan: An exploratory case study. *Human Resource Development Quarterly, 18*(2), 211–228. doi:10.1002/hrdq.1200

Lin, C.-P. (2007). To share or not to share, modeling tacit knowledge sharing, its mediators and antecedents. *Journal of Business Ethics, 70*, 411–428. doi:10.1007/s10551-006-9119-0

Lin, H.-F., & Lee, G.-G. (2006). Effects of sociotechnical factors on organizational intention to encourage knowledge sharing. *Management Decision, 44*(1), 74–88. doi:10.1108/00251740610641472

Lin, L., & Kwok, L. (2006). Challenges to KM at Hewlett Packard China. *Knowledge Management Review, 9*(1), 20–23.

Liu, C.-C. (2006). Modeling the transfer of technology to Taiwan from China. *International Research Journal of Finance and Economics, 7*, 48–66.

Liu, Y. W., Pucel, D. J., & Bartlett, K. R. (2006). Knowledge transfer practices in multinational corporations in China's information technology industry. *Human Resource Development International, 9*(4), 529–552. doi:10.1080/13678860601032635

Lundberg, C. C. (1996). Managing in a culture that values learning. In S. A. Cavaleri & D. S. Fearson (Eds.), *Managing in organizations that learn.* Cambridge, MA: Blackwell.

Luo, Y. (1999). Dimensions of knowledge: comparing Asian and Western MNEs in China. *Asia Pacific Journal of Management, 16*(1), 75–93. doi:10.1023/A:1015410219287

March, J. G. (1991). Exploration and exploitation in organization learning. *Organization Science, 2*, 71–87. doi:10.1287/orsc.2.1.71

Marquardt, J. (1996). *Building the learning organization.* New York: McGraw Hill.

Martinsons, M. G., & Martinsons, A. B. (1996). Conquering cultural constraints to cultivate Chinese management creativity and innovation. *Journal of Management Development, 15*(9), 18–35. doi:10.1108/02621719610146239

McEvily, B., & Zaheer, A. (1999). Bridging ties: A source of firm heterogeneity in competitive capabilities. *Strategic Management Journal, 20*, 1133–1156. doi:10.1002/(SICI)1097-0266(199912)20:12<1133::AID-SMJ74>3.0.CO;2-7

Mead, R. (1994). *International management.* Oxford, UK: Blackwell.

Mei, S., & Nie, M. (2007). Relationship between knowledge sharing, knowledge characteristics, absorptive capacity and innovation: An empirical study of Wuhan optoelectronic cluster. *Business Review (Federal Reserve Bank of Philadelphia)*, 7(2), 154–160.

Michailova, S., & Hutchings, K. (2006). National cultural influences on knowledge sharing: a comparison of China and Russia. *Journal of Management Studies*, 43(3), 383–405. doi:10.1111/j.1467-6486.2006.00595.x

Miesing, P., Kriger, M. P., & Slough, N. (2007). Towards a model of effective knowledge transfer within transnationals: The case of Chinese foreign invested enterprises. *The Journal of Technology Transfer*, 32, 109–122. doi:10.1007/s10961-006-9006-y

Miner, A. S., & Mezias, S. J. (1996). Ugly duckling no more: Pasts and futures of organizational learning research. *Organization Science*, 7(1), 88–99. doi:10.1287/orsc.7.1.88

Morgan, N. A., Zou, S., Vorhies, D. W., & Katsikeas, C. S. (2003). Experiential and informational knowledge, architectural marketing capabilities, and the adaptive performance of export ventures: a cross-national study. *Decision Sciences*, 34(2), 287–321. doi:10.1111/1540-5915.02375

Mullen, T. P., & Lyles, M. A. (1993). Toward improving management development's contribution to organizational learning. *Human Resource Planning*, 16(2), 35–49.

Murray, P. (2002). Knowledge management as a sustained competitive advantage. *Ivey Business Journal*, 66(4), 71–76.

Nadler, D., & Nadler, M. (1996). *Champions of change*. San Francisco: Jossey-Bass.

Nadler, D., & Tushman, M. (1997). *Competing by design*. New York: Oxford University Press.

Nahapiet, J., & Ghoshal, S. (1998). Social capital, intellectual capital, and the organizational advantage. *Academy of Management Review*, 23, 242–266. doi:10.2307/259373

Nelson, K., & Cooprider, J. (1996). The contribution of shared knowledge to IS group performance. *MIS Quarterly*, 20(4), 409–429. doi:10.2307/249562

Newell, S. (1999). The transfer of management knowledge to China: Building learning communities rather than translating Western textbooks? *Education + Training, 41*(6/7), 286-293.

Nonaka, I. (1994). A dynamic theory of organizational knowledge creation. *Organization Science*, 5(1), 14–37. doi:10.1287/orsc.5.1.14

Osborn, R. N., & Hagedoorn, J. (1997). The institutionalization and evolutionary dynamics of interorganizational alliances and networks. *Academy of Management Journal*, 40, 261–278. doi:10.2307/256883

Pablos, P. O. D. (2002). Knowledge management and organizational learning: typologies of knowledge strategies in the Spanish manufacturing industry from 1995 to 1999. *Journal of Knowledge Management*, 6(1), 52–62. doi:10.1108/13673270210417691

Paulson, D. S. (2002). *Competitive business, caring business: An integral business perspective for the 21st century*. New York: Paraview Press.

Pearson, T. (1999). Measurements and the knowledge revolution. *Quality Progress*, 32(9), 31–37.

Peng, J., Li-Hua, R., & Moffett, S. (2007). Trend of knowledge management in China: Challenges and opportunities. *Journal of Technology Management in China*, 2(3), 198–211. doi:10.1108/17468770710825142

Peng, M. W. (2003). Institutional transitions and strategic choices. *Academy of Management Review*, 28(2), 275–296.

Ramasamy, B., Goh, K. W., & Yeung, M. C. H. (2006). Is Guanxi (relationship) a bridge to knowledge transfer? *Journal of Business Research, 59,* 130–139. doi:10.1016/j.jbusres.2005.04.001

Reed, R., & DeFillippi, R. J. (1990). Causal Ambiguity, barriers to imitation, and sustainable competitive advantage. *Academy of Management Review, 15*(1), 88–102. doi:10.2307/258107

Rodan, S., & Galunic, C. (2004). More than network structure: How knowledge heterogeneity influences managerial performance and innovativeness. *Strategic Management Journal, 25,* 541–562. doi:10.1002/smj.398

Saint-Onge, H. (1999). *Developing an effective knowledge strategy.* Paper presented at Chief Learning Officer Conference, Boston.

Schein, E. H. (1985). *Organizational culture and leadership: A dynamic view.* San Francisco: Jossey-Bass.

Schick, S. (2002). Bleak future painted for KM projects. *Computing Canada, 28*(9), 1–4.

Si, S., & Bruton, G. (1999). Knowledge transfer in international joint ventures in transitional economies: The China experience. *The Academy of Management Executive, 13*(1), 83–90.

Standfield, K. (2002). *Intangible management: tools for solving the accounting and management crisis.* Boston: Academic Press.

Sullivan, P. H. (2000). *Value-driven intellectual capital: how to convert intangible corporate assets into market value.* New York: Wiley.

Szulanski, G. (1996). Exploring internal stickness: Impediments to the transfer of best practice within the firm. *Strategic Management Journal, 17,* 27–43.

Therin, F. (2002). Organizational learning and innovation in high-tech small firms. In *Proceedings of the 36th Hawaii International Conference on System Sciences,* Hawaii.

Thong, J., Yap, C., & Raman, K. (1996). Top management support, external expertise and information systems implementation in small business. *Information Systems Research, 7*(2), 248–267. doi:10.1287/isre.7.2.248

Tsang, E. W. K. (2002). Acquisition knowledge by foreign partners for international joint ventures in a transition economy: Learning-by-doing and learning myopia. *Strategic Management Journal, 23*(9), 835–854. doi:10.1002/smj.251

Tsui, A. S., & Farh, J. L. (1997). Where guanxi matters. *Work and Occupations, 24,* 56–79. doi:10.1177/0730888497024001005

Tyre, M. J., & Von Hippel, E. (1997). The situated nature of adaptive learning in organizations. *Organization Science, 8,* 71–83. doi:10.1287/orsc.8.1.71

Uzzi, B. (1999). Embeddedness in the making of financial capital: How social relations and networks benefit firms seeking financing. *American Sociological Review, 64,* 481–505. doi:10.2307/2657252

Van de Ven, A. H., Polley, D., Garud, R., & Venkatraman, S. (1999). *The innovation journey.* New York: Oxford University Press.

Voelpel, S. C., & Han, Z. (2005). Managing knowledge sharing in China: The case of Siemens ShareNet. *Journal of Knowledge Management, 9*(3), 51–63. doi:10.1108/13673270510602764

Wang, P., Wong, T. W., & Koh, C. P. (2004). An integrated model of knowledge transfer from MNC parent to China subsidiary. *Journal of World Business, 39,* 168–182. doi:10.1016/j.jwb.2003.08.009

Wang, X. F., & Lihua, R. (2006). Examining knowledge management factors in the creation of new city. *Journal of Technology Management in China, 1*(3), 243–261. doi:10.1108/17468770610704921

Wang, Y., & Nicholas, S. (2005). Knowledge transfer, knowledge replication, and learning in non-equity alliances: Operating contractual joint ventures in China. *Management International Review, 45*(1), 99–118.

Warner, M. (1993). Human resource management with Chinese characteristics. *International Journal of Human Resource Management, 4*, 45–65.

Weir, D., & Hutchings, K. (2005). Cultural embeddedness and contextual constraints: knowledge sharing in Chinese and Arab cultures. *Knowledge and Process Management, 12*(2), 89–98. doi:10.1002/kpm.222

Wiig, K. M. (1995). *Knowledge management methods. Practical approaches to managing knowledge.* Arlington, TX: Schema Press.

Wiig, K. M. (1997). Knowledge management: Where did it come from and where will it go? *Expert Systems with Applications, 13*(1), 1–14. doi:10.1016/S0957-4174(97)00018-3

Wiig, K. M. (1999). What future knowledge management users may expect. *Journal of Knowledge Management, 3*(2), 155–166. doi:10.1108/13673279910275611

Wiig, K. M., de Hoog, R., & van der Spek, R. (1997). Supporting knowledge management: A selection of methods and techniques. *Expert Systems with Applications, 13*(1), 15–27. doi:10.1016/S0957-4174(97)00019-5

Wong, Y.-Y., Maher, T. E., & Luk, S. T. K. (2002). The hesitant transfer of strategic management knowledge to international joint ventures in China: Greater willingness seems likely in the future. *Management Research News, 25*(1), 1–15. doi:10.1108/01409170210782981

Wu, X. B., Liu, X. F., & Du, J. (2007). Local firm's knowledge acquisition in the global manufacturing network: Evidence from Chinese samples. *International Journal of Innovation and Technology Management, 4*(3), 267–281. doi:10.1142/S0219877007001119

Xing, W. (2006). Knowledge capitalism put into practice as an operational mechanism. *Journal of Knowledge Management, 10*(1), 119–130. doi:10.1108/13673270610650157

Yan, Y., & Zhang, J. A. (2003). Performance of high-tech firms' resource and capability-based development: Knowledge acquisition, organizational utilization and management involvement. *International Journal of Business Studies, 11*(1), 45–67.

Yang, J. (2005). Knowledge integration and innovation: Securing new product advantage in high technology industry. *The Journal of High Technology Management Research, 16*, 121–135. doi:10.1016/j.hitech.2005.06.007

Yao, L. J., Kam, T. H. Y., & Chan, S. H. (2007). Knowledge sharing in Asian public administration sector: The case of Hong Kong. *Journal of Enterprise Information Management, 20*(1), 51–69. doi:10.1108/17410390710717138

Yeh, Y. J., Lai, S. Q., & Ho, C. T. (2006). Knowledge management enablers: a case study. *Industrial Management & Data Systems, 106*(6), 793–810. doi:10.1108/02635570610671489

Yin, E., & Bao, Y. (2006). The acquisition of tacit knowledge in China: an empirical analysis of the 'supplier-side individual level' and 'recipient-side' factors. *Management International Review, 46*(3), 327–348. doi:10.1007/s11575-006-0050-5

Zander, U., & Kogut, B. (1995). Knowledge and the speed of transfer and imitation of organizational capabilities: an empirical test. *Organization Science, 6*, 76–92. doi:10.1287/orsc.6.1.76

Zhang, L., Tian, Y., & Li, P. (2005). Organizational knowledge sharing based on the ERP implementation of Yongxin Paper Co., Ltd. In M. Jennex (Ed.), *Case studies in knowledge management.* Hershey, PA: Idea Group Publishing.

Zhang, L., Tian, Y., & Qi, Z. (2006). Impact of organizational memory on organizational performance: an empirical study. *Business Review (Federal Reserve Bank of Philadelphia), 5*(1), 227–232.

Zhang, Q., Lim, J. S., & Cao, M. (2004). Innovation-driven learning in new product development: A conceptual model. *Industrial Management & Data Systems, 104*(3), 252–261. doi:10.1108/02635570410525799

Zhang, Q. P., Chintakovid, T., & Sun, X. N. (2007). Saving face or sharing personal information? A cross-cultural study on knowledge sharing. *Journal of Information & Knowledge Management, 5*(1), 73–79. doi:10.1142/S0219649206001335

This work was previously published in International Journal of Knowledge Management, Volume 6, Issue 1, edited by Murray E. Jennex, pp. 1-22, copyright 2010 by IGI Publishing (an imprint of IGI Global).

Chapter 2
Supporting Knowledge Evaluation to Increase Quality in Electronic Knowledge Repositories

Lena Aggestam
University of Skövde, Sweden

Per Backlund
University of Skövde, Sweden

Anne Persson
University of Skövde, Sweden

ABSTRACT

Knowledge forms an important asset in modern organizations. In order to gain and sustain competitive advantage knowledge has to be managed. One aspect of this is to use Electronic Knowledge Repositories (EKR) to enhance knowledge sharing, reuse and learning. The success of an EKR is dependent on the quality of its content. For knowledge to be stored in an EKR, it has to be captured. One crucial part of the capture process is to evaluate whether the identified knowledge should be incorporated in the EKR or not. Therefore, to increase quality in an EKR, the evaluation stage of the capture process must be successfully carried out. Based on an interpretive field study and an extensive literature review, this paper identifies and characterizes Critical Success Factors (CSF) in the evaluation stage and presents guidance aiming to support implementation of the evaluation stage with the purpose to increase the quality of an EKR. In particular, the guidance supports the decision whether identified knowledge should be stored or not and it highlights the importance of performing evaluation addressing correctness, relevance, protection and redundancy. The characterization of the capture process contributes mainly to KM theory, and the guidance to KM practice.

DOI: 10.4018/978-1-4666-0035-5.ch002

1. INTRODUCTION

To gain and sustain competitive advantage organizations must manage their knowledge resources, i.e. they need a conscious strategy for Knowledge Management (KM). Successful KM that contributes to improved organizational effectiveness requires that the appropriate knowledge is provided to those that need it when it is needed (Jennex, Smolnik & Croasdell, 2007). One way to do this is to implement Electronic Knowledge Repositories (EKR), a key form of KM (Kankanhalli, Tan & Wei, 2005). EKR prevent knowledge from being lost when a specific employee leaves the organization and, furthermore, according to Aggestam (2006a), they are a feasible start for an organization that desires to achieve maturity as a Learning Organization (LO).

The success of an EKR is dependent on whether or not the repository is actually used. For a knowledge repository to be used the users must perceive that its usage will greatly enhance their performance at work (Sharma & Bock, 2005). Hence, *what* is stored in the repository is critical for success. In order for knowledge to be stored in the repository it needs to be captured. Thus, to be able to manage knowledge, the ability to capture it is a key aspect (Matsumoto, Stapleton, Glass and Thorpe, 2005). Furthermore, according to Jennex et al. (2007), capturing the *right* knowledge is necessary for KM success. This is also corroborated by Sharma and Bock (2005) who manifest that quality, for example reliability and relevance, in the knowledge repository has to be high for knowledge re-use to take place. Hence, we consider the process of capturing the "right" knowledge to be critical for the success of an EKR. One problem related to capturing knowledge is a lack of awareness of the complex issues related to an effective knowledge capture process and the benefits achieved through it (Hari, Egbu & Kumar, 2005). Also, there is a lack of systematic support for implementing KM in organizations

(see Wong & Aspinwall, 2004). This paper aims to decrease these lacks.

Knowledge capture can be defined as a two stage process involving 1) the *identification* of knowledge to be captured, and 2) the *evaluation* of identified knowledge for possible storage in the EKR. Storing all identified knowledge causes information overflow and low quality in the EKR resulting in problems to find the required knowledge. "It's difficult to make people remember that they don't need to store everything." as put by an HR manager in a large Swedish company. Hence, evaluation of identified knowledge is crucial when capturing the "right" knowledge. It is well known in the KM literature that too many KM projects fail. From the perspective of what we store in the EKR is critical for success, it is clear how complicated it must be to perform the evaluation stage efficiently.

Storing the "right" knowledge requires knowledge and understanding about what conditions those need to be met in the evaluation stage of the capture process, but here we have a problematic gap in the literature. In the literature, the topic of Success Factors (SF) in knowledge management work is frequently discussed, for example, by Davenport and Prusak (1998), Hung et al. (2005), Montequin (2006), and Storey and Barnett (2000). We can also find studies identifying SF with regard to employee contribution of knowledge to EKR (e.g., Kankanhalli et al., 2005; Jan & Jeffres, 2006). However, since employee contribution of knowledge is only one aspect of the knowledge capture process, more research is needed to identify and understand SF for this important knowledge process, i.e. here is a problematic gap. With the purpose to decrease this gap and increase the body of knowledge concerning conditions in the evaluation stage as well to provide support in this stage of the capture process, the goal of this paper is twofold: *1) To define and characterize Critical Success Factors (CSF) for the evaluation stage of the capture process and, based on these, 2) present guidance for systematic implementation of the evaluation stage with the purpose to increase the quality of an EKR.* To achieve the paper's goal we carried out a qualitative analysis including a theoretical analysis and an interpretive field study. This research work resulted in two contributions, one to KM theory and one to KM practice:

- *A description of CSF in the evaluation stage of the capture process.* This contribution extends the existing KM theory by describing success factors for a specific stage in the capture process. By doing so, the factors can be more detailed and concrete described which also enhances practical use. This is mainly a contribution to KM theory and hence the main target group is the KM research community.
- *Guidance for the evaluation stage.* This is a contribution to KM practice and hence the main target groups are project leaders for a KM implementation project aiming to result in an EKR and employees responsible for evaluating whether identified knowledge should be stored or not.

We want to emphasise that capturing the "right" knowledge is not enough for ensuring success. The way in which the captured knowledge is packaged, stored and made accessible to the users is also crucial, since it must be possible to find the knowledge when needed. However, failure in capturing the "right" knowledge can never be compensated by successful packaging. Hence, this paper is focused on the evaluation stage in the capture process. Furthermore, the way of working, that was adopted when developing the guidance, could be applicable when developing implementation support for other parts of the KM process.

2. POINTS OF DEPARTURE

The setting of the paper is Knowledge Management (KM), or more precisely Electronic Knowledge Repositories (EKR). Based on an extensive literature review, we in this section define relevant concepts and give an overview of KM. Finally, we describe EKR more carefully.

KM aims to create value for the organization by enabling learning. Even if learning and accumulation of (new) knowledge always start from the perspective of an individual (Jensen, 2005), there are different types of KM. One type accumulates knowledge outside people in order to disseminate knowledge to support learning (Wiig, 1994); this is the type to which EKR refers. EKR enable both individual and organizational learning, and hence support the other two types of KM identified by Wiig (1994): to accumulate knowledge inside people and to embed knowledge in processes, routines etc. With respect to Binney's (2001) six elements, developing EKR includes both a product and a process perspective. There must be processes associated with the management of the knowledge repository and improvements of work processes in order to support different types of knowledge conversions as described by Nonaka and Takeuchi (1995). The application of technology when building the repository embeds knowledge in the application and the use of it. Binney (2001) terms this transactional KM, which is a side-effect of building knowledge repositories.

There are different types of knowledge. Wiig (1993) terms knowledge that people hold in their minds internal knowledge. Knowledge in, for example, books and IT systems is referred to as external knowledge. From the perspective of an employee, external knowledge is organizational knowledge, i.e. knowledge that remains in the organization even if employees quit. An EKR is a part of the organizational knowledge. Another common distinction in the literature is between tacit and explicit knowledge (see Gore & Gore 1999; Loermans, 1993; Nonaka & Takeuchi,

1995; Wiig, 1993). Tacit knowledge is difficult to identify and to express since it is highly personal and concerns insights and intuition (Nonaka & Takeuchi 1995; Blodgood & Salisbury, 2001). Explicit knowledge is easier to express and can, in contrast to tacit knowledge, also be processed by a computer (Blodgood & Salisbury 2001; Nonaka & Takeuchi, 1995). From an organization's perspective organizational knowledge stored in a repository can be regarded as explicit and organizational knowledge stored in the culture and embedded in work routines as tacit. Figure 1 summarizes our conceptualization of KM.

Knowledge derives from information (Davenport & Prusak, 1998; Wiig, 1993), and knowledge also has a function to produce new information (Schreiber et al., 1999). Activities aiming to create knowledge take place within or between people (Davenport & Prusak, 1998), but the real transformation process, when information changes to knowledge, is an individual one. Thus it is impossible to store "knowledge"; it is information that supports knowledge transformation that is stored. However, we have experienced that people regard stored information as knowledge, because this is the way it is used, and thus we can also refer to such stored information as external knowledge.

An EKR requires capturing, packaging and storing of relevant knowledge. These processes take place when a knowledge repository is created for the first time in a KM implementation project, as well as every time new knowledge that has potential relevance for incorporation in an existing EKR is generated. The latter is critical for ensuring that the EKR is updated and furthermore for maintaining usefulness and trust in the repository over time. Hence, the importance of the capture process is apparent. The Framework for IT-supported KM (FIT-KM) (Aggestam, 2006b), see Figure 2, describes KM work using an EKR. FIT-KM visualizes how the capture process, our research focus, relates to other processes and flows in this context.

One way to start KM work is to review already stored information (Gore and Gore 1999), and FIT-KM clearly indicates that this is one entrance to the process "Capture new knowledge". The Capture process together with packaging and storing are the organizational processes in FIT-KM. The process to "Capture new knowledge" aims to capture *new* knowledge compared to existing content in the EKR. "Capture New Knowledge" uses external and internal knowledge and already stored information as input. For knowledge to be captured it must first be identi-

Figure 1. Different parts of KM and their relations (developed from Aggestam and Backlund, 2007)

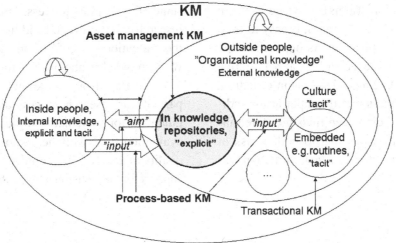

Figure 2. FIT-KM describing KM work using Electronic Knowledge Repositories (Aggestam, 2006b)

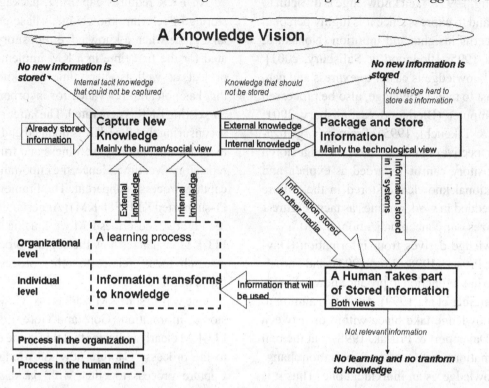

fied. The knowledge identified must be evaluated in order to support a decision whether or not it should be passed on to the process of packaging and storing the captured knowledge. *Thus, to support the evaluation stage means to support the decision whether or not to store the knowledge identified.* "Package and Store Information" uses the output from the "Capture new knowledge" process as input; i.e. identified knowledge that passed the evaluation. It aims to package and store information in such a way that it is easy to find, share, use and complement. As opposed to the capturing process, the technological perspective dominates in packaging and storing information. The stored information is the input at the individual level. If an employee finds the stored information relevant according to both a task at hand and earlier knowledge, the information will be used.

3. RESEARCH PROCESS

Our research process includes a qualitative analysis based on both an interpretive field study and a theoretical review. Therefore, the results can be described as a synthesis emerging from a combination of theoretical and empirical data. The first part of the research process aimed to identify and characterize CSF in the evaluation stage of the capture process. This first part of the research process reveals conditions for performing the evaluation successfully and hence provides us with knowledge about what the guidance must support. Based on this knowledge, the second part of our research process aimed to develop guidance for systematic implementation of the evaluation stage with the purpose to increase the quality of an EKR. This guidance should include support for the decision whether to store identified knowledge or not.

The purpose of our research is to increase the body of knowledge concerning CSF in the evaluation stage as well to support the evaluation stage in the capture process including the decision whether or not to store the knowledge identified. Hence, the results emerging from this research should also contribute to practice. A *pragmatic approach* implies an interest for actions in their context; what are the practical consequences, as well as what works and what does not work (Goldkuhl, 2004). Thus, we must gain knowledge about implementing EKR in practice. This knowledge can be gained through social construction, such as, e.g., language, consciousness, shared meanings and documents. This is in accordance with how Klein and Myers (1999) classify an interpretive study. Furthermore, since the literature lacks the topic of CSF for this specific stage in KM work, empirical data must be an important input to our qualitative analysis. Thus, an interpretive field study of an implementation of a knowledge repository was performed in the EKLär project (see 3.1).

A review of prior, relevant literature is an essential feature of any academic project. An effective review creates a firm foundation for advancing knowledge. It facilitates theory development... *(Webster and Watson, 2002, p.xiii).*

Hence, our theoretical review has focused on success factors for KM work and how they are described in the literature. These factors have then been analyzed with respect to if, and in that case how, they influence the evaluation stage in the capture process. As this work plays an important role in our analysis, it implies that our results are theoretically grounded.

A single case study can be justified if it is purposeful and provides a large amount of information (Gummesson, 2001), which is the case in the EKLär project. Furthermore, the theoretical review is not limited to the health sector and with regard to the EKP approach used being based on experiences in earlier projects, as, for example, ELEKTRA

(ELEKTRA Consortium, 1999; Rolland, Stirna, Prekas, Loucopoulos, Grosz and Persson, 2000) and Hyperknowledge (Stirna, Persson and Kaindl, 2002; Persson, Stirna, Dulle, Hatzenbichler and Strutz, 2003) and accordingly revised, the way of working in EKLär is well grounded in other projects. To increase the credibility and dependability activities such as prolonged engagement, persistent observation, and triangulation have been used (Lincoln and Guba, 1985). There are two main types of triangulations, method triangulation and source triangulation (Williamson et al., 2002). Efforts towards both have been made, e.g. we have used different types of data collection and data collection techniques, as well as collected data at different times and from different people with regard to profession and location. Two techniques that aim to strengthen credibility are member checking and referential adequacy (Lincoln and Guba, 1985). By sending documents such as protocols, models, and the report back to members of the project group, our intention was to test our interpretations and conclusions.

Before summarizing the steps included in the qualitative analysis, we describe the interpretive field study.

3.1 Interpretive Field Study

The interpretive field study was conducted through participation in an EKR implementation project called *Efficient Knowledge Management and Learning in Knowledge Intensive Organizations (EKLär)* which ran for three years and was completed in 2007. To assess the quality in this interpretive study, the work was guided by ideas that are conceptualized in the principles proposed by Klein and Myers (1999).

EKLär was a Swedish project that took place in the health care domain and that focused on knowledge about the prevention and treatment of leg ulcers. Three types of health care organizations were included in the project: Home Healthcare, Primary Care and Hospital. The objective of these

Figure 3. A fraction of the knowledge map (Persson, Stirna & Aggestam, 2008)

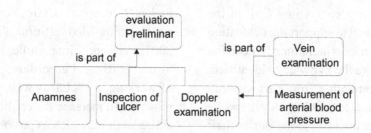

stakeholders is to provide the patient with the best possible treatment at all times. One of the most important resources in achieving this objective is knowledge about the latest evidence based medical findings and empirically tested practices, and the sharing of them. Hence, one purpose of the EKLär project was to develop an EKR for learning and sharing of best practices with respect to treatment and prevention methods for leg ulcers[1]. The KM approach used in EKLär, Enterprise Knowledge Patterns (EKP), combines Enterprise Modelling (EM) with organizational patterns (Stirna, Persson & Aggestam, 2006). The approach is characterized by a strong emphasis on stakeholder participation and the use of Organizational Patterns to package knowledge.

The EKLär project was carried out in three phases, preparation, implementation and evaluation. The work concerning the capture process was performed in the implementation phase and thus we briefly describe how we worked in this phase.

The implementation phase was completed in approximately fifteen months and aimed to 1) develop an EKR prototype, and 2) prepare the hospital for long term EKR maintenance. This phase involved daily efforts by the researchers to develop the repository and hands-on learning to help stakeholders learn how to manage knowledge by using the EKR. Data were collected mainly at project team meetings. An average of one meeting a month was performed, with each meeting spanning four to eight hours. The meetings aimed to develop the prototype were documented by models, purpose-built patterns and detailed written notes, and the meetings about repository main-

tenance were mainly documented by recording, transcribing and note-taking methods. Meeting notes were summarised and sent to the participants for confirmation. Additional data was collected in the form of relevant documents and documents of similar projects from other hospitals. Initial project team meetings aimed to identify key knowledge areas for the project. This work was carried out through enterprise modelling using a participatory approach (Bubenko, Persson and Stirna, 2001). The result was a "Knowledge map" in the form of a conceptual model (Figure 3).

The areas identified were an integration of the knowledge needs of the intended knowledge users identified in the preparation phase and the knowledge bearers' (hospital personnel) views of the most important knowledge to be shared and learned. On this basis the project team proceeded to capture relevant knowledge, and to package and store it. As the project proceeded, nurses became increasingly independent and carried out more and more work autonomously in between monthly project team meetings. As a technological tool the project team chose an existing technical solution already in use by the hospital for other projects. An important part when preparing for long term EKR maintenance was defined as the identification of situations where key knowledge with the potential for storage might be created. Much effort was invested in order to identify these situations. Data from project meetings about repository maintenance were mainly collected by recording, transcribing and note-taking methods.

3.2 Six Steps Included in the Analysis

To analyze the data collected from the interpretive field study as well as from the literature study the following six steps have been carried out:

1. Summary of Success Factors (SF) in KM work already described in the literature. Output: An account of SF for KM work
2. Analysis of SF with a specific focus on how they influence the capture process. Output: An account of SF for the capture process based on theoretical data.
3. Analysis of data collected in EKLär in order to identify SF that influence the capture process. Output: An account of SF for the capture process based on empirical data.
4. Analysis of the SF specific to the capture process aiming to extract those success factors that influence the evaluation stage. Output: An account and description of SF for the evaluate stage based on both theoretical and empirical data.
5. Identification of CSF for the evaluation stage. At this stage we have a large number of SF for the evaluate activity, All SF cannot be CSF. If there are too many factors, more than 4-6, they are probably too detailed and all of them are probably not critical (Avison & Fitzgerald, 1998); hence CSF is a *limited* number of factors. Thus, aiming to identify the *critical* SF, we conceptually analyzed, organized and grouped the SF with regard to *how* they influence the evaluate activity as well as each other. Output: An account and a characterization of CSF for the evaluate stage. The characterization also includes a conceptual model showing factors that influence the CSF. *This is our contribution to KM theory.*
6. Development of KM guidance based on the characterization of CSF. Output: Guidance aiming to support the guidance of the evalu-

ations stage in the capture process. *This is our contribution to KM practice.*

In the next section we summarize how data, i.e. the identified SF for the evaluations stage, output from Step 4, influence the evaluation stage and hence our findings.

4. IDENTIFYING SUCCESS FACTORS FOR THE EVALAUTION STAGE

In order to enhance traceability to Step 2 and Step 3 in the analysis, the forthcoming section includes references to the literature and illustrative examples as well as quotations from the interpretive field study. With regard to illustrative quotations from the case study, Orlikowski (1993) and Persson (2001) use a similar way of writing. All quotations are our own translations from Swedish. To enhance reading, we end this section with a summary where key words are italicized.

In the EKLär case we explicitly discussed and analyzed "How do we evaluate knowledge and related to what?" To store everything results in information overflow and problems finding the required knowledge. In EKLär, different people, i.e. from different work professions, performed the evaluation. Who did the evaluation was dependant on the perspective from where the knowledge was evaluated. It was the nurses who evaluated if the knowledge was relevant with respect to what knowledge they wanted to share through the repository. Here the Knowledge map was an important tool to evaluate against. Doctors evaluated if the packaged knowledge was correct, and they signed each chunk of knowledge as an act of quality assurance. This division of labour was the main reason for us to identify that evaluation with respect to both relevance and correctness is a SF. Regardless of the kind of evaluation, it must be systemized and the evaluation task must be included in work role descriptions, meaning that employees must have time for performing this task, if it is to be performed regularly. This is another SF. Further analysis shows that the literature supports both types of evaluation, but the difference was not as obvious in the studied literature. In the following we discuss each type of evaluation separately:

Evaluate with respect to relevance: If knowledge is to be incorporated in the repository it must be in line with the purpose of the repository. This is a SF. As Davenport and Prusak (1998) put it: What business goals should the codified knowledge serve? The importance of the knowledge vision is well stated in the literature (see Remus & Schub, 2003; Wong & Aspinwall, 2004; Blodgood & Salisbury, 2001). In the EKLär case, the importance of the knowledge goal, in the form of the Knowledge map, when evaluating identified knowledge, was revealed. The users´ needs that were discovered in the preparation phase of the EKLär case is an important part of the knowledge goal. Important aspects for the users are knowledge about treatment materials and images to compare with in order to identify leg ulcer type as well as to describe a leg ulcer. Thus, one valuable evaluation criterion in the beginning, and a SF, was that the first version of the prototype had to reflect these needs. Otherwise there was a great risk that the first impression of the intended users will be negative. Some illustrative quotations from the preparation phase about relevance of knowledge about materials:

Material costs a lot of money... Good if the repository contains information about material and what material, bought by different purchasers, are equivalent. Even dressing techniques are good to find information about, sometimes you can not do it as the instruction says." ... "Are we allowed changing bandage material? ... New bandage, and alternative products (from the interviews in the pre study).

And some about the pictures:

Pictures in the repository to compare with would be good. ... Good with pictures of different types of leg ulcers because when a leg ulcer is to be described it will be possible to relate to a picture. (from the interviews in the pre study)

Pictures as a means of enhancing stored knowledge with regard to the tacit dimension is described by Polanyi (1983).

Even though legal aspects were not an issue in the EkLär project, due to the generic nature of the knowledge stored, they are likely to appear in most settings, thus being a relevant SF. If legislation prohibits storing a specific type of information, the knowledge cannot be deemed relevant for the repository. Another important evaluation criterion, and a SF, is protection (Carlsson, 2001) which concerns both value erosion and imitation by competitors. The latter was not topical in the EKLär case, because it is a project in the area of public healthcare. We note that legal aspects can be regarded as another perspective of protection (Aggestam & Backlund, 2007). Value erosion concerns the transformation from knowledge to information and hence requires some sort of packaging.

An EKR provides knowledge that is already captured (Chua & Lam, 2005). Thus we must capture *new* knowledge, i.e. an important evaluation criterion is what is already stored in the repository. When storing new knowledge, this can result in removing already stored knowledge or updating it. An example from the EKLär case is when, every third year, a new purchase of treatment materials is done.

Evaluate with regard to correctness: The correctness of the knowledge is a SF. In the EKLär case doctors evaluated identified knowledge with regard to correctness. This requires that the knowledge is documented, i.e. "packaged" in some way. Identified knowledge, after some initial packaging, may need to return to the capturing process; thus revealing an iterative element.

We do the [packaging] job and then present it to the medically responsible person who can say 'yes' or 'no'. If everything is ok, he/she signs his/her name underneath... (nurse in the project team)

In the EKLär case the EKP approach (Persson & Stirna, 2002) has been used for packaging. After checking, the knowledge chunk went back to the nurses including comments about how to update it or, if everything was correct, the responsible doctor's signature and date of approval was given. Considering that people judge information on the basis of who provides it (Davenport & Prusak, 1998), this also contributed to credibility.

Is there any person who can quality assure all patterns or is it that way that some patterns are so complex that more than one person is needed? Do we need a doctor for doing this? Is it a role or a person who should do this job? (nurse in the project team)

With respect to the credibility of the EKR it is important that a person who the users have faith in does this type of evaluation. This is a SF. The main target group is nurses in primary care and home health care who know and have faith in the individual doctors at the hospital that work with leg ulcers. Therefore, we decided that the person rather than the role was important and as a consequence each doctor puts his/her name on the stored knowledge chunks (patterns). The observations performed in the evaluation phase showed that this was the wrong decision, and we then complemented the name with the role.

I wonder who this is... The role increases trustworthiness ... I want to know who this person is. (from two of the observations in the evaluation phase)

The main users of the EKR in the EKLär case, nurses in primary care and in the municipality, belong to the group that Markus (2001) identifies as "Shared work practitioners". According to Markus (2001) this group selects available knowledge documents, among other things, based on the reputation of the person who contributes

the document. That the current knowledge has been committed to by some sort of management, in the EKLär case the doctors, is also important with regard to political processes. It is important to realize that individuals can act in order to reach personal objectives and that everybody does not act in a rational manner in order to reach the common objectives (Bastöe & Dahl, 1996). Political processes between different stakeholders must be managed (Chua & Lam, 2005), and authority is one among many forms of power (Bolman & Deal, 1997). In the area of health care, e.g., doctors have a legible and visible authority.

Summary: The evaluate activity aims to select what to store. Evaluating with respect to *correctness* influences the *reliability*, and a person who the users have faith in should do this kind of evaluation. For this, *the role* is as important as *who* did it, and, from a political perspective, this is also a sign of *commitment*. Other types of evaluation concerns judging whether the knowledge is *relevant* with regard to the *knowledge goal and intended users*, if it is *already stored* or not, and if it can be stored with regard to *legal aspects* and the organization's *protection policy*. One valuable evaluation criterion in the beginning is what the *end users regard as most important* to find in the first prototype of the repository. This presupposes knowledge about the needs of the users already in the beginning of the project and the need of *preparation* work including finding this out is clear. Some evaluation criteria, e.g. correctness, require that the actual knowledge *is packaged* in some way and an iterative element between the capture process and the process of package and store is here revealed. All these different *types of evaluation* require different types of criteria to value against and thus require different types of competences. Different roles can be responsible for all or parts of the evaluation, but regardless of this, it must be defined which role ("who") is responsible for which part and corresponding *work role descriptions* must be accordingly revised. This is the management's responsibility.

As described previously, Step 5, we conceptually analyze, organize and group the SF with regard to *how* they influence the evaluate activity as well as each other. The result was an account and a characterization of CSF for the evaluate stage, which is presented in the next section. How the SF described in this section relates to the identified CSF is summarized in Table 1.

Table 1. How SF and identified CSF relates

SF's influence	CSF1	CSF2	CSF3	CSF4	CSF5	CSF6
The KM project goal, e.g. in the form of a Knowledge map, decides if identified knowledge is relevant				X		X
The first version must includes the uesrs' main needs						X
Different kinds of evaluation must be performed and hence different competences are needed, i.e. different people must be involved	X					
Restrictions for what kind of knowledge is allowed to be stored exist			X			
If the knowledge already includes the identified knowledge it should not be stored again					X	
Storing new identified knowledge may imply deleting/revising already stored information					X	
There must be employees who can decide if the identified knowledge is correct or not		X				
Who signed if the knowledge is correct or not influence the credibility		X				
When transforming knowledge to information there is a risk that critical knowledge element/s will be lost, i.e. value erosion			X			
Storing the identified knowledge may enhance imitation by external actors			X			
Management's commitment to the KM project	X					
The maturity of integration between daily work processes and the capture process	X					
Employees' allocated time for performing KM work	X					

5. CRITICAL SUCCESS FACTORS FOR THE EVALUATE STAGE WHEN CAPTURING NEW KNOWLEDGE

This section characterizes CSF for the evaluation stage in the capture process, i.e. conditions that need to be met in this stage from the perspective of high quality in the EKR, and it includes hence our contribution to KM theory. The purpose with this contribution is to characterize CSF, related to the evaluation stage of an effective knowledge capture process, and hence increase the awareness of them as well as the benefits achieved through an effective knowledge capture process.

As a result of Step 5 in our analysis work, the following six CSF have been identified:

- CSF1: The evaluate activity is included in relevant work role descriptions
- CSF2: Evaluation addressing correctness is performed
- CSF3: Evaluation addressing protection of organizational knowledge is performed
- CSF4: Evaluation addressing relevance is performed
- CSF5: Evaluation addressing redundancy is performed
- CSF6: The repository satisfies most important knowledge needs of the users

To further characterize these CSF we have developed a conceptual model, Figure 4, showing how these CSF influence the evaluation of identified knowledge as well as factors that in turn influence the CSF.

The capture process takes place when a knowledge repository is created for the first time, and every time new knowledge is generated that has potential relevance for an existing repository. It is crucial to understand that new knowledge is not regularly generated, e.g., once or twice a week, and, accordingly, knowledge must be *continuously* captured. To enable that identified knowledge is continuously evaluated, somebody must be responsible for doing it. This in turn facilitates the work with integrating this activity in daily work process by using the work role description as "a link" between the individual and organizational level (CSF1). However, it is not enough to perform the evaluate activity, the evaluation must be performed in such a way that it increases the quality of the EKR and hence increases its usefulness. High quality from a capture perspective means that employees, when using the captured knowledge, perceives that it supports and facilitates their work performance and hence also satisfies their most important needs (CSF6). We want to emphasise that our experience from the EKLär project is that CSF6 is one of the most critical factors in the first prototype since the first impression is crucial for future success. This is the main reason why CSF6 is an separate CSF even if the users' needs should be included in the knowledge goal and hence also in CSF4.

CSF2-CSF6 characterize different perspectives that must be taken into consideration when performing the evaluation. These perspectives require different competences and, hence, no single individual can normally perform all these different types of evaluations. However, having too many people involved results in a slower process in which the risk of losing knowledge increases. This is something the guidance must take into consideration. Our analysis also shows that some types of evaluation, namely those focusing on correctness and value erosion, require some sort of initial packaging. This means that those types of evaluation should be performed as late as possible in order to avoid unnecessary packaging.

Successful evaluation includes managing CSF for the evaluate activity. Thus, we use the work presented in this section as a basis when developing guidance for the evaluation stage, which is presented in the next section.

Figure 4. CSF for the evaluation stage and their influence factors

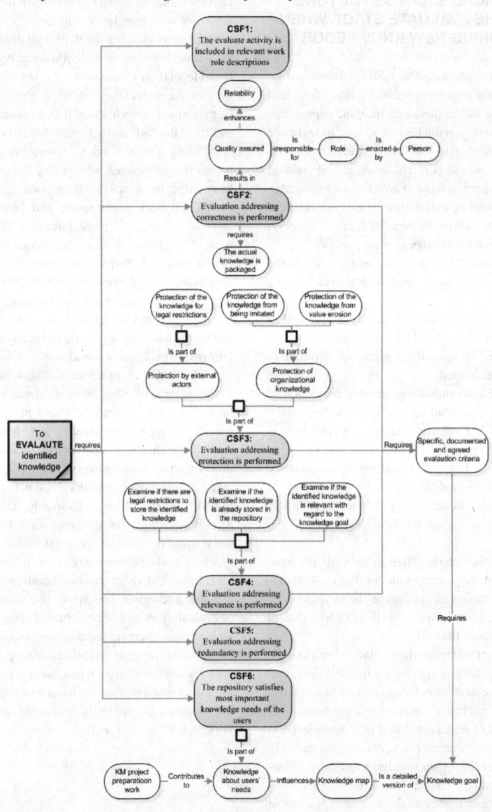

6. GUIDANCE FOR IMPLEMENTATION OF THE EVALUATION STAGE IN THE CAPTURE PROCESS

This section presents guidance aiming to support the implementation of the evaluations stage in the capture process in order to increase the quality of an EKR. It aims to be used by KM implementation project leaders.

Before proceeding, we want to remind the reader that Critical Success Factors (CSF) in this paper refer to "…the conditions that need to be met to assure success of the system" (Poon & Wagner, 2001, p. 395). This means that in order to be *sure* of success for the evaluation stage in the capture process when starting a KM implementation project, all CSF have to be already met at the beginning. However, since this is more or less never the fact, the critical issue is to carry out the project in such a way that these factors are met when it is concluded and KM is supposed to become institutionalised. Hence, the guidance must take the CSF into consideration.

The main part of the guidance is six evaluation criteria based on CSF2-CSF6 and a template (Appendix 1) in order to enhance documentation of the evaluation according to these criteria. As described in the former section, normally no single person can perform all the different types of evaluation. On the other hand, too many involved actors will inherently slow down the capture process. This is also something that the guidance takes into consideration by including advice for how to think when including the different types of evaluation in relevant work role descriptions (CSF1). Furthermore, in order to avoid unnecessary work, it is important to decide as early as possible whether the identified knowledge should be stored or not. This means that those types of evaluation that require some sort of packaging should be performed after the other types. To support this, the third part of the guidance is a model showing the order in which the different types of evaluation should be performed.

Hence, as a result of Step 6 in our analysis work, the guidance consists of the following three parts:

- Advice for including the evaluation task in relevant work role descriptions
- A model showing the order in which the different types of evaluation should be performed
- Six evaluation criteria including a template for documentation

Because the criteria are used in the two other parts of the guidance, we for clarity reasons describe the evaluation criteria first.

6.1 Six Evaluation Criteria Including a Template for Documentation

Knowledge which is not relevant and correct should not be stored because it jeopardizes the quality of an EKR. This means that for knowledge to be stored, it must pass the evaluation process. The proposed evaluation criteria aim to support the decision whether or not identified knowledge should be stored or not.

The six evaluation criteria are as follows:

1. *Is the identified knowledge relevant?* Evaluate if the identified piece of knowledge contributes to achieving the goal of the knowledge repository. If it does not, it should not be incorporated in the knowledge repository. Notably, the evaluation performed when building the knowledge repository must also examine if the knowledge to be stored satisfies the most important needs of the users.

2. *Is the identified knowledge already stored?* Evaluate if the identified piece of knowledge is already stored in the repository. If so, examine if it needs to be revised/updated according to the newly identified piece of knowledge. If storing the particular piece

of knowledge means that already stored knowledge should be revised in some way, it is important to pass this information onto the package and store process.

3. *Is there a risk for imitation?* Evaluate if storing the identified piece of knowledge enhances the risk of imitation by external actors in such a way that may diminish the organization's competitive advantage. If this is the case, the organization must examine if there are other ways of solving the problem, for example, by storing information about where the actual knowledge can be found or limiting access rights to the knowledge repository. It is critical to pass on information that influences how the actual piece of knowledge should be stored to the package and store process.

4. *Does the organization have the right to store/share the identified knowledge?* Evaluate if the identified piece of knowledge is protected by external actors. If this is the case, the degree of protection decides whether the knowledge should be stored or not. For example, if it is against the law it should not be incorporated in the repository. However, perhaps information about the knowledge owner could be stored.

5. *Is there a risk for value erosion?* Evaluate if storing the knowledge results in losing critical knowledge elements. However, before this can be done, different storage formats, e.g., text, picture, or film, must be evaluated. If storing results in the loss of critical knowledge elements, the organization must evaluate whether it is worth storing the knowledge at all. Perhaps an alternative is to store information about the knowledge owner. We recommend evaluating value erosion in the package and store process also, since the packaging itself may influence this criterion.

6. *Is the identified knowledge correct?* Evaluate if the identified piece of knowledge is cor-

rect. For reliability reasons and as a quality assurance measure, it is of critical importance that the employee who makes this evaluation signs the actual piece of knowledge with both name and work role/title. Since storing may involve losing knowledge elements, this evaluation criterion, in accordance with criterion number 5, assumes some form of packaging. We recommend that it should be performed again in the package and store process.

It is important to document the evaluation activity in order to ensure traceability and to enable information that has been revealed during the evaluation work and which is relevant for the package and store process to be passed on to this process. In order to support this documentation, a template can be found in Appendix A. The criteria in the template are in the same order as in the model showing the order of the different types of evaluation (Figure 5). Furthermore, to support traceability, the template includes a column for an id number. With regard to the id number, we recommend a system that provides information about the type of knowledge, e.g. a system in which one letter that indicates knowledge type is followed by a unique number. The id number for each piece of knowledge can also be used if additional comments that the template does not have space for are needed.

6.2 Including the Evaluation Activity in Relevant Work Role Descriptions

1. Identify potential work roles for performing evaluation concerning each of the evaluation criteria. Concerning criterion 6 about correctness, we want to remind about the importance of choosing a person that employees have faith in.

2. In order to avoid too many involved people examine if there is any role which can perform more than one type of evaluation. At

Figure 5. The order of different types of evaluation

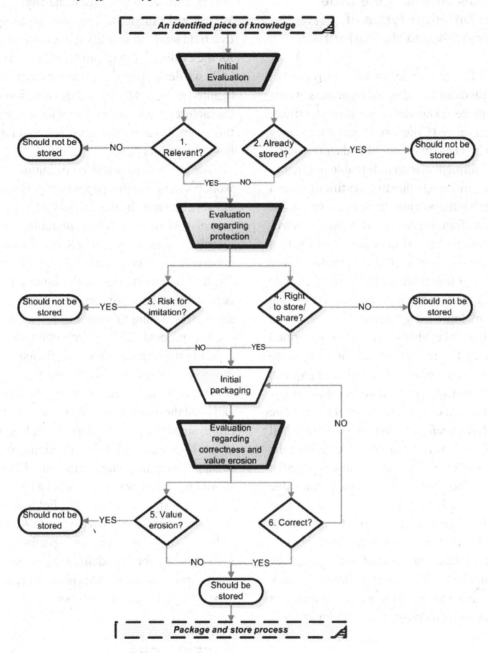

least, criteria 1 and 2 should be performed by the same person. Include the evaluation task in the identified work role descriptions.

3. For the remaining criteria, choose the most suitable work role/s and include the evaluation task in these work role descriptions.

Note, that evaluation regarding correctness and value erosion often requires different persons with regard to what specific subject that is in focus.

6.3 A Model Showing the Order in which Different Types of Evaluation Should Be Performed

Two types of evaluation do not require any form of packaging and can be addressed regardless of how the actual piece of knowledge has been identified, namely relevance (Criterion 1) and redundancy (Criterion 2). These two types of evaluation should thus be performed as soon as possible in order to quickly determine whether the identified piece of knowledge has the potential to be stored or not. We claim that performing this initial evaluation saves resources in the form of man-hours. Evaluation addressing protection, i.e. the right to store/share and the risk of imitation, probably require some specialist knowledge, but do not require storing the piece of knowledge. Hence, we argue that these two types of evaluation should be performed in the middle of the evaluate activity. Checking for potential value erosion (Criterion 5) requires specialist knowledge, since this concerns identifying if, and in that case which, critical knowledge elements have been lost when storing the actual piece of knowledge. Furthermore, checking the correctness (Criterion 6) also requires specialist knowledge. The aspects of correctness and value erosion are closely linked, because value erosion may result in the knowledge not being correct anymore. In addition, since both these types of evaluation require some sort of packaging, they should hence be performed last. The model visualizing this can be found in Figure 5. The numbers in the model correspond to the evaluation criteria.

7. CONCLUSION

High quality in the knowledge that aimed to be share, is a crucial factor for all KM work and hence also for organizations' competitiveness. With the purpose to increase quality in EKR, this paper characterizes CSF in the evaluation stage as well as presents guidance for facilitating the implementation of this stage in the capture process. We utilized a theoretical review and an interpretive field study to identify and characterize CSF for the evaluation stage, and then, based on these CSF, we developed the guidance. This approach resulted in a set of CSF for the evaluation stage of the capture process and guidance for implementing this stage. Thus, we can conclude that this paper has achieved its purpose and goals.

The main theoretical contribution from the work presented in this paper is that it extends the existing literature by describing CSF for a specific part of KM work. Existing literature frequently discusses success factors in KM work on a more generic level. By specifically discussing CSF for the evaluation stage in the capture process it is possible to be more concrete, which enhances the understanding of what has to be done in the capture process. This is important in order to perform the capture process efficiently and to develop a successful EKR in practice.

One important part of future work is to empirically test the guidance in other domains. Furthermore, since the presented guidance has its roots in the KM area, and the evaluation criteria aim to support deciding whether identified knowledge should be stored or not, we believe that they will benefit from the literature in the fields of Decision Support System and Expert Systems. Another part of future work is that we plan to perform the same type of work for the identification stage in the capture process in order to achieve more complete support for the capture process.

REFERENCES

Aggestam, L. (2006a, September 4-8). Towards a maturity model for learning organizations – the role of Knowledge Management. In *Proceedings of the 7th International Workshop on Theory and Applications of Knowledge Management (TAKMA 2006), 17th International Conference on Database and Expert Systems Applications (DEXA 2006)*, Krakow, Poland (pp. 141-145).

Aggestam, L. (2006b, May 21-24). Wanted: A framework for IT-supported KM. In *Proceedings of the 17th Information Resources Management Association (IRMA) Conference,* Washington, DC (pp. 46-49).

Aggestam, L., & Backlund, P. (2007). *Strategic knowledge management issues when designing knowledge repositories.* Paper presented at the 15th European Conference on Information Systems (ECIS).

Avison, D. E., & Fitzgerald, G. (1998). *Information systems development: Methodologies, techniques and tools* (2nd ed.). New York: McGraw Hill

Bastøe, K., & Dahl, P. (1996). *Organisationsutveckling i offentlig verksamhet.* Lund, Sweden: Utbildningshuset Studentlitteratur.

Binney, D. (2001). The knowledge management spectrum – understanding the KM landscape. *Journal of Knowledge Management, 5*(1), 33–42. doi:10.1108/13673270110384383

Blodgood, J. M., & Salisbury, W. D. (2001). Understanding the influence of organizational change strategies on information technology and knowledge management strategies. *Decision Support Systems, 31,* 55–69. doi:10.1016/S0167-9236(00)00119-6

Bolman, L. G., & Deal, T. E. (1997). *Nya perspektiv på organisation och ledarskap.* Lund, Sweden: Andra upplagan, Studentlitteratur.

Bubenko, J. A., Jr., Persson, A., & Stirna, J. (2001). *User guide of the knowledge management approach using enterprise knowledge patterns* (Deliverable D3, IST Project No. IST-2000-28401). Stockholm, Sweden: Department of Computer and Systems Sciences, Royal Institute of Technology.

Carlsson, S. A. (2001, June 27-29). *Knowledge management in network context.* Paper presented at the Ninth Conference on Information Systems, Bled, Slovenia.

Chua, A., & Lam, W. (2005). Why KM projects fail: A multi-case analysis. *Journal of Knowledge Management, 9*(3), 6–17. doi:10.1108/13673270510602737

Davenport, T. H., & Prusak, L. (1998). *Working knowledge.* Cambridge, MA: Harvard Business School Press.

ELEKTRA Consortium. (1999). *Newton: Validated ESI knowledge base* (ELEKTRA Project Deliverable Document, ESPRIT Project No. 22927). Cologne, Germany: ELEKTRA Project.

Gore, C., & Gore, E. (1999). Knowledge management: The way forward. *Total Quality Management, 10*(4,5), 554-560.

Gummesson, E. (2001). Are current research approaches in marketing leading us astray? *Marketing Theory, 1*(1), 27–48. doi:10.1177/147059310100100102

Hari, S., Egbu, C., & Kumar, B. (2005). A knowledge capture awareness tool An empirical study on small and medium enterprises in the construction industry. *Engineering, Construction, and Architectural Management, 12*(6), 533–567. doi:10.1108/09699980510634128

Hung, Y., Huang, S., Lin, Q., & Tsai, M. (2005). Critical factors in adopting a knowledge management system for the pharmaceutical industry. *Industrial Management & Data Systems, 105*(2), 164–183. doi:10.1108/02635570510583307

Jennex, E. M., Smolnik, S., & Croasdell, D. (2007). Towards defining knowledge management success. In *Proceedings of the 40th Hawaii International Conference on Systems Science* (pp. 193c).

Jennex, M. E., & Olfman, L. (2006). A model of knowledge management success. *International Journal of Knowledge Management, 2*(3), 51–68.

Jensen, P. E. (2005). A contextual theory of learning and the learning organization. *Knowledge and Process Management, 12*(1), 53–64. doi:10.1002/kpm.217

Kankanhalli, A., Tan, B. C. Y., & Wei, K.-K. (2005). Contributing knowledge to electronic knowledge repositories: an empirical investigation. *MIS Quarterly, 29*(1), 113–143.

Klein, H. K., & Myers, M. D. (1999). A set of principles for conducting and evaluating interpretive field studies in information systems. *MIS Quarterly, 23*(1), 67–94. doi:10.2307/249410

Lincoln, Y. S., & Guba, E. G. (1985). *Naturalistic inquiry*. Newbury Park, CA: SAGE Publications.

Loermans, J. (2002). Synergizing the learning organization. *Journal of Knowledge Management, 6*(3), 285–294. doi:10.1108/13673270210434386

Markus, L. M. (2001). Toward a theory of knowledge reuse: Types of knowledge reuse situations and factors in reuse success. *Journal of Management Information Systems, 18*(1), 57–93.

Matsumoto, I. T., Stapleton, J., Glass, J., & Thorpe, T. (2005). A knowledge capture report for multidisciplinary design environments. *Journal of Knowledge Management, 9*(3), 83–92. doi:10.1108/13673270510602782

Monk, A., Wright, P., Haber, J., & Davenport, L. (1993). *Improving your human-computer interface*. New York: Prentice Hall.

Montequin, V. R., Fernandez, F. O., Cabal, V. A., & Gutierrez, N. R. (2006). An integrated framework for intellectual capital measurement and knowledge management implementation in small and medium-sized enterprises. *Journal of Information Science, 32*(6), 525–538. doi:10.1177/0165551506067127

Nonaka, I., & Takeuchi, H. (1995). *The knowledge-creating company*. Oxford, UK: Oxford University Press.

Orlokowski, W. J. (1993). CASE tools as organizational vhange investigating incremental and radical changes in systems development. *MIS Quarterly, 17*(3).

Patton, M. Q. (2002). *Qualitative research & evaluation methods* (3rd ed.). Thousands Oaks, CA: Sage Publications. ISBN: 0-7619-1971-6.

Persson, A. (2001). *Enterprise Modelling in Practice: Situational Factors and their Influence on Adopting a Participative Approach*, Ph.D. Thesis, Department of Computer and System Sciences, Stockholm University, ISSN 1101-8526

Persson, A., & Stirna, J. (2002). Creating an organisational memory through integration of enterprise modelling, patterns and hypermedia: The HyperKnowledge approach. In M. Kirikova et al. (Eds.), *Information systems development – advances in methodologies, components and management* (pp. pp. 181-192). New York: Kluwer Academic.

Persson, A., Stirna, J., & Aggestam, L. (2008). How to disseminate professional knowledge in health care – the case of Skaraborg hospital. *Journal of Cases on Information Technology, 10*(4), 41–64.

Persson, A., Stirna, J., Dulle, H., Hatzenbichler, G., & Strutz, G. (2003). Introducing a pattern based knowledge management approach - the Verbundplan Case. In *Proceedings of the 4th International Workshop on Theory and Applications of Knowledge Management (TAKMA'03), 14th International Workshop on Database and Expert Systems Applications (DEXA'03)*, (pp. 1529-4188/03). Washington, DC: IEEE Computer Society.

Polanyi, M. (1983). *The tacit dimension*. Glouster, MA: Peter Smith Publisher. ISBN: 0-8446-5999-1.

Poon, P., & Wagner, C. (2001). Critical success factors revisited: success and failure cases of information systems for seniior executives. *Decision Support Systems, 30*, 393–418. doi:10.1016/S0167-9236(00)00069-5

Remus, U., & Schub, S. (2003). A blueprint for the implementation of process-oriented knowledge management. *Knowledge and Process Management, 10*(4), 237–253. doi:10.1002/kpm.182

Rolland, C., Stirna, J., Prekas, N., Loucopoulos, P., Grosz, G., & Persson, A. (2000). Evaluating a pattern approach as an aid for the development of organisational knowledge: An empirical study. In In *Proceedings of the 12th International Conference on Advanced Information System Engineering (CAiSE)* (LNCS 1789, pp. 176-191). ISBN 3-540-67630-9.

Schreiber, G., Akkermans, H., Anjewierden, A., de Hoog, R., Shadbolt, N., Van de Velde, W., et al. (2000). *Knowledge engineering and management the CommonKADS Methodology.* Cambridge, MA: MIT Press. ISBN: 0-262-19300-0

Sharma, S., & Bock, G.-W. (2005). Factor's influencing individual's knowledge seeking behaviour in electronic knowledge repository. In D. Bartmann, F. Rajola, J. Kallinikos, D. Avison, R. Winter, P. Ein-Dor, et al. (Eds.), *Proceedings of the Thirteenth European Conference on Information Systems,* Regensburg, Germany (pp. 390-403). ISBN 3-937195-09-2.

Stirna, J., Persson, A., & Aggestam, L. (2006, June 12-14). Building knowledge repositories with enterprise modelling and patterns – from theory to practice. In *Proceedings of the 14th European Conference on Information Systems (ECIS),* Gothenburg, Sweden (No. 239).

Stirna, J., Persson, A., & Kaindl, H. (2002). *Evaluation of the trial applications* (Deliverable D7, IST Project no. IST-2000-28401). Stockholm, Sweden: Department of Computer and Systems Sciences, Royal Institute of Technology.

Storey, J., & Bernett, E. (2000). Knowledge management initiatives: Learning from failures. *Journal of Knowledge Management, 4*(2), 145–156. doi:10.1108/13673270010372279

Webster, J., & Watson, R. T. (2002). Analyzing the past to prepare for the future: Writing a literature review. *MIS Quarterly, 26*(2), xiii–xxiii.

Wiig, K. M. (1993). *Knowledge management foundations – thinking about thinking – how people and organizations create, represent, and use knowledge.* Arlington, TX: Schema Press LTD.

Wiig, K. M. (1994). *Knowledge management the central management focus for intelligent-acting organizations.* Arlington, TX: Schema Press LTD.

Williamson, K., Bow, A., Burstein, F., Darke, P., Harvey, R., Johanson, G., et al. (2002). *Research methods for students, academics and professionals.* Wagga Wagg, New South Wales, Australia: Quick Print. ISBN: 1 876 938 42 0.

Wong, K. Y., & Aspinwall, E. (2004). Knowledge management implementation frameworks: A review. *Knowledge and Process Management, 11*(2), 93–104. doi:10.1002/kpm.193

APPENDIX 1. AN TEMPLATE FOR DOCUMENTATION OF THE EVALUATION STAGE IN THE CAPTURE PROCESS(TABLE 2)

Id	Identified: who and date	Knowledge description	Relevant? Yes/No +sign and date	Already stored? Yes/Yes, but must be updated/ Partly/No +sign and date	Risk for imitation? Yes/ No, but store information about the knowledge owner/No +sign and date	Right to store/share? Yes/No inclusive with regard to what and if storing information about the knowledge owner.+ sign and date	Value erosion? Yes inclusive in what ways/No, but store information about the knowledge owner/No +sign and date	Correct? Yes/No inclusive what to correct +sign and date	Decision regarding storing: Write date and sign. If decision to store: - Needed re-evaluation in the next process? - Storing influences already stored information? Not store/ Pass+relevant Store who owns information the knowledge

[1] The resulting EKR can be found at http://www.vgregion.se/skassarwebben (in Swedish)

This work was previously published in International Journal of Knowledge Management, Volume 6, Issue 1, edited by Murray E. Jennex, pp. 23-43, copyright 2010 by IGI Publishing (an imprint of IGI Global).

Chapter 3
The Outcome of Knowledge Process for Customers of Jordanian Companies on the Achievement of Customer Knowledge Retention

Amine Nehari Talet
King Fahd University of Petroleum & Minerals, Saudi Arabia

Samer Alhawari
Applied Science Private University, Jordan

Haroun Alryalat
The Arab Academy for Banking and Financial Sciences, Amman-Jordan

ABSTRACT

Organizations have increasingly recognized the importance of managing customer relationships, and Knowledge Management (KM) from the perspective of a process approaches assure positive impact on customer retention. Many organizations are turning to Customer Relationship Management (CRM) to better serve customers and facilitate closer relationships. This paper investigates how Knowledge Process for customers is used in practice by Jordanian companies to achieve Customer Knowledge Retention. The current practice is based on the data collected from 156, randomly drawn and reported from a survey of CRM applications and evaluation of CRM analytical functions provided by three software business solution companies working in the CRM area, and four companies that used the CRM system. Based on data collected from the companies, results from the analysis indicated that the knowledge process for customers had a positive effect on customer knowledge retention. The paper also verified the hypotheses of the effect of knowledge processes for customers on customer retention. The findings shed light on the potential relationship between the knowledge processes for customers and customer retention. It also provides guidance for the Information Technology (IT) industry as to how an analytical knowledge process for customers should be taken into account in developing countries to support to achieve customer knowledge retention due to cultural, social and educational differences.

DOI: 10.4018/978-1-4666-0035-5.ch003

1. INTRODUCTION

The globalization of business has highlighted the need of IT to understand the rapid growth customers' demands, due to the global competition; defensive marketing is becoming more attractive and popular. Obviously, this trend is magnified by the rapid development of CRM systems and the adoption of the customer-centric orientation (Stefanou et al., 2003). Knowledge has become strategic resource of organization and the foundation of competitive advantage; In addition, it has been recognized as an important asset for sustaining a competitive advantage (Papoutsakis & Vallès, 2006). Consequently, many organizations lost sight of it to grow and compete with domestic and global competitors. Thus, organizations try to achieve it from managing knowledge. Since the 1980s, researchers have been talking more and more about an era of focusing on customer retention Sheth (2002). In addition, the organization has been using KM to decrease the time to process customer requests, improve ongoing service, and better structure deals to meet customer retention.

Undoubtedly, Customer Knowledge Management (CKM) creates new knowledge sharing platforms and processes between companies and their customers. It is a continuous strategic process by which companies enable their customers to move from passive information sources and recipients of products and services to empowered knowledge partners (Gibbert et al., 2002). Through review and study of selected fundamentals related literature, that focused on developed countries and accordingly based on cultural, educational, technological, social and economical factors applicable to advanced Western societies rather than developing countries.

Our study is therefore distinctive in that, it addresses one of the important issues in Middle Eastern area because the use of IT is new for them. We strongly believe that our study will help and provide guidance for the IT industry, and researchers as to how an analytical knowledge process for customers should be taken into account in developing countries to support to achieve customer knowledge retention.

This paper is organized as follows. In the next section, we review relevant literature; section three proposes the research model and hypotheses, section four is about the research methodology in which we discuss the design of the questionnaire, sample, data collection, hypotheses analysis and results. The last segment of this paper is our conclusion, limitations of the study, and areas for further research.

2. LITERATURE REVIEW

KM, as a discipline, is designed to provide strategy, process, and technology to increase organizational learning (Satyadas et al., 2001). The various system designs attempt to capture and capitalize on the existing explicit, implicit and, in some cases, tacit knowledge of organizations. This emphasis on technology hides the range of knowledge available in an organization and processes that facilitates the flow of knowledge. Organizations must develop an integrative approach to KM that covers all potential components of knowledge and leverages specific components strategically aligned to their business objectives. In addition, KM is not something new; it is going to be something tangible and, in other words, there is a type of revolution on this topic today. Therefore it can be useful for the success of CRM activity. As a concept, it is one of the important factors for achievement of customer knowledge retention in the long term. Study of the KM process is important for the organization to validate the objective. Therefore, CRM process can be considered as knowledge oriented process with the characteristics of knowledge intensity and process complexity (Lin et al., 2006). Customer knowledge managers seek opportunities for partnering with their customers as equal co-creators of organizational value. This is also in stark contrast to the desire to maintain and nurture an existing customer base (Gibbert et al., 2002). Goh (2005) describes KM as an expertise that is widely recognized as having a significant impact on business performance. It is an approach that is used to capture, create, and apply knowledge to make the CRM process successful (Alryalat et al., 2007). The literature shows that managers focus on how to produce growth for the corporation through acquiring new customers and through engaging in an active and value-creating dialogue with them, and are much less concerned with customer retention information. Furthermore, it has been maintained that CRM and KM have been gaining recently wide interest in business environment (Gebert et al., 2002).

In this new era, companies are focusing on managing customer relationship in order to efficiently maximize customer retention. Most jobs are becoming ever more knowledge intensive and a majority of employees are moving to customer retention. Deng and Yu (2006) view the managing of the knowledge as a kind of asset, corporate needs developing corresponding criteria to control the knowledge assets. Additionally, organization should put a great deal of emphasis on discovering who its best customers are and how to find new customers who will be similarly loyal and profitable (Cao & Gruca, 2005). As a result, organizations start thinking of how to develop process to enhancement customer knowledge retention. Nowadays, customer retention is a critical issue in the success of any business system. Customer retention affects the company's profitability because it is more efficient to maintain an existing customer relationship than create a new one (Payne et al., 1999; Reichheld, 1996). Therefore, to sustain the competitive advantage, an organization needs to understand how to achieve the retention of customers.

2.1. Customer Knowledge Flows

Salomann et al. (2005) distinguish between three kinds of knowledge flows that play a vital role in the interaction between an organization and its customers: knowledge for, from and about customers. Knowledge for customers to support customers in their buying cycle, a continuous knowledge flow directed from the company to its customers. Knowledge from customers has to be incorporated by the company for product and service innovation, idea generation as well as for the continuous improvement of its products and services. Knowledge about customers is collected in CRM service and support processes and analyzed in CRM analysis processes. Additionally, Bueren et al. (2005) note that organizations need to focus on three sorts of knowledge in CRM processes. Firstly, they need to understand the requirements of customers in order to address them. This is referred to as knowledge about customers. Secondly, the information needs of the customers in their interaction with the enterprise require knowledge for customers. Thirdly, customers possess knowledge about the products and services they use as well as about how they perceive the offerings they purchased. This knowledge from customers is valuable as it feeds into measures to improve products and services. Efforts need to be made to channel this knowledge back into the organizations.

2.2 Knowledge Management Capabilities Needed for Customer Relationship Management

The CRM research highlights the importance of KM, culture change to develop a customer-oriented organization, and technological readiness essentially CRM is about customer interaction and about learning about customers' needs and preferences in order to provide more appropriate products and services to customers in the future. The importance of technology in enabling CRM is demonstrated by the attempts at defining the concept. One view of CRM is the utilization of customer related information or knowledge to deliver relevant products or services to customers

(Levine, 2000). Newell (2000) discusses a range of CRM case studies that used customer knowledge to deliver relevant products and services. CRM has been also defined as the alignment of business strategies and processes to create customer loyalty and ultimately corporate profitability enabled by technology (Rigby, Reichheld, & Schefter, 2002). In a similar vein, Ryals (2002) defines it as the lifetime management of customer relationships using IT.

Firestone and McElroy (2005) noted that the operational processes are those that use knowledge but, apart from routinely produced knowledge about specific events and conditions, don't produce or integrate it. Examples of outcomes are Sales Revenue, Market Share, Customer Retention and Environmental Compliance. In this note, CRM can also be defined as the management approach that involves identifying, attracting, developing and maintaining successful customer relationships over time in order to enhance retention of profitable customers (Bradshaw & Brash, 2001; Massey et al., 2001). A high degree of CRM process implementation is characterized as where firms are able to adjust their customer interactions based on the life-cycle stages of their customers and their capacity to influence or shape the stages i.e., extending relationships (Reinartz et al., 2004). E-CRM is defined as the application of CRM processes utilizing IT and relies on technology such as relational databases, data warehouses, data mining, computer telephony integration, the Internet, and multi-channel communication platforms in order to get closer to customers (Chen & Chen, 2004; Fjermestad & Romano, 2003). Interestingly, the level of technological sophistication of CRM technology makes no contribution to economic performance and supports the view that CRM is more than just software Reinartz et al., (2004). CRM can be conceptualized at three levels: (1) company wide, (2) functional, and (3) customer facing (Buttle, 2004).

KM can be useful for the success of CRM activity. As a concept, it is one of the important factors for achievement of CRM in the long term. Study of the KM process is important for the organization to verify the objective and how achieve this objective. The CRM process can be considered as knowledge oriented process with the characteristics of knowledge intensity and process complexity (Lin et al., 2006). Furthermore, CRM has emerged as one of the most demanded issues in business because of the value expected from carrying out CRM in organizations. CRM became an important business process because it touches the most important asset of all organizations that is the customer. Also, CRM itself is not a new idea but it is turning out to become a practice due to recent advances in organizations software technology. Customer relationship marketing techniques focus on single customers and require the organization to be organized around the customer rather than the product (Chen & Popovich, 2003). Bhaskar and Zhang (2005) confirm that the most significant changes in the practice of marketing during the last decade are the shift in emphasis from a transaction orientation customer interaction to the CRM. However, in large organizations, it is not very easy to collect and to transform the customer data necessary for creating systems to support it as the basis of the organizations wide customer relationship strategy, In terms of marketing strategies, CRM systems allow organizations to manage customer data, analyze customer relationships to keep existing customers and attract potential new customers. Therefore, the goal of every organization is to get new customers and keep customers involved in organization Also, retention existing customer within the organization, and enhancing the relationship with customers to develop the expansion of customer relationship. The enhancement of existing relationships is important to organizations, since attracting new customers is known to be more expensive. Therefore, as part of their CRM strategy, the need to understand and react to changes of customer behavior is an inevitable aspect of surviving in a competitive and mature market (Lariviere & Poel, 2004).

2.3 Phases of Process for Knowledge

Alavi and Leidner (2001) suggest that knowledge creation process is concerned with combining new sources of knowledge just in time learning. Knowledge creation that supports generation and creation of knowledge to development of new knowledge in an organization focuses on creating new products, better ideas, more efficient services or new skills (Sun & Gang, 2006). Therefore, to achieve the process for knowledge (knowledge creation); we need to go through six sub stages see Table 1 (Alkhaldi et al., 2006).

The first stage is rationalization the knowledge. A huge amount of information can be obtained, some are relevant and some are not. The rationalization stage can help in obtaining the relevant information for a specific subject. Moreover, rationalization is a method of employing logic or reason by removing unnecessary things in order to think thoroughly, reveal, clarify and ensure the reliability of the knowledge captured. Additionally, Rationalization is a cognitive process that is

concerned with forming something that seems to be consistent with or based on reason. Furthermore, rationalization is a practical application of knowledge to attain a preferred end. It leads to coordination, efficiency and control over both the physical and social environment. Viewed this way, rationalization can help in defending, explaining and clarifying a way or making excuses for something by reasoning. Lai and Chu (2000) describe that generation is concerned with identifying what sort of knowledge exists in the organization, who owns it, and who are thought leaders, or gather and importing knowledge from outside or learning from existing knowledge. Knowledge acquisition supports to obtain knowledge. The importance of knowledge acquisition depends on organization culture and objectives (Sun & Gang, 2006).

The second stage is about understanding of knowledge. Once knowledge is captured by organizations or individuals, a process of knowledge analysis is carried out to comprehend the content, meaning, importance and purpose of certain knowledge. Moreover, knowledge creation process concerned with combining new sources of Knowledge Just in time learning (Alavi & Leidner, 2001). Also, the Creation process contains production of new knowledge, which can

Table 1. Taxonomy of process for knowledge

Main dimension/ KM main process		Sub dimension/ Parts of process	References
Process for Knowledge	Knowledge Creation	Rationalization	*Lai and Chu (2000) Sun and Gang (2006)*
		Understanding	*Alavi and Leidner (2001) Bouthillier and Shearer (2002).*
		Inspection	*Sunassee and Sewry (2002) Deng and Yu (2006)*
		Development of Confidence	*Miltiadis and Pouloudi, (2003) Sun (2004)*
		Experimentation	*Sun and Gang (2006)*
		Validation	*Lai and Chu (2000) Sun and Gang (2006)*

be accomplished in several ways. First, internal knowledge may be combined with other internal knowledge to create new knowledge. And secondly, information may be analyzed to create new knowledge (Bouthillier & Shearer, 2002).

The third stage is inspection knowledge. It focuses on carrying out a careful examination of the content of knowledge in a way to guarantee its accuracy and correctness. This stage focuses on exposing knowledge to a methodical examination in order to inspect it with close attention. Moreover, each organization should emphasize on selecting suitable knowledge that meets the demands of its requirements. Additionally, organizations also need to identify old and existing knowledge as well as any new knowledge which it might need during the course of the KM effort, and for the business in general (Sunassee & Sewry, 2002). Consequently, identifying which knowledge is relevant to the organizations in terms of its KM strategy and its business strategy. It is also essential that the knowledge which has been chosen to be included in the repository is verified, in terms of its relevancy and importance to the organization. Knowledge selection means assessing knowledge relevance, value, and accuracy (Deng & Yu, 2006).

The fourth stage concerns itself with developing confidence in the knowledge. Once it is inspected and finally proves high standards of accuracy and correctness, the individual or organization starts developing feelings of trust and confidence towards the captured knowledge. Confidence builds up a strong feeling of assurance that facilitates the process of adaptation of knowledge. Enable reuses phase support to adapt and create the knowledge (Miltiadis & Pouloudi, 2003). Also, generating the knowledge includes adaptation and or creation new knowledge in the organization (Sun, 2004).

The fifth stage is concerned with experimentation of knowledge. It can go through certain experiment for purposes of testing and updating. It is an act of conducting a controlled test or investigation of an idea or concept to examine its reliability. It focuses on performing a procedural

test under certain conditions to cover up certain functions such as revealing a recognized truth, examining the validity of a theory, determining the effectiveness of something that has been previously tried, or establishing the efficiency of something that has never been tried before in order to gain experience. Additionally, Sun and Gang (2006) describe knowledge ontology design is to formalize the existing knowledge and offer a format for adding new knowledge. Consequently, its generation is concerned with producing new knowledge. Knowledge generation also occurs when the knowledge cannot be acquired from outside the organization.

The sixth stage is knowledge validation. This stage refers to the process of validating the knowledge sources and the information obtained. Many pieces of incorrect information could be found among people based on certain assumptions or unexamined sources to the extent in which they are viewed sometimes as being facts, realities or justified true beliefs. Additionally, Validation is defined as testing and evaluation of knowledge claims and beliefs. In this regard, the goal of validation is centered on finding out or testing the truth of something to satisfy a certain criterion. Any un-validated knowledge will be subjected to the experimental stage for more testing measurements to discover its truth. The modeling phase is concerned with justifying the generated knowledge (Lai & Chu, 2000). Also, knowledge evaluation needs to be conducted after the knowledge has been generated internally or acquired from outside (Sun & Gang, 2006).

3. RESEARCH MODEL AND HYPOTHESIS

Customer knowledge retention processes refers to the process of retaining existing customers within the organization. CRM is often described as a strategy or a set of activities the organizations employs to gain a competitive advantage. Also, CRM helps organizations make sense of

Figure 1. Research model

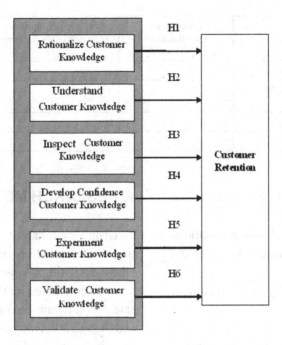

customer needs and help organizations manage these relationships and helps to predict the future. Therefore, customer knowledge retention is very important for the survival of organizations to achieve the competitive advantage.

Based on the theoretical background and literature review shown in Figure 1, we have developed a conceptual model represented in Figure 1 to examine the role of knowledge process for customer (Rationalization of Customer Knowledge, Understanding Customer Knowledge, Scrutinizing Customer Knowledge, Developing Confidence Customer Knowledge, Experimentation Customer Knowledge, and Validation of Customer Knowledge) on Customer Retention.

The main objective of customer knowledge retention is customer knowledge creation. It contains six sub-stages: The first stage is concerned with rationalization of the customer knowledge. A huge amount of information can be obtained, some are relevant and some are not. It can help obtain the relevant information for a specific subject.

The second stage deals with understanding of customer knowledge. Once knowledge is captured by organization or individuals, this process is conceived by understanding the content, meaning, importance and purpose of the knowledge.

The third stage is inspecting customer knowledge. It focuses on careful examination of the content of knowledge to ensure its accuracy and correctness. It concentrates on exposing knowledge to a methodical examination in order to inspect it with close attention.

The fourth stage is concerned with developing confidence of the customer knowledge. Once it is inspected by individuals, it yields accuracy and correctness. The individual or organization starts developing a feeling of trust and confidence into the captured knowledge. Confidence builds up a feeling of assurance.

The fifth stage is concerned with the experimentation of customer knowledge. It can go through experiments for testing and updating. It is an act of conducting a controlled test or investigation of an idea to find or discover the truth of something.

The sixth stage is interested in validation of customer knowledge. Any incorrect information could exist among people based on certain as-

Table 2. Summary of the pilot study

Category	Number of Questionnaire Distributed	Number of Completed Questionnaires Returned	Number of Questionnaires Unreturned
Software Business Solution Companies	7	6	1
Organizations which Applied the CRM System	4	4	0
Total	11	10	1
Total Rate		91%	9%

sumptions or sources, which become facts and reality or justified true belief.

Six hypotheses addressed the associations between knowledge processes for customer and customer retention.

The six hypotheses which guided this line of inquiry are as follows:

H01: There is no direct positive relationship between Rationalization Customer Knowledge and Customer Retention.

H02: There is no direct positive relationship between understanding of Customer Knowledge and Customer Retention.

H03: There is no direct positive relationship between Inspection of Customer Knowledge and Customer Retention.

H04: There is no direct positive relationship between Development of Confidence Customer Knowledge and Customer Retention.

H05: There is no direct positive relationship between Experimentation of Customer Knowledge and Customer Retention.

H06: There is no direct positive relationship between the Validation of Customer Knowledge and Customer Retention.

4. RESEARCH METHODOLOGY

To ensure the reliability and validity of the questionnaire, several criteria have been considered when designing a questionnaire survey. Pilot test was conducted on the practitioners from the selected software business solution companies, and organizations which apply the CRM system to reduce and minimize any misunderstanding or ambiguous questions and procedures that will be used in conducting the survey. Ten completed questionnaires were received from the three software business solution companies and four organizations which apply the CRM system. This selection helps to give the best feedback about the content of the questionnaire and research. Table 2 shows a summary of the pilot sample.

The questionnaire starts with a brief description of the meaning of the main concepts and it gives the instructions on how to answer each section of the questionnaire and these are what make it of consistent style. An initial draft was developed based on an extensive literature review. It includes many questions which are in line with the research that aims at achieving several objectives. Therefore, the research survey could be described as being comprehensive.

It is divided into two parts. The first part includes personal information of the respondents such as age, gender, area of profession, and years of experience. The second part includes the questions related to variables that affect the integrated process for customer and customer retention.

Based on the feedback from the pilot study test, a few questions on companies' information that were not strictly relevant for testing the hypotheses were deleted.

4.1 Sample

The sample of the survey was divided into two categories in the Jordanian Companies, the three software business solution companies, and four companies which apply the CRM system. The software business solution companies represented those working in the CRM area. The organizations which apply the CRM system represented those used the CRM in organization. A total of 176 questionnaires were sent. A total of 168 questionnaires were returned, of which of 156 completed questionnaires were also returned and 12 uncompleted questionnaires were also returned. A total of 8 questionnaires were unreturned. To increase the return rate, each company was assigned a contact person to collect and return the questionnaires. Table 3 shows the summary of the sample size.

4.2 Data Collection

The researchers accepted the premise that even though all the relevant variables could not be studied simultaneously nor rigorously controlled, they must plunge in somewhere. Bernard (1988) suggests that all researchers operate under assumptions that enable them to see some things while preventing them from seeing others. The researcher should make assumptions as explicit as possible. Furthermore, Van Maanen's (1988) observation that behavior will depend on the respondent's definition of the situation seems to be a valid one.

The structural questionnaire design was applied to develop the survey instrument. Each was operationalized on a five points *Likert-type scale* where 1="strongly agree", and 5= "strongly disagree". In order to ensure the variables selected for this study are relevant to the respondents, a pilot study has been conducted to increase the validity and reliability of the questionnaire, experts were invited to review the questionnaire and pilot tests were administered before designing the final one. This pilot study has helped to identify the participants' opinions and experiences from their point of view.

This study relies on a quantitative approach of collecting information from the respondents. The research focuses on how the organizations understand and of view the purpose and importance of the process for knowledge to enhancement

Table 3. Summary of the sample size

Category		No of Questionnaire Distributed	No of Completed Questionnaires Returned	No of Uncompleted Questionnaires Returned	No of Questionnaires Unreturned
Software Business Solution Companies	First Company	25	22	2	1
	Second Company	9	9	0	0
	Third Company	7	7	0	0
Companies that Applied CRM System	First Company	45	38	5	2
	Second Company	30	26	1	3
	Third Company	40	36	2	2
	Fourth Company	20	18	2	0
Total		176	156	12	8

customer retention based on their experience or understanding. The data required for fulfilling this aim has been acquired using the quantitative approach. Surveys are a suitable research instrument for this research. The surveys allow for the collection of a large amount of data from a sizeable population in a highly economical way. As a general survey that aims at explanation, the survey of this research is concerned with the relationships between variables. The factor analysis was adopted to test construct validity.

The construct was subjected to the scale reliability procedure of SPSS 11.0, using the Cronbach's Alpha Cronbach (1951) criterion to assess the internal consistency of the studied construct. The Cronbach' Alpha coefficient is above 0.73 the value exceeds the accepted cut-off value of .70, as suggested by Nunnally (1978). This indicates that each individual item is internally consistent and highly reliable.

4.3 Data Analysis and Result

This study contains 113 males with a percentage of 72.4% and 43 females with a percentage of 27.6%. The largest group of respondents' (55 or 35.3%) indicates that their age ranges between 20-25 years, additionally, the smallest group of respondents' was between (36-40 years). The largest group of respondents' (55 or 35.3%) indicates that their area of specialization is Information Technology. The smallest group area of specialization of respondents' indicates MIS (4 or 2.6%). The largest group of respondents' (93 or 59.6%) indicates that their years of experience range from (1-5 years). Also, the smallest group of respondents' (13 or 8.3%) indicates that their years of experience range from (16-20 years). The demographic data are detailed in Table 4.

Based on the objectives and hypotheses of the study, the researcher applied the Analysis (ANOVA). The following in Table 5 represents the test of hypotheses by using Analysis of variance (ANOVA), based on the significant level of (0.05).

Table 4. Demographic data

Description	Variable	Result	Percentage
Gender	Male	113	72.4%
	Female	43	27.6%
Age	20-25 years	55	35.3%
	26-30	54	34.6%
	31-35	18	11.5%
	36-40	13	8.3
	40 and above	16	10.3
Area of specialization	Information Technology	55	35.3%
	MIS	4	2.6%
	Marketing	44	28.2%
	CRM	43	27.6%
	Others	10	6.4%
Experience	1-5 year	93	59.6%
	6-10	30	19.2%
	11-15	20	12.8%
	16-20	13	8.3%

Table 5. Regression test of hypotheses

Hypotheses	Independent variables	dependent variables	R square	T	Sig
H01	Rationalize Customer Knowledge	Customer Retention	0.18	8.77	0.00
H02	Understand Customer Knowledge	Customer Retention	0.29	4.78	0.00
H03	Inspect Customer Knowledge	Customer Retention	0.00	11.86	0.00
H04	Develop Confidence Customer Knowledge	Customer Retention	0.26	4.89	0.00
H05	Experiment Customer Knowledge	Customer Retention	0.38	10.45	0.00
H06	Validate Customer Knowledge	Customer Retention	0.15	3.69	0.00

The hypothesis is accepted if the significant level is more than (0.05).

Referring to Table 5, 18% of the variance in customer retention accounted by *Rationalize Customer Knowledge,* the *t* value is 8.77 with a significance equal 0.000, which is less than (0.05). Therefore, we reject the null hypothesis. The alternative hypothesis indicates that there is an effect of rationalize customer knowledge on customer retention the results are supported by previous studies. Bueren et al., (2004) explain the use of modern IT to provide knowledge support to CRM processes. This knowledge support allows for performance enhancement in customer oriented business processes.

Twenty-nine percent of the variance in customer retention accounted by Understand Customer Knowledge, the *t* value equal 4.78 with a significance equal 0.000, which is less than (0.05); therefore, we reject the null hypothesis. The alternative hypothesis indicates that Understand Customer Knowledge has an effect on customer retention. Bueren et al.., (2005) reported that, the CRM business process needs the processing of customer knowledge to understand the customer behavior and customer needs.

Zero percent of the variance in customer retention accounted by Inspect Customer Knowledge,

the *t* value equal 11.68 with significance equal to 0.000, which is less than (0.05); therefore, we reject the null hypothesis. The alternative hypothesis indicates that this has an effect of customer retention Ocker & Mudambi (2002*)* pointed out that the organizations require exploring CRM and KM methods to add value to the organization by the retention of the customer.

Twenty-six percent of the variance in customer retention accounted by Develop Confidence Customer Knowledge, the t value equal 4.89 with a significance equal to 0.000, which is less than (0.05); therefore, we reject the null hypothesis. The result is supported by Belbaly et al., (2007) who propose a new category of Information System referred to which enables the management knowledge to be embedded in the new product development processes.

Thirty-eight percent of the variance in customer retention accounted by Experimentation Customer Knowledge, the *t* value equal 10.45 with a significance equal to 0.000, which is less than (0.05); therefore, we reject the null hypothesis. The independent variable has a significant effect on customer retention. *Lin et al., (2006)* present the Knowledge CRM model which facilitates the examination of the relationship among the three dimensions: customer knowledge sources,

Customer Knowledge Management, and customer knowledge performance measurement.

Fifteen percent of the variance in customer retention accounted by Validation Customer Knowledge, the *t* value is 3.69 with a significance equal 0.000, which is less than (0.05); therefore, we reject the null hypothesis. The alternative hypothesis indicates that there is an effect of Validation Customer Knowledge on customer retention. It is supported by Gebert et al., (2002) who pointed out that, Knowledge for customers is required in CRM processes to satisfy knowledge needs of customers.

The relation between the knowledge processes for customer and the customer retention was confirmed in this study and the findings are summarized as follows:

1. Rationalize Customer Knowledge had a positive impact on the customer retention.
2. Understand Customer Knowledge had a positive impact on the customer retention.
3. Inspect Customer Knowledge had a positive impact on the customer retention.
4. Develop Confidence Customer Knowledge had a positive impact on the customer retention.
5. Experimentation Customer Knowledge had a positive impact on the customer retention.
6. Validation Customer Knowledge had a positive impact on the customer retention.

5. CONCLUSION

The results for this study show that all the selected factors have a significant impact on customer retention. Consequently, the paper describes the role of process for knowledge to accomplish customer knowledge retention. These processes help retain customers by providing the members of the organization with real information to react and make the right decisions to gain the competitive advantage.

The authors tried to address some voids in literature by proposing an empirically new conceptual model for the evolution of customer satisfaction in one of developing countries. The proposed model is based on a set of processes to achieve customer retention. Hopefully, these findings will shed some light for the policy makers to integrate knowledge processes for customers and customer retention to improve customer satisfaction in Jordanian companies.

However, there are limitations to this study and therefore the results cannot be generalized due to the sample size because the organizations that developed CRM system in Jordan is still low and the number of users is still small. The use of questionnaire as the only mean of the data collection can be considered as another limitation. The last limitation of this research is that this research has been undertaken in medium size Jordanian companies; therefore, this research is restricted to a certain context—Jordanian companies

In order to get a better understanding of knowledge processes for customers on Customer Retention, future research endeavors should focus on a big sample of respondents and several other developing countries for comparative purposes and significant analysis. Additionally, one major direction for further research would be geared towards replicating this study across a broader range of other countries in large organizations.

REFERENCES

Alavi, M., & Leidner, D. (2001). Review: Knowledge management and knowledge management system: Conceptual foundations and research issues. *MIS Quarterly, 25*(1), 107–136. doi:10.2307/3250961

AlKhaldi, F., Karadsheh, L., & Alhawari, S. (2006). *Knowledge management life cycle: An investigative methodology toward a conceptual framework.* Paper presented at the Sixth Annual international Conference for Business Ethics and Knowledge Society, Al-Zaytoonah Private University of Jordan.

Alryalat, H., & Alhawari, S. (2008, January 4-6). A review of theoretical framework: How to make process about, for, from knowledge work. In *Proceedings of the 9th International Business Information Management Association Conference (IBIMA) in the Information Management in Modern Organization*, Marrakech, Morocco (pp. 37-50). ISBN: 0-9753393-8-9.

Alryalat, H., Alhawari, S., & Al-Omoush, K. (2007, June 20-22). An integrated model for knowledge management and customer relationship management. In *Proceedings of the 8th International Business Information Management Association Conference (IBIMA) in the Networked Economy,* Dublin, Ireland (pp. 446- 453). ISBN: 0-9753393-7-0.

Belbaly, N., Benbya, H., & Meissonier, R. (2007). An empirical investigation of the customer knowledge creation impact on NPD performance. In *Proceedings of the 40th Hawaii International Conference on System Sciences* (pp. 193a). Washington, DC: IEEE Computer Society.

Bernard, R. (1988). *Research methods in cultural anthropology.* Newbury Park, CA: Sage.

Bhaskar, R., & Zhang, Y. (2005). CRM systems used for targeting market: A case at Cisco Systems. In *Proceedings of the International Conference on e-Business Engineering* (pp. 183-186). Washington, DC: IEEE Computer Society.

Bouthillier, F., & Shearer, K. (2002). Understanding knowledge management and information management: the need for an empirical perspective. *Information Research Journal, 8*(1), 1–39.

Bradshaw, D., & Brash, C. (2001). Management customer relationships in the e business world: how to personalise computer relationships for increased profitability. *International Journal of Retail & Distribution Management, 29*(12), 520–530. doi:10.1108/09590550110696969

Bueren, A., Schierholz, R., Kolbe, L., & Brenner, W. (2004). Customer knowledge management improving performance of customer relationship management with knowledge management. In *Proceedings of the 37th Hawaii International Conference on System Sciences* (pp. 70172b). Washington, DC: IEEE Computer Society.

Bueren, A., Schierholz, R., Kolbe, L., & Brenner, W. (2005). Improving performance of customer processes with knowledge management. *Business Process Management Journal, 11*(5), 573–588. doi:10.1108/14637150510619894

Buttle, F. (2004). *Customer relationship management.* Oxford, UK: Elsevier Butterworth-Heinemann.

Cao, Y., & Gruca, T. S. (2005). Reducing adverse selection through customer relationship management. *Journal of Marketing, 69,* 219–229. doi:10.1509/jmkg.2005.69.4.219

Chen, I. J., & Popovich, K. (2003). Understanding Customer Relationship Management (CRM) people, process and technology. *Business Process Management Journal, 9*(5), 672–688. doi:10.1108/14637150310496758

Chen, Q., & Chen, H. (2004). Exploring the success factors of eCRM strategies in practice. *Database Marketing & Customer Strategy Management, 11*(4), 333–343. doi:10.1057/palgrave.dbm.3240232

Cronbach, L. J. (1951). Coefficient alpha and the internal structure of tests. *Psychometrika, 16,* 297–333. doi:10.1007/BF02310555

Deng, Q., & Yu, D. (2006). An approach to integrating knowledge management into the product development process. *Journal of Knowledge Management Practice, 7*(2).

Dous, M., Salomann, H., Kolbe, L., & Brenner, W. (2005). Knowledge management capabilities in CRM: Making knowledge For, from and about customers work. In *Proceedings of the Eleventh Americas Conference on Information Systems,* Omaha, NE (pp. 167-178).

Firestone, J. M., & McElroy, M. W. (2005). Doing knowledge management. *The Learning Organization Journal, 12,* 1–29.

Fjermestad, J., & Romano, N. C. (2003). Electronic customer relationship management revisiting the general theories of usability and resistance: An integrative implementation framework. *Business Process Management Journal, 9*(5), 572–591. doi:10.1108/14637150310496695

Gebert, H., Geib, M., Kolbe, L., & Riempp, G. (2002). Towards customer knowledge management: Integrating customer relationship management and knowledge management concepts. In *Proceedings of the 2nd International Conference on Electronic Business,* Taipei, Taiwan.

Gibbert, M., Leibold, M., & Probst, G. (2002). Five styles of customer knowledge management and how smart companies use them to create value. *European Management Journal, 20*(5), 459–546. doi:10.1016/S0263-2373(02)00101-9

Goh, A. L S. (2005). Adoption of Customer Relationship Management (CRM) solutions as an Effective Knowledge Management (KM) tool: A systems ValueDiagnostic. *Journal of Knowledge Management Practice, 6*. Retrieved from http://www.tlainc.com/jkmpv6.htm. ISSN 1705-9232.

Kamakura, W., Mela, C., Ansari, A., Bodapati, A., Fader, P., & Iyengar, R. (2005). Choice models and customer relationship management. *Marketing Letters, 16*(3), 279–291. doi:10.1007/s11002-005-5892-2

Lai, H., & Chu, T. H. (2000). Knowledge management: A review of theoretical frameworks and industrial cases. In *Proceedings of the 33rd Hawaii International Conference on System Sciences* (pp. 3022). Washington, DC: IEEE Computer Society.

Lariviere, B., & Poel, D. V. D. (2004). investigating the role of product features in preventing customer churn, by using survival analysis and choice modeling: The case of financial services. *Expert Systems with Applications, 27,* 277–285. doi:10.1016/j.eswa.2004.02.002

Levine, S. (2000). The rise of CRM. *America's Network, 104*(6), 34.

Lin, Y., Su, H.-Y., & Shihen, C. (2006). A knowledge enabled procedure for customer relationship management. *Industrial Marketing Management, 35,* 446–456. doi:10.1016/j.indmarman.2005.04.002

Massey, A. P., Montoya-Weiss, M., & Holcom, K. (2001). Re-engineering the customer relationship: Leveraging knowledge assets at IBM. *Decision Support Systems, 32*(2), 155–170. doi:10.1016/S0167-9236(01)00108-7

Miltiadis, D. L., Pouloudi, A., & Poulymenakou, A. (2002). Knowledge management convergence expanding learning frontiers. *Journal of Knowledge Management, 6*(1), 40–51. doi:10.1108/13673270210417682

Newell, F. (2000). *Loyalty.com: Customer relationship management in the new era of internet marketing.* New York: McGraw-Hill, New York.

Nunnally, J. C. (1978). *Psychometric theory* (2nd ed.). New York: McGraw-Hill.

Ocker, R. J., & Mudambi, S. (2002). Assessing the readiness of firms for CRM: A literature review and research model. In *Proceedings of the 36th Hawaii International Conference on System Sciences* (pp. 10). Washington, DC: IEEE Computer Society.

Papoutsakis, H., & Vallès, R. S. (2006). Linking knowledge management and information technology to business performance: A literature review and a proposed model. *Journal of Knowledge Management Practice, 7*(1).

Payne, A., Christopher, M., Clark, M., & Peck, H. (1999). *Relationship marketing for competitive advantage* (2nd ed.). Oxford, UK: Butterworth Heinemann.

Reichheld, F. (1996). *The loyalty effect.* Cambridge, MA: Harvard Business School Press.

Reinartz, W., Krafft, M., & Hoyer, W. (2004). The customer relationship management process: Its measurement and impact on performance. *JMR, Journal of Marketing Research, 61*(1), 293–305. doi:10.1509/jmkr.41.3.293.35991

Rigby, D., Reichheld, F., & Schefter, P. (2002). Avoid the four perils of CRM. *Harvard Business Review, 80*(2), 101.

Ryals, L., & Knox, S. (2001). Cross functional issues in the implementation of relationship marketing through customer relationship management. *European Management Journal, 19*(5), 534. doi:10.1016/S0263-2373(01)00067-6

Salomann, H., Dous, M., Kolbe, L., & Brenner, W. (2005). Rejuvenating customer management: How to make knowledge for, from and about customers work. *European Management Journal, 23*(4), 392–403. doi:10.1016/j.emj.2005.06.009

Satyadas, A., Harigopal, U., & Cassaigne, N. P. (2001). Knowledge management tutorial: An editorial overview. *IEEE Transactions on Systems, Man and Cybernetics. Part C, Applications and Reviews, 31*(4), 429–437. doi:10.1109/5326.983926

Saunders, M., Lewis, P., & Thornhill, A. (2007). *Research methods for business students* (4th ed.). Upper Saddle River, NJ: Prentice Hhall.

Sheth, N. J. (2002). The future of relationship marketing. *Journal of Services Marketing, 16*(7), 590–593. doi:10.1108/08876040210447324

Stefanou, J., Sarmaniotis, C., & Stafyla, A. (2003). ACRM and customer-centric knowledge management: An empirical research. *Business Process Management Journal, 9*(5), 617–634. doi:10.1108/14637150310496721

Sun, Z. (2004). A waterfall model for knowledge management and experience management. In *Proceedings of the 4th International Conference on Hybrid Intelligent Systems,* Kitakyushu, Japan, (pp. 472-475). Washington, DC: IEEE Computer Society.

Sun, Z., & Gang, G. (2006). HSM: A Hierarchical Spiral Model for knowledge management. In *Proceedings the 2nd International Conference on Information Management and Business,* Sydney, Australia (pp. 542-551).

Sunassee, N. N., & Sewry, D. A. (2002). A theoretical framework for knowledge management implementation. In *Proceedings of the Annual Research Conference of the South African Institute of Computer Scientists and Information Technologists (SAICSIT) on Enablement through Technology* (pp. 235-245).

Van Maanen, J. (1988). Tales of the field: On writing ethnography. Chicago: *University of Chicago Press.*

Wong, Y. K. (2006). Issues of software quality and management in practice: An empirical investigation of use of explicit documents in software review. *International Journal of Internet and Enterprise Management, 4*(1), 37–53. doi:10.1504/IJIEM.2006.008864

Yin, R. K. (1994). *Case study research: Design and methods* (2nd ed.). Thousand Oaks, CA: Sage.

APPENDIX: QUESTIONNAIRE DESIGN

Part One: Personal Information

1. Which gender are you?

Male		❑
Female		❑

2. How many years old were you on the 1st of January 2008?

20 or less		❑
21-30		❑
31-40		❑
41-50		❑

3. Area of specialization

Information Technology		❑
Management Information System		❑
Marketing		❑
Customer Relationship Management		❑
Other		❑

4. How many years in professional life?

Less than 1 year		❑
1-2 years		❑
3-5 years		❑
6-10 years		❑
11 years or more		❑

Part Two: Information on Customer Knowledge Retention

Please put √ under level of agreement you have for each of the following questions					
Questions	**Strongly Agree**	**Agree**	**Neutral**	**Disagree**	**Strongly Disagree**
1. Knowledge Process for customer is important in attaining Customer retention					
2. Knowledge Process for customer produces customer knowledge creation					
3. Rationalization stage helps to obtain the relevant information for a specific subject					
4. Understanding customer knowledge stage is important to understand the content					
5. Understanding customer knowledge stage is important to understand the meaning					
6. Understanding customer knowledge stage is important to understand the importance and purpose of the knowledge					
7. Inspecting customer knowledge stage focuses on careful examination of the content of knowledge to tests its accuracy.					
8. Inspecting customer knowledge stage focuses on careful examination of the content of knowledge to tests its correctness					
9. Developing confidence about the customer knowledge builds up a feeling of trust about the captured knowledge					
10. Developing assurance about the captured knowledge					
11. Knowledge can go through experiment for testing					
12. Knowledge can go through experiment for updating					
13. Knowledge for Customer includes the Knowledge of customers need in their interaction with the organization					
14. Verification ensures that the phase of "knowledge for Customer" verifies retaining customers					
15. Retention phase is considered to be a way of preserving a relationship with existing customers					
16. Retention phase focuses on supporting and raising a long-lasting relationship with customer					
17. Retention phase builds its success on customer satisfaction					

This work was previously published in International Journal of Knowledge Management, Volume 6, Issue 1, edited by Murray E. Jennex, pp. 44-61, copyright 2010 by IGI Publishing (an imprint of IGI Global).

Chapter 4
Using Knowledge Management to Create Self-Reliant Communities in Thailand

Chalard Chantarasombat
Mahasarakham University, Thailand

Boonchom Srisa-ard
Mahasarakham University, Thailand

Matthew H. S. Kuofie
University of Central Michigan, USA

Murray E. Jennex
San Diego State University, USA

ABSTRACT

Many look at knowledge management as an organizational initiative. However, can KM also be used to assist low technology situations such as rural villages? This paper describes the application of KM to the creation of a self-reliant community in Thailand. Changing demographics are threatening the ability of rural villages to sustain their viability as traditional methods of passing knowledge from one generation to the next are circumvented by the movement of the young to more urbanized areas of Thailand. KM is seen as a way of changing the traditional knowledge transfer process to something that assists those who remain in the villages. The KM approach investigated consisted of five stages: 1) Preparation, 2) Create motivation, awareness, promote participation, 3) Develop the KM plan, 4) Implement the KM plan, and 5) Evaluation. The approach was assessed and found to be successful by using eight organizations over an 8-month period.

INTRODUCTION

The world is experiencing fast economic, social and technological changes and global competition relies on knowledge. Society not only relies on funds, labor, natural resources and raw materials for creating production values but also needs knowledge for creating innovation and intellectual property. Development of this body of knowledge can affect competition and the strength of community, organization, and institute which are regarded as the foundation of the process of country development (Patthamasiriwat, 2004). Sharing this body

DOI: 10.4018/978-1-4666-0035-5.ch004

of knowledge improves the ability of knowledge workers to further innovate. An important element of knowledge management (KM) is the process of knowledge sharing (Kuofie, 2005; Wichainpanya, 2005). Therefore, Thai society should promote knowledge creators and users to generate added value and competitive capability within a social context of improving Thai society, raising living standards, and general well being by using five religious principles. These five principles are morality, intelligence, right economy, right state, and strong society. These are in accordance with the National Plan for Economic and Social Development 9 (2002-2006). This plan determines development vision based on these five principles (Watthanasiritham, 2003).

In Thai society, the most important thing is not resources such as labor or money; the most important resource is knowledge. Thai society is constantly learning. KM and learning processes are very important. Management of the leaning process for the community can help it discover and develop human potential until it can rely on itself. A strong Thai community which can rely on itself must support these four basic principles: 1) create reliability, 2) rehabilitate relationships, 3) develop management systems, and 4) learning process (Phongphit, Nanthasuwan, & Raekphinit, 2001).

All strong Thai communities and organizations must be ready to learn. Self-reliant communities in the Changwat (administrative province) of Maha Sarakham have various types of groups including cooperative groups, occupation groups and local wisdom groups. There are interesting areas of learning, particularly in the Tambon (sub-district) of Na kha and the Tambon (sub-district) of Pracha Phatthana in the Amphoe (district) of Wapi Pathum (Chantarasombat, 2004) These communities regard principles of community welfare and community enterprises as guidelines for self-reliance. They began activities by forming occupation groups, using available local raw materials to be transformed into products and using local

wisdom to adjust to current situations. Thailand is attempting to create jobs and occupations for community people to rely on themselves. However, they still lack systematic KM/KM mechanisms to support the communities to work efficiently and continuously. Thus the researchers were interested in conducting this study to develop a KM model for self-reliant communities in the Changwat (administrative province) of Maha Sarakham by applying a mix of participatory research, quantitative and qualitative research techniques. If a Thai community successfully implements the KM model for self-reliant communities, the community becomes self-reliant and loves one another better than before the implementation.

This paper presents the lessons and experience gained in developing KM and KMS for building self reliant communities in Thailand. The purpose of this paper is three-fold:

1. To develop a KM process model for creating self-reliant communities in Thailand,
2. To examine success and satisfaction with KM and KMS developed for creating self-reliant communities implementing the KM model
3. To identify success factors for KM and KMS for creating self-reliant communities.

BACKGROUND

Jennex (2005) defines KM as the practice of selectively applying knowledge from previous experiences of decision making to current and future decision making activities with the express purpose of improving the organization's effectiveness. Also, Jennex (2005) viewed a KM system, KMS, as that system created to facilitate the capture, storage, retrieval, transfer, and reuse of knowledge. The perception of KM and KMS is that they holistically combine organizational and technical solutions to achieve the goals of knowledge retention and reuse to ultimately improve organizational and individual decision making. This is a Churchman (1979) view of KM that allows KMS to take whatever form necessary to accomplish these goals. Another key definition of KM includes Holsapple and Joshi (2004) who consider KM as an entity's systematic and deliberate efforts to expand, cultivate, and apply available knowledge in ways that add value to the entity, in the sense of positive results in accomplishing its objectives or fulfilling its purpose. The entity's scope may be individual, organizational, tran organizational, national, etc. Finally, Alavi and Leidner (2001) in their seminal work concluded that KM involves distinct but interdependent processes of knowledge creation, knowledge storage and retrieval, knowledge transfer, and knowledge application.

Davenport and Prusak (1998) view knowledge as an evolving mix of framed experience, values, contextual information and expert insight that provides a framework for evaluating and incorporating new experiences and information. They found that in organizations, knowledge often becomes embedded in documents or repositories and in organizational routines, processes, practices, and norms. They also say that for knowledge to have value it must include the human additions of context, culture, experience, and interpretation. Nonaka (1994) expands this view by stating that knowledge is about meaning in the sense that it is context-specific. This implies that users of knowledge must understand and have experience with the context, or surrounding conditions and influences, in which the knowledge is generated and used for it to have meaning to them. This also implies that for a knowledge repository to be useful it must also store the context in which the knowledge was generated. That knowledge is context specific argues against the idea that knowledge can be applied universally, however it does not argue against the concept of organizational knowledge. Organizational knowledge is considered to be an integral component of what organizational mem-

bers remember and use meaning that knowledge is actionable. This paper applies these concepts in the Thai culture and illustrates how knowledge and KM can be culturally applied.

METHODOLOGY

The study was divided into five phases:

- **Phase 1: Literature Review.** The literature review involved the study of KM literature for basic concepts and definitions as well as relevant models. Formulated the conceptual framework used to generate the KM model for Thai self reliant communities.

- **Phase 2: Focus Group Selection.** Two villages were selected, Ban Nam Kliang and Ban Lao Rat Phatthana. These villages were selected because they had established community organization groups and had begun self reliant community development activities but had not implemented KM. Additionally, eight community organizations were selected for the study: agricultural cooperative group, mulberry and silk raising group, biofertilizer group, Thai traditional massage group, toxin-free rice production group, herbal Thai noodles group, cultural conservation group, and savings group. The requirements for group selection included three dimensions: establishment, sizes, and activity types. Establishment dimension had 2 types: established by the state and established by each community itself. Size dimension had large size, medium size, and small size. Dimension of activity types had various types such as cooperative, occupation group, and local wisdom.

- **Phase 3: KM Process Model Development.** A tentative process model for KM in self-reliant communities in Thailand was generated based on the research conceptual framework generated in phase 1 and based on the scope of major activities for KM (Nanaka & Takeuchi, 1995; Panich, 2005; Wiig, 1993). The tentative KM model was submitted to five experts for review based on appropriateness, feasibility, and congruence with KM plans and group development plans. Their comments were used to revise the KM model for self-reliant communities in Thailand and improve it.

- **Phase 4: Implementation of the KM process in the two villages.**
- **Phase 5: Assessment of the effectiveness of the KM Process Model.** An assessment questionnaire was developed using American Productivity & Quality Center and Arthur Andersen. (2005) and David Skyrme Associates (2005). The questionnaire consisted of two parts: Part 1: General data of the evaluator and Part 2: Operation of knowledge management of community organization groups. To improve the response rate and to reduce the likelihood of unusable responses, each part also included simple instructions for completing it. The questionnaire was then piloted by surveying a random sample of some of the communities. The questionnaire was adjusted based on the result of the pilot test (see appendix A for the final questionnaire). The final questionnaire was distributed to eight community organizational groups: 1) agricultural cooperative group of Nam Kliang Wiang Chiang, 2) mulberry and silk raising group, 3) biofertilizer group, 4) Thai traditional massage group, 5) toxin-free rice production group, 6) herbal Thai noodles group, 7) civic-society--cultural conservation group, 8) and savings group. Forty evaluation/questionnaire forms were sent to the identified group members. There

were 20 group members in each of the two villages: Ban Nam Kliang and Ban Lao Rat Phatthana. A total of 34 responses were received; 16 responses from Ban Nam Kliang and 18 responses from the Ban Lao Rat Phatthana. Eight months were spent evaluating the KM process model with the groups. The questionnaires consisted of 25 5-point Likert scale items. Responses were analyzed by determining the mean and standard deviation for each of the villages.

THE KM APPROACH

The developed KM process model for self-reliant communities in Thailand is shown in Figure 1. As can be seen in Figure 1, the KM Process Model for Self-Reliant Community in Thailand has 18 activities grouped into five stages.

The KM process was implemented in the two selected villages with the support of a KM advising team from Mahasarakham University in northern Thailand. The advising team provided support throughout the period of the study. It is interesting to note that all the community organizations still continued using KM in the issues they were interested in and desired to develop their work process body of knowledge even after the KM study was completed.

FINDINGS AND OBSERVATIONS

Both villages were able to implement the KM process model. Each functional group was able to form a KM team consisting of community knowledge managers that served as facilitators, group work performers, record keepers, and coordinators. Lessons learned were generated through work performance and with knowledge obtained from solving problems and answering questions to create the appropriate body of knowledge. The community learning process occurred through

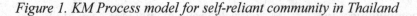

Figure 1. KM Process model for self-reliant community in Thailand

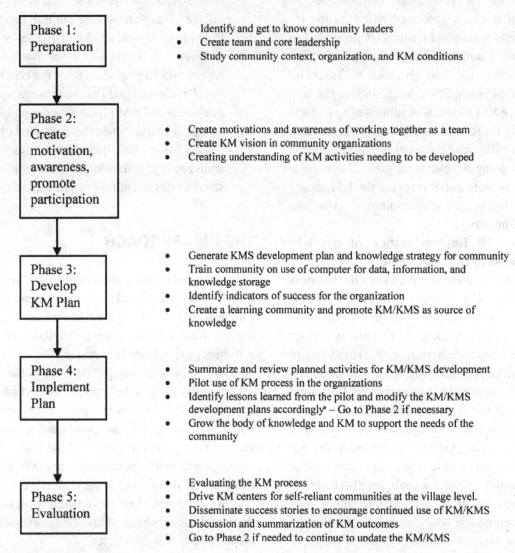

| Phase 1: Preparation | • Identify and get to know community leaders
 • Create team and core leadership
 • Study community context, organization, and KM conditions |

| Phase 2: Create motivation, awareness, promote participation | • Create motivations and awareness of working together as a team
 • Create KM vision in community organizations
 • Creating understanding of KM activities needing to be developed |

| Phase 3: Develop KM Plan | • Generate KMS development plan and knowledge strategy for community
 • Train community on use of computer for data, information, and knowledge storage
 • Identify indicators of success for the organization
 • Create a learning community and promote KM/KMS as source of knowledge |

| Phase 4: Implement Plan | • Summarize and review planned activities for KM/KMS development
 • Pilot use of KM process in the organizations
 • Identify lessons learned from the pilot and modify the KM/KMS development plans accordingly – Go to Phase 2 if necessary
 • Grow the body of knowledge and KM to support the needs of the community |

| Phase 5: Evaluation | • Evaluating the KM process
 • Drive KM centers for self-reliant communities at the village level.
 • Disseminate success stories to encourage continued use of KM/KMS
 • Discussion and summarization of KM outcomes
 • Go to Phase 2 if needed to continue to update the KM/KMS |

building, classifying, storing, implementing, sharing, and evaluating knowledge. KM centers were created and served to be drivers for the groups to meet and share knowledge in each village. Additionally web based KM centers were created as repositories and sources for disseminating KM outcomes and knowledge.

The community organizations/groups were highly satisfied with KM operation for self-reliant communities as a whole. When accessed at the village level Ban Lao Rat Phatthana had more satisfaction with operation of community organization knowledge management than Ban Nam Kliang. Ban Lao Rat Phatthana had an average satisfaction of 3.70 compared to Ban Nam Kliang's 3.32. This was determined to be due to greater top management support as at Ban Lao Rat Phatthana, all the community organization groups were greatly satisfied with KM operation because the community leaders were interested in and had participatory administration, distributed work for all members to do according to the functional roles of KM centers, leading to operation to achieve the goals, visions, and mis-

Table 1. Satisfaction with operation of community organization KM as a whole

Aspect	Ban Nam Kliang			Ban Lao Rat Phatthana		
	$\overline{X}$	S.D.	Satisfaction	$\overline{X}$	S.D.	Satisfaction
Knowledge management process	3.32	0.70	medium	3.70	0.25	high
Knowledge management leadership	3.41	0.61	medium	3.91	0.34	high
Knowledge management culture	3.56	0.74	high	4.11	0.42	high
Knowledge management technology	3.21	0.82	medium	3.81	0.49	high
Knowledge management evaluation	3.52	0.58	high	3.86	0.38	high
As a Whole	3.40	0.58	medium	3.88	0.23	high

Table 2. Satisfaction with operation of community organization KM in the aspect of KM process

Evaluation Item	Ban Nam Kliang			Ban Lao Rat Phatthana		
	$\overline{X}$	S.D.	Satisfaction	$\overline{X}$	S.D.	Satisfaction
Your community organization group has a systematic analysis for finding out flaws in knowledge and uses the process with clear stages to correct the flaws.	3.22	0.88	medium	4.06	0.57	high
Your community organization group seeks knowledge systematically.	3.50	0.86	medium	3.56	0.63	high
All of your community organization group members participate in seeking new ideas/concepts.	3.11	0.90	medium	3.31	0.60	medium
Your organization group transfers knowledge and teaches work to members to learn systematically.	3.28	1.07	medium	3.56	0.63	high
Your organization group appreciates knowledge available in itself.	3.50	0.71	medium	4.00	0.63	high
As a Whole	3.32	0.70	medium	3.70	0.25	high

sions. However, three community organization groups at Ban Nam Kliang had satisfaction with KM operation at a high level and one group at a medium level because the community leaders who were KM center heads had not yet realized the importance of group forming and participatory work performance and because they did not participate in activities continuously. Tables 1-6 summarize the findings on satisfaction.

The success factors for the KM Process Model for Self-Reliant Communities in Thailand are summarized as follows:

A. The inclusion of the KM research advisory team as participant, learner, instructor, and manager reinforced the use of the KM process model.

B. Provision of opportunities for participants to participate in all stages and activities of the KM Process Model contributed to the participants viewing themselves as owners of the KM process. This factor generated continuity and commitment to perform work by them. Also, it generated reliability in their own organizational body of knowledge and

Table 3. Satisfaction with operation of community organization KM in the aspect of KM leadership

Evaluation Item	Ban Nam Kliang			Ban Lao Rat Phatthana		
	$\overline{X}$	S.D.	Satisfaction	$\overline{X}$	S.D.	Satisfaction
Knowledge management is an important strategy of your organization group.	3.28	0.67	medium	4.13	0.72	high
Your organization group understands potentials in production and products of its own.	3.56	0.86	high	4.06	0.57	high
Your organization group members can adjust themselves to catch up with present situations.	3.22	0.73	medium	3.88	0.72	high
Your organization group members use learning to add to available capability of the organization group for strength.	3.56	0.86	high	3.63	0.72	high
Having an evaluation and giving compensations to group members are done by considering participation in building the body of knowledge of the organization.	3.17	0.71	medium	3.94	0.68	high
Your organization group members share learning with one another.	3.67	0.77	high	3.81	0.91	high
As a Whole	3.41	0.61	medium	3.91	0.34	high

Table 4. Satisfaction with operation of community organization KM in the aspect of KM culture

Evaluation Item	Ban Nam Kliang			Ban Lao Rat Phatthana		
	$\overline{X}$	S.D.	Satisfaction	$\overline{X}$	S.D.	Satisfaction
Your organization group has climate of openness and trust in one another.	3.78	0.81	high	3.81	0.91	high
Members of your organization group operate knowledge management of creating value to the products.	3.39	0.78	medium	4.19	0.66	high
Your organization group members learned from the outcomes that occurred, and then improved the work.	3.61	0.85	high	4.06	0.77	high
All of the members are responsible for knowledge management in the organization.	3.44	0.98	medium	4.38	0.62	high
As a Whole	3.56	0.74	high	4.11	0.42	high

more overall self-reliance in themselves and the village.

C. Learning by practicing, improving and developing work, raising new questions, and implementing in practices to achieve the goals could be caused by participatory action research (PAR), which could originate interactions with one another in their own group and other groups in the village.

D. People and self-reliant communities were enthusiastic to learn. For work performance in their own groups and sharing learning at the group, village, and cross-village levels, they tried to use tacit knowledge through practice and trying out until they were confident. There were documentation of lessons and record keeping as explicit documents. Then the meaningful body of knowledge of the community organizations occurred.

E. There were supporting mechanisms of KM centers of community organizations, which Tambon Administrative Organizations of

Table 5. Satisfaction with operation of community organization KM in the aspect of KM technology

Evaluation Item	Ban Nam Kliang			Ban Lao Rat Phatthana		
	$\overline{X}$	S.D.	Satisfaction	$\overline{X}$	S.D.	Satisfaction
Computer is used to benefit data storage.	3.00	1.28	medium	3.88	0.81	high
Data are classified according to the knowledge base in the community.	3.22	1.06	medium	3.75	0.68	high
The use of web site at the Knowledge Management Center is for studying and dissemination.	2.89	1.02	medium	3.88	0.89	high
The information systems of the organization group can provide information and the information can be utilized.	3.50	0.71	medium	3.75	0.86	high
Knowledge sharing from database leads to work development.	3.44	0.86	medium	3.81	0.75	high
As a Whole	3.21	0.82	medium	3.81	0.49	high

Table 6. Satisfaction with operation of community organization KM in the aspect of KM evaluation

Evaluation Item	Ban Nam Kliang			Ban Lao Rat Phatthana		
	$\overline{X}$	S.D.	Satisfaction	$\overline{X}$	S.D.	Satisfaction
Your organization group invented new techniques affecting operation in continuity.	3.61	0.92	high	3.50	0.89	medium
Your organization group determines and uses indicators of success in supplement to knowledge management and work development.	3.33	0.84	medium	3.56	0.89	high
Indicators of success balance with operation of your organization group.	3.33	0.69	medium	3.94	0.85	high
Resources are sought for the Knowledge Management Center of your organization group.	3.67	0.77	high	4.06	0.68	high
The group members have works or pieces of work to be proud of.	3.67	0.69	high	4.25	0.58	high
As a Whole	3.52	0.58	high	3.86	0.38	high

these villages had been partnerships. These Tambon organizations allotted budgets to support some activities based on the plans/projects, and their representatives participated in the research as participants.

DISCUSSION

The KM Model for Self-Reliant Communities in Thailand was found to be successful and able to originate expected outcomes. This was because

in developing the model, the researchers used the conceptual framework from analyzing and synthesizing concepts and research results of qualified persons at an international level both in the part of KM and the part of techniques of development such as the KM concepts of Nonaka and Takeuchi (1995), Panich (2005), and the KM process of Wiig (1993). Integration into development techniques included the use of principles of working of His Majesty (HM) the King of Thailand involving self-reliance, participation; and knowing, love, and, unity. These were community preparation, after-action recording, questioning, and knowledge sharing both on real and unreal forums. Also, there were mechanisms supporting KM: village KM centers as centers for operational sources and as websites, resulting in integrated KM for self-reliant communities.

Some evidence indicating success which should be discussed included the following:

A. Important learning persons. Every organization had four groups of knowledge managers: facilitators, practitioners, note takers, and network managers. This is in accordance with Nonaka and Takeuchi (1995). Members of each organization understood their own functions in KM: the real knowledge manager was the practitioner; the medium-level administrators were interpreters who transformed tacit knowledge to explicit knowledge on paper. The group of knowledge managers determined goals, created the climate to help in sharing knowledge, and extracted knowledge to originate values (Panich, 2005).

B. Learning together with practices. Sources of knowledge were problems, question raising, problem solving by real practitioners until the proper body of knowledge emerged, leading to KM based on the issues the members were interested in. The KM issues included classifying, storing, implementing, and sharing knowledge; and evaluation. This is in congruence with the principles of working of King Bhumibol Adulyadej (Office of Special committee for coordination in Projects from H.M. the King's considerations). The King considers that for knowing, love and unity, people and the group of people must know by knowing that before beginning to do anything, we must know it first, know all the factors, know the problems, and know how to solve those problems. We must have love to have to consider beginning to act in solving those problems. Also, we must

have unity in practice. We should always remember that nobody can work alone. We must work collaboratively and spiritedly as an organization or a staff to have power to solve the problems successfully, This is in accordance with Wasi (2002) who says that anybody's learning is not sufficient to make a task successful because other involved people, organizations, and institutes have not learned; and only learning together in practice will bring success which must manage knowledge through practices as package of knowledge of each group of organizations. Also, it is in congruence with Phlainoi (2003) who says that after-action recording (AAR) is regarded as important learning in extraction of proper knowledge gist and findings of persons or organizations.

C. KM centers as drivers. KM centers were drivers for groups to meet and share learning at each village and to operate work to achieve the established visions, missions, goals, and purposes. Each center administrative committee followed up the progress in work development through the real monthly meeting forum and the realities forum. There were web sites in the Internet system as sources of disseminating KM works and as sources of storing knowledge and sharing learning. This is in accordance with the concept of Nonaka and Takeuchi (1995) and Panich (2005) that KM must rely on utilization of information technology and communication to support KM and on instruments or technology to use in KM.

The self-reliant communities had satisfaction with KM operation of community organizations as a whole at a high level. When classified into villages, it was found that three community organization groups at Ban Nam Kliang had satisfaction with KM operation at a high level and one group at a medium level because the community leaders who were KM center heads had not yet realized the importance of group forming and participatory work performance and because they did not participate in activities continuously. However, at Ban Lao Rat Phatthana, all the community organization groups had satisfaction with KM operation at a high level because the community leaders were interested in and had participatory administration, distributed work for all members to do according to the functional roles of KM centers, leading to operation to achieve the goals, visions, and missions.

Some significant success factors of the KM model which should be discussed were as follows.

A. For the important persons in KM of self-reliant communities when this research was being conducted in the last phase, the team of participants intended to work for the public advantages to originate success according to their functional roles, expressed their sense of belonging to activities and plans/work, and sought more cooperation from persons and organizations both in and outside their communities.

B. Providing opportunities for participants to have participation from the beginning; thinking together, planning together, performing together, checking together, and being responsible for conducting research together. This is in congruence with Sinlarat (1998). The principles of administration of organization leaders which trusted these leaders were having prestige and having high influences on the organization. Therefore, if the leader built understanding and cooperatively determined assumptions on participatory working together and then it would affect working together, satisfaction with working and having good work climate; and would push work to be successful.

C. Learning by practicing is the way of life. It is practiced by actual action. Experience in the new body of knowledge emerges, which can help in actual applications. There

occurred connection and relationships with one another between persons and groups of organizations. Integrated KM and participatory research emerge' this is in accordance with the research work of Yawanut Thinnalak (2006). She conducted a study entitled Building Knowledge of Thai Society for Permanent Development. She found that building knowledge appropriately in accordance with Thai society was regarded as the way of self-reliance; developed the learning innovations in which they had aptitudes, could build the body of knowledge for solving problems and living joyfully in the society.

D. Mechanisms supporting working together: KM centers for self-reliant comminuting under management by the team of participants to follow up the progress in operation of self-reliant communities to originate continuity and connection and relationships among one another. There were web sites and utilization of the Internet system as sources of seeking knowledge and disseminating KM works and as sources of storing other finds of knowledge and sharing knowledge of community people.

RECOMMENDATIONS AND FUTURE RESEARCH

After completion of the KM Process Model assessment, the KM research team reflected on possible lessons learned and improvements. The following are recommendations of the KM research team.

Recommendations for Implementing the KM Process Model

For implementation of the developed KM model for self-reliant communities to obtain full benefits, it is necessary to operate all the 5 stages and 18 major activities. In case the self-reliant communities have ongoing KM operations, they can begin operation from Activity 11, summarize and review plans and activities for developing KM. KM operation of the organization groups may begin together with activities for group development which are not quite difficult, or may operate upgrading the body of knowledge and KM in the issues in which the groups are interested. Additionally, Activities 16-18 are important for the KM centers at the village level and must be implemented to create continuity in the KM process.

The team of participants regarded as real knowledge managers including facilitators, group practitioners, note takers, and coordinators should prepare readiness in the academic aspects: participatory planning, community master plans, learning together with practices in utilizing Internet and web sites. (Note: neither of the subject villages had Internet access prior to the KM project.)

The KM centers of self-reliant communities regarded as mechanisms driving the team of participants to share knowledge of what they have found and summarized lessons with conclusions should take after-action records for summarizing to the appropriate body of knowledge of the organization groups as obtained from practices on both real forum and realistic forum.

Support and promote self-reliant communities to use community plans as plans for determining the direction of community development based on the visions and strategies for developing the determined areas. There must be continuous follow-ups and evaluation. Also, there must be objective indicators of KM success for KM of self-reliant communities.

Areas for Future Research

Learning processes should be examined together with practices of self-reliant communities in individuals and groups. Particular attention needs to be paid to determining the appropriate frequency and type of knowledge artifact. Examples of knowledge artifacts include summaries, narra-

tions, transcription of lessons, knowledge sharing, and note-taking.

There should be research in and development of activity curricula for developing capacity for community leaders, organization group leaders, and local knowledge managers. This training should enable these persons to be efficient in KM so that they can serve as process resources and facilitators in the community to generate learning leading to healthy and joyful villages.

There should be research and development for upgrading KM centers of self-reliant communities to better enable community organization network involving practices of knowledge managers leading to transference of experiences and working standards as a part of learning difference course in providing education.

This research should be replicated in more villages to ensure the KM Process Model can be generalized to all of Thailand.

CONCLUSION

Can KM be used in a low technology environment to assist traditional social structures in changing the way knowledge is transferred? This paper suggests it can. While applied in a Thai rural context, the practical implication of this research is that any social process that relies on a traditional, family based, knowledge pass down approach (father to son, mother to daughter, parent to child) can be maintained by changing the knowledge transfer process to a more social basis per Nonaka and Takeuchi (1995) (in particular by applying the socialization process). The key to success is in creating local social structures to replace broken family structures. This paper looks at rural villages in Thailand where the youth are migrating away from the rural villages to the opportunities in the urban centers. The remaining villagers are facing economic decline as the traditional family structures are failing to pass knowledge to villagers outside of the family. Researchers used a KM Process Model that was based on the creation of social "families"—groups forged on common interest in a knowledge area. Each group identified knowledge leaders and knowledge capture processes that led to the creation of group specialized bodies of knowledge. These bodies of knowledge served as replacement knowledge repositories for traditional family repositories and were made available to all in the social group. The two villages where the KM Process Model was piloted experienced economic success. This leads to the conclusion that this research is successful in helping to create economically sustainable rural villages.

Limitations to this research are an unclear understanding of the impact of Thai culture on the success of the KM Process Model. Further research is needed to determine if the reason the KM Process Model was successful is due to unique characteristics of Thai culture. If Thai culture is found to be a significant contributor to the KM Process Model then this may limit the ability to generalize the research results to other contexts.

ACKNOWLEDGMENT

Our greatest appreciation to Royal Grace of His Majesty. King Bhumibol Adulyadej for royally conferring "Bhumibol Scholarship" to support this research. Our thanks to Mahasarakham University for also financially supporting this research project. Our thanks to Dr. Matthew H. S. Kuofie for serving as an external Doctoral Dissertation Committee member

REFERENCES

Alavi, M., & Leidner, D. E. (2001). Review: Knowledge management and knowledge management systems: Conceptual foundations and research issues. *MIS Quarterly, 25*(1), 107–136. doi:10.2307/3250961

American Productivity and Quality Center. Arthur Andersen. (2005). *The Knowledge Management Assessment Tool (KMAT)*. Retrieved July 17, 2009, from http://kwork.org/White_Papers/KMAT_BOK_DOC.pdf

Boonmatthaya, R., Benjathum, C., Pomdong, P., Witaporn, S., Jimmee, S., & Paireenart, S. (2005). *Synthesizing the local body of knowledge concerning knowledge management for Joyful Communities in Northeast Thailand: A case study of Indra Paeng Network, Isan Folk Sages and Si Sa Asok community*. Bangkok, Thailand: Office of Research Supporting Fund.

Chantarasombat, C. (2004). *Constructing and developing networks for self-reliant communities*. Maha Sarakham, Thailand: Network Center for Learning and Creating Community and Grassroot Economy, Faculty of Education, Mahasarakham University.

Churchman, C. W. (1979). *The systems approach*. New York: Dell Publishing.

Davenport, T. H., & Prusak, L. (1998). *Working knowledge*. Cambridge, MA: Harvard Business School Press.

David Skyrme Associates. (2005). *Know-all 10: A quick KM assessment*. Retrieved July 17, 2009, from http://www.skyrme.com/tools/know10.htm

Epstein, L. D. (2000). *Sharing knowledge in organization: How people use media to communication*. Unpublished Doctoral Dissertation, University of California, Berkeley.

Gruber, H. G. (2000). *Does organizational culture affect the sharing of knowledge? The case of a department in a high-technology company*. Unpublished master's thesis, Carleton University.

Hanphanit, B. (2003). *Developing a knowledge management model at Thai higher educational institutes*. Unpublished doctoral dissertation, Chulalongkorn University, Bangkok, Thailand.

Holsapple, C. W., & Joshi, K. D. (2004). A formal knowledge management ontology: Conduct, activities, resources, and influences. *Journal of the American Society for Information Science and Technology*, *55*(7), 593–612. doi:10.1002/asi.20007

Jennex, M. E. (2005). What is knowledge management? *International Journal of Knowledge Management*, *1*(4), i–iv.

Kuofie, M. H. S. (2005). E-management: E-knowledge management for optimizing rural medical services. *The International Journal of Management and Technologies*, *1*(1), 37–50.

Nonaka, I. (1994). A dynamic theory of organizational knowledge creation. *Organization Science*, *5*(1), 14–37. doi:10.1287/orsc.5.1.14

Nonaka, I., & Takeuchi, H. (1995). *The knowledge-creating company: How Japanese companies create the dynamics of innovation*. New York: Oxford University Press.

Office of Special Committee for Coordination in Projects from H.M. the King's Considerations. (n.d.). *The Working Principles of H.M. the King*. Bangkok, Thailand: King Chulalongkorn's Cadet School.

Panich, V. (2005). *Knowledge management, a practitioner's version*. Bangkok, Thailand: Institute of Knowledge Management Promotion for the Society (IKMPS).

Patthamasiriwat, D. (2004). Public policy for good quality of life by decentralization to the local and people participation. *The Good Public Policy, 4*(8).

Phongphit, S., Wichit, N., & Jumnong, R. (2001). *Community enterprises, master plan, concepts, model guidelines*. Bangkok, Thailand: Tai Wisdom.

Plainoi, N. (2007). An analysis of learning process in transcribing lessons: Using after-action review instruments. In *Supplement to training* (pp. 2-5).

Sinlarat, P. (1998). *Principle and general higher education*. Bangkok, Thailand: Chulalongkorn University.

Thinnalak, Y. (2006). *Riddles of local wisdom*. Bangkok, Thailand: Withithat Institute.

Udompaichitkul, T. (2005). *Sustainable economy based on the king's permanent ideas*. Bangkok, Thailand: Srinakharinwirot University.

Wasi, P. (2002). *Knowledge management*. Bangkok, Thailand: The Knowledge Management Institute.

Watthanasiritham, P. (2003). *Social administration: Science of the century for Thai society and global society*. Bangkok, Thailand: Institute for Community Organization Development (Public Organization).

Wichianpanya, C. (2005). *Document in supplement to workshop meeting on librarians/information scientists and knowledge management*. Changwat Nonthaburi, Thailand: Mental Health Department.

Wiig, K. (1993). *Knowledge management foundations*. Arlington, TX: Schema Press.

APPENDIX A: SATISFACTION EVALUATION FORM FOR IMPLEMENTATION OF THE KNOWLEDGE MANAGEMENT OF COMMUNITIES IN THAILAND

INSTRUCTIONS:

1. This evaluation form evaluates satisfaction with operating knowledge management of the community organization group to which you are attached.
2. Please give your responses in actuality.
3. Your responses will be confidential without any effect on you.
4. This evaluation form is divided into 2 parts:

Part 1 is the general data of the respondent.
    Part 2 is operation of knowledge management of the community organization group.

Part 1. General Data of the Evaluator

Instruction: For each item please make a tick (✓) in the circle which is true to you.

1. Sex ○ Male ○ Female
2. Position ○ community leader/member of tambon orgamization memeber
    - group leader
    - group member
3. Village member and group member
    - At Ban Nam Kliang, group member of
    - Ban Nam Kliang civic agricultural cooperative
    - biofertilizer
    - Thai traditional massage
    - others (Please identify.) ……………………………………………..
    - At Ban Lao Rat Phatthana, group member of
    - Thai noodles
    - word-keeping savings
    - biofertilizer
    - others (Please identify.) ……………………………………………..

Part 2. Operation of Knowledge Management of Community Organization Groups

Instruction: Please consider and evaluate (Tables 7 and 8) at which level your organization group operated knowledge management of the community organization group in each item: the most, high, medium, low, the least. Then place make only one tick (✓) in the box to show the level of your satisfaction.

No.	Evaluation Item	Level of Satisfaction				
		Most	High	Medium	Low	Least
0	The organization group stored the data to be updated.		✓			

No.	Evaluation Item	Level of Satisfaction				
		Most	High	Medium	Low	Least
1	Your community organization group has a systematic analysis for finding out flaws in knowledge and uses the process with clear stages to correct the flaws.					
2	Your community organization group seeks knowledge systematically.					
3	All of your community organization group members participate in seeking new ideas/concepts.					
4	Your organization group transfers knowledge and teaches work to members to learn systematically.					
5	Your organization group appreciates knowledge available in itself.					
6	Knowledge management is an important strategy of your organization group.					
7	Your organization group understands potentials in production and products of its own.					
8	Your organization group members can adjust themselves to catch up with present situations.					
9	Your organization group members use learning to add to available capability of the organization group for strength.					
10	Having an evaluation and giving compensations to group members are done by considering participation in building the body of knowledge of the organization.					
11	Your organization group members share learning with one another.					
12	Your organization group has climate of openness and trust in one another.					
13	Members of your organization group operate knowledge management of creating value to the products.					
14	Your organization group members learned from the outcomes that occurred, and then improved the work.					
15	All of the members are responsible for knowledge management in the organization.					
16	Computer is used to benefit data storage.					
17	Data are classified according to the knowledge base in the community.					
18	The use of web site at the Knowledge Management Center is for studying and dissemination.					
19	The information systems of the organization group can provide information and the information can be utilized.					
20	Knowledge sharing from database leads to work development.					
21	Your organization group invented new techniques affecting operation in continuity.					
22	Your organization group determines and uses indicators of success in supplement to knowledge management and work development.					
23	Indicators of success balance with operation of your organization group.					
24	Resources are sought for the Knowledge Management Center of your organization group.					
25	The group members have works or pieces of work to be proud of.					

Example:

From No.0 in the example above, the respondent ticked (✓) in the "high" box, showing that the respondent viewed that his/her community organization group stored the data to be updated at a high level of his/her satisfaction.

This work was previously published in International Journal of Knowledge Management, Volume 6, Issue 1, edited by Murray E. Jennex, pp. 62-78, copyright 2010 by IGI Publishing (an imprint of IGI Global).

Chapter 5
A Project Staffing Model to Enhance the Effectiveness of Knowledge Transfer in the Requirements Planning Phase for Multi-Project Environments

Donald P. Ballou
State University of New York, USA

Salvatore Belardo
State University of New York, USA

Harold L. Pazer
State University of New York, USA

ABSTRACT

When the systems analysis phase produces faulty requirements, it can often be traced to the failure of the requirements determination team and the client to communicate effectively. This failure is frequently a consequence of inadequate knowledge of the client's domain possessed by the development team. This paper presents concepts and procedures designed to facilitate communication between requirements determination teams and clients across a full set of IS projects with potentially differing priorities. A systematic framework for staffing requirements determination teams is provided. The importance and interdependence of two types of knowledge, explicit and tacit, to the success of the requirements determination phase is extensively explored. A metric for explicit knowledge coupled with a model that captures the impact of various levels of tacit knowledge upon the acquisition rate of explicit knowledge serve as key inputs to our Project Staffing Model. The appropriately weighted area under an explicit knowledge curve captures the totality of explicit knowledge. Summing such values, weighted to reflect project importance, provides a mechanism for evaluating alternative staffing assignments. An illustrative case highlights implementation issues and suggests procedures when uncertainty exists concerning key inputs. A research agenda is recommended for the estimation of factors required by the analysis.

DOI: 10.4018/978-1-4666-0035-5.ch005

INTRODUCTION

A continuing problem in the IS field is the large number of projects that are deemed by the client to be failures. "Despite good faith efforts by organizations, analysts, and users, a majority of systems are either abandoned before completion or fail to meet user requirements ..." (Browne & Rogich, 2001). As far back as the 1960s it has been recognized that a major reason for system failure is that more often than not the requirements determination phase produces faulty requirements (Davis, 1998; Vessey & Conger, 1994; Wand & Weber, 2002; Zmud et al., 1993). It has long been known that for many projects this can be traced to the failure of the requirements determination team and the client to communicate effectively during the requirements gathering phase (Churchman & Schainblatt, 1965; Kaiser & King, 1982; Bostrom, 1989; Agarwal & Tanniru, 1990; Holtzblatt & Beyer, 1995). Thus even if the client has full knowledge of how his or her business operates, and even if the IS team has full knowledge of the technology required for the project, that does not by any means guarantee success, because communication between the two parties may not be effective. To a substantial degree this failure to communicate is a consequence of inadequate knowledge of the client's domain possessed by the development team (Churchman & Schainblatt, 1965; Byrd et al., 1992). A number of methods designed to improve communication between end users and system developers during the requirements analysis phase of the systems development effort have been proposed, including semantic structuring (Marakas & Elam, 1998), and collaborative elaboration (Chin et al., 2005). Similarly, Bloom's Taxonomy helps facilitate communication by helping the questioner employ a critical thinking approach to his/her questioning strategy. Bloom's Taxonomy has been shown to be extremely successful in teaching systems analysis (Yadin, 2007). It has also been successfully employed by the accrediting organization AACSB to help business school professors improve their ability to communicate and learn. As a result, it might be more intuitive for many business school graduates who work in systems development.

Traditionally, IS consulting firms or internal IS groups simultaneously undertake multiple projects for a disparate set of clients. This paper presents a set of concepts and procedures that are designed to facilitate communication between requirements determination teams and clients so as to enhance the likelihood that in some overall sense the full *set* of IS projects will be completed successfully. The focus is on staffing these projects so as to facilitate knowledge transfer between these parties. The material presented should be of value to IS management having the responsibility to staff and then manage coincident, multiple IS requirements determination teams in either external or internal systems development contexts. IS management is aware of the need to assign personnel resources to the requirements determination teams so as to assure to the greatest degree possible successful completion of these projects. This implies that although the most critical projects may receive a disproportionate share of available resources, in general no project can receive an ideal allocation. The usual process is to staff each project with a mix of senior and experienced personnel and relatively inexperienced personnel with the importance of the projects factored into such assignments. Although some IS management does a good job of balancing the needs of multiple projects, the process is frequently ad hoc. In light of the high failure rate noted above, a more systematic approach is appropriate and desirable.

Most research related to requirements determination has focused on techniques and procedures to ensure the success of this phase in the context of a specific project (Marakas & Elam, 1998; Zmud et al., 1993). Our work, however, provides a systematic framework for selecting that staffing composition, from among a set of possibilities, for the requirements determination teams. The goal is to maximize the likelihood of success across the set of projects to be undertaken by maximizing, from among the set of staffing alternatives, the transfer of knowledge from the clients to the requirements determination teams. We maintain that although a successful requirements determination is not sufficient to guarantee project success, it is a necessary condition (Cooper & Swanson, 1979; Kydd, 1989). We focus solely on knowledge transfer from the client to the developer. The reverse transfer also takes place, of course, but to simplify the model we do not include this, since it is viewed as being much less critical for requirements determination (Coughlan et al., 2003; Marakas & Elam, 1998).

It is intuitive that the more experienced the IS requirements determination team and the more knowledgeable the team is with the client's environment, the more effective the communication between client and analyst would be (van der Meij, 1990; Marakas & Elam 1998). Our work provides a systematic approach to staffing multiple teams so as to enhance overall effectiveness. Effective communication, however, is much more than getting suitable answers to the right questions. It is also important for the requirements determination team to be able to correctly interpret or understand the client's response. The more experience the IS developer has had working in the client's domain the better the chance that communication will be effective (Coughlan et al., 2003). To fully understand what the client is saying, the developer needs knowledge of the client's domain. This knowledge is of two types, explicit and tacit. Although these terms have somewhat varying meaning depending on the context, our use of them (to be discussed more fully later) is as follows. Explicit knowledge relates to information the systems analyst has concerning the client's domain *relevant to the project* and enables the analyst to transform data provided by the client into information. Tacit knowledge is the mental model used by the analyst to assimilate facts provided by the client. Having tacit knowledge essentially allows the analyst to *think* like the client thereby allowing the analyst to better understand knowledge embedded in business rules. Consequently, while it is explicit

knowledge that is needed to derive the information required by the requirements determination process, it is tacit knowledge that allows the correct assimilation of this explicit knowledge.

The ideal for an IS analysis team is to have both high explicit knowledge (The analyst knows a lot about the project domain of the client.) and high tacit knowledge (The analyst would be able to internalize quickly and correctly information from the client.) We posit that for the requirements determination phase to be successful, the IS team must have or acquire a high level of explicit knowledge of that part of the client's domain relevant to the project. This is facilitated by the requirements determination team having a high level of tacit knowledge.

Our work is in the context of multiple projects that are to be undertaken in parallel; these projects can have differing start times and of course can last for differing lengths of time. It is assumed that these projects are for various clients, who may be internal to the organization or external, and that the body of explicit and tacit knowledge possessed by the IS group is not sufficient to assure a high level of explicit and tacit knowledge for all projects. It is further assumed that whatever initial explicit knowledge regarding the client's project domain is possessed by a particular requirements determination team, that knowledge will increase over the course of the requirements determination phase. We measure the likelihood of success of the requirements determination phase of a particular project by the totality of explicit knowledge of the client's domain relevant to the project possessed or acquired by the requirements determination team over the course of this phase. We assume that the technical skills of the IS team are at a sufficiently high level that they do not contribute substantially to any deficiencies. Our work incorporates the possibility that differing projects may require a relatively high level of explicit knowledge early as opposed to late in the requirements determination phase.

Implicit in our approach is the need to quantify over time the totality of explicit knowledge possessed by the IS team of the client's domain. For this we use Bloom's taxonomy (Bloom, 1956), which posits six levels of knowledge acquisition ranging from the most fundamental, Vocabulary, to the most advanced, Evaluation. As discussed in more detail in the next section, these are cross-referenced with several key dimensions of knowledge quality to provide a framework for estimating the quantity and quality of explicit knowledge possessed by the developer throughout the requirements determination phase.

The next section of this paper presents Bloom's taxonomy, which provides our metric for the evaluation of explicit knowledge. This is used in conjunction with several descriptors of the quality of knowledge to formulate the Knowledge Quality Evaluation Model and the Knowledge Transfer Model. These serve as basis of out approach, described in section after that for evaluating alternative staffing assignments for a set of multiple projects so as to select that one which will most effectively facilitate knowledge transfer across the set of projects during the requirements determination phases. After that we illustrate the use of this model for various scenarios. The final section contains concluding remarks but focuses on implementation of this research.

THEORETICAL FOUNDATION

This paper makes extensive use of the concepts of explicit and tacit knowledge, which we now consider more fully. Explicit knowledge (Nonaka, 1991) is also referred to as objective knowledge (Ambrosini & Bowman, 2001) and as declarative knowledge (Kogut & Zander, 1992). The key aspect of explicit knowledge, as discussed in Ambrosini and Bowman (2001), is that it is knowledge that can be shared, which implies that such knowledge can be "written down, encoded, explained, or understood" (Sobol & Lei, 1994).

Although explicit knowledge can be transferred from communicator to recipient, it does not follow that the recipient necessarily absorbs nuances and inferences that are meaningful to the communicator.

Tacit knowledge is also called know-how knowledge (Kogut & Zander, 1992) and is knowledge that is "context specific" (Ambrosini & Bowman, 2001). Such knowledge is gained through experience and is imbedded in culture and context (Sternberg, 1994). Thus one would assume that the client would have tacit knowledge of the environment for which the proposed system is to be developed whereas those on the requirements determination team would have such knowledge only if they had previously worked in a similar environment or developed systems for such an environment. While it can be reasoned that someone with a high degree of tacit knowledge should have a high degree of explicit knowledge, this does not necessarily follow. For example, a person with high tacit knowledge may not yet have absorbed the explicit knowledge contained in a recent piece of legislation that impacts his or her field of expertise. More importantly, a person's tacit knowledge of a field, even if high, may not include explicit knowledge relevant to the project in question. (Few programmers, no matter how accomplished, would know the minutia of every programming language. But such a person could learn them quickly.) A related issue is that people may know how to do something without being able to articulate how they do it (Goguen, 1997).

Bloom's taxonomy provides a convenient metric to evaluate over time the level of explicit knowledge of the client's domain possessed by the development team. A synopsis of it is given in the next subsection. It turns out, however, that although this framework is very useful, it does not capture for our purposes the nuances of knowledge. For this we introduce descriptors of knowledge that capture its quality analogous to those long associated with data quality. We next combine Bloom's taxonomy and the quality descriptors of knowledge into a common framework, which we refer to as a Knowledge Quality Evaluation Model, which in turn serves as the basis for modeling the Knowledge Transfer Rate. The latter model is used to optimize the composition of requirements development teams from among a set of identified alternatives in the context of multiple projects for which management is responsible.

Bloom's Taxonomy

Bloom's taxonomy consists of six levels of intellectual skills now listed in ascending order: knowledge, comprehension, application, analysis, synthesis, and evaluation. Bloom's use of "knowledge" is analogous to vocabulary, i.e., awareness of the meaning of the basic terms, which in our context would be the language used by the client to discuss his or her domain. To avoid confusion we use "vocabulary" in place of Bloom's first level, "knowledge", a word used by us in other contexts (explicit and tacit knowledge). Comprehension implies that the individual not only knows the vocabulary but also has internalized it to a degree that the individual's use of it is both correct and automatic. Thus at this level the developer can explain client concepts in his or her own words.

Application involves the ability to reclassify or restructure a problem so as to solve new problems or find new ways to solve old problems. It implies that the individual is sufficiently knowledgeable about the client's domain that he or she can anticipate the effect that a given change would have on the overall system. Analysis would imply that a developer operating at this level would be able to discern unstated assumptions and would comprehend how various components would fit together. This is analogous to problem solving capabilities associated with the case method.

Synthesis requires the learner to be able to draw upon previous knowledge and comprehension to devise new solutions to unfamiliar problems. Basically the developer is able to apply his or her store of knowledge to new uses. Evaluation implies

the developer is able to make correct judgments regarding the worth or value of some course of action. It implies the ability to choose correctly from among several alternative approaches and to use the correct tools and techniques to address the problem.

It is important to draw the distinction between the higher levels of Bloom's Taxonomy and the concept of tacit knowledge. For example, explicit knowledge for the synthesis of design flexibility could involve the specification of interface formats of potential plug-in modules while tacit knowledge may relate to management's preference for flexibility or efficiency. In terms of evaluation explicit knowledge of critical success factors will allow the specification of data to be collected for the evaluation process while tacit knowledge of management's use of subjective criteria will permit further refinement of the evaluation process.

Operationalization of Tacit Knowledge

The model we present requires values for the level of explicit knowledge over a period of time, namely the duration of the requirements determination phase. However, for the purpose of making staffing assignments, estimates are required prior to the start of the project for the level of explicit knowledge over the time frame for requirements determination. Using our adaptation of Bloom's taxonomy, it is feasible to provide a value for the explicit knowledge prior to the start of the project for each of the alternative staffing assignments specified. To predict how explicit knowledge will increase over the duration of the requirements determination phase for a specific staffing alternative, we need to have a measure of the level of tacit knowledge related to the staffing alternative in question. The basic principle is that the greater the level of tacit knowledge possessed by a team, the faster that team will be able to acquire explicit knowledge.

For the illustrative example we present in this paper, it is sufficient to know the level of tacit knowledge in a macro sense. However, for more refined modeling it is important to be able to operationalize tacit knowledge. Although most work related to tacit knowledge has been of a conceptual nature, the paper by Ambrosini and Bowman (2001) presents a set of ideas based on cognitive maps that do serve as a vehicle for operationalization of tacit knowledge. We refer the reader to this paper for additional information.

Descriptors of Knowledge

Since the term "knowledge" is inherently broad, we have found it desirable to use several descriptors of knowledge that capture various aspects of its quality. As mentioned, doing this is analogous to using descriptors in the field of data quality (Wang & Strong, 1996). Although there are potentially many such descriptors, we focus on four that are widely found in the literature, namely, accuracy, completeness, timeliness and consistency (e.g., Ballou & Pazer, 1985; Zmud, 1978). Each of these terms has an interpretation that depends on the particular level in Bloom's taxonomy under consideration. To illustrate the appropriate meaning, we consider in detail the implications of each of these descriptors for the first level, vocabulary.

At the first level, accuracy is the proportion of terms regarding the client's domain known by the developer of the system that the analyst can define correctly. Completeness is the ratio of the vocabulary regarding the client's domain known to the analyst to the total set of vocabulary the client could use. At each level timeliness has two aspects, currency and durability. At the vocabulary level currency measures the age of the analyst's knowledge regarding the terms. The durability aspect relates to the shelf life of the meaning, i.e., how long the meaning stays relevant. The final descriptor, consistency, measures the degree to which terms have the same meaning in different environments. The first two measures, accuracy

and completeness, involve the analyst's preparation. The last two form a measure of how this preparation should be evaluated in the context of the client's environment.

Some of the material needed for the project-staffing model can be found in earlier work by the authors (Belardo et al., 2004). In particular the Knowledge Quality Evaluation Model and the Knowledge Transfer Model, both of which are described below, appeared in that paper.

Knowledge Quality Evaluation Model

The material found in the previous two subsections is now combined to form a model or framework for evaluating the level of explicit knowledge possessed by the requirements determination team of the client's domain. One could evaluate each of Bloom's six levels on each of the four descriptors of knowledge, but this would lead to a cumbersome 24 states. To reduce the number of states to a more manageable level, we group in a pair-wise fashion the six levels and similarly, as suggested above, combine accuracy with completeness and timeliness with consistency. Since Bloom's Taxonomy is a critical thinking approach to learning and communication we thought it appropriate to collapse the taxonomy according to a critical thinking framework that consists of three levels, summary/definition, analysis, hypothesis/evaluation. We grouped Bloom's levels of vocabulary and comprehension according to the critical thinking framework category of summary/definition, application and analysis according to the critical thinking category analysis, and Bloom's Taxonomy last two levels synthesis and evaluation according to hypothesis/evaluation. Together with the quality dimension the result yields six states, as displayed in Figure 1. The purpose of the weights w_{ij} displayed in Figure 1 is explained below.

For each of these cells, the actual evaluation could be either qualitative (an ordinal scale) or quantitative (a percentage of an ideal). The infor-

Figure 1. Knowledge quality evaluation model with weights

Knowledge Levels	Quality	
	Accuracy and Completeness	Timeliness and Consistency
Vocabulary & Comprehension	w_{11}	w_{12}
Application & Analysis	w_{21}	w_{22}
Synthesis & Evaluation	w_{31}	w_{32}

mation found in the Knowledge Quality Evaluation Model (KQEM) is needed for the Knowledge Transfer Model, described in the next subsection. For that model it is necessary to transform the information contained in the KQEM to a numerical value from 0 to 1, and thus it is natural to evaluate each of the six cells of the KQEM using the same scale. This of course does not preclude qualitative evaluations, as Low Medium, High, for example, would be mapped to 1/6, 1/2 and 5/6 (the midpoints of the unit interval subdivided into thirds) respectively. Bloom's taxonomy is a hierarchy of knowledge possession, and in general one cannot function at Stage 2 unless one has mastered Stage 1, and so forth. However, for the requirements determination phase it may well not be the case. For example, the requirements determination team may have considerable experience with developing IS projects and thus rank high on Evaluation and yet be unfamiliar with the client's environment, and so rank low on Vocabulary. One would anticipate that for a given project some of the six cells would be of greater importance for the successful completion of the requirements analysis phase than others. To accommodate this likelihood we form the weighted sum of the various evaluations in the six cells of the KQEM using weights w_{ij}, ($i = 1, 2, 3, j = 1, 2$) which capture the relative importance of the grouped levels of Bloom's taxonomy and grouped descriptors of knowledge. As usual the weights sum to 1. If V_{ij} denotes the evaluation for the ijth cell, then the input required by the Knowledge Transfer Model described below would be the number $\sum w_{ij}*V_{ij}$, which can be thought of as an evaluation of explicit knowledge as appropriate

for a specified project at some point in time. This number is the ordinate in Figure 2, introduced in the next subsection. The implementation process we describe and use for enhancing knowledge transfer in multi-project environments requires this number be known only at time t = 0. For other, possible implementation strategies, it may well be required at subsequent points of time.

Knowledge Transfer Model

A major premise of this work is that the quantity of explicit knowledge of the client's domain increases over the course of the requirements determination phase, and that it is the totality of such knowledge that is a critical component in the success of this phase. We need a mechanism for capturing or representing the increase of explicit knowledge and also a measure for the totality of explicit knowledge over the course of the requirements determination phase. The four diagrams found in Figure 2 (see Belardo et al., 2004) illustrate both these needs. The vertical scale captures the level of explicit knowledge possessed by the development team of the client's domain at various points in time. The symbol K_0 represents the initial level of explicit knowledge. ($K_0 = \sum w_{ij}*V_{ij}$ at time t = 0.) The vertical scale is between 0 and 1 with 0 representing no explicit knowledge and 1 complete knowledge. Issues regarding how to operationalize this model are discussed using, the Illustrative Example.

The horizontal axis represents time, with 0 signifying the start time for the requirements determination phase and 1 the scaled completion time. Each of the situations displayed in Figure 2

Figure 2. Illustrative knowledge transfer environment

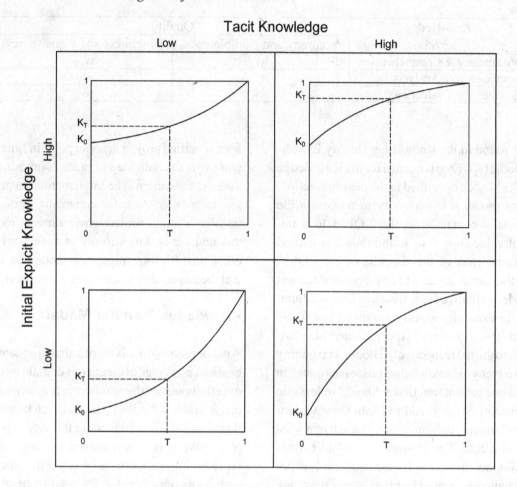

implies that the requirements determination team possesses full explicit knowledge of the client's domain by the end of the requirements determination phase of the project. This of course does not have to be the case, but if the requirements determination team does not possess a high level of explicit knowledge by this time, then there should be concern as to whether this phase had been successfully concluded. It would seem that having the level of explicit knowledge close to 1 by the end of the requirements determination phase in general is a necessary but not sufficient condition for project success.

The focus of this paper is how to optimize from among a set of staffing alternatives a priori the likelihood that a set of projects will have suc-

cessful requirements determination phases. For each of the projects the value K_0 for that project is but the initial level of explicit knowledge and does not by itself indicate how the proposed team will do for the duration of the requirements determination phase. A low initial value could be more than compensated for by the team's ability to learn rapidly, while a high initial value could be negated by an inability to acquire additional explicit knowledge. For any specific project and staffing of the requirements determination team we assume that that team's explicit knowledge of the client's domain will increase over the course of the requirements determination phase. However, the rate at which this explicit knowledge is acquired will vary across teams, and hence even if some proposed staffing assignments for a particular project should have the same initial value K_0, the quantity of explicit knowledge of the client's domain acquired over the requirements determination phase could vary substantially across the teams.

The key to determining the rate of acquisition of explicit knowledge during the requirements determination phase is the level of tacit knowledge of the client's domain possessed by a proposed requirements determination team. It has been shown (e.g., Ambrosini & Bowman, 2001) that when the level of tacit knowledge is high, learning takes place rapidly, and conversely. We capture the level of tacit knowledge possessed by a proposed requirements determination team regarding the client's domain by means of the convexity of the explicit knowledge curve. The higher the level of tacit knowledge the more concave down the curve. The lower the level of tacit knowledge the more concave up the curve. This captures the fact that the higher the level of tacit knowledge, the more readily the requirements determination team acquires explicit knowledge, and conversely. The four diagrams found in Figure 2 represent four possible combinations of low and high explicit knowledge combined with low and high tacit knowledge.

Our model is driven by the assumption that the greater the quantity of explicit knowledge possessed by the development team over the course of the requirements determination phase, the greater the likelihood that this phase will be successful. The area under the explicit knowledge curve captures this totality of explicit knowledge. Thus to determine which of several possible team assignments is most likely to lead to a successful requirements determination phase for a given project, project management would generate curves analogous to those displayed in Figure 2 for each possible team assignment. In the context of exactly one project the staffing assignment that produced the greatest area under the explicit knowledge curve is the one that should be chosen, as that team would possess for the totality of the

requirements determination phase the largest quantity of explicit knowledge.

The assumption that the area under the explicit knowledge curve is an appropriate metric for comparing potential staffing assignments is fundamental to our work and thus requires detailed consideration. We posit that for a successful requirements determination the level of explicit knowledge is important throughout, not just the level at the end of this phase. Thus our situation is *not* analogous to courses for which the course grade is based only on a final exam, and it does not matter whether one acquires the needed knowledge just before the exam or over the course of the semester. It is more analogous to a grading scheme that is based solely on how well one does on weekly quizzes and that one needs to accumulate knowledge to do well on future quizzes.

To justify the assumption regarding the impact of the totality of explicit knowledge on successful completion of the requirements determination phase, we consider various cases. We argue that at the extremes this assumption is clearly reasonable. If, for example, the requirements determination team has had from the start 100% of the needed explicit knowledge of the client's domain, there is no reason, assuming adequate time is available, why the requirements determination phase would not be completely successful. (The issue of time duration of requirements determination is addressed at the end of model development section) Clearly the area under the explicit knowledge curve in this case is the largest possible. On the other hand if the development team has no explicit knowledge of the client's domain and never acquires any, the likelihood of success is 0, which is the area under the explicit knowledge curve in this case.

A pair-wise examination of the six possible pairs of the cases illustrated in Figure 2 further justifies this assumption. By comparing, say, the top two horizontal cases, high explicit, low tacit with high explicit, high tacit knowledge, intuitively we would expect the likelihood of a successful requirements determination phase for the high explicit, high tacit case to be greater than for the high explicit, low tacit case. (For each horizontal pair considered separately the starting level K_0 and ending level at time $t = 1$ of explicit knowledge are the same and the lengths of time for the requirements determination phase are the same.) Clearly the area under the high-high case is greater than that for the high-low case. Similar conclusions hold for several of the other possible pairs. However, for the high-low and low-high pair (upper left and lower right) it is not intuitively obvious which is more likely to lead to successful completion. Our metric, the area under the explicit knowledge curve, would remove that ambiguity.

MODEL TO ENHANCE THE EFFECTIVENESS OF KNOWLEDGE TRANSFER IN MULTI-PROJECT ENVIRONMENTS

Analytical Framework

In this section we present a model that can be used to analyze alternative staffing of projects in a multi-project environment so as to maximize the totality of the transfer of knowledge from the client groups to the development groups from among a set of identified alternatives. The projects to be staffed can have varying importance. The purpose of the model is to evaluate the efficacy of a particular staffing assignment in the context of alternative staffing assignments. Whenever personnel with a high level of explicit and/or tacit knowledge are assigned to a particular project, that project benefits, but other projects where such individuals could have contributed would suffer. The goal is to determine on balance which of the possible staffing assignments under consideration would maximize the quantity of explicit knowledge transferred and hence enhance the likelihood of successful requirements determination phases across all projects being undertaken.

The analytical framework assumes that management wishes to assign IS developmental personnel to N projects. As is usually the case, these projects do not need to start or stop at the same time. We scale the earliest of the start times to 0 and let T represent the latest anticipated completion time. Let $t_k(s)$ and $t_k(c)$ represent respectively the projected start and completion times for the requirements determination phase of the kth project. As discussed in the previous section, the area under the explicit knowledge curve is a measure of the totality of explicit knowledge possessed by the development team regarding the client's domain. To capture this quantity analytically, let $f_k(t)$ represent the level of explicit knowledge over time ($t_k(s) \leq t \leq t_k(c)$) for the requirements determination phase of the kth project. For this work it is necessary to have actual, analytic expressions for the explicit knowledge curves $f_k(t)$. Various procedures are described below for estimating these functions.

For some projects it may be more important to have a high level of explicit knowledge early on; for others having a high level is more important at the end. To capture the varying importance of having explicit knowledge at various times during the requirements determination phase, we introduce a function $w_k(t)$ to capture the relative importance of having explicit knowledge at time t. With this notation the time-weighted quantity of explicit knowledge F_k possessed by the development team over the course of the requirements determination phase for the kth project is given by

$$F_k = \left[1 \Big/ \int_{t_k(s)}^{t_k(c)} w_k(t)dt \right] * \int_{t_k(s)}^{t_k(c)} w_k(t)f_k(t)dt \tag{1}$$

The purpose of the first factor is to normalize the weighting function $w_k(t)$.

The projects in general will differ in importance. To capture this, let W_k represent the relative importance of the kth project. Then the weighted Totality of Explicit Knowledge possessed by the development teams for all N projects from time 0 to time T is given by

$$TEK = \sum_{k=1}^{N} W_k F_k \, . \qquad (2)$$

The goal of project management is to choose the best staffing assignment from a set of potential, alternative staffing possibilities. In practice those responsible for staffing a set of projects would not consider all possible permutations and combinations of personnel available to staff these projects, nor do we. To select the best staffing assignment, management should evaluate the TEK value for each of the identified alternatives and then select that one which yields the largest number.

In practice IS management must with or without a model such as ours make assignments of requirements determination teams. For this management must incorporate issues such as differing importance of projects, overall budget and personnel constraints, need to complete by differing times, and so forth. Management will consider alternative ways of staffing the teams. The question arises: Which of the alternatives IS management can visualize is most effective in an overall sense? The role of this model is to provide a quantitative determination of which alternative is best. Also, it would be useful for management to do a sensitivity analysis on the importance of the various projects. The weights W_k capture management's estimate of the relative importance of the projects. By systematically varying the values for these parameters, management can determine using this model how sensitive staffing requirements determination teams is to these estimates of project importance. (See Figure 4 and accompanying explanatory material found in illustrative case study section) This type of analysis would be particularly useful should the importance of the projects change with time. For example, even though a project may have become less important, it does not follow that the require-

ments determination teams should be changed. The model assists in making such a determination. An example of this is found in Figure 4.

Issues

It should be kept in mind that this framework uses three different sets of weights. The first set introduced, w_{ij}, captures the relative importance of levels of knowledge coupled with descriptors of knowledge as displayed in Figure 1. The second set, $w_k(t)$ (see expression (1)), represents the importance of explicit knowledge during the requirements determination phase. The third, W_k, allows for projects to have varying importance. Clearly identifying values for all these weights is a non-trivial implementation issue. In the final section we return to this need. To simplify implementation, management always has the option of assuming that for one or more of these sets the weights are equal.

This framework allows for considerable flexibility in identifying project staffing alternatives. Different combinations of personnel can be assigned to the projects. Key personnel can be taken from one project in midcourse and transferred to a different project. This would be natural if, for example, certain expertise is needed early on for one project and later for another one running concurrently. Although this would result in discontinuities for the explicit knowledge curves $f_k(t)$ of the projects involved, it presents no difficulties for the modeling framework. In general personnel can be added to or removed from a given project midcourse. Disruptions caused by people joining or leaving the team clearly affect the team's learning ability. IS managers intuitively assess this impact. For this model it would be necessary for management to reevaluate the level of explicit knowledge possessed by the team at the time an individual joins or leaves the team. If a person should join the team, presumably at that time the learning curve would jump to a new, higher level. It would also be necessary to assess whether the team's rate of learning (slope of the learning curve) is impacted. Since the definite integral permits discontinuities in f(t), expression (1) is valid in such cases. The model can also handle qualitative issues such as changes in moral resulting from the addition or departure of a team member. For example, suppose a new member adds to the team's level of explicit knowledge (the learning curve jumps to a new, higher level), but the new member's personality inhibits the team's effectiveness. This would cause the learning curve to rise less rapidly. How in practice the learning curve can be specified originally and whenever there is a midcourse correction is discussed below.

The duration of the requirements determination phase for one or more projects can be either lengthen or shortened. The start times for one or more of the projects can be changed, as can the completion times. This very large number of possible alternatives precludes identifying the true optimal scenario. Thus our work is in the context of a satisficing model rather than an optimizing one. (Simon, 1960)

Implicit in our modeling approach is the fact that the greater the amount of time devoted to the requirements determination phase, all other factors being equal, the greater the F_k value for that project. This agrees with common sense. However, various constraints on resources preclude long-duration requirements determination phases. One feature of this modeling framework is that IS management can test out the implications of bringing additional resources to bear by computing the TEK with current resources and also with additional resources.

Another aspect that is implicitly required by this model is the need for IS management to have an inventory of the explicit and tacit knowledge possessed by personnel who are available for the various projects. As will be described in the next subsection, the Knowledge Quality Evaluation Model is used to determine in essence the $f_k(t)$ curves. This work assumes that the development teams are small enough that they function as one unit, i.e., the totality of explicit knowledge and the

level of tacit knowledge possessed by the team is the union (in a set-theoretic sense) of the explicit and tacit knowledge of the individual members. Thus it is sufficient for only one member of the term to possess the relevant knowledge.

Implementation of Model

The key to implementing the model described above is to have expressions for each of the $f_k(t)$ functions. Due to the inherent difficulties of measuring knowledge, obtaining a value for a team's explicit knowledge of a client's domain at even one specific point in time is difficult at best. This problem is compounded by the apparent need to predict the level of explicit knowledge for all t, $t_k(s) \le t \le t_k(c)$, for each of the N explicit knowledge functions $f_k(t)$. These practical constraints argue for the need to use approximations for the true explicit knowledge curves. This is the approach we adopt. An example in the IS domain of an application of Bloom's taxonomy to capture explicit knowledge is found in Niehoff and Whitney-Bammerlin (1995).

It seems reasonable that those responsible for staffing the N projects would wish to know how knowledgeable a possible team is for a specific project at the start of that project, that is, given a possible staffing for a specific project, how much explicit knowledge does that team have of the client's domain at the start of the project? As indicated in the second section, we use $\sum w_{ij} * V_{ij}$ evaluated at $t = t_k(s)$ for the value $K_0 = f_k(t_k(s))$, namely, the level of explicit knowledge at the start of the project.

As discussed earlier, by the end of the requirements determination phase one would expect that the value for $f_k(t_k(c))$ would be 1 or close to it, that is, the requirements determination team would possess full explicit knowledge of the client's domain. Although realistically this will often not be the case, if the value of $f_k(t_k(s))$ is not reasonably close to 1, it would seem that there is a real danger that the requirements determination phase was not done well. Since one would expect that management would not consciously staff a project with the expectation that $f_k(t_k(c))$ would be substantially less than 1 (which would all but ensure project failure), we will assume that for viable staffing assignments $f_k(t_k(c)) = 1$ holds.

As mentioned, this modeling approach permits reassignment of staff from one project to another in mid-course for one or all projects. This would introduce discontinuities into the $f_k(t)$, which is not a problem, but does significantly complicate discussing generic functions. Thus the following discussion is in the context of project teams that do not change over the course of the requirements determination phase.

If the composition of the team does not change over the course of the requirements determination phase, one would expect that the level of its explicit knowledge would keep increasing. Thus $f_k(t)$ should be a monotone increasing function. Although any class of such functions could be used for the $f_k(t)$, the simplest class that contains sufficient flexibility to model various levels of tacit knowledge is the set of quadratic functions. As indicated, we use convexity to capture the level of tacit knowledge. With the values of $f_k(t)$, namely K_0 and 1, known at the end points $t_k(s)$ and $t_k(c)$ respectively, to specify a quadratic it suffices to identify the value of $f_k(t)$ at one more point. Although any point between $t_k(s)$ and $t_k(c)$ would suffice, it is natural to estimate $f_k(t)$ at the midpoint mid_k. The value at the midpoint is basically a function of the tacit knowledge possessed by the proposed team. Thus $f_k(mid_k)$ controls the convexity of the quadratic. In practice this value would be estimated by IS management.

The applicability of the model depends upon IS management being able to estimate quantities such as K_0 and $f_k(mid_k)$. Also, should there be a midcourse correction, then to determine the resulting impact on the learning curve, it would be necessary for management to estimate the new level of explicit knowledge and also the equivalent of $f_k(mid_k)$, i.e., the midpoint for the remaining time. We have discussed this need with

senior managers at a top five consulting firm and at a top-three software company. In both cases we were assured that it is common practice for project managers to make estimates of this sort.

ILLUSTRATIVE CASE STUDY: HIKE, CAMP, AND CANOE, INC.

We apply the main concepts discussed above to Hike, Camp, and Canoe, Inc., a rapidly growing East Coast manufacturer and distributor of "mid-ticket items for the serious outdoorsman". Until recently both production and distribution were centralized in the mid-Atlantic region. Two years ago major distribution centers were added in the northeast and southeast. At the time of this expansion, an in-house system development group was established and is continuing to expand. For the coming year the manager of this group has committed to the following three projects to be completed within a year. The case and the description of each system were obtained from an experienced manager familiar with the case, using a method similar to the reflective methodology described by Schon (1983).

Design and Build a Packaged Payroll Processing System

After consultation it was determined that the establishment of this system was a prerequisite to the development of a more ambitious human resources planning and control system desired by the V.P. of Human Resources. Designers must have or quickly acquire substantial knowledge concerning a payroll-processing environment. They must understand the need to have strong financial controls integrated into the design of this system. Consequently "front end" knowledge is highly desired.

Design and Build a Computer-Based Production Capacity Planning Simulation System

This system is to provide inputs for mid-to-long-term investment decisions for expanded production facilities. The production area has been the leading customer for the in-house development group since its creation. The design and implementation, over the past year, of a MRP-based production scheduling system is considered to be the group's greatest accomplishment. For the capacity planning simulation system, while knowledge of the production environment is important from the start, it is equally important to have a firm understanding of the type of questions that managers will pose to this system in order to design output formats and options.

Design and Build an Inventory Optimization System

At earlier stages of the firm's development, inventory control was primarily driven by "stockout avoidance". It is now generally agreed that inventory investment has become excessive. At the same time the substantial seasonality of demand in the Northeast and the Southeast has lead to unacceptable stockout occurrences.

While the basic concepts of inventory control are widely known and/or easy to acquire for the initial stages of the design, understanding demand seasonality, interactive dimensions and the dynamics of the market require a high degree of sophistication by the time that this project would be complete.

Changing Importance of Explicit Knowledge Over Time

While the Project Staffing Model can easily handle non-linear variation in the importance of explicit knowledge for the projects over time, for simplicity this example will use a linear model to represent the changing importance of explicit knowledge, namely

$$w = mt + b. \tag{3}$$

A negative value for m indicates a declining importance and a positive value increasing importance of explicit knowledge over time for the project in question. To simplify the expression for F_k, expression (1), we choose the intercept b so that the weighting factor will equal one, i.e., the average weight over time is one (the integral of $w_k(t)$).

As shown in Figure 3 the formula for the declining weight for the payroll processing project gives three times the weight to knowledge relating to the first stage as to the last. The converse is true for the inventory optimization project with weight increasing by a factor of three over the duration of this requirements determination. It would, of course, have been easy to use any other ratio that management wished to specify for the difference between initial and ending stage weights. For the production capacity simulation system the importance of explicit knowledge is constant throughout the requirements determination phase.

To simplify the presentation, we assume that all three projects run concurrently with the same start and stop times, which are scaled to the interval [0,1]. Furthermore, as mentioned, we assume for each project that the level of explicit knowledge at time $t = 1$ is 1, that the value at time $t = 0$ ($y_0 = K_0$) can be any value between 0 and 1, and that a value for y_0 is provided by management using the Knowledge Quality Evaluation Model. To specify a quadratic curve representing the increase of explicit knowledge over time, namely $f_k(t)$, an additional point is required. We use the midpoint, $t = \frac{1}{2}$. The value for y at the midpoint, namely $y = y_1$, essentially determines the convexity. We assume that managerial judgment is involved in providing an estimate for y_1. The final section provides some ideas as to how such numbers could be estimated.

Figure 3. Time weighted quantity of expected knowledge (F) for three projects

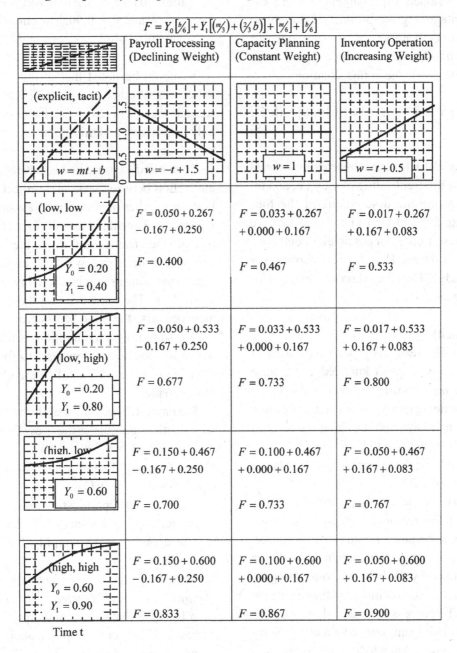

Time t

To determine the quadratic curve for a particular project, evaluate the generic expression $y = a + bt + ct^2$ at each of the points $(t,y) = (0, y_0)$, $(\frac{1}{2}, y_1)$ and $(1,1)$. This results in three equations in the three unknowns a, b, and c, which can then be solved simultaneously to yield

$$y = y_0 + (4y_1 - 3y_0 - 1)\, t + (2y_0 - 4y_1 + 2)\, t^2.$$

(4)

Here $0 \leq t \leq 1$ and $0 \leq y_0 < y_1 < 1$. For this application the above quadratic is the function $f_k(t)$ that appears in expression (1).

Next we evaluate expression (1) for this example by integrating the product of the above quadratic (our $f_k(t)$) and $y = mt + b$ (our $w_k(t)$) over the interval 0 to 1 to produce the expression for total explicit knowledge in this situation:

$$F = y_0[b/6] + y_1[(m/3) + (2/3)b] + [m/6] + [b/6]. \quad (5)$$

The material that follows evaluates this expression for F for different values of y_0, y_1, b, and m.

The following are descriptions of the four cases for explicit and tacit knowledge that we examine. These are the four possible combinations of the values Low and High for both explicit and tacit knowledge. Thus they represent extreme or bounding cases.

(Explicit, Tacit)

(Low, Low) The team starts with only 0.20 of the required explicit knowledge. Because of low tacit knowledge, only a quarter of the remaining required knowledge is gained by the halfway point, bringing the level of explicit knowledge to 0.40. Thus $y_0 = 0.20$ and $y_1 = 0.40$; the explicit knowledge curve is $y = 0.20 + 0.80t^2$.

(Low, High) The team also starts with only 0.20 of the required explicit knowledge. However, because of high tacit knowledge, three-quarters of the remaining knowledge is obtained by the halfway point, bringing the level to 0.80. Thus $y_0 = 0.20$ and $y_1 = 0.80$. The curve is $y = 0.20 + 1.60t - 0.80t^2$.

(High, Low) This team starts with 0.60 of the required explicit knowledge. Due to low tacit knowledge, only a quarter of the knowledge deficit is filled by the halfway point, bringing the level to 0.70. Thus $y_0 = 0.60$ and $y_1 = 0.70$. The curve is $y = 0.60 + 0.40t^2$.

(High, High) In this best (but most expensive) of the four cases, the team starts with 0.60 of the required explicit knowledge and since it also has high tacit knowledge, quickly moves to

the 0.90 level by the half-way point. Thus $y_0 = 0.60$ and $y_1 = 0.90$. The curve is $y = 0.60 + 0.80t - 0.40t^2$.

It should be noted that in order to identify these or any other members of this family of second-degree curves, the manager need specify only the starting and mid-point levels of explicit knowledge.

To avoid obscuring key issues relating to the interaction between team and project characteristics, a number of simplifying assumptions are incorporated into this example. First among these is, that when teams are formed, the incremental cost of moving from low to high explicit knowledge is the same as moving from low to high tacit knowledge. The second is that these cost increments are also the same across projects.

A result of these assumptions is the simplifying of the cost/benefit analysis to follow. Also, referring to Figure 3 the following observations can be made:

For Payroll Processing the (High Explicit, Low Tacit) options dominates the (Low Explicit, High Tacit) choice. F = 0.700 > 0.667.

For Capacity Planning the two options are equal. F = 0.733 = 0.733.

For Inventory Optimization the (Low Explicit, High Tacit) option dominates. F = 0.800 > 0.767.

These observations simplify the cases displayed in Figure 4.

Recalling that F represents *time-weighted quantity of explicit knowledge*, it can be noted from Figure 3 that even though the F values are highest for the Inventory Optimization project, the change between (Low, Low) and (High, High) is smallest for this project. The change in F with the largest of these values corresponds to the Payroll Processing project (F = 0.367 < 0.400 < 0.433).

Figure 4 makes use of the simplifying assumptions discussed above to explore the costs and benefits of various ways of staffing the three projects. Four points along the cost-benefit curve are identified corresponding to: no incremental ex-

Figure 4. Cost and benefits of various ways of staffing three projects

$	Team (explicit, tacit)	Project	TEK			
	(Payroll), (CapPlan), (InvOpt)	Payroll, CapPlan, InvOpt	W= (1/3, 1/3,1/3)	W= (2/3, 1/6,1/6)	W= (1/6, 2/3,1/6)	W= (1/6, 1/6,2/3)
0.0	(L,L),(L,L),(L,L)	.400, .467, .533	.467	.433	.467	.500
1/3	(H,H), (L,L), (L,L)	.833, .467, .533	.611	.722*	.539	.572
	(L,L), (H,H), (L,L)	.400, .867, .533	.600	.500	.734*	.567
	(L,L), (L,L), (H,H)	.400, .467, .900	.589	.464	.528	.745*
	(L,L), (L,H), (L,H)	.400, .733, .800	.644	.522	.689	.722
	(H,L), (L,L), (L,H)	.700, .467, .800	.656*	.678	.561	.728
2/3	(H,L), (L,H), (L,L)	.700, .733, .533	.656*	.678	.694	.594
	(H,H), (H,H), (L,L)	.833, .867, .533	.744	.789	.806	.639
	(H,H), (L,L), (H,H)	.833, .467, .900	.733	.783	.600	.817
	(L,L), (H,H), (H,H)	.400, .867, .900	.722	.561	.795	.811
	(H,H), (L,H), (L,H)	.833, .733, .800	.789*	.811*	.761	.794
	(H,L), (H,H), (L,H)	.700, .867, .800	.789*	.745	.828*	.794
1.0	(H,L), (L,H), (H,H)	.700, .733, .900	.778	.739	.755	.839*
	(H,H), (H,H), (H,H)	.833, .867, .900	.867	.850	.867	.883

penditure, one-third of the maximum expenditure, two-thirds of this expenditure, and the maximum expenditure. The last option yields teams of both high explicit and high tacit knowledge for all three projects. Without the simplification there would have been thirty-two options each with a potentially different cost.

Next, Total Explicit Knowledge (TEK) was calculated from the previously discussed formula: TEK $= \Sigma W_i F_i$. This was recorded for the four weighting schemes and recorded in Figure 4.

W $= (1/3, 1/3, 1/3)$. The three projects are equally important to management.

W $= (2/3, 1/6, 1/6)$. The Payroll Processing project is four times as important as each of the other two projects.

W $= (1/6, 2/3, 1/6)$. The Capacity Planning project is four times as important.

W $= (1/6, 1/6, 2/3)$. The Inventory Optimization project is four times as important.

It is seen that for no incremental investment the TEK is the lowest, 0.433, as the case of

the front-end loaded Payroll Processing project has a heavy weight. It is highest, 0.500, for the situation where the heavy weight is assigned to the back-end loaded Inventory Optimization project.

An investment in one-third of the maximum allows two of the six team descriptors to be moved from Low to High. When weights were equal, then all of the "share the wealth" strategies, which moderately improved two of the teams, were superior to all of the strategies which concentrated improvement on a single team. For the cases of unequal weights, not surprisingly, the clearly superior strategy was to put both the eggs in the high priority basket.

When an investment of two-thirds of the maximum was made, four of the team descriptors were High. For the case of equally weighted projects, the strategies which left one team at the (Low, Low) level were clearly inferior to those which spread the investment across all three. For the cases of unequal project weights all of the preferred solutions had the structure that the heavily weighted

Figure 5. Incremental gains in TEK achieved for incremental costs

Δ $	Δ TEK			
	$W = (\frac{1}{3}, \frac{1}{3}, \frac{1}{3})$	$W = (\frac{2}{3}, \frac{1}{6}, \frac{1}{6})$	$W = (\frac{1}{6}, \frac{2}{3}, \frac{1}{6})$	$W = (\frac{1}{6}, \frac{1}{6}, \frac{2}{3})$
First 1/3	0.189	0.289	0.267	0.245
Second 1/3	0.133	0.089	0.094	0.094
Last 1/3	0.078	0.039	0.039	0.044
Total	0.400	0.417	0.400	0.383

project would be moved to (High, High) while the other the other two project teams would be improved in one of the two descriptors.

For maximum investment the TEK's are arrayed in a manner parallel to the no incremental investment case with the lowest value corresponding to the Payroll Processing project and the highest for Inventory Optimization.

It can be seen that for intermediate expenditure levels that all of the cases that heavily weight one of the projects outperform the case where the projects are of equal importance. For example, when Δcost = 1/3, the TEK's for the cases where a project is heavily weighted range from 0.722 to 0.745 compared to a TEK of 0.656 for the case where the projects are equally weighted.

Figure 5 presents, in tabular format, the incremental gains in TEK that can be achieved for each incremental increase in cost. Substantial diminishing returns are observed even for the case of equal project weights, with the first cost increment providing 2.4 times the gain in TEK as does the last cost increment (0.189/0.078 = 2.42). This difference is much more pronounced for the cases where one project is heavily weighted and is equal to 7.4 (0.289 / 0.039 = 7.41) for the case where the payroll project received two-thirds of the weight.

If management has determined that an increase in TEK of 0.100 justifies the expenditure of an additional cost increment, then for equal weights, both the first and second cost increments would be justified, while for the cases of unequal weights only the first cost increment would meet this criterion.

Assume that management knows that the Payroll Project is more important but is unsure of the exact weight. If, however, they are sure that the weight is between 1/3 and 2/3, then by referring to Figure 5 the following observations can be made:

1. If the required increase in TEK is greater than 0.289, then no incremental expenditure should be made to upgrade the teams.
2. If the required increase in TEK is less than 0.189, then at least the first cost increment should be incurred and the analysis continued as discussed below.
3. If the required increase is greater than 0.133, then only the first cost increment is prescribed.
4. If the required increment is less than 0.089, then the second cost increment should also be incurred and the analysis continued.

Only if the TEK increment falls between the above action limits would a more refined estimate of the importance of the Payroll Project be required.

While the preceding analysis has focused primarily on uncertainty concerning project weights, once the model has been developed for a specific set of projects, it can be used to explore the impact of uncertainty on many other dimensions. Equation (5) can provide a powerful tool for exploring the impact of uncertainty regarding the following dimensions:

1. Initial explicit knowledge through varying y_0,

2. Tacit knowledge through varying y_1 for a given level of y_0,
3. Changing importance of explicit knowledge over time through varying m, and
4. The ratio of the importance of early vs. late acquisition of explicit knowledge through the varying of the combination of b and m.

The results could be displayed in formats similar to Figures 3 and 4.

IMPLEMENTATION ISSUES AND CONCLUDING REMARKS

The full implementation of the project-staffing model requires further research in three areas, discussed below. An empirical study to accomplish this is beyond the scope of this paper.

First, to employ the Knowledge Quality Evaluation Model the weights w_{ij} indicated in Figure 1 must be estimated. For example, an application in a technical production environment designed to reduce product cost may require knowledge of an extensive technical vocabulary while evaluation will be straight-forward cost minimization. An application related to estimating the impact of product mix modification in a dynamic market place may require only a standard vocabulary but may require the understanding of a complex and changing evaluation methodology. The use of equal weights across the six KQEM cells will seldom be the best allocation; consequently it will be necessary to have a model which can estimate in advance the appropriate weights for each project being considered.

Secondly, the shape parameters for the knowledge transfer curve must be estimated. While the shape of the curve is a function of the level of tacit knowledge possessed by the team, it is also likely to vary with certain project characteristics. For example, it may be found that for complex environments the knowledge transfer rate increases dramatically when a team possesses high tacit

knowledge, while, perhaps, in environments of low complexity little difference exists between teams of high and low tacit knowledge.

Thirdly, the changing importance of explicit knowledge over time must be estimated. It may prove that projects in unique and/or complex environments may depend on quickly understanding the appropriate vocabulary. Projects that may require a variety of output formats may be most dependent on the explicit knowledge level late in the requirements determination phase. If both conditions exist, weights for the importance of explicit knowledge may remain constant over time.

In order to establish a sufficient historical base for these predictive models, a large number of completed projects must be reviewed and classified by a general framework. Two of the authors have previously presented one such framework "Scope/Complexity: A Framework for the classification and Analysis of Information-Decision Systems" (Belardo & Pazer, 1985). Each project in the historical database could be assigned a score on each of the principle components. Cluster analysis could then be employed to define groups of similar projects. For each project cluster in the historical database typical weights and shape parameters can be estimated. Determining which cluster provides the best fit to each new project being considered will provide values for the required parameters to be used in the analysis. In some cases these values could be used directly, in other cases additional information may exist which will allow improvement of these estimates for the projects being considered.

The need to implement something like the project-staffing model is attested to by the fact that projects continue to be developed that are deemed by the client to be failures. By some estimates the cost of these failures is on the order of one percent of the United States' gross domestic product (Ewusi-Mensah, 1997). Although many things must go well for a project to be successful, for most projects a necessary condition is that the requirements determination team and the client need to communicate effectively. Realistically management cannot and does not consider all possible staffing permutations and combinations, but it does identify various alternative possibilities, from which one is selected.

The purpose of this paper is to present a framework and set of supporting concepts and techniques for evaluating the likely level of knowledge transfer during the requirements determination phase for each possible staffing scenario that management has identified. This work is in the context of multiple, coincident projects for which personnel resources are constrained or limited. The measure we use to determine the likelihood of a successful requirements determination phase is the totality of explicit knowledge of the client's project domain acquired by the team during the requirements determination phase. The team's level of tacit knowledge captures how rapidly the team can acquire this explicit knowledge.

The model would lend itself to "what–if" investigation. For example, the impact of lengthening some requirements determination phases at the expense of others could be investigated, as could shifting personnel from one team to another. The value of adding or removing personnel in mid-course or of bringing additional resources to bear could also be analyzed.

The framework presented includes a metric based on Bloom's well–established taxonomy for evaluating the level of explicit knowledge possessed by a team. We couple Bloom's taxonomy with several descriptors of knowledge quality. This serves as input to the Knowledge Transfer Model, which in turn is used by the Project Staffing Model, the basis for our approach. Together these provide a framework for operationalizing the staffing of requirements determination teams. An Illustrative Case Study applies the concepts presented in the paper and highlights those parameters that management needs to provide to implement the Project Staffing Model. Full implementation would require additional research in several areas, which are discussed, as are various approaches for conducting this research.

REFERENCES

Agarwal, R., & Tanniru, M. R. (1990). Knowledge acquisition using structured interviewing: An empirical investigation. *Journal of Management Information Systems*, 7(11), 123–140.

Ambrosini, V., & Bowman, C. (2001). Tacit knowledge: Some suggestions of operationalization. *Journal of Management Studies*, 38(6), 811–829. doi:10.1111/1467-6486.00260

Ballou, D. P., & Pazer, H. L. (1985). Modeling data and process quality in multi-input, multi-output information systems. *Management Science*, 31(2), 150–162. doi:10.1287/mnsc.31.2.150

Belardo, S., Ballou, D. P., & Pazer, H. L. (2004). Analysis and design of information systems: A knowledge quality perspective. In Anderson, K. V., & Vendelo, M. T. (Eds.), *The Past and Future of Information Systems* (pp. 43–59). New York: Elsevier.

Belardo, S., & Pazer, H. L. (1985). Scope/Complexity: A framework for the classification and analysis of information-decision systems. *Journal of Management Information Systems*, 2(2), 55–72.

Bloom, B. S. (1956). *Taxonomy of Educational Objectives*. New York: David McKay Co.

Bostrom, R. P. (1989). Successful application of communication techniques to improve the systems development process. *Information & Management*, 16(5), 279–295. doi:10.1016/0378-7206(89)90005-0

Browne, G. J., & Rogich, M. B. (2001). An empirical investigation of user requirements elicitation: Comparing the effectiveness of prompting techniques. *Journal of Management Information Systems*, 17(4), 223–249.

Byrd, T. A., Cossick, K. L., & Zmud, R. W. (1992). A synthesis of research on requirements determination and knowledge acquisition techniques. *Management Information Systems Quarterly*, 16(1), 117–138. doi:10.2307/249704

Churchman, C. W., & Schainblatt, A. H. (1965). The researcher and the manager: A Dialectic of Implementation. *Management Science, 11*(4), B69–B87. doi:10.1287/mnsc.11.4.B69

Cooper, R. B., & Swanson, E. B. (1979). Management information requirements assessment: The state of the art. *Database, 10,* 5–16.

Coughlan, J. M., Lycett, M., & Macredie, R. D. (2003). Communication issues in requirements elicitation: A content analysis of stakeholder experiences. *Information and Software Technology, 45*(8), 525–537.

Davis, A. M. (1988). A comparison of techniques for specification of external systems behavior. *Communications of the ACM, 31*(9), 1098–1115. doi:10.1145/48529.48534

Ewusi-Mensah, K. (1997). Critical issues in abandoned information systems projects. *Communications of the ACM, 40*(9), 74–80. doi:10.1145/260750.260775

Goguen, J. A. (1997). Toward a social, ethical theory of information. In Bowker, G. C., Star, S., Turner, W., & Gasser, L. (Eds.), *Social Science, Technical Systems and Cooperative Work: Beyond the Great Divide* (pp. 27–56). Mahwah, NJ: Lawrence Erlbaum Associates.

Holtzblatt, K., & Beyer, H. R. (1995). Requirements gathering: The human factor. *Communications of the ACM, 38*(5), 31–32. doi:10.1145/203356.203361

Kaiser, K. M., & King, W. R. (1982). The manager analyst interface in systems development. *Management Information Systems Quarterly, 6*(1), 49–59. doi:10.2307/248754

Kogut, B., & Zander, U. (1992). Knowledge of the firm, combinative capabilities, and the replication of technology. *Organization Science, 3,* 383–396. doi:10.1287/orsc.3.3.383

Kydd, C. T. (1989). Understanding the information content in MIS management tools. *Management Information Systems Quarterly, 13*(3), 277–290. doi:10.2307/249002

Majchrzak, A., Beath, C. M., Lim, R. A., & Chin, W. W. (2005). Managing Client Dialogues During Information Systems Design to Facilitate Client Learning. *Management Information Systems Quarterly, 29*(4), 653–672.

Marakas, G. M., & Elam, J. J. (1998). Semantic structuring in analyst acquisition and representation of facts in requirements analysis. *Information Systems Research, 9*(1), 37–63. doi:10.1287/isre.9.1.37

Niehoff, B. P., & Whitney-Bammerlin, D. L. (1995). Don't let your training process derail your journey to total quality management. *S.A.M. Advanced Management Journal, 60*(1), 39–45.

Nonaka, I. (1991). The knowledge creating company. *Harvard Business Review, 69*(6), 96–104.

Schon, D. A. (1983). *The Reflective Practitioner: How Professionals Think in Action.* New York: Basic Books.

Simon, H. A. (1960). *The New Science of Management Decision.* New York: Harper and Row.

Sobol, M. G., & Lei, D. (1994). Environment, manufacturing technology, and embedded knowledge. *The International Journal of Human Factors in Manufacturing, 4*(2), 167–189. doi:10.1002/hfm.4530040205

Sternberg, R. J. (1994). Tacit knowledge and job success. In Anderson, N., & Herriot, P. (Eds.), *Assessment and Selection in Organizations: Methods and Practice for Recruitment and Appraisal* (pp. 27–39). London: John Wiley.

Van der Meij, H. (1990). Question Asking: To know that you do not know is not enough. *Journal of Educational Psychology, 82*(3), 505–512. doi:10.1037/0022-0663.82.3.505

Vessey, I., & Conger, S. (1994). Requirements specification: learning object, process, and data methodologies. *Communications of the ACM, 37*(5), 102–113. doi:10.1145/175290.175305

Wand, Y., & Weber, R. (2002). Research Commentary: Information systems and conceptual modeling--A research agenda. *Information Systems Research, 13*(4), 363–376. doi:10.1287/isre.13.4.363.69

Wang, R. Y., & Strong, D. (1996). Beyond Accuracy: What data quality means to data consumers. *Journal of Management Information Systems, 12*(4), 5–34.

Yadin, A. (2007). *Implementation of Bloom's Taxonomy on Systems Analysis Workshops.* Paper presented at the AIS SIG-ED IAIM 2007 Conference.

Zmud, R. W. (1978). An empirical investigation of the dimensionality of the concept of information. *Decision Sciences, 9,* 187–195. doi:10.1111/j.1540-5915.1978.tb01378.x

Zmud, R. W., Anthony, W. P., & Stair, R. M. (1993). The use of mental imagery to facilitate information identification in requirements analysis. *Journal of Management Information Systems, 9*(4), 175–191.

This work was previously published in International Journal of Knowledge Management, Volume 6, Issue 2, edited by Murray E. Jennex, pp. 1-21, copyright 2010 by IGI Publishing (an imprint of IGI Global).

Chapter 6
Sustaining Organizational Innovativeness:
Advancing Knowledge Sharing During the Scenario Process

Hannu Kivijärvi
Aalto University School of Economics, Finland

Kalle Piirainen
Lappeenranta University of Technology, Finland

Markku Tuominen
Lappeenranta University of Technology, Finland

ABSTRACT

This paper aims to provide a conceptual basis for creating semi-virtual communities that facilitate knowledge creation and sharing that seeks to promote organizational innovativeness. In addition, based on the theoretical discussion, the paper proposes a concrete context that supports and stimulates the conversion of personal knowledge into new innovations and organizational decisions. As a methodological means, scenario driven innovation process is employed as a way to enhance creativity and knowledge convergence within an organization. The authors discuss that in its deepest sense knowledge is the capability to make decisions. Scenarios aim to increase that capability, and are thus a piece of organizational knowledge. The practical implementations of the contexts and the experiences with these implementations are evaluated by two real case studies in real life contexts.

1. INTRODUCTION

Innovativeness, an organization's ability to initiate and implement innovations, is a critical resource for prosperity in the long term. The notion that innovation and the utilization of knowledge assets provide a source of competitive advantage has gained attention in recent discussions (Wiggins & Ruefli, 2005). Every innovation requires exploration of new knowledge, in addition to the exploitation of existing knowledge, personal as well as organizational. This has led to a search to find means to enhance creativity and knowledge

DOI: 10.4018/978-1-4666-0035-5.ch006

convergence from personal to organizational use in the innovation process.

Knowledge and knowledge sharing are important facets of any innovative activity. The quality of innovations depends on creation, transformation and integration of knowledge across individuals and organizational groupings. As organizations have become larger and more diversified, and as individual roles and tasks have become more specialized, there is a growing need to convert personal knowledge to common usage. In addition, there is a need to turn and align personal or local inventions into broader systems of organizational innovations. The question is: 'What kinds of organizational arrangements are capable of increasing organizational innovativeness?' or in other words 'How to support organizations as they strive towards integrated innovations?'

Information and communication technology (ICT) offers many instruments for knowledge management and thus for the stimulation of the innovation process (Sher & Lee, 2004; Cody, Kreulen, Krishna, & Spangler, 2002). Although the means for sharing information, communicating and expressing ideas have broadened considerably during the last decades, much of the relevant knowledge in an organizational context remains unmined, unshared, and underutilized.

The focus and contribution of this paper is first to provide a theoretical basis for a support context and, second, to propose a concrete system that supports and stimulates the conversion of personal knowledge into innovations and organizational decisions. This system forms a set of artificial conditions that quasi-exercise organizational skills and capabilities, by employing Group Support Systems (GSS), different mapping techniques, and cluster analyses in order to increase the communication between individuals, and increase the trust in the outcomes of the process.

Concepts such as community of practice (Lave & Wengler, 1991), ba (Nonaka & Konno, 1998), and networks of practice (Brown & Duguid, 2001a) are used to explain the organizational conditions favoring knowledge creation and shar-

ing, and innovation. The most favorable contents of these arrangements depend on factors such as the organizational context, the experiences and other capabilities of the members, the management style applied.

The initial validity of the developed system is evaluated empirically by two real life cases. The cases have been built relying on Yin (2003) as a frame of reference. Based on the conceptual discussion, an actual environment is demonstrated where the creation of new knowledge can be stimulated and managed, and personal knowledge can be converted into organizational decisions. It is shown how even hidden, tacit aspects of individual knowledge can be externalized into an explicit form and generalized for organizational use. The large amount of new and innovative knowledge created is potential evidence of the value of the proposed approach. The developed system forms a set of artificial conditions to exercise organizational skills and capabilities.

The remainder of the paper is organized around the key concepts described in Figure 1. The contents of each concept and the relationships between them are discussed in the second section. The third section proposes a support context for scenario driven innovation processes. The fourth section describes the practical implementations of the context and the experiences with these implementations. The fifth section presents the evaluation of the semi-virtual community, based on the presented cases. The final section discusses the results and presents conclusions at theoretical and practical levels.

2. CONCEPTUALIZING THE KEY ELEMENTS OF SCENARIO DRIVEN INNOVATIONS

2.1 Knowledge and Knowing

Knowledge is traditionally interpreted as a singular, independent object. Another, processual interpretation of knowledge is to consider it as

Figure 1. Conceptual structure of the study

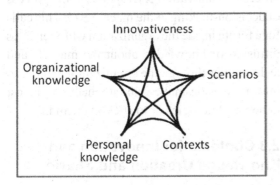

a path consisting of related steps (Carlile & Rebentisch, 2003). A wider interpretation is viewing knowledge as a network or a system where each element is related directly or indirectly to each other. This latter definition leads to the conclusion that totally new knowledge cannot be created; only the attributes of the knowledge system can be changed, or new relations between the elements created.

Defining knowledge, Tsoukas and Vladimirouv (2001, p. 979) refer to a person's ability to draw distinctions: "Knowledge is the individual ability to draw distinctions, within a collective domain of action, based on an appreciation of context or theory, or both." According to this definition, a person is more knowledgeable if she/he can draw fine distinctions. Making distinctions and judgments, classifying, structuring, giving order to chaos, are capabilities of an expert who has knowledge. Kivijärvi (2008) has elaborated the characterization of knowledge further, and defines knowledge as the individual or organizational ability to make decisions; all actions are consequences of decisions.

If, as Simon (1960) argued, decision-making is not a synonym for management, it is still undoubtedly at the core of all managerial functions. When a decision is made, the epistemic work has been performed and the physical work to implement the decision can start. Jennex and Olfman (2006, p.53) note that "...decision making is the

ultimate application of knowledge". The value of knowledge and information is ultimately evaluated by the quality of the decisions made. Making decisions also involves making distinctions, categorizations and judgments – the need to search for and structure alternatives.

In his later works, Polanyi (1966) talks of knowledge, and particularly when discussing tacit knowledge, he really refers to a process rather than objects. Consequently, there is a need to pay more attention to tacit *knowing* rather than tacit knowledge. Zeleny (2005) characterizes the relationship of explicit and tacit knowledge much in the same way. He observes that although people may appear knowledgeable, knowledge is embedded in the process of 'knowing', in the routines and actions that come naturally for a person who *knows.*Cook and Brown (1999) also emphasize that knowing is an important aspect of all actions, and thus, tacit knowledge most easily becomes evident when it is used; that is, it will manifest itself during the knowing process.

Tsoukas and Vladimirou (2001, p. 981-983) state "Organizational knowledge is the set of collective understanding embedded in a firm … [it is] the capability the members of an organization have developed to draw distinctions in the process of carrying out their work, in particular concrete contexts, by enacting sets of generalizations (propositional statements) whose application depends on historically evolved collective understandings and experiences". Similar to the way the definition of personal knowledge was extended, the definition of organizational knowledge above has been extended to capture the capability the members of an organization have developed to make decisions in the process of carrying out their work in organizational contexts (Kivijärvi, 2008).

2.2. Innovation and Innovativeness

Innovation is generally defined as an idea which is commercialized. The organizational aspect of innovation is that an idea is rarely an organizational item, it is a product of individual creativeness, but an innovation most often requires the organization and division of tasks before the idea is ready to be produced commercially. At a more practical level, an innovation can be defined as a novel product, service or even a way of organizing. In the context of this paper, drawing on Luecke and Katz (2003), innovation is primarily, an embodiment, combination, or synthesis of knowledge.

An important aspect of innovation is that revolutionary technologies can often lay dormant for a number of years before an actor recognizes the potential and develops a novel artifact which offers superior performance and value compared to the dominant technology and design. Paap and Katz (2004) have noted that on many occasions the incumbents are aware of the revolutionary technology, but fail to act upon it until the market is reformed. Another perspective to this phenomenon is that in order to recognize the market potential of a technology an organization has to have a certain knowledge base and expertise to be able to assess the potential of new technologies (Cohen & Levinthal 1990). Kogut and Zander (1992) stress combinative capability, the ability to combine knowledge about market and customer needs with technological knowledge, which together create an innovation, for example a commercially successful novel product, service or organization.

Considering innovation in the organizational context, the discussion outlined above amounts to the proposition that knowledge is a capability to make decisions, and is tied to the process of knowing. Thus, innovation is dependent on the organization's ability to integrate knowledge assets with innovative artifacts, and to choose the final commercial offerings from these artifacts. This may be a mechanistic view, but this proposal corresponds to modern industrial practices, where waterfall-type innovation processes in which a large number of product ideas are developed to concepts which are all screened, and a few are selected to become product development projects, and the best end up as commercial products. The

process of innovation corresponds to the process of decision-making at the macro level. This calls for a forum inside the organization which enables diffusion of knowledge about the markets and technologies through the organization in order to inform decision-makers about whether to invest in new technologies or to stick to the old.

2.3 Contexts for Innovation and Knowledge Creation and Sharing

Lave and Wengler (1991, p. 98) introduced the concept of *community of practice* which they regard as "an intrinsic condition for the existence of knowledge". Communities of practice have been identified as critical conditions for learning and innovation in organizations, and they are formed spontaneously by work communities without the constraints of formal organizations. According to Lesser and Everest (2001, p. 41) "Communities of practice help foster an environment in which knowledge can be created and shared and, most importantly, used to improve effectiveness, efficiency and innovation". In other words, a community of practice can form the shared context, which supports the recipient decoding a received message with the same meaning as the sender who coded it (Gammelgaard & Ritter, 2008). Although the communities develop informally and spontaneously, in some cases spontaneity can be structured (Brown & Duguid, 2001b).

When people are working together in communities, knowledge sharing is seen as a social process, where the members participate in communal learning at different levels and create a kind of 'community knowledge'. According to studies on communities of practice, new members learn from the older ones by being allowed to first participate in certain 'peripheral' tasks of the community. Later the new members are approved to move to full participation. The participation of the members is most fundamental to the existence and development of a community.

Since the original introduction of the concept of community of practice, a number of attempts have been made to apply the concept to business organizations and managerial problems (Brown & Duguid, 1996; Wengler, 1998; Gammelgaard & Ritter, 2008). Recent studies on communities of practice have paid special attention to the manageability of the communities (Swan, Scarborough, & Robertson, 2002), alignment of different communities, and the role of virtual communities (Kimble, Hildreth, & Wright, 2001). Gammelgaard and Ritter (2008), for example, propagate virtual communities of practice for knowledge transfer in multinational companies.

The concept of ba has some similarities to that of 'community of practice'. Nonaka and Konno (1998) introduced the concept to the western community as a multi-context place for knowledge creation. Nonaka, Toyama and Konno (2001, p. 22) define ba as "a shared context in which knowledge is shared, created and utilized". It is a time-place location where physical, virtual, and mental spaces are incorporated to increase the interaction between individuals. In this regard it is the context where knowledge sharing takes place.

Although ba and 'community of practice' have obvious similarities, Nonaka, Toyama and Konno (2001, p. 23) emphasize the differences between these concepts:

While a community of practice is a place where the members learn knowledge that is embedded in the community, ba is a place where new knowledge is created. While learning occurs in any community of practice, ba needs energy to become an active ba where knowledge is created. The boundary of a community of practices is firmly set by the task, culture and history of the community. Consistency and continuity are important for a community of practice, because it needs an identity. In contrast, the boundary of ba is fluid and can be changed quickly as it is set by the participants. Instead of being constrained by history, ba has a 'here and now' quality as an emerging relationship. It is constantly moving; it is created, functions and disappears according to need.

The organizational context forms the circumstances required for bas. In the organizational context, different kinds of working groups and teams, their roles and rules, offer natural settings for bas. In those groups, the interacting participants activate knowledge creation. Like organizations in general, bas can also be arranged hierarchically, forming greater bas or bashos (Nonaka & Konno, 1998).

Brown and Duguid (2001a, p. 205), dissatisfied with the concept of community of practice, introduced the notion of *networks of practice* in which "relations among networks members are significantly looser than those within a community of practice". In a network of practice, members can share professional knowledge through conferences, workshops, newsletters, listserves, web pages, and the like (Brown & Duguid, 2001a; 2001b). Networks of practice are considered crucial to innovations as they allow the local knowledge of particular groups to be accessible to others who are within the broader set of similar practitioners (Ziman, 1968; Brown & Duguid, 2001a). What distinguishes virtual communities from on-line communities is a shared working history, bi-directional knowledge exchange between the community and an individual participant, and a common goal and common interest (Gammelgaard & Ritter, 2008). Despite well developed electronic means for communication, virtual communities have significant challenges. The geographical dispersion of the group and the potentially relatively small shared context and knowledge overlap compared to a traditional community, poses a challenge for message decoding (Gammelgaard & Ritter, 2008)

In summary, the general requirements for a community are a common interest, a strong shared context; including own jargon, habits, routines, and informal ad hoc relations in problem-solving and other communication (Amin & Roberts, 2008).

An important facet of a community of practice is that the community is emergent and is formed by individuals who are motivated to contribute by a common interest and sense of purpose. A cautious researcher might be inclined to use the term quasi-community or a similar expression in the case of artificial set-ups, but in the interest of being succinct, the word community in used in this paper to also include non-emergent teams.

2.4 Scenarios and the Scenario Process

Kahn and Wiener (1967, p. 33) define scenarios as "Hypothetical sequences of events constructed for the purpose of focusing attention to causal processes and decision points". Added to this is the further need that the development of each situation is mapped step by step, and the decision options of each actor are considered along the way. The aim of scenarios is to answer the questions "What kind of chain of events leads to a certain event or state?" and "How can each actor influence the chain of events at each time?"

Schwartz (1996) describes scenarios as plots that tie together the driving forces and key actors of the environment. In his view, the story gives a meaning to the events, and helps the strategists to see the trend behind seemingly unconnected events or developments. Some writers (Schwartz, 1996; Blanning & Reinig, 2005), use the concept 'drivers of change' to describe forces such as influential interest groups, nations, large organizations and trends, which shape the operational environment of organizations. We assume in this study that these drivers create movement in the operational field, which can be reduced to a chain of related events. These chains of events are in turn labeled as scenarios, leading from the present *status quo* to the defined end state during the time span of the respective scenarios.

One of the key questions in the scenario process is how to organize and transform available knowledge into logical and coherent scenarios which are relevant to the decision-makers of the organization. The literature on scenario planning describes a multitude of techniques, methods and processes (Bradfield, Wright, Burt, Cairns, & van der Heijden, 2005). The methods range from the intuitive approach, which largely relies on logical thinking in constructing scenarios, to statistical Trend and Cross Impact Analysis methods. Heuristic methods form the intermediate approach in that they are more structured than intuitive approaches, but are less methodologically restricting than those which employ statistical techniques. The method adopted in our study is the intuitive decision-oriented scenario method, which, in the process, uses Group Support Systems to mediate group work.

2.5. Relationships Between the Conceptual Elements

The discussion above has shown that organizations can benefit from creating (semi-) virtual communities in order to facilitate knowledge creation and knowing to promote innovativeness. The discussion has also tied knowing to action and decision-making through the notion that, in its deepest sense, knowledge is the capability to make decisions. Scenarios, as such, aim to increase that capability, and are thus an element of organizational knowledge. As discussed above, knowledge is tied to action. Scenarios are a kind of 'quasi-action' where knowledge items can be tested in relation to other items. In the scenario literature, it is sometimes claimed that one of the major benefits of the scenario process is the process itself - in the sense that it also helps the decision-makers to consider the effects of change in ways that are not written down in the actual scenarios (Bergman, 2005).

Fenwick (2003, p. 123) argues that "innovation is ... a significant and complex dimension of learning in work, involving a mix of rational, intuitive, emotional and social processes embedded in activities of a particular community of practice". Thus, innovation process is a knowing activity embedded deeply in activities of a particular community of practice. Knowledge management can be seen as a medium to support innovation process, or as an innovation process in its own right (Scarbrough, 2003). Swan (2002, p. 168) perceives the community of practice as a "discursive strategy to promote innovation in a context where necessary knowledge and experience and the locus of power is widely distributed across different professional groups". The role of knowledge management in 5th generation innovation processes has been seen as of special importance. As Huang (2006, p. 384-385) describes "In the current 5th generation, knowledge management plays an important supporting role for facilitating the process of innovation through organizational learning and knowledge sharing". In practice, 63% percents of companies use knowledge management to accelerate innovations (KPMG, 2002, 2003).

It is generally accepted that all knowledge has value: "All knowledge is of itself of some value"[1]. However all knowledge does not have value that is based in its real world or market application. Rather, it is innovation that is that kind of knowledge that always owes itself to utilization or aspects of the market.

The quality on innovations depends on the creation, transformation and integration of knowledge across individuals and organizational groupings. As organizations have become larger and more diversified, and as individual roles and tasks have become more specialized, there is a growing need to convert personal knowledge into common use.

Through the scenario process there is a possibility to create alternative futures. The alternative future images can be significant sources for creativity and innovation. Particularly when an organization is seeking breakthrough innovations for future markets, scenarios can stimulate experts to think creatively and to share and explicate their personal knowledge (Ringland, 2008). Scenario driven innovation process is a means to enhance creativity and knowledge convergence within an organization.

The next section introduces a proposed artificial context for a semi-virtual community to support organizational innovativeness. The proposed context is built on the concepts discussed above, and the main practical implication is to develop a concrete context that supports and stimulates the conversion of personal knowledge into new innovations and organizational decisions. The core of the context is a Group Support System integrated with a number of mapping methodologies.

3. SUPPORTING SCENARIO DRIVEN INNOVATIVENESS: A SEMI-VIRTUAL COMMUNITY

The most complex decisions in organizations, particularly strategic decisions, are made by groups. The increasingly competitive environment also increases the complexity of decisions and the need for meetings and group work. Groups combine knowledge and create new knowledge, and the members become committed to the implementation of the decisions (Turban, Aronson, & Liang, 2005). A Group Support System (GSS) support a group of people engaged in a decision-related meeting. Through GSS it is possible to approximate the interpersonal relationships of the social world within the organization. It is a virtual environment for knowledge accumulation and sharing. GSSs typically include tools such as electronic brainstorming, electronic conferencing or meetings, group scheduling, planning, conflict resolution, model building, videoconferencing, electronic document sharing, voting. The typical process of a group meeting includes idea generation, idea organization, prioritizing of alternatives, and policy development.

Bhatt and Zhaveri (2002) argue that fundamentally, decision support systems have an enabling role in organizational learning, and GSS particularly enables information and knowledge sharing.

When weighing up the benefits and challenges of using GSS, the literature supports the potential for facilitating the scenario process effectively by means of a GSS. In many instances, GSS has been deemed effective in facilitating communication and, to some extent, improving group cohesion and idea generation (Huang, Wei, Watson, & Tan, 2002; Blanning & Reinig, 2005). Other benefits are commitment and consensus creation through anonymity and knowledge sharing, and when the participants' roles outside the session do not influence interaction, the focus would more likely turn to the substance than in a traditional face-to-face situation. Kwok and Khalifa (1998), for example, claim that GSS enhances group learning through active participation and cooperative working practices. Other researchers have picked up these propositions and have experimented with the use of GSS in the scenario process with encouraging results, (e.g. Piirainen et al., 2010; Lindqvist, Piirainen, & Tuominen, 2008).

The scenario processes can be supported by a number of other methodologies. If the scenario process is considered as a learning experience, there might be a demand for techniques enhancing knowledge representation. For some time now, mapping techniques have been offered as a means for knowledge representation. The most widely featured types of maps are the mind map, which has even been registered as a trademark, the concept map, the cognitive map and the causal map. The main differences between these variations are that a mind map pictures a central concept and the outward spreading branches of related concepts, whereas the other maps can be used to describe multiple concepts with intertwining relationships and causalities.

The value of maps is that with mapping techniques, relatively large volumes of complex data can be presented in an illustrative manner. For the scenario process, it can be suggested that the drivers and their relations can be formed into a map fairly easily, and perhaps the information value and usability of such map can be higher than a written document about the same subject.

The big question for a manager is that if the community in the case is not emergent, but purposefully set up, is still a community? According to Amin and Roberts (2008) the answer would most likely be 'yes and no', and the short-lived community that is presented in this paper would be classified as a 'creative community', where the base of trust is professional, and the purpose is to solve a problem collectively. The backbone of the experimental community in our study is a group support system, which is employed to mediate the interaction and to support the community in the task of composing scenarios.

4. EXPERIENCES WITHIN THE SEMI-VIRTUAL COMMUNITY

The discussion above presented the premises for the argument that using a scenario process would form a community that encourages knowledge sharing and promotes innovativeness. This section describes two cases which aim to investigate whether the semi-virtual community presented above is a practical method to encourage knowledge sharing and to promote innovativeness. The cases are designed after Yin's (2003) framework. The data presented below was collected through questionnaires and interviews after the actual scenario sessions. The first case focuses on strategic planning and positioning in a university; the second case is taken from a project where the objective was to develop measures to identify and assess business opportunities at an intersection of industries. To add insight and depth to reporting, one of the authors was present in the case sessions to facilitate and observe the communities at work. The descriptions of the scenario process past the workshop are first hand accounts of the authors who were working on finalizing the scenarios in the first case. The cases both use the same context although the communities are different.

4.1 Case 1: University Management

This case is based on large scale experiments conducted in a medium-sized university to discover administrative and service types of innovation. The members of the semi-virtual community hold personal knowledge and experience in a number of areas such as research, teaching, and administration in different departments and in the administration of the whole university. The purpose was to discover new opportunities for the future position and operational environment of the university over the following ten years. The community was composed of individuals most of whom had met but who were not very familiar with each other. Thus, the most apparent link between most of the individuals was the presented problem of creating scenarios for the organization.

After the preparation, definition, and briefing of the problem, the actual work within the community started by brainstorming the key external uncertainties and drivers of change. This phase comprised an idea generation with a brainstorming tool, followed by a period for writing comments about the ideas and clarification of the proposed drivers. Unclear items were rephrased or explained by verbal comments, and overlapping items were removed or merged. After the discussion, the drivers were prioritized through a process of voting.

The drivers form the backbone of the scenarios. The scenarios were composed by adopting the method proposed by Blanning and Reinig (2005). The phase comprises brainstorming of events which will or could be triggered by the drivers. The resulting event sets were once again discussed and commented upon, and overlapping events were merged or removed. After discovering the events, the group votes on (or otherwise assigns) a subjective probability and impact factor for each event. The original proposition is that the scenarios are formed by selecting three groups of 10-20 events: the most probable events form a realistic scenario, medium to high probability events with a positive impact form a positive scenario, and the events with medium to high probability and a negative impact form a negative scenario. The events were grouped into initial scenarios by qualitative graphical clustering and discussed during the meeting. Later however, to adjust the final grouping of the event to scenarios, the expectation-maximization *clustering method* was used rather than graphical clustering proposed in the original method.

The GSS-workshop phase of the process ended in the evaluation of the events and graphical grouping, from which the data was moved to the remainder of the process as a GSS-log file. The log contained the input items and voting outcome, the drivers, events and their ranks, impacts and probabilities. After the workshop the first task was to examine the log, clean the data and commence mapping the drivers and the events.

Also after the workshop, the scenario authors used the principles of systems thinking to ponder the cause and effect between drivers and events inside the scenarios. Using this analogy, the drivers of the scenarios form a system with feed-back relations. Figure 2 illustrates the feedback loops identified from a cognitive map drawn from the drivers in this particular case.

After mapping the drivers and the data clean-up, the events were organized into a concept map and tied together as logical chains with appropriate linking phrases; these described the connection and transition between the events. The names for the scenarios were picked after examining the general theme in the scenarios. In this case, in order to test the reactions and validate the logical structure of the maps, after the initial maps were drawn they were presented to some of the closer colleagues familiar with the sessions in the form of a focus group interview. Figure 3 shows one of the final concept maps from the case; this was used to illustrate the logic and the paths of the scenarios.

The final scenario stories were written around the logic of the concept maps. Other than some minor adjustment to the maps, the writing up was

Figure 2. An abstracted cognitive map of the drivers in the case 1

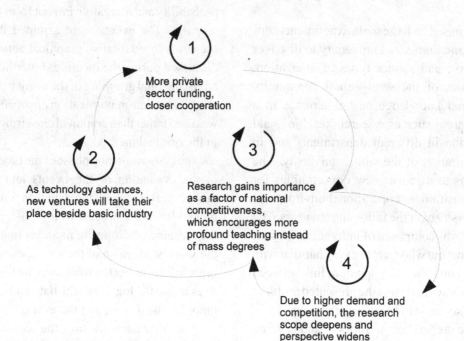

a straightforward process of tying the events together as a logical story, from the present to a defined state in the future. The process might be characterized as iterative, a resonance between the drivers and the scenario maps conducted by the writer. Figure 4 provides a window to the scenarios.

4.2 Case 2: Opportunity Recognition at an Intersection of Industries

The purpose of the second case was to discover new opportunities at the intersection of a manufacturing industry and a complementary industry. For this case, the members of the semi-virtual community were 'selected' from each industry, as well as from academics and general experts in the field. The working process followed the same outline as the previous case described above.

Working within the community started with a presentation of the aims of the innovation project

and scenarios in general, followed by the more detailed outline and working objectives. The identification of the drivers of change was also carried out with the same principles as in the first case. When the drivers had been sorted, the work proceeded to identifying events, or in this case, business opportunities. The ideas for events were generated in two phases. In order to better tie the idea generation with the drivers, the participants first generated and noted events while examining the drivers and then moved on to using GSS. The basic questions to aid the event recognition were "What kind of business opportunities can the identified trends open up in ten years' time?" "What events will these opportunities create?" The events were also discussed and clarified in the group.

As the evaluations form the basis for grouping the events to scenarios the evaluation phase is of paramount importance to the final scenarios. Un-

Figure 3. An example of a scenario map in case 1

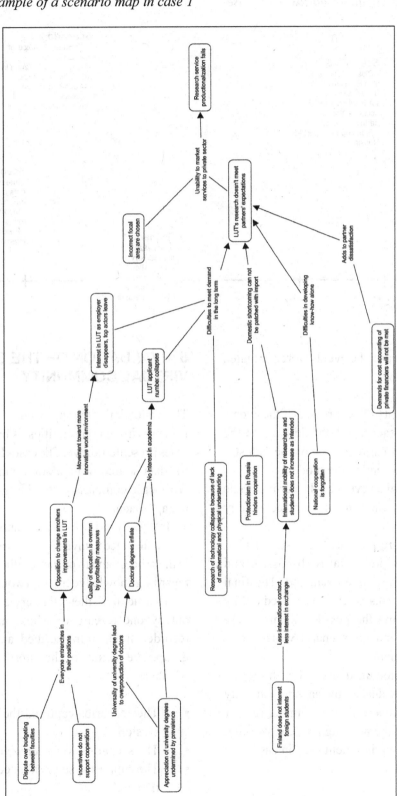

Figure 4. Overview of the scenarios in the case 1

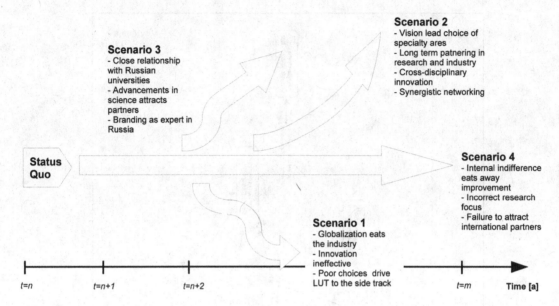

like the previous case, the events were evaluated in three dimensions:

1. The probability of occurrence of the events
2. The impact each event should have on the business and earning logic of the industry that is implementing the product
3. The impact of an event on the earning logic of the industry and on dominant technology

The events were presented as a scatter plot, the grouping was preliminarily discussed, and the voting outcomes were examined. The final grouping of the scenario sets was carried out by cluster analysis, but the possible themes were discussed freely and the scenario writers took notes of the comments.

At the conclusion the quality of each session with GSS was evaluated by an automatically generated questionnaire. As an example, Table 1 provides detail of the working process, working methods, and the environment used in case 2.

5. EVALUATION OF THE SEMI-VIRTUAL COMMUNITY

The evaluation of the approach, which is grounded in semi-virtual communities, is based on the two cases presented above. The cases formed the basis for data-source triangulation and enabled basic cross-case comparison to address the validity of the approach.

Interviews with the participants of the first case were conducted to investigate possible weaknesses in the process and to probe whether the arguments regarding knowledge creation would be supported. Semi-structured, themed interviews were carried out by one researcher. These interviews were recorded and later transcribed, and analyzed in a group. The themes of the interviews considered whether:

- The scenarios captured the essence of the session
- The scenarios were perceived as reliable
- The support system enhanced communication and

Table 1. Questionnaire items and basic statistics

Questionnaire items	Avg	Md	Mo	Std. Dev.	Conf.
Have you used or tried GSS tools previously?					
I have worked with a GSS previously (1 never - 10 regularly)	5.71	8.00	8.00	3.09	2.29
How do you think the environment affected the results (1 extremely negatively, 10 extremely positively)	7.86	8.00	8.00	0.90	0.67
The brainstorming process (1 completely disagree - completely agree 10)					
The goals of the session were clear	8.57	9.00	10.00	1.40	1.04
The goals were reached	8.14	8.00	7.00	1.21	0.90
Do you feel that the process included the most important factors	8.00	8.00	8.00	1.00	0.74
Do you consider the results as realistic and relevant to your company	7.86	8.00	7.00	1.35	1.00
Are the results trust-inspiring to you	8.00	8.00	8.00	0.82	0.60
The results are trustworthy because of the used work methods	7.29	8.00	8.00	1.38	1.02
Work methods (1 completely disagree - completely agree 10)					
The process helped in getting and outlining ideas	7.71	8.00	8.00	1.25	0.93
The ideas were clear and understood	7.43	8.00	8.00	1.13	0.84
GSS-environment in the process (1 completely disagree - completely agree 10)					
GSS systematized the process	8.86	9.00	10.00	1.21	0.90
GSS helped in observing different perspectives	7.57	8.00	8.00	2.64	1.95
GSS helped in getting committed to the process	7.29	8.00	6.00	1.60	1.19

- There was knowledge sharing or creation during the process

The interviews were conducted some time after the sessions, so the novelty of the situation did not affect the interviewees' reports. Generally, the members of the communities saw the GSS-context in a positive light because they felt that the knowledge sharing was effective, and promoted open-minded consideration. A factor is that when other peoples' contributions can be seen, this can create different connotations and mindsets. Interpreting the statements, interviewees appear to reflect that the context formed a community, which facilitated interaction in the group and promoted knowledge transfer as well as shared knowing.

Although the process was generally perceived by the interviewees as a positive working concept, some minor areas of criticism were recounted. The goals of the process or the process itself were sometimes somewhat unclear to the participants or were forgotten during the process in the first case. The identification of drivers of change was sometimes not integrated to the process well enough, or the identified drivers were not adequately connected to the future events. Even though the participants were presented with a list of the prioritized drivers, they felt that the events were not connected to the drivers clearly enough.

All in all, the interviewees in the first case generally saw the approach as a viable and practical tool for large and important decisions, even with its minor flaws. One finding was that in addition to the concrete scenarios, some interviewees saw the process as a kind of learning experience, promoting open-minded consideration of different options and ideas, and as a possibility to create consensus on large issues and goals in a large heterogeneous organization. The interviews did not provide as straightforward an answer to the question of knowledge creation, as was perhaps hoped for. One factor influencing the outcome was that the definition of 'knowledge' or knowledge creation was not too familiar to the subjects; the definitions being somewhat equivocal. However, notwithstanding the above, the findings from the first case still point to the fact that the subjects in the sessions formed a community, exchanged, and diffused knowledge through the system; this provides support for the argument put forward in this paper.

The contribution of the second case is that the findings are similar to the first case and this suggests that the process is indeed practicable and replicable to different contexts. The similarity of the findings between cases is an indication that the argument is not solely valid in special, one-of-a-kind circumstances, and therefore provides analytical generalization (Yin, 2003) for the proposed approach. The second case also provides some insight to the practical applicability of the approach because the participating industrial managers felt that the process provided trustworthy outcomes in the context of promoting recognition of business opportunities.

The artificial semi-virtual community can also be evaluated as a knowledge management system (KMS) by using well-established evaluation measures (Jennex & Olfman, 2006). The model can be used as a framework for qualitative evaluation. The evaluation dimensions include knowledge quality, system quality, and service quality; these positively contribute to the intention to use and user satisfaction, and the whole chain contributes to the net benefit. The challenges are slightly different in a semi-virtual community compared to other KMSs; for example, the community is facilitated and temporary, so the usual challenges for acquiring critical mass and penetrations do not apply. By the criteria set by Jennex and Olfman (2006) the technical system quality is average, but the user experience is better, and this arguably provides a balance. The quality of knowledge is hard to assess, but the process and community facilitate storing the correct knowledge in the system, and

the community surrounding the group will, with discussion, ensure an appropriate social context. The service quality in the system is exceptional compared to a usual KMS. This is because the facilitator is present for the whole session and supports the user experience. Given this consideration, the basic premises should be considered as appropriate for a semi-virtual community.

We have discussed user satisfaction and perceived benefits above. To summarize the findings, satisfaction with the system and the scenarios was excellent, and the community was perceived as useful for complex decision situations. The final link in the chain is the net benefit, which, alas, must remain open in this study. This is because the benefits are, in the first instance, not easy to measure, and were not attempted to be measured in this research. However, there is evidence to support the preceding chain as solid enough to propose that there are significant benefits to be achieved by using the semi-virtual community for knowledge creation and sharing, innovation stimulation, and scenario planning.

6. CONCLUSION AND DISCUSSION

In this paper we conceptualize a semi-virtual community which enhances innovativeness by promoting knowledge creation and knowledge sharing among the community members through the shared context and information and knowledge diffusion. The premises are that knowledge is, ultimately, a capability to make decisions, and that innovation is tied to combining knowledge and choosing the right solutions which are to be commercialized. Furthermore, the shared context can be provided in a community of practice, or in the absence of a community of practice, in a semi-virtual facilitated community. Figure 5 integrates the theoretical concept discussed in section 2 and the properties of the approach proposed in this paper. Generally, the proposed approach fits the conceptual requirements. The empirical experi-

Figure 5. Integrating the theoretical concepts, properties of the supporting system, and the respective tools and techniques

Theoretical concept	Properties of the supporting system	Respective tools and techniques
Personal knowledge		
1. Object	• Supports to make categories and distinctions and to organize primary knowledge elements from the huge mass of knowledge and information overflow.	Categorizer, outliner
2. Path	• Supports to create for procedural knowledge by related steps.	Successive sessions
3. Network	• Helps to create new relations between the knowledge elements and to relate participants over organization.	Electronic bainstorming, distributed meetings, outliner
4. Tacit	• Stimulates the sharing and usage of tacit knowledge by providing a shared context for social processes; accepts personal experience.	Visualization, all tools and tecniques
5. Explicit	• Supports codification and sharing/diffusing of explicit knowledge assets.	Record keeping, group writing, whitebords, briefcases
6. Knowing	• Integrates subjective, social, and physical dimensions of knowledge in the epistemic process of knowing. • Supports the interplay between the different types of knowledge and knowing.	All phases
Organizational knowledge		
1. Knowledge	• Supports to create organizational knowledge withing the organization and with value chain partners.	Consensus and accepted decisions, Group ouliner
2. Knowing	• Supports organizational decision making. Organizational rules of actions are applied.	All phases
Innovation		
1. Idea, insight, invention	• Sustains individual creativity and idea generation.	Brainstorming, topic commenter
2. Innovation	• Supports "bringing ideas to life".	Discussion, leapfrogging from others' ideas
3. Organizational innovation	• Supports to create business structures and processes, practices, etc. to implement innovations in organizational context. Helps to evaluate the value and meaning of single innovation in larger frameworks.	Shared context and process
4. Innovation process	• Supports the different phases of the innovation process and knowledge flow between the phases.	Facilitation, discussion and GSS tools
Context		
1. Participation	• Allows equal opportunity for participation.	Team building, shared, parallel inputs
2. Spontaneity	• Diminishes bureaucracy but allow to structure spontaneity. Keeps feeling of voluntarity. • Possibility to choose the time of participation.	Verbal discussions
3. Self-motivation	• Supports self-determination of goals and objectives.	Different time, free participation.
4. Freedom from organizational constraints	• Explicates clear causality between personal efforts, group outcomes and personal outcomes.	Anonymous work, free contribution
5. Networking	• Manages participants from different organizational units at various organizational levels. • Allows traditional face to face communication to promote mutual assurance between participants. Allows freedom of expression, verbal and non-verbal communication. Maintains social networking among participants.	Distributed meetings, internet enabled
Scenario		
1. Driver	• Electronic dicussion, and voting tools enable identification of important drivers	Discussion, categorizer
2. Event	• Discussion and voting tools enable	Discussion, categorizer
3. Chains of events	• Maps and other representations support organizing the knowledge of future drivers and events to scenarios	Mapping tools, discussions
4. Phases of the process	• Information about the future accumulates and coverges toward shared knowledge toward the end of the process	Discussions, meetings

ences with the system suggest that the process is able to promote knowledge creation, sharing, and sustaining organizational innovativeness.

An examination of the findings suggests that the cases uphold the theoretical propositions concerning support for the semi-virtual community. In addition the argument for using the GSS-supported scenario process to facilitate (semi-) virtual communities was also upheld. The evidence for this is that the group worked as a community toward a common goal and was satisfied with the outcomes. The first case indicated that knowledge was diffused in the group, and the participants felt that they had learned in the process, which in turn would increase the quality of decisions.

In the light of the findings, it appears that the concept of utilizing the supported scenario process to create actionable knowledge is feasible. On the one hand, it appears that the execution of the process needs further development in order to achieve optimal performance and outcomes from the setting, although the empirical testing was rather small, at least in sample size, and therefore the statistical generalizability of the findings is somewhat problematic. On the other hand, in terms of analytical generalization (Yin, 2003), the findings correspond reasonably well with the theoretical premises, and are fairly reliable in the sense that the findings are similar between the two cases. The chain between the premises, the main argument and the empirical findings is hardly seamless, so the results may be handled as a sort of proof-of-concept rather than definitive validation.

To conclude the paper, we propose that knowledge is manifested in decision-making, and that managers benefit from a forum where they can quasi-act and simulate their decisions to gain knowledge. The approach appears to be a feasible and practicable way to integrate multidisciplinary groups to create new knowledge in the form of scenarios, which could be used to promote *knowing* future opportunities and decision options. The properties of scenarios promote, and even require,

open minded consideration of the plausible, rather than of the known, and probable or the usual norm. Taken together, the case experiences suggest that the approach was at least partially able to engage the group in a semi-virtual community and to facilitate knowledge creation in the innovation context.

In the academic arena, the paper has contributed to the discussion about communities of practice and tested the use of communities for promoting innovation and knowledge creation. The main contribution is the practical insight on the matter. With regard to practical implications, the findings suggest that GSS can facilitate semi-virtual communities in diverse epistemic tasks. In its original conception a community of practice is an informal and emergent community; however this paper presents a successful semi-virtual community, which has the potential to combine some of the advantages of communities of practice to the advantages of facilitated group work. Further research on the subject would be the investigation of virtual communities and the motivation to contribute in different settings. This is important because motivation and a shared sense of purpose are some of the most important precedents for communities.

REFERENCES

Amin, A., & Roberts, J. (2008). Knowing in action, beyond communities of practice. *Research Policy*, *37*, 353–369. doi:10.1016/j.respol.2007.11.003

Bergman, J.-P. (2005). *Supporting Knowledge Creation and Sharing in the Early Phases of the Strategic Innovation Process (Tech. Rep.)*. Lappeenranta, Finland: Lappeenranta University of Technology.

Bhatt, G. D., & Zaveri, J. (2002). The enabling role of decision support systems in organizational learning. *Decision Support Systems*, *32*, 297–309. doi:10.1016/S0167-9236(01)00120-8

Blanning, R. W., & Reinig, B. A. (2005). A Framework for Conducting Political Event Analysis Using Group Support Systems. *Decision Support Systems*, *38*, 511–527. doi:10.1016/j.dss.2003.09.006

Bradfield, R., Wright, G., Burt, G., Cairns, G., & van der Heijden, K. (2005). The origins and evolution of scenario techniques in long range business planning. *Futures*, *37*, 795–812. doi:10.1016/j.futures.2005.01.003

Brown, J. S., & Duguid, P. (1996). Organizational Learning and Communities-of-Practice: Toward a Unified View of Working, Learning, and Innovation. In Cohen, M. D., & Sproull, L. S. (Eds.), *Organizational Learning* (pp. 58–82). Thousand Oaks, CA: Sage.

Brown, J. S., & Duguid, P. (2001a). Knowledge and organization: A social-practice perspective. *Organization Science*, *12*(2), 198–213. doi:10.1287/orsc.12.2.198.10116

Brown, J. S., & Duguid, P. (2001b). Structure and Spontaneity: Knowledge and Organization. In Nonaka, I., & Teece, D. (Eds.), *Managing Industrial Knowledge* (pp. 44–67). London: Sage.

Carlile, P., & Rebentisch, E. S. (2003). Into the Black Box: The Knowledge Transformation Cycle. *Management Science*, *49*(9), 1180–1195. doi:10.1287/mnsc.49.9.1180.16564

Cody, W. F., Kreulen, J. T., Krishna, V., & Spangler, W. S. (2002). The integration of business intelligence and knowledge management. *IBM Systems Journal*, *41*(4), 697–713.

Cohen, W. M., & Levinthal, D. A. (1990). Absorptive Capacity: A new Perspective on Learning and Innovation. *Administrative Science Quarterly*, *35*, 128–152. doi:10.2307/2393553

Cook, S. D. N., & Brown, J. S. (1999). Bridging Epistemologies: The Generative Dance Between Organizational Knowledge and Organizational Knowing. *Organization Science*, *10*(4), 381–400. doi:10.1287/orsc.10.4.381

Fenwick, T. (2003). Innovation: examining workplace learning in new enterprises. *Journal of Workplace Learning*, *15*(3), 123–132. doi:10.1108/13665620310468469

Gammelgaard, J., & Ritter, T. (2008). Virtual Communities of Practice: A Mechanism for Efficient Knowledge Retrieval in MNCs. *International Journal of Knowledge Management*, *4*(2), 46–51.

Huang, W. (2006). Acquiring Innovative Knowledge via Effective Process Management. In *Proceedings of IEEE International Conference on Management of Innovation and Technology* (pp. 384-388).

Huang, W. W., Wei, K.-K., Watson, R. T., & Tan, B. C. Y. (2002). Supporting virtual team-building with a GSS: an empirical investigation. *Decision Support Systems*, *34*, 359–367. doi:10.1016/S0167-9236(02)00009-X

Jennex, M. E., & Olfman, L. (2006). A Model of Knowledge Management Success. *International Journal of Knowledge Management*, *2*(3), 51–68.

Kahn, H., & Wiener, A. J. (1967). *The Year 2000: A Framework for Speculation on the Next Thirty-Three Years*. London: Collier-Macmillan Limited.

Kimble, C., Hildred, P., & Wright, P. (2001). Communities of Practice: Going Virtual. In Malhotra, Y. (Ed.), *Knowledge Management and Business Model Innovation* (pp. 220–234). Hershey, PA: IGI Global.

Kivijärvi, H. (2008). Aligning Knowledge and Business Strategies within an Artificial Ba. In Abou-Zeid, E.-S. (Ed.), *Knowledge Management and Business Strategies: Theoretical Frameworks and Empirical Research*. Hershey, PA: IGI Global.

Kivijärvi, H., Piirainen, K., Tuominen, M., Elfvengren, K., & Kortelainen, S. (2008). A Support System for the Strategic Scenario Process. In Adam, F., & Humphreys, P. (Eds.), *Encyclopedia of Decision Making and Decision Support Technologies*. Hershey, PA: IGI Global.

Kogut, B., & Zander, U. (1992). Knowledge of the Firm, Combinative Capabilities, and the Replication of Technology. *Organization Science, 3*(5), 383–397. doi:10.1287/orsc.3.3.383

KPMG. (2003). *Insights from KPMG's European Knowledge Management Survey 2002/2003.* KPMG Knowledge Advisory Services.

Kwok, R. C. W., & Khalifa, M. (1998). Effect of GSS on Knowledge Acquisition. *Information & Management, 34*, 307–315. doi:10.1016/S0378-7206(98)00062-7

Lave, J., & Wengler, E. (1991). *Situated learning: Legitimate peripheral participation*. New York: Cambridge University Press.

Lesser, E., & Everest, K. (2001). *Using Communities of Practice to manage Intellectual Capital'*. *Ivey Business Journal*. March/April.

Lindqvist, A., Piirainen, K., & Tuominen, M. (2008). Utilising group innovation to enhance business foresight for capital-intensive manufacturing industries. In *Proceedings of the 1st ISPIM Innovation Symposium*. Singapore.

Luecke, R., & Katz, R. (2003). *Managing Creativity and Innovation*. Boston, MA: Harvard Business School Press.

Nonaka, I., & Konno, N. (1998). The concept of 'Ba': Building a Foundation for Knowledge Creation. *California Management Review, 40*(3).

Nonaka, I., Konno, N., & Toyama, R. (2001). The Emergence of "Ba": A Conceptual Framework for the Continuous and Self-transcending Process of Knowledge Creation. In Nonaka, I., & Nishiguchi, T. (Eds.), *Knowledge Emergence, Social, Technical, and Evolutionary Dimensions of Knowledge Creation* (pp. 13–29). Oxford, NY: University Press.

Paap, J., & Katz, R. (2004). Anticipating Disruptive Innovation: Predicting the "unpredictable". *Research & Technology Management*, (Sept.-Oct.), 13-22.

Piirainen K., Kortelainen S., Elfvengren K., & Tuominen, M. (in press). A scenario approach for assessing new business concepts, *Management Research News, 32*(7).

Polanyi, M. (1966). *The Tacit Dimension*. Gloucester, MA: Peter Smith.

Ringland, G. (2008). Innovation: scenarios of alternative futures can discover new opportunities for creativity. *Strategy and Leadership, 36*(5), 22–27. doi:10.1108/10878570810902086

Scarbrough, H. (2003). Knowledge management, HRM and the innovation process. *International Journal of Manpower, 24*(5), 501–516. doi:10.1108/01437720310491053

Schwartz, P. (1996). *The Art of the Long View: Planning for the Future in an Uncertain World*. New York: Doubleday Dell Publishing Inc.

Sher, P. J., & Lee, V. C. (2004). Information technology as a facilitator for enhancing dynamic capabilities through knowledge management. *Information & Management, 41*(8), 933–945. doi:10.1016/j.im.2003.06.004

Simon, H. A. (1960). *The New Science of Management Decisions*. New York: Harper Brothers.

Swan, J., Scarborough, H., & Robertson, M. (2002). The Construction of 'Communities of Practice' in the Management of Innovation. *Management Learning, 33*(4), 477–496. doi:10.1177/1350507602334005

Tsoukas, H., & Vladimirou, E. (2001). What is Organizational Knowledge? *Journal of Management Studies, 38*(7), 973–993. doi:10.1111/1467-6486.00268

Turban, E., Aronson, J., & Liang, T.-P. (2005). *Decision Support Systems and Intelligent Systems* (7th ed.). A Simon & Schuster Company.

Wiggins, R. F., & Ruefli, T. W. (2005). Schumpeter's Ghost: Is Hypercompetition Making the Best of Times Shorter? *Strategic Management Journal, 26*, 887–911. doi:10.1002/smj.492

Yin, R. K. (2003). *Case Study Research, Design and Methods*. Thounsand Oaks, CA: Sage.

Zeleny, M. (2005). *Human Systems Management: Integrating Knowledge, Management and Systems*. World Scientific Publishing.

Ziman, J. M. (1968). *Public knowledge*. Cambridge, UK: Cambridge University Press.

ENDNOTES

[1] Sam. Johnson in Boswell. 1775. Gross, ed. Oxford Book of Aphorisms.

This work was previously published in International Journal of Knowledge Management, Volume 6, Issue 2, edited by Murray E. Jennex, pp. 22-39, copyright 2010 by IGI Publishing (an imprint of IGI Global).

Chapter 7
A Viewpoint–Based Approach for Understanding the Morphogenesis of Patterns

Pankaj Kamthan
Concordia University, Canada

ABSTRACT

An understanding of knowledge artifacts such as patterns is a necessary prerequisite for any subsequent action. In this article, as an initial step for formulating a theoretical basis for patterns, a conceptual model of primitive viewpoints is proposed and, by exploring one of the viewpoints, a conceptual model for stakeholders of a pattern is presented. This is followed by the description of a conceptual model of a process, namely P3, for the production of patterns. The workflows of P3 highlight, as appropriate, the interface of patterns to humans and/or machines. The implications of the Semantic Web and the Social Web towards P3 are briefly discussed.

INTRODUCTION

The reliance on the knowledge acquired from past experience can be crucial for solving problems that occur in any development. A *pattern* is one such kind of conceptually reusable knowledge based on 'best practice' that has been found to be useful in different ways. In particular, from their foundations in urban planning and architecture in the 1970s (Alexander, Ishikawa, & Silverstein, 1977), followed by object-oriented software design in the 1980s and the 1990s (Gamma et al., 1995), patterns have been applied in various domains of

interest (Rising, 2000). These domains include distributed software architectures, electronic commerce systems, mobile interaction design, security engineering, and use case modeling, to name a few. For novices, patterns have served as means of guidance; for experts, they have served as means of reference.

The purpose of this article is establishing a theoretical basis for patterns for the purpose of contributing to and improving upon the current understanding of patterns. Indeed, such an understanding is necessary for developing means to describe patterns, for managing patterns, and for making appropriate use of patterns. To do that,

DOI: 10.4018/978-1-4666-0035-5.ch007

this article identifies basic concerns pertaining to patterns and, by means of conceptual modeling, studies each concern separately. It proposes a conceptual model for viewing a pattern from certain relevant, different but related, perspectives and, by examining one of the viewpoints, proposes a conceptual model for stakeholders of a pattern. These models then form a requisite input to a conceptual model for producing patterns.

The rest of the article is organized as follows. First, the background necessary for subsequent discussion is outlined, and related work is presented. Then, conceptual models for viewpoints of a pattern, for stakeholders of patterns, and for a pattern production process are proposed. Next, challenges and directions for future research are outlined. Finally, concluding remarks are given.

BACKGROUND AND RELATED WORK

This section presents the necessary terminology specific to patterns and a brief analysis of related work.

Basic Concepts of the Pattern Domain

The *pattern domain* is the universe of discourse for all things related to patterns. The *pattern body of knowledge (PBOK)* is the set of fundamental concepts, activities, and results that characterize the pattern domain. The *pattern concept space* or simply *pattern space* is the collection of basic concepts in the PBOK.

In the last two decades or so, the PBOK has grown and the scope of concepts in it has broadened. There is currently no single source, reference model, or standard for the PBOK. Therefore, for the terminology related to the pattern space, this section relies on selected publications (Appleton, 1997; Meszaros & Doble, 1998; Buschmann, Henney, & Schmidt, 2007) that can be considered as authoritative.

There are a number of members in the pattern space that are of interest. A *pattern* is an empirically proven solution to a recurring problem that occurs in a particular context. The advantages and disadvantages of patterns have been highlighted (Wesson & Cowley, 2003), a detailed discussion of which is beyond the scope of this article.

A *pattern description* is a set of indicative statements that specify a pattern. A pattern description, if structured, typically consists of a number of elements. The name element of a pattern is an identifier that often reflects the nature of the solution; the author element gives the identity of the pattern author(s); the context element provides the situation or pre-conditions within which the problem occurs; the forces element provides the constraints that are resolved to arrive at a solution; the solution element provides an abstract, general, and reusable solution to the problem and is shown to work in practice via an examples element; the resulting context element provides the consequences or post-conditions of applying the solution; and the related patterns element outlines any other pattern(s) to which a pattern is related to in some way. At times, the element labels may vary across community, and other (optional) elements, such as those related to metadata, may be included to enrich the description. A *pattern form* is a prescription of a specific set of pattern elements that are expected to appear in a pattern description. There are a number of pattern forms available (Appleton, 1997; Coplien, 1996), and they are often named after their originators. It is this explicit structure that makes patterns more than a mere collection of problem-solution pairs, and makes them unique and more practical in their applicability among other kinds of experiential knowledge such as principles, guidelines, and heuristics.

A pattern is usually referred to by its name. In this article, the name of a pattern is presented in uppercase in order to distinguish it from the surrounding text.

There are other members in the pattern space that are of interest. An *anti-pattern* suggests a 'negative' solution to a given problem, and occurs when the context of the problem is not understood or the underlying forces are not optimally balanced. It may not be feasible to provide a single solution to a 'large' problem. In such a case, the problem is considerately partitioned into a manageable collection of smaller problems. A *pattern language* is a collection of patterns that are closely related to each other through their individual contexts and contribute towards a common goal. Thus, a pattern language solves a larger problem than that possible by any individual pattern.

The notion of *pattern engineering* is inspired by that of conventional engineering fields: it is a systematic and disciplined approach to (1) the definition, subsequent use and maintenance, and (2) interface to humans, machines, and other entities of knowledge, of a member of the pattern space within the given constraints of available resources. A *pattern production process* (P3) is a collection of activities and their interrelationships for developing a pattern. There are some activities of P3 that must be conducted socially; the others can be conducted either individually or socially. Figure 1 illustrates P3 within the larger context of elements of pattern engineering.

Related Work on the Production of Patterns

The P3 proposed in this article is based on collation, abstraction, and extension of past work. There are a few initiatives that outline P3 for specific domains, a brief chronological analysis of which is given in the rest of this section.

The possibility of a "process for developing patterns" has been raised (Meszaros & Doble, 1998). However, no details are given.

It has been shown (May & Taylor, 2003) that object-oriented software design patterns can be used for articulating and recording an organization's implicit knowledge. In doing so, it has been proposed that the activities in P3 can fit in the milieu of knowledge management, specifically that of knowledge creation and transformation as given by the Socialization, Externalization, Combination, Internalization (SECI) process (Nonaka & Takeuchi, 1995). However, the study has the following limitations: the differences between tacit and implicit knowledge have not been considered; the transition of knowledge between the four stages, namely Socialization, Externalization, Combination, and Internalization that occurs in form of a spiral has not been emphasized; the crucial role of '*Ba*', namely, the shared context for knowledge creation and transformation, used alongside the SECI process

Figure 1. An abstract model of the elements of pattern engineering that situates P3

is not discussed; even though the SECI process has garnered some acceptance in the knowledge management community (Bjørnson & Dingsøyr, 2008), it has its shortcomings due to its basis on empirical validation in a restricted environment (Gourlay, 2003) that are not pointed out; the human and social perspective of patterns in general and the role of stakeholders in particular are not taken into account; certain activities (such as planning and maintenance) are not considered; and the details of certain activities, such as description of patterns, especially the aspects of representation and presentation, are not given.

A pattern capture and reuse (PattCaR) method is proposed in (Seruca & Loucopoulos, 2003). PattCaR focuses on the elicitation of patterns for processes involved in the domain of small-and-medium sized clothing manufacturing enterprises in Portugal. These business processes include inventory management, order processing, customer relationship management, and so on. There is a strong emphasis on domain analysis in PattCaR. However, PattCaR has the following limitations: it is tied to a specific domain (and is therefore not general), it does not highlight the role of people involved in PattCaR, and it does not pay any attention to the need for evaluating patterns.

A list of activities for eliciting e-learning patterns and pattern languages has been given (Retalis, Georgiakakis, & Dimitriadis, 2006). However, the activities in it have not been described completely or rigorously.

An approach for specifying use case patterns that includes phases for maintenance and quality control has been given (Issa, Odeh, & Coward, 2006). However, this study has the following limitations: it focuses on the template for describing use case patterns in its first phase, it does not define the meaning of quality of a collection of patterns, it does not cover certain origins (such as discovery of new relationships among patterns, internal or external to the collection of use case patterns, or discovery of duplicate patterns upon comparison of multiple collections of patterns) for

the need of maintenance, and it does not take into consideration the people involved in the process.

A process for developing pattern languages by partitioning specific domains such as online auction has been proposed (Braga, Ré, & Masiero, 2007). The idea is to create an object-oriented model of a domain using the Unified Modeling Language (UML) and then develop a pattern for each problem in the domain (represented by a sub-graph of the domain model graph). However, this study does not consider certain crucial viewpoints of a pattern, address essential activities like planning or publishing patterns in the process, or identify all relevant stakeholders of a pattern or a pattern language.

A multidisciplinary, interdisciplinary, and participatory methodology called Identification-Development-Refinement (IDR) for interaction design patterns in the context of technology-enhanced learning has been proposed (Winters & Mor, 2008). IDR includes three stages, namely pattern identification, pattern development, and pattern refinement. There is a strong emphasis on incorporating the social aspects in the production of a pattern. However, IDR has the following limitations: it commits rather early to the structure of a pattern, classification of patterns, and relationships between patterns; it claims to be 'participatory' but does not precisely identify stakeholders or provide details of their involvement; and it uses a pattern template that does not have a solution element.

Finally, a "method for pattern development" for interactive television (iTV) applications has been proposed (Kunert, 2009). This 'method' goes through the identification of problems, the contexts of their occurrence, identification of corresponding solutions, and evaluation. There is a detailed treatment of user context and a strong emphasis on usability of the pattern solution. However, this 'method' has the following limitations. It assumes that the expertise derived from experience is (at best) a co-requisite rather than a prerequisite. Therefore, a pattern author does not have to be aware of the pattern solution a priori; rather this solution can be 'constructed' as a result of this 'method'. In other words, this 'method' makes it possible to develop patterns for new domains. The evaluation of iTV design patterns is based on the criteria of clarity, relevance, and completeness, none of which are defined. The evaluation is based on the opinions of those with expertise in iTV domain but not necessarily an expertise in patterns, a stark contrast to shepherding (Harrison, 2000). Furthermore, this 'method' advocates the use of Pattern Language Markup Language (PLML) for representing patterns. It is known (Kamthan, 2006) that PLML suffers from a number of technical issues.

TOWARDS ESTABLISHING A THEORETICAL BASIS FOR PATTERNS: USE OF VIEWPOINTS AND THEIR IMPLICATIONS

This section presents necessary viewpoints of a pattern followed by stakeholders of a pattern. These are subsequently used in describing a conceptual model for P3. The remainder of the article rests on the following interrelated hypothesis:

Hypothesis: An improvement in the process for development can bring about improvement in the quality of the product (Nelson & Monarchi, 2007).

Hypothesis: A preventative approach to addressing quality is at least as significant as a curative approach (Dromey, 2003).

A Model for Viewpoints of a Pattern

The purpose of a viewpoint model is to create an understanding of viewpoints of a thing (say, an object, property, or an event) and views that originate from it. The use of viewpoints and/ or views is known in requirements elicitation, software architecture, and software quality modeling; they can be applied to other areas as well, including patterns.

There are a number of possible views of a pattern emanating from different viewpoints. Let $\mathbf{P_V}$ be the set of all viewpoints of a pattern. The viewpoints of concern in this article are *epistemological*, *contactual*, *axiological*, and *semiotical*. These viewpoints are motivated by the basic or primitive questions of *what* (is it), *who* (comes in contact with it or for whom does it exist), *why* (does it exist), and *how* (does it exist), respectively. Figure 2 illustrates this subset of $\mathbf{P_V}$.

Figure 2. A collection of viewpoints of a pattern relevant to P3

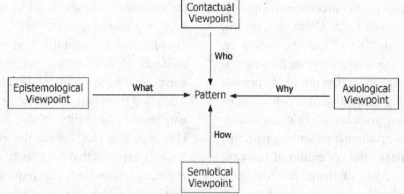

Epistemological Viewpoint

This viewpoint is crucial for understanding the inception of a pattern. A view emanating from the epistemological viewpoint is that a pattern is a kind of *knowledge asset* or *knowledge artifact*.

The pursuit of understanding patterns has led to studies of patterns from the perspective of the theories of knowledge. It has been posited (Devedžic, 2002; Garzás & Piattini, 2005) that object-oriented software design patterns (Gamma et al., 1995) are, from an ontological viewpoint, a kind of object-oriented software design knowledge. There are similar arguments about electronic learning (e-learning) patterns (Baggetun, Rusman, & Poggi, 2004), interaction design patterns (Van Welie & Van der Veer, 2003), and management patterns (Jessop, 2004). However, an in-depth analysis of these statements has not been carried out.

A pattern is a result of making the implicit knowledge derived from past experience explicit. This is explored further in a later section.

Contactual Viewpoint

This viewpoint is crucial for understanding those who are involved in the realization and subsequent use of a pattern. A view emanating from the contactual viewpoint is that a pattern is a kind of *social entity*. A pattern encounters other animate entities (such as humans) or inanimate entities (such as machines, specifically computers, or programs) in the world. This is explored further in a later section.

Axiological Viewpoint

This viewpoint is crucial for understanding the need for a pattern. There is a presumed valuative aspect to any human creation. A view emanating from the axiological viewpoint is that a pattern is useful to somebody for some purpose, that is, a pattern has *value*.

For example, a professor may question if applying a pattern leads to better teaching or learning, a project manager may question whether applying a pattern leads to cost savings, or a software engineer may question whether applying a pattern leads to 'improved' productivity (in the sense of higher process quality) or to a 'better' software system (in the sense of higher product quality).

Indeed, patterns have been found useful in various instances in both academia and industry (Appleton, 1997).

Semiotical Viewpoint

This viewpoint is crucial for understanding a description of a pattern. A view emanating from the semiotical viewpoint is that a pattern is a kind of *sign*. A denotation of a sign is that it has a *signifier* and a *signified*. In case of a pattern, for example, the pattern's name is the linguistic signifier and the description of the pattern is the signified (Noble & Biddle, 2002). A pattern language is then a *semiotic system*.

This view can help address a variety of issues in PBOK such as the need for multiple different elements of a pattern; for understanding the existence of two patterns with the same name; for understanding misinterpretations of the notion of a pattern such as equating a pattern to its name, or equating a pattern to its solution; for understanding the need for the different levels of a representation of a pattern description; and so on.

Organization of Viewpoints

It is possible to have a hierarchy of viewpoints. A viewpoint can have a sub-viewpoint that again is-a-kind-of a viewpoint. For example, *applicational* viewpoint, *commercial* viewpoint, and *pedagogical* viewpoint are three possible sub-viewpoints of the axiological viewpoint. They are motivated by the prospects of use of a pattern for some purpose (including development), positive return on investment (ROI) (or making a profit), and teaching/

Figure 3. A taxonomy of viewpoints of a pattern relevant to P3

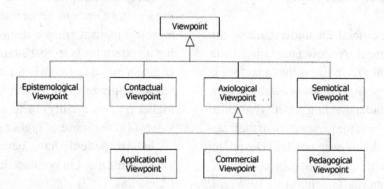

learning, respectively. Figure 3 illustrates a subset of P_v by means of a UML Class Diagram.

Potential Uses of the Pattern Viewpoint Model

There are a number of potential uses of the pattern viewpoint model. A pattern viewpoint model can help explain the reason for the existence of some of the multiple different definitions as well as misconceptions of the notion of a pattern. It can also help clarify and understand certain properties of a pattern stated in the current literature.

For example, identifying a (design) pattern as a 'predefined (design) decision' (Kruchten, 2004) is related to a developmental viewpoint; equating a pattern to a 'format' (Granlund, Lafrenière, & Carr, 2001) is related to a semiotical viewpoint; suggesting that a pattern is a 'learning aid,' an 'encyclopedia' (Gamma et al., 1995), or a 'problem solving approach' is related to a pedagogical viewpoint; and labeling a pattern as 'organizational memory' for developing mobile applications (Ahlgren, & Markkula, 2005) is related to an intersection of epistemological and applicational viewpoints.

Characteristics of the Pattern Viewpoint Model

There are certain unique characteristics of the pattern viewpoint model that can be highlighted.

Relationships between Pattern Viewpoints. The viewpoints in P_v are not necessarily mutually exclusive in the sense that it is not possible to completely describe some viewpoints without referring to other viewpoints.

For example, the epistemological and axiological viewpoints are related since the value of a pattern (Derntl & Botturi, 2006) is determined by the usefulness of the knowledge it encapsulates; the axiological and contactual viewpoints are related since a value judgment of a pattern can not be made in absence of the (human) recipient of the value; the contactual and semiotical viewpoints are related since (1) the *signification* (namely, the relationship between a signifier and a signified) depends on a pattern stakeholder (such as a pattern reader) and (2) the author element in the description of a pattern needs the knowledge of the pattern author(s), conversely, a classification of stakeholders can depend on the nature of contact of a stakeholder with a pattern that, in turn, requires some knowledge of the description of that pattern; the axiological and semiotical viewpoints are related since for a reader to determine the value of a pattern, the pattern needs to be first described in some manner that is perceivable by that reader and, conversely, the value of a pattern (a sign) depends on its relationship to other patterns (other signs) in a pattern language (a semiotic system).

Need for Multiple Pattern Viewpoints. The four primitive viewpoints are minimal in the sense that a proper subset of these is not sufficient for establishing a theoretical basis for patterns. In some practical cases, a single viewpoint of a pattern may not be sufficient, and it may be necessary to consider multiple viewpoints. For example, in the actual development of a software system both the applicational and pedagogical viewpoints of a pattern need to be considered. In the description of a pattern, all relevant viewpoints must be considered.

A Model for Stakeholders of a Pattern

The contactual viewpoint of a pattern suggests focusing on humans that come in contact with a pattern. The purpose of a stakeholder model is to create an understanding of stakeholders and, in doing so, that of the pattern community at-large.

The *pattern community* is the group of people in society that are interested in patterns or pattern-related activities for some reason. A *pattern person* is a member of the pattern community. A *pattern stakeholder* is a person who has interest in a specific pattern for some purpose.

The stakeholders of patterns can be classified using different perspectives. For example, the possible stakeholders of patterns can be identified and classified into *pattern producers* and *pattern consumers* based upon their roles with respect to a pattern. The union of the set of pattern producers and pattern consumers is equal to the set of pattern stakeholders.

- *Pattern Producers:* There are four essential pattern producers that can be identified. A *pattern author* is a person responsible for authoring a pattern. It is expected that a pattern author typically owns the intellectual property rights (IPR) to the pattern. A *pattern evaluator* is a person responsible for evaluation and feedback on a pattern. A *pattern engineer* is a person responsible for providing means for describing a pat-

tern. A *pattern administrator* is a person responsible for maintenance and management of patterns.

- *Pattern Consumers:* There are four essential pattern consumers that can be identified. A *pattern perceiver* is a person targeted for perceiving a pattern. A *pattern browser* is a person targeted for browsing a pattern. A *pattern reader* is a person targeted for reading a pattern. A *pattern user* is a person targeted for using a pattern.

The same person can take upon different roles, and the same role can be taken upon by different persons. For example, a person reading a pattern plays the role of a pattern reader but, given the write permission, can (at least in part) play the role of a pattern administrator.

Let P_C be the set of members of the pattern community and let P_{SI} be the set of all stakeholders of a pattern. Then, P_{SI} is a proper subset of P_C. For example, a pattern person may belong to P_C but, for any given pattern, may neither be a pattern producer, nor a pattern consumer.

Let P_{SC} be the set of all stakeholder classes of a pattern. Figure 4 illustrates a subset of P_{SC} by means of a UML Class Diagram.

Characteristics of the Pattern Stakeholder Model

There are certain unique characteristics of the pattern stakeholder model that can be highlighted.

Relationships between Pattern Stakeholders. The pattern stakeholders are not necessarily mutually exclusive. For the sake of this article, browsing is a form of casual scanning (of the description of a pattern) that may not have a predetermined, specific goal. Thus, browsing is a weaker form of reading. Furthermore, for information to be browsed or read, it is necessary that it be first perceived in some modality. Therefore, a pattern browser or a pattern reader is always a pattern perceiver; the converse is not necessarily true.

Figure 4. A taxonomy of stakeholders of a pattern

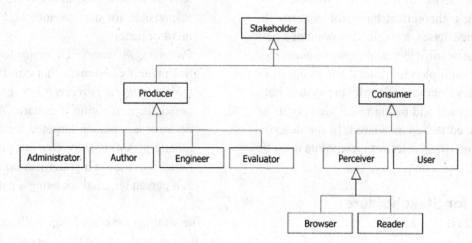

In addition, a pattern evaluator or a pattern user is always a pattern reader; the converse is not necessarily true.

Extensions of the Pattern Stakeholder Model. Figure 4 is based on an Open World Assumption. The taxonomy of stakeholders in Figure 4 is intentionally limited and could be extended in both 'horizontal' and 'vertical' directions. For example, a person sponsoring, financing, or supervising a pattern engineering project could be considered as a producer (specifically, say, a *pattern manager*) but has not been included as one of the sub-classes of pattern stakeholders. Indeed, if there is a need to manage a large number of pattern stakeholders (say, multiple collaborating pattern authors) and there is a need to manage a large number of patterns (say, using a *pattern management system* (PMS)), a separate role of a pattern manager may be required. In such a case, some of the responsibilities of a pattern administrator would also be delegated to the pattern manager.

The granularity of the pattern evaluator class could be increased. The pattern evaluator class could be sub-classed, say, based on the avenue of evaluation of a pattern, into pattern shepherd and pattern Writers' Workshop participant. *A pattern shepherd* is responsible for mentoring a pattern author, and evaluating and providing feedback on a pattern. A *pattern Writers' Workshop participant*

is responsible for evaluating and providing feedback on a pattern.

The granularity of the pattern user class could also be increased, say, by sub-classing it based on their level of knowledge and skill of usage of the pattern into *beginner pattern user* and *advanced pattern user*, or based on their context of usage of the pattern into *work-related pattern user* and *non-work-related pattern user*. For example, a person using a pattern for developing software as an academic exercise at an educational institution or developing open source software (OSS) as a hobby is a non-work-related pattern user.

Concretization of Pattern Stakeholders. The pattern stakeholder model is abstract: it only constitutes a starting point for a pattern stakeholder model in general and a pattern user model in particular. A systematic construction of such models requires taking other factors including individual human characteristics, (computational) environmental characteristics, and personal preferences into consideration. For example, in a real-world setting, it can not in general be assumed that certain pattern stakeholder classes are homogeneous. Indeed, pattern consumers vary in many ways including in their demographical and geographical distribution and (client-side) computing environment. In such a case, for a pattern (or a pattern language), a concrete user model, say, a persona or a user profile, could be constructed to create a more in-depth understanding of members of that stakeholder class. Further discussion of this aspect is beyond the scope of this article.

Actors of a Pattern. The definition of a stakeholder presented here is intentionally limited. A stakeholder is, by definition, human. An organization (say, supporting a pattern engineering project) is not considered a stakeholder. The notion of an *actor* (in the sense of use cases, for example) includes humans and non-humans and is thereby an extension of the notion of a stakeholder as given above. For example, a computer program used for authoring a pattern is an actor but not a stakeholder. Further discussion of this aspect is beyond the scope of this article.

A Model for a Process for the Production of a Pattern

This section presents a process, the resulting product of which is a pattern. Even though patterns have conventionally been produced informally, based on Hypothesis 1, it is evident that some

degree of predictability and control is necessary for the result to exhibit 'high-quality.' In doing so, striking a balance between agility and discipline in the process is critical, and in turn forms the motivation for P3.

A *workflow* of P3 is a high-level organization unit that consists of one or more activities. There are a number of workflows in P3, including [P3-W1] *Planning*, [P3-W2] *Developing*, [P3-W3] *Describing*, [P3-W4] *Evaluating and Revising*, [P3-W5] *Publishing and Outreaching*, and [P3-W6] *Maintaining*. These are prefixed by [P3-W0] *Acquiring Sapience and Assessing Viability*, which is a prerequisite to the workflows that follow. It is evident that P3, and by reference its workflows therein, should be feasible in order to be practical. In the following, unless otherwise stated, the associated identifier is used to indicate the corresponding workflow.

Let P3(W) be the set of all workflows of P3. Figure 5 illustrates the order of execution of the workflows in P3 by means of a UML Activity Diagram.

Figure 5. The collection of workflows in P3 and their interrelationships

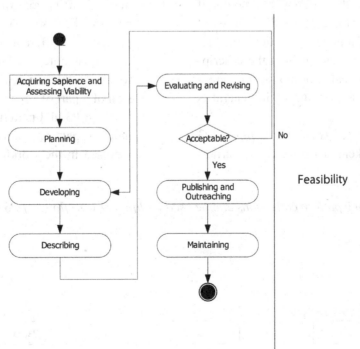

Characteristics of Workflows of P3

The workflows of P3 have a number of characteristics. A workflow can be either mandatory or optional. The workflows [P3-W0], [P3-W2], the presentational aspect of [P3-W3], [P3-W4], and [P3-W5] are mandatory; the workflows [P3-W1], the representational aspect of [P3-W3], and [P3-W6] are highly recommended but optional. The decision to include any optional workflows must be made at the initiation of [P3-W1].

The transition from [P3-W4] to [P3-W5] is conditional. This is because it is not automatic that a pattern may pass the evaluation.

The workflows [P3-W0] and [P3-W2] are the least mechanical and cognitively most demanding among the workflows, and thus require more attention compared to other workflows of P3.

Nature of P3

The nature of P3 is reflected in the following observations, each of which is elaborated further in the sections that follow:

- *Observation 1 [P3 is Viewpoint-Based]:* P3 is based on the different viewpoints of a pattern as it progresses, and the different viewpoints of a pattern are 'tied' together by P3. Then, as evident from the description of individual workflows, the mapping between P3(W) and P_V in general is many-to-many.
- *Observation 2 [P3 is Human-Centric]:* P3 aims to be stakeholder-centric. The partici-

pation by stakeholders of a pattern in P3 varies across its workflows. The mapping between P3(W) and P_{SI} in general is many-to-many. The human-centeredness of P3 is motivated by a number of reasons.

- *Observation 3 [P3 is Socially-Conscious]:* There are a number of social relationships that are fostered in a successful execution of P3. The relationship between a pattern author and a pattern consumer is built on the value that a pattern provides. The needs of pattern consumers (including human factors) are a 'first-class' consideration for a pattern author during P3. A pattern is a shared resource or 'commons' (Hess & Ostrom, 2007) during and after P3. The relationship between a pattern author and a pattern evaluator (particularly, a pattern shepherd) is built on mutual trust. For P3 and, by reference, the pattern itself, to be successful, enabling an environment for communication among stakeholders is critical.
- *Observation 4 [P3 is Pattern-Oriented]:* An execution of P3 can benefit from past experiences. There are patterns that can help P3 in its goal of producing ('new') patterns. For example, Figure 6 illustrates patterns for different purposes. These patterns constitute a subset of the resources for P3. In this sense, Figure 6 is an extension of a part of Figure 1. The relationship between P3 and patterns is therefore *symbiotic*. If patterns from existing collections are used in the workflows of P3 then, by

Figure 6. The existing pattern collections can be used in different workflows of P3

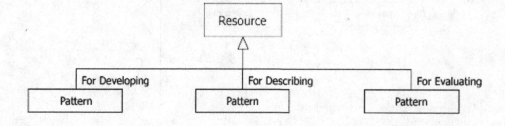

virtue of commitment, the orientation of P3 is determined by the selection of those patterns.

- *Observation 5 [P3 is Evolutionary]:* The experiences in authoring patterns have shown that, in general, a pattern is not produced linearly in a single pass. This could be seen as a consequence of the *review/extend principle* of problem solving (Pólya, 1945). Indeed, P3 needs to support the development of a pattern in a manner that is both *iterative* (to revisit the past) and *incremental* (to make progress-by-addition in the future).

The following sections provide descriptions of the workflows of P3. The descriptions of the workflows that occur in later stages of P3 are intentionally brief and, if necessary, could be elaborated further.

[P3-W0] Acquiring Sapience and Assessing Viability

Goal: The purpose of this 'pseudo-workflow' is for a person to reflect on personal experience, to assess personal capabilities and interest to become a pattern author, and to be able to justify the production of a pattern.

There are different ways of classifying knowledge (Gašević, Djuric, & Devedžic, 2006; Nickols, 2000). Table 1 presents a classification of knowledge used in subsequent discussion.

The two potential approaches for acquiring internal knowledge are *individual* and *sociological*.

1. *Individual Approach:* In the individual approach, there is a single person who relies on *retrospection* arising from personal experiences. For example, the person may reflect upon successes and failures of developing computer programs individually or may reflect upon successes and failures of developing software systems collectively, as part of a team.

2. *Sociological Approach:* In the sociological approach, there are multiple persons relying on personal experiences and *extrospection* based on each other's experiences. For example, these persons may discuss the positive and negative experiences of solving the same problem.

For the sake of discussion, consider the individual approach. It is assumed in this article that practice involves action (doing). It is also assumed that there is a person who is aware of the existence of the pattern domain and is interested in it. In other words, the person belongs to the pattern community in the role of a pattern person. The practice over a period of time by a person of repeatedly solving a problem in some domain D leads to experiences. (It can be noted that a pattern is always specific to some domain. For example, D could be mobile interaction design, object-oriented software design, use case

Table 1. A multifaceted classification of knowledge

	Dimension I	Dimension II		Dimension III
Knowledge	Internal Knowledge	Tacit Knowledge	Cognitive Tacit Knowledge	Experiential Knowledge
			Technical Tacit Knowledge	
		Implicit Knowledge		
	External Knowledge	Explicit Knowledge		Conceptual Knowledge
				Systemic Knowledge

modeling, and so on.) These experiences in turn, contribute towards acquisition of knowledge that, in turn, is necessary for understanding that again, in turn, is necessary for learning.

There are different cognitive and logistical challenges pertaining to each approach. For example, the sociological approach requires convergence of the mental models (Van Welie & Van der Veer, 2003) of the authors with respect to a given pattern. This, in turn, necessitates collaboration among the authors involved (for collective decision making, and so on). This again, in turn, necessitates communication, cooperation, negotiation, and consensus among the authors involved. For example, deciding upon the name of a pattern in the sociological approach requires consensus.

Experiential Learning

It is known that different people, including potential pattern authors, learn differently. There are a number of learning theories (Jordan, Carlile, & Stack, 2008) based on different approaches to educational psychology as well as epistemological and philosophical beliefs.

For example, the learning theories related to direct experience in general and relevant to [P3-W0] in particular are: action learning, active learning, problem-based learning, learning-by-doing, individual constructivism, problem solving, social constructivism, and social constructionism. These learning theories are different but not necessarily competing at the exclusion of the others. The possibility that multiple learning theories are applicable to experiential learning can not be excluded. Therefore, this article does not advocate a single, specific learning theory.

However, learning alone is not sufficient for expertise. In other words, there is more than learning from experience to be expected of a potential pattern author.

From Experience to Sapience

An insight can be considered as a cognitively high-level of understanding and, according to Gestalt psychology, is a result of productive thinking. The knowledge acquired from ensemble of the experiences themselves, and of the retrospective after each experience along with other factors (such as motivation), lead to *insight*. The insight of the pattern person can consist of one or more of the following: knowing how to solve the problem more effectively than done so previously, knowing which solution is better than others and why, being able to identify frequent recurrences of certain problem-solution pairs in similar situations, and so on.

The experiences may also lead to acquisition of a *skill* such as abstracting, diagramming, typing, and so on. This is important for any practical development.

The experiences may also lead to the appreciation of relativism, for example, exercising *discretion* in problem solving. This is important for an understanding of the context of a problem and the constraints of its solution.

It is then experiential knowledge, insight, and skills, along with sound judgment of using them that leads to *sapience*. (For the sake of this article, sapience is a kind of expertise.)

From Internal to External Knowledge

The experiential knowledge (specifically, a posteriori and situated knowledge) internalized by the pattern person is either *implicit* or *tacit*. At this stage, the internal knowledge resides only in the mind of the pattern person. For example, from an individual constructivist viewpoint (Kohls & Scheiter, 2008; Piaget, 1952), the knowledge is organized and structured in the mind of a pattern person in form of a *mental model* or a *mental schema*.

The pattern person realizes that the internal knowledge can have value for others, and thereafter may voluntarily decide to share the implicit knowledge in the schemata with others. For that, the implicit knowledge needs to be communicated, and to do that, it needs to be externalized (articulated) in form of explicit knowledge (Nickols, 2000). (It is not possible to articulate tacit knowledge (Polanyi, 1983). It is possible to communicate tacit knowledge, for example, by demonstration.)

Figures 7 and 8 illustrate certain elements of knowledge creation and transformation.

The pattern person determines the viability of proposing a 'new' pattern (or *proto-pattern*) to

the pattern community at-large, including potential pattern readers and potential pattern users that are being targeted. This is done based on (1) the sapience gained from personal experiences and extrospections based on others' experiences and (2) research on existing patterns.

The appropriateness of the size of the problem-solution pair is a concern: if the problem-solution is rather large to describe in a single setting, then the original problem needs to be split into parts and each smaller sub-problem is to be dealt separately. For example, 'a customer should be able to find a product in a shopping system' may be

Figure 7. The experience of a person in solving problem in some domain contributes to the acquisition of experiential knowledge

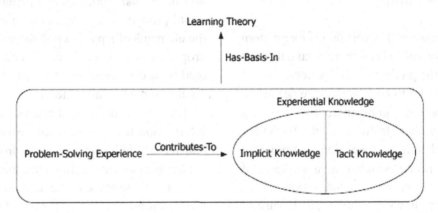

Figure 8. The implicit experiential knowledge of a person can be shared with others by making it explicit in some form

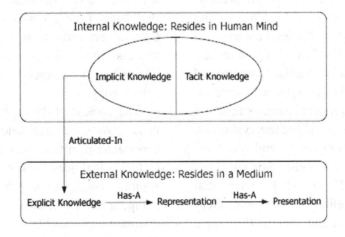

too large a problem to tackle in a single pattern. These sub-problems are interrelated, and eliciting relationships between sub-problems is the inception of a pattern language.

The pattern person also checks for the existence of *pattern complements*, that is, patterns that may be similar or variants, of the one being proposed. The pattern person may also look for reports on the 'discoveries' of patterns during pattern 'mining'.

This workflow concludes with a favorable decision to proceed with a definition of the proto-pattern. It is at this point that the pattern person takes upon the role of a (potential) pattern author. It is expected prerequisite that an aspiring pattern author must be an expert in the domain D.

[P3-W1] Planning

Goal: The purpose of this workflow is for a pattern author to get organized and thereby take the first step towards the production of a pattern.

In order for P3 to be effective, the definition of the proto-pattern requires appropriate planning by the pattern author. (In this sense, this workflow is similar to planning any development project.) The planning needs to include an assessment of the availability of resources including time, effort, expert body of knowledge, and tools. In case of multiple pattern authors, schedules for meetings also need to be decided upon.

There is a cost factor associated with P3. In particular, if the author seeks a 'formal' analysis of the pattern, there is cost involved in attending one of the members of the Pattern Languages of Programming (or *PLoP) 'family' of conferences. There can perhaps also be ancillary costs related to publishing and administering the proto-pattern. The exceptions to this are the voluntary time and effort of the pattern authors and pattern evaluators.

There are a few commercial and non-commercial resources at the pattern author's disposal to assist during P3. These include experiential knowledge like guidelines (Buschmann, Henney, & Schmidt, 2007) and patterns (Meszaros

& Doble, 1998; Harrison, 2003) for describing patterns. There are patterns for shepherding (Harrison, 2000), and patterns for Writers' Workshops (Coplien, 2000). There are tools available for representing and presenting patterns; however, aside from the coverage in [P3-W3] and [P3-W5], a detailed discussion of these is beyond the scope of this article.

[P3-W2] Developing

Goal: The purpose of this workflow is for a pattern author to be able to take the first step (of the three steps) in conveying past experience semiotically.

In pursuit of the goal of this workflow, a pattern author needs to address both functional and non-functional properties of a pattern. The functional properties are especially concerned with the elements of a pattern and the non-functional properties are especially concerned with (1) the quality of each element of a pattern and (2) the quality of the overall pattern.

From a morphological analysis of the given information, the pattern author abstracts the problem and, guided by retrospection from [P3-W0], explicitly places the problem in a specific context that reflects the scope of the problem. The author tries to ensure that the statement of the problem is, as far as possible, context-free.

Next, a general and (conceptually) reusable solution for the problem needs to be devised. This is achieved via abstraction of instances of the solution from [P3-W0]. The solution describes both the process *and* the thing (created by the process) (Buschmann, Henney, & Schmidt, 2007). The purpose of the process aspect of the solution is pedagogy.

The context of the problem imposes certain constraints on the formulation of a solution. These constraints manifest themselves as a collection of forces that need to be resolved to arrive at a solution. The forces may or may not be mutually compatible. The nature of these forces may be qualitative or quantitative. These forces can be seen as statements of desirable quality attributes of a solution (Lea, 1994; Taibi & Ngo, 2002).

If the forces are mutually compatible, then, in theory, it is possible that a given solution completely resolves all forces and there is a unique solution to the problem. However, in practice, this is unlikely since the forces usually are not mutually compatible. The result is that the problem has more than one solution such that each solution takes a proper subset of the forces into consideration and resolves them at the expense of other forces. In other words, each solution has its own advantages and disadvantages.

The 'best' solution is chosen based on an optimal balance (or equilibrium) of forces. The pattern author outlines the thought process, including the rationale, for arriving at the selected solution.

It follows from the above discussion that even the seemingly 'best' solution is not absolute. Therefore, the pattern author examines the consequences (or implications, including negative side-effects) of applying the solution. These consequences could include forces that are ignored, not entirely resolved, as well as, new forces that may arise. Indeed, this can result in a new context and new problems, attempts to solve which may lead to the need for other pattern(s). This is the inception of a pattern language.

The solution proposed by the pattern must be generative (Lea, 1994), that is, it must be demonstrably proven to work. Therefore, based on the 'Rule of Three' (Meszaros & Doble, 1998), the pattern author elicits three examples (or instances of the solution) that best demonstrate the feasibility of the proposed solution. The examples could possibly be from earlier personal experiences and extrospections based on others' experiences from [P3-W0]. However, since the proto-pattern is based on empirical knowledge (by virtue of the fact that the knowledge is experiential), it is prone to subjectivity. Therefore, to lend some degree of objectivity, these examples should not exclusively be internal, that is, they should not be all from pattern author's personal experiences. In other words, there must be at least one external example.

Finally, the proto-pattern is placed in its social context. To do that, related patterns (if any) along with the nature of their relationships to the proto-pattern are listed.

For the purpose of communication (including, but not limited to, identification, signification, and citation), the pattern author assigns a unique, evocative, and pronounceable name to the proto-pattern. The name of a pattern often mimics the nature of the solution of that pattern.

This marks the end of the 'zeroth' iteration of the proto-pattern. However, following Observation 5, further iterations are likely and increments are possible.

[P3-W3] Describing

Goal: The purpose of this workflow is for a pattern author to be able to take the second step (of the three steps) in conveying past experience semiotically.

In order for the information in form of a proto-pattern as in [P3-W2] to become explicit, there is a need for a suitable means of description. It is preferable, although not necessary, that the proto-pattern description have an expressive pattern form.

The *representation* and *presentation* are two distinct aspects of a pattern description, and need to be considered separately. From a semiotic viewpoint, a pattern is a kind of sign, and a sign can have one or more representations. Then, for example, a representation can be presented in one or more ways to a pattern stakeholder.

In this workflow, the pattern author selects one of the available means for describing (representing and presenting) the proto-pattern. The means for pattern description is usually a natural language or an artificial language (or more generally an information technology (IT)) that is either already available or is made possible by a pattern engineer. Figure 9 illustrates the relationship between explicit knowledge, its representation, and the language of representation.

Figure 9. The basis for selecting a language for representation is rationalized by the semiotic properties of the language

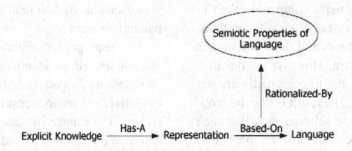

The rationale for selecting an IT for describing a proto-pattern needs to be based on some criteria. The criteria can be derived from the concerns at different semiotic levels (Shanks, 1999), namely physical, empirical, syntactical, semantical, pragmatical, and social.

For example, the input to the criteria can be one or more of the following semiotic properties of an IT: the amenability of the representation based on the IT to both humans as well as machines; the affordances of the IT that enable desired use cases (activities) related to patterns; formality of the IT (such as the spectrum of informal, semi-formal, and formal); expressiveness of the IT; decidability of the IT; sensory modality of the IT (such as visual, aural, and so on), including the possibility of multimodality; sign type (such as linguistic, symbolic, graphic, and so on); degree of access of the IT to public in the sense of rights (such as the language specification being open or closed), in the sense of finance (such as the IT being commercial or free), and in the sense of agreement (such as the IT being proprietary or an international standard); and so on.

Use of Natural Language

The use of a natural language (usually, English) remains the most broadly used means to articulate the implicit knowledge in a proto-pattern. There a number of advantages of the use of a natural language in situations that involves humans. For example, it has been suggested (Coplien, 1996)

that a pattern is work of literature, and the use of a natural language remains the most effective means to preserve and communicate the literary nature of a pattern to its stakeholders.

However, there are also a number of limitations of the use of a natural language in situations that involve machines. For example, an unstructured natural language text fragment lends itself only to limited possibilities of (automatic) machine processing (Kamthan & Pai, 2006a) including effective reuse during authoring, ease of transformation, and ease of manipulation (such as extraction and/or reorganization of text). These, in turn, can adversely affect a number of use cases such as navigating, querying (for the purpose of searching), and sorting (such as indexing) that are relevant for effective communication and dissemination of a pattern to its consumers.

From Representation to Presentation

There are a number of IT currently available for representations that can reside in the electronic medium. For example, a proto-pattern (and even an entire proto-pattern language) may be represented (Kamthan & Pai, 2006a; Kamthan & Pai, 2006b) in the Extensible Markup Language (XML), the Resource Description Framework (RDF), Topic Maps, or the Web Ontology Language (OWL), each intended for a different purpose. The representations themselves may be archived in a PMS.

Then, depending on the nature of the client request, including the type of computing device and

Figure 10. The normative source of the representation of a (proto-)pattern is transformed for the purpose of presentation onto one or more abstract targets

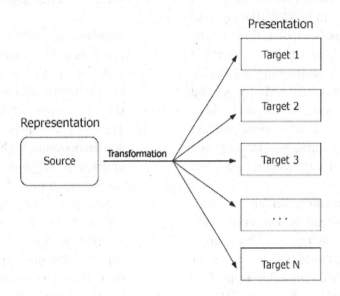

preferences of the pattern consumer, a representation can be (down-)transformed and presented appropriately. In doing so, the needs of the pattern consumers (Meszaros & Doble, 1998; Harrison, 2003) should to be kept into consideration. The result of the transformation can be either temporary or permanent. Figure 10 illustrates the relationship between a representation and an abstract presentation of a (proto-)pattern.

Figure 11 illustrates some concrete presentation possibilities. For the sake of this article, a notebook computer is synonymous with a laptop computer, and a personal digital assistant (PDA) or a smartphone is a kind of information appliance.

Figure 11. The representation of a (proto-)pattern is transformed for the purpose of presentation onto one or more concrete targets

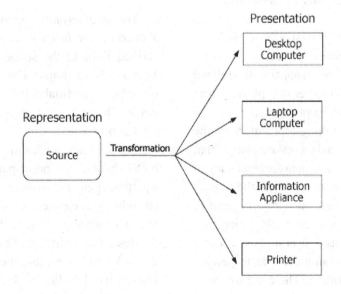

There are a number of IT currently available for carrying out the intended transformation of a representation of a pattern in XML (the input) to a presentation (the output) including, for example, the Cascading Style Sheets (CSS), Extensible Stylesheet Language Transformations (XSLT), Streaming Transformations for XML (STX), and XQuery. If the output is such that none of these special-purpose options are viable, then a program in some general-purpose programming language for carrying out the intended transformation needs to be written.

To be able to successfully perceive a proto-pattern, its appropriate presentation is necessary. There are a number of alternatives for presentation, depending on the target. These include, for example, a profile of the Extensible HyperText Markup Language (XHTML) such as XHTML 1.1 and XHTML Basic 1.1, which are targeted for the Web and the Mobile Web, respectively; the (Wiki) Creole 1.0, which is targeted for the Social Web (Kamthan, 2009a); an electronic book reader format or the Windows Help File format, which are targeted for a desktop computer; and the Portable Document Format (PDF), which is targeted for a printer. This 'one-representation-to-many-presentations' is a typical manifestation of the single source approach.

[P3-W4] Evaluating and Revising

Goal: The purpose of this workflow is for a pattern author to be able to reflect on previous workflows and to share the responsibilities related to the proto-pattern with other role players so as to ensure the quality of the proto-pattern.

The acceptance of a thing as a pattern by the pattern community depends on establishing if that thing is in fact a pattern. To reach the candidacy of a pattern, a proto-pattern must satisfy the properties of a pattern. There are currently no general, automatic, or mathematical means for doing that.

Based on Hypothesis 2, it is suggested that a proto-pattern go through an audit for an inspection of its properties as a pattern. There are currently two common and related approaches for such an audit, namely shepherding and Writers' Workshop:

1. *Shepherding (Individual Evaluation):* The prime example of audit is submission of a proto-pattern to one of the members of the *PLoP 'family' of conferences. If a submission is accepted, it leads to shepherding. The process of shepherding is an informal, non-anonymous, highly recommended but optional, review process. It includes a one-on-one mentoring of the pattern author by another person, namely the pattern shepherd. Based on the DOMAIN EXPERTISE IN SHEPHERDS pattern (Harrison, 2000), it is expected that the shepherd is familiar with the underlying domain to which the pattern belongs to and is experienced in PBOK. The role of the pattern author during shepherding is that of an apprentice (or sheep).

2. *Writers' Workshop (Group Evaluation):* The shepherding is usually followed by participation in a Writers' Workshop that is an informal, face-to-face, and structured peer review process. A Writers' Workshop typically requires the pattern author to present the proto-pattern in front of a group of individuals that are experts in the underlying domain D and in PBOK.

The shepherding together with the Writers' Workshop can last a few days. There is no prescribed limit to the scope of shepherding and Writers' Workshops. The non-anonymity and personal contact makes them more human, though not any less rigorous compared to conventional review processes.

The evaluation may involve directly or indirectly checking the proto-pattern for properties of a pattern against an instrument such as guidelines (Buschmann, Henney, & Schmidt, 2007) or patterns (Meszaros & Doble, 1998; Harrison, 2003) for describing patterns. This may lead to a few iterations of the proto-pattern and thereby a revisitation of [P3-W2] and [P3-W3]. The THREE

ITERATIONS pattern (Harrison, 2003) suggests that it takes three iterations during shepherding. At the end of the evaluation, the proto-pattern may reach the candidacy of a pattern.

The experience of shepherding and Writers' Workshops may lead to a change in the pattern author's understanding of the pattern since the occurrence of [P3-W0]. If that is indeed the case, then according to social constructivism (Vygotsky, 1978), there is a shift in the Zone of Proximal Development (ZPD) of the pattern author.

The pattern author, individually or otherwise as a result of the evaluation, may associate a rating reflecting the confidence or maturity level of the pattern. The pattern author may also optionally associate metadata information such as that related to configuration management, copyright/licensing, keywords, and so on, with the description of the pattern to enable better opportunities for processing.

There have been reports of other avenues for submitting, evaluating, and subsequently revising a proto-pattern (Leacock, Malone, & Wheeler, 2005; Winters & Mor, 2008), a discussion of which is beyond the scope of this article.

[P3-W5] Publishing and Outreaching

Goal: The purpose of this workflow is for a pattern author to be able to take the third step (of the three steps) in conveying past experience semiotically.

Publishing

The pattern up until now is limited to internal consumption. In order for the pattern to reach a broader community, that is, beyond the pattern author and pattern evaluator(s), it needs to be published in a public environment.

The pattern can be published in some physical (usually print) and/or virtual (usually electronic) medium that is deemed reachable to the pattern community. In the current electronic environment, the Web is one candidate medium for the publication of patterns (Kamthan, 2008).

Outreaching

The pattern author may feel the need for outreach once the pattern is published. For example, the pattern community at-large may need to be informed of the existence of the pattern. The need for awareness of the pattern on the Web can be satisfied in one of the two ways: *client-pull* or *server-push*.

In case of client-pull, the news of the publication of the pattern could be announced to the pattern consumers by some means, for example, using one of the current syndication technologies like Atom or Really Simple Syndication (RSS). In case of server-push, the news could be announced by some means, for example, posting on a blog, a mailing list, or a newsgroup.

[P3-W6] Maintaining

Goal: The purpose of this workflow is for a pattern author to delegate the responsibilities related to the pattern to other role players so as to ensure sustenance of the pattern.

In theory, a pattern aspires to be immune to any future changes. It is expected that a pattern is described at the level of abstraction that makes is 'timeless' (Alexander, 1979). However, timelessness of a pattern is a global, not local, property. Therefore, to stay current and relevant, and to avoid obsolescence, a pattern may need to evolve.

In practice, there a number of sources of potential change to a pattern.

Origins of Change

The need for maintaining a pattern arises from a number of sources that can necessitate change:

- *To Err is Human:* In spite of the due care during evaluation, followed by revision, certain errors may have crept into the description of a pattern. These must be rectified.

- *Technological Indirection:* The solution of a pattern, and the examples used to illustrate the solution, may depend on certain technology or technologies that need not be, temporally or otherwise, invariant. This is particularly the case for patterns in technically-inclined domains such as software engineering and human-computer interaction. For example, the notations used in a number of examples used to illustrate the solutions of object-oriented software design patterns (Gamma et al., 1995) have become obsolete.
- *Re-Organization:* It is possible that after publication of a given pattern P, 'new' patterns related to P are 'discovered', new types of relationships between P and other patterns are 'discovered' or, based on a new classification scheme, P needs to be reclassified. For example, these circumstances led to a revision of patterns in an existing pattern language for the user interface design of safety-critical systems and their inclusion in a new classification scheme (Connelly et al., 2001).
- *Re-Presentation:* The single source approach ensures that the representation model of a pattern is not modified in a fundamental manner. The presentation model of a pattern may need to be modified due to previously unforeseen presentation prospects. For example, this is the case for presentation of a pattern on new devices.

Therefore, if needed, a pattern administrator carries out corrective, adaptive, and/or perfective maintenance of pattern(s) on a timely basis. Furthermore, these pattern(s) may also be integrated (into a larger collection) and organized (say, classified and indexed) in some way. This concludes the conventional P3 from the viewpoint of the pattern producers.

Remarks on P3

In the following, certain unique characteristics of P3 are highlighted.

Remark 1: The workflows of P3 can be seen as a refinement of the four principles of problem solving (Pólya, 1945): understand the problem, devise a plan, carry out the plan, and review/extend.

Remark 2: The description of P3 shows that it is nonlinear. The temporal order on P3(W) is partial. The workflows of P3 are not necessarily mutually exclusive in the sense that some of them can (at least in part) overlap temporally. For example, [P3-W3] can commence in parallel to (but not necessarily concurrently with) [P3-W2]. For example, in case of multiple authors, some authors may devote more time to developing, while other may commit more time to describing (representing and presenting) what has already been developed.

Remark 3: The quality of execution of the workflows of P3 can have a direct impact on subsequent executions of P3. In particular, the success of seeking pattern complements in [P3-W0], seeking related patterns in [P3-W2], seeking desirable patterns for representing and presenting in [P3-W3], and seeking relevant patterns for shepherding and Writers' Workshop in [P3-W4], depends intimately on how well existing collection of patterns have been described and published. Therefore, [P3-W3] and [P3-W5] are not only relevant to the pattern consumers but also to (other, future) pattern authors: if a pattern is described and published appropriately, then a pattern author's task of finding any relevant patterns becomes easier. This aids repeatability of P3.

P3 in Perspective

In this section, known limitations of P3 are highlighted. P3 does not address the following cases: patterns that are produced by revising existing patterns for some domain to suit a different domain or patterns that are produced by combining existing patterns.

It is evident that some of the workflows of P3 (such as [P3-W1] and [P3-W3]) could be strengthened further by making them more 'formal'. For example, P3 could benefit from process workflow patterns (Dumas, Van der Aalst, & Ter Hofstede, 2006). However, there are side-effects of formality.

P3 relies on human creativity (Gabriel, 1996; Iba, 2007) and can not be completely automated. In particular, even though the transition from representation to presentation in [P3-W3] can, in general, be automated, the automability of [P3-W0] is unlikely.

Finally, it is evident that P3 is not universally applicable. The workflows of P3 and the activities therein present a *sufficient* but not necessary condition for a pattern. This relaxation is intentional. For example, the resources and skills required for [P3-W3]–[P3-W5] can be prohibitively demanding on some pattern producers.

DIRECTIONS FOR FUTURE RESEARCH

In this section, certain directions in which P3 can be strengthened as well as extended are briefly outlined. The quality of knowledge artifacts is an important consideration (Rech et al., 2007). The value of a pattern to its stakeholders depends on the semiotic quality of its description (Kamthan, 2009b). For that, a quality model for description of patterns is desirable. Indeed, such a quality model must include a mapping of relevant quality attributes to specific stakeholder classes. For example, maintainability of a representation is a concern to a pattern administrator and usability of a presentation is a concern to a pattern reader.

P3 is limited in this article to a pattern, the most widely known member of the pattern space. From a knowledge management perspective, it would also be of interest to recast P3 to other members of the pattern space, specifically to a pattern language.

The workflows [P3-W3], [P3-W5], and [P3-W6] would be strengthened by a conceptual model for a PMS. There are initiatives that explore the use the Web for dissemination of patterns, anti-patterns, and pattern languages (Kamthan, 2008; Manolescu et al., 2007). However, a comprehensive effort in this direction is lacking. Furthermore, it would be of interest to specify the requirements and design of a PMS that utilizes the knowledge representation infrastructure provided by the confluence of the extensions of the current Web, namely the Semantic Web (Hendler, Lassila, & Berners-Lee, 2001) and the Social Web (O'Reilly, 2005). Figure 12 illustrates the extensions of the Web and situates a PMS, a representation and the corresponding presentation of a (proto-)pattern in

Figure 12. A PMS based within the environment of the Web and its directions of evolution, namely the Semantic Web and the Social Web

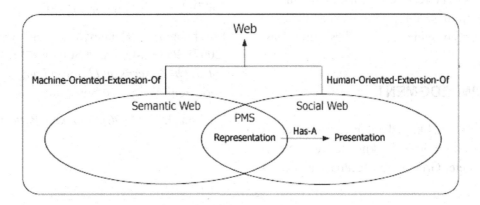

it. It can be noted that a representation belongs to an intersection of the Semantic Web and the Social Web, while a presentation of a (proto-) pattern belongs to the Social Web.

CONCLUSION

It is likely that knowledge garnered through past experience will continue to play a role in any constructive endeavor such as engineering. In particular, the quest for practical knowledge that is time-invariant, can be passed from one generation to another, and enables the development of 'high-quality' systems, is an important goal.

The members of the pattern space in general and patterns in particular are uniquely situated among entities of knowledge that are available for conceptual reuse during development. It is therefore only natural that a theoretical basis for patterns be established for their subsequent practical use. To do that, it is crucial to focus on essential rather than accidental concerns pertaining to patterns.

In conclusion, an understanding of patterns from different viewpoints, in particular from the perspective of knowledge management, can be helpful in their subsequent use by both humans and machines. For that, the process of production of patterns from inception to conclusion needs to be outlined. In doing so, the human and social aspects of the process are an imperative, and need to be embraced. The value of production of patterns to its stakeholders needs to be highlighted. For patterns to be reachable to their community, the means for describing patterns need to be investigated. P3 provides a step in these directions.

ACKNOWLEDGMENT

The author would like to thank Frederick Nickols for insight into models for knowledge management, and Peter Grogono for feedback and comments on P3.

REFERENCES

Ahlgren, R., & Markkula, J. (2005, June 13-15). *Design Patterns and Organisational Memory in Mobile Application Development*. Paper presented at the Sixth International Conference on Product Focused Software Process Improvement (PRO-FES 2005), Oulu, Finland. Alexander, C. (1979). *The Timeless Way of Building*. New York: Oxford University Press.

Alexander, C., Ishikawa, S., & Silverstein, M. (1977). *A Pattern Language: Towns, Buildings, Construction*. New York: Oxford University Press.

Appleton, B. A. (1997). Patterns and Software: Essential Concepts and Terminology. *Object Magazine Online*, 3(5), 20–25.

Baggetun, R., Rusman, E., & Poggi, C. (2004, June 21-26). Paper presented at the 2004 World Conference on Educational Multimedia, Hypermedia and Telecommunications (ED-MEDIA 2004), Lugano, Switzerland.

Bjørnson, F. O., & Dingsøyr, T. (2008). Knowledge Management in Software Engineering: A Systematic Review of Studied Concepts, Findings and Research Methods Used. *Information and Software Technology*, 50(11), 1055–1068. doi:10.1016/j.infsof.2008.03.006

Braga, R., Ré, R., & Masiero, P. C. (2007, May 27-30). *A Process to Create Analysis Pattern Languages for Specific Domains*. Paper presented at the Sixth Latin American Conference on Pattern Languages of Programming (SugarLoafPLoP 2007), Porto de Galinhas, Brazil.

Buschmann, F., Henney, K., & Schmidt, D. C. (2007). Pattern-Oriented Software Architecture: *Vol. 5. On Patterns and Pattern Languages*. New York: John Wiley and Sons Inc.

Coplien, J. O. (1996). *Software Patterns*. SIGS Books.

Coplien, J. O. (2000). A Pattern Language for Writers' Workshops. In Harrison, N. B., Foote, B., & Rohnert, H. (Eds.), *Pattern Languages of Program Design 4*. Reading, MA: Addison-Wesley.

Derntl, M., & Botturi, L. (2006). Essential Use Cases for Pedagogical Patterns. *Computer Science Education, 16*(2), 137–156. doi:10.1080/08993400600768182

Devedžic, V. (2002). Understanding Ontological Engineering. *Communications of the ACM, 45*(4), 136–144. doi:10.1145/505248.506002

Dromey, R. G. (2003). Software Quality - Prevention Versus Cure? *Software Quality Journal, 11*(3), 197–210. doi:10.1023/A:1025162610079

Dumas, M., van der Aalst, W. M., & ter Hofstede, A. H. (2006). *Process-Aware Information Systems: Bridging People and Software through Process Technology*. New York: John Wiley and Sons Inc.

Gabriel, R. P. (1996). *Patterns of Software: Tales from the Software Community*. New York: Oxford University Press.

Gamma, E., Helm, R., Johnson, R., & Vlissides, J. (1995). *Design Patterns: Elements of Reusable Object-Oriented Software*. Reading, MA: Addison-Wesley.

Garzás, J., & Piattini, M. (2005). An Ontology for Microarchitectural Design Knowledge. *IEEE Software, 22*(2), 28–33. doi:10.1109/MS.2005.26

Gaševic, D., Djuric, D., & Devedžic, V. (2006). *Model Driven Architecture and Ontology Development*. New York: Springer Verlag.

Gourlay, S. (2003, September 18-19). *The SECI Model of Knowledge Creation: Some Empirical Shortcomings*. Paper presented at the Fourth European Conference on Knowledge Management (ECKM 2003), Oxford, England.

Granlund, Å., Lafrenière, D., & Carr, D. A. (2001, August 5-10). *A Pattern-Supported Approach to the User Interface Design Process*. Paper presented at the Ninth International Conference on Human-Computer Interaction (HCI International 2001), New Orleans, Louisiana, USA.

Harrison, N. B. (2000). The Language of Shepherding: A Pattern Language for Shepherds and Sheep. In Harrison, N. B., Foote, B., & Rohnert, H. (Eds.), *Pattern Languages of Program Design 4*. Reading, MA: Addison-Wesley.

Harrison, N. B. (2003, June 25-29). *Advanced Pattern Writing*. Paper presented at the Eighth European Conference on Pattern Languages of Programs (EuroPLoP 2003), Irsee, Germany.

Hendler, J., Lassila, O., & Berners-Lee, T. (2001). The Semantic Web. *Scientific American, 284*(5), 34–43. doi:10.1038/scientificamerican0501-34

Hess, C., & Ostrom, E. (2007). *Understanding Knowledge as a Commons: From Theory to Practice*. Cambridge, MA: MIT Press.

Iba, T. (2007, December 3). *Creation toward Quality Without a Name - Sociological Analysis of Pattern Language*. Paper presented at the First International Workshop on Software Patterns and Quality (SPAQu 2007), Nagoya, Japan.

Issa, A., Odeh, M., & Coward, D. (2006). Using Use Case Patterns to Estimate Reusability in Software Systems. *Information and Software Technology, 48*(9), 836–845. doi:10.1016/j.infsof.2005.10.005

Jessop, A. (2004). Pattern Language: A Framework for Learning. *European Journal of Operational Research, 153*(2), 457–465. doi:10.1016/S0377-2217(03)00165-6

Jordan, A., Carlile, O., & Stack, A. (2008). *Approaches to Learning: A Guide for Teachers*. New York: McGraw-Hill.

Kamthan, P. (2006). A Critique of Pattern Language Markup Language. *Interfaces*, *68*, 14–15.

Kamthan, P. (2008). A Situational Methodology for Addressing the Pragmatic Quality of Web Applications by Integration of Patterns. *Journal of Web Engineering*, *7*(1), 70–92.

Kamthan, P. (2009a). A Framework for Integrating the Social Web Environment in Pattern Engineering. *International Journal of Technology and Human Interaction*, *5*(2), 36–62.

Kamthan, P. (2009b, October 25). *On the Symbiosis between Quality and Patterns*. Paper presented at the Third International Workshop on Software Patterns and Quality (SPAQu 2009), Orlando, FL, USA.

Kamthan, P., & Pai, H.-I. (2006a). Knowledge Representation in Pattern Management. In Schwartz, D. (Ed.), *Encyclopedia of Knowledge Management*. Hershey, PA: IGI Global.

Kamthan, P., & Pai, H.-I. (2006b). Representation of Web Application Patterns in OWL. In Taniar, D., & Rahayu, J. W. (Eds.), *Web Semantics and Ontology*. Hershey, PA: IGI Global.

Kohls, C., & Scheiter, K. (2008, October 18-20). *The Psychology of Patterns*. Paper presented at the Fifteenth Conference on Pattern Languages of Programs (PLoP 2008), Nashville, TN, USA.

Kruchten, P. (2004, December 2-3). *An Ontology of Architectural Design Decisions in Software-Intensive Systems*. Paper presented at the Second Gröningen Workshop on Software Variability Management: Software Product Families and Populations, Gröningen, The Netherlands.

Kunert, T. (2009). *User-Centered Interaction Design Patterns for Interactive Digital Television Applications*. New York: Springer-Verlag.

Lea, D. (1994). Christopher Alexander: An Introduction for Object-Oriented Designers. *ACM*, *19*(1), 39–46.

Leacock, M., Malone, E., & Wheeler, C. (2005, March 3-7). *Implementing a Pattern Library in the Real World: A Yahoo! Case Study*. The 2005 American Society for Information Science and Technology Information Architecture Summit (ASIS&T IA 2005), Montreal, Canada.

Manolescu, D., Kozaczynski, W., Miller, A., & Hogg, J. (2007). The Growing Divide in the Patterns World. *IEEE Software*, *24*(4), 61–67. doi:10.1109/MS.2007.120

May, D., & Taylor, P. (2003). Knowledge Management with Patterns. *Communications of the ACM*, *46*(7), 94–99. doi:10.1145/792704.792705

Meszaros, G., & Doble, J. (1998). A Pattern Language for Pattern Writing. In Martin, R. C., Riehle, D., & Buschmann, F. (Eds.), *Pattern Languages of Program Design 3* (pp. 529–574). Reading, MA: Addison-Wesley.

Nelson, H. J., & Monarchi, D. E. (2007). Ensuring the Quality of Conceptual Representations. *Software Quality Journal*, *15*(2), 213–233. doi:10.1007/s11219-006-9011-2

Nickols, F. W. (2000). The Knowledge in Knowledge Management. In Cortada, J. W., & Woods, J. A. (Eds.), *The Knowledge Management Yearbook 2000-2001* (pp. 12–21). Woburn, MA: Butterworth-Heinemann.

Noble, J., & Biddle, R. (2002, June 10-14). *Patterns as Signs*. Paper presented at the Sixteenth European Conference on Object-Oriented Programming (ECOOP 2002), Malaga, Spain.

Nonaka, I., & Takeuchi, H. (1995). *The Knowledge-Creating Company: How Japanese Companies Create the Dynamics of Innovation*. New York: Oxford University Press.

O'Reilly, T. (2005, September 30). *What Is Web 2.0: Design Patterns and Business Models for the Next Generation of Software*. O'Reilly Network.

Piaget, J. (1952). *The Origins of Intelligence in Children*. Madison, CT: International University Press. doi:10.1037/11494-000

Polanyi, M. (1983). *The Tacit Dimension*. Gloucester, MA: Peter Smith.

Pólya, G. (1945). *How to Solve It: A New Aspect of Mathematical Method*. Princeton, NJ: Princeton University Press.

Rech, J., Decker, B., Ras, E., Jedlitschka, A., & Feldmann, R. L. (2007). The Quality of Knowledge: Knowledge Patterns and Knowledge Refactorings. *International Journal of Knowledge Management*, 3(3), 74–103.

Retalis, S., Georgiakakis, P., & Dimitriadis, Y. (2006). Eliciting Design Patterns for E-Learning Systems. *Computer Science Education, 16*(2), 105–118. doi:10.1080/08993400600773323

Rising, L. (2000). *The Pattern Almanac 2000*. Reading, MA: Addison-Wesley.

Seruca, I., & Loucopoulos, P. (2003). Towards a Systematic Approach to the Capture of Patterns within a Business Domain. *Journal of Systems and Software, 67*(1), 1–18. doi:10.1016/S0164-1212(02)00083-3

Shanks, G. (1999, September 29). *Semiotic Approach to Understanding Representation in Information Systems*. Information Systems Foundations Workshop, Sydney, Australia.

Taibi, T., & Ngo, C. L. (2002, July 14-18). *A Pattern for Evaluating Design Patterns*. Paper presented at the Sixth World Multiconference on Systemics, Cybernetics and Informatics (SCI 2002), Orlando, FL, USA.

Van Welie, M., & Van der Veer, G. C. (2003, September 1-5). *Pattern Languages in Interaction Design: Structure and Organization*. Paper presented at the Ninth IFIP TC13 International Conference on Human-Computer Interaction (INTERACT 2003), Zürich, Switzerland.

Vygotsky, L. S. (1978). *Mind in Society: The Development of Higher Psychological Processes* (Cole, M., John-Steiner, V., Scribner, S., & Souberman, E., Eds.). Boston, MA: Harvard University Press.

Wesson, J., & Cowley, L. (2003, September 1-2). *Designing with Patterns: Possibilities and Pitfalls*. Paper presented at the Second Workshop on Software and Usability Cross-Pollination, Zürich, Switzerland.

Winters, N., & Mor, Y. (2008). IDR: A Participatory Methodology for Interdisciplinary Design in Technology Enhanced Learning. *Computers & Education, 50*(2), 579–600. doi:10.1016/j.compedu.2007.09.015

This work was previously published in International Journal of Knowledge Management, Volume 6, Issue 2, edited by Murray E. Jennex, pp. 40-65, copyright 2010 by IGI Publishing (an imprint of IGI Global).

Chapter 8

Qualitative Analysis of Semantically Enabled Knowledge Management Systems in Agile Software Engineering

Jörg Rech
Semantic Technologies, Germany

Christian Bogner
Technical University of Kaiserslautern, Germany

ABSTRACT

In many agile software engineering organizations there is not enough time to follow knowledge management processes, to retrieve knowledge in complex processes, or to systematically elicit knowledge. This chapter gives an overview about the human-centered design of semantically-enabled knowledge management systems based on Wikis used in agile software engineering environments. The methodology – developed in the RISE (Reuse in Software Engineering) project – enables and supports the design of human-centered knowledge sharing platforms, such as Wikis. Furthermore, the paper specifies requirements one should keep in mind when building human-centered systems to support knowledge management. A two-phase qualitative analysis showed that the knowledge management system acts as a flexible and customizable view on the information needed during working-time which strongly relieves software engineers from time-consuming retrieval activities. Furthermore, the observations gave some hints about how the software system supports the collection of vital working experiences and how it could be subsequently formed and refined.

DOI: 10.4018/978-1-4666-0035-5.ch008

INTRODUCTION

The development of complex software systems is based on company- and domain- specific knowledge that has to be constantly cultivated among the employees, because the resulting quality of manufactured software systems depends on what degree the needed knowledge is actually available (Decker et al., 2005).

Typically, knowledge management (KM) platforms are used to support the knowledge capturing, management, or sharing processes within companies. However, in agile software engineering (SE) organizations there is not enough time to follow KM processes, retrieve knowledge in complex processes, or systematically elicit knowledge (e.g., using post-mortem analyses (Birk et al., 2002)). The technical KM platform for agile software organizations should release Software Engineers as much as possible from time-consuming retrieval processes.

Today, due to the various possibilities of searching and browsing through software engineering artifacts, it is assumed that users feel overwhelmed just by the flood of information: while the increasing amount of information itself might not be a problem, an unfiltered and unrated access to it is. When using KM systems, we should never forget that the main goal is to ensure that Software Engineers can deal with their daily tasks without burdening them with additional work.

Hence, we developed a semantically-enabled knowledge management system for SMEs based on a Wiki. This system not only supports the easy retrieval but also acquires valuable pieces of information from users, who publish their problems and experiences during work. Out of the day-to-day work, company- and product-specific knowledge can be built and refined without interfering too much with the daily work. Our approach, which concentrates on essential aspects of an artifact, considers the previous knowledge as well as the interests of the targeted users – provided by semantics encoded in metadata, concept structures

and user profiles. It can be used to arrange artifacts in a flexible way depending on the users' needs (e.g., artifacts written/read by the user and given interests or tasks of the user). Besides that searching the whole system for certain artifacts will present results in a nested or context-based way (e.g. the artifact describing "Pair Programming" is arranged under its parent concept "Extreme Programming" (Beck, 1999a)). This solution is based on underlying Ontologies (Gruber, 1995). After the whole process of selecting certain aspects and restructuring them, users may be provided with complete, self-contained and motivating knowledge.

Our contribution touches several fields, such as Human-Centered Interfaces, Education, and knowledge management with a special focus on Wikis. We tackled the objectives to reduce learning barriers, improve the quality of knowledge, and improve the structure as well as interconnection of knowledge within KM systems. Our contributions comprises of knowledge elicitation techniques, SE-specific didactically improved templates, and semantic relations for SE documents.

In this paper, we present the research methodology (section 2) used in our project to build and evaluate a human-centered and semantically enabled knowledge management system (section 4) as well as the necessary background (section 3) from SE and KM. Several methods to support the users by means of an intelligent application are discussed within in the paper. The qualitative evaluation conducted in the project RISE – including baseline and delta evaluation – is then described in section 5. We give a summary and conclusion in section 6.

METHODOLOGY

In order to support the reuse of software engineering products such as requirement documents, we build the semantically enabled knowledge management system Riki (Reuse-oriented Wiki).

Figure 1. Human-centered design processes for interactive systems (ISO-13407, 1999)

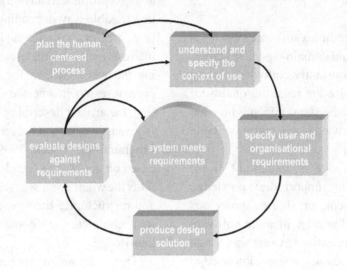

The Riki was targeted towards ease of use and improved the acceptance by the users (Höcht & Rech, 2006). The methodology and technology developed make it possible to share knowledge in the form of software artifacts, experiences, or best practices based on pedagogic approaches.

Development Methodology

Our methodology to develop the Riki was based on the principles of a Human-Centered Design Process according to the international standard ISO 13407, as depicted in Figure 1. It expects that users take an active part in the development process in order to get a clear idea of what might be specific requirements (ISO-13407, 1999).

The early phase of our research project RISE (Rech et al., 2007b), therefore, was dominated by context-analyses within the participating companies. Qualitative-centered studies delivered deep insight into organizational aspects and users' special needs. Two focus groups dealt with the drawbacks and opportunities of using conventional Wiki-systems which were formerly introduced by the associated companies. Furthermore, the analysis of existing artifacts allowed allocat-

ing functions among the technical system and respectively the users themselves.

For example, the analysis of individually built file structures showed that an automatically enabled structuring of existing artifacts might be critical because people tend to use structures in different ways (hierarchical, time-based, priority-based, people-based etc.) and with different granularity. This includes accessing existing artifacts as well as creating new ones. Teevan et al. discovered in a comparable study that people even use hierarchical organized structures if they do not maintain their individual structures hierarchically (Teevan et al., 2004). This example shows, how important it is, to allocate functions between users and intelligent systems. But it also gets clear that definite answers could not be found until final tests of the application.

Evaluation Methodology

The objective of our explorative evaluation was to show its effectiveness in a specific application context. In our evaluation the tailored instances of the Riki system were evaluated to identify the usefulness to the users, the examined applicability, the evolvability, as well as economic factors.

As *subjects* two companies participated in the evaluation: empolis GmbH – an enterprise with a development team of 40 developers and brainbot technologies AG – a micro-enterprise with 5 developers.

While we mainly conducted an explorative evaluation about the use of knowledge in agile organizations without specific hypotheses, one very important *hypothesis* of the RISE project was that software development teams collaboratively using a Riki, are actually about to create a semantic structure – with users not necessarily to be aware of. This structure called "Wikitology" can be considered as a weakly formalized ontology with three main characteristics: a) the *maintenance of content and metadata (i.e., the ontology)* is not considered as extra activity, b) *ontologies* (as seen/build by the users) may always grow behind the content, and c) maintenance of these Ontologies can be *supported efficiently.*

The evaluation itself was split into two *phases*. The baseline evaluation was purely evaluative and used to elicit the context and current state of knowledge transfer. The delta evaluation later helped to measure the effect of the introduced Riki system. The baseline and delta evaluations have been carried out with the same teams and managers.

In both phases we used the following three *techniques* to elicit valuable information from the organizations and potential end-users:

- Goal-oriented, questionnaire-based *interviews* were used to query the previously listed questions with three to ten persons in two to four sessions. The collected answers were summarized and validated by the participants via email.
- *Group discussions* were done at every company to collect any additional information, opinions, ideas, etc. that were not covered by the interviews. The discussion

was started with a specific topic (e.g., why had the old Wiki not worked for you as a KM system?) and every person could state what they expected from an improved knowledge management infrastructure.

- *Artifact analyses* were conducted to identify knowledge sources, the type of knowledge within, as well as how the people structure their documents and knowledge in existing storage systems (e.g., the hierarchy of directories in personal file systems or in pre-existing Wiki systems).

These evaluation techniques helped to cover the evaluation of a) the t*echnology* used by the companies (e.g., technical infrastructure, existing KM systems, and other software systems) that might be integrated into the Riki system, b) the *methodology* applied in the companies for software development and knowledge management, and c) the *knowledge* available in the companies as well as their characteristics and interrelation (e.g., for the development of an ontology).

A more detailed description of the baseline and delta evaluation as well as some results of the two evaluation phases are described in section 5.

BACKGROUND

The RISE Project

The research project "RISE" (Reuse In Software Engineering) was part of the research program "Software Engineering 2006" funded by the German Federal Ministry for Education and Research (BMBF) that started in June 2004 and ended in December 2005. The goal of this research project, in general, was to improve the reuse of artifacts in software engineering (with a focus on the requirement phase) and brought together researchers from social science (the Department of Educational Sciences and Professional Development at the Technical University of Kaiserslautern) and computer science (Fraunhofer Institute for Experimental Software Engineering (IESE) and the German Research Center for Artificial Intelligence (DFKI)) with industrial partners (empolis GmbH – a small enterprise with a development team of about 40 developers and brainbot technologies AG – a micro-enterprise with approx. 4 developers).

Software Engineering and Reuse

Software engineering (SE) as a field in computer science is concerned with the systematic development of high-quality software systems. During the planning, definition, development and maintenance of software systems the people involved generate and require any information and knowledge to support them in their work or to back up their decisions. This includes source code as well as information about processes, products, or technologies. Knowledge reuse and code reuse, from our point of view, is equivalent as the user has to internalize the meaning of the reusable object (e.g., a code fragment or a how-to guideline) and apply it in a new context.

This reuse of existing knowledge and experience is one of the fundamental parts in many sciences. Engineers often use existing components and apply established processes to construct complex systems. Without the reuse of well proven components, methods, or tools we had to rebuild and relearn them again and again.

In the last thirty years the fields software reuse and experience management (EM) (Althoff et al., 2001) are gaining increasingly importance. The roots of EM lie in Experimental Software Engineering (e.g., the "Experience Factory"), in Artificial Intelligence (e.g., "Case-Based Reasoning"), and in knowledge management. EM is comprised of the dimensions methodology, technical realization, organization, and management. It includes technologies, methods, and tools for identifying, collecting, documenting, packaging, storing, generalizing, reusing, adapting, and evaluating experience knowledge, as well as for development, improvement, and execution of all knowledge-related processes.

The Experience Factory (EF) is an infrastructure designed to support experience management (i.e., the reuse of products, processes, and experiences from projects) in software organizations (Basili et al., 1994). It supports the collection, preprocessing, and dissemination of experiences the organizational learning and represents the physical or at least logical separation of the project and experience organization as shown in Figure 2. This separation is meant to relieve the project teams from the burden to find, adapt, and reuse

Figure 2. The experience factory

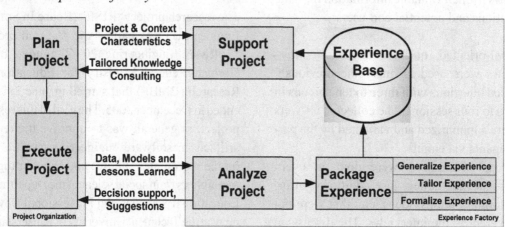

knowledge from previous projects as well as to support them to collect, analyze, and package valuable new experiences that might be reused in later projects.

Traditional, Process-Oriented Software Development and Reuse

Since its beginning several research directions developed and matured in field SE. Figure 3 shows the software development reference model integrating important phases in a software lifecycle. *Project Engineering* is concerned with the acquisition, definition, management, monitoring, and controlling of software development projects as well as the management of risks emerging during project execution. Methods from *Requirements Engineering* are developed to support the formal and unambiguous elicitation of software

requirements from the customers, to improve the usability of the systems, and to establish a binding and unambiguous definition of the resulting system during and after software project definition. The research for *Software Design & Architecture* advances techniques for the development, management, and analysis of (formal) descriptions of abstract representations of the software system as well as required tools and notations (e.g., UML). Techniques to support the professional *Programming* of software are advanced to develop highly maintainable, efficient, and effective source code. *Verification & Validation* is concerned with the planning, development, and execution of (automated) tests and inspections (formal and informal) in order to discover defects or estimate the quality of parts of the software.

Research for Implementation & Distribution is responsible for the development of methods for

Figure 3. Software development reference model

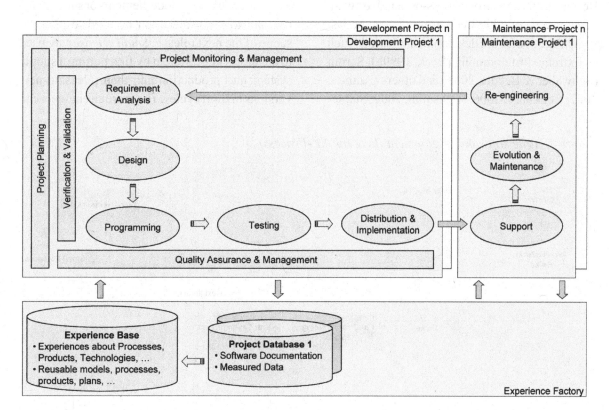

the introduction at the customer's site, support during operation, and integration in existing IT infrastructure.

After delivery to the customer software systems typically switch into a *Software Evolution* phase. Here the focus of research lies on methods in order to add new and perfect existing functions of the system. Similarly, in the parallel phase *Software Maintenance* techniques are developed for the adaptation to environmental changes, prevention of foreseeable problems, and correction of noticed defects. If the environment changes dramatically or further enhancements are impossible the system either dies or enters a *Reengineering* phase. Here techniques for software understanding and reverse engineering of software design are used to port or migrate a system to a new technology (e.g., from Ada to Java or from a monolithic to a client/server architecture) and obtain a maintainable system.

Agile Software Development and Reuse

Beside the traditional or process-oriented software development another trend arose during the last years. Agile software development methods such as Extreme Programming (Beck, 1999b), Scrum (Schwaber & Beedle, 2001) and others (Ambler, 2002; Cockburn, 2006; Highsmith, 2000; Staple-

ton, 1999), impose as little overhead as possible in order to develop software as fast as possible and with continuous feedback from the customers. Agile methods have in common that small releases of the software system are developed in short iteration in order to give the customer a running system with a subset of the functionality needed. Therefore, the development phase is split into several activities that are followed by small maintenance phases.

Today, Extreme Programming (XP) (Beck, 1999a) is the best-known agile software development approach. Figure 4 shows the general process model of XP that is closely connected to refactoring and basically its cradle (Beck & Fowler, 1999). Extreme programming (XP) is based upon 12 principles (Beck, 1999a). We mention four of these principles as they are relevant to our work. *The Planning Game* is the collective planning of releases and iterations in the agile development process and necessary to quickly determine the scope of the next release. Knowledge about the existence of existing code elements or subsystems relevant to the project can be used to plan the scope of the next release. *Small releases* are used to develop a large system by first putting a simple system into production and then releasing new versions in short cycles. The more an engineer can

Figure 4. Agile software development (here the XP-Process)

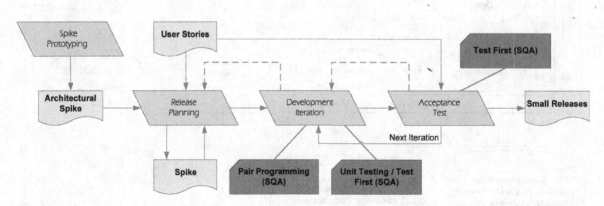

reuse the faster his work is done and the quicker the customer gets feedback. *Simple design* means that systems are built as simple as possible, and complexity in the software system is removed if at all possible. The more libraries are used and identified (via code retrieval) the less functionality has to be implemented in the real system. *Refactoring* or the restructuring of the system without changing its behavior is necessary to remove quality defects that are introduced by quick and often unsystematic development. Decision support during refactoring helps the software engineer to improve the system (Rech, 2007).

In contrast to traditional, process-oriented SE where all requirements and use cases are elicited, the agile methods focuses on few essential requirements and incrementally develops a functional system in several short development iterations. Agile software processes, rely on direct face-to-face communication between customers and developers for knowledge sharing and, therefore, reduce the information loss in in-team and team-to-customer communication (Chau et al., 2003). Pair programming activities improve the exchange of knowledge and experience between two team members and results in fewer bugs, spreading code understanding, and producing overall higher quality code (Begel & Nagappan, 2008). In general, many positive benefits of agile approaches have been reported including shorter development cycle, higher customer satisfaction, lower bug rate, and quicker adaptation to changing business requirements (Barry & Richard, 2003). For the Scrum method, (Cho, 2008) identified the five challenges including reduced documentation, malfunctioning communication, missing user involvement, closed working environment, and superfluous team information exchange.

Traditional software reuse initiatives and approaches that were developed for process-driven software development are inadequate for highly dynamic and agile processes where the software cannot be developed for reuse and reuse cannot be

planned in advance. KM in agile methods apply a personalization strategy with (1) reliance on proficient people (e.g., individual development), (2) orientation towards tacit knowledge (e.g., emergent solutions), (3) knowledge transfer through conversation (e.g., dialogue and discussion), (4) channeling of expertise (e.g., access to experts), and (5) focus on effectiveness (e.g., through flexibility) (Wendorff & Apshvalka, 2005). The main point why agile organizations need new KM approaches (and tools) are the lack of time and the rejection of formal processes by the developers.

Teams and organizations developing with agile methods need automated tools and techniques that support their work without consuming much time. Therefore, *agile software reuse* is a fairly new area where minimally invasive techniques are researched to support software engineers (Cinneide et al., 2004).

HUMAN-CENTERED DESIGN OF SEMANTICALLY-ENABLED KM SYSTEMS

Important Challenges in Software Development

The development of complex software systems requires specific knowledge. The quality of the outcomes depends strongly on how successful existing knowledge and expertise of the employees can be provided and actually applied.

Software engineering in general aims at engineering-like development, maintenance, adjustment and advancement of complex software systems. One characteristic of software engineering compared with classical engineering lies in the prevalent immateriality and the complexity and abstractness of software resulting from it. For this reason experts point out the difficulty to gain vital working-experiences and stress deficits in the field of further training (Broy & Rombach, 2002). Although many companies apply (agile) methods of software engineering, the transfer of the underlying complex knowledge still represents a crucial problem.

Considering this challenging situation, the German research project RISE aimed at a holistic support of software engineering tasks. Software Engineers should be enabled to deal with their tasks and thus act more professional. Furthermore, the transfer of existing knowledge within software-related companies has to be optimized. This should be accomplished by systematic reuse of experiences, methods and models in different application contexts.

The vision of RISE is to develop a user-friendly knowledge management application for software developers that makes fun and requires minimum effort. Software developers are gently supported during teamwork and their re-use of working-experiences and knowledge. Consequently, the organization itself should profit from improved productivity increases.

Based on the stated special problems and situations, research also focuses on how high the impact of an Intranet-based platform could be, in order to ensure the individual capacity to act successfully through re-use of experiences, methods and models. Thus, RISE tries to find answers to the question what are main requirements for a knowledge management platform from the view of employees

- …In order to keep complex knowledge manageable
- …So that knowledge can be used individually and updated during work

It has to be clarified, in what respect a technical platform may allow an individually focused view of the information needed (knowledge management) and might facilitate (*usability*) use of it.

The participating companies already used wiki-systems (Leuf & Cunningham, 2001) as our project started. They provided initial data for the empirical study in the early project-phase. In our case, we had to deal with technically and functionally rather different wiki-systems, which can all be summarized under the wide term "Social Software".

Such web-based content management systems allow users not only to access content but also to add own pieces of information or to edit already available artifacts with as little effort as possible.

The underlying rationale is based on a strongly decentralized way of editing content. Early results of the evaluation showed however that a sophisticated methodology is required to successfully implement "Social software" at the intranets of software-firms, in order to ensure a broad acceptance.

As observed, acceptance might decrease rapidly if the application system no longer represents a source of information which is usable as described within the international standard ISO 9241-11: "extent to which a product can be used by specified users to achieve specified goals with effectiveness, efficiency and satisfaction in a specified context of use" (ISO-9241-11, 1998). So, if the systems fail to be usable neither contents are published or edited nor even read in the worst case. The communication amongst software engineers will not be intensified – as intended – but stagnates to a total deadlock.

Understanding Context-of-Use for KM Systems in Agile Organizations

It seems to be obvious that employees are responsible for an individual development of a vital knowledge basis. Not only that this requires special abilities, resources and strategies. Moreover, employees increasingly have to gather information and subsequently learn new things just besides their main work focus. These working-related information and knowledge gathering activities are conducted in peaks.

The main kind of peak being considered is caused by strict deadlines which temporarily raise the working load to a maximum. Besides those hard and rather ordinary kinds of peaks, a more elementary one is considered: the problem-orientation that many software engineers cling to. The term "problem-orientation" refers to the view that software development, viewed superficially, is a rather trivial process: developers are provided with certain requirements and try to realize them in the software development process.

But from time to time that "trivial" process gets disturbed by tricky problems developers stuck in. Those hard problems represent another kind of peak, which has fatal consequences for knowledge management in software companies: developers which run into that peak are often highly motivated to solve the problem and try to solve it on their own. They spend hours and hours with their problem and often don't bother about existing and proven solutions, concepts or methods. In this case, re-use does not exceed accidental or sporadic access to available knowledge in available knowledge repositories (e.g., internet forums). Considering that the knowledge collected by means of a content management system, it seems to be almost impossible to build a shared repository. The result would be a collection of various problems (hopefully including a solution) which might resemble each other more or less. The so called "Experience Factory" approach has to be mentioned which is considered as one answer to that challenge: "the Experience Factory approach was initially designed for software organizations and takes into account the software discipline's experimental, evolutionary, and non-repetitive characteristics" (Basili et al. 2001, p. 1). Basili et al. propose that the company has to release its experts from the burden of managing the knowledge: "Experts in the organization have useful experience, but sharing experience consumes experts' time. The organization needs to systematically elicit and store experts' experience and make it available in order to unload the experts" ((Basili et al., 2001), p. 2).

Accordingly, employees with huge expertise are no longer considered like a means to an end but rather the core of the technical knowledge management system with the following characteristics:

- *First*, this application system acts as a flexible and customizable view (like a window) on the information needed during working-time. This system strongly relieves software engineers from time-consuming retrieval activities.
- *Second*, the system supports the collection and storage of vital working experience which has to be subsequently formed and refined.

These are the two main factors of the RISE methodology, which were optimized during project time.

Riki: A Semantically Enabled Knowledge Management System

We approached the before mentioned challenges by developing an enhanced Wiki-centered Framework (Louridas, 2006) that was targeted to act as a knowledge sharing platform for software development teams with fast and liberal access to deposit, mature, and reuse experiences made in software projects.

The content in the Riki (Reuse-oriented Wiki) consists of information on products (requirements, designs, documentations, component interactions, presentations, demo systems), projects (use cases, user stories, test cases, ideas), contacts (employees, customers, partners, suppliers), as well as individual blogs of the employees about software technologies, software development, etc. Furthermore, we extended it by two main components:

- First, the Riki was extended by search technologies using case-based reasoning technology and ontologies to provide a formal and consistent framework for the description of knowledge and experiences. As a consequence, software developers are now not only able to search the content of Wiki pages, but are also able to find files within other information repositories such as the shared file system.

- Second, the Riki contains a unified content system that allows software developers to annotate any type of content with so-called "tags". Tags have become very popular with the rise of Web 2.0 and various new applications are adopting this principle. Using the Riki tags can be easily attached to any type of content. In our project, we decided to use shared tags: once a tag has been attached, it can be seen and modified by all users. This solution was favored in order to support a common vocabulary about artifacts within software development teams. Although this has been considered as being crucial for successful development processes, employees still have the opportunity to use their own "language" by using private tags.

Ontologies and templates enrich the Riki content with semantics that enable us to didactically augment the knowledge within the Riki with additional information and documented experiences. Additionally, the usage of metadata enables the users to build up and use their own individual ontology (in the form of individual tags) that is not bound to compromises or constraints from universal ontologies that might have been constructed in advance. Furthermore, metadata from the universal ontology (i.e., specified beforehand or as defined by other users) was partially used in their own ontology.

Within the Riki, the results are clustered by this metadata and the metadata can be used to refine search queries. Annotated pages that were listed in search results remind the users that they have already read them or that they are highly valuable and should be read again.

EVALUATION OF SEMANTICALLY-ENABLED KM SYSTEMS

The objective of an explorative evaluation of a KM system such as the Riki is to show its effectiveness in a specific application context. In our evaluation the tailored instances of the Riki system were evaluated to identify the usefulness to the users, the examined applicability, the evolvability, as well as economic factors. As mentioned previously two companies participated in the evaluation: empolis GmbH – an enterprise with a development team of 40 developers and brainbot technologies AG – a micro-enterprise with 5 developers.

While we mainly conducted an explorative evaluation about the use of knowledge in agile organizations without specific hypotheses, one very important hypothesis of the RISE project was that software development teams collaboratively using a Riki, are actually about to create a semantic structure – with users not necessarily to be aware of. This structure called "Wikitology" can be considered as a weakly formalized ontology with three main characteristics: a) the *maintenance of content and metadata (i.e., the ontology)* is not considered as extra activity, b) *ontologies* (as seen/build by the users) may always grow behind the content, and c) maintenance of these Ontologies can be *supported efficiently.*

The evaluation itself was split into two *phases*. The first phase – called *baseline evaluation* – at the start of the project was purely evaluative and used to elicit the context and current state of knowledge transfer. From the information we gathered in this phase we designed and developed the Riki system considering the people, processes, and available technologies. The second phase – called *delta evaluation* – at the end of the project helped to measure the effect of the introduced Riki system. The baseline and delta evaluations have been carried out with the same project managers, who represented small teams of five to twenty people, and software developers of the companies. These people used the Riki system during real projects within their companies.

- Goal-oriented, questionnaire-based *interviews* were used to query the previously listed questions with three to ten persons in two to four sessions. The collected answers were summarized and validated by the participants via email.
- *Group discussions* were done at every company to collect any additional information, opinions, ideas, etc. that were not covered by the interviews. The discussion was started with a specific topic (e.g., why had the old Wiki not worked for you as a KM system?) and every person could state what they expected from an improved knowledge management infrastructure.
- *Artifact analyses* were conducted to identify knowledge sources, the type of knowledge within, as well as how the people structure their documents and knowledge in existing storage systems (e.g., the hierarchy of directories in personal file systems or in pre-existing Wiki systems).

These evaluation techniques helped to cover the evaluation of the following three topics:

- *Technology*: Elicitation of the existence and characteristics of the technical infrastructure, existing KM systems, and other software systems that might be integrated into or used as the KM system (i.e., the Riki system). Furthermore, these technological systems potentially have valuable information that can be utilized in a KM system.
- *Methodology*: Elicitation of the applied methodology for production (e.g., software development) and knowledge management (esp. knowledge transfer processes). This gives further information about how the KM system should be integrated into the social system of the organization and where, when and by whom knowledge is produced or consumed.

- *Knowledge*: Elicitation of the existing knowledge components available in the organization as well as their characteristics and interrelation (e.g., for the development of an ontology). Furthermore, the typical structure of documents that might be didactical enriched.

A more detailed description as well as some results of the two evaluation phases are described in this the following sections. They address persons, who want to evaluate a KM system such as the Riki in an organization.

Baseline Evaluation

The baseline evaluation is concerned with the determination of the organizational context a socio-technical knowledge management should be embedded in. The core goal of the baseline evaluation is to measure and analyze the current status of the implicitly or explicitly performed KM processes, the used knowledge carrying or KM systems as well as the knowledge culture itself. Baseline evaluations are typically applied only once to get a consistent view of the KM in the organization before larger changes. This section describes the basic process for the evaluation of a KM system as well as a summary of our baseline evaluation.

Baseline Evaluation process

The baseline evaluation process (and similarly the delta evaluation) is structured into three sub-phases problem-determination, context-determination, and knowledge-determination. The baseline evaluation was used to capture the working process before the intervention (i.e., the introduction of a Riki). As depicted in Figure 5 the steps in these sub-phases define a process that results in several documents (e.g., a problem description) usable for the specification of a socio-technical KM system integrated into the surrounding organizational context.

Figure 5. Plan for baseline and delta evaluation

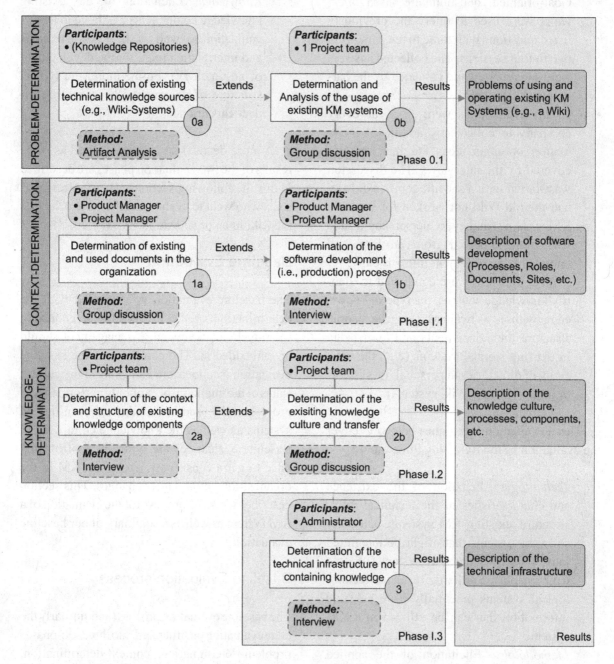

- *Problem-Determination*: The problem determination serves to identify existing knowledge sources (e.g., in the case of the partner empolis a Wiki system named MASE) as well as emerged problems and challenges with it. Step 0a is used to determine existing information systems and technical knowledge sources using a sys- tematic analysis method. By means of a group discussion in step 0b the exchange of knowledge via existing technical (KM) systems in a typical project team is illuminated.

- *Context-Determination*: This sub-phase is concerned with the determination of the context the socio-technical KM system is embedded in. The context determination produces information about the production processes, roles, documents, or sites that might be used in the KM system. The three steps in this sub-phase are concerned with the development processes which are to be supported by the KM initiative. Step 1a uses a group discussion technique to determine existing documents, templates, and other potentially reusable elements. To elicit or update the development process in use we applied an interview with several product and project managers in step 1b.

- *Knowledge-Determination*: The knowledge determination sub-phase targets the core information that should be made reusable via the KM system. The content, context, and structure of reusable elements is determined in step 2a using an interview. Based on this information the knowledge transfer processes and the knowledge culture itself is analyzed in step 2b using a group discussion with several members of project teams.

Finally, step 3 is used to identify the technical infrastructure of tools and systems not used for knowledge management but might be integrated and connected with the new or improved KM system (i.e., a new Riki or an improved Riki).

Results from the Baseline Evaluation

In the context of the RISE project we applied step 0a to step 3 of the evaluation plan as depicted in Figure 5. For the execution of the baseline evaluation one period we required a time -span of approx. 3 months taken into account that not all employees are continuously available. Based on different vacation planning, holidays in summer, autumn, and Christmas as well as other projects one should take into account more time during such an evaluation.

During the group discussion concerning the usage of existing KM systems (cf. Figure 5, 0b)

as well as the knowledge culture and transfer (cf. Figure 5, 2b) we determined the following status in the organization:

- The organization used a Wiki that few people used and contained partially documented concepts, ideas, comments, and larger documentations about planned as well as already developed software systems. Other information in the Wiki included: Customer information, dates, To-do-lists, addresses, and absent lists.
- Important information about the software system itself is documented in the source code (in this case: Python and ePyDoc (ePyDoc, 2005)). To extract this information one has to check-out the whole software system from the versioning system and search for relevant information on file level.
- Important information about changes to the software system is documented in the used versioning system (in this case: Subversion). Changes at the software system are sent to all interested users by email. To extract this information without the eMails one has to analyze every check-in into the system and the appropriate comments.
- Internal information sources (i.e., Repositories) with other project-relevant information are: Change tracking system, project folders, universal and private network drives, eMails, and chat tools (e.g. ICQ) with information in files such as plain text or MS Word documents. Furthermore, task cards at a physical blackboard.
- External information sources are distributed over the whole internet but the employees had a focus on MSDN and Google if they required further information.

Positive Characteristics: What runs well?

- The co-operation between two people closely working together, but who were distributed physically over two cities, worked very well over the old Wiki.
- The local teams worked on one floor and had only short distances to their colleagues. The face-to-face communication was very good (i.e. everybody was in "shouting" distance).

Negative Characteristics: What runs badly?

- The Wiki was not used anymore at the start of the evaluation and the feedback indicates that most people were not pleased with the structure of the knowledge base.
- Neither the old WIKI nor the documentation language for Python (ePyDoc) permitted the integration of pictures or graphics.
- The search for information in the WIKI and file system is term-based (i.e., no stemming or Boolean operators). This was perceived as insufficient and de-motivating by the users. Furthermore, the search in the Wiki was impeded by the use of camel case (e.g., "MyProjectDescription") in the page names.
- The discovery of relevant information is perceived as complicated as they are distributed over multiple repositories that all use different (or none) search mechanisms.
- Access to the Wiki from a text editor (e.g. emacs under Linux/Unix) or a shell (i.e. command line interface) is impossible and/or uncomfortable. Nevertheless, some developer are bias or required to use these and are not willing to install or use other operating systems (or web browsers such as internet explorer™).
- Neither were the authors (resp. other observers) informed about changes done to the content in the Wiki nor were they informed about changes to the navigational or divisional structures (i.e., chapters and sections) of the content.
- It was not clear were to store information as they could be spread or duplicated in multiple repositories, for example, in the versioning system, change tracking system, or the code itself.

In summary, the knowledge transfer and management processes as they were lived in the organization previously to the Riki introduction were determined by the baseline evaluation as follows:

- *Recording* of information is limited to few people in the organization and the documented information is only partially complete, consistent, or valid. The informal storage, e.g., of user requirements, opens the door for inconsistent, incomplete, and generally low-quality documents. Nevertheless, most users embraced the Wiki idea and recorded even preliminary information that is revised and improved by themselves or other users over time. In order to improve this quality, approach such as incentive systems (Feurstein et al., 2001) can be used to motivate the sharing as well as improvement of knowledge. Paul Duguid examined the "laws of quality" and found that peer-produced projects constantly change: "What is flawed today may be flawless tomorrow" (Duguid, 2006). However, during the RISE project, we could not address this topic thoroughly enough. But our findings indicate that the overall quality or value of an information space is judged by the users themselves and was acceptable. The users were able to comment about artifacts and incomprehensible, out-of-date, misleading, or unhelpful documents were often directly improved or commented.

- *Reuse* of content is minimal as the information is distributed over several sources with different search interfaces and techniques. Furthermore the content of the documents have inconsistent structures, incomplete descriptions, or are plain outdated.
- *Workflow* for reuse of content and getting an *overview* is slow and typically demotivating as multiple sources have to be searched manually and documents belonging together are not grouped or linked.
- *Sharing knowledge* is cumbersome, there are no templates, guidelines, or checklists to validate if the recorded information has some quality and might be easily reused by the colleagues.
- *Confidence* in the knowledge transfer system and *motivation* to share is low, as only few people are creating shareable documents and the documents are sometimes not accurate or up-to-date. Nevertheless the participants stated that they would like to share their knowledge in a more persistent way.
- *Face-to-face communication* is strong esp. as most employees have short distances to their colleagues, are roughly of the same age, and see not need to hide their information (i.e., egghead's syndrome).

Delta Evaluation

The core goal of a delta evaluation is to measure and analyze the changes a KM system has inflicted on the affected organization. Delta evaluations can be applied multiple times during the lifecycle of a KM system (e.g., every year) to evaluate the effect on the organization.

Delta Evaluation Types

Since KM systems are usually used only irregularly in the beginning and not yet a firm part of the working process, the delta evaluation phase can be applied in three different types:

1. *Applicability*: The first type serves to examine how frequently the system is used, if it integrates into the socio-technical infrastructure and if it helps the users in their daily work. In order to keep the costs of the evaluation down to a minimum, a light-weight evaluation is planned by reusing existing plans and other technology assessment or acceptance models.
2. *Usefulness*: In the second type the results and experiences from the first type serve to concretize the requirements and improvement goals. The system has already demonstrated that it is applicable in the organization and represents an integral component of the regular work routine. By means of structured evaluation processes a formal evaluation plan is constructed to examine, in particular, the aspect of the usefulness, ease-of-use, and usability for the direct users and management.
3. *Economy*: Finally the third type serves to examine the economical aspects of the KM system. The system is already integrated into the regular work routine and users share and reuse the knowledge within. An adaptive evaluation, reaction, and risk plan are developed to continuously monitor and improve the system. The focus of this type is the evaluation of the system and forecast of the usefulness regarding the Return on Investment (ROI) and Total Cost of Ownership (TCO).

To identify existing or potential problems the entire system is continuously monitored during the start-up phase. Log-files help to drill-down into specific problems if the users observe a problem while using the system.

Results from the Delta Evaluation

In the context of the RISE project we could only apply the first sub-phase and evaluate the applicability of the Riki system. Due to the short amount of time the system was used (2 month) we could only get little insight into the usefulness of the system for the users in their daily routine. During the group discussion concerning the usage of the Riki (cf. Figure 5, 0b) as well as knowledge culture and transfer (cf. Figure 5, 2b) we noted the following characteristics the users liked very much about the Riki:

- Metadata elements that can be placed by every user (such as keywords in form of tags) can be very helpful in indexing the content of a Riki and the users reacted very positively that they were able to *index every page* with their own metadata.
- The usage of metadata enabled the users to build up and use their own *individual ontology* (in form of individual tags) that is not bound to compromises or constraints from universal ontologies that might have been constructed in advance. Furthermore, metadata from the universal ontology (i.e., specified beforehand or as defined by other users) was partially used in their own ontology.
- *Searching* the information stored in the Riki is more accepted by the users when the metadata might be integrated into the search process. In the Riki the results are *clustered* by this metadata and the metadata might be used to *refine* the search query. The search technology exploit co-occurring metadata from multiple users and applies "collaborative filtering" techniques (i.e., "metadata x you search for is also called y").
- Annotated pages that were listed in search results reminded the users that they already read them or were highly valuable and should be read again. Similar to the

Memex concept by Vannevar Bush (Bush, 1945) (cf. http://en.wikipedia.org/wiki/Vannevar_Bush) the metadata might even be used to record a reading sequence for oneself.
- The integrated view a Riki gives over the information in the organization enables the user to send links that are not subject to change as, for example, mounted devices in the windows file system.

In comparison to the status as determined by the baseline evaluation the usage of the Riki system had the following subjective effect on the organization:

- *More recording* of information into the Riki than before as barriers (technological and social) are reduced.
- *More reuse* of content from the Riki as users are more likely to share and search for content.
- *Faster workflow* for reuse of content and an *improved overview* due to the integrative view over multiple systems (e.g., file system, eMail, etc.) in a central integrated repository.
- *Less barriers for sharing knowledge* as it easier and faster to enter information but this typically results in a *low quality* of the content. Most users embrace the Wiki idea and record even preliminary information that is revised by oneself or others over time.
- *Higher confidence* in the system and *increased motivation* as content is easier to find and more people are participating in the sharing process.
- *Consistent face-to-face communication* even as more information is reused from the technical system.

Further and more quantitative results about the usefulness and economical aspects esp. of the more SE specific features of a Riki such as ontology-based templates for requirements will be elicited in later evaluations.

Evaluation of Design Solutions against Requirements

The evaluation of the design solutions was dominated by qualitative methods and revealed valuable insights about requirements of users and organizations. Two focus groups were dedicated to explore usage problems with the knowledge management platforms introduced in earlier stages. The gathered qualitative data is characterized by high validity, which means that a common understanding of user requirements was developed and the involved users agreed which user requirements should be realized in favor (DA-Tech 2004, P. 76).

In order to classify the collected data, the so called "Munich knowledge management model" has been used with its four categories: knowledge-representation, knowledge-usage, knowledge-communication and knowledge-creation (Reinmann-Rothmeier, 2000, pp. 18).

Knowledge-Representation: Some employees tend to write down a minimum of information. It was observed that some of them document just as little as possible so that they will be able to find out later what was meant by the given artifact. The main disadvantage of that behavior is that the saved data becomes hard or even almost impossible to understand for other employees accessing that content because they don't have the necessary knowledge to »decode« and to classify it. However, it seems to be a kind of game those developers are playing when doing some documentation: they rather puzzle together pieces of information than writing down supposedly redundant or superfluous information.

Use of Knowledge: Crucial information about projects, products or customers is distributed across various databases. This means, that useful knowledge is hard to find and thus hard to be transferred in other contexts like new projects for example.

Communication about Knowledge: Employees who browse or search through wiki-content in order to find some special piece of information have to spend a lot of time. Moreover, editing content in most Wikis is rather uncomfortable: for example, adding a chart, a table or even a picture to wiki pages requires a special handling if it is not even impossible. As a consequence, information is being transferred by mail under pressure of time and not added to the wiki-site.

Creation of Knowledge: With increasing activity in a wiki, it becomes harder for authors to integrate their piece of information into the existing structure. So, it is very likely that no new content is being added and already saved content gets orphaned.

Basically, using metadata is a good idea to keep heterogeneous and complex structures describable and thus technically manageable. But the problem is that users often fail to provide useful metadata or simply don't bother about complex sets of metadata.

DISCUSSION

During the RISE project, qualitative evaluation activities have been preferred, because they helped to specify the context of use as well as user and organizational requirements. In general, empirical data gathered by means of qualitative research methods is characterized by its high validity. Unfortunately, it is rather difficult to extract requirements out of those data or to check to what extent those "implicit" requirements have been considered during the development process of the software system.

Following user-centered design approaches that problem could not be bypassed. It is rather necessary to provide prototypes as soon as possible which contain as much functionality as necessary in order to check current implementations against more or less "implicit" requirements.

In terms of a rather comprehensive meaning of *usability* it was not only about developing user interfaces and improving them. In fact, usability engineering is considered as a vital concept in software development. So, it is not only about to describe, design or produce design solutions for user interfaces. It is rather about to understand and facilitate human-engineered socio-technical systems (DATech, p. 77).

CONCLUSION

One very important hypothesis of the RISE project was, that software development teams that use a wiki, collaboratively, to build knowledge repositories are actually about to *create a semantic structure* – with users not necessarily to be aware of. This structure called "Wikitology" can be considered as a weakly formalized ontology. This user-generated content and ontology has three main advantages.

- The *maintenance of content and metadata (i.e., the ontology)* is not considered as extra activity.
- *Ontologies* (as seen/build by the users) may always grow behind the content.
- Maintenance of these Ontologies can be *supported efficiently*

Nevertheless, the quality of the ontology – as well as the content – depends always on the expertise and knowledge of the contributors. Therefore, similar to Wikipedia or the Experience Factory system special administrators are required that inspect, assess, and correct (i.e., "refactor" (Rech et al., 2007a)) the ontology and content from time to time.

Another crucial approach of the RISE project is the *use of tags* as a very minimalistic but rather effective way of providing metadata. Any tags may be assigned individually to content-pages in the Riki. So, each user is able to create his view on any artifact by using his own depiction. Since in our approach all users are able to see the tags provided by the others, it is of course very probable that teams members manage to create a shared set of tags as well. Later these tags can be analyzed (e.g., using data mining techniques) in order to automatically extract or semi-automatically build ontologies for specific topics (e.g., software engineering or specific software projects)

Furthermore, *templates* for special types of content (bug report, use case, user story etc.) help to provide a minimum of required information. Readers as "consumers" of the artifact can be satisfied, too. For example, the given structure helps them to browse faster through the content in order to find only some pieces of information being of interest. Finally, this results in a higher acceptance of the system which motivates the employees of adding more content to the repository.

Additionally, a *blog-component* was added to the system. The blog contains not only news. In fact, the blog can be considered as an active filter on the wiki-content. For example users might link to a certain Riki-page and provide some extra information along with the link. So, other users get useful assistance with the evaluation of artifacts.

ACKNOWLEDGMENT

Our work is part of the project RISE (Reuse in Software Engineering), funded by the German Ministry of education and science (BMBF) grant number 01ISC13D.

REFERENCES

Althoff, K.-D., Decker, B., Hartkopf, S., Jedlitschka, A., Nick, M., & Rech, J. (2001, July 24-25). *Experience Management: The Fraunhofer Institute for Experimental Software Engineering (IESE) Experience Factory*. Paper presented at the Industrial Conference Data Mining: Data Mining, Data Warehouse and Knowledge Management, Leipzig, Germany.

Ambler, S. (2002). *Agile Modeling: Effective Practices for eXtreme Programming and the Unified Process*. John Wiley & Sons, Inc.

Barry, B., & Richard, T. (2003). Using Risk to Balance Agile and Plan-Driven Methods. *Computer, 36*(6), 57–66. doi:10.1109/MC.2003.1204376

Basili, V. R., Caldiera, G., & Rombach, H. D. (1994). Experience Factory. In Marciniak, J. J. (Ed.), *Encyclopedia of Software Engineering* (*Vol. 1*, pp. 469–476). New York: John Wiley & Sons.

Basili, V. R., Lindvall, M., & Costa, P. (2001, June 13-15). *Implementing the Experience Factory concepts as a set of Experience Bases*. Paper presented at the 13th Int. Conf. on Software Engineering & Knowledge Engineering, Buenos Aires, Argentina.

Beck, K. (1999a). *Extreme programming explained: embrace change*. Harlow, UK: Addison-Wesley.

Beck, K. (1999b). *eXtreme Programming eXplained: Embrace Change*. Reading, MA: Addison-Wesley.

Beck, K., & Fowler, M. (1999). Bad Smells in Code. In Booch, G., Jacobson, I., & Rumbaugh, J. (Eds.), *Refactoring: Improving the Design of Existing Code* (1st ed., pp. 75–88). Reading, MA: Addison-Wesley.

Begel, A., & Nagappan, N. (2008). *Pair programming: what's in it for me?* Kaiserslautern, Germany: ACM.

Birk, A., Dingsøyr, T., & Stålhane, T. (2002). Postmortem: Never Leave a Project without It. *IEEE Software, 19*(3), 43–45. doi:10.1109/MS.2002.1003452

Broy, M., & Rombach, H. D. (2002). Software Engineering. Wurzeln, Stand und Perspektiven. *Informatik-Spektrum, 25*(6), 438–451. doi:10.1007/s002870200266

Bush, V. (1945). As We May Think. *The Atlantic Online, 176*, 101–108.

Chau, T., Maurer, F., & Melnik, G. (2003). *Knowledge Sharing: Agile Methods vs. Tayloristic Methods*. Washington, DC: IEEE Press.

Cho, J. (2008). Issues and Challenges of Agile Software Development with Scrum. *Issues in Information Systems, 9*(2), 188–195.

Cinneide, M. O., Kushmerick, N., & Veale, T. (2004, July). Automated Support for Agile Software Reuse. *ERCIM News*.

Cockburn, A. (2006). *Agile Software Development: The Cooperative Game* (2nd ed.). Reading, MA: Addison-Wesley.

DATech. (2004). DATech-Prüfungshandbuch. Usability-Engineering-Prozess. Leitfaden für die Evaluierung des Usability-Engineering-Prozesses bei der Herstellung und Pflege von interaktiven Systemen auf der Grundlage von DIN EN ISO 13407. Frankfurt a. M.: Deutsche Akkreditierungsstelle Technik e.V.

Decker, B., Ras, E., Rech, J., Klein, B., Reuschling, C., Höcht, C., et al. (2005). *A Framework for Agile Reuse in Software Engineering using Wiki Technology*. Paper presented at the Conference Professional Knowledge Management - Experiences and Visions, Kaiserslautern, Germany.

Duguid, P. (2006). Limits of self–organization: Peer produc-tion and 'laws of quality'. *First Monday, 11*(10). ePyDoc. (2005). *Epydoc website*. Retrieved 5 October, 2005 from http://epydoc.sourceforge.net/

Feurstein, M., Natter, M., Mild, A., & Taudes, A. (2001, January 3-6). Incentives to share knowledge. In *Proceedings of Hawaii International Conference on System Sciences* (p. 8). Los Alamitos, CA, USA: IEEE Computer Society.

Gruber, T. R. (1995). Toward principles for the design of ontologies used for knowledge sharing. *International Journal of Human-Computer Studies, 43*(Nov), 907. doi:10.1006/ijhc.1995.1081

Highsmith, J. A. III. (2000). *Adaptive software development: a collaborative approach to managing complex systems.* New York: Dorset House Publishing Co., Inc.

Höcht, C., & Rech, J. (2006). Human-centered Design of a Semantically Enabled Knowledge Management System for Agile Software Engineering. In Lytras, M. D., & Naeve, A. (Eds.), *Open Source for Knowledge and Learning Management: Strategies beyond Tools.* Hershey, PA: IGI Global.

http://www.wissensmanagement.net/ download/ muenchener_modell.pdf

ISO-13407. (1999). *Human-centred design processes for interactive systems (Standard ISO).ISO.* International Organization for Standardization.

ISO-9241-11. (1998). *Ergonomic requirements for office work with visual display terminals (VDTs) -- Part 11: Guidance on usability* (Standard No. ISO 9241-11:1998(E), ISO TC 159/SC 4/WG 5). ISO (the International Organization for Standardization).

Leuf, B., & Cunningham, W. (2001). *The Wiki Way: Quick Collaboration on the Web.* Reading, MA: Addison-Wesley.

Louridas, P. (2006). Using Wikis in Software Development. *IEEE Software, 23*(2), 88–91. doi:10.1109/MS.2006.62

Rech, J. (2007). Handling of Software Quality Defects in Agile Software Development. In Stamelos, I., & Sfetsos, P. (Eds.), *Agile Software Development Quality Assurance.* Hershey, PA: IGI Global.

Rech, J., Decker, B., Ras, E., Jedlitschka, A., & Feldmann, R. L. (2007a). The Quality of Knowledge: Knowledge Patterns and Knowledge Refactorings. [IJKM]. *International Journal of Knowledge Management, 3*(3), 74–103.

Rech, J., Ras, E., & Decker, B. (2007b). RIKI: A System for Knowledge Transfer and Reuse in Software Engineering Projects. In Lytras, M. D., & Naeve, A. (Eds.), *Open Source for Knowledge and Learning Management.* Hershey, PA: IGI Global.

Reinmann-Rothmeier, G. (2000). *Wissen managen: Das Münchener Modell.* Retrieved from.

Schwaber, K., & Beedle, M. (2001). *Agile Software Development with Scrum.* Upper Saddle River, NJ: Prentice Hall.

Stapleton, J. (1999). *DSDM: Dynamic Systems Development Method.* Washington, DC: IEEE.

Teevan, J., Alvarado, C., Ackerman, M. S., & Karger, D. R. (2004). *The perfect search engine is not enough: a study of orienteering behavior in directed search.* Vienna, Austria: ACM.

Wendorff, P., & Apshvalka, D. (2005). *The Knowledge Management Strategy of Agile Software Development.*

This work was previously published in International Journal of Knowledge Management, Volume 6, Issue 2, edited by Murray E. Jennex, pp. 66-85, copyright 2010 by IGI Publishing (an imprint of IGI Global).

Chapter 9
Critical Success Factors and Outcomes of Market Knowledge Management:
A Conceptual Model and Empirical Evidence

Subramanian Sivaramakrishnan
University of Manitoba, Canada

Marjorie Delbaere
University of Saskatchewan, Canada

David Zhang
University of Saskatchewan, Canada

Edward Bruning
University of Manitoba, Canada

ABSTRACT

In this paper, the authors examine critical success factors and outcomes of market knowledge management, which is the management of knowledge pertaining to a firm's customers, competitors, and suppliers. Using data collected from 307 managers in 105 businesses across Canada, the authors show that a firm's extent of information technology adoption, its analytical capabilities, and market orientation are critical success factors for the firm's market knowledge management. An important outcome of market knowledge management is the organization's financial performance, mediated by customer satisfaction and customer loyalty. Results of this study indicate that superior business performance depends not only on the effective management of knowledge, but also on what type of knowledge is managed. Finally, implications of results and avenues for future research are discussed.

DOI: 10.4018/978-1-4666-0035-5.ch009

INTRODUCTION

Knowledge Management is a broad construct that encompasses the interdependent yet distinct processes of creation, storage and retrieval, transfer, and application of knowledge (Alavi & Leidner, 2001). This paper focuses on one particular component of organization-wide knowledge management, Market Knowledge Management (MKM), which is defined as the creation, sharing, and application of knowledge pertaining to the organization's customers, competitors, and suppliers in order to inform key strategic decisions (Li & Calantone, 1998). Essentially, MKM focuses on managing market knowledge that would enable the firm to satisfy its customers better than the competition.

The important role of market knowledge has been shown in several different contexts such as innovation (Marinova, 2004), new product development (Li & Cavusgil, 1999), export performance (Toften & Olsen, 2003), sales force performance (Chen, 2005), market entry timing (Mitra & Golder, 2002), and retailing (Conant & White, 1999). Knowledge about an organization's markets, including customers and competitors, is a key resource for sustainable competitive advantage in the future (Srivastava, Shervani, & Fahey, 1998; Achrol & Kotler, 1999).

Several prior studies have presented models that elucidate critical success factors (CSF) for, and consequences of, knowledge management (e.g., Davenport & Prusak, 1998; Janz & Prasarnphanich, 2003; Jennex & Olfman, 2005, 2006; Liebowitz, 1999; Lindsey, 2002; Massey, Montoya-Weiss, & Driscoll, 2002; Trussler, 1998). As these studies generally support the notion that knowledge management leads to superior performance for the organization, we would expect that MKM would also have a positive impact on the firm's performance. Therefore, it is important to understand the CSFs of MKM as well as the outcomes from it. Moreover, although researchers have posited superior business performance as a

benefit of MKM, or organization-wide knowledge management in general, much of the extant literature on this subject has been theoretical (e.g., Jennex & Olfman, 2005, 2006; Plessis, 2007) and the empirical evidence to substantiate this proposition qualitative in nature, such as a case study of a single firm (Akhavan, Jafari, & Fathian, 2006). While multi-case studies provide opportunities for more systematic investigations (e.g., Akhavan, Jafari, & Fathian, 2006; Oltra, 2005), Lin and Tseng (2005) and Oltra (2005) argue that quantitative survey methods would provide more robust validation. Jennex and Adelakun (2003) and Jennex, Amoroso, and Adelakun (2004) systematically examined CSFs using survey methods in the specific context of offshore software development companies and small companies in developing countries, respectively. To date, little is known on the CSFs of the MKM component of knowledge management. Our research attempts to fill this gap by proposing three key CSFs for MKM and empirically substantiating their role in enabling superior results for the firm in regard to market performance and financial returns.

A question that may arise is whether the CSFs for MKM are likely to be different from those for KM. Although MKM is a subset of KM, it is an application of KM that specifically deals with the firm's markets, namely its customers, competitors, and suppliers (Glazer, 1991; Moorman, 1995). Therefore, it can be expected that CSFs for KM in general may not adequately capture the specific nature of the CSFs for MKM. Although the CSFs for KM will apply to MKM also, the reverse is not necessarily true. For example, the market knowledge creation component of MKM requires a systematic monitoring of competitor actions that may not be addressed by CSFs for organization-wide KM. In this research, we empirically demonstrate technology adoption and analytical capabilities within the firm as important CSFs for MKM. Furthermore, we show that the firm's market orientation (MO), which is the extent to which the firm is customer- and competitor-oriented (Kohli & Jaworksi, 1990; Narver & Slater, 1990), is also a CSF of MKM.

Most models of CSFs for generic knowledge management do not adequately address this specific cultural orientation of the firm. Although Narver and Slater (1990) and Kohli and Jaworski (1990) argue that having a market orientation improves business performance, Armario, Ruiz, and Armario (2008) suggest that MO's influence on organizational performance might be moderated by knowledge acquisition (Armario, Ruiz, & Armario, 2008). It is our contention that the link between MO and performance is in fact mediated by MKM. The results of our research demonstrate that a firm's MKM results in greater customer satisfaction and loyalty, which in turn leads to superior financial performance for the firm.

LITERATURE REVIEW

Market Knowledge Management

Morgan and Turnell (2003) have demonstrated the important role that market-based organizational learning plays in firms' performance gains. They regard market-based organizational learning as a core competency that results in a market-based competitive advantage for the firm. Their model draws the linkage from customer orientation and competitive orientation directly to market performance. We believe the market knowledge generated as a result of market-based organizational culture needs to be effectively managed. Accordingly, this paper aims to demonstrate the central role that MKM plays in transforming market knowledge to business performance.

Two concepts closely related to MKM are Customer Relationship Management (CRM) and Customer Knowledge Management (CKM). Both CRM and CKM focus on the relationship between a firm and its customers, not competitors or suppliers (Rollins & Halinen, 2005; Rowley, 2004; Tzokas & Saren, 2004). Although recent articles have

presented the similarities and synergies among CRM, CKM, and KM (Rollins & Halinen, 2005; Smith & McKeen, 2005; Tzokas & Saren, 2004; Xu & Walton, 2005), Rowley (2004) recommends that KM needs to embrace many other domains in addition to customer knowledge. Our conceptualization of MKM maintains a distinction between the focus on a particular pool of knowledge (about customers, competitors, and suppliers) and the more general organization-wide KM.

Another concept closely related to MKM is market intelligence (Jagetia & Patel, 1981; Moyer, 1972), which has been around longer than MKM. Market Intelligence, which is a subset of Business Intelligence, is a system of gathering information pertaining to a firm's markets. Business Intelligence focuses specifically on explicit information and knowledge whereas MKM encompasses both explicit and tacit knowledge (Herschel & Jones, 2005; Nonaka, 1994; Nonaka, Reinmoeller, & Senoo, 1998). Cody, Kreulen, Krishna, and Spangler (2002) suggest that Business Intelligence and KM will eventually fuse into one entity, consistent with the views of Griffin and Jennex in Corral, Griffin, and Jennex (2005). MKM is more than the explicit content of market intelligence as it also includes the tacit market knowledge embedded in the process of knowledge acquisition, dissemination, and application.

It is generally accepted that the ability to manage market knowledge is a potential source of competitive advantage (Drucker, 1993; Nonaka, 1991; Nonaka & Takeuchi, 1995). There are different theoretical approaches to studying competitive advantage (e.g., resource-based view of the firm and stakeholder theory), with each approach suggesting specific domains of knowledge as critical to achieving that advantage (Tzokos & Saren, 2004). The theory on market orientation suggests that firms which systematically seek and manage knowledge of customers and competitors realize superior business performance (Jaworski & Kohli, 1993; Narver & Slater, 1990). Several researchers have examined the outcomes of MKM.

Marinova (2004) shows that MKM propels a firm's innovation efforts and thereby improves firm performance. Similarly, it has been shown that competence, in the form of market knowledge, helps firms develop more successful new products due to a better understanding of their markets (Li & Cavusgil, 1999) and also to improve retail performance (Conant & White, 1999). Moreover, Chen (2005) proposes ways in which firms can improve MKM using one of their primary sources of market knowledge – their salespeople. In an international marketing context, Toften and Olsen (2003) suggest that market knowledge of one's export markets results in superior export performance. Along these lines, Mitra and Golder (2002) demonstrate that market knowledge helps firms time their entry into a foreign market better. These studies all point to a common finding: MKM helps firms perform better.

Gold, Malhotra, and Segars (2001) approach KM from an organizational capabilities perspective, viewing it as a collection of infrastructures and processes that are concerned with how information is collected, distributed, analyzed, and shared as knowledge. According to Davenport, Harris, De Long, and Jacobson (2001), firms use information technology to generate data and information, which is subsequently converted to knowledge through analytical processes. From Gold et al.'s (2001) perspective of organizational capabilities, it can be seen how the availability of information technology and analytical capabilities within the firm can support the creation, storage, retrieval, and transfer of market knowledge. Without these critical components, it can be expected that the extent of MKM that the firm can practice would be rather limited. Therefore, in the following section, we propose that an organization's extent of information technology adoption and its analytical capabilities are two key CSFs for MKM.

Critical Success Factors of Market Knowledge Management

Analytical Capabilities: In Morgan and Turnell's (2003) model, organizational strategic analysis was considered as an integral part of market-based organizational learning. Similarly, we believe the organization's analytical capability is a necessary condition for effective MKM. We define an organization's analytical capabilities as the degree to which it has the necessary resources (people with analytical skills) to be able to analyze and interpret market as well as organizational information. This definition is consistent with Huber (1991) and Sinkula's (1994) conceptualization of organizational learning, where interpretation is considered an essential part of the organizational learning process.

According to the hierarchical and value-added approach toward the development of knowledge (Davenport et al., 2001), raw data is processed into meaningful information through analysis. The information then becomes knowledge through a process of further analysis and interpretation (Grover & Davenport, 2001). Davenport et al. (2001) explicated the importance of developing analytical capabilities within an organization, and the critical role analytical capabilities play in the creation of knowledge. As they propose in their model, while an organization can generate huge volumes of data, whether these data get converted to information and subsequently to knowledge depends on the analytical capabilities existent within the firm–in terms of people with the necessary analytical skills to convert data to information and then to knowledge.

In a broader context of KM research, DeLone and McLean's (2003) revised information systems (IS) success model suggests that information quality is one of the key CSFs. Jennex and Olfman's (2006) knowledge management systems (KMS) success model further refines what contributes to knowledge/information quality. They argue that the combination and interaction of knowledge strategy, process, and the richness and linkages add to knowledge/information quality. In a marketing context, we believe that employees' analytical capabilities would add to the richness of knowledge, and enhance the strategizing aspect of the knowledge process. This proposition is consistent with prior research findings that recognize human skills as of one of the most important CSFs. For example, Oltra (2005) argues that KM must work in conjunction with human resources to be effective. Hung, Huang, Lin, and Tsai (2005) demonstrate that employee involvement and training is one of the CSFs for KM adoption. Jennex and Adelakun (2003) and Jennex, Amoroso, and Adelakun (2004) also rate workers' skills as the top CSF for KM success. Wei, Choy, and Yeow (2006) reveal that while this aspect of critical skill in knowledge audit is perceived as important, ironically, it is often the least implemented.

In this paper, we focus in from broader concepts of "human factors" (Oltra, 2005) and workers' skills (Jennex & Adelakun, 2003) to a specific skill set, analytical capabilities, and test it in the context of MKM.

We argue that the organization's analytical capability limits and regulates the MKM process. We propose, therefore, that the firm's analytical capability is a CSF for MKM.

H_1: An organization's analytical capability is antecedent to, and positively related to, its market knowledge management.

Information Technology Adoption: In today's information technology (IT) world, one's analytical abilities can be put to little use without the hardware and software needed to convert the data to information and knowledge and then manage it. Hence, a firm would need to complement its analytical capabilities with the necessary technologi-

cal support for its personnel to apply their analytical skills. The availability of low-cost, high-power computational processing has allowed for data and information generation and dissemination on a scale that was unimaginable in the past (Roberts, 2000). Moreover, information technology can greatly enhance an organization's ability to communicate and share knowledge among departments and units.

Several researchers have examined the antecedents to IT adoption. The Technology Acceptance Model (Davis, 1989) suggests that IT adoption is primarily influenced by its perceived usefulness and perceived ease of use. Recent efforts in this line of research have helped us better understand other antecedent influences such as trust (Pavlou & Fygenson, 2006), switching costs (Chen & Forman, 2006), and network effects (Zhu, Kraemer, Gurbaxani, & Xu, 2006). By comparison, as observed by Kim and Malhotra (2005), much less systematic effort has gone into providing insights into the consequences of IT adoption. From a strategic perspective, IT adoption is presumed to have a value-adding ability for firms (McFarlan, 1984; Porter & Millar, 1985). From a resource-based view of the firm, an organization's IT skills can be considered a potential source of competitive advantage (Mata, Fuerst, & Barney, 1995).

IT adoption has been widely accepted as one of the CSFs to general KM strategies. DeLone and McLean's (2003) information system success model specifies "system quality" as one of the CSFs for information system success. Jennex and Olfman's (2006) Knowledge Management System (KMS) success model further expands the aspect of "system quality" to include technological resources, and the levels and forms of KMS. The notion that acquiring technological resources and adopting appropriate levels and forms of KMS would enhance the success of KMS has received considerable empirical support. For example, Orzano et al. (2007) show that sophisticated technical tools such as electronic health records can help medical practices to manage knowledge. Hung, Huang, Lin and Tsai (2005) also demonstrate that IT is one of the top CSFs in KM implementation. Lin, Chang, and Chang (2004) and Lin, Tan, and Chang (2002) illustrate that IT helps intra- and inter- organizational interaction, and hence, enhances knowledge transfer. Jennex and Adelakun (2003) and Jennex, Amoroso, and Adelakun (2004) rate telecommunication and technical infrastructure as one of the most important factors for firm success.

In contrast to studies that examine antecedents to technology acceptance, in this research we examine the beneficial consequences of IT adoption—specifically on MKM. It has been argued that IT enhances organizational memory, knowledge dissemination, and retrieval by establishing electronic bulletin boards, knowledge repositories, and databases (Alavi & Leidner, 2001). Therefore, it can be seen that IT allows a firm to realize its analytical potential by effectively converting data to knowledge, disseminating that knowledge, and making it accessible when needed across the organization. Accordingly, we propose that information technology adoption is a CSF for MKM.

H₂: An organization's information technology adoption is antecedent to, and positively related to, market knowledge management.

Market Orientation: Market Orientation (MO) deals primarily with the use of market-related knowledge to obtain a competitive advantage. Since Kohli and Jaworski (1990) and Narver and Slater (1990) defined and operationalized the construct in their seminal papers, MO has received considerable attention in the literature. Kohli and Jaworksi (1990) define MO as the organization-wide generation of market intelligence pertaining to current and future customer needs,

dissemination of the intelligence across departments, and the organization-wide responsiveness to customers. This perspective considers market-oriented firms as embracing a collection of systems and procedures aimed at obtaining a competitive edge by managing intelligence pertaining to customers. Narver and Slater (1990) conceptualize MO as an organizational culture that enhances the firm's response to its markets by encouraging and facilitating the activities involved in acquiring information about customers and competitors and disseminating that information throughout the organization. Although the two conceptualizations of MO are somewhat different, both concur in signifying that MO requires managing market knowledge.

A suitable organizational culture has been considered as one of the most important CSFs for KM success (Hung, Huang, Lin, & Tsai, 2005). Orzano et al. (2007) argue that in order to foster effective knowledge management, firms must develop a knowledge-driven culture, where employees are involved and encouraged to talk to each other about things that benefit the firm. Market-oriented firms encourage an organizational culture of high levels of interfunctional coordination, which requires employees from various functional areas to communicate with each other and coordinate concerted actions.

Based on the theory of planned behavior (Ajzen, 1991; Ajzen & Fishbein, 1977), which states that culture, norms, and attitudes precede behavior, we hypothesize that possessing a MO is antecedent to the organization's MKM; that is, an organization's MO is a CSF for its MKM. We contend that for the right knowledge to be managed (created, shared, and utilized), MO is necessary. We believe that knowledge without a MO, albeit knowledge of some sort, is not likely to be useful for enabling superior business performance. Accordingly, we hypothesize:

H₃: An organization's market orientation is antecedent to, and positively related to, market knowledge management.

Performance Outcomes

Although there have been several studies confirming the link between MO and business performance (Deng & Dart, 1994; Jaworski & Kohli, 1993; Narver & Slater, 1990), there have also been studies that have failed to find evidence of a relationship between market orientation and performance (Diamantopoulos & Hart, 1993; Greenley, 1995). Some researchers have responded to this lack of consensus by advocating a broader definition of business performance that includes short-term customer satisfaction and long-term customer loyalty, in addition to financial performance (Gray, Matear, Boshoff, & Matheson, 1998). Gray et al. (1998) found a stronger link between MO and customer satisfaction than they did between market orientation and financial performance. Accordingly, we will employ measures of market performance, operationalized as customer satisfaction and customer loyalty, along with measures of financial performance.

Based on both Narver and Slater's (1990) and Kohli and Jaworksi's (1990) definitions of MO, it is clear that having a MO requires systematic procedures for managing knowledge. There is empirical evidence for the effects of MO on performance (Jaworski & Kohli, 1993; Narver & Slater, 1990; Slater & Narver, 1994) and KM on performance (Sivaramakrishnan, Delbaere, & Bruning, 2004). It can be expected that an organizational culture of being market-oriented should lead the firm to establish MKM systems and procedures that would subsequently provide the competitive advantage to result in improved business performance, as measured by the satisfaction and loyalty among the organization's customers. Further, we expect that it is market performance that subsequently leads to greater financial performance. Therefore, we hypothesize:

H₄: *An organization's market orientation positively impacts market performance (customer satisfaction and loyalty) mediated by market knowledge management.*

H₅: *An organization's extent of market knowledge management positively impacts financial performance mediated by market performance.*

Our hypothesized model is shown in Figure 1.

Figure 1. Hypothesized model

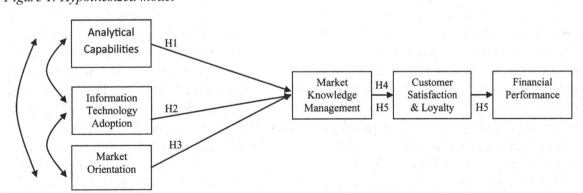

METHODOLOGY

Choice of Research Method

A cross-sectional survey method is well suited for testing our hypotheses. Data from a large number of organizations can be collected systematically via this method, especially using a mail or web survey. The constructs and relationships being examined do not lend themselves to qualitative research or experimental manipulation. Therefore, the survey method is considered most appropriate for this study.

Sample

Data to test our hypotheses were collected by surveying managers in 500 companies that were randomly drawn from a database of Canadian businesses. Respondents were top- or middle-level managers from various functional areas spanning several industries. We restricted our data collection to top- and middle-level managers considering that junior managers may not have had adequate experience in the firm to accurately respond to our questionnaire items. Rather than rely on a key informant, questionnaires were administered to multiple respondents within each company, as recommended by Kohli, Jaworksi, and Kumar (1993). Our questionnaire was administered through either a web or a mail survey, depending on which method the contact person preferred (subsequent t-tests on all the measured constructs showed no statistically significant difference in method of data collection). Follow-up calls were conducted on all non-responses. Usable responses were obtained from 307 managers from 105 businesses representing a 21% response rate. Tests comparing early with late respondents on their responses and organizational characteristics yielded no significant differences. To check for non-response bias, we compared company characteristics such as size, industry type, and geographic location of the companies that responded with those that did not and found no significant differences. As per Kohli et al. (1993), responses from individuals within the same company were averaged to give one response per company, as our unit of analysis was the company and not the individual. Subsequent analyses were run with the aggregated data that represented 105 companies.

Independent Variables

- **Information Technology Adoption (ITA):** Was measured with a six-item, seven-point semantic-differential scale (see Appendix). The specific items were adapted from Lewis, Snyder, and Rainer (1995) to measure the extent to which information and communication technology (hardware and software) had been adopted by departments within an organization to store and analyze data and communicate information, as well as top management's support of the use of this technology. Factor analysis revealed one clear factor as expected. The items were averaged into one ITA index score (coefficient alpha=0.87).

- **Analytical Capability (AC):** Was measured with a two-item, seven-point Likert scale. To our knowledge, there is no established scale to measure an organization's analytical capability. Therefore, we constructed the items based on the model proposed by Davenport et al. (2001). Consistent with the "transformation of data to knowledge" component in their model, the items were developed to capture whether the organization possessed the requisite analytical skills and the actual engagement of employees in information analysis activities, respectively. The two items were then averaged to form an AC index score (r=0.65, p<.001).

- **Market Orientation (MO):** Was measured using items from Narver and Slater's (1990) market orientation scale. Customer and competitor orientation were tested using five-item and three-item, seven-point Likert scales, respectively. Narver and Slater's (1990) MO scale also includes items measuring interfunctional coordination. For our research, however, this aspect of communication is better captured under the MKM construct rather than MO, as sharing of knowledge is an important component of knowledge management. Interfunctional coordination, therefore, was not included in our market orientation construct to avoid duplication of measurement. As has been traditionally done in the MO literature, the eight items were averaged to form a MO index (coefficient alpha=0.86). This is further justified by the significant correlation between the customer- and competitor orientation constructs (r=0.58, p<0.001).

- **Market Knowledge Management (MKM):** Was measured with a seven-item, seven-point Likert scale. Although there is a growing body of research on knowledge management, there is no single validated and widely-accepted scale used to measure the construct. We therefore developed our items based on work by Gold et al. (2001). The items were grouped into three subscales to measure market knowledge acquisition, dissemination, and application. Factor analysis revealed two highly correlated factors (r=0.6, p<.001). One of the factors represented the knowledge acquisition dimension, while the other factor represented both the dissemination and application dimensions. Due to the high correlation between the two factors, they were treated as representing one dimension. Therefore, the seven items were averaged into one MKM index (coefficient alpha = 0.85).

- **Customer Satisfaction and Loyalty (CSL):** These were measured with a six-item, seven-point Likert scale from Kohli and Jaworski's (1990) conception of the two constructs. A confirmatory factor analysis revealed that

customer satisfaction and loyalty can be considered uni-dimensional. Therefore, the six items were averaged into a CSL index (coefficient alpha=0.87).

- **Financial performance (FP):** Was a seven-point, three-item measure of the performance of the firm relative to competition. Respondents were asked to indicate their firm's overall sales revenue, return on investment, and return on assets relative to major competitors. As data were collected from different industries that could vary considerably in terms of what is considered good or poor financial performance, relative financial measures are more appropriate than absolute measures for comparison across industries. Such measures have been used by Jaworski and Kohli (1993). The three FP items were factor-analyzed revealing a one-factor construct. The three items on the scale had statistically significant correlations, which is not surprising, considering that a firm that has higher revenue than competitors could be expected to have higher ROI and ROA as well. Therefore, they were averaged into one FP index (coefficient alpha=0.80).

Figure 2 summarizes the means and variances of each measured variable and the covariances among all the variables.

ANALYSIS AND RESULTS

Reliability and Validity: Confirmatory factor analysis (CFA) was used to examine the reliability and validity of our scales. A scale would be reliable if the items load onto the intended factor and yield a Cronbach's alpha of at least 0.70 (Nunnally, 1978) for each factor. This was established for all our scales.

Figure 2. DescriptiveStatistics and Pearson correlations among variables

Variables	Means	Variance	Covariance (sig.)					
			ITA	AC	MO	MKM	CSL	FP
IT Adoption (ITA)	5.32	0.76	1.00					
Analytical Capability (AC)	4.61	1.95	0.55 (0.00)	1.00				
Market Orientation (MO)	5.04	0.89	0.35 (0.00)	0.61 (0.00)	1.00			
Market Knowledge Management (MKM)	4.81	0.78	0.36 (0.00)	0.68 (0.00)	0.56 (0.00)	1.00		
Customer Satisfaction & Loyalty (CSL)	5.65	0.66	0.13 (0.08)	0.21 (0.07)	0.41 (0.00)	0.44 (0.00)	1.00	
Financial Performance (FP)	5.43	0.66	0.14 (0.54)	0.23 (0.05)	0.39 (0.00)	0.41 (0.00)	0.60 (0.00)	1.00

Next, we wished to confirm that MKM and MO were indeed two distinct constructs. Discriminant validity is achieved if the 90% confidence interval of the covariance (squared correlation coefficient) between the constructs does not include the value 1. Discriminant validity was demonstrated by using CFA with structural equation modeling and by a confidence interval around the correlation between the constructs. The structural equation model used to test these measurement issues is illustrated in Figure 3.

All measured items load onto the intended construct significantly, and all standardized regression weights are greater than 0.50 (see Figure 4). Further, the covariance between MO and MKM was moderate (Cov=0.38, standard error=0.11), and the 90% confidence interval for the covariance between MO and MKM did not contain the value of 1, indicating discriminant validity (Kline, 2005). Thus, we conclude that the discriminant validity between MO and MKM is achieved.

Test of our hypothesized model: Each individual hypothesis was tested with ordinary least square (OLS) regression. Furthermore, the predicted relationships may exist and operate simultaneously. Hence, path analysis with structural equation modeling (SEM) was used to test the simultaneous multiple

Figure 3. Discriminant validity model

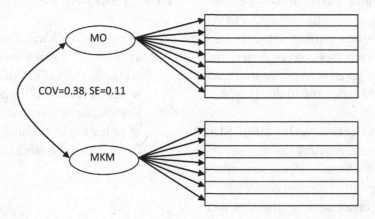

Figure 4. Loadings in discriminant validity analysis

Latent Construct	Measured Items	Loading	Sig.
Market Orientation	Our principal business goal is to satisfy the needs of our customers.	0.51	0.00
	We use customers as an important source of service ideas.	0.72	0.00
	We constantly monitor our level of commitment to our customers.	0.76	0.00
	Our strategy for competitive advantage is based on our customers' needs.	0.82	0.00
	We do not measure customer satisfaction systematically.	0.50	0.00
	We regularly share information within our company concerning competitor strategies.	0.57	0.00
	We respond rapidly to competitive actions that threaten us.	0.66	0.00
	Our company regularly scans competitors' strengths and weaknesses.	0.65	0.00
Market Knowledge Management	Our company converts data/information about our markets to useful knowledge.	0.61	0.00
	Our company converts data/information about our suppliers to useful knowledge.	0.54	0.00
	Our company absorbs knowledge from individuals into the company.	0.81	0.00
	Our company does not distribute acquired knowledge throughout the company.	0.53	0.00
	Our company makes knowledge accessible to those employees who need it.	0.78	0.00
	Our company converts knowledge into action (decisions).	0.82	0.00
	Our company does not match sources of knowledge to challenges we face.	0.70	0.00

relationships. All hypothesis tests were conducted at the 0.05 level of significance.

First, we examined our hypoheses that AC and ITA are critical success factors for MKM (hypotheses 1 and 2 respectively). MKM was regressed on ITA and AC individually. Both ITA and AC were significant predictors of MKM. Following this, MKM was regressed on both ITA and AC simultaneously, to confirm that they predict MKM when included in the model together. Both ITA and AC remained significant predictors of MKM (see Figure 5), thereby confirming hypotheses 1 and 2 that they are CSFs for MKM.

Next, we examined hypothesis 3 that a market-orientation is also a critical success factor for market knowledge management. This hypothesis is supported by the results that MO has a positive and significant influence on MKM ($\beta=0.67$, $p<0.001$), as well as the increased explanatory power by including MO in the model (adjusted $R^2=0.52$). Interestingly, after MO was introduced in the regression model, ITA lost its significance ($p=0.09$), which suggests that market-oriented organizational culture and employee analytical capabilities are even more important than the hardware-based adoption of information technologies.

Figure 5. CSFs to market knowledge management

IV	DV	Adj. R^2	Beta	t-Value	p-value
ITA	MKM	.18	.43	4.80	.001
AC	MKM	.30	.55	6.66	.001
ITA	MO	.24	.23	2.39	.02
AC			.36	3.80	.001
MO	MKM	.44	.67	9.09	.001
ITA			.14	1.72	.089
AC	MKM	.52	.27	3.27	.001
MO			.49	6.14	.001

Table 1. Analysis of mediation by market knowledge management

IV	DV	Adj. R^2	Beta	t-Value	p-value
MO	CSL	.209	.466	5.24	.001
MO	MKM	.444	.671	9.09	.001
MKM	CSL	.354	.601	7.48	.001
MO MKM	CSL	.357	.123 .519	1.15 4.87	.251 .001

Next, the mediation relationship among market orientation, market knowledge management, and customer satisfaction and loyalty were examined with a series of regression analyses as recommended by Baron and Kenny (1986). First, CSL was regressed on MO. Second, MKM was regressed on MO. Third, a regression of CSL on MKM showed a significant relation indicating that CSL is an outcome of MKM. Finally, CSL was regressed on both MO and MKM. As can be seen from the results presented in Table 1, MO remained significant even after MKM was introduced in the model, indicating that MKM partially mediates the link between MO and CSL, lending partial support to hypothesis 4. Similarly, we examined whether CSL mediates the relation between MKM and financial performance. Our results, shown in Table 2, confirm hypothesis 5 that MKM leads to financial performance by enabling higher customer satisfaction and loyalty.

To further confirm our results, in addition to OLS regression analysis, we also tested all of our hypotheses simultaneously by specifying a path model with AMOS 16 (Arbuckle, 2007). The estimated model is shown in Figure 6. All paths were significant except for the path from ITA to MKM. The model fit the data well ($\chi^2=2.637$, df=1, p=0.104; CFI=0.999; RMSEA=0.127).

These results confirm our hypotheses that analytical capability, information technology adoption, and market orientation are all critical success factors for market knowledge management. The impact of IT adoption and analytical capability on market knowledge management are further augmented by the firm's market-oriented organizational culture. Market knowledge management by the firm results in enhanced customer satisfaction and loyalty, which in turn leads to greater financial returns. Our results indicate, therefore, that an organization's market knowledge management is a key factor that ties together the firm's technology, analytical capabilities, and market-orientation culture, and makes significant contribution to the firm's financial success.

DISCUSSION

This empirical research contributes to our understanding of critical success factors and outcomes

Table 2. Analysis of mediation by customer satisfaction and loyalty

IV	DV	Adj. R^2	Beta	t-Value	p-value
MKM	FP	.10	.34	3.33	.001
MKM	CSL	.38	0.62	7.94	.001
CSL	FP	.13	.37	3.67	.001
MKM CSL	FP	.12	.11 .30	0.88 2.30	.38 .03

Figure 6. Estimated path model (standardized path coefficients)

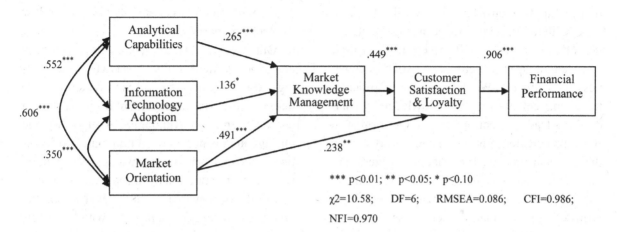

*** p<0.01; ** p<0.05; * p<0.10

$\chi 2=10.58$;   DF=6;   RMSEA=0.086;   CFI=0.986; NFI=0.970

of market knowledge management. Several researchers have discussed critical success factors for knowledge management. Delone and McLean (2003) posit that the CSFs for IS success include three categories - information quality, system quality, and service quality. Jennex and Olfman's (2005, 2006) KMS success model further investigated the subsets embedded in each of these three categories, and introduce more elaborate feedback loops among these factors. These CSF models have received considerable empirical support (e.g., Tsai & Chen, 2007; Kulkarni, Ravindran, & Freeze, 2006; Wei, Choy, & Yeow, 2006). However, the CSFs for the management of market knowledge in particular have not been adequately addressed in the literature. As shown by our data, market knowledge management is very important to the firm, because it impacts customer satisfaction and loyalty, which are critical for realizing higher sales and profit.

Further, our results show that organizations increase their likelihood of improving business performance by adopting appropriate information technology and possessing the capabilities to analyze information to gain a richer understanding of their customers and competitors. We demonstrate that the extents to which the organization has adopted information technology

and has the necessary analytical capabilities are critical success factors for its market knowledge management. This is mediated by the organization's market orientation, wholly in the case of technology adoption and partially in the case of analytical capability, indicating market –orientation as a key CSF for MKM. This suggests that information technology does little for effective market knowledge management unless the firm has a market orientation. Without this orientation, it is easy to imagine how the organization can generate large quantities of information that would never be converted to knowledge, or knowledge that would never be applied to decision-making.

Traditional market orientation models (Jaworski & Kohli, 1993; Narver & Slater, 1990) suggest that having a market orientation results in superior business performance. In this research, we demonstrate that a market orientation does not automatically result in higher performance. We show that having a market orientation, along with IT adoption and analytical capability, generally results in greater inclination to engage in market knowledge management, which in turns leads to higher customer satisfaction and loyalty among the organization's customers. This implies that to reap greater benefits of a market orientation, firms would have to manage the gathering, dissemination, and application of knowledge within the firm.

The literature in knowledge management suggests that firms which effectively manage their knowledge reap the benefits in terms of better business performance. We demonstrate empirically that management of market knowledge by itself does not lead to superior financial performance. It leads to greater satisfaction and loyalty among the firm's customers, presumably by catering to their needs better using the knowledge gained. This in turn leads to the firm reaping benefits in terms of superior financial performance.

Our results have normative implications for managers. In today's competitive business world, it can be expected that a good understanding (knowledge) of customers and competitors is necessary for a firm to survive. Our research shows that a firm needs to have the necessary organizational culture (market orientation) and capabilities (information technology and analytical capabilities) for effective management of knowledge on the firm's markets. Without these, the firm could still perform some market knowledge management, although how effective it will be in producing superior business performance is questionable.

Our research is not without limitations. We measured market knowledge management and analytical capability with scales we developed, as there are no accepted published scales for these constructs. Although our scales demonstrated good reliability and face validity, further research could examine these constructs with a different set of scale items. Our data were collected in Canada. Although we would expect Canadian and American organizations to be quite similar, whether our results would hold in a country with a considerably different management style (e.g., Japan or India) is not clear. It is possible that in certain cultures, market knowledge management may be done in an informal yet effective way. Although we collected data from firms in diverse industries, our sample size did not allow us to examine if there are differences among industries in terms of our

theoretical model. Further research could test our model with much larger sample sizes that allow for such comparisons.

Our theoretical model and results present several opportunities for future research. An interesting question is whether a firm can have an effective market knowledge management without having a market orientation. Although market knowledge management is possible without market orientation, whether that market knowledge management will result in superior business performance is doubtful. Moreover, is a high level of market knowledge management possible with low levels of information technology and analytical capability? Our data indicates that it is not. However, anomalous firms that effectively manage their market knowledge without much use of information technology or analytical personnel could serve as interesting case studies. Future research could examine moderators of the relationships in our proposed model. For example, it can be seen that factors such as industry characteristics (some industries are more technology-intensive than others) or organizational characteristics (centralized versus decentralized) could be possible moderators in the model. The area of knowledge management is rich in terms of research potential. In this paper, we have presented the important role played by the market knowledge management component of an organization-wide knowledge management system. Further research could examine the role of other such knowledge management components to provide us with an insight into the role each of them plays in providing the organization with a competitive advantage through the effective management of its knowledge.

REFERENCES

Achrol, R. S., & Kotler, P. (1999). Marketing in the network economy. *Journal of Marketing, 63,* 146–163. doi:10.2307/1252108

Ajzen, I. (1991). The theory of planned behavior. *Organizational Behavior and Human Decision Processes*, *50*, 179–211. doi:10.1016/0749-5978(91)90020-T

Ajzen, I., & Fishbein, M. (1977). Attitude-behavior relations: A theoretical analysis and review of empirical research. *Psychological Bulletin*, *84*, 888–918. doi:10.1037/0033-2909.84.5.888

Akhavan, P., Jafari, M., & Fathian, M. (2006). Critical success factors of knowledge management systems: A multi-case analysis. *European Business Review*, *18*(2), 97–113. doi:10.1108/09555340610651820

Alavi, M., & Leidner, D. E. (2001). Review: Knowledge management and knowledge management systems: Conceptual foundations and research issues. *Management Information Systems Quarterly*, *25*(1), 107–136. doi:10.2307/3250961

Arbuckle, J. (2007). *Amos 7.0 User's Guide. Spring House*. PA: Amos Development Corporation.

Armario, J. M., Ruiz, D. M., & Armario, E. M. (2008). Market Orientation and Internationalization in Small and Medium-Sized Enterprises. *Journal of Small Business Management*, *46*(4), 485–511. doi:10.1111/j.1540-627X.2008.00253.x

Baron, R. M., & Kenny, D. A. (1986). The moderator-mediator variable distinction in social psychological research: Conceptual, strategic, and statistical considerations. *Journal of Personality and Social Psychology*, *51*(6), 1173–1182. doi:10.1037/0022-3514.51.6.1173

Chen, F. (2005). Salesforce incentives, market information, and production/inventory planning. *Management Science*, *51*(1), 60–75. doi:10.1287/mnsc.1040.0217

Chen, P., & Forman, C. (2006). Can vendors influence switching costs and compatibility in an environment with open standards? *Management Information Systems Quarterly*, *30*, 541–562.

Cody, W. F., Kreulen, J. T., Krishna, V., & Spangler, W. S. (2002). The integration of business intelligence and knowledge management. *IBM Systems Journal*, *41*(4), 697–713. doi:10.1147/sj.414.0697

Conant, J. S., & White, J. C. (1999). Marketing program planning, process benefits, and store performance: An initial study among small retail firms. *Journal of Retailing*, *75*(4), 525–541. doi:10.1016/S0022-4359(99)00017-2

Corral, K., Griffin, J., & Jennex, M. E. (2005). BI experts' perspective: The potential of knowledge management in data warehousing. *Business Intelligence Journal*, *10*(1), 36–40.

Davenport, T. H., Harris, J. G., De Long, D. W., & Jacobson, A. L. (2001). Data to knowledge to results: Building an analytical capability. *California Management Review*, *43*(2), 117–138.

Davenport, T. H., & Prusak, L. (1998). *Working Knowledge*. Cambridge, MA: Harvard Business Press.

Davis, F. D. (1989). Perceived usefulness, perceived ease of use, and user acceptance of information technology. *Management Information Systems Quarterly*, *13*(3), 319–340. doi:10.2307/249008

Delone, W. H., & McLean, E. R. (2003). The Delone and McLean model of information systems success: A ten-year update. *Journal of Management Information Systems*, *19*(4), 9–30.

Deng, S., & Dart, J. (1994). Measuring market orientation: A multi-factor multi-item approach. *Journal of Marketing Management*, *10*(8), 725–742. doi:10.1080/0267257X.1994.9964318

Diamantopoulos, A., & Hart, S. (1993). Linking market orientation and company performance: Preliminary evidence on Kohli and Jaworski's framework. *Journal of Strategic Marketing*, *1*, 93–121. doi:10.1080/09652549300000007

Drucker, P. F. (1993). *Post-Capitalist Society.* New York: HarperCollins Publishers.

Glazer, R. (1991). Marketing in an information-intensive environment: Strategic implications of knowledge as an asset. *Journal of Marketing, 55,* 1–19. doi:10.2307/1251953

Gold, A. H., Malhorta, A., & Segars, A. H. (2001). Knowledge management: An organizational capabilities perspective. *Journal of Management Information Systems, 18*(1), 185–214.

Gray, B., Matear, S., Boshoff, C., & Matheson, P. (1998). Developing a better measure of market orientation. *European Journal of Marketing, 32,* 884–903. doi:10.1108/03090569810232327

Greenley, G. E. (1995). Market orientation and company performance: Empirical evidence from UK companies. *British Journal of Management, 6,* 1–13. doi:10.1111/j.1467-8551.1995.tb00082.x

Grover, V., & Davenport, T. H. (2001). General perspectives on knowledge management: Fostering a research agenda. *Journal of Management Information Systems, 18*(1), 5–21.

Herschel, R. T., & Jones, N. E. (2005). Knowledge management and business intelligence: The importance of integration. *Journal of Knowledge Management, 9*(4), 45–55. doi:10.1108/13673270510610323

Huber, G. P. (1991). Organizational learning: The contributing processes and the literatures. *Organization Science, 2,* 88–115. doi:10.1287/orsc.2.1.88

Hung, Y. C., Huang, S. M., Lin, Q. P., & Tsai, M. L. (2005) Critical factors in adopting a knowledge management system for the pharmaceutical industry. *Industrial Management + Data Systems, 105*(1/2), 164-183.

Jagetia, L. C., & Patel, D. M. (1981). Developing an end-use intelligence system. *Industrial Marketing Management, 10*(2), 101–107. doi:10.1016/0019-8501(81)90003-1

Janz, B. D., & Prasarnphanich, P. (2003). Understanding the antecedents of effective knowledge management: The importance of a knowledge-centered culture. *Decision Sciences, 34*(2), 351–384. doi:10.1111/1540-5915.02328

Jaworski, B., & Kohli, A. (1993). Market orientation: Antecedents and consequences. *Journal of Marketing, 57,* 53–70. doi:10.2307/1251854

Jennex, M. E., & Adelakun, O. (2003). Success factors for offshore information system development. *Journal of Information Technology Cases and Applications, 5*(3), 12–31.

Jennex, M. E., Amoroso, D., & Adelakun, O. (2004). E-commerce infrastructure success factors for small companies in developing economies. *Electronic Commerce Research, 4*(3), 263–286. doi:10.1023/B:ELEC.0000027983.36409.d4

Jennex, M. E., & Olfman, L. (2005). Assessing knowledge management success. *International Journal of Knowledge Management, 1*(2), 33–49.

Jennex, M. E., & Olfman, L. (2006). A model of knowledge management success. *International Journal of Knowledge Management, 2*(3), 51–68.

Kim, S. S., & Malhotra, N. K. (2005). A longitudinal model of continued IS use: An integrative view of four mechanisms underlying post-adoption phenomena. *Management Science, 51*(5), 741–755. doi:10.1287/mnsc.1040.0326

Kohli, A., & Jaworski, B. (1990). Market orientation: The construct, research propositions, and managerial implications. *Journal of Marketing, 54,* 1–18. doi:10.2307/1251866

Kohli, A., Jaworski, B. K., & Kumar, A. (1993). MARKOR: A Measure of Market Orientation. *JMR, Journal of Marketing Research, 30*(4), 467–477. doi:10.2307/3172691

Kulkarni, U., Ravindran, S., & Freeze, R. (2006). A knowledge management success model: Theoretical development and empirical validation. *Journal of Management Information Systems, 23*(3), 309–347. doi:10.2753/MIS0742-1222230311

Lewis, B. R., Snyder, C. A., & Rainer, K. R. (1995). An empirical assessment of the information resource management construct. *Journal of Management Information Systems, 12*(1), 199–210.

Li, T., & Calantone, R. J. (1998). The impact of market knowledge competence on new product advantage: Conceptualization and empirical examination. *Journal of Marketing, 62*(4), 13–29. doi:10.2307/1252284

Li, T., & Cavusgil, S. T. (1999). Measuring the dimensions of market knowledge competence in new product development. *European Journal of Innovation Management, 2*(3), 129–146. doi:10.1108/14601069910289068

Liebowitz, J. (1999). Key ingredients to the success of an organization's knowledge management strategy. *Knowledge and Process Management, 6*(1), 37–40. doi:10.1002/(SICI)1099-1441(199903)6:1<37::AID-KPM40>3.0.CO;2-M

Lin, C., Chang, S., & Chang, C. S. (2004). The impact of technology absorptive capacity on technology transfer performance. *International Journal of Technology Transfer & Commercialisation, 3*(4), 384–409. doi:10.1504/IJTTC.2004.005610

Lin, C., Tan, B., & Chang, S. (2002). The critical factors for technology absorptive capacity. *Industrial Management + Data Systems, 102*(5/6), 300-308.

Lin, C., & Tseng, S. M. (2005). The implementation gaps for the knowledge management system. *Industrial Management + Data Systems, 105*(1/2), 208-222.

Lindsey, K. (2002). Measuring knowledge management effectiveness: A task-contingent organizational capabilities perspective. *Eighth Americas Conference on Information Systems*, 2085-2090.

Marinova, D. (2004). Actualizing innovation effort: The impact of market knowledge diffusion in a dynamic system of competition. *Journal of Marketing, 68*(3), 1–20. doi:10.1509/jmkg.68.3.1.34768

Massey, A. P., Montoya-Weiss, M. M., & O'Driscoll, T. M. (2002). Knowledge management in pursuit of performance: Insights from Nortel Networks. *Management Information Systems Quarterly, 26*(3), 269–289. doi:10.2307/4132333

Mata, F. J., Fuerst, W. L., & Barney, J. B. (1995). Information technology and sustained competitive advantage: A resource-based analysis. *Management Information Systems Quarterly, 19*(4), 487–505. doi:10.2307/249630

McFarlan, F. W. (1984). Information technology changes the way you compete. *Harvard Business Review, 62*(3), 98–103.

Mitra, D., & Golder, P. N. (2002). Whose culture matters? Near-market knowledge and its impact on foreign market entry timing. *JMR, Journal of Marketing Research, 39*(3), 350–365. doi:10.1509/jmkr.39.3.350.19112

Moorman, C. (1995). Organizational marketing information processes: Cultural antecedents and new product outcomes. *JMR, Journal of Marketing Research, 32*, 318–335. doi:10.2307/3151984

Morgan, R. E., & Turnell, C. R. (2003). Market-based organizational learning and market performance gains. *British Journal of Management, 14*, 255–274. doi:10.1111/1467-8551.00378

Moyer, M. S. (1972). Market intelligence for modern merchants. *California Management Review, 14*(4), 3–69.

Narver, J. C., & Slater, S. F. (1990). The effect of a market orientation on business profitability. *Journal of Marketing, 54,* 20–35. doi:10.2307/1251757

Nonaka, I. (1991). The knowledge-creating company. *Harvard Business Review, 69,* 96–104.

Nonaka, I. (1994). A dynamic theory of organizational knowledge creation. *Organization Science, 5*(1), 14–37. doi:10.1287/orsc.5.1.14

Nonaka, I., Reinmoeller, P., & Senoo, D. (1998). The 'ART' of knowledge: Systems to capitalize on market knowledge. *European Management Journal, 16*(6), 673–684. doi:10.1016/S0263-2373(98)00044-9

Nonaka, I., & Takeuchi, H. (1995). *The Knowledge-Creating Company.* New York: Oxford University Press.

Nunnally, J. C. (1978). *Psychometric Theory.* New York: McGraw-Hill.

Oltra, V. (2005). Knowledge management effectiveness factors: The role of HRM. *Journal of Knowledge Management, 9*(4), 70–86. doi:10.1108/13673270510610341

Orzano, A. J., Tallia, A. F., McInerney, C. R., McDaniel, R. R. Jr, & Crabtree, B. F. (2007). Strategies for developing a knowledge-driven culture in your practice. *Family Practice Management, 14*(4), 32–34.

Pavlou, P. A., & Fygenson, M. (2006). Understanding and predicting electronic commerce adoption: An extension of the theory of planned behavior. *Management Information Systems Quarterly, 30*(1), 115–143.

Plessis, M. D. (2007). Knowledge management: What makes complex implementations successful? *Journal of Knowledge Management, 11*(2), 91–101. doi:10.1108/13673270710738942

Porter, M. E., & Millar, V. E. (1985). How information gives you competitive advantage. *Harvard Business Review, 63*(4), 149–160.

Roberts, J. (2000). From know-how to show how? Questioning the role of information and communication technologies in knowledge transfer. *Technology Analysis and Strategic Management, 12,* 429–443. doi:10.1080/713698499

Rollins, M., & Halinen, A. (2005). Customer knowledge management competence: Towards a theoretical framework. In *Proceedings of the 38th Hawaii International Conference on System Sciences.* Washington, DC: IEEE. DOI: 0-7695-2268-8/05. Retrieved from www.hicss.hawaii.edu

Rowley, J. (2004). Partnering paradigms? Knowledge management and relationship marketing. *Industrial Management & Data Systems, 104*(2), 149–157. doi:10.1108/02635570410522125

Sinkula, J. M. (1994). Market information processing and organizational learning. *Journal of Marketing, 58,* 35–45. doi:10.2307/1252249

Sivaramakrishnan, S., Delbaere, M., & Bruning, E. (2004). The role of knowledge management in the market orientation–business performance linkage. *International Journal of Knowledge, Culture, and Change Management, 4,* 775–783.

Slater, S., & Narver, J. (1994). Does competitive environment moderate the market orientation-performance relationship? *Journal of Marketing, 58,* 46–55. doi:10.2307/1252250

Smith, H. A., & McKeen, J. D. (2005). Customer knowledge management: Adding value for our customers. *Communications of the Association for Information Systems, 16,* 744–755.

Srivastava, R. K., Shervani, T. A., & Fahey, L. (1998). Market-based assets and shareholder value: A framework for analysis. *Journal of Marketing, 62*, 2–18. doi:10.2307/1251799

Toften, K., & Olsen, S. O. (2003). Export market information use, organizational knowledge, and firm performance: A conceptual framework. *International Marketing Review, 20*(1), 95–110. doi:10.1108/02651330310462284

Trussler, S. (1998). The rules of the game. *The Journal of Business Strategy, 19*, 16–19. doi:10.1108/eb039904

Tsai, C. H., & Chen, H. Y. (2007). Assessing knowledge management system success: An empirical study in Taiwan's high-tech industry. *Journal of American Academy of Business, 10*(2), 257–262.

Tzokas, N., & Saren, M. (2004). Competitive advantage, knowledge and relationship marketing: where, what and how? *Journal of Business and Industrial Marketing, 19*(2), 125–135. doi:10.1108/08858620410524007

Wei, C. C., Choy, C. S., & Yeow, P. H. P. (2006). KM implementation in Malaysian telecommunication industry: An empirical analysis. *Industrial Management + Data Systems, 106*(8), 1112-1132.

Xu, M., & Walton, J. (2005). Gaining customer knowledge through analytical CRM. *Industrial Management & Data Systems, 105*(7), 955–971. doi:10.1108/02635570510616139

Zhu, K., Kraemer, K. L., Gurbaxani, V., & Xu, S. X. (2006). Migration to open-standard interorganizational systems: Network effects, switching costs and path dependency. *Management Information Systems Quarterly, 30*, 515–539.

APPENDIX: VARIABLES AND THEIR MEASUREMENT SCALES

Information Technology Adoption (α=0.87)

To what extent does your company use information technology (hardware and software) to:	*Not at All*		*Very Great Extent*		*Don't Have*
Store data	1 2 3	4	5 6 7		☐
Analyze data	1 2 3	4	5 6 7		☐
Communicate information	1 2 3	4	5 6 7		☐
To what extent does your management encourage the use of information technology (hardware and software) to:	*Not at All*		*Very Great Extent*		*Don't Have*
Store data	1 2 3	4	5 6 7		☐
Analyze data	1 2 3	4	5 6 7		☐
Communicate information	1 2 3	4	5 6 7		☐

Analytical Capability (r=0.65)

	Strongly Disagree		*Strongly Agree*		*Don't Know*
Our company does not have people with advanced data analysis skills to analyze *data/information*.	1 2 3	4 5	6 7		☐
Our company has people who analyze market *data/information* to make effective decisions.	1 2 3	4 5	6 7		☐

Market Orientation (α=0.86)

	Strongly Disagree		*Strongly Agree*		*Don't Know*
Our principal business goal is to satisfy the needs of our customers.	1 2 3	4 5	6 7		☐
We use customers as an important source of service ideas.	1 2 3	4 5	6 7		☐
We constantly monitor our level of commitment to our customers.	1 2 3	4 5	6 7		☐
Our strategy for competitive advantage is based on our understanding of our customers' needs.	1 2 3	4 5	6 7		☐
We do not measure customer satisfaction systematically.	1 2 3	4 5	6 7		☐
We regularly share information within our company concerning competitor strategies.	1 2 3	4 5	6 7		☐
We respond rapidly to competitive actions that threaten us.	1 2 3	4 5	6 7		☐
Our company regularly scans competitors' strengths and weaknesses.	1 2 3	4 5	6 7		☐

Market Knowledge Management (α=0.85)

	Strongly Disagree		*Strongly Agree*	*Don't Know*
Our company converts data/information about our markets to useful *knowledge*.	1 2 3 4 5 6 7			❏
Our company converts data/information about our suppliers to useful knowledge.	1 2 3 4 5 6 7			❏
Our company absorbs knowledge from individuals into the company.	1 2 3 4 5 6 7			❏
Our company does not distribute acquired knowledge throughout the company.	1 2 3 4 5 6 7			❏
Our company makes knowledge accessible to those employees who need it.	1 2 3 4 5 6 7			❏
Our company converts knowledge into action (decisions).	1 2 3 4 5 6 7			❏
Our company does not match sources of knowledge to problems and challenges we face.	1 2 3 4 5 6 7			❏

Customer Satisfaction & Loyalty (α=0.87)

	Strongly Disagree		*Strongly Agree*	*Don't Know*
Our customers are satisfied with their relationship with our firm.	1 2 3 4 5 6 7			❏
Our customers are not satisfied with the products our company offers them.	1 2 3 4 5 6 7			❏
Our customers are satisfied with the service our company provides them.	1 2 3 4 5 6 7			❏
Our customers would repeat their purchases with our firm rather than a competitor.	1 2 3 4 5 6 7			❏
Our customers would not recommend our company to others.	1 2 3 4 5 6 7			❏
Our customers rely on us as their supplier.	1 2 3 4 5 6 7			❏

Financial Performance (α=0.80)

	Very Much Below	*Same*	*Very Much Above*	*Don't Know*
What has your company's overall sales revenue been over the last 3 years relative to major competitors?	1 2 3 4 5 6 7			❏
What has your company's overall Return on Investment (ROI) been over the last 3 years relative to major competitors?	1 2 3 4 5 6 7			❏
What has your company's overall Return on Assets (ROA) been over the last 3 years relative to major competitors?	1 2 3 4 5 6 7			❏

This work was previously published in International Journal of Knowledge Management, Volume 6, Issue 3, edited by Murray E. Jennex, pp. 1-21, copyright 2010 by IGI Publishing (an imprint of IGI Global).

Chapter 10
Linking Business Strategy and Knowledge Management Capabilities for Organizational Effectiveness

Trevor A. Smith
University of the West Indies, Jamaica

Annette M. Mills
University of Canterbury, New Zealand

Paul Dion
Susquehanna University, USA

ABSTRACT

The effective management of knowledge resources is a key imperative for firms that want to leverage their knowledge assets for competitive advantage and improved performance. However, most firms do not attain the required performance levels even when programs are in place for managing knowledge resources. Research suggests this shortcoming can be addressed by linking knowledge management to business strategy. This study examines a model that links business strategy to knowledge management capabilities and organizational effectiveness. Using data collected from 189 managers, the results suggest that business strategy is a key driver of knowledge capabilities, and that both business strategy and knowledge capabilities impact organizational effectiveness. Additionally, the authors' findings indicate that knowledge infrastructure capability is a key imperative for effective knowledge process capability. Managerial implications, limitations and opportunities for future research are also discussed.

INTRODUCTION

It is well-recognized that effective knowledge management leads to improvements in business performance. Knowledge management has therefore assumed a great sense of importance

and urgency as firms come to recognize the potential for competitive advantage that the firms' knowledge assets possess. Despite the value that knowledge management projects are expected to accrue to businesses, as many as 84% of knowledge management projects do not have a significant effect on the organizations that invest in these

DOI: 10.4018/978-1-4666-0035-5.ch010

initiatives (Lucier & Torsilieri, 1997). Even if the projects are well-resourced and appear to have the support of top management, researchers suggest that many are still predisposed to failure (Storey & Barnett, 2000).

Notwithstanding these negative prospects, executives still believe that knowledge management systems are a key source of competitive advantage and business success (Bohn, 1994; Broadbent, 1998; Clarke, 2001; Felton, 2002; Grover & Davenport, 2001; Lucier & Torsilieri, 1997). This is further substantiated by Gold, Malhotra and Segars (2001) in a survey of senior executives which found that having appropriate knowledge infrastructure and process capabilities within the firm improves organizational effectiveness.

Researchers also argue that additional improvements in firm performance can be attained by linking knowledge management initiatives to the firm's business strategy (Clarke, 2001; Maier & Remus, 2002; Zack, 1999). Indeed, Clarke (2001) argues that knowledge programs are unlikely to succeed unless they are closely linked to the business strategy. Thus, it can be argued that business strategy is not only a key factor impacting firm performance; it is also indispensable when it comes to maximizing the return on technology investments. Although researchers have discussed the importance of linking business strategy to knowledge management (Clarke, 2001; Maier & Remus, 2002), there has been little research examining the link between business strategy and knowledge management (Maier & Remus, 2002). For example, while many studies have shown that knowledge management capabilities significantly impact firm performance (Gold et al., 2001), the role of business strategy vis-à-vis a firm's knowledge management capabilities has not been evaluated.

Drawing on prior research that suggests knowledge management should be linked to business strategy (Clarke, 2001; Lang, 2001; Maier & Remus, 2002; Zack, 1999), and that knowledge infrastructure capability and knowledge process

capability are additive and collectively determine the knowledge management construct (Grant, 1996; Gold et al., 2001; Kelly & Amburgey, 1991; Law, Wong, & Mobley, 1998), this study examines the role of business strategy as this relates to knowledge management and organizational effectiveness. More specifically, this study addresses a gap in the literature by investigating a modified version of the Gold et al. (2001) model of knowledge management capabilities, that incorporates business strategy as an antecedent of knowledge management capabilities and organizational effectiveness.

The knowledge management capabilities framework (Gold et al., 2001) offers a useful context to examine the role of business strategy. The Gold et al. (2001) model brings together two widely recognized dimensions of knowledge management in organizations – the process perspective which focuses on a set of activities (or knowledge management process capabilities) related to knowledge acquisition, knowledge conversion, knowledge application and knowledge protection; and the infrastructure perspective which focuses technology, organizational structure, organizational culture. Researchers in both streams suggest these activities and structures as necessary preconditions for effective knowledge management capabilities (Alavi & Leidner, 2001; Davenport, Delong, & Beers, 1998), and these are in turn posited as key antecedents of organizational effectiveness (Gold et al., 2001; Stein & Zwass, 1995).

A review of the prior research also shows that few have examined the relationship between knowledge capabilities, more specifically knowledge infrastructure and knowledge process capabilities, and at best, the results have been mixed. For example, while some suggest that knowledge infrastructure underpins knowledge process (Lee & Choi, 2003) others suggest that knowledge process is an antecedent of knowledge infrastructure (Paisittanand, Digman, & Lee, 2007). Hence, the relative roles of knowledge infrastructure and knowledge process capabilities are not well understood. To address this gap, this study will also assess the role of knowledge infrastructure capability as an antecedent to knowledge process capability, in combination with business strategy with a view to clarifying the role and relative importance of infrastructural considerations vis-à-vis knowledge process capability.

The findings of this study are expected to contribute to research and practice, by elaborating the relationships among business strategy, knowledge management capabilities, and firm performance. Researchers can also use the modified framework to examine other factors linked to knowledge management and firm performance, such as knowledge quality, organizational learning, and user satisfaction (Jennex & Olfman, 2005, 2006). Practitioners, on the other hand, can benefit from the insights into the link between a firm's knowledge management capabilities and the strategic posture required for advancing key performance variables such as competitive advantage.

LITERATURE REVIEW

The management literature is replete with references to knowledge as an important source of competitive advantage and, consequently, a key ingredient to business successes (Bohn, 1994; Broadbent, 1998; Clarke, 2001; Felton, 2002; Grover & Davenport, 2001; Lucier & Torsilieri, 1997). In spite of this insight, the business impact of most knowledge management programs is moderate at best. For example, it is estimated that one-sixth of these knowledge management programs achieve significant business impact within the first two years, one-half achieve small but important benefits and the remaining one-third are failures with little impact (Lucier & Torsilieri, 1997). Storey and Barnett (2000) also argue that knowledge management programs are predisposed to failure even when they are reasonably well resourced and appear to have the support of top management.

Despite the negative performances on knowledge management programs, Ruggles (1998) submitted that 94% of executives believe "it would be possible, through more deliberate management, to leverage the knowledge existing in [his or her] organization to a higher degree" (p. 81). Gold et al. (2001) supported this claim and found that the appropriate knowledge infrastructure capability and knowledge process capability within the firm will improve organizational effectiveness. Researchers have also argued that further improvement in the firm's performance could be attained by linking knowledge management initiatives to the business strategy (Clarke, 2001; Maier & Remus, 2002; Zack, 1999).

According to these observations there is a strong theoretical tie between a firm's knowledge capabilities (i.e., knowledge process capability and knowledge infrastructure capability), business strategy and organizational effectiveness. The following sections will therefore examine the nature of these capabilities, and develop the theoretical foundation that underpins the links between business strategy, knowledge capability and organizational effectiveness.

Theoretical Foundation

Knowledge management activities are theoretically grounded in the theories of the firm, with particular emphasis on the social capital theory, the knowledge-based view of the firm and the resource-based view of the firm (Gold, Malhotra, & Segars, 2001).

Nahapiet and Ghoshal (1998) defined social capital as "the sum of actual and potential resources embedded within, available through, and derived from the network of relationships possessed by the individual or social unit" (p. 243). They stated that social capital theory offers a valuable perspective for understanding and explaining intellectual capital, where the term *intellectual capital* refers to the knowledge and knowledge capability of the social collectivity.

The knowledge-based view also offers insight into the strategic and managerial issues which drive inter-firm collaboration (Grant & Baden-Fuller, 1995). Developing a knowledge-based theory of the firm not only requires an understanding of the propositions relating to the firm, but also an understanding of the term *knowledge* as "there are many types of knowledge relevant to the firm" (Grant, 1996, p. 110). Grant also argued that different types of specialist knowledge possessed by individuals within the firm are ultimately coordinated in the production process.

The resource-based theory seeks to explain and predict sustainable competitive advantage and performance of the firm. In addition, it suggests that the firm is a unique bundle of individual capabilities and resources and that the primary role of management is "to maximize value through the optimal deployment of existing resources and capabilities, while developing the firm's resource base for the future" (Grant, 1996, p. 110). Similar to Grant (1996), Nonaka and Takeuchi (1995) concluded that the resource-based view sees competencies, capabilities, skills, or strategic assets as the source of sustainable competitive advantage within the firm.

In the context of knowledge management, it has long been recognised that firms need to develop appropriate capabilities to manage their knowledge resource. Where knowledge possesses characteristics such as valuable, rare, inimitable and non-substitutability (Grant, 1996) it is an asset that has potential for competitive advantage. A firm's knowledge management capabilities may therefore have potential to contribute directly to firm performance or indirectly through its effect on other resources or outcomes linked to firm performance (Gold et al., 2001; Stein & Zwass, 1995; Wade & Hulland, 2004).

Taken altogether these theoretical perspectives suggest that knowledge management resources when leveraged appropriately can enhance organizational effectiveness. Researchers also suggest that additional benefits may accrue if knowledge management initiatives are linked to the firm's business strategy (Clarke, 2001; Maier & Remus, 2002). This link between knowledge and strategy is supported by research which suggests that "the most important context for guiding knowledge management is the firm's strategy" (Zack, 1999, p. 125). This study therefore investigates the relationship between business strategy, knowledge management capabilities and organizational effectiveness. More specifically, this study aims to address the question: What is the relationship between business strategy, knowledge management capabilities, and organizational effectiveness?

While there has been much speculation concerning the importance of business strategy for ensuring the success of knowledge management initiatives in businesses, there has been little empirical assessment of the role of business strategy in relation to knowledge management capabilities and organizational performance. To address the research aim, this study investigates a research model that is adapted from Gold et al.'s (2001) model of knowledge management capabilities which theorizes the link between knowledge management capabilities and organizational effectiveness. In the adapted model, business strategy is incorporated as an antecedent of knowledge management capabilities and organizational effectiveness.

The Gold et al., (2001) model provides a useful starting point for the current research, as it brings together many of the key aspects of knowledge management capabilities identified in the literature (e.g., Alavi & Leidner, 2001; Stein & Zwass, 1995; Lee & Choi, 2003). The resultant framework consists of two broad types of knowledge management capabilities (i.e., knowledge infrastructure capability and knowledge process capability). The Gold et al. model has been successfully used by many researchers to assess the links between knowledge management capabilities, and outcome variables such as organizational performance, knowledge management success, knowledge transfer success and strategy implementation (Chan & Chao, 2008;

Jennex & Olfman, 2005; Laframboise, Croteau, Beaudry, & Manovas, 2007; Paisittanand, Digman, & Lee, 2007). The next section looks more closely at these capabilities, and their impact on organizational performance.

Knowledge Management Capabilities

Grant (1991) posited that a capability or competence is an integrated, linked and networked set of resources. Following on this, Grant (1996) stated that organizational capabilities are outcomes of knowledge integration and that organizational capability analysis offers insight into the linkage between capabilities and competitive advantage. Grant also noted that "the extent to which a capability is 'distinctive' depends upon the firm accessing and integrating the specialized knowledge of its employees" (Grant, 1996, pp. 116-117).

Knowledge management capabilities can be categorized into two broad types - knowledge process capability and knowledge infrastructure capability (Gold et al., 2001). Collectively, these capabilities represent the firm's ability to establish internal structures and processes to create organizational competencies (Ulrich & Wiersema, 1989).

Knowledge management supports the integration of resources into organizational capabilities (Maier & Remus, 2002). Drawing on the organizational behavior literature on the additive property of *capability* and *resources* (Kelly & Amburgey, 1991; Law, Wong, & Mobley, 1998), Gold et al. (2001) suggests that knowledge infrastructure capability and knowledge process capability are combination of additive sum of their various factors and not higher-level abstractions of their underlying dimensions.

Knowledge Infrastructure Capability

Knowledge infrastructure capability refers to modular products and organizational designs which enable knowledge management activities in an organization (Sanchez & Mahoney, 1996).

Referred to also as knowledge enablers, these support elements typically include organizational culture, organizational structure, and information technology (Davenport et al., 1998; Gold et al. 2001; Lee & Choi, 2003). For example, Davenport et al. (1998) studied 31 knowledge management projects in 24 firms and concluded that knowledge projects are more likely to succeed in those firms with effective technical and organizational infrastructure. Gold et al. (2001) also concluded that *technology*, *organizational culture* and *organizational structure* are the key building blocks of knowledge infrastructure capability.

In the rolling out of knowledge management efforts, organizations generally "start with the implementation of a technological capability, which allows them [at least in principle] to capture and share corporate know-how" (Ruggles, 1998, p. 87). In this study the technology infrastructure will include the IT required for an organization to allow a firm to carry out its knowledge management activities.

Organizational culture can be a key inhibitor to effective knowledge sharing. Indeed, it is argued that cultural obstacles to sharing knowledge "have more to do with how you design and implement your knowledge management effort than with changing your culture" (McDermott & O'Dell, 2001, p. 84). Turban and Aronson (2001) added that "the ability of an organization to learn, develop memory, and share knowledge is dependent on its culture" (p. 355). Thus, culture is a key component of a firm's knowledge infrastructure capability and an important imperative for successful knowledge management.

Finally, in respect of organizational structure, Beveren (2003) stated that many knowledge management authors have suggested that "organizations need to change from hierarchical departmentalized structures to flatter networked forms in order to transfer and create knowledge for the firm" (p. 91). It is therefore expected that successful organizations will be characterized by simplicity and flexibility of organizational design.

Knowledge Process Capability

Knowledge process capability represents the organization's ability to create new knowledge through the process of converting tacit knowledge into explicit knowledge and eventually transforming it to organizational knowledge (Nonaka & Takeuchi, 1995); this new knowledge stems from a firm's combinative processes (Kogut & Zander, 1992). Process capabilities and competencies are also the key leverage points to business success and should be "the primary focus for improvements that will actualize a business strategy" (Cascella, 2002, p. 63).

When it comes to conceptualizing knowledge process capability, there is general agreement that process capability is multifaceted, and that various practices (or activities) make up the knowledge process capability (Alavi & Leidner, 2001; Stein & Zwass, 1995; Zack, 1999). As such, when examining knowledge processes, different combinations of practices have been addressed in the literature. For example, Alavi and Leidner (2001) identified creation, storage/retrieval, transfer and application as key aspects of the knowledge management process; Stein and Zwass (1995) identified the acquisition, retention, maintenance, search and retrieval as fundamental for knowledge management; and Zack (1999) referred to acquisition, refinement, storage, retrieval and distribution. Sifting through the different activities (and terms used) identified in the knowledge management process literature, Gold et al. (2001) concluded that these could be grouped into four broad dimensions of process capability, namely knowledge acquisition, knowledge conversion, knowledge application and knowledge protection. Consistent with the prior research, this study will incorporate these four processes (i.e. acquisition, creation, application and protection) as conceptualized by Gold at al. (2001) into the research model.

The first consideration is to acquire knowledge aimed at managing and controlling the interest of stakeholders and to influence the participation of these stakeholders in the knowledge management

process (Lee & Suh, 2003). Lee and Suh (2003) added that knowledge is not only to be acquired and shared, but something to be converted for use in the business environment.

In a knowledge management environment, knowledge is typically extracted from individuals who originally created the knowledge. The knowledge is made independent of the original creator, and then used/applied in various ways (Mathiassen & Pourkomeylian, 2003). Bhatt (2001) stated that "knowledge application means making knowledge more active and relevant for the firm in creating value" (pp. 72-73); and that knowledge within an organization needs to be applied to a company's products, processes and services.

Protection of knowledge from illegal and inappropriate use is also essential for a firm to establish and maintain a competitive advantage (Porter-Liebskind, 1996). In explaining the inherent difficulties in knowledge protection, Porter-Liebskind noted that property laws are deficient in their definition of *knowledge*. Deficiencies in property legislation are also brought into sharp focus by Everard (2001) who submitted that copyright laws, for example, are limited in their treatment of resources in the online world and that legal jurisdictions are not fully established in the environment of the Internet. Gold et al. (2001) cautioned that despite the difficulties in the knowledge protection process, the protection of knowledge should not be abandoned or marginalized.

In summary, for this study, knowledge management capabilities will be conceptualized in terms of two dimensions and their respective factors, namely knowledge process capability (consisting of knowledge acquisition, knowledge conversion, knowledge application and knowledge protection) and knowledge infrastructure capability (consisting of *technology, organizational culture* and *organizational structure*). The next section will now examine the theoretical links between these dimensions and business strategy, an organizational effectiveness.

RESEARCH MODEL AND HYPOTHESES

Knowledge Management Capabilities and Business Strategy

The importance of aligning a firm's business strategy with their information technology has been well-documented (Henderson & Venkatraman, 1993; Sabherwal & Chan, 2001). Likewise, when it comes to the role of knowledge management, it is believed that the successful deployment of knowledge management resources is linked to alignment with business strategy (Clarke, 2001; Maier & Remus, 2002; Zack, 1999). For example, Lam and Chua (2005) in a study of five failed knowledge management projects found that a key cause of failure was lack of alignment between the knowledge management initiative and organizational strategy.

Maier and Remus (2002) argue that the highest benefits incurred by organizations from the knowledge – strategy link are in the areas of improved customer satisfaction and improved speed of innovation. In a review of empirical studies that investigate knowledge management initiatives in organizations, Maier and Remus found that some researchers consider knowledge management as a type of business strategy that firms adopt in order to gain competitive advantage, while others treated knowledge management initiatives as a separate business strategy, in parallel with other strategies. Still others identify business strategy as a separate factor impacting the success of knowledge management initiatives (Maier & Remus, 2002; Zack, 1999).

For example, Zack (1999) found that the most important context for guiding knowledge management is the firm's strategy. The organization's strategic context is therefore seen as a vehicle for identifying knowledge management initiatives that support its purpose or mission, strengthen its competitive position, and create stakeholder value. Zack also argued that every strategic position is linked to a set of intellectual resources and capabilities and that whatever the firm believes it must do to compete (i.e., employment of its strategies), there is a corresponding set of things that it must know and know how to do (i.e., management of knowledge). Hence, this study proposes that:

H1: Business strategy is positively related to knowledge infrastructure capability.

H2: Business strategy is positively related to knowledge process capability.

Business Strategy and Organizational Effectiveness

The finding that business strategy influences firm performance has been repeated so often in the management and IS literature that it is commonly accepted that business strategy influences organizational performance (Bergeron, Raymond, & Rivard, 2004). For example, Afiouni (2007) found that organizational effectiveness and value will result when strategies that exploit organizational resources and capabilities are employed. In an empirical assessment of manufacturing firms, Lo and Wang (2007) also concluded that managers should analyze the industrial environment more closely to ensure that the business strategy employed will improve organizational performance. Hence, it is expected that:

H3: Business strategy is positively related to organizational effectiveness

Knowledge Management and Organizational Effectiveness

Unlike financial ratios which are easily defined, organizational effectiveness is not well defined and is therefore complex in terms of description and dimension (Chakravarthy, 1987). Gold et al. (2001) therefore utilized both practitioners' statements and the general literature to operationalize this nebulous concept. They noted that organizational effectiveness includes activities such as improved ability to innovate, improved coordination of efforts, and rapid commercialization of new products; and that external factors (e.g., overall economic growth, industry growth and profitability, level and intensity of competition, consumer preferences) as well as factors internal to the firm (e.g., cost structure, revenue, firm size, efficiency) can contribute to overall effectiveness. Their study provided strong empirical support for the link between knowledge management capabilities and organizational effectiveness.

Other studies also confirm the knowledge management – organizational effectiveness link. For example, Gosh and Scott (2007) argued that knowledge infrastructural capabilities related to culture, structure and technology should be considered along with knowledge process capabilities (such as actual flow and use of knowledge) for improvements in effectiveness. Ho (2008) also demonstrated a positive relationship between knowledge management capabilities and innovation. Lee and Choi (2003) also found that knowledge creation is positively related to organizational creativity, and concluded that firms could achieve significant benefits through effective knowledge creation.

The management literature also associates knowledge management capabilities with organizational effectiveness (Davenport & Prusak, 1998; Nonaka & Takeuchi, 1995). For example, in a survey of over 200 manufacturing firms, empirical support was found for the proposition that knowledge capabilities have a positive impact on the financial performance of firms (Germain, Droge, & Christensen, 2001). Liu, Chen, and Tsai (2005) also suggested that knowledge management capabilities positively influence new product strategy. Thus, it is suggested that:

H4: Knowledge infrastructure capability is positively related to organizational effectiveness.

H5: Knowledge process capability is positively related to organizational effectiveness.

Knowledge Process Capability and Knowledge Infrastructure Capability

Although researchers have examined the links between knowledge infrastructure capability, knowledge process capability and organizational performance (Gold et al., 2001; Jennex & Olfman, 2005), it is not yet apparent how knowledge infrastructure capability might relate to knowledge process capability. For example, some studies suggest that knowledge infrastructure capability might mediate the link between knowledge process capability and organizational performance (Paisittanand, Digman, & Lee, 2007), yet others suggest knowledge infrastructure capability is a precondition for knowledge process capability (Lee & Choi, 2003). As such, the role of knowledge infrastructure capability as an enabler of knowledge process capability is yet to be clarified.

A dominant theme that emerges from the literature suggests that knowledge management infrastructure is an important precondition for knowledge management processes (Gosh & Scott, 2007; Lee & Choi, 2003), and can thus be viewed as a key antecedent of the knowledge process. For example, research suggests that infrastructural factors such as culture, structure and appropriate technology are key imperatives for successful knowledge management (Davenport et al., 1998), and are likely to play a significant role in supporting and advancing knowledge management processes and activities. While Gosh and Scott (2007) concur that knowledge infrastructural capability should be considered along with knowledge process capability for improvements in effectiveness, they also suggest that infrastructural dimensions such as culture and structure will play a significant role in advancing process capabilities (such as an individual's ability to create and share knowledge). Goh (2002) also found that an organizational culture that emphasizes collaboration and problem

Figure 1. Research model

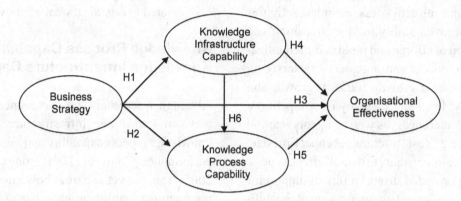

seeking and solving are important conditions for knowledge management processes such as knowledge transfer to take place. In an empirical study of knowledge creation processes, Lee and Choi (2003) found that knowledge enablers had a significant impact on knowledge creation.

It can therefore be argued that firms need to have appropriate structures and technologies as well as a supportive culture for various knowledge management processes (such as, creation, storage/retrieval, transfer and application) to be executed successfully. Hence it is expected that:

H6: Knowledge infrastructure capabilities are positively related to knowledge process capabilities.

In summary, a consensus exists in the literature that for knowledge management initiatives to be highly successful, they should be linked to the business strategy, and to measures of organizational effectiveness such as economic value and competitive advantage for these initiatives to be a sustained effort (Lam & Chua, 2005; Maier & Remus, 2002). This study therefore examines the role of business strategy in relation to knowledge management capabilities and organizational effectiveness; the link between knowledge infrastructure capability and knowledge process capability

is also explored. The associated hypotheses are summarized in the research model in Figure 1.

METHODOLOGY

Sample

To assess the research model, data was collected by surveying students enrolled in a number of MBA, EMBA and M.Sc. (business elective) programs offered in Jamaica. The facilitators of these programs were contacted and permission sought to administer the survey among the targeted participants. The individual's willingness to participate, current employment by a private organization, and sufficient insight into the organization were key criteria for inclusion (Germain, Droge, & Christensen, 2001). Although respondents could come from anywhere in the organization, similar to Gold et al. (2001), it was determined that the ideal participant should hold a management position in the firm as they are likely to be more cognizant than others, of the firm's business strategy, organizational structure and other knowledge infrastructural and process capabilities.

Approximately 500 surveys were distributed and 265 responses (53%) were returned. Of these, 189 responses (71%) were received from persons in management positions and the remainder (76 responses) from persons in non-management positions (e.g., technical or support staff). An analysis of the responses using t-tests showed significant differences between the responses from management and non-management staff in respect of knowledge management capabilities and business strategy. Given that managers (in comparison with non-management staff) are often more aware of the broader practices, policies and processes in their organization, and consistent with prior research (Gold et al., 2001), the 76 responses from non-management staff were excluded from the data analysis.

Of the 189 responses from management personnel, 86.8%, (n=164) represented the service sector, while the remaining 13.2% (n=25) were from manufacturing. 80.4% of the firms employed 100 persons or more; only 6.3% (12) of the firms were considered very small with 10 or fewer employees.

Instrument

A multi-section survey instrument was used to collect demographic information and to measure knowledge management capabilities, business strategy and organizational effectiveness. In support of surveys, Dillman (2000) argues that the survey is the preferred option among the field methods as it is efficient (in terms of speed and cost) and offers the potential of reaching a large sample of the target population.

Consistent with prior research, the survey instrument was pilot tested with over 40 respondents; the minimum internal reliability of .707 (Chin, 1998) was exceeded for each subscale. No changes were made to the survey instrument, thus the pilot participants were included in the final dataset as they were a part of the target population (Lewis, Agarwal, & Sambamurthy, 2003).

Measures

The measurement model consisted of four main constructs: knowledge infrastructure capability, knowledge process capability, organizational effectiveness and business strategy. Knowledge infrastructure capability and knowledge process capability was operationalized using existing scales and the constructs modeled as second-order latent variables (Gold et al., 2001; Laframboise et al., 2007). Knowledge infrastructure capability comprised of three first-order variables namely, technology, organizational structure, and organizational culture; and knowledge process capability comprised of four first-order variables, namely knowledge acquisition, knowledge conversion, knowledge application, and knowledge protection. Organizational effectiveness was also modeled as a latent variable and measured using six items taken from an existing scale (Gold et al., 2001). The fourth construct - business strategy - consisted of five items and was developed based on the prior literature (Bryson & Alston, 1996). Items included: "My organization examines the environment in which it exists and operates"; "My organization explores the factors and trends that effect the way it does business and carry out its roles". Finally, all four constructs were assessed using 7-point Likert-type scales, anchored with 'Strongly Agree' and 'Strongly Disagree' as the end-points.

DATA ANALYSIS AND RESULTS

Structural equation modeling (SEM) using Partial Least Squares (with PLS-Graph 3.0 Build 1130) and SPSS version 17.0 were used for model testing. PLS-graph was used to assess the measurement model and the theorized relationships between knowledge management capabilities, business strategy and organizational effectiveness. The bootstrapping re-sampling method (using PLS-Graph and 200 samples) was used to test the significance of the paths. These methods are widely used in IS research and have been used to assess similar research models (Laframboise et al., 2007); thus it was considered appropriate to use the Partial Least Squares approach to assess the research model in this study.

Structural equation modeling assessment in PLS-Graph includes assessment of the measurement model and of the structural model. In this study, business strategy and organizational effectiveness are assessed as first-order factors, and knowledge infrastructure capabilities and knowledge process capabilities assessed as second-order factors.

To assess construct reliability, factor loadings and composite reliabilities were examined. First, the measurement models for all first-order constructs were assessed (Table 1). Ideally, item loadings should exceed 0.707; loadings of 0.60 can also be accepted if there are additional indicators for comparison (Chin, 1998); however, items that load below 0.50 should be reconsidered. One item (AQ2) returned a loading of 0.400, and was therefore dropped from the measurement model. Of the remaining items, TC5 and ST6 returned loadings below 0.707 but above 0.60, hence these items were retained. Composite reliabilities were well above the recommended threshold of 0.70, exceeding 0.90 and (Fornell & Bookstein, 1982).

To assess convergent validity, the average variance extracted (AVE) was examined. The results showed the AVEs exceeded 0.60 so this criterion was met for knowledge infrastructure and knowledge process capabilities (Fornell & Larcker, 1981). The AVE for each construct was also higher than the variance shared between the constructs satisfying the criterion for discriminant validity (Chin, 1998).

Discriminant validity can also be established by examining item loadings and cross-loadings for each construct (Table 3). The results (Tables 2 and 3), show this criterion was satisfied for each variable, as each item loaded more on its associated construct than on other constructs in the model.

Following the assessment of the first-order constructs, the latent variable scores were extracted and used to create second-order constructs for knowledge infrastructure and knowledge process capabilities. The final measurement model was then assessed. The results (Table 4) show that the factor loadings exceeded the recommended threshold of 0.707; composite reliabilities were also well above the cut-off of 0.70, and convergent validity satisfactory with the AVEs for all constructs exceeding 0.70 (Fornell & Bookstein, 1982; Fornell & Larcker, 1981).

For discriminant validity, the results (Table 5) showed that the AVE for business strategy and organizational effectiveness as before, exceeded the shared variance suggesting items loaded more on their own construct than others in the substantive model (Chin, 1998). However, this criterion was not satisfied for knowledge infrastructure capability and knowledge process capability, using this test. Loadings and cross-loadings were then compared for knowledge infrastructure capability and knowledge process capability. The results (Table 6) showed that technology, culture and structure components were loaded marginally more on knowledge infrastructure capability than on knowledge process capability; likewise, acquisition, conversion, application and protection were loaded marginally more on knowledge process capability than on knowledge infrastructure capability. Taken altogether, the results suggest that while the respondents could distinguish sufficiently between the constructs at the component level (see Tables 2 and 3) this distinction was less clear at the higher-order level (Tables 5 and 6).

Next, PLS-Graph was used to assess the paths in the structural model and the results examined. As shown in Figure 2, the results indicate a positive relationship between business strategy and knowledge infrastructure capability (β=0.749; p$\leq$0.001) and knowledge process capability (β=0.284; p$\leq$0.001). Hypotheses H1 and H2 were therefore supported. The results also confirmed the relationship between knowledge infrastructure

Table 1. Item loadings, composite reliabilities and average variance extracted for first-order constructs

Latent Constructs (No of Items)	Item Loadings	Composite Reliability (CR) / Average Variance Extracted (AVE)	Latent Constructs (No of Items)	Item Loadings	Composite Reliability (CR) / Average Variance Extracted (AVE)
Knowledge Infrastructure Capability			**Knowledge Process Capability**		
Technology (TC)			Acquisition (AQ)		
TC5	0.702	CR = 0.921	AQ1	0.823	CR = 0.923
TC6	0.923	AVE = 0.747	AQ3	0.807	AVE = 0.707
TC7	0.917		AQ5	0.863	
TC9	0.897		AQ8	0.856	
			AQ12	0.855	
Culture (CU)			Application (AP)		
CU1	0.774	CR = 0.918	AP3	0.849	CR = 0.963
CU2	0.757	AVE = 0.651	AP4	0.923	AVE = 0.789
CU4	0.802		AP5	0.894	
CU9	0.850		AP6	0.896	
CU10	0.853		AP7	0.903	
CU13	0.798		AP8	0.906	
			AP10	0.843	
Structure (ST)			Protection (PT)		
ST3	0.811	CR = 0.924	PR1	0.894	CR = 0.948
ST4	0.855	AVE = 0.635	PR2	0.874	AVE = 0.724
ST5	0.779		PR3	0.886	
ST6	0.669		PR4	0.851	
ST7	0.851		PR7	0.861	
ST10	0.728		PR8	0.757	
ST11	0.865		PR10	0.828	
			Conversion (CN)		
Business Strategy			CN3	0.834	CR = 0.950
BS1	0.858	CR = 0.951	CN4	0.881	AVE = 0.759
BS2	0.918	AVE = 0.795	CN5	0.850	
BS3	0.842		CN8	0.884	
BS4	0.937		CN9	0.906	
BS5	0.898		CN10	0.871	
Organizational Effectiveness					
OE1	0.780	CR = 0.951			
OE2	0.897	AVE = 0.763			
OE3	0.897				
OE4	0.906				
OE5	0.866				
OE6	0.890				

Table 2. Inter-construct correlations and discriminant validity (for first-order constructs)

	ST	CU	TC	AQ	CN	AP	PT	BS	OE
Knowledge Infrastructure Capabilities									
Structure (ST)	0.797								
Culture (CU)	0.744	0.807							
Technology (TC)	0.560	0.483	0.864						
Knowledge Process Capabilities									
Acquisition (AQ)	0.640	0.668	0.565	0.841					
Conversion (CN)	0.721	0.748	0.637	0.735	0.871				
Application (AP)	0.715	0.753	0.604	0.724	0.813	0.888			
Protection (PT)	0.596	0.593	0.599	0.588	0.643	0.643	0.851		
Business Strategy (BS)	0.659	0.718	0.532	0.669	0.714	0.774	0.559	0.873	
Organizational Effectiveness (OE)	0.742	0.722	0.575	0.718	0.752	0.822	0.671	0.822	0.892

Note: Shaded items represent the square-root of the variance shared between the constructs and their measures; the off-diagonal elements are the correlations among the constructs.

Table 3. Item loadings and shared-loadings for first-order constructs

	ST	CU	TC	AQ	CN	AP	PR	OE	BS
ST3	.811	.581	.357	.490	.550	.563	.455	.596	.547
ST4	.855	.587	.462	.544	.593	.574	.526	.624	.531
ST5	.779	.559	.406	.435	.483	.569	.442	.554	.438
ST6	.669	.539	.396	.409	.536	.465	.425	.481	.429
ST7	.851	.652	.550	.546	.605	.593	.485	.623	.608
ST10	.727	.506	.353	.462	.542	.532	.475	.572	.403
ST11	.865	.700	.560	.643	.691	.670	.513	.670	.663
CU1	.606	.774	.343	.464	.560	.556	.417	.516	.486
CU2	.620	.757	.342	.468	.591	.593	.435	.585	.469
CU4	.607	.802	.305	.465	.581	.576	.480	.545	.531
CU9	.571	.850	.457	.581	.632	.627	.535	.590	.644
CU10	.566	.853	.469	.604	.627	.639	.508	.603	.669
CU13	.642	.798	.398	.616	.621	.645	.483	.642	.639
TC5	.419	.310	.701	.406	.471	.440	.326	.364	.384
TC6	.506	.449	.923	.491	.578	.533	.575	.527	.453
TC7	.532	.446	.917	.523	.556	.537	.575	.543	.501
TC9	.474	.449	.896	.522	.591	.571	.559	.531	.491
AQ1	.430	.470	.465	.822	.509	.577	.434	.590	.577
AQ3	.466	.484	.446	.807	.566	.537	.480	.557	.519
AQ5	.580	.614	.510	.863	.703	.636	.554	.634	.552
AQ8	.569	.597	.411	.856	.594	.663	.512	.582	.571
AQ12	.636	.633	.536	.855	.708	.626	.491	.650	.590
CN3	.642	.650	.482	.667	.834	.681	.501	.677	.609

continued on following page

Table 3. Continued

	ST	CU	TC	AQ	CN	AP	PR	OE	BS
CN4	.685	.699	.561	.648	.880	.670	.537	.641	.604
CN5	.639	.608	.569	.546	.850	.734	.534	.628	.620
CN8	.569	.622	.602	.680	.884	.670	.548	.625	.576
CN9	.606	.654	.559	.657	.906	.727	.588	.656	.643
CN10	.626	.671	.558	.642	.871	.758	.643	.695	.671
AP3	.594	.662	.542	.622	.680	.849	.614	.728	.707
AP4	.615	.653	.481	.655	.751	.923	.539	.729	.712
AP5	.701	.660	.586	.676	.768	.894	.637	.757	.672
AP6	.599	.671	.476	.625	.697	.896	.518	.694	.646
AP7	.624	.695	.551	.651	.701	.903	.558	.731	.748
AP8	.664	.703	.571	.667	.763	.906	.577	.768	.690
AP10	.645	.635	.546	.601	.690	.843	.553	.695	.628
PR1	.529	.517	.520	.517	.548	.544	.894	.565	.457
PR2	.502	.471	.499	.554	.524	.481	.873	.537	.408
PR3	.460	.472	.530	.513	.531	.475	.886	.526	.427
PR4	.467	.453	.492	.464	.522	.456	.851	.496	.384
PR7	.463	.502	.507	.458	.543	.525	.861	.586	.505
PR8	.584	.546	.472	.460	.572	.670	.757	.659	.579
PR10	.503	.533	.536	.527	.556	.613	.828	.570	.506
EF1	.537	.556	.509	.618	.571	.619	.539	.780	.623
EF7	.652	.636	.515	.616	.679	.777	.558	.897	.718
EF8	.659	.631	.482	.619	.650	.775	.569	.897	.793
EF12	.701	.676	.502	.678	.661	.729	.633	.906	.725
EF13	.658	.619	.470	.592	.658	.677	.588	.866	.724
EF14	.673	.662	.540	.643	.716	.720	.627	.890	.714
SG1	.569	.625	.411	.550	.587	.689	.492	.738	.858
SG2	.614	.662	.518	.616	.688	.726	.528	.754	.918
SG3	.508	.595	.456	.577	.625	.603	.363	.666	.842
SG4	.622	.673	.481	.633	.670	.728	.550	.785	.937
SG5	.615	.643	.501	.603	.609	.695	.545	.714	.898

capability and knowledge process capability ($\beta=0.661$; p$\leq$0.001) supporting hypothesis H6. Taken together, knowledge infrastructure capability and business strategy explained 0.799 of the variance observed for knowledge process capability.

Turning to organizational effectiveness, the results showed that the research model accounted for 0.788 of the variance observed for organizational effectiveness. More specifically, these findings provide strong support for the hypothesized relationship between organizational effectiveness and business strategy ($\beta=0.388$; p$\leq$0.001), knowledge infrastructure capability ($\beta=0.139$; p$\leq$0.05), and knowledge process capa-

Table 4. Descriptive statistics, loadings, composite reliabilities and average variance extracted (ave) for the substantive model

Latent Constructs	Factor Loadings	Composite Reliability	AVE	Mean	StDev
Knowledge Infrastructure Capability (KIC)		0.891	0.732	4.733	1.268
Structure (ST)	0.908				
Culture (CU	0.885				
Technology (TC)	0.768				
Knowledge Process Capability (KPC)		0.930	0.770	5.082	1.264
Acquisition (AQ)	0.868				
Conversion (CN)	0.915				
Application (AP)	0.915				
Protection (PN)	0.807				
Business Strategy (BS)	See Table 1	0.951	0.795	5.471	1.382
Organizational Effectiveness (OE)	See Table 1	0.951	0.763	4.810	1.478

Table 5. Inter-construct correlations and discriminant validity

	BS	KIC	KPC	OE
Business Strategy (BS)	0.892			
Knowledge Infrastructure Capability (KIC)	0.749	0.856		
Knowledge Process Capability (KPC)	0.779	0.874	0.877	
Organizational Effectiveness (OE)	0.822	0.799	0.847	0.873

Note: Shaded represent the square-root of the variance shared between the constructs and their measures; the off-diagonal elements are the correlations among the constructs.

Table 6. Loadings and shared loadings for knowledge infrastructure capability and knowledge process capability

	Knowledge Infrastructure Capability (KIC)	Knowledge Process Capability (KPC)
Structure (ST)	.908	.764
Culture (CU	.885	.791
Technology (TC)	.768	.685
Acquisition (AQ)	.731	.868
Conversion (CN)	.822	.915
Application (AP)	.811	.915
Protection (PN)	.694	.807

bility (β=0.423 p$\leq$0.001). Hypotheses H3, H4 and H5 were therefore supported.

An analysis of the path coefficients (using the bootstrap results) further showed that for organi-zational effectiveness, knowledge infrastructure capability was the weakest contributor of the three determinants; there was no significant difference in the path weights for knowledge process capa-

Figure 2. The results

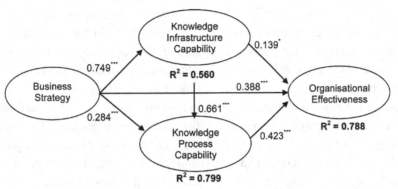

Key: *** p≤0.001; ** p≤0.05; * p≤0.10

bility and business strategy. On the other hand, knowledge infrastructure capability was by far the more important factor (p≤0.001) in relation to knowledge process capability when compared with business strategy. Business strategy also had a stronger effect (p≤0.001) on knowledge infrastructure than on knowledge process capability.

DISCUSSION AND IMPLICATIONS

Consistent with expectations, the study results provided strong empirical support for the Gold et al. (2001) model, suggesting that altogether technology, organizational culture, organizational structure, knowledge acquisition, knowledge conversion, knowledge application and knowledge protection are important preconditions for effective knowledge management capabilities. The results also showed that together with business strategy, these factors accounted for 0.788 of the variance observed for organizational effectiveness.

Although the literature provides strong theoretical arguments for a link between knowledge management capabilities and business strategy (Clarke, 2001; Maier & Remus, 2002; Zack, 1999), there has been little elaboration of the role that business strategy plays vis-à-vis knowledge capabilities or empirical assessment. This study addresses this gap by testing the link between

business strategy and knowledge management capabilities, and providing empirical support of a positive relationship between business strategy and knowledge management capabilities. In particular, the study confirms the role of business strategy as an antecedent of knowledge management capabilities, and that both business strategy and knowledge management capabilities impact organizational effectiveness. Given the lack of consensus regarding the placement of business strategy in relation to knowledge management capabilities, this study contributes to the literature by suggesting that business strategy is an important factor impacting knowledge management capability (Zack, 1999).

Knowledge infrastructure capability was also shown to have a moderate and positive impact on organizational effectiveness (similar to the findings of Gold et al., 2001). Although, it is highly unlikely that infrastructure by itself would strongly influence effectiveness, the results suggest that knowledge infrastructure capability in tandem with knowledge process capability will have a positive and more meaningful impact on effectiveness (Jennex & Olfman, 2005).

Alongside knowledge infrastructure, knowledge process capability was also shown to have a strong and positive impact on organizational effectiveness. As expected, the direct impact of the process capability on organizational effectiveness was higher than that of infrastructure capability (Gold et al., 2001). This is also an important finding, as firms often focus too much attention on their technology at the expense of other aspects of their knowledge systems (Davenport & Prusak, 1998). Thus, this study confirms the need for firms to attend to both aspects of knowledge management to realize improvements in organizational performance (Gold et al., 2001).

The results also showed that knowledge infrastructure capability influences knowledge process capability (Gosh & Scott, 2007), suggesting that a key imperative for the deployment of successful processes lies with the development of appropriate infrastructure (Lee & Choi, 2003). This supports a widely-held view that infrastructure is a key enabler of the knowledge process (Davenport et al., 1998; Gosh & Scott, 2007; Lee & Choi, 2003).

Together with business strategy, knowledge infrastructure capability accounted for 0.799 of the variance observed for knowledge process capability. More specifically, the results suggest that knowledge infrastructure capabilities of technology, structure and culture together with business strategy impact the process capabilities of knowledge acquisition, knowledge application, knowledge conversion and knowledge protection. Furthermore, the study showed that knowledge infrastructure capability was by far the more important factor vis-à-vis knowledge process, when compared with the influence of business strategy. This implies that while business strategy might play an important role in respect of knowledge process capabilities, a large proportion of the difference in knowledge process capabilities across firms can be explained by the infrastructural imperatives of technology, culture, and structure.

Implications for Practice

For business managers, the results show that effective knowledge management requires an integrative approach that considers the interrelationships between business strategy, knowledge

infrastructure capability and knowledge process capability. Foremost, the results confirm what has been speculated in the literature – that business strategy is a key imperative for effective knowledge management, and that business strategy linked to knowledge management initiatives is important for organizational effectiveness. Thus firms need to align their knowledge management initiatives with the organization's business strategy. Investments should therefore not be made into infrastructure or processes without first considering the fit with business strategy.

Effective knowledge management also requires managers to develop a holistic as well as a pragmatic understanding of how a firm's technological, cultural and structural capabilities impact and support their knowledge management processes (Davenport et al., 1998; Gold et al., 2001; Jennex & Olfman, 2006). To pursue the path of improved organizational effectiveness, management should commence their knowledge management initiatives by putting measures in place to improve the knowledge infrastructure capabilities of the firm, paying attention to all three aspects of infrastructure, namely technology, structure and culture. Although basic knowledge management often begins with the capture of explicit data, the highly effective organization will need to develop mechanisms that enable the sharing and capture of intangible (tacit) forms of knowledge that are in people's heads and which are critical to the organization. Thus, in addition to addressing the more obvious elements of technology requirements, firms need to adapt their organizational structure and redesign their cultures to ensure adequate support for knowledge sharing. For example, as organizations begin to embrace new digital platforms such as Web 2.0, effective integration of these technologies will require management to radically rethink many other aspects of their existing infrastructure (e.g. culture, policies) as well as their knowledge management practices (McAfee, 2006). Appropriate infrastructure capabilities will in turn provide a sustainable and effective platform for improving their knowledge process capabilities, and the process capabilities will drive improvements in organizational effectiveness. While improving infrastructure capabilities by themselves may lead to some improvements in organizational effectiveness, greater effectiveness can be attained if the infrastructure is first improved then the processes.

CONCLUSION

Studies shows that a high proportion knowledge management projects fail to deliver the benefits expected. Much of this failure has been attributed to the lack of alignment between a firm's business strategy and their knowledge management initiatives. However, while there is general agreement that business strategy is important (Maier & Remus, 2002), there is little evidence as to what that role might be.

This study directly addresses this gap and contributes to knowledge management theory by conceptualizing and assessing a framework that links business strategy as an antecedent to knowledge capabilities and organizational effectiveness. The results show that business strategy together with knowledge management capabilities (both infrastructure and process) impact organizational effectiveness and that of the three factors, knowledge process capability and business strategy have the greater direct impact. The study also shows that business strategy is an important antecedent of knowledge process capability, impacting process capability both directly and indirectly through its effect on knowledge infrastructure capability. Knowledge process capability is further impacted by a firm's knowledge infrastructural capabilities.

This study is one of the first to explore the theoretical role of business strategy as an antecedent of knowledge capabilities, as well as the joint impact of business strategy and knowledge capabilities on organizational effectiveness. Using the Gold et al (2001) model, this study offers a theoretical

framework that can be used by future research to further examine the links between business strategy and knowledge capabilities. Three areas for future research are elaborated next.

First, the literature shows that knowledge process capability is a multifaceted concept, and thus there is no commonly agreed conceptualization of which components (or practices) should comprise knowledge process capability (Alavi & Leidner, 2001; Gold et al., 2001; Stein & Zwass, 1995; Zack, 1999). Assessing the role of business strategy in relation to other conceptualizations of knowledge capability may therefore yield different outcomes.

Second, prior research suggests that different relationships may exist at the factor-level, when it comes to particular components (Lee & Choi, 2003). Thus while business strategy may exert a general effect on knowledge infrastructure and process capabilities at the construct level, the enablers and processes that make up these capabilities may be differentially impacted. Future research could therefore examine the relationships among the factors that make up knowledge capabilities and business strategy.

Finally, the literature calls for further research into the links between knowledge capabilities and organizational effectiveness (Jennex & Olfman, 2005, 2006). Although this study goes some way in addressing this call, there are opportunities to further explore the effect of business strategy and knowledge capabilities on other success measures such as user satisfaction, intention to use, and perceived benefits (Jennex & Olfman, 2005), and of other antecedents (such as user capabilities, task characteristics, and alignment of business strategy with knowledge management strategy) on knowledge management success.

Limitations

This research yielded many useful outcomes. However, there are some limitations to consider when interpreting and applying the findings. First, the sample of firms was not randomized; in addition the data was collected from firms in a single country – Jamaica. This may call into question the extent to which the findings are generalized outside the research context. Notwithstanding context, the findings are a strong indicator of the link between business strategy (as an antecedent) and knowledge management capabilities, and of the joint impact of knowledge management capabilities and business strategy on organizational effectiveness. However, the model should be retested to determine generalization in context to other settings.

Second, the unit of analysis is the firm. Similar to prior research the study targeted managers as the most likely to have a good understanding of the knowledge management resources of the firm, business strategy and organizational effectiveness. However, not all of the respondents may have had a holistic view of their firm's resources and processes - there may therefore be some inaccuracies (such as under- or over-reporting) in the responses. Conducting more in-depth research into the relationships identified in this study, alongside triangulation of the data will help future work overcome this constraint..

Finally, to ensure a good response rate, the number of items used in the scales was reduced. Although all constructs were measured using at least four items which is considered adequate for convergent validity (Chin, 1998), further validation of the reduced measures is recommended.

REFERENCES

Afiouni. (2007). Human resource management and knowledge management: A road map toward improving organizational performance. *Journal of American Academy of Business, 11*(2), 124-130.

Alavi, M., & Leidner, D. E. (2001). Review: Knowledge Management and knowledge Management Systems: Conceptual Foundations and research Issues. *Management Information Systems Quarterly, 25*(1), 107–136. doi:10.2307/3250961

Bergeron, F., Raymond, L., & Rivard, S. (2004). Ideal patterns of strategic alignment and business performance. *Information & Management, 41*(8), 1003–1020. doi:10.1016/j.im.2003.10.004

Beveren, J. V. (2003). Does healthcare for knowledge management? *Journal of Knowledge Management, 7*(1), 90–95. doi:10.1108/13673270310463644

Bhatt, G. D. (2001). Knowledge management in organizations: Examining the interaction between technologies, techniques, and people. *Journal of Knowledge Management, 5*(1), 68–75. doi:10.1108/13673270110384419

Bohn, R. E. (1994). Measuring and managing technological knowledge. *Sloan Management Review*, 61–73.

Broadbent, M. (1998). The phenomenon of knowledge management: What does it mean to the information profession? *Information Outlook, 2*(5), 23–33.

Bryson, J. M., & Alston, F. K. (1996). *Creating and implementing your strategic plan: A workbook for public and nonprofit organizations*. San Francisco, CA: Josssey-Bass.

Cascella, V. (2002). Effective strategic planning. *Quality Progress, 35*(11), 62–67.

Chakravarthy, B. S. (1987). On tailoring a strategic planning system to its context: some empirical evidence. *Strategic Management Journal, 8*(6), 517–534.

Chan, I., & Chao, C. (2008). Knowledge management in small and medium-sized enterprises. *Communications of the ACM, 51*(4), 83–88. doi:10.1145/1330311.1330328

Chin, W. W. (1998). The partial least squares approach to structural equation modeling. In Marcoulides, G. (Ed.), *Modern Methods for Business Research* (pp. 295–336). Camberley, UK: LEA Publishers.

Clarke, T. (2001). The knowledge economy. *Education + Training*, *43*(4/5), 189–196. doi:10.1108/00400910110399184

Davenport, T., Delong, D., & Beers, M. (1998). Successful knowledge management programs. *Sloan Management Review*, *39*, 43–57.

Davenport, T. H., & Prusak, L. (1998). *Working knowledge: How organizations manage what they know*. Boston: Harvard Business School Press.

Dillman, D. (2000). *Mail and Internet surveys: The tailored design method*. New York: John Wiley & Sons.

Everard, J. (2001). We are Plato's children. *Library Management*, *22*(6/7), 297–302. doi:10.1108/EUM0000000005594

Felton, S. M. (2002). Knowledge is capital, the rest is just money. *Strategy and Leadership*, *30*(3), 41–42.

Fornell, C., & Bookstein. (1982). Two structural equation models: LISREL and PLS applied to consumer exit-voice theory. *JMR, Journal of Marketing Research*, *19*(4), 440–452. doi:10.2307/3151718

Fornell, C., & Larcker, D. F. (1981). Evaluating structural equation models with unobservable variables and measurement error. *JMR, Journal of Marketing Research*, *18*(1), 39–50. doi:10.2307/3151312

Germain, R., Droge, C., & Christensen, W. (2001). The mediating role of operations knowledge in the relationship of context with performance. *Journal of Operations Management*, *19*, 453–469. doi:10.1016/S0272-6963(00)00067-X

Goh, S. C. (2002). Managing effective knowledge transfer: an integrative framework and some practice implications. *Journal of Knowledge Management*, *6*(1), 23–30. doi:10.1108/13673270210417664

Gold, A. H., Malhotra, A., & Segars, A. H. (2001). Knowledge management: An organizational capabilities perspective. *Journal of Management Information Systems*, *18*(1), 185–214.

Gosh, B., & Scott, J. E. (2007). Effective knowledge management systems for a clinical nursing setting. *Information Systems Management*, *24*(1), 73–84. doi:10.1080/10580530601038188

Grant, R. M. (1991). The resource-based theory of competitive advantage: Implication for strategy formulation. *California Management Review*, *33*(3), 114–135.

Grant, R. M. (1996). Toward a knowledge-based theory of the firm. *Strategic Management Journal*, *17*, 109–122.

Grant, R. M., & Baden-Fuller, C. (1995). A knowledge-based theory of inter-firm collaboration. *Academy of Management Journal*, 17–21.

Grover, V., & Davenport, T. H. (2001). General perspectives on knowledge management: Fostering a research agenda. *Journal of Management Information Systems*, *18*(1), 5–21.

Henderson, J. C., & Venkatraman, N. (1999). Strategic alignment: Leveraging information technology for transforming organizations. *IBM Systems Journal*, *38*(2-3), 472–484. doi:10.1147/SJ.1999.5387096

Ho, L. (2008). What affects organizational performance? The linking of learning and knowledge management. *Industrial Management & Data Systems*, *108*(9), 1234–1254. doi:10.1108/02635570810914919

Jennex, M. E., & Olfman, L. (2005). Assessing knowledge management success. *International Journal of Knowledge Management*, *1*(2), 33–49.

Jennex, M. E., & Olfman, L. (2006). A model of knowledge management success. *International Journal of Knowledge Management, 2*(3), 51–68.

Kelly, D., & Amburgey, T. (1991). Organizational inertia and momentum: A dynamic model of strategic change. *Academy of Management Journal, 34*(3), 591–612. doi:10.2307/256407

Kogut, B., & Zander, U. (1992). Knowledge of the firm, combinative capabilities, and the replication of technology. *Organization Science, 3*(3), 383–397. doi:10.1287/orsc.3.3.383

Laframboise, K., Croteau, A., Beaudry, A., & Manovas, M. (2007). Interdepartmental knowledge transfer success during information technology projects. *International Journal of Knowledge Management, 3*(2), 47–67.

Lam, W., & Chua, A. (2005). Knowledge management project abandonment: An exploratory examination of root causes. *Communications of the Association for Information Systems, 16*, 723–743.

Lang, J. C. (2001). Managerial concerns in knowledge management. *Journal of Knowledge Management, 5*(1), 43–57. doi:10.1108/13673270110384392

Law, K. S., Wong, C., & Mobley, W. H. (1998). Toward a taxonomy of multidimensional constructs. *Academy of Management Review, 23*(4), 741–753. doi:10.2307/259060

Lee, H., & Choi, B. (2003). Knowledge Management Enablers, Processes, and Organizational Performance: An Integrative View and Empirical Examination. *Journal of Management Information Systems, 20*(1), 179–228.

Lee, H., & Suh, Y. (2003). Knowledge conversion with information technology of Korean companies. *Business Process Management Journal, 9*(3), 317–336. doi:10.1108/14637150310477911

Lewis, W., Agarwal, R., & Sambamurthy, V. (2003). Sources of influence on beliefs about information technology use: An empirical study of knowledge workers. *Management Information Systems Quarterly, 27*(4), 657–678.

Liu, P. L., Chen, W. C., & Tsai, C. H. (2005). An empirical study on the correlation between the knowledge management method & new product development strategy on product performance in Taiwan's industries. *Technovation, 25*(7), 637–644.

Lo, C., & Wang, J. (2007). The relationship between defender and prospector business strategies and organizational performance in two different industries. *International Journal of Management, 24*(1), 174–183.

Lucier, C. E., & Torsilieri, J. D. (1997). Why knowledge programs fail: A C.E.O.'s guide to managing learning. *Strategy & Business, 9*(4), 14–28.

Maier, R., & Remus, U. (2002). Defining process-oriented knowledge management strategies. *Knowledge and Process Management, 9*(2), 103–118. doi:10.1002/kpm.136

Mathiassen, L., & Pourkomeylian, P. (2003). Managing knowledge in a software organization. *Journal of Knowledge Management, 7*(2), 63–80. doi:10.1108/13673270310477298

McAfee, A. P. (2006). Enterprise 2.0: The Dawn of Emergent Collaboration. *MIT Sloan Management Review, 47*(3), 21–28.

McDermott, R., & O'Dell, C. (2001). Overcoming cultural barriers to sharing knowledge. *Journal of Knowledge Management, 5*(1), 76–85. doi:10.1108/13673270110384428

Nahapiet, J., & Ghoshal, S. (1998). Social Capital, Intellectual Capital, and the Organizational Advantage. *Academy of Management Review, 23*(2), 242–266. doi:10.2307/259373

Nonaka, I., & Takeuchi, H. (1995). *The knowledge creation company: How Japanese companies create the dynamics of innovation*. New York: Oxford University Press.

Paisittanand, A., Digman, L. A., & Lee, S. M. (2007). Managing Knowledge capabilities for strategy implementation effectiveness. *International Journal of Knowledge Management*, *3*(4), 84–110.

Porter-Libskind, J. (1996). Knowledge, strategy, and the theory of the firm. *Strategic Management Journal*, *17*, 93–107.

Ruggles, R. (1998). The state of the notion: Knowledge management in practice. *California Management Review*, *40*(3), 80–89.

Sabherwal, R., & Chan, Y. E. (2001). Alignment between business and IS strategies: A study of prospectors, analyzers, and defenders. *Information Systems Research*, *12*(1), 11–33. doi:10.1287/isre.12.1.11.9714

Sanchez, R., & Mahoney, J. T. (1996). Modularity, flexibility, and knowledge management in product and organization design. *Strategic Management Journal*, *17*, 63–76.

Stein, E. W., & Zwass, V. (1995). Actualizing Organizational Memory with Information Systems. *Information Systems Research*, *6*(2), 85–117. doi:10.1287/isre.6.2.85

Storey, J., & Barnett, E. (2000). Knowledge management initiatives: Learning from failures. *Journal of Knowledge Management*, *4*(2), 145–156. doi:10.1108/13673270010372279

Turban, E., & Aronson, J. E. (2001). *Decision support systems and intelligent systems* (6th ed.). Upper Saddle River, NJ: Prentice Hall.

Ulrich, D., & Wiersema, M. (1989). Gaining strategic and organizational capability in a turbulent business environment. *The Academy of Management Executive*, *3*(2), 115–122.

Wade, M., & Hulland, J. (2004). Review: The resource-based view and information systems research: Review, extension, and suggestions for future research. *Management Information Systems Quarterly*, *28*(1), 107–142.

Zack, M. H. (1999). Developing a knowledge strategy. *California Management Review*, *41*(3), 125–145.

This work was previously published in International Journal of Knowledge Management, Volume 6, Issue 3, edited by Murray E. Jennex, pp. 22-43, copyright 2010 by IGI Publishing (an imprint of IGI Global).

Chapter 11
The Impact of Supporting Organizational Knowledge Management through a Corporate Portal on Employees and Business Processes

Kamla Ali Al-Busaidi
Sultan Qaboos University, Oman

ABSTRACT

Due to corporate portal playing a major role on organizational knowledge management (KM), this study was conducted to assess the impact of supporting KM processes through a corporate portal on business processes and employees at an academic institution. This paper specifically assesses the impact of knowledge acquisition, knowledge conversion, knowledge application and knowledge protection on business processes' effectiveness, efficiency and innovation, and employees' learning, adaptability, and job satisfaction. Findings suggest that the ending KM process, knowledge application, produces the highest impact on business processes and employees. First, supporting knowledge application through a corporate portal was positively associated with business processes' effectiveness and innovation and employees' learning, adaptability, and job satisfaction. Second, supporting knowledge conversion was positively associated with business processes' effectiveness and employees' learning, whereas supporting knowledge protection was positively associated with business processes' effectiveness and efficiency but negatively associated with employees' learning. Finally, supporting knowledge acquisition was positively associated with only business processes' innovation.

INTRODUCTION

In the knowledge age, knowledge what creates value to individuals and organizations. Governments, organizations and individuals that manage knowledge and harness it are the ones that most likely achieve competitive advantage. Therefore, knowledge management (KM) is essential for organizations; KM improves organizations' learning and innovative performance (Chang & Lee, 2007; Jiang & Lia, 2008), which consequently enables organizations to differentiate themselves and achieve competitive advantage. KM involves

DOI: 10.4018/978-1-4666-0035-5.ch011

several processes starting from knowledge acquisition to knowledge application.

Deploying information technologies (IT) that facilitate knowledge management and exchange are imperative for the development of a knowledge-based economy. Knowledge management systems (KMS) improve the effectiveness and efficiency of organizational KM. KM and KMS result in employees' and business processes' benefits such as productivity, learning, innovation, effectiveness, efficiency and many others (Alavi & Lidner, 1999; Becerra-Fernandez, Gonzalez, & Sabherwal, 2004; Davenport & Prusak, 1998).

Several information technologies have been used to support one or several KM processes, including databases, data warehouses, document management systems, and artificial intelligence techniques such as expert systems, neural network and case-based reasoning. One of the new web-based technologies that provide a gateway into integrated internal and external data, information and knowledge sources is portal. Corporate portal is a type of portals that provides a gateway into corporate internal and external information and knowledge resources. Corporate portal plays a major role on supporting organizational knowledge management processes. Several researchers have conceptually illustrated the strengths of using corporate portal to support organizational KM processes (Benbya, Passiante, & Belbaly, 2004). Goh, Chua, Luyt, and Lee (2008) validated a model for the use of corporate portal to support KM processes. The literature, however, lacks the empirical evaluation of the impacts of using corporate portal to support KM processes. Most of the claimed benefits of corporate portals are intuitive; a more rigorous methodology is needed to verify these benefits through real case studies (Dias, 2001). A Review of the portals literature shows that there are very limited studies investigating the impacts and returns of using portals especially for organizational KM. Most previous studies have focused on issues related to the service quality or the Web design quality (Yang,

Cai, Zhouc, & Zhou, 2005); hence future research should explore and examine the benefits of corporate portals (Daniel & Ward, 2006). There are some studies in the KM literature, such as Chang and Lee (2007), Liu and Tsai (2007), Jiang and Liab (2008), Tiwana (2004) and Norman (2002), that have investigated the impact of KM, but at very limited KM processes and/or benefits scales. Assessing the specific impact of each KM process independently, a crucial aspect of KM has not been addressed adequately. Investigating the activities required for the systematic handling of knowledge resources is necessarily (Heisig, 2009; Holsaple & Joshi, 2002).

Linking KM and business processes, and the support of senior managers are two critical success factors for KM (Heisig, 2009) and for effective deployment of corporate portal (Benbya et al., 2004). Gaining senior managers' support can be achieved by linking the deployment of information technologies to economic and productivity values (Turban, Leidner, McLean, & Wetherbe, 2008). Likewise, end users' perceived KMS benefits are a significant determinant of their use (Wu & Wang, 2006). Therefore, it is vital for organizations to recognize the impact of supporting organizational KM processes through corporate portals on employees and business processes.

Therefore, this study aims to examine the impact of supporting organizational knowledge management processes, as identified by Gold, Malhotra and Segars (2001), through corporate portal on employees and business processes, as identified by Becerra-Fernandez et al. (2004), in an academic institution. It specifically assesses the specific impact of supporting knowledge acquisition, knowledge conversion, knowledge application and knowledge protection on employees' learning, adaptability, and job satisfaction and business processes' effectiveness, efficiency and innovation.

The use of corporate portals in academic institutions is gaining momentum worldwide. They are getting a wide-spread attention in the academic world (Li & Wood, 2005). In the academic context, there is some literature on the use of corporate portal, with topics such as the strengths and weaknesses of academic portal (Al-Busaidi, 2009; Pinto & Doucet, 2007), the status of portals in the academic world (Li & Wood, 2005), and the success factors of academic portal implementations (Masrek, 2007). Furthermore, Tikhomirova, Gritsenko and Pechenkin (2008) demonstrated a model of using information technologies to support KM at a university, and recommended that other technologies such as portals can be also utilized for KM at universities. However, empirical studies that assess the impact of supporting KM processes through corporate portal on business processes and employees in the academic context are also very limited. School portals have not been formally evaluated yet (Li & Wood, 2005).

BACKGROUND LITERATURE

Knowledge Management Processes

Knowledge management systems (KMS) are systems that manage knowledge throughout the organization; they are developed to assist individuals and organizations to store, retrieve, transfer and distribute knowledge. Structured or unstructured explicit knowledge from internal or external sources can be stored in an Organizational KMS (Davenport & Prusak, 1998; Turban et al., 2008). Knowledge management is "the organized and systematic process of generating and disseminating information, and selecting, distilling, and deploying explicit and tacit knowledge to create unique value that can be used to achieve a competitive advantage in the marketplace by an organization" (Hult, 2003, p. 189). Several empirical studies in different countries provided evidence on the significance of KM and KMS such as Gold et al. (2001), and Jennex (2008a) in the US, Chong (2006) in Malaysia, Liu, and Tsai

(2007) and Wu and Wang (2006) in Taiwan, and Al-Busaidi and Olfman (2005) in Oman.

Knowledge management processes have been classified in the literature in several dimensions, which are more or less the same. KM starts with knowledge acquisition (or creation/generation) and ends with knowledge application (or utilization). According to Davenport and Prusak (1998), KM consists of three major processes: knowledge generation, knowledge codification and knowledge utilization. Based on the same perspective, Alavi and Leidner (2001) and Becerra-Fernandez et al. (2004) made there classifications of KM processes. Alavi and Leidner (2001) classified KM processes as knowledge creation, knowledge codification/storage, knowledge transfer, and knowledge application; whereas Becerra-Fernandez et al. (2004) classified them as knowledge discovery, knowledge capture, knowledge sharing, and knowledge application. Gold et al. (2001) also provided a similar classification, but with a new KM dimension. They indicated that the capability of organizational KM is assessed by incorporating tools and mechanisms that support not only knowledge acquisition, knowledge conversion, knowledge application, but also knowledge protection. Several other frameworks of KM processes were summarized by Holsaple and Joshi (2002), Benbya et al. (2004) and Heisig (2009). Heisig's (2009) analysis of 160 KM frameworks from 1995 to 2003, indicated that the most frequent categorization of KM processes are share, create, apply, store and identify knowledge.

Recently, new classifications are proposed for KM processes from different perspectives. From a knowledge engineering perspective on KM, Lai (2007) proposed the following processes: knowledge modelling, knowledge verification, knowledge storage, knowledge querying and knowledge update. Kjaegaard and Kautz (2008) proposed a KM venturing process that includes knowledge creation, negotiation and formalization.

This study adopts Gold et al.'s (2001) classification to evaluate the KM processes as it has been highly tested in the KM research and it is more comprehensive than other classifications. According to Gold et al. (2001), knowledge acquisition process is the process of obtaining knowledge from internal and external sources. Knowledge conversion is the process of making existing knowledge useful by organizing, integrating, combining, structuring, coordinating and distributing knowledge. Knowledge application is the process of using the knowledge to solve problems and make decisions. Knowledge protection is related to the protection of the organization knowledge from illegal or inappropriate use.

Corporate Portal and Knowledge Management

Portals offer a common gateway into multiple distributed repositories. Portals enable an efficient access to relevant and accurate information and knowledge (Gurugé, 2002; Turban et al., 2008). Corporate portal is a type of portals that provides a gateway into the organization's knowledge resources. Corporate portal provides a single web-based entry to corporate information and knowledge located inside and outside the organization; it synchronizes knowledge and provides a single integrated view of the organizational intellectual capital (Benbya et al., 2004). The deployment of a corporate portal improves employees' productivity by improving corporate information access (Aneja, Rowan, & Brooksby, 2000; Gurugé, 2002).

There are several architectures proposed for corporate portals. According to Aneja et al. (2000), a corporate portal incorporates internal and external information resources. Internal information resources include internal websites, collaboration products, documents, organizational knowledge bases, and data warehouses; whereas, external information resources may include external websites, external content, news and news feeds, and external services. Furthermore, Benbaya et al. (2004) indicated that portals offer a number

of features including core capabilities, supportive capabilities and web services. Core capabilities of the portal include collaboration, integration, publication, search, personalization and taxonomy; while supportive capabilities include security, scalability and profiling. Based on these features, a portal can play a major role on organizational knowledge management. It provides tools for knowledge creation (acquisition), knowledge conversion and storage, and knowledge transfer and application. Moreover, corporate portal provides tools to protect and secure organizational intellectual capital.

According to Detlor (2000), corporate portal provides employees with a rich shared information work space to create, exchange, store, retrieve, share and reuse knowledge; it has content space for information access and retrieval, communication space for conversation and negotiations, and coordination space for cooperative work tasks.

Thus, corporate portal includes several features and tools that support organizational KM processes: knowledge acquisition, knowledge conversion, knowledge application and knowledge protection. First, with corporate portal, knowledge can be acquired through corporate knowledge sources or collaborations between individuals as well as linkages between the organization and other alliances. Corporate portal provides a rich content space that enables searching, accessing and retrieving content from internal and external sources. It also includes collaboration and communication tools. Second, two core capabilities of corporate portal that enables knowledge conversion are content integration and personalization; corporate portal consolidates and synchronizes knowledge from internal and external sources and provides a single personalized integrated view of the organizational intellectual capital (Benbya et al., 2004). Third, knowledge application can be more efficient with the use of corporate portal. Corporate portal includes rich content that can be applied by users to solve problems and make decisions; corporate portal integrates corporate websites, corporate documents, business content, external content, websites and news. Finally, corporate portal protects corporate internal and external knowledge by including authentication tools such as users' names and passwords. Another way to protect corporate content is that corporate portal customizes and displays corporate information and knowledge according to the users' authorization level. Thus, corporate portal plays a major role on organizational knowledge management for any organization. For instance, in the context of e-government portal, Goh et al. (2008) validated a model of how a portal can be used to support knowledge access, creation and transfer.

KM and Corporate Portal Benefits

The literature indicated that the use of KMS results in several individual and organizational benefits. These benefits can be tangible or intangible benefits. However, not much empirical research has focused on the benefits of KMS (Teo & Men, 2008). Based on qualitative study, Alavi and Lidner (1999) found that the perceived benefits of KMS can be categorized as process outcomes and organization outcomes. Process outcomes include communication (enhanced communication and increased staff participation); and efficiency (reduced problem solving time and proposal times and improved results, delivery to market, and overall efficiency). Organization outcomes include financial (increased sales, decreased cost and improved profitability); marketing (improved customer service and marketing); and general (consistent proposals to multinational clients, improved project management and personnel reduction). Another qualitative Delphi study indicated that the expected benefits of KMS are improved productivity, effectiveness, efficiency, responsiveness, communication innovation and market share (Nevo & Chan, 2007).

Becerra-Fernandez et al. (2004) provided a comprehensive categorization of KM benefits;

these benefits are classified as employees benefits (such as learning, adaptability, and job satisfaction); business processes benefits (such as efficiency, effectiveness, and innovation); products benefits (such as value-added products and knowledge-based products); and organizational benefits (such as return on investment as a direct impact, and economies of scale and scope and sustainable competitive advantage as indirect impacts). This study adopted the Becerra-Fernandez et al.'s (2004) classification as it is more comprehensive and covers all entities that might be affected by KMS implementation. Products and organizational benefits were not assessed in this study as they are better assessed at managers' level not users level; thus employees benefits and business processes benefits were assessed. Indicators of KMS benefits can be soft and non-financial as most of KMS benefits are intangible and indirect (Wu & Wang, 2006).

According to Gurugé (2002), the deployment of corporate portal provides several benefits. Corporate portal increases corporate reach, reduces operational cost, bolsters customer loyalty by eliminating delays, improves online productivity through online tools, enhances corporate competitiveness through effective web mechanisms, accelerates decision making through rapid access to relevant information and knowledge sources, and expedites and reduces the cost of business processes.

Prior Empirical Studies on KM Processes and Benefits

The literature has very limited empirical studies that provided in depth investigations of the benefits of supporting KM processes through a corporate portal. However, there are several empirical quantitative studies that generally examined the impact of KM and KMS. For instance, Gold et al. (2001) found that knowledge infrastructure capability (technology, structure, and culture) and knowledge process capability (acquisition, conversion, application and protection) improves organizational effectiveness in terms of innovation, adaptability, efficiency and market responsiveness. Lee and Choi (2003) found also that KM improves organizational effectiveness measured by organizational members' perceptions of the degree of the overall success, market share, profitability, growth rate, and innovativeness of the organization in comparison with key competitors. In a case study, Newell, Huang, Galliers, and Pan (2003) found that the implementation of enterprise resource planning (ERP) and KM systems simultaneously promotes flexibility and innovation as well as efficiency.

Nevertheless, very limited empirical studies examined the specific impact of each of the KM processes independently. Few studies conducted such investigation at very limited KM processes and/or benefits scales. There are a number of empirical studies that investigated the impact of knowledge acquisition. For instance, Chang and Lee (2007) empirically verified the effects of knowledge acquisition, knowledge storage, and knowledge diffusion on organizational innovation. Liu and Tsai (2007) found that KM (knowledge acquisition, knowledge creation, knowledge storage and knowledge sharing) through KMS positively improve organizations' operating performance. Jiang and Lia (2008) confirmed the effects of knowledge sharing and knowledge creation on firms' innovative performance.

An empirical study that might shed light on the impact of knowledge conversion is Tiwana (2004). Based on an empirical study, Tiwana (2004) detected a significant impact of knowledge integration on various dimensions of software development performance; Knowledge integration lowers density of warrant stage defects, lowers defect density throughout the development trajectory, enhances software development efficiency, and improves design effectiveness.

On the impact of knowledge application, Liu (2003) empirically found that knowledge application as a dimension of KMS use improves

individual learning. Al-Busaidi (2005) empirically found that knowledge utilization results in individual benefits, which was assessed by measurements related to effectiveness, efficiency, innovation and learning. Jennex and Olfman (2006) identified that the utilization of KMS results in improved individual productivity in terms of decision making, root cause analysis, problem resolution, timeliness, and operability assessment documentation; this improved individual productivity further positively impacts organizational productivity. In the context of knowledge portal, Teo and Men (2008) found that the utilization of knowledge portal improves firms' performance. Also, De Carvalho, Ferreira, Choo, and Da Silva (2007) found that the usage of enterprise portal improves sense making, knowledge creation and decision making.

Very limited studies have examined the impact of knowledge protection. In the context of strategic alliances, Norman (2002) indicated that knowledge protection is essential for the success and effectiveness of strategic alliances.

The above cited empirical studies showed that knowledge acquisition (or creation) and knowledge sharing are the most investigated KM processes. Moreover, the benefits, highlighted in these cited studies fall within Becerra-Fernandez et al.'s (2004) benefits classification.

FRAMEWORK

Framework Development

System use is a measure of an information system (IS) success (DeLone & McLean, 1992; DeLone & McLean, 2003) including KMS (Jennex, 2008b; Jennex & Olfman, 2006; Wu & Wang, 2006); consequently system use results in net benefits. System use is determined by information quality, system quality and service quality (DeLone & McLean, 2003). Jennex and Olfman (2006) proposed detailed dimensions of the determinants of

Figure 1. The study model

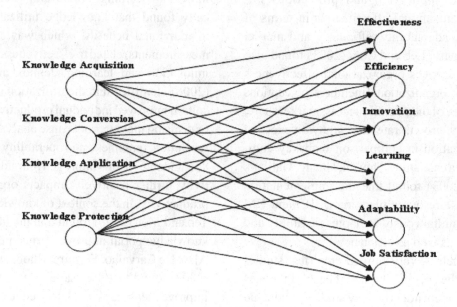

KM success based on the DeLone and McLean's IS success model, and suggested that the net benefits of KMS use can be assessed by improved individual and organizational productivity. Likewise, Wu and Wang (2006) re-specified DeLone and McLean's constructs and their interrelationships for measuring KMS success. This study closely examines the use of corporate portal based on its support for organizational KM processes, and the net benefits of corporate portal based on its impact on employees and business processes. For organizational knowledge management, an organization can utilize a corporate portal to support KM processes, which may result in net benefits. Thus, this study aims to assess the impact of using corporate portal to support KM processes on business processes and employees. This study adopts Gold et al.'s (2001) classification of KM processes: knowledge acquisition, knowledge conversion, knowledge application and knowledge protection. As for the benefits, this study adopts the Becerra-Fernandez et al.'s (2004) classification: business processes' benefits (efficiency, effectiveness, and innovation) and employees' benefits (learning, adaptability and

job satisfaction). Figure 1 illustrates the model of this investigation.

KM enables improvements in organizational business processes such as marketing, manufacturing, accounting, engineering, and public relations. For academic institutions, KM enables improvements in basic academic business processes such as consulting, education, research, publishing, and courses manufacturing (Tikhomirova et al., 2008). These improvements in business processes can be seen along three major dimensions: Effectiveness, efficiency and innovation (Becerra-Fernandez et al, 2004). Effectiveness is performing the most suitable processes and making the best possible decisions; whereas efficiency is performing the processes quickly and at a low-cost. Innovation, on the other hand, is performing the processes in a creative and novel manner that improves marketability

Furthermore, KM has several impacts on employees; they are measured by three dimensions: Learning, adaptability and job satisfaction (Becerra-Fernandez et al., 2004). KM can facilitate employees' learning through externalization, internalization, socialization, and communities of practice. KM makes employees to most likely accept change, and be prepared to respond to change. KM also provides employees with solutions to problems they face in case those same problems have been encountered earlier, which consequently affects their job satisfaction.

Hypotheses Development

Knowledge Acquisition

Knowledge acquisition process is the process of obtaining knowledge from internal and external sources. Several terms are used to describe this process such as acquire, seek, generate, create, capture and collaborate (Gold et al., 2001); all these terms referred to knowledge accumulation. Providing tools for knowledge creation and acquisition is important for the deployment of KMS as it creates an organizational knowledge repository for future organizational reuse. Knowledge capture and acquisition is essential for the establishment of organizational memory (Becerra-Fernandez et al., 2004; Davenport & Prusak, 1998). Corporate portal provides a rich content space that enables searching, accessing and retrieving content from internal and external sources. It also includes collaboration and communication tools. Corporate portal speeds up business processes through rapid access to relevant and accurate corporate information and knowledge (Gurugé, 2002; Turban et al., 2008). It eliminates delays, frustration and inefficiency. Thus, corporate portal enables efficient and effective knowledge acquisition. Empirical studies found that knowledge acquisition significantly improves performance and innovation (Chang & Lee, 2007; Jiang & Lia, 2008). Knowledge acquisition through corporate portal also promotes learning. Knowledge might be created and acquired through corporate knowledge sources or collaborations between individuals as well as linkages between the organization and other alliances. Along with rich content space for corporate information and knowledge ac-

cess, corporate portal integrates collaboration and communication tools (email system, discussion forums etc). Collaborations and interactions between individuals promote learning (Teece, 1998). Employees' adaptability is highly related to their learning capability. As knowledge acquisition from corporate portal enables employees to learn from each other, and from organizational knowledge repositories, employees will most likely gain sufficient knowledge that enables them to adapt to new tasks and circumstances at their work (Becerra-Fernandez et al., 2004). Likewise, innovation is closely related to learning. The higher the learning is the greater the innovation (Weerawardena, O'Cass, & Julian, 2006). With all these perceived business processes' benefits and employees' benefits, knowledge acquisition through corporate portal may contribute to employees' job satisfaction. Users' satisfaction may result from net benefits resulted from the system use (Becerra-Fernandez et al., 2004; DeLone & McLean, 2003; Jennex, 2008a; Jennex & Olfman, 2006). Thus, I hypothesize that:

Hypothesis 1a: Supporting knowledge acquisition through a corporate portal is positively associated with business processes' effectiveness.

Hypothesis 1b: Supporting knowledge acquisition through a corporate portal is positively associated with business processes' efficiency.

Hypothesis 1c: Supporting knowledge acquisition through a corporate portal is positively associated with business processes' innovation.

Hypothesis 1d: Supporting knowledge acquisition through a corporate portal is positively associated with employees' learning.

Hypothesis 1e: Supporting knowledge acquisition through a corporate portal is positively associated with employees' adaptability.

Hypothesis 1f: Supporting knowledge acquisition through a corporate portal is positively associated with employees' job satisfaction.

Knowledge Conversion

Knowledge conversion process is the process of making existing knowledge useful; it is the process of organizing, integrating, combining, structuring, coordinating, and distributing knowledge (Gold et al., 2001). This KM process is critical because it standardizes and integrates organizational knowledge, and makes it consistent and useful for utilization. It sets the stage for a successful knowledge application, and consequently improves the efficiency and effectiveness of the organizational knowledge. Two core capabilities of corporate portal are content integration and personalization; corporate portal synchronizes knowledge from internal and external sources and provides a single personalized integrated view of the organizational intellectual capital (Benbya et al., 2004). Combining and integrating knowledge reduces redundancy and improves efficiency (Davenport & Prusak, 1998). Structuring and organizing knowledge makes it easier to access and disseminate it. In the context of software development, Tiwana (2004) found that knowledge integration improves product development effectiveness, reduces defect density, lowers warranty defects, and increases software development efficiency. Furthermore, the process of combining, integrating and converting knowledge through corporate portal impacts business processes' innovation. Firm's innovativeness results from growing its knowledge base or integrating its existing knowledge into new syntheses (Nonaka & Takeuchi, 1995). In a case study, Newell et al. (2003) found the implementation of ERP, which standardizes and integrates organizational knowledge and information, and KM systems simultaneously, promotes both innovation as well as efficiency. Innovation is also closely related to learning (Weerawardena et al., 2006). Consequently, as indicated above, improved employees' learning enhances employees' adaptability; and all these perceived benefits may result in enhanced employees' job satisfaction. Thus, I hypothesize that:

Hypothesis 2a: Supporting knowledge conversion through a corporate portal is positively associated with business processes' effectiveness.

Hypothesis 2b: Supporting knowledge conversion through a corporate portal is positively associated with business processes' efficiency.

Hypothesis 2c: Supporting knowledge conversion through a corporate portal is positively associated with business processes' innovation.

Hypothesis 2d: Supporting knowledge conversion through a corporate portal is positively associated with employees' learning.

Hypothesis 2e: Supporting knowledge conversion through a corporate portal is positively associated with employees' adaptability.

Hypothesis 2f: Supporting knowledge conversion through a corporate portal is positively associated with employees' job satisfaction.

Knowledge Application

The value of KMS is recognized by the knowledge application process. Knowledge application is the process of using (applying) knowledge to solve business problems and make business decisions. It includes the retrieval and application of knowledge. Corporate portal includes rich content that can be accessed and retrieved by users to solve problems and make decisions; corporate portal integrates corporate websites, corporate documents, business content, external content, websites and news. Knowledge utilization from corporate portal improves sense making and decision making (De Carvalho et al., 2007), and firms' performance (Teo & Men, 2008). This application of relevant knowledge for problem solving and decision making improves individuals' learning, decision-making and innovation capabilities (Davenport & Prusak, 1998; Liu, 2003). It improves their judgments and skills and consequently enable them make better decisions (i.e., improved effectiveness) and accomplish their work more efficiently. Also, knowledge application helps organizations improve their efficiency and reduce costs (Davenport & Prusak, 1998). Furthermore, knowledge application plays a major role on innovation. Drucker (1993) defined innovation as "the application of knowledge to produce new knowledge". Thus, innovation in business processes results from the individual's application of knowledge. The higher the learning is the greater the innovation (Weerawardena et al., 2006). In an empirical study in Oman, Al-Busaidi (2005) found that knowledge utilization results in individual benefits, which was assessed by measurements related to effectiveness, efficiency, innovation and learning. Moreover, as indicated above, improved employees' learning enhances employees' adaptability. Employees' awareness of new ideas and knowledge prepares them to respond to change and accept it (Becerra-Fernandez et al., 2004). All these perceived benefits may result in enhanced employees' job satisfaction. Thus, I hypothesize that:

Hypothesis 3a: Supporting knowledge application through a corporate portal is positively associated with business processes' effectiveness.

Hypothesis 3b: Supporting knowledge application through a corporate portal is positively associated with business processes' efficiency.

Hypothesis 3c: Supporting knowledge application through a corporate portal is positively associated with business processes' innovation.

Hypothesis 3d: Supporting knowledge application through a corporate portal is positively associated with employees' learning.

Hypothesis 3e: Supporting knowledge application through a corporate portal is positively associated with employees' adaptability.

Hypothesis 3f: Supporting knowledge application through a corporate portal is positively associated with employees' job satisfaction.

Knowledge Protection

Knowledge protection process is related to the protection of the organization knowledge from illegal or inappropriate use. Corporate portal protects corporate internal and external knowledge by including authentication tools such as users' names and passwords. Another way to protect corporate content is that corporate portal customizes and displays corporate information and knowledge according to the users' authorization level. Protecting organizational knowledge provides a competitive advantage (Gold et al., 2001). To achieve a competitive advantage through organizational knowledge, knowledge should be rare and inimitable (Barney, 1991). Securing organizational information and knowledge improves organizational information quality, and consequently organizational efficiency and effectiveness (Turban et al., 2008). Information and knowledge quality is improved by having only authorized employees exchange knowledge and information through the corporate portal. Very limited empirical studies assessed the direct impact of knowledge protection on business processes and employees. However, in the context of strategic alliances, Norman (2002) indicated that knowledge protection is essential for the success and effectiveness of strategic alliances. Knowledge protection might positively impact the quality of knowledge, and business processes' efficiency and effectiveness, but it may negatively impact employees' learning, adaptability, and business processes' innovation. Restricting access to the system and organizational knowledge may also restrict and hinder employees' learning, and consequently their business processes' innovation. Likewise, providing employees with limited information and knowledge sources may improve their performance of existing business processes, but it reduces their capability to respond and adapt to new job demands and tasks and consequently their job satisfaction. Cautious knowledge protection approaches may improve the organization effectiveness, but it brings potentially serious disadvantages; limiting information and knowledge flows will likely slow communication and limit flexibility of the organization (Norman, 2002). Thus, I hypothesize that:

Hypothesis 4a: Supporting knowledge protection through a corporate portal is positively associated with business processes' effectiveness.

Hypothesis s 4b: Supporting knowledge protection through a corporate portal is positively associated with business processes' efficiency.

Hypothesis 4c: Supporting knowledge protection through a corporate portal is negatively associated with business processes' innovation.

Hypothesis 4d: Supporting knowledge protection through a corporate portal is negatively associated with employees' learning.

Hypothesis 4e: Supporting knowledge protection through a corporate portal is negatively associated with employees' adaptability.

Hypothesis 4f: Supporting knowledge protection through a corporate portal is negatively associated with employees' job satisfaction.

METHODOLOGY

Investigated Corporate Portal

The participants of this study represent users of a corporate portal in a public academic institution, Sultan Qaboos University (SQU), in Oman. The SQU portal is a dynamic web-based electronic gateway on the university internal and external data, information and knowledge resources. The portal has several features such as content management, information aggregation, searching and indexing, personalization, single sign and bi-lingual interface and content. The SQU portal enables employees to acquire information and knowledge from different resources and applications. It aggregates and converts them into one single interface. Aggregated information and knowledge are customized and personalized according to the type of users, and their authorization level. Users, including instructors, login into

their personal pages using access authorization (username and password).

The main home page of the SQU portal provides links to general services data and general information such as the university's scientific publications, universities magazines, staff publications; main library resources, vacancy notices and other useful links. The main home page also has login space to allow users including instructors to login into their personal pages using access authorization (usernames and password). The content and services of the portal varies according to the users types. For instance, instructors', which represent the majority of participants in this study, main page includes three main sections: general section, academic section and services section. In the "general section", instructors can: view information about university regulations, coming training courses, workshops, conferences, and other university activities; (2) use and search the university on-line telephone directory; and (3) link to relevant external websites. In the "academic section", instructors can: (1) find information about their academic work (i.e. class details and time tables, teaching survey results, students, advisees etc); (2) communicate through email with students and advisees; and (3) view and share their publication records. In the "services section", instructors can: (1) view several information and content such as employment details, training courses, official trips, borrowed and overdue books etc; (2) communicate with several university units and request vehicle, road permits, visa, wireless services, help desk services; and (3) link to the university learning management systems and email system.

Data Collection and Sample Profile

Data was collected through email from employees in an academic institution, SQU, in Oman. The author emailed the questionnaire in MS Word format to the study participants, the end users of the university portal. The email was sent to academic and administrative staff in the university's colleges and supporting centers in the university. A reminder email was sent after two weeks of the first email.

The total respondents were 100, which represents about 17.7% of the invited portal users. This 100 sample size represents end users, mainly instructors. About 78% of the sample was male, and all the participants had above average computer skills. About 88% of the sample size had academic positions: About 10% of the participants were lecturers, 46% were assistant professor, 24% were associate professors and 8% were full professors. About 79% of the sample had at least 2 years work experience, and about 83% had at least a year of portal-use experience, and only 16% of them had less than one year portal-use experience. The majority of the participants, 67%, were PhD holders; while 29% of them were MSc holders and 4% of them were BSc holders.

Research Questionnaire

The questionnaire included the study's constructs, needed for quantitative analysis, along with demographic questions (e.g., gender, age, degree, portal usage experience, work experience, and job title). Construct measurements items were phrased according to a 5–point Likert scale (1= strongly disagree; 2=disagree; 3=Neutral; 4=agree and 5=strongly agree).

To evaluate this study's model, the questionnaire included 24 items that formed the independent (endogenous) constructs and dependent (exogenous) constructs (see Table 2). Exogenous constructs (KM processes) were each assessed by three indicators; while endogenous constructs (KM benefits) were each assessed by two indicators. Constructs related to KM processes were adopted from Gold et al. (2001), while constructs related to benefits were self-developed based on Becerra-Fernandez et al. (2004), and relevant literature. The questionnaire was reviewed by a couple of experts in the field to check the relevancy and clarity of the measurements. The question-

naire was also pre tested by a small number of portal users (with different backgrounds) to check the clarity of the measurements. Appendix A illustrates the measurements that were included in the questionnaire.

DATA ANALYSIS AND RESULTS

PLS Analysis Methodology

Data was analyzed by PLS-Graph 3.0 software. PLS (partial least square) is a variance-based structural equation model (SEM) technique that allows path analysis of models with latent variables. The evaluation of the model was based first on the assessment of the model measurements by assessing their validity and reliability. Second, it was based on the analysis of the paths of the structural model. The model included 10 constructs (4 exogenous and 6 endogenous) with 24 indicators. The total sample size used for analysis was 100. This sample size is more than sufficient to conduct SEM paths analysis of the research model according to Chin and Newsted's (1999) recommendations.

Constructs' Validity and Reliability

With PLS, the reliability of the measurements was evaluated by internal consistency, and the validity was measured by the average variance extracted (AVE), which refers to the amount of variance in a latent variable captured from its indicators. The recommended level for internal consistency reliability is at least 0.70, while for AVE, is at least 0.50 (Chin, 1998). Table 1 shows that the study constructs' reliability and AVE are above the recommended levels. The factor loadings from the confirmatory factor analysis (CFA) provide evidence for convergent validity as all items load sufficiently high on the corresponding constructs (see Table 2). They all exceed the threshold value of 0.50 suggested by Peterson (2000).

To achieve the discriminant validity of the constructs, Fornell and Larcker (1981) suggest

Table 2. Measurements statistics

	MEAN	STD	LOADING
Knowledge Acquisition			
ACQU1	2.820	0.892	0.7370
ACQU2	2.750	0.880	0.7673
ACQU3	2.900	0.927	0.7494
Knowledge Conversion			
CONV1	3.020	1.073	0.8698
CONV2	2.220	0.917	0.8910
CONV3	2.560	0.914	0.9337
Knowledge Application			
APPL1	2.620	0.850	0.8482
APPL2	2.920	0.849	0.8341
APPL3	2.670	0.682	0.9089
Knowledge Protection			
PROT1	3.250	1.086	0.8991
PROT2	3.430	1.103	0.9565
PROT3	3.300	0.893	0.9219
Effectiveness			
EFFE1	3.410	0.753	0.9745
EFFE2	3.250	0.770	0.9659
Efficiency			
EFFI1	3.480	0.904	0.9593
EFFI2	3.390	0.803	0.9584
Innovation			
INNO1	2.590	0.753	0.9578
INNO 2	2.420	0.699	0.9738
Learning			
LEAR1	2.910	0.996	0.9238
LEAR2	3.240	0.955	0.8652
Adaptability			
ADAP1	3.110	0.863	0.9261
ADAP2	3.130	0.960	0.9316
Satisfaction			
SATI1	3.260	0.824	0.9333
SATI2	3.230	0.815	0.9539

that the square root of the average variance extracted (AVE) of each construct should exceeds the correlations shared between the constructs and the other constructs in the model. Table 3 shows that the model constructs satisfy that rule, as the square root of the AVE (on the diagonal) for each construct is greater than the correlations with the other constructs. Thus, all the model's constructs have a satisfactory reliability and validity measurements.

Table 1. Constructs' validity and reliability

Construct	Total items	Reliability	AVE
Acquisition(ACQU)	3	0.795	0.565
Conversion(CONV)	3	0.926	0.807
Application(APPL)	3	0.898	0.747
Protection(PROT)	3	0.948	0.858
Effectiveness(EFFE)	2	0.747	0.941
Efficiency(EFFI)	2	0.958	0.919
Innovation(INNO)	2	0.965	0.933
Learning(LEAR)	2	0.889	0.801
Adaptability(ADAP)	2	0.926	0.863
Satisfaction(SATI)	2	0.942	0.890

Table 3. Construct' correlations and discriminant validity

Constructs	ACQU	CONV	APPL	PROT	EFFE	EFFI	INNO	LEAR	ADAP	SATI
ACQU	**0.752**									
CONV	0.407	**0.898**								
APPL	0.366	0.456	**0.864**							
PROT	0.153	0.646	0.389	**0.926**						
EFFE	0.195	0.505	0.401	0.535	**0.970**					
EFFI	0.272	0.442	0.295	0.440	0.826	**0.959**				
INNO	0.355	0.208	0.372	0.131	0.356	0.477	**0.966**			
LEAR	0.330	0.439	0.654	0.159	0.377	0.409	0.498	**0.895**		
ADAP	0.299	0.144	0.549	0.050	0.405	0.490	0.461	0.772	**0.929**	
SATI	0.207	0.233	0.532	0.213	0.530	0.669	0.454	0.669	0.844	**0.943**

Model Evaluation and Paths Analysis

With PLS, R-square values are used to evaluate the predictive relevance of a structural model for the dependent latent variables, and the paths coefficients are used to assess the effects of the independent variables. The significance of the model paths were tested by T-tests. Bootstrapping technique was utilized with a re-sampling of 200 to test the significance of the PLS estimates of path coefficients. Based on PLS-Graph user's guide, this resample size provides reasonable standard error estimates.

Table 4 shows the R2 values of the endogenous constructs. The model explains 50.9% of variance in employees' learning, 35.4% of variance in busi-

ness processes' effectiveness, 34.8% of variance in employees' adaptability, 28.4% in employees' job satisfaction, 21.6% in the business processes' efficiency and 19.5% in the business processes' innovation.

Table 4 also shows that the paths' coefficients analysis between the exogenous constructs (KM processes) and the endogenous constructs (benefits). The statistical significance of paths' coefficients was measured by t-values. The analysis shows that, first, providing tools that support knowledge acquisition through a corporate portal was significantly positively associated with only business processes' innovation (Beta-β of 0.261 and p-value of <0.05); thus *Hypothesis 1c* was only supported for knowledge acquisition. Second,

Table 4. Model evaluation and paths analysis

Constructs (R²)	Effectiveness (0.354)	Efficiency (0.216)	Innovation (0.195)	Learning (0.509)	Adaptability (0.348)	Satisfaction (0.284)
Acquisition	-0.0080	0.1730	0.261[b]	0.0090	0.1400	0.0230
Conversion	0.214[a]	0.0450	0.0280	0.359[e]	0.0920	0.0340
Application	0.179[a]	0.0890	0.291[c]	0.608[e]	0.595[e]	0.529[e]
Protection	0.328[e]	0.314[d]	-0.0040	-0.311[b]	-0.1430	0.0250
a. p-value < 0.1 **b.** p-value < 0.05 **c.** p-value < 0.01 **d.** p-value <.0025 **e.** p-value < 0.0005						

providing tools that support knowledge conversion through a corporate portal was significantly positively associated with business processes' effectiveness (β =0.214; p < 0.1); and employees' learning (β =0.359; p < 0.0005). Thus, *Hypothesis 2a* and *Hypothesis 2d* were only supported for knowledge conversion. Third, providing tools for knowledge application was significantly positively associated with business processes' effectiveness (β =0.179; p < 0.1), business processes' innovation (β =0.291; p < 0.01), employees' learning (β =0.608; p < 0.0005), employees' adaptability (β =0.595; p < 0.0005) and employees' job satisfaction (β =0.529; p < 0.0005). Thus,

Hypothesis 3a, Hypothesis *3c*, *Hypothesis 3d*, *Hypothesis 3e* and *Hypothesis 2f* were supported for knowledge application. Fourth, providing tools for knowledge protection portal was significantly positively associated with business processes' effectiveness (β =0.328; p < 0.0005) and the business processes' efficiency (β =0.314; p < 0.0025), but negatively associated with employees' learning (β =-0.311; p < 0.1). Thus, *Hypothesis 4a*, *Hypothesis 4b* and *Hypothesis 4d* were supported for knowledge protection. Figure 2 shows the model with only the significant paths.

Figure 2. The study model with only significant paths

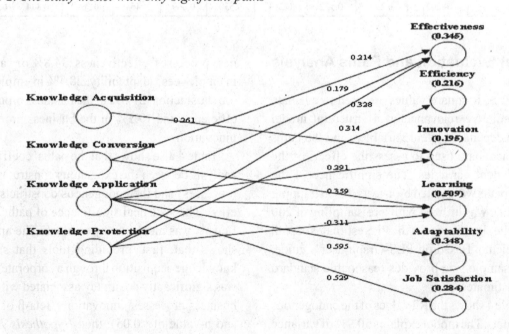

DISCUSSION OF FINDINGS

A corporate portal provides a gateway into corporate internal and external information and knowledge resources. Corporate portals are playing a major role on organizational knowledge management by incorporating tools for efficient access of organizational information/knowledge, communication and collaboration. The objective of this study was to identify the impact of supporting knowledge management processes (acquisition, conversion, application and protection) through a corporate portal on business processes' efficiency, effectiveness and innovation, and employees' learning, adaptability and job satisfaction.

The results suggested that supporting knowledge management through corporate portal had significant impacts on organizational business processes and employees. Consistent with the literature and previous research, the knowledge application has the highest impact on business processes and employees, compared to the other KM processes. The benefit of a KM tool is achieved by the application of its knowledge to solve problems and make decisions. First, knowledge application had a significantly positive impact on employees' learning (β =0.608), employees' adaptability (β =0.595) and employees' job satisfaction (β =0.529). Knowledge application also had a significantly positive impact on business processes in terms of innovativeness (β =0.291), and effectiveness (β =0.179), but not efficiency. These significant findings are consistent with Al-Busaidi (2005), Davenport and Prusak's (1998), and Liu (2003).

Second in order of impact on employees and business processes was knowledge protection. Knowledge protection, consistent with Gold et al.'s (2001) empirical research and Turban et al.'s (2008) suggestion, had a significantly positive impact on business processes' effectiveness (β =0.328) and efficiency (β =0.314). However, knowledge protection had a significantly negative impact on employees' learning (β =-0.311).

These results illustrated that even though knowledge protection may improve the quality of the knowledge and consequently business processes' effectiveness and efficiency, it may restrict employees' learning. Restricting access to the system and organizational knowledge may also restrict and hinder employees' learning, and consequently employees' adaptability and job satisfaction. Norman (2002) indicated that cautious knowledge protection approaches may improve the organization effectiveness, but it brings potentially serious disadvantages; Besides, limiting information flows will likely slow communication and decision-making and result in bottlenecks and schedule delays, and limit flexibility of the organization.

Knowledge conversion is the third in order of impacting business processes and employees. Providing tools that support knowledge conversion through a corporate portal had a significantly positive impact on employees' learning (β =0.359), consistent with Weerawardena et al. (2006), and business processes' effectiveness (β =0.214), consistent with Gold et al. (2001) and Tiwana (2004).

Finally, knowledge acquisition had the lowest impact on business processes and employees, compared to the other KM processes. The analysis showed that providing tools that support knowledge acquisition through a corporate portal had a significantly positive impact on only the business processes' innovation (β =0.261), consistent with Chang and Lee (2007) and Jiang and Lia (2008).

In conclusion, the sequence of the significance of KM processes' impact on business processes and employees makes a logical sense. KM core processes starting from knowledge acquisition (creation/generation), moving to knowledge conversion and ending with knowledge application (or utilization) is a systematic sequence of KM lifecycle. The ending process, knowledge application is the one that accumulates most of the KM lifecycle benefits; while the starting KM process, knowledge acquisition, makes the lowest impact. Knowledge protection is a supporting process for the KM lifecycle; it ensures the right quality, effectiveness and efficiency of organizational knowledge throughout the KM lifecycle. However, too much protection and restriction procedures may restrict and hinder employees' learning.

Furthermore, the correlations analysis in Table 3 provided some insights on this KM investigation. First, the high correlations between the employees' job satisfaction and the other business processes' and employees' benefits, suggest that the employees' job satisfaction may be associated with the net benefits gained from the system use. Thus, supporting KM processes through a corporate portal does not directly impact employee's job satisfaction (except for knowledge application), but indirectly through the other perceived net benefits (business processes' and employees' benefits). This is similar to DeLone and McLean's (2003), Jennex's (2008a) and Jennex and Olfman's (2006) proposition of user satisfaction and net benefits. Second, the high correlation between employees' learning and adaptability, r=0.77, indicated the strength of the relationship between the two. Employees' adaptability is highly related to their learning capability; learning provides employees with sufficient knowledge that enables them to adapt to new tasks and circumstances at their work (Becerra-Fernandez et al., 2004). Third the high correlation between efficiency and effectiveness, r=0.826, illustrated a strong relationship between business processes' efficiency and effectiveness. Effective application of knowledge also improves organizations' efficiency and reduces costs (Davenport & Prusak, 1998).

CONCLUSION

Study Implications

In conclusion, this study provided some implications for practitioners and researchers. First, this study tackled an under investigated area in portals and KM literature, the impact of support-

ing KM through corporate portal on employees and business processes. The study confirmed for practitioners and researchers that the deployment of organizational KMS, specifically corporate portals, results in numerous benefits for business processes and employees. The study also provided measurements for evaluating such benefits. Second, the study empirically showed that corporate portal is a promising technology for organizational knowledge management as it can be used as a tool to acquire, convert, apply and protect organizational knowledge. A corporate portal provides employees with a rich shared information work space to create, exchange, store, retrieve, share and reuse knowledge. Third, the study showed that the major impact of KMS results from the application of its managed knowledge. The benefits of KMS are achieved by the application of its knowledge to carry out business processes, solve business problems and make business decisions. Providing mechanisms and tools to support knowledge acquisition and knowledge conversion are important, but not sufficient to fully harness the benefits of a knowledge management system. Supporting and ensuring knowledge application will do that. Also, throughout the knowledge management lifecycle, providing tools to protect organizational knowledge is essential for its effectiveness and efficiency. However, practitioners need to ensure that these protection tools and mechanisms do not restrict and hinder employees' learning. Fourth, this study was conducted in under investigated area, the Middle East. Knowledge is a power for any national economy including developing countries. Developing countries needs to increase their knowledge base, invest in educating their people, and take advantage of new technologies for acquiring and disseminating knowledge (World Bank, 1998). This study showed that corporate portal is a promising technology for organizational knowledge management at a Middle Eastern organization. Fifth, the study illustrated the utilization of corporate portal for organizational KM at an academic institution. For academic institutions,

KM enables improvements in basic academic business processes such as consulting, education, research, publishing, and courses manufacturing (Tikhomirova et al., 2008). Corporate portal enables efficient and effective KM for academic institution. Li and Wood (2005) indicated that most schools have not formally evaluated their portals. Thus, this study provided measurements for academic institutions to evaluate the capability of their portals to support their organizational knowledge management.

Limitations and Future Research

There is no study without limitations. First, this study investigated KM processes based on Gold et al.'s (2001) classification and benefits based on Becerra-Fernandez et al.'s (2004) classification. Future research might conduct this investigation based on different KM processes and benefits classifications. Second, this study assessed the benefits of corporate portal from end users' perspective; Organizational benefits were not assessed in this study as they are better assessed from managers' perspective not users' perspective. Third, this investigation of the impact of supporting KM processes on employees and business processes was done in the context of corporate portal, and the sample was from one academic institution in one country, Oman. Before generalizing the findings, further investigations are needed across different KM systems and from different organizations and countries.

REFERENCES

Al-Busaidi, K., & Olfman, L. (2005). An Investigation of the Determinants of Knowledge Management Systems Success in Omani Organizations. *Journal of Global Information Technology Management*, *8*(3), 6–27.

Al-Busaidi, K. A. (2005). *A Socio-Technical Investigation of the Determinants of Knowledge Management Systems Usage*. Unpublished doctoral dissertation, Claremont Graduate University, Claremont, CA.

Al-Busaidi, K. A. (2009). Strengths and Weaknesses of Corporate Portal. In K. Soliman (Ed.), *Proceedings of the 13th International Business Information Management Association Conference: Knowledge Management and Innovation in Advancing Economies* (pp. 875-882). International Business Information Management Association (IBIMA).

Alavi, M., & Leidner, D. (1999). Knowledge Management Systems: Issues, Challenges, and Benefits. *Communication of the AIS*, *1*(7), 2–37.

Alavi, M., & Leidner, D. (2001). Review: Knowledge management and knowledge management systems: Conceptual foundations and research issues. *Management Information Systems Quarterly*, *25*(1), 107–136. doi:10.2307/3250961

Aneja, A., Rowan, C., & Brooksby, B. (2000). Corporate portal framework for transforming content chaos on Intranets. *Intel Technology Journal*, *Q1*, 1-7.

Barney, J. (1991). Firm resources and sustained competitive advantage. *Journal of Management*, *17*(1), 99–120. doi:10.1177/014920639101700108

Becerra-Fernandez, I., Gonzalez, A., & Sabherwal, R. (2004). *Knowledge management: Challenges, solutions and technologies* (1st ed.). Upper Saddle River, NJ: Pearson Education Inc.

Benbya, H., Passiante, G., & Belbaly, N. (2004). Corporate portal: a tool for knowledge management synchronization. *International Journal of Information Management*, *24*, 201–220. doi:10.1016/j.ijinfomgt.2003.12.012

Chang, S., & Lee, M. (2007). The Effects of Organizational Culture and Knowledge Management Mechanisms on Organizational Innovation: An empirical study in Taiwan. *The Business Review-Cambridge, 7*(1), 295–301.

Chin, W. (1998). The partial least square approach to structural equation modelling. In Marcoulides, G. A. (Ed.), *Modern Methods for Business Research* (pp. 295–336). London: Lawrence Erlbaum Associates.

Chong, S. (2006). KM critical success factors: A comparison of perceived importance versus implementation in Malaysian ICT companies. *The Learning Organization, 13*(3), 230–256. doi:10.1108/09696470610661108

Daniel, E., & Ward, J. (2006). Integrated service delivery: Exploratory case studies of enterprise portal adoption in UK local government. *Business Process Management Journal, 12*(1), 113–123. doi:10.1108/14637150610643805

Davenport, T. H., & Prusak, L. (1998). *Working knowledge*. Boston: Harvard Business School Press.

De Carvalho, R. B., Ferreira, M. A., Choo, C. W., & Da Silva, R. V. (2007). The Effects of Enterprise Portals on Knowledge Management Projects. In Tatnall, A. (Ed.), *Encyclopedia of Portal Technologies and Applications* (pp. 296–303). Hershey, PA: IGI Global.

DeLone, W., & McLean, E. (1992). Information Systems Success: The quest for the dependent variable. *Information Systems Research, 3*, 60–95. doi:10.1287/isre.3.1.60

DeLone, W., & McLean, E. R. (2003). The DeLone and McLean model of information systems success: A ten-year update. *Journal of Management Information Systems, 19*(4), 9–30.

Detlor, B. (2000). The corporate portal as information infrastructure: towards a framework for portal design. *International Journal of Information Management, 20*, 91–101. doi:10.1016/S0268-4012(99)00058-4

Dias, C. (2001). Corporate portals: a literature review of a new concept in Information Management. *International Journal of Information Management, 21*, 269–287. doi:10.1016/S0268-4012(01)00021-4

Drucker, P. F. (1993). *Post-capitalist Society*. New York: Butterworth Heineman.

Fornell, C., & Larcker, D. (1981). Evaluating structural equation models with unobservable variables and measurement error. *JMR, Journal of Marketing Research, 18*, 39–50. doi:10.2307/3151312

Goh, D., Chua, A., Luyt, B., & Lee, C. (2008). Knowledge access, creation and transfer in e-government portals. *Online Information Review, 32*(3), 348–369. doi:10.1108/14684520810889664

Gold, A. H., Malhotra, A., & Segars, A. H. (2001). Knowledge management: An organizational capabilities perspective. *Journal of Management Information Systems, 18*(1), 185–214.

Gurugé, A. (2002). Living and Breathing Portals. *Corporate Portals Empowered with XML and Web Services*, 273-284.

Heisig, P. (2009). Harmonisation of Knowledge Management – Comparing 160 KM Frameworks around the Globe. *Journal of Knowledge Management, 13*(4), 4–31. doi:10.1108/13673270910971798

Holsapple, C. W., & Joshi, K. D. (2002). Knowledge Manipulation Activities: Results of a Delphi study. *Information & Management, 39*, 477–490. doi:10.1016/S0378-7206(01)00109-4

Hult, G. T. M. (2003). An integration of thoughts on knowledge management. *Decision Sciences, 34*, 189. doi:10.1111/1540-5915.02264

Jennex, M. (2008a). Impacts From Using Knowledge: A longitudinal study from a nuclear power plant. *International Journal of Knowledge Management, 4*(1), 51–64.

Jennex, M. (2008b). Exploring System Use as a Measure of Knowledge Management Success. *Journal of Organizational and End User Computing, 20*(1), 50–63.

Jennex, M., & Olfman, L. (2006). A Model of Knowledge Management Success. *International Journal of Knowledge Management, 2*(3), 51–68.

Jiang, X., & Lia, Y. (2008). An empirical investigation of knowledge management and innovative performance: The case of alliances. *Research Policy, 38*(2), 358–368. doi:10.1016/j.respol.2008.11.002

Kjaegaard, A., & Kautz, K. (2008). A process model of establishing knowledge management: Insights from a longitudinal field study. *Omega, 36*, 282–297. doi:10.1016/j.omega.2006.06.009

Lai, L. (2007). A knowledge engineering approach to knowledge management. *Information Sciences, 177*, 4072–4094. doi:10.1016/j.ins.2007.02.028

Lee, H., & Choi, B. (2003). Knowledge management enablers, process, and organizational performance: an integrative view and empirical examination. *Journal of Management Information Systems, 20*(1), 179–228.

Li, S., & Wood, W. (2005). Portals In The Academic World: Are They Meeting Expectations? *Journal of Computer Information Systems, 45*(4), 50–55.

Liu, P., & Tsai, C. (2007). Effect of Knowledge Management Systems on Operating Performance: An Empirical study of hi-tech companies sing the balanced scorecard approach. *International Journal of Management, 24*(4), 734–744.

Liu, S. (2003). *A study of factors that facilitate use of knowledge management systems and the impact of use on individual learning.* Unpublished doctoral dissertation, Claremont Graduate University, Claremont, CA.

Masrek, M. (2007). Measuring campus portal effectiveness and the contributing factors. *Campus-Wide Information Systems, 24*(5), 342–354. doi:10.1108/10650740710835760

Nevo, D., & Chan, Y. E. (2007). A Delphi study of knowledge management systems: Scope and requirements. *Information & Management, 44*, 583–597. doi:10.1016/j.im.2007.06.001

Newell, S., Huang, J., Galliers, R., & Pan, S. (2003). implementing enterprise resource planning and knowledge management systems in tandem: fostering efficiency and innovation complementarily. *Information and Organization, 13*, 25–52. doi:10.1016/S1471-7727(02)00007-6

Nonaka, I., & Takeuchi, H. (1995). *The Knowledge-creating Company: How Japanese Companies Create the Dynamics of Innovation.* New York: Oxford University Press.

Norman, P. (2002). Protecting knowledge in strategic alliances: Resource and relational characteristics. *The Journal of High Technology Management Research, 13*, 177–202. doi:10.1016/S1047-8310(02)00050-0

Peterson, R. (2000). A meta-analysis of variance accounted for and factor loadings in exploratory factor analysis. *Marketing Letters, 11*, 261–275. doi:10.1023/A:1008191211004

Pinto, M., & Doucet, A. (2007). An educational resource for information literacy in higher education: Functional and users analyses of the e-COMS academic portal. *Scientometrics, 72*(2), 225–252. doi:10.1007/s11192-007-1725-9

Teece, D. (1998). Capturing Value from Knowledge Assets: the new economy, markets for Know-How and Intangible Assets. *California Management Review, 40*(3), 55–79.

Teo, T., & Men, B. (2008). Knowledge portals in Chinese consulting firms: A task–technology fit perspective. *European Journal of Information, 17*, 557–574. doi:10.1057/ejis.2008.41

Tikhomirova, N., Gritsenko, A., & Pechenkin, A. (2008). University Approach to Knowledge Management. VINE. *The journal of information and knowledge management systems, 38*(1), 16-21.

Tiwana, A. (2004). An empirical study of the effect of knowledge integration on software development performance. *Information and Software Technology, 46*(13), 899–906. doi:10.1016/j.infsof.2004.03.006

Turban, E., Leidner, D., McLean, E., & Wetherbe, J. (2008). *Information Technology for Management: Transforming organizations in the digital economy*. New York: Wiley & Sons, Inc.

Weerawardena, J., O'Cass, A., & Julian, C. (2006). Does industry matter? Examining the role of industry structure and organizational learning in innovation and brand performance. *Journal of Business Research, 59*(1), 37–45. doi:10.1016/j.jbusres.2005.02.004

World Bank. (1998). *World Development Report 1998/99: Knowledge for Development*. Retrieved from http://www.worldbank.org/wsr/wsr98/contents.htm.

Wu, J.-H., & Wang, Y.-M. (2006). Measuring KMS success: A respecification of the DeLone and McLean's model. *Information & Management, 43*, 728–739. doi:10.1016/j.im.2006.05.002

Yang, Z., Cai, S., Zhouc, Z., & Zhou, N. (2005). Development and validation of an instrument to measure user perceived service quality of information presenting Web portals. *Information & Management, 42*, 575–589. doi:10.1016/S0378-7206(04)00073-4

APPENDIX A: MEASUREMENTS

Knowledge Acquisition Tools- Corporate portal has tools for:
ACQU1.generating new knowledge(info) from existing knowledge
ACQU2. identifying best practices
ACQU3. acquiring new knowledge(information) from external sources
Knowledge Conversion Tools-Corporate portal has tools for:
CONV1.integrating different sources and types of knowledge(info)
CONV2. converting competitive intelligence into plans of action
CONV3. filtering knowledge(information)
Knowledge Application Tools-Corporate portal has tools for:
APPL1. using knowledge(information) to solve new problems
APPL2.locating and applying knowledge(information) to critical competitive needs
APPL3. matching sources of knowledge(information) to problems and challenges
Knowledge Protection Tools-Corporate portal has tools for:
PROT1.protecting knowledge(information) from inappropriate use inside the organization
PROT2. protecting knowledge(information) from inappropriate use outside the organization
PROT3. restricting access to some sources of knowledge(information)
Effectiveness- The use of corporate portal:
EFFE1. improves the effectiveness of my work
EFFE 2. improves the quality of my work
Efficiency- The use of corporate portal:
EFFI1. helps me complete my work quickly
EFFI 2. helps me complete my work at lower cost
Innovation- The use of corporate portal:
INNO1. improves my creativity at work
INNO 2. Improves my innovation at work
Learning- The use of corporate portal:
LEAR1. improves my learning process
LEAR 2. enhances my personal knowledge
Adaptability- The use of corporate portal:
ADAP1. enhances my adaptability level at work
ADAP 2. helps me be responsive to new job demands
Satisfaction- The use of corporate portal:
SATI1. enhances my job satisfaction
SATI2. makes me more satisfied with my job

This work was previously published in International Journal of Knowledge Management, Volume 6, Issue 3, edited by Murray E. Jennex, pp. 44-64, copyright 2010 by IGI Publishing (an imprint of IGI Global).

Chapter 12

Foot-Printing E-Learners' Activity:
A First Step to Help their Appropriation of the Training System?

Magali Ollagnier-Beldame
Chambéry Management School, France

ABSTRACT

Information and communication technologies have invaded the field of training, though their performances have been judged by companies to be insufficient. Among the origins of this state of affairs, the author considers that the lack of knowledge of what happens in a "real use situation" plays an important role. Indeed, understanding what is involved in learners-system interactions is fundamental to improve the system appropriation and its efficient usage. This appropriation is a dual necessity for learners as they must take over the offered possibilities of interactions and acquire the necessary knowledge. As appropriation is made through offered interactions, the author considers computer interactions traces as potential appropriation facilitators. This conceptual article presents bibliographical research concerning the use of computer interactions traces and proposes a classification of 'tracing systems'. Additionally, the links between these works and the process of appropriation in an instrumented training situation is provided, while the author also presents an experimental study conducted on the role of traces of interactions in a collaborative mediated task by using a numerical environment.

INTRODUCTION

As in innumerable other fields of activity, information and communication technologies have invaded the field of teaching and training. A recent study of Bersin (2006) shows that North American industries' budget for e-learning and instrumented training amounts to 46.6 billion dollars. The amount spent on external technologies, products and services represents around 14.8 billion dollars. The amount concerned with tele-learning (Learning Management Systems - LMS) represents 3 to 7% of the total expenditure on

DOI: 10.4018/978-1-4666-0035-5.ch012

training in an organisation. In the last few years, a large number of big industrial groups have tried to improve and consolidate the usage that is made of LMSs. According to (Bersin, 2006), in the next 12 months, a third of companies plan to increase the number of systems used within their organisations. Virtual class systems have been adopted in numerous sectors. In Bersin (2006) we can read that 60% of the companies listed in the study use virtual classes for company training. In another study from the same group, published in January 2006, the global budget of the LMSs was 480 million dollars.

Moreover, the performances of e-learning solutions have up until now, been judged to be insufficient by the companies. In particular, they do not have a real idea of the results of the implementation of such solutions. Among the reasons for this state of affairs, we think that a lack of knowledge of what happens in a "real use situation" plays an important role. In fact, an understanding of what is involved in the interaction between learner(s) and system(s) is fundamental for improving the appropriation of these systems and for their efficient use. The researchers in the technology enhanced learning field, who study instrumented learning situations, discover flaws in the conceptualization of interactions between learner(s) and system(s), particularly as multiple learners are involved with them: the learner himself, the system designer *etc.* In this context, it seems to us that the fact of tracing the learner-environment interactions is a very interesting path to follow, so that they can be later used to help learners appropriate the system. Besides, it appears to be both relevant and urgent that a typology is proposed for computer assisted learning situations which already use computer traces of the interactions between learner(s) and system(s). This is precisely what this conceptual article is concerned with.

We will firstly present the context of the intelligent learning environments, followed by a classification of the systems tracing interactions.

We will finally explain how traces can facilitate the learner's appropriation of the environment.

Technology Enhanced Learning

The research field on instrumented learning and digital environments for human learning has mainly dealt with interactions between learners and technical devices, in particular with regard to digital environments. This therefore concerns digital environments designed with the aim of *'aiding human learning; that is to say, increasing the learner's knowledge'* (Tchounikine, 2002, p. 3). This type of environment enables learners to interact with others, to interact with artificial agents, to gain access to all types of teaching elements which are the resources for the learning activity. They aim to facilitate the building up of a sense, in particular through the collective processes where a sense emerges.

We consider that the question of learner's appropriation of this type of environment is central. In fact, intelligent learning environments are complex environments that are rarely 'intuitive' despite the efforts of their designers. The question of their appropriation and their 'recognition' as instruments by learners, fundamentally motivated our work.

The learners spontaneously 'instrument' their activity *via* their digital environment, using the possibilities of 'available interactions' as a basis. Traces of these interactions should therefore 'naturally' reveal this appropriation to 'provide a sense' for learners.

In the case of an activity which instruments interactions, as it is the case in a situation where an intelligent learning environment is used, a part of these interactions becomes tangible and likely to be observed both by the human (learner) and by the environment (system). A certain number of digital environments make it possible to retain computer traces of interactions which are tangible for a human observer, whether he is the one observed (learner, person who produces traces) and /or an observer of the activity in progress, for example an analyst of the situation. The use of these traces for the means of analysis is quite common in the field of intelligent learning environments when the observer is a teacher or a designer of educative activities (learner follow-up, tutoring), whereas it is an exception when the observer is himself the producer. Therefore, although the theoretical challenges, in terms of design of 'user centred' environments are very important, the research field concerning the 're-use' of experience in the form of a visualization of interaction traces is a field of research that has seldom been explored, and in particular, in the context of human learning.

We therefore think that presenting computer traces of interactions to learners, as 'inscribed knowledge' in the system, can facilitate their appropriation of intelligent learning environments.

Below, we present a classification of the digital environments, which traces the interactions between the learner(s) and the digital environment(s).

Classifying the 'Tracing Systems'

For the rest of this conceptual article, we have retained the following definition for 'computer traces of interactions'. They are '*sequences of information registered by and included in the environment relating to uses a person made of it*'. In the domain of human-computer interaction, tracing learner-environment interactions and using these traces as research tools has existed for a

long time (Szilas & Kavakli, 2004). These traces are 'histories', used to understand the interaction situation or to help the learner with his task.

We propose to classify situations related to the use of 'history of interactions' according to the way they are used, and in particular, according to whether they are presented to learners or not. We present here the different situations where computer traces are used and classify them according to the possibilities and the type of operations the tracing environment makes it possible to carry out on these traces.

Figure 1 summarizes our classification grid.

In this conceptual article, we are more particularly interested in the use of computer traces of interactions when they are sent back with visualization to learners who produced them during their activity, as shown in Figure 1.

In the next sections, we illustrate the grid, classify systems according to it, and show that the grid can be an operational tool to distinguish numerical environments.

Environments Using Interactional History without Presenting it to Learners

The first group of environments we can identify is those which do not present histories of interactions to learners. These environments use learners' environment traces of interactions but they do not exploit them in the form of visualizations. These

Figure 1. The proposed grid to classify Tracing Systems

Computer traces	For learners	For observers : analysts, tutors, teachers
Without visualization	*Personalization*	*Indicators*
	Indicators	*Profiles*
With visualization	*Activities facilitators*	*Processes analysis*
	Explicit instrumentation	*Abstractions*

traces called 'log files' are calculated with the aim of predicting, according to an implicit model, the future actions of learners, and thus modifying the interface so that it corresponds to the 'predicted' behaviour. The interactions' information, on which calculations are made, corresponds to the information of the following type: access to resources, screen consultations, clicks made, time spent on operations, choices made, answers given to possible questions *etc*. These processes are automatic and are provided for in the programme. In these environments, learners' actions are compared to a model of anticipated actions.

Such environments are thus concerned with the learners' preferences when personalizing the interface. Some of these environments propose interfaces which 'give and take advice' (Lieberman, 2001) by interacting with learners. These interfaces reflect the calculations made on learners-environment interactions stored in memory, by suggesting possible actions to users. The web browser *Letizia* (Lieberman, *op.cit.*), 'gives advice' and proposes assistance to the learner by trying to undertake actions s/he is undertaking for him. The learner can accept, disregard or reject the proposition. While the learner is 'surfing' in the left-hand window, *Letizia* also 'surfs' and proposes advice in the right-hand window. The graphic editor *Mondrian* (Lieberman, *op.cit.*) asks for advice from learners, using concrete and visual examples to show what they are expecting, associated with actions, so that the *Mondrian* environment can interpret the examples. In their state of the art on the question of environments guiding and supporting collaborative learning, Jermann, Soller and Mühlenbrock (2001) qualify these environments as 'advisors' and 'moderators'. These environments analyse the state of collaboration among learners by using an interaction model and offering advice to improve the actual learning. The environmental coach (human or artificial) has the role of guiding learners in a collaborative and effective learning process. According to these authors, since a satisfying collaborative learning process includes as much learning to collaborate, as collaborating in order to maintain the learning process, the environment has to be able to propose advice of a social or collaborative nature as much as advice on the learning task.

Environments Offering a Visualization of Interactional History to Situation Observers

The second group of environments concerns environments offering a visualization of learner-environment interaction traces to the situation observer who is not the learner of the environment. In the context of uses analysis in interactional situations, it can be interesting for the situation analyst (for example a researcher) to have access to traces of the interactions between learners and environments. For a long time, computer traces have been used by researchers to 'spy on' the way 'subjects' behave in a given situation, or use an environment. These types of studies exist in ergonomics, educational sciences, psychology and communication. Després (2001) developed an environment for an instrumented learning situation, based on interaction traces, enabling a tutor to detect the state of advancement of the learners' work. Another well-known 'spy' used for man-machine interactions, is that of *PlayBack* (Neal & Simons, 1983). A recording of interaction traces can lead to diverse counting procedures: time spent, frequencies of use, functionalities used or not used, errors, rates of success *etc*. (Dubois et al., 2000) cite other, more specific, measures such as the rate of repetition, the rate of composition and the locality (Greenberg and Witten, 1988). For a classification based on traces, methodologies are applied, based on works from the recognition of forms: neural networks and data mining. These methods analyze sequences appearing in traces or all transitions of sequences. (op. cit., Dubois et al., 2000), with the aim of taking a large variety of different types of information into consideration, propose a method to analyze use traces in their context, in order to make an ergonomic validation of web sites. They carried out an automatic processing based on the degrees of similitude and correlation in the reference matrix. (Georgeon, Mille, & Bellet, 2006) propose the *Abstract* environment (Analysis of Behaviour and Situation for menTal Representation Assessment and Cognitive acTivity modelling) to trace car drivers' actions and to analyze them. Five sources of data are integrated into traces: video data from different cameras on the vehicle, measures from the vehicle's interior, information from a telemeter, navigation data from a GPS and events triggered by the investigator. In the context of a learning process, the files obtained from a learner can be used to characterize interactions and make a model of the learner by the researcher. According to Renié (2000), interaction traces give information on the operations which can be correlated with other parameters, such as the results obtained in tests, and the characteristics of learners, to obtain 'profiles'. In these environments, an objective can be to discover certain 'motives of actions' for the learners through the means of statistical calculations.

Environments Offering a Visualization of Interactional History to Learners and Proposing Possibilities of Browsing Actions

The third group of environments offers a visualization of interaction traces to learners and enables them to browse in this information. These environments present the interactional history to learners to make their activities easier. The possibilities for learners to interact with this history are limited to the browsing and do not concern the undertaking of new actions nor the entering of information which triggers these actions. Certain environments concern browsing, others are intended to learning situations.

Web Browsing Environments

Reviewing past events is useful in numerous contexts. Greenberg and Witten (1988) were interested very early in the fact that users repeat their actions when using computers. They noticed that users repeated certain operations and took an interest in the possibilities offered by environments to encourage re-using (e.g., teletypewriters, graphic selections, editions, browsing in menus, predictions and programming). A study of web browsing shows, for example, that 58% of the URLs consulted by users had already been consulted by these same users (Tauscher & Greenberg, 1997), and that, consequently, web browsing could gain considerable benefit from tools presenting histories. These authors in fact analyzed six weeks of use of a browser by 23 users with the following objectives: to understand the way in which the users revisit web pages, to see if 'repeated motives' exist for reusing them, to assess the types of existing histories in the current browsers, and to create design indications for the new 'historical environments' associated with browsers. They showed that users frequently revisit the pages they have already visited, but also that they continue to visit new ones, often just once. Concerning the pages that were visited several times, they showed that the last visited pages were often re-solicited - 30% of browsing actions consisting in using the 'Back' button of the browser. Unfortunately, whereas most of the browsers propose historical functions, they are in general limited and not very satisfying.

There has also been a debate on the representation of the history: in a linear form, in a tree structure, in a network or other forms (Hightower et al., 1998; Greenberg & Cockburn, 1999). *Webmap* (Doemel, 1994) is a browser extension which provides a graphical link between web pages. The *PadPrints* environment (Hightower et al., 1998) is a 'companion' of the browser which dynamically constructs a map of the history of visited web pages. The map represents the consulted

URLs in a tree structure to be read from left to right. According to these authors, the web pages are revisited, but the users do not use the history proposed by the browser. They prefer the 'Back' button of the browser. The authors explain that this is because of the three main limitations which are the incompleteness, the textual form and the cumbersome aspect of the histories. Greenberg and Cockburn (1999), while studying the field of web browsing and the implication of the histories, considered the role of the 'Back' button of the browser. They showed that the 'Back' and 'Forward' buttons are frequently used in order to revisit pages, more than the histories and the bookmarks. These results were confirmed by Cockburn and Jones (2000) who developed the web browsing aid environment, *WebNet*, using a graphical and dynamic representation of user's browsing actions. With the *Specter* environment, Schneider, Bauer and Kröner (2005), propose an 'artificial memory' to help users by increasing their perception. The idea is a dual one. Firstly, such a memory could provide support by taking the context into account, and considering the previous experiences connected with similar situational contexts. Secondly, this memory could supplement the subject's 'natural' memory and could be used to find the information again. Based on a memory model, inspired by the cognitivist models of human memory, this support proposes cooperation between the user and the environment based on ontologies. It proposes reviewing certain of the users' actions, then carrying them out again and posting them. In this environment, the question of the format of traces is considered, which has to be understandable for the *Specter* environment and the users. The environment of Wexelblat and Maes (1999), *Footprints*, proposes to link information relating to the various uses of the web browser to the objects manipulated by the user who is browsing. It analyzes the http logs of a server in order to make a graph of the browsing done by users. The *Footprints* environment is one of the 'social browsing' support environments. Social browsing is a process which consists of using signals or traces originating from other people, for example by using posting or classifying, to make the task easier. It is a way of 'finding information in the activities of others', through communication and interactions. It can be direct, *i.e.* explicit, for example someone says 'You should go to another cinema', or indirect *i.e.* implicit, for example someone who is in the queue for the cinema. It can be planned *versus* fortuitous (Svensson, 2000) according to the relationship with the other person. The idea is to use the history of interactions from previous uses of environments as part of the learner interface, that is to say, to use the traced information that is useful for the task in hand. The interactional history between users and the learning environment emerges in the interface between these learners, where interactions take place. In fact, digital environments lack historical traces and the representations do not integrate traces of use or interactions into the environment which are visible for learners. However, the richness as well as the form of these traces modify the way learners perceive the objects of interaction, the way they appropriate, consider and reuse them.

Environments Dedicated to Learning

Histories of interactions can be beneficial to learners in numerous fields. They can help learners to improve their skills, through research in digital libraries, word processing tasks, computer-assisted design tools, environments which aid electronic performance and web browsers (Hill & Hollan, 1993; Wexelblat & Maes, 1999). According to Plaisant et al. (1999), proposing an understandable recording of their actions can help learners to regulate their activities by considering their progression and their experiences. This can also help the collaboration between learners. In fact, an ability to record the activities can be beneficial for learners: a complete session can be recorded, in such a way that peers or tutors can analyze the work carried out. The *SimPLE* (Simulated Process in a Learning Environment) environment replaces learning histories by a learning environment based on simulations (Plaisant et al., 1999). *SimPLE* includes a module called a 'visual historian' which provides learners with the means of interacting with the recorded histories: possibility of posting, replaying, editing parts of the history or the complete history. Carroll et al. (1996) and Guzdial et al. (1996) suggest that learning histories are useful because they encourage cognitive activities concerning cognitive processes (we are here speaking of 'metacognitive' activities) because of the support that they provide to learners in terms of control of their activity and reflections made on their progress. According to these authors, giving learners access to their past experiences can help them to understand what they have done, to correct/ modify an event, to replay their history, to save their histories so that they can replay them later, to consult them with their peers or tutors or to search for events in these histories.

In the field of digital environments for human learning, tools exist for visualizing learners' click stream, developed to support reflective activities and learners' 'metacognitive' adjustments. These tools are based on the idea that using computer traces of learners' activities is a means which helps in the understanding of the learning process. This reflection with regard to the task, called 'reflective follow up' (Katz & Lesgold, 1992), enables learners to visualize traces of their actions and performance, leading them to an awareness which makes it possible to carry out the 'metacognitive' adjustments. In this approach, the principal difficulties involved are to be able to detect, trace, model and represent actions that are significant for the learner, as Gama (2003) showed. *Sherlock II* (op. cit., Katz & Lesgold, 1992) is an example of an environment using this type of reflective incitation. Carroll et al. (1996) developed an environment, called the 'Journal for Assessing Learning', which is based on all the information recorded during learning sessions, an that is then proposed to support reflective activities.

Environments Offering a Visualization of Interactional History to Learners and Proposing Possibilities for Actions other than Browsing

The last group of environments we can identify concerns environments presenting a visualization of learners' interactions history and offering them the possibility to act on it. These environments use the history of interactions as a tool for learners, allowing them to enter their data or commands. We will rapidly describe three of these environments, *Histview*, *Collagen* and *Sherlock*.

In the *Histview* environment of Terveen, McMackin, Amento, and Hill (2002), the history of interactions cannot only be visualized and browsed, but it can also enable users to inform the environment of what corresponds the most to their preferences among the propositions made to them. The example showed in the article of Terveen et al. (2002) concerns an environment processing musical play lists. The user is invited to define his preferences according to his personal history or that of others. A histogram of musical style is proposed to him. In this histogram, two sliding bars represent each style and each artist: one bar for what has been played in the past and one bar for the current choice. The user can act on the second bar, increasing it or reducing it, which means that he requests more or less music of this type. The modification of one bar leads to a modification of the other choice bars, so that the number of pieces of music continues to be numbered. These authors carried out experiments to empirically test two types of interfaces for their environment, by implementing them into computers and mobile telephones. They also tested the role of the 'historicalness' of the situation according to three situations: the participants had to select pieces of music to be played. A third party of participants had access to the history of their use of the environment, *i.e.* the pieces already listened to as well as the sequences that had been played.

Another third party had access to the history of the group, *i.e.* the pieces listened to by all the learners. In the last group, the subjects did not have access to any information of a historical nature. The results of this research are as follows; first, having access to the history made it easier for subjects to select the titles they wished to program. Then, this was done more rapidly that in the situation where there was no access to the history. Finally, it was shorter that in the situation where there was access to the group history.

In a certain number of systems from the fourth group, the history of interactions had been used to replay or to elude the command sequences, with possible variations between the former sequence and the new one. For example, the interface of the *Collagen* environment, described in (Rich & Sidner, 1997), enables an element to be selected in the history of interactions called a 'segment'. This makes it possible to create new commands in a menu linked to the achievement of an objective. The facts of presenting an interactional history to the learner that is explicit and can be manipulated, and the fact that this can be structured according to the preferences of the learner, offer the possibility of transforming the format of the problem to be solved, in the application. Three categories of action can be envisaged. The first one is to stop the course of actions being carried out. The second one is to go backwards (retrying, revisiting or undoing), which makes it possible to go back to the previous level in the problem-solving process. And the third one is to replay the action, therefore making it possible to reuse the previous work in a new context.

Regarding the test interface developed for the *Sherlock* environment (Lesgold et al., 1992), which is an environment for training technicians in avionics, Lemaire and Moore (1994) used as a basis the idea that past human-computer dialogues are sources of knowledge. In this tutoring environment, the history of interactions is used to improve the explanations given to the learner. He can select a past explanation, provided by the environment, and ask the environment to compare it with the current explanation. The environment therefore automatically produces a text comparing the two situations to support the learner's task. When the *Sherlock* environment refers to a previous explanation, it scrolls through the dialogue history to the appropriate point and shows the learner the portion of the dialogue in question. When the learner wishes to refer to another part of the dialogue and asks a question about it, it enables him to locate the zone of the dialogue and ask a question from a range of standard questions. In this environment, the history of the human-computer dialogues can therefore be shown to the learner, but also manipulated by him, and its representation on the screen can be modified according to his preferences.

All the works we have just presented here consider the role played by computer traces in learners' activities. Among these researches, the environments developed for learners presenting a visualization of the history of interactions are based on the hypothesis that this presentation will enable learners to distance themselves from their activity and in this way, would create an activity within an activity, of a reflective nature.

From the classification of 'tracing systems' for learning that we have proposed, and following our first definition of 'traces of interactions', we would now like to specify the role of traces in the appropriation process.

In fact, we would like to have a better understanding of the role that computer traces can play in the particular context of the use of intelligent learning environments. On the question of the role of such systems traces, we would like to underline the fact that, in a 'learning context', learners must first appropriate the environment, before being able to carry out their main task, which consists in assimilating the pedagogical content the system offers.

Traces of Interactions as Appropriation Facilitators

In a situation with a digital environment, the difference between the designer logic and the user logic can be the cause of large disparities and lead to difficulties in the usage that users make of the environment. These disparities correspond to the difference between the functions within the artefacts, i.e., previously defined functions whose creation is the basis for the design of the artefact, and the constituted functions, *i.e.* functions created during the usage of the artefacts (Folcher & Rabardel, 2004). This distance that ergonomists have noticed between the recommended usage and the real usage of digital environments, causes problems for users when appropriating the environment. With regard to these difficulties, which, in our opinion, constitute obstacles preventing the 'good' use of intelligent learning environments, we consider that activity traces, when presented to learners can further the understanding that they have of the environment. We therefore put forward the hypothesis that computer traces of interactions, presented to learners, can facilitate learners' appropriation of the digital environment by enhancing the understanding they have of the environment and the possibilities it offers.

Few researches have focused on the appropriation process as such, and we note that even the term 'appropriation' is often used in the "common sense of the word". However, we present below the works of certain authors concerning this process of appropriation.

Millerand et al. (2001) define the process of appropriation as being connected with the process of learning and human development and envisage the sense of the term in the same way as Vygotsky. In their view, appropriation is '(…) *the manner in which an individual acquires, masters, transforms or translates the codes, the protocols, the knowledge and the know-how necessary for "correctly" coming to terms with the material objects'*. They propose necessary elements for a

socio-cognitive approach of usages, in order to understand the way in which the appropriation of technical devices is achieved. When observing appropriation, they reintroduced the experience concerning the materiality of technique by considering technical devices as partners in learners' activity. They proposed an operating definition of appropriation that could, in their opinion, only be compromised in the context of a temporal process implying transformations of the situation on the part of the learners. Thus according to this perspective, '*learners choose or redefine functions of the device to give a sense to its use until it becomes the object of a new definition.*' And the 'changes of usage' observed can thus be understood as 'elements revealing the dynamics of differentiated appropriation that takes place when practical experience is gained'. According to these authors, it is 'during' the learner's experience of the device that appropriation comes into play, i.e. during the implementation of technique. For Dourish (2003), appropriation is the '*process by which people adopt and adapt technologies, adjusting them to their own practices*'. The process, which is of a reflective nature, is thus, in his view, similar to that of 'personalizing', but which relates to the types of adoption of the technology, and a transformation of the practices, so that they are of a higher level. For (Rabardel & Samurçay, 2001), appropriation corresponds to what Wertsch calls 'mastery' (skills when using a tool, acquired during its usage, and in a given context), and results from a progressive process of instrumental creation. Wertsch (1998) defines appropriation as the process in which a subject takes something which belongs to another to make it his own. It is a non-linear process, which is difficult, and which leads to tensions between the object of the appropriation and the usage made of it in a particular context, tensions which lead to resistances.

We retain the idea that appropriation is an iterative process where sense negotiation, which is involved when a person uses an object, enables the adoption and the adaptation of the object. Appropriation is, in a certain way, the action of giving a sense to a situation which 'does not have one'. Therefore, the process of appropriation is situated, in our view, between the two moments where the sense is stabilized, in the 'intermediate' periods. We also accept the view, expressed in the works presented here, that appropriation is a process which is linked to a reflective point of view of the person on his activity.

We have here made the connection with some works cited in our classification of tracing environments; this concerns tracing environments which present a visualization of interactional history to learners, proposing different possibilities for browsing or acting on it. These environments offer visualization of interactions to learners, based on meta-cognitive hypothesis, and aim at furthering the learners' reflective awareness of their activity. By 'reflective activity' we mean an activity that has been reflected on, i.e., self-orientated. We are referring to an activity considering itself as the object. The idea is that the digital environment can serve as a 'mirror with a memory' for learners, presenting traces. These latter can incite learners to distance themselves from their activities which is at the origin of a meta-type awareness. An example of the use of these principles for sharing knowledge can be found in Komlodi (2002) who applied it to the legal domain through a process of annotation and re-memorization.

Some Experimental Results on the use of Traces of Interactions

We have conducted a study on the use of traces of interactions in a collaborative mediated task (Ollagnier-Beldame, 2006; Heili & Ollagnier-Beldame, 2008), using a numerical environment and conducting to a vygotskian development of users. Another experimental work is also in progress (Heili & Ollagnier-Beldame, 2008; Héraud, 2008; Gendron et al., 2008; Cram et al., 2008). In this study, we observed dyads of users using

a digital artefact to carry out the task that we assigned to them (a co-redaction of a procedural text). 'Raw' traces of their activity appeared on the environmental interface during the course of the activity. These traces appeared in fact as 'imprints' of the users' activities inscribed by and in the environment. We observed if users used the traces or not.

The main result is that traces were used and that they could be qualified differently according to two dimensions: First, depending on the user 'at the origin' of the traces and depending on the user who used them. Second, depending on the 'digital area' of the environment where users left the traces and let them be seen. These traces of interactions proved to be objects aiding the negotiation of activity, objects that were in continuous evolution during the development of the activity. This study provided us with elements for understanding the relationship existing between traces of interactions and knowledge jointly constructed between users. These traces were supports during the communication between users, and they were also the means of interacting with the other person and with oneself, *via* reflexive activity.

This study took the point of view of considering traces of interactions as potential aids in the sense-construction, such as in the process appropriation of computer environments, in particular when the activity is collective. It also permits us to consider design paths we could use for the creation of 'tracing systems'. These types of system in which the interactions only appear because of the interface have been explicitly developed to trace the interactions between users and interactions between users and the environment, and to present them on the interface. The conceptual literature and experiments show clearly that the use of 'tracing systems' has great potential, but also shows the difficulties in offering 'appropriated' means of exploiting this 'mine' of experience (episodes of activity) to be discovered during the activity, reused, shared and capitalised etc. We are mainly thinking of the design of systems that provide users with the immediate history of their interactions in real time according to the 'points of view', which would open the way for us to look back over the user's activity and the associated processes of human development. In our opinion, it is very likely that the fact of making explicit the user's history of his interactions with the system, with the possibility of acting on it, is an element to consider as a principle to be followed within the same human-centred design process for digital artifacts and, in particular for devices concerned with learning processes.

CONCLUSION

This conceptual article gave us the opportunity to make a bibliographical research concerning the use of computer traces of interactions in activities mediated by a digital environment. We have distinguished the uses of computer traces according to whether they can be visualized as traces or not. We have also considered the 'addressees' of the visualization, and shown different uses of traces: Firstly, traces 'for' learners but without visualization or personalization. Secondly, traces 'for' learners and with reflective actions in their activity. Thirdly, traces for an observer-analyst and with calculations of indicators. And fourthly, traces 'for' an observer-analyst, with reformulations and abstractions for the purpose of analyzing activities. We have then presented the importance of the appropriation process when it was concerned with sense-construction, in particular in a situation of human learning. Finally, we showed that experimental results confirm our hypothesis concerning the role of interactions traces in a collaborative mediated activity.

With regard to the setting up of mediated learning situations, we suggest that the choice of digital devices offering a *de facto* visualisation of the interaction traces could enable learners to take stock of their activity and have a better control of their learning process as a process situated in the

time limit and the 'digital spaces' proposed. In fact, we think that in a learning context, situations where there are collective activities have really a great deal to gain from the implementation of digital environments enabling the exploitation of computer traces of interactions. In fact, in these types of situations, the sense-construction is an explicit necessity and we imagine that argumentative negotiation could really benefit from an aid provided by explicit traces of the interactions among learners and between learners and computers environment (Dillenbourg, 1999).

As a conclusion, the strong dynamic of the current research into computer traces of interactions leaves us confident that a 'knowledge-orientated' research programme will be developed in very good conditions. And we think that this type of research will be able to give us information on the processes occurring when a digital environment is used for human learning. We think that this understanding is, in fact, a necessity for improving the performances of the e-learning solutions that have been implemented, particularly in companies.

REFERENCES

Bersin., & Associates. (2006). *New study looks at US corporate learning market. Institute for Competitive Intelligence*. Retrieved from http://www.trainingreference.co.uk/ news/gn060329a.htm

Carroll, S., Beyerlein, S., Ford, M., & Apple, D. (1996). The Learning Assessment Journal as a tool for structured reflection in process education. In [Washington, DC: IEEE.]. *Proceedings of Frontiers in Education, 96*, 310–313.

Cockburn, A., & Jones, S. (2000). Which way now? Analysing and easing inadequacies in WWW navigation. *International Journal of Human-Computer Studies, 45*, 105–129. doi:10.1006/ijhc.1996.0044

Cram, D., Fuchs, B., Prié, Y., & Mille, A. (2008, June 8-12). *An approach to User-Centric Context-Aware Assistance based on Interaction Traces.* Paper presented at the Fifth International Workshop Modeling and Reasoning in Context (MRC 2008), Delft, The Netherlands.

Després, C. (2001). *Modélisation et Conception d'un Environnement de Suivi Pédagogique Synchrone d'Activités d'Apprentissage à Distance.* Thèse de Doctorat, Université du Maine, Le Mans.

Dillenbourg, P. (1999). What do you mean by collaborative learning? In Dillenbourg, P. (Ed.), *Collaborative-learning: Cognitive and Computational Approaches* (pp. 1–19). Oxford, UK: Elsevier.

Doemel, P. (1994). WebMap - A Graphical Hypertext Navigation Tool. In *Proceedings of 2nd International Conference on the World Wide Web*, Chicago, IL (pp. 785-789).

Dourish, P. (2003). The Appropriation of Interactive Technologies: Some Lessons from Placeless Documents. *Computer-Supported Cooperative Work: Special Issue on Evolving Use of Groupware*, *12*, 465–490. doi:10.1023/A:1026149119426

Dubois, J.-M., Dao-Duy, J.-M., & Eldika, S. (2000). L'analyse des traces informatiques des usages: un outil pour valider la conception d'un site web. In *Proceedings of Dans Actes des rencontres jeunes chercheurs en Interaction Homme-Machine* (pp. 85-89).

Folcher, V., & Rabardel, P. (2004). Hommes, artefacts, activités: perspective instrumentale. In Falzon, P. (Ed.), *Ergonomie*. Paris: PUF.

Gama, C. (2003). *Towards a model of Metacognition Instruction in Interactive Learning Environments.* Unpublished doctoral dissertation, University of Sussex, England.

Gendron, E., Carron, T., & Marty, J.-C. (2008, October 16-17). *Collaborative Indicators in Learning Games: an immersive factor.* Paper presented at the 2nd European Conference on Games Based Learning, Barcelona, Spain.

Georgeon, O., Mille, A., & Bellet, T. (2006). Analyzing behavioral data for refining cognitive models of operator. In *Proceedings of the Philosophies and Methodologies for Knowledge Discovery*, Krakow, Poland. Washington, DC: IEEE.

Greenberg, S., & Cockburn, A. (1999, June 3). Getting Back to Back: Alternate Behaviors for a Web Browser's Back Button. In *Proceedings of the 5th Annual Human Factors and the Web Conference*, Gaithersburg, MD.

Greenberg, S., & Witten, I. H. (1988, June 15-19). How Users Repeat Their Actions on Computers: Principles for Design of History Mechanisms. In E. Soloway, D. Frye, & S. B. Sheppard (Eds.), *Proceedings of the ACM CHI 88 Human Factors in Computing Systems Conference* (pp. 171-178). Washington, DC: IEEE.

Guzdial, M., Kolodner, J., Hmelo, C., Narayanan, H., Carlso, D., & Rappin, N. (1996). The collaboratory notebook. *Communications of the ACM*, *39*(4), 32–33. doi:10.1145/227210.227218

Heili, J., & Ollagnier-Beldame, M. (2008). *Analyse de l'activité et complexité des interactions homme-machine: Pour une revalorisation des études de cas.* Actes 13eme conférence AIM 2008, Paris.

Heili, J., Ollagnier-Beldame, M., & Héraud, J.-M. (2008). Traces d'utilisation, utilisation de traces: Application à l'adaptation des IHM. In *Proceedings of the 13ème Conférence AIM 2008*, Paris.

Hightower, R., Ring, L., Helfman, J., Bederson, B., & Hollan, J. (1998). Graphical multiscale web histories: A study of PadPrints. In. *Proceedings of Hypertext*, *98*, 58–65.

Hill, W. C., & Hollan, J. D. (1993). History-enriched digital objects. In *Proceedings of Third ACM Conference on Computers, Freedom and Privacy*, San Francisco, CA (pp. 917-920). New York: ACM.

Jermann, P. R., Soller, A., & Mühlenbrock, M. (2001). From mirroring to guiding: A review of state of the art technology for supporting collaborative learning. In *Proceedings of European Perspectives on Computer-Supported Collaborative Learning*, Bergen, Norway (pp. 324-331).

Katz, S., Lesgold, A., Eggan, G., & Gordin, M. (1992). Modelling the student in Sherlock II. *Artificial Intelligence in Education, 3*(4), 495–518.

Lemaire, B., & Moore, J. (1994). An improved interface for tutorial dialogues: browsing a visual dialogue history. In *Proceedings of the Conference on Human Factors in Computing Systems* (pp. 16-22).

Lesgold, A., Lajoie, S., Bunzo, M., & Eggan, G. (1992). Sherlock A Coached Practice Environment for an Electronics Troubleshooting Job. In Larkin, J., & Chabay, R. (Eds.), *Computer Assisted Instruction and Intelligent Tutoring Systems: Shared Goals and Complementary Approaches*. Hillsdale, NJ: Lawrence Erlbaum Associates.

Lieberman, H. (2001). Interfaces that Give and Take Advice. In Carroll, J. (Ed.), *Human-Computer Interaction for the New Millenium* (pp. 475–485). New York: ACM Press.

Millerand, F., Giroux, L., & Proulx, S. (2001). La culture technique dans l'appropriation cognitive des TIC. Une étude des usages du courrier électronique, Dans *Actes du colloque international ICUST 2001*, Paris (pp. 400-410).

Neal, A. S., & Simons, R. M. (1983). Playback: A method for evaluating the usability of software and its documentation. In *Proceedings of CHI '83* (pp. 78-82).

Ollagnier-Beldame, M. (2006). *Traces d'interactions et processus cognitifs en activité conjointe: Le cas d'une co-rédaction médiée par un artefact numérique*. Thèse de Doctorat, Université Lumière Lyon2, France.

Plaisant, C., Rose, A., Rubloff, G., Salter, R., & Shneiderman, B. (1999). The Design of History Mechanism and Their Use in Collaborative Educational Simulations. In *Proceedings of the Computer Support for Collaborative Learning*, Palo Alto, CA (pp. 348-359).

Rabardel, P., & Samurçay, R. (2001, March 21-23). From Artifact to Instrument-Mediated Learning. In *Proceedings of International symposium on New challenges to research on Learning*, Helsinki, Finland.

Renié, D. (2000). Apport d'une trace informatique dans l'analyse du processus d'apprentissage d'une langue seconde ou étrangère. In Duquette, L., & Laurier, M. (Eds.), *Apprendre une langue dans un environnement multimédia* (pp. 281–301). Outremont, Canada: Les Éditions Logiques.

Rich, C., & Sidner, C. L. (1997). Segmented Interaction History in a Collaborative Interface Agent. In *Proceedings of International Conference on Intelligent User Interfaces*, Orlando, FL (pp. 23-30).

Schneider, M., Bauer, M., & Kröner, A. (2005). Building a personal memory for situated user support. In *Proceedings of the First International Workshop on Exploiting Context Histories in Smart Environments (ECHISE 2005)* at Pervasive 2005, Munich.

Svensson, M. (2000). *Defining and designing social navigation*. Unpublished doctoral dissertation, Stockholm University, Department of computer and system sciences.

Szilas, N., & Kavakli, M. (2006, January 29-February 1). PastMaster@Strorytelling: A Controlled Interface for Interactive Drama. In *Proceedings of IUI 2006: International Conference on Intelligent user Interfaces*, Sydney, Australia (pp. 288-290).

Tauscher, L., & Greenberg, S. (1997). How People Revisit Web Pages: Empirical Findings and Implications for the Design of History Systems. *International Journal of Human-Computer Studies, 47*(1), 97–138. doi:10.1006/ijhc.1997.0125

Tchounikine, P. (2002). Pour une ingénierie des Environnements Informatiques pour l'Apprentissage Humain. *Revue I3 information – interaction – intelligence, 2*(1). Retrieved from www.revue-i3.org

Terveen, L. G., McMackin, J., Amento, B., & Hill, W. (2002, April). Specifying Preferences Based On User History. In *Proceedings of CHI'2002*, Minneapolis MN (pp. 315-322). New York: ACM Press.

Wertsch, J. (1998). *Mind as Action*. Oxford, UK: Oxford University Press.

Wexelblat, A., & Maes, P. (1999). Footprints: History-rich tools for information foraging. In *Proceedings of ACM CHI 99 Conference on Human Factors in Computing Systems* (pp. 270-277).

This work was previously published in International Journal of Knowledge Management, Volume 6, Issue 3, edited by Murray E. Jennex, pp. 65-77, copyright 2010 by IGI Publishing (an imprint of IGI Global).

Chapter 13
A Knowledge Framework for Development:
Empirical Investigation of 30 Societies

Ravi S. Sharma
Nanyang Technological University, Singapore

Ganesh Chandrasekar
Nanyang Technological University, Singapore

Bharathkumar Vaitheeswaran
Nanyang Technological University, Singapore

ABSTRACT

In this article, the authors investigate the diverse dimensions of a knowledge society. First, the relevant literature on post industrial societies is reviewed to identify the key constituents of successful growth and development. The authors then propose a 10-dimension framework within political, economic, social and technological parameters that describe the state of evolution of a given knowledge society. Knowledge assessment scores, human development indices, technology readiness scores and competitiveness scores are selected as composite indicators of knowledge societies. Proxy indicators are assigned for the dimensions, and secondary data was gathered from reputed international sources. Partial Pearson Correlation Analysis was done between the proxy indicators and the composite scales to determine the direction and strength of relationships. Hygiene factors and competitive factors of a knowledge society are distilled from the empirical results and recommendations are suggested to address some areas of concern when pursuing policies for knowledge based development.

INTRODUCTION

"Development is neither smooth nor linear—at any geographic scale. Growth comes earlier to some places than to others" declared a World Bank (2009, p. 8) report. Indeed waves of development do not appear to reach all societies alike, and so are their growth and development cycles. This article examines why sustainable development comes to some societies earlier for reasons other than natural advantages. Field research has shown that knowledge based economies are directly based

DOI: 10.4018/978-1-4666-0035-5.ch013

on the effective production, distribution and use of knowledge and information (OECD, 1996; UNDP, 2007; World Bank, 2009). In these economies, knowledge is created, shared and transferred as commodities for the welfare of society and hence it requires a change in other facets of life (Kahin & Foray, 2006). Unlike land and capital wherein sharing results in diminished wealth for its owners, knowledge is a non diminishing resource. In fact knowledge owners liberally share for reputation and reciprocity (Davenport & Prusak, 2000), and profit commercially by diffusion through licensing or franchising.

This article considers knowledge globally pervasive, inviting enabled individuals and societies to adopt and apply knowledge to solve real problems. The concept of a knowledge society is incomplete without taking globalization into consideration because knowledge is ubiquitous. Gupta and Govindarajan (2000) have studied barriers of knowledge flows within multi-national corporations while work of Simard and Rice (2007) analyzed the linkages between best practice transfer and knowledge creation. Friedman (2007) has proposed ten *flatteners* which drive knowledge exchange and concludes that the convergence of new platform, new processes and new players have made developing countries compete and excel in chosen sectors of the knowledge economy. Prahalad (2005) suggested that once societies evolve as knowledge societies there is a real possibility that the flow of knowledge from developed to developing countries will be complimented by reverse flows as well. While knowledge creation is a requisite for knowledge society, it should make efforts to understand the nuances of making knowledge flow to absorb external knowledge and penetrate internal knowledge. A knowledge society needs to have virtues of creation, absorption and mobilization.

Technology infrastructure and usage is the basis for a knowledge society and the penetration of technology is hence critical (OECD, 2004; Sharma & Mokhtar, 2006). According to Prahalad

and Krishnan (2008), the growth of future businesses invariably depends on accessing global assets to co create with customers which requires social and technical architectures as fundamental building blocks. Technology in itself does not lead to knowledge creation and but provides a universal platform for sharing knowledge. Porter (1998) argues that such a platform is part of the business environment for competing firms and plays a major role to attract fresh players and help existing players to leverage their competitive advantages. Though monopoly and state control are major inhibitors for innovation (Kotler et al., 1997), in the post-industrial society, governments have an important role of empowering the individuals by providing education, infrastructure and consistency in national policy.

From a knowledge based economy there is a natural evolution to transform into a knowledge society wherein knowledge is the key differentiator and has penetrated not only high technology sectors but also traditional industries (Foray, 2006). To achieve such a society, a combination of social, political, technological and business assets should coalesce to achieve critical mass. A goal driven strategy to develop a state as a knowledge society along the lines of the Millennium Development Goals (Spence, 2008) would lead to a flatter world, where increased knowledge transfer and unleashed markets help economies create, share and transfer knowledge equitably.

It is therefore relevant and timely to attempt to construct and measure macro indicators for knowledge creation and diffusion that supplement general indicators like Gross Domestic Product and Annual Growth rate. The World Bank Knowledge Assessment Methodology (World Bank, 2008a) and the United Nations Human Development Index (2007) account for many such non-economic factors and give a composite score. However, the knowledge society rests on other blocks as well – for example, infrastructure, governance, human capital and culture and each block has supporting columns (Sharma et al., 2008,

2009). This article presents a framework to analyze and measure the knowledge capital of a society and gives leads on its embrace of future shocks from external elements. In the remainder of the article, dimensions from the four categories of the well-known PEST (political, economic, social and technological) framework are constructed. A thorough review of the research literature revealed proxy indicators for each dimension. Secondary data for the proxy indicators was collected from reputed sources such as the World Bank, United Nations and World Economic Forum. Partial Pearson Correlations between the proxy indicators, and development scales were computed to validate the measures. The analysis revealed hygiene factors which are common across the developed and evolving knowledge societies as well as core dimensions for developed societies. Based on these patterns, competitive factors were also identified and within them causal analysis was performed to identify lead and lag indicators. It is theorized that hygiene and competitive factors would help acadamics and policy makers to perform a status checks and formulate policies to develop competitive advantage.

BACKGROUND REVIEW

According to The Growth Report (Spence, 2008), countries that have recorded growth rates in excess of 7% growth over 25 years since have 5 significant similarities – exploitation of global economy, macroeconomic stability, high rates of savings and investment, market allocation of resources and committed, credible and capable governments. The World Bank's Knowledge Assessment Methodology (2008a) is a benchmarking tool developed with 83 structural and qualitative variables to help countries identify challenges and opportunities in their evolution to knowledge based economies. The World Development Report (World Bank, 2009) identifies density of economic activity, geographic proximity to economic cen-

ters and barriers to economic interactions as the key dimensions for the transformation of such economies. The geographic proximity to markets is a key factor for development and factors like being sea locked, landlocked and area size of the country play a major role not only in the case of industrial economies, but also for knowledge economies (Sharma et al., 2008). Clustering of industries for knowledge flows, infrastructural improvements to improve mobility of workforce and trade agreements which are the characteristics of industrialized countries are major focus areas for growth (Kotler et al., 1997; Porter, 1998). Apparently, there are no short cuts to development and most societies have to thread similar evolutionary paths involving tough policy choices (Spence, 2008). This section reviews the major literature on the subject and attempts to synthesize a single model to benchmark the performance of economies as knowledge societies.

To begin the pursuit of a unified model for benchmarking and analysis factors that identify knowledge flows and facilitators within knowledge societies, we adopt the framework of Kotler et al. (1997) as illustrated in Figure 1. Kotler et al. (1997, p. 22) claim, after an extensive analysis of sustainable development, that "A nation's wealth creation, to a great extent, should be both a physical reality and a state of mind in which society has the drives and means to pursue a better life. People of all nations aspire to a good economy, a good society, and a good political process." While formulating a strategic vision, they suggest that a nation's capabilities be categorized into five major facets: (1) culture, attitudes and values; (2) social cohesion; (3) factor endowments; (4) industrial organization; and (5) government leadership. Corroborating this, the Legatum Prosperity Index (http://www.prosperity.com/) is a notable global assessment of wealth and wellbeing. In contrast to the KAM and KEI that rank countries by actual levels of wealth, life satisfaction or development, the LPI produces rankings based upon the very foundations of prosperity – those

Figure 1. The 5 blocks of a knowledge society

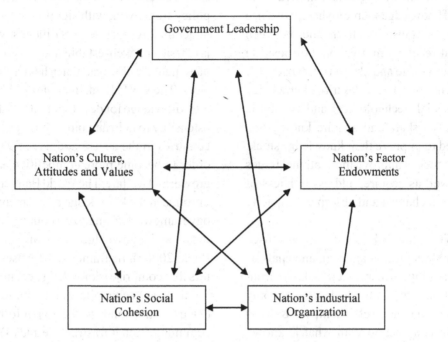

Source: Adapted from Kotler et al. (1997).

factors that help drive economic growth and produce happy citizens over the long term. These are: Economic Fundamentals, Entrepreneurship & Innovation, Democratic Institutions, Safety & Security, Governance, Personal Freedom, Education, Social Capital, and Health (not in any order of precedence).

The knowledge level of a society can hence be taken as the accumulation of everything that is known and used in carrying out its economic and social activities (Smith & Weber, 2000). This is a view that is consistently shared by development economists and scholars (Foray, 2006; Kahin, 2006; Spence, 2008). Dixon (2000) argues that to reinvent and update knowledge, organizations should create knowledge from experience and share knowledge across time and space. This applies to societies as well – enabling knowledge creation and knowledge sharing is the hallmark of a developed knowledge economy. Foray (2006) defines such dispersion on an open, distributed

platform as "public knowledge". This notion of forum or knowledge exchange is known as a 'ba' – a multi-context space to define the communication and effect five key enablers – autonomy, creative chaos, redundancy, requisite variety, trust and commitment (Nonaka et al., 2000).

Such work has shifted the focus from individuals to the environment with the implication that individuals are creative at all times and the environment is the key to transforming creative ideas into valuable knowledge (Kates et al., 2005; Prahalad & Krishnan, 2008). Similarly, sharing knowledge within the system and from outside the society involves a set of qualities. Knowledge transfer is a one-off activity wherein a strategy to acquire specific knowledge is crafted and the transfer effected. Such knowledge flows refer to the broader concept which accounts for factors that facilitate or inhibit knowledge diffusion. Gupta and Govindarajan's (2000) study of knowledge within global organizations as dependent on 5 characteristics – value of knowledge share, motivational disposition of knowledge source to share, existence and richness of transmission channel between source and at receiver, motivational disposition to acquire knowledge and absorptive capacity of receiver. Their model hence describes knowledge sharing on social, technological and economic perspectives. To share and acquire knowledge, societies need to improve their knowledge stock, address the issues to improve motivational issues to share as well as acquire, address richness of communication channel and absorptive capacity of receiver.

The PEST framework is a commonly used approach for strategic management and analysis which offers a comprehensive view of the environment in which an entity (individual, firm, economy or trading bloc) operates (cf. Thompson & Martin, 2005). In conjunction with what is known as a SWOT Analysis (cf. Porter, 1998), PEST may be used to get an outside-in view wherein the society builds on expectations from external forces whereas Kotler's (1997) framework gives an inside-out perspective where the society builds on its internal strengths. To also include the competitive perspective, a synthesis of the two with focus on elements that facilitate knowledge creation and knowledge sharing, is necessary. In other words, for a society to continuously evolve as a knowledge society it should nurture its political, economic, social and technological factors while addressing external expectations as well as leveraging on internal strengths. The factors derived from such a synthesis could be interpreted as drivers for knowledge flow processes. This is described in the next section.

KNOWLEDGE POLICY FRAMEWORK

Using political, economic, social and technological blocks to derive a more precise characterization of a knowledge society resulted in a search of the research and policy literature. Figure 2 shows a summary of the synthesized knowledge policy framework with significant factors nested under their respective PEST blocks. While PEST is classic and well-established, this framework is incremental in the sense that it has built on previous work. The World Bank Institute (2007) developed the 'knowledge for development' (K4D) program ostensibly to help and build the capacity of client countries in the access and use of knowledge in order to become more competitive and improve growth and welfare. The World Bank subsequently introduced the knowledge assessment methodology framework to analyze a country's knowledge index and knowledge economy index (World Bank, 2008b). Its framework focuses on the factors that comprise a knowledge economy and has 4 pillars: (1) economic and institutional regime, (2) education and skills, (3) information and communication infrastructure and (4) innovation system. Using this as the basis, Sharma et al. (2008, 2009) refined the 4 pillar framework (Infrastructure, Governance, Human Capital and Culture) and derived a condensed set of 13 dimensions as defining characteristics of knowledge societies. In retrospect, it was apparent that the factors derived from both of these could have been categorized under PEST classes. In this section, each of these blocks will be elaborated on further to provide a comprehensive characterization of knowledge societies for benchmarking and analysis.

Block 1: Political

It has been noted that political leadership is required for establishing a strong vision for knowledge based development and pursuing appropriate policies to achieve the same is a consequence of this (Spence, 2008). Friedman (2007) considers able politicians with skills of persuasion and inspiring charisma as a critical need, even for developed countries. Control of corruption is another key factor for development as corruption leads to inefficient use of resources (Kotler et al., 1997). Nonaka et al. (2000) suggest autonomy as

Figure 2. Blocks and dimensions of knowledge society

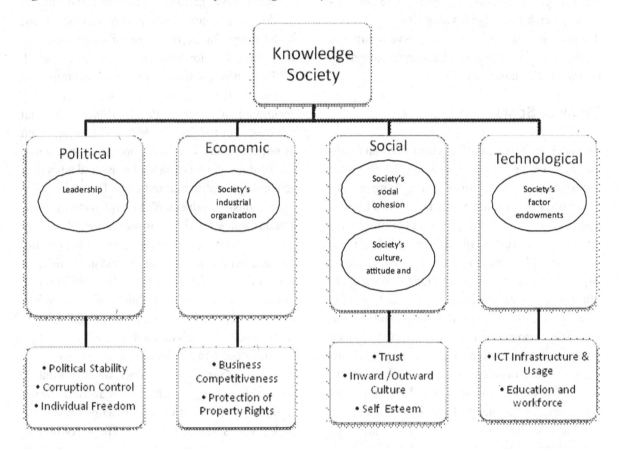

an enabler for knowledge creation. The political system should hence offer individual rights and liberties which give autonomy to individuals. In short, the political system should have a vision to develop a knowledge society, policies to develop it and the resilience to implement it while providing the social context for individuals to create knowledge.

Block 2: Economic

The economic and business environment plays a crucial role in the development of knowledge society. Competing forces are the key drivers for dynamic changes and improvement of existing systems (Kotler et al., 1997). Classical economics suggests that the greater the local competition, more capable the industry becomes to innovate

and compete with other countries and drive the frontiers further (Porter, 1998; Prahalad & Krishnan, 2008). As competition increases, another key driver for knowledge creation – creative chaos (Nonaka et al., 2000) – is creeps into the structure of society. Strong local competition leads to the formation of new business enterprises, jobs and general well-being (Porter, 1998) and introduces requisite variety to the industry, yet another enabler for knowledge creation. Protection of private property and intellectual rights is another driver for knowledge based development (Kotler et al., 1997; Huang, 2009). Legal protection for ownership provides a secure marketplace for knowledge owners to trade their knowledge. Protection of rights thus drives elements of society to be more creative for personal gain and also makes it mandatory for knowledge seekers to value the knowledge and obtain it by appropriate due process. When knowledge is valued, there is greater disposition to share as well as receive it with the market ensuring the needed absorptive capacity (Gupta & Govindarajan, 2000).

Block 3: Social

Social characteristics affect economics and conversely changes in economic conditions alter social structure. So a proper synergy with society is required to exploit the best benefits of knowledge economics. Social norms and cultures give elements like trust, commitment and thriftiness which provide competitive advantage to nations. Trust enables knowledge creation (Nonaka et al., 2000) and also results in saving transaction costs (Fukuyama, 1995). Cultural openness and internal solidarity – postulated by Friedman (2007) as a competitive advantage in globalizing environment – often provides societies with requisite variety for knowledge creation and also improves the absorption capacity of receiver. Trust based on shared values, norms and behavior improves motivational disposition on their side and improves the richness of communication channel (Gupta & Govindarajan, 2000).

Block 4: Technological

Technology, particularly information-communications technologies, have been well-studied as a key differentiator between competing nations (OECD, 2004; The Economist Group, 2008b; World Bank Institute, 2007; World Economic Forum, 2008; United Nations, 2008). It is generally accepted that Information and Communication Technology (ICT) has contributed to sustained competitive advantage of institutions and societies alike. Technological capability generally includes the infrastructure as well as the skills base as key metrics of measurement. As this implies that the human capital necessary for infrastructure design, maintenance and usage, many of the above cited

research have included education and trained workforce as technological indicators. Conversely, technology forms the core of education and workforce in knowledge societies. Kotler et al. (1997) conjecture that the higher the average skill of people, the easier it is to process and absorb technological progress. Porter (1998) argues that the classifier for firms as low tech and high tech is not the industry of their operation, but based on the deployment of skilled work and advanced technology within that industry. Technology is a cross industry enabler which can provide competitive advantage for players in the market. The ability to train a large number of skilled workers would cause a certain amount of redundancy which is one of the enablers for knowledge creation. ICT structures also improve richness of communication between the knowledge source and receiver and hence improve knowledge sharing.

From the 4 major blocks outlined above, the research examined a number of authoritative sources for the construction of what would be the defining characteristics of knowledge societies to be known as dimensions. As well, proxy indicators were also formulated that could quantify these dimensions. The methodology with which these dimensions were constructed and indicators selected is discussed in the next section.

EMPIRICAL METHODOLOGY

A study of post industrial economics was the starting point of this research. Peter Drucker (1993) provided a framework of the post industrial society and the integration of economic and social aspects of life. He also enunciated the attributes of the knowledge society such as the type of work and worker expectations. Kotler et al. (1997) developed a framework to measure the capability of societies based on five constructs – government leadership, nation's culture, attitudes and values, nation's social cohesion, nation's industrial organization and nation's factor production. This model was adapted as the building block of the framework and dimensions of analysis developed in this article and presented in Figure 2.

Competitiveness as a dimension of a knowledge society was obtained from the works of Michael Porter (1998) where an industry perspective of clustering and competition is identified as a key driver for growth and better productivity. Francis Fukuyama (1995) and Robert Putnam (2001) provide the social attributes such as culture and trust, which impact all facets of a society including business, enterprise and competition. CK Prahalad (2005) and Thomas Friedman (2007) explored the qualities which give developing countries the capability to absorb technological know-how from more advanced economies. Publications of the OECD (2004) and Mckinsey Quarterly (2009) provided technological and economic dimensions that operationalise the framework as shown in Figure 2. The work of Davenport and Prusak (2000) and Dixon (2000) provided an overview of knowledge management and the processes of knowledge creation and knowledge sharing was adopted from Nonaka et al. (2000). Simard and Rice (2007) provided the facilitators of knowledge creation whereas the model proposed by Gupta and Govindarajan (2000) provided facilitators for knowledge flows.

In this manner, we extracted development drivers and knowledge flow facilitators as building blocks and categorized then into political, economic, social and technological blocks as shown in Figure 2. Hence, dimensions within each block were derived from theoretical foundations while proxy indicators assigned to each dimension were obtained from examining various authoritative sources such as the World Bank Knowledge Assessment Methodology 2008 (World Bank, 2008a), United Nations Development Programme Human Development Report 2007-08 (UNDP, 2007), World Economic Forum's Global Competitiveness Report 2008 (WEF, 2008), World Bank Migration and Remittances Factbook 2008 (World Bank, 2008b), Economist Intelligence Unit Democracy

Index 2008 (The Economist Group, 2008a), United Nations E-readiness report 2008 (United Nations, 2008) and Economic Intelligence Unit E readiness report 2008 (The Economist Group, 2008b). The link between dimensions and proxy indicators was made on the basis of a match between their respective definitions (obtained from the literature and databases respectively).

As published, data from UNDP's HDI, UN E readiness and EIU E readiness databases were on a 0-1 scale; WEF's GCR data was in a 0-7 scale; and KAM & EIU democracy indexes were in 0-10 scales. Despite scores being in different scales, correlation analysis was done to determine the strength of relationships between indicators across some 30 societies without normalization of scales. 30 societies were selected as representative of high, medium and low income countries to avoid any data bias. The cross section of representative societies include large geographic countries and city-states; early developers and late developers; stable democracies to centrally ruled states; resource rich countries to lesser endowed countries; and individual driven and community driven states.

Table 1 summarizes the dimensions of a knowledge society that was derived from the literature using the framework in Figure 2 and their corresponding proxy indicators obtained from the authoritative sources of published data. In the next section, we test the validity of the dimensions and indicators in terms of characterizing and benchmarking the development of knowledge societies.

RESULTS AND DISCUSSION

The full data set that was used for the empirical analysis and its component sources are reproduced in the appendix. The computations of values and the scales used to derive the scores of both the composite as well as the proxy indicators is beyond the scope of this article as they were adopted from their respective sources. We first computed the Pearson Partial Correlation Coefficients among

Table 1. Dimensions and proxy indicators of knowledge societies

No	Dimensions	Description	Reference	Proxy indicators
1	Trust	The ability of members of a society to trust each other and work in groups for common purposes.	Fukuyama, 1995; Nonaka et al., 2000	Cooperation in labor-employer relations, Willingness to delegate authority
2	Inward/outward culture	Openness of culture to accept foreign ideas and solidarity to work together for national progress	Friedman, 2007	Inward Remittance as % of GDP, Brain drain
3	Social Esteem	Self respect and hope for a better future, and inherent values of competence and work ethics.	Friedman, 2007	Gender empowerment measure, Reliance on Professional Management
4	Political Effectiveness	The stability of institutions, vision of national leadership and its impact.	Drucker, 1993; Spence, 2008	Political Stability, Government Effectiveness
5	Individual Freedom	Freedom in society to express individual views and the community's ability to put up with divergent individual opinions.	Friedman, 2007	Civil Liberty
6	Control of Corruption	Increased transparency improves resource allocations and adherence to processes leads to better utilization of all resources.	Kotler et al., 1997	Control of Corruption
7	Business Competitiveness	A monopoly is a great inhibitor to innovation. Competition creates a dynamic climate and continuous productivity improvements.	Kotler et al., 1997	Intensity of Local Competition
8	Protection of Knowledge Assets	Protection of intellectual property rights is a motivator for individuals to innovate and share it for repute, credibility or monetary benefits.	Kotler et al., 1997; Huang, 2009	Property Rights, Intellectual Property Protection
9	ICT Infrastructure & Usage	ICT is a major driver for business which not only results in increased knowledge sharing, but also an enables knowledge creation by itself.	OECD, 2004	Tele-density, Price Basket for Internet in US$/ month, Internet Users/1000 Population
10	Education & Workforce	Enabled, skilled and mobile individuals contribute purposefully to growth in the knowledge economy.	Kotler et al., 1997	Quality of the Educational System, Availability of Scientists and Engineers

the various composite indicators (KAM, HDI, UN-E, EIU-E, and GCR) to test for internal consistency among the dependent variables themselves. Pearson correlations are used when all the fields represent real values which are continuous and non-atomic (as opposed to ranks, ordinal values or enumerated types). Partial correlations are used when the analysis is more on relationship than inter-dependencies. Partial correlations measure the degree of association between two variables with control variable effects removed. Table 2 gives a summary of the results. Generally, Pearson Coefficients were found to be high, ranging from 0.79 to 0.96 at p=0.01. Hence we conclude that

there is a basis for surmising that the composite indicators are internally consistent and reliable.

More specifically, from Table 2 it is observed that the World Bank's knowledge assessment score 2008, Economic Intelligence Unit's e-readiness score 2008, United Nation's E-readiness score 2008, World Economic Forum's competitiveness score 2008 and United Nations Development Programme's human development index 2007-08 are correlated at a confidence level of 99%. A high degree of correlation between the scales shows internal validity among the scales selected. This seemingly justifies the use of all the above

Table 2. Pearson partial correlation coefficients among composite indicators

Correlation	KAM Score	HDI Value	UN E- Readiness	EIU E- Readiness	GCR Score
KAM score	1				
HDI Value	.931*	1			
UN E-Readiness	.957*	.933*	1		
EIU E -Readiness	.958*	.869*	.941*	1	
GCR Score	.872*	.791*	.868*	.885*	1

* indicates correlated at 99% confidence

5 measures as composite indicators of the level of development in knowledge societies.

We next computed Pearson Partial Correlation Coefficients between composite indicators above and the proxy indicators that were identified for each of the 10 dimensions of our 4-block framework. Since there was overlap between the secondary sources of data and the composite indicators used for evaluation in a few of the cases, correlations were not computed between scales and indicators that came from same source in order to avoid bias.

Table 3 shows Pearson Partial Correlation Coefficients of the 18 proxy indicators of the 10 dimensions with each of the composite measures. Pearson correlation is taken since all data are continuous and non-atomic. Partial correlation was preferred over multiple correlations as we were concerned with the strength of relationship between the indicators and composite measures rather than inter-dependencies. In Table 3, proxy indicators from same source as the composite indicator are ignored and those blocks which are not correlated at 99% confidence are gray scaled. We consider variables that are correlated at a confidence level of 99% across all composite measures as being consistently correlated and hence key indicators. Those indicators which are correlated at 99% confidence with any 4 of the 5 (i.e., 80%) composite measures are termed partially correlated and hence considered support indicators. The proxy indicators which have a 99% confidence in 2 or less of the 5 composite measures are termed as mostly no correlation.

We may observe that the political indicators – political stability, government effectiveness and control of corruption are all correlated at 99% confidence with all composite measures. This confirms our proposition that political stability and effectiveness are definitive characteristics of knowledge societies. We may also note that government performance is a key indicator for any knowledge society. Among the economic indicators, we observe that private property and intellectual property protection rights are correlated at 99% confidence with all the composite measures while intensity of local competition is mostly not correlated with them. With regard to social indicators, we observe that brain drain, gender empowerment measure and reliance on professional management are correlated at 99% confidence across all the composite measures, while willingness to delegate authority is correlated at 99% confidence with 80% of them. Technology usage – telecommunications and Internet usage - and quality of the education system are correlated at 99% confidence with all the composite measures and hence are the key contributors to the technological block.

From Table 3 we may conclude that since brain drain, gender empowerment measure, reliance on professional management, political stability, government effectiveness, control of corruption, intellectual property protection, property rights, tele-density, internet usage, quality of the educational system are consistently correlated with all five indices, they may be termed *key factors* that measure the state of evolution of knowledge society. Willingness to delegate authority is cor-

Table 3. Pearson partial correlation coefficients between composite and proxy indicators

Proxy indicator	KAM score	GCR Score	HDI Value	UN E-Readiness score	EIU E-Readiness Score	Comments
Cooperation in labor-employer relations	0.353		0.305	0.266	0.377	Mostly no correlation
Willingness to Delegate Authority	.587**		.469*	.609**	.672**	Partially correlated
Inward Remittance as % of GDP	-.407*	-0.357	-0.3	-0.303	-0.389	Mostly no correlation
Brain Drain	.564**		.581**	.554**	.464*	Consistently correlated
Gender Empowerment Measure (GEM)	.760**	.621**		.727**	.736**	Consistently correlated
Reliance on Professional Management	.599**		.473**	.570**	.659**	Consistently correlated
Political Stability		.630**	.630**	.635**	.885**	Consistently correlated
Government Effectiveness		.874**	.779**	.835**	.938**	Consistently correlated
Civil Liberty	.528**	0.353	.461*	.471*	.559**	Mostly no correlation
Control of Corruption		.783**	.743**	.773**	.900**	Consistently correlated
Intensity of Local Competition (1-7)		.770**	.379*	.476*	.632**	Mostly no correlation
Intellectual Property Protection (1-7)		.869**	.662**	.783**	.894**	Consistently correlated
Property rights	.755**		.566**	.683**	.830**	Consistently correlated
Price basket for Internet, US$ per month		-0.249	-.394*	-0.183	0.07	Mostly no correlation
Tele-Density		.795**	.884**	.884**	.869**	Consistently correlated
Internet Users per 1000 Population		.834**	.812**	.910**	.904**	Consistently correlated
Quality of the Educational system	.598**		.497**	.565**	.676**	Consistently correlated
Availability of Scientists and Engineers	.404*		0.351	.450*	0.318	Mostly no correlation

** indicates correlated at 99% confidence; * indicates correlated at 95% confidence; Blank field indicates indicator is from same source and hence ignored; Shaded blocks indicate not correlated at 99% confidence.

related in most cases and hence it is a key enabler for a knowledge society. It is also clear that all four blocks – political, economic, social and technological – contribute in terms of defining dimensions of the knowledge society.

To probe further, we divided the societies of interest into 2 categories depending on the distribution of scores obtained from the proxy indicators. We used median scores to categorise societies into areas of concern (below average) and comfort zones (above average). For indicators such as brain drain, reliance on professional management, intellectual property protection, property rights, quality of the educational system, willingness to delegate authority and intensity of local competition which are rated between 1 and 7 we consider 1-3.99 as areas of concern and 4-6.99 as comfort zones. For gender empowerment measure we consider below .50 as area of concern and above .50 as comfort zone. For political stability, government effectiveness and control of corruption we consider positive as comfort zones and negative as area of concerns. For internet and telecommunications usage below 500 is considered areas of concern and above 500 is considered comfort zones. In short, we were trying to discern stronger and weaker performance grades in the proxy indicators for the 30 societies. This was done as a sort of SWOT analysis in order to understand the characteristics of growth drivers and inhibitors. Tables 4, 5 and 6 show the results of such an analysis. In all 3 of the tables, cells which fall in the areas of concern are gray scaled.

A close inspection of Table 4 reveals that the dimensions - willingness to delegate authority, gender empowerment measure, reliance on professional management, intensity of local competition, property rights and tele-density have high degrees of similarity across countries and an overwhelming majority of societies score well on these factors. These dimensions may be considered as prerequisites broadly addressed by all countries and no longer offer competitive advantage. They are hygiene factors and in proceeding with the comparison between OECD and evolving societies, we ignore the above fields which are important yet do not provide discernible characteristics of analysis.

A close inspection of Table 5 reveals that among OECD countries with less than 3 areas of concern, most score well on brain drain, political stability, government effectiveness, control of corruption, intellectual property protection and quality of educational system with minor differences in Internet usage. An inspection of Table 6 shows that among evolving countries having more

than 3 areas to be addressed we observe a pattern. Among these dimensions an overwhelming majority of societies under-perform with respect to political stability, control of corruption, intellectual property protection and Internet usage while they under-perform in 60% to 80% of the cases for brain drain, government effectiveness and quality of education system. A valid finding is that political stability, control of corruption, intellectual property protection and Internet usage are key competitive factors of a knowledge society, and these factors along with brain drain, gender empowerment measure, government effectiveness and quality of education system provide competitive advantage to countries as they evolve as knowledge societies. Factors like willingness to delegate authority, reliance on professional management, intensity of local competition, property rights and telephone usage are prerequisites for evolution of knowledge society but do not seemingly provide competitive advantage.

CONCLUDING REMARKS

Based on the results reported in this research, we may conclude that the competitive factors of a knowledge society are the dimensions of *political effectiveness, open culture* and *control of corruption* whose proxy indicators are wholly and strongly correlated with the composite indicators. Our research suggests that these should be the fundamental drivers of knowledge policy. As well, the hygiene factors of a knowledge society were found to be *trust, social esteem* and *business competiveness.* Our research suggests that the lack or absence of these characteristics in knowledge policy would be inhibitors of knowledge based development. Other dimensions such as protection of *knowledge assets, education & workforce,* and *ICT infrastructure & usage* were found to be competitive as well as hygiene factors in parts. Their proxy indicators were so divided.

Hence, contrary to the general perception that knowledge societies reduce the role of the state

Table 4. Key indicators having common scores across all levels of societies

Country	Willingness to delegate authority	Gender empowerment measure (GEM)	Reliance on professional management	Intensity of Local Competition (1-7)	Property rights	Tele-Density - Total Telephones per 1,000 People
Argentina	4.2	0.728	4.9	4.2	3.2	1,050.00
Australia	5.1	0.847	6.1	5.7	6.3	1,430.00
Brazil	4.6	0.49	5.4	5.3	4.6	730
Canada	5.3	0.82	5.9	5.7	6.4	1,170.00
Republic of Chile	4.6	0.519	5.6	5.7	5.4	960
People's Republic of China	4.2	0.534	5	5.3	5	630
Egypt, Arab Rep. of	4.6	0.263	3.5	4.7	4.7	390
France	4.6	0.718	5.5	5.8	6.1	1,390.00
Federal Republic of Germany	5.4	0.831	6	6.3	6.5	1,680.00
Republic of Ghana	4.5	n/a	5	5.1	4.4	250
Hong Kong SAR	4.8	n/a	5.4	6	6.3	1,920.00
Republic of India	4.8	n/a	5.4	5.9	5	190
Republic of Indonesia	4.7	n/a	5	5.5	3.5	360
State of Israel	4.8	0.66	5.4	5.6	5.2	1,620.00
State of Japan	4.9	0.557	5.6	6	6.3	1,230.00
Republic of Kenya	4.2	n/a	4.9	5.1	4.2	190
Malaysia	4.9	0.504	5.5	5.7	5.5	920
United Mexican States	4.2	0.589	4.5	4.9	4.1	740
New Zealand	5.3	0.811	6.2	5.4	6.2	1,270.00
Republic of the Philippines	4.6	0.59	5.2	5	4	540
Russian Federation	3.8	0.489	4.8	4.5	3.3	1,120.00
Republic of Singapore	5.1	0.761	6	5.5	6.5	1,480.00
Republic of South Africa	4.8	n/a	5.7	5.1	6	820
Republic of South Korea	4.7	0.51	5.1	5.6	5.4	1,380.00
Taiwan	4.6	n/a	5.2	5.8	5.6	1,660.00
Thailand	4.1	0.472	4.8	5.3	4.7	750
Republic of Turkey	3.6	0.298	4.1	5.5	4.2	980
United Kingdom	5	0.783	5.6	6	5.5	1,700.00
United States of America	5.5	0.762	6	5.9	5.8	1,350.00
Eastern Republic of Uruguay	4.1	0.525	4.1	4.2	4.9	1,000.00
Cutoff	4	0.5	4	4	4	500

Shaded cells are areas of concern

Table 5. Key indicators for developed countries

Country	Brain drain	Political Stability	Government Effectiveness	Control of Corruption	Intellectual Property Protection (1-7)	Internet Users per 1000 People	Quality of the educational system
Australia	4.1	0.85	1.94	1.99	5.9	740	5.5
Canada	4.9	0.94	2.03	1.9	5.7	680	5.6
Republic of Chile	5.3	0.85	1.25	1.31	4	250	3.2
France	4	0.46	1.2	1.44	5.9	490	5
Federal Republic of Germany	4.6	0.83	1.52	1.78	6.5	470	4.9
Hong Kong SAR	5	1.16	1.76	1.71	5.5	550	4.9
State of Israel	3.4	-1.18	1.1	0.83	5.1	270	4
State of Japan	5	1.11	1.29	1.31	5.6	690	4.5
Malaysia	4.5	0.35	1.02	0.38	5.1	430	5
New Zealand	2.8	1.27	1.94	2.38	5.8	760	4.9
Republic of Singapore	5	1.3	2.2	2.3	6.2	380	6.2
Republic of South Korea	4.3	0.42	1.05	0.31	5.4	700	4.6
Taiwan	4.6	0.51	1.11	0.53	4.9	640	4.8
United Kingdom	4.6	0.46	1.83	1.86	6	550	4.6
United States of America	6.1	0.31	1.64	1.3	5.4	690	5
Cutoff	4	0	0	0	4	500	4

Shaded cells are areas of concern

Table 6. Key indicators for evolving countries

Country	Brain drain	Political Stability	Government Effectiveness	Control of Corruption	Intellectual Property Protection (1-7)	Internet Users per 1000 People	Quality of the educational system
Argentina	3.4	-0.03	-0.19	-0.47	2.8	210	2.9
Brazil	4.3	-0.09	-0.11	-0.33	3.3	230	2.7
People's Republic of China	4.2	-0.37	-0.01	-0.53	3.4	100	3.8
Egypt, Arab Rep.	2.1	-0.87	-0.41	-0.41	3.5	80	2.4
Republic of Ghana	1.3	0.23	0.05	-0.12	3.8	30	3.4
Republic of India	3.7	-0.84	-0.04	-0.21	4	50	4.3
Republic of Indonesia	4.9	-1.17	-0.38	-0.77	3.1	70	4.2
Republic of Kenya	3	-1.09	-0.69	-0.97	3	80	4.4
United Mexican States	3.4	-0.4	0.16	-0.35	3.5	180	2.8
Republic of the Philippines	2.5	-1.26	-0.01	-0.69	3.1	50	4
Russian Federation	4	-0.74	-0.43	-0.76	2.6	180	4.3
Republic of South Africa	3.1	-0.07	0.78	0.56	5.2	110	2.8
Thailand	4.4	-0.99	0.29	-0.26	4.1	130	3.8
Republic of Turkey	3.3	-0.65	0.23	0.06	3.4	170	3.4
Eastern Republic of Uruguay	2.9	0.73	0.48	0.8	3.9	230	3.7
Cutoff	4	0	0	0	4	500	4

Shaded cells are areas of concern

to mere facilitator, we note that functions of state such as political stability, government effectiveness and control of corruption in fact play a major role in evolving knowledge societies. Political indicators remain a key differentiator between developed states and evolving ones. This finding corroborates with the central thesis of The Growth Report (Spence, 2008) which concluded that among countries performing consistently well over an extended period strong political vision is a critical component.

The emergence of Japan and Canada as knowledge societies is yet another case of societies transforming as power centers through a sustained, national policy. The case of Brazil, South Korea, China leapfrogging their competitors are credited mainly to the vision and will of its political class. Economic and business factors such as intensity of competition and ownership of property rights must be addressed by all aspiring knowledge societies. It seems that these dimensions are driven more by competition than by government policies. Hence, as a result of globalization, the competitive advantage of developed societies over evolving ones is diminishing. Nevertheless these dimensions are dynamic and all societies need to grow and sustain their business competitiveness and social cohesion in order to evolve further and remain competitive.

Social issues such as trust, culture and self esteem are addressed by all countries with brain drain seemingly the only differentiating factor. The emergence of evolving societies to a level on par with developed societies on this facet is noticeable. Societies need to build a positive climate for people to engage socially and professionally. Naturally social cohesion and strong civic institutions are needed to support such activities. While the embrace of modern telecommunication is passé, Internet penetration remains low in evolving societies. This is mitigated by the trend of falling prices for Internet services and devices globally. Focus on quality education is yet another area which differentiates the societies. The emergence of globalization has resulted in increased mobility

of natural resources, human workforce and access to cross national markets. This has given evolving countries an opportunity to catch up with the developed societies at a rate never possible before the advent of ICT-enabled globalization. Quality of education needs to be addressed by reforms to encourage public private partnerships and the transfer of best practices from foreign institutions. Efforts to decentralize control yet improve coordination within societies with global outreach, and increased interfaces with business communities can improve the quality of the education system. An entire summit discussed ways and means of brining forth Internet usage and application (cf. Sharma & Mokhtar, 2006). Implementation of information technology in government services can spur the demand for Internet and allied communication industries.

A cause effect analysis between the evolution of knowledge societies and the dimensions proposed in this research indicates that political dimensions are the key drivers for evolution of a knowledge society. This is based on the observation that not a single developed society has more than one area of concern whereas among evolving states we observe cases of societies having political dimensions in comfort zone. The above conclusion is corroborated anecdotally by pointing to the evolution of societies such as South Korea, Singapore, Malaysia, Brazil and China under visionary leadership. Other competitive dimensions of knowledge societies such as technology usage follow the evolution of knowledge society since even among the developed societies we observe these issues as areas of concern. Hence we may conclude from this that governments are the key architects of knowledge based development and growth.

Thus, we posit that the world is not flat, but is flattening at a faster pace than ever before in the history of civilization. The advantage is no longer based on natural resources or geographic area. Countries with stable political systems and visionary leadership enjoy competitive advantage over nations with weaker governance sturctures.

Evolving countries can step up their pace of development by leveraging on the increased cross border flow of personnel and technology. It is hoped that this work is a step towards what Foray (2006) calls "evidence-based knowledge policy". More specifically, this is predicated on a belief that "given the characteristics of knowledge as an economic good, it is possible to identify resource allocation mechanisms, socioeconomic institutions, that can in principle produce and allocate knowledge in an efficient manner" (p. 14). The dimensions stated in our framework that characterize a knowledge society are intended serve such a purpose.

ACKNOWLEDGMENT

The authors are part of an informal, irreverent knowledge research factory (styled on the Bourbaki group) at the Nanyang Technological University, Singapore. Ravi S. Sharma is Associate Professor of KM at NTU. Ganesh Chandrasekar and Bharat Vaitheeswaran are recent graduates of the MSc in KM program at NTU and are now KM professionals. The findings reported in this article are part of the on-going efforts to develop a formal understanding of knowledge management methods and policies. The authors are grateful to the World Bank, UNDP and EIU for the access to authoritative country data. Many thanks are also due to Murray Jennex and the anonymous reviewers for their thoughtful review of an early draft which has led to a much improved paper.

REFERENCES

Davenport, T. H., & Prusak, L. (2000). *Working Knowledge: How organizations manage what they know*. Boston: Harvard Business School Press.

Dixon, N. M. (2000). *Common Knowledge: How Companies Thrive by Sharing What They Know*. Boston: Harvard Business School Press.

Drucker, P. F. (1993). *Post-Capitalist Society*. Oxford, UK: Butterworth-Heinemann.

Foray, D. (2006). Optimizing the Use of Knowledge. In Kahin, B., & Foray, D. (Eds.), *Advancing Knowledge and the Knowledge Economy* (pp. 9–16). Cambridge, MA: MIT Press.

Friedman, T. L. (2007). *The World Is Flat: A brief history of the twenty-first century*. New York: Farrar, Straus and Giroux.

Fukuyama, F. (1995). *Trust: The Social Virtues and the Creation of Prosperity*. New York: The Free Press.

Fukuyama, F. (2004). *State-Building: Governance and World Order in the 21st Century*. New York: Cornell University Press.

Gupta, A. K., & Govindarajan, V. (2000). Knowledge flows within multinational corporations. *Strategic Management Journal, 21*, 473–496. doi:10.1002/(SICI)1097-0266(200004)21:4<473::AID-SMJ84>3.0.CO;2-I

Huang, Y. (2009). Private Ownership: The real source of China's economic miracle. *The McKinsey Quarterly, (1)*: 148–155.

Kahin, B. (2006). Prospects for knowledge policy. In Kahin, B., & Foray, D. (Eds.), *Advancing Knowledge and the Knowledge Economy* (pp. 1–8). Cambridge, MA: MIT Press.

Kates, R., Parris, T., & Leiserowitz, A. (2005). What is Sustainable Development? *Environment, 47*(3), 8–21.

Kotler, P., Jatusripitak, S., & Maesincee, S. (1997). *The Marketing of Nations: A Strategic Approach to Building National Wealth*. New York: The Free Press.

Nonaka, I., Toyama, R., & Konno, N. (2000). SECI, *Ba* and Leadership: A unified model of dynamic knowledge creation. *Long Range Planning, 33*, 5–34. doi:10.1016/S0024-6301(99)00115-6

OECD. (1996). *The Knowledge Based Economy.* Paris: OECD.

OECD. (2004). *The Economic Impact of ICT: Measurement, Evidence and Implications.* Paris: OECD.

Porter, M. E. (1998). Clusters and the New Economics of Competition. *Harvard Business Review*, 77–90.

Prahalad, C. K. (2005). *The Fortune at the Bottom of the Pyramid: Eradicating Poverty Through Profits.* Philadelphia: Wharton School Publishing.

Prahalad, C. K., & Krishnan, M. S. (2008). *The new age of innovation: driving co-created value through global networks.* New York: McGraw-Hill Professional.

Putnam, R. D. (2001). *Bowling alone: the collapse and revival of American community.* New York: Simon & Schuster.

Sharma, R., & Mokhtar, I. (2006). Bridging the Digital Divide in Asia. *The International Journal of Technology. Knowledge and Society, 1*(3), 15–30.

Sharma, R., Ng, E. W. J., Dharmawirya, M., & Lee, C. K. (2008). Beyond the Digital Divide: A Conceptual Framework for Analyzing Knowledge Societies. *Journal of Knowledge Management, 12*(5), 151–164. doi:10.1108/13673270810903000

Sharma, R. S., Ekundayo, M. S., & Ng, E. W. (2009). Beyond the digital divide: policy analysis for knowledge societies. *Journal of Knowledge Management, 13*(5), 373–386. doi:10.1108/13673270910988178

Simard, C., & Rice, R. E. (2007). The practice gap: Barriers to the diffusion of best practices. In McInerney, C. R., & Day, R. E. (Eds.), *Re-thinking knowledge management: From knowledge objects to knowledge processes* (pp. 87–124). Dordrecht, The Netherlands: Springer-Verlag.

Smith, J. M., & Webster, L. (2000). The knowledge economy and SMEs: a survey of skills requirements. *Business Information Review, 17*(3), 138–146. doi:10.1177/0266382004237656

Spence, M. (2008). *The Growth Report – Strategies for Suatainable Growth and Inclusive Development.* Washington, DC: The World Bank.

The Economist Group. (2008a). *Economist Intelligence Unit Index of Democracy 2008.* London: Author.

The Economist Group. (2008b). *E-readiness rankings 2008: Maintaining momentum.* London: The Economist Group.

Thompson, J. L., & Martin, F. (2005). *Strategic Management: Awareness & Change.* London: South-Western Cengage Learning.

UNDP. (2007). *Human Development Report 2007/ 2008.* Retrieved January 12, 2008, from http://hdr. undp.org/en/media/ HDR_20072008_EN_Complete.pdf

United Nations. (2008). *UN E-Government Survey 2008.* Retrieved March 13, 2009, from http://unpan1.un.org/intradoc/ groups/public/documents/ UN/UNPAN028607.pdf

World Bank. (2007). *Building Knowledge Economies: Advanced Strategy for Development.* Retrieved October 14, 2008, from http:// siteresources.worldbank.org/ KFDLP/Resources/4611971199907090464/ BuildingKEbook.pdf

World Bank. (2008a). *World Bank Knowledge Assessment Methodology*. Retrieved February 1, 2009, from http://web.worldbank.org/WB-SITE/EXTERNAL/ WBI/WBIPROGRAMS/ KFDLP/EXTUNIKAM/ 0,menuPK:1414738 ~pagePK:64168427~ piPK:64168435~theSite PK:1414721,00.html

World Bank. (2008b). *Migration and Remittances Factbook 2008*. Retrieved January 30, 2009, from http://econ.worldbank.org/WBSITE/ EXTERNAL/EXTDEC/EXTDECPROSPECTS/ 0,contentMDK:21352016~menuPK:3145470~ pagePK:64165401~piPK:64165026~ theSitePK:476883~isCURL:Y,00.html

World Bank. (2009). *World Development Report 2009*. Retrieved March 1, 2009, from http://econ.worldbank.org/WBSITE/ EXTER-NAL/EXTDEC/EXTRESEARCH/ EXTW-DRS/EXTWDR2009/ 0,menuPK:4231145~ pagePK:64167702~ piPK:64167676~theSite PK:4231059,00.html

World Economic Forum. (2008). *The Global Competitiveness Report 2008-2009*. Retrieved February 3, 2009, from http://www.weforum. org/ en/initiatives

APPENDIX 1.

Table A1. Social and political indicators

Country	Social indicators						Political Indicators			
	Trust		Inward/outward culture		Self esteem		Political Stability		Individual Freedom	Governance
	Cooperation in labor-employer relations	Willingness to delegate authority	Inward Remittance as % of GDP	Brain drain	Gender empowerment measure (GEM)	Reliance on professional management	Political Stability	Government Effectiveness	Civil Liberty	Control of Corruption
Argentina	3.7	4.2	0.3	3.4	0.728	4.9	-0.03	-0.19	8.24	-0.47
Australia	4.8	5.1	0.4	4.1	0.847	6.1	0.85	1.94	10	1.99
Brazil	4.3	4.6	0.4	4.3	0.49	5.4	-0.09	-0.11	9.41	-0.33
Canada	4.9	5.3	.	4.9	0.82	5.9	0.94	2.03	10	1.9
Republic of Chile	4.7	4.6	0.002	5.3	0.519	5.6	0.85	1.25	9.71	1.31
People's Republic of China	4.5	4.2	0.9	4.2	0.534	5	-0.37	-0.01	1.18	-0.53
Egypt, Arab Republic	4.7	4.6	5	2.1	0.263	3.5	-0.87	-0.41	4.12	-0.41
France	3.4	4.6	0.6	4	0.718	5.5	0.46	1.2	9.12	1.44
Federal Republic of Germany	5	5.4	0.2	4.6	0.831	6	0.83	1.52	9.41	1.78
Republic of Ghana	4.2	4.5	0.8	1.3	.	5	0.23	0.05	5.88	-0.12
Hong Kong SAR	5.6	4.8	0.2	5	.	5.4	1.16	1.76	9.41	1.71
Republic of India	4.7	4.8	2.8	3.7	.	5.4	-0.84	-0.04	9.41	-0.21
Republic of Indonesia	5.1	4.7	1.6	4.9	.	5	-1.17	-0.38	6.76	-0.77
State of Israel	4.7	4.8	0.9	3.4	0.66	5.4	-1.18	1.1	5.29	0.83
State of Japan	5.7	4.9	0.03	5	0.557	5.6	1.11	1.29	9.41	1.31
Republic of Kenya	4.3	4.2	.	3	.	4.9	-1.09	-0.69	5	-0.97
Malaysia	5.3	4.9	1	4.5	0.504	5.5	0.35	1.02	6.18	0.38
United Mexican States	4.5	4.2	2.9	3.4	0.589	4.5	-0.4	0.16	8.82	-0.35
New Zealand	4.9	5.3	0.6	2.8	0.811	6.2	1.27	1.94	10	2.38

continued on following page

Table A1. Continued

	Social indicators						Political Indicators			
Republic of the Philippines	4.4	4.6	13	2.5	0.59	5.2	-1.26	-0.01	9.12	-0.69
Russian Federation	4.3	3.8	0.3	4	0.489	4.8	-0.74	-0.43	5	-0.76
Republic of Singapore	6.2	5.1	.	5	0.761	6	1.3	2.2	7.35	2.3
Republic of South Africa	3.7	4.8	0.3	3.1	.	5.7	-0.07	0.78	8.82	0.56
Republic of South Korea	4.2	4.7	0.1	4.3	0.51	5.1	0.42	1.05	8.24	0.31
Taiwan	5.4	4.6	.	4.6	.	5.2	0.51	1.11	9.71	0.53
Thailand	5.2	4.1	0.6	4.4	0.472	4.8	-0.99	0.29	7.06	-0.26
Republic of Turkey	3.7	3.6	0.3	3.3	0.298	4.1	-0.65	0.23	5	0.06
United Kingdom	4.9	5	0.3	4.6	0.783	5.6	0.46	1.83	8.82	1.86
United States of America	5.2	5.5	0.02	6.1	0.762	6	0.31	1.64	8.53	1.3
Eastern Republic of Uruguay	3.5	4.1	0.5	2.9	0.525	4.1	0.73	0.48	9.71	0.8
Source	GCR 2008-09	GCR 2008-09	WB MGR 2008	GCR 2008-09	UNDP HDR 2007-08	GCR 2008-09	WB KAM 2008	WB KAM 2008	EIU Democracy index 2008	WB KAM 2008

APPENDIX 2.

Table A2. Economic & technological indicators

	Economic & Business indicators			Technology & Workforce indicators				
	Business competitiveness	Protection of property rights		ICT Infrastructure & Usage			Education and workforce availability	
Country	Intensity of Local Competition (1-7)	Intellectual Property Protection (1-7)	Property rights	Price basket for Internet, US$ per month	Total Telephones per 1,000 People	Internet Users per 1000 People	Quality of the educational system	Availability of scientists and engineers
Argentina	4.2	2.8	3.2	14.37	1,050.00	210	2.9	4
Australia	5.7	5.9	6.3	11.93	1,430.00	740	5.5	4.8
Brazil	5.3	3.3	4.6	25.98	730	230	2.7	4.4
Canada	5.7	5.7	6.4	8.9	1,170.00	680	5.6	5.5
Republic of Chile	5.7	4	5.4	25.63	960	250	3.2	4.7

continued on following page

Table A2. Continued

	Economic & Business indicators			Technology & Workforce indicators				
People's Republic of China	5.3	3.4	5	9.75	630	100	3.8	4.5
Egypt, Arab Republic.	4.7	3.5	4.7	4.97	390	80	2.4	4.5
France	5.8	5.9	6.1	12.43	1,390.00	490	5	5.6
Federal Republic of Germany	6.3	6.5	6.5	7.4	1,680.00	470	4.9	4.9
Republic of Ghana	5.1	3.8	4.4	23.56	250	30	3.4	3.6
Hong Kong SAR	6	5.5	6.3	3.86	1,920.00	550	4.9	4.2
Republic of India	5.9	4	5	6.78	190	50	4.3	5.7
Republic of Indonesia	5.5	3.1	3.5	17.26	360	70	4.2	4.9
State of Israel	5.6	5.1	5.2	22.02	1,620.00	270	4	5.5
State of Japan	6	5.6	6.3	13.79	1,230.00	690	4.5	5.9
Republic of Kenya	5.1	3	4.2	75.93	190	80	4.4	4.6
Malaysia	5.7	5.1	5.5	7.39	920	430	5	5
United Mexican States	4.9	3.5	4.1	20.05	740	180	2.8	3.5
New Zealand	5.4	5.8	6.2	22.82	1,270.00	760	4.9	4
Republic of the Philippines	5	3.1	4	1.81	540	50	4	3.8
Russian Federation	4.5	2.6	3.3	12.72	1,120.00	180	4.3	4.8
Republic of Singapore	5.5	6.2	6.5	20.48	1,480.00	380	6.2	5
Republic of South Africa	5.1	5.2	6	63.21	820	110	2.8	3.4
Republic of South Korea	5.6	5.4	5.4	32.62	1,380.00	700	4.6	5.1
Taiwan	5.8	4.9	5.6	7.9	1,660.00	640	4.8	5.5
Thailand	5.3	4.1	4.7	6.95	750	130	3.8	4.4
Republic of Turkey	5.5	3.4	4.2	11.61	980	170	3.4	4.3
United Kingdom	6	6	5.5	27.25	1,700.00	550	4.6	4.8
United States of America	5.9	5.4	5.8	14.95	1,350.00	690	5	5,5
Eastern Republic of Uruguay	4.2	3.9	4.9	23.87	1,000.00	230	3.7	3.9
Source	WB KAM 2008	GCR 2008-09	WB KAM 2008	WB KAM 2008	WB KAM 2008	WB KAM 2008	GCR 2008-09	GCR 2008-09

APPENDIX 3

Table A3. Selected compsite scales

Country	KAM 2008 score	GCR 2008 Score	HDI 2007-08	UN E-readiness score 2008	Ereadiness score 2008
Argentina	5.49	3.87	0.869	0.5844	5.56
Australia	9.05	5.2	0.962	0.8108	8.83
Brazil	5.57	4.13	0.8	0.5679	5.65
Canada	9.21	5.37	0.961	0.8172	8.49
Republic of Chile	6.92	4.72	0.867	0.5819	6.57
People's Republic of China	4.35	4.7	0.777	0.5017	4.85
Egypt, Arab Republic	4.03	3.98	0.708	0.4767	4.81
France	8.47	5.22	0.952	0.8038	7.92
Federal Republic of Germany	8.87	5.46	0.935	0.7136	8.39
Republic of Ghana	2.5	3.62	0.553	0.2997	
Hong Kong SAR	8.2	5.33	0.937	.	8.91
Republic of India	3.12	4.33	0.619	0.3814	4.96
Republic of Indonesia	3.23	4.25	0.728	0.4107	3.59
State of Israel	8.22	4.97	0.932	0.7393	
State of Japan	8.56	5.38	0.953	0.7703	8.08
Republic of Kenya	2.82	3.84	0.521	0.3474	
Malaysia	6.06	5.04	0.811	0.6063	6.16
United Mexican States	5.45	4.23	0.829	0.5893	5.88
New Zealand	8.87	4.93	0.943	0.7392	8.28
Republic of the Philippines	4.25	4.09	0.771	0.5001	4.9
Russian Federation	5.4	4.31	0.802	0.512	4.42
Republic of Singapore	8.24	5.53	0.922	0.7009	8.74
Republic of South Africa	5.55	4.41	0.674	0.5115	5.95
Republic of South Korea	7.68	5.28	0.921	0.8317	8.34
Taiwan	8.69	5.22		.	8.05
Thailand	5.44	4.6	0.781	0.5031	5.22
Republic of Turkey	5.61	4.15	0.775	0.4834	5.64
United Kingdom	9.09	5.3	0.946	0.7872	8.68
United States of America	9.08	5.74	0.951	0.8644	8.95
Eastern Republic of Uruguay	6.35	4.04	0.852	0.5645	
Source	WB KAM 2008	GCR 2008-09	UNDP HDR 2007-08	UN E readiness report 2008	EIU 2008 E readiness score

WB KAM 2008: World Bank KAM Report 2008
UNDP HDR 2007-08: United Nations Development Report Human Development Index 2007-08
GCR 2008-09: Global Competitiveness Report 2008-09
WB MGR 2008: World Bank Migration and Remittances Factbook 2008

This work was previously published in International Journal of Knowledge Management, Volume 6, Issue 4, edited by Murray E. Jennex, pp. 1-23, copyright 2010 by IGI Publishing (an imprint of IGI Global).

Chapter 14
Exploring the Extent and Impediments of Knowledge Sharing in Chinese Business Enterprise

Wen Bing Su
Nanjing University, China

Xin Li
Nanjing University, China

Chee W. Chow
San Diego State University, USA

ABSTRACT

This study explores the extent and impediments of knowledge sharing in Chinese firms because they are becoming dominant entities in the global economy, yet limited research exists on this important aspect of their operations. Survey data are obtained from experienced managers of 164 Chinese firms from a wide range of industries, sizes, and ownership types. The responses indicate that knowledge sharing is not open and complete in Chinese firms. Similar to findings from developed economies in the West, a large number of factors impede knowledge sharing in Chinese firms. These range from Chinese cultural values—which had been identified as being important by prior China-based studies—to attributes of the firm (e.g., incentive system, communication channels, organizational culture), as well as those of knowledge holders and potential recipients (e.g., judgment ability, organizational commitment). Implications of these findings for practice and research are discussed.

1. INTRODUCTION AND OVERVIEW

Knowledge is increasingly being viewed as a key source of competitive advantage, economic growth, and corporate value (Volberda, 2005; Lev, 2001; Stenmark, 2000). Many large global corporations have launched formal initiatives to promote knowledge sharing among employees (e.g., CIGNA, Dow Chemical, Hewlett-Packard, Shell, Xerox), and articles addressing the topic have proliferated in the professional literature (e.g., Robinson et al., 2006; Weick, 2005; Sharp,

DOI: 10.4018/978-1-4666-0035-5.ch014

2003; Alavi & Leidner, 2001; Stimpson, 1999). This widespread attention to knowledge sharing is based on the belief that bringing together the full range of employees' skills, knowledge, and experience increases the effectiveness with which firms can solve problems, avoid repeating mistakes, and spread the adoption of best practices (Collins & Smith, 2006; Husted & Michailova, 2002).[i]

Yet total and full knowledge sharing is not a naturally-occurring phenomenon in most organizations. A large body of research in developed economy settings, especially in organizational learning (e.g., Argote, 1999; Hedlund, 1994; Epple et al., 1991; Huber, 1991) and cognitive psychology (e.g., Kraiger et al., 1993), has found that knowledge transfers within organizations typically are both limited and difficult to achieve (Szulanski, 1994, 2000, 2003; von Hippel, 1994). Consistent with this finding from academic studies, a survey of high-level executives by Ernst & Young has found that while 87 percent of the participants named knowledge as being critical to competitiveness, fully 44 percent considered knowledge transfers within their organizations to be either poor or very poor (Stimpson, 1999, p. 36). The literature also has identified a wide range of factors that can impede knowledge sharing in organizations. These range from macro-level factors like organizational culture (Long & Fahey, 2000), reward systems (Bonner et al., 2000) and use of information technology (Banker et al., 2002), to more micro-level variables like workload pressure (DeZoort & Lord, 1997), closeness of supervision (Brazel et al., 2004), organizational commitment (Putti et al., 1990), and apprehension about being evaluated (Irmer et al., 2002).[ii]

In this study, we explore the extent and impediments of knowledge sharing in Chinese firms. These firms are becoming increasingly important in the global economy as suppliers, customers, competitors, partners, and investment targets (OECD, 2005; Roberts & Engardis, 2006), yet only a few studies have investigated the knowledge sharing aspect of their operations. While a large literature does exist on knowledge sharing, it is almost entirely focused on developed Western economies and may not be directly generalizable to the Chinese setting. Our study engages a rather large sample that encompasses Chinese firms of different sizes, industry types, state vs. private ownership, and domestic vs. foreign ownership. The findings indicate that knowledge sharing in Chinese firms is far short of being completely open, and that a wide range of factors, ranging from Chinese cultural values to attributes of the firm and individual employees, affect the extent of knowledge sharing. In addition to advancing understanding of an important aspect of Chinese firms' operations, these findings can augment general knowledge about factors that influence knowledge sharing in our increasingly global economy.

The remainder of this article is organized as follows. The next section reviews the Western literature to illustrate the wide range of factors that have been found to impede knowledge sharing in organizations. Then we provide examples of factors that may affect knowledge sharing in Chinese firms. Some of these overlap ones already reported in the Western literature, while others are relatively unique to the Chinese setting. We also review several prior studies in the Chinese context to show the need for further inquiry. Following this, we explain how we developed and used a survey to collect data from experienced Chinese managers, then present the data and findings. The final section concludes the paper with a summary and discussion of the results.

2. POTENTIAL DETERMINANTS OF KNOWLEDGE SHARING

The factors suggested by the extant (Western) literature as having an effect on knowledge sharing can be grouped under a number of general headings, including the attributes of the knowledge itself, attributes of the knowledge holders and potential recipients and their relationship, characteristics of the organization, and characteristics of the environment in which the organization operates (Szulanski, 1996, 2003; Ardichvili, 2008). We briefly describe some of these factors below. The objective is not to provide a comprehensive listing of all the factors that had been identified. Rather, its more modest aim is to provide a structure for understanding our empirical investigation.

- *Knowledge attributes:* Students of knowledge sharing commonly distinguish between explicit and tacit knowledge (Ambrosini & Bowman, 2001; Ancori et al., 2000; Ipe, 2003; Nonaka & Takeuchi, 1995). Explicit knowledge is not specific or idiosyncratic to the firm or person possessing it, and can be articulated in written language or symbols (Richter & Vettel, 1995). As such, explicit knowledge can be readily communicated in the form of hard data, or codified rules and procedures that have evolved over time (Sobol & Lei, 1994, p. 170).

In contrast, tacit knowledge consists of mental models that individuals follow in certain situations, and is context-specific because it typically is acquired on the job or in the situation where it is used (Sternberg, 1994, p. 28; Polanyi, 1976). As such, tacit knowledge can be difficult to put into words, and usually requires joint, shared activities in order to transmit it (Stenmark, 2000; Nonaka, 1991). The uncodifiable nature of tacit knowledge means that, in contrast to explicit knowledge, it is not possible for an organization or its members to unambiguously identify who has such knowledge, in turn making it very difficult to use formal systems and processes to assure that it is shared. Nevertheless, companies do try to overcome this obstacle by developing directories of knowledge, skills and abilities to help employees find those with key tacit knowledge.

- *Attributes of knowledge holders and potential recipients.* For knowledge sharing to be worthwhile to a knowledge holder, the potential benefits have to exceed the costs. If sharing his/her knowledge may reduce the holder's competitive advantage and/or performance evaluation, then there will be a reduced tendency to share (Garfield, 2006; Connelly & Kelloway, 2003). In addition, lack of awareness, or uncertainty about the value of the knowledge also could curtail the propensity to share it with others (Riege, 2005; DeLong & Fahey, 2000). Wasko and Faraj (2000) indicate that mastering the application of expertise takes experience, and individuals with longer tenure are likely to better understand how their expertise is relevant, and are thus better able to share knowledge with others. Related to this, individuals who feel that their expertise is inadequate, or lack confidence in their knowledge are less likely to contribute (Wasko & Faraj, 2000). Likewise, potential recipients' lack of awareness or uncertainty about the knowledge's usefulness could impede sharing via reducing their pro-active efforts to seek or encourage such sharing (Garfield, 2006; Davenport & Prusak, 1998). But even when they have a receptive mindset, people still may be impeded by their cognitive capacity, or ability to absorb knowledge (Alavi & Leidner, 2001; Hinds & Pfeffer, 2003).

- *Relationship between knowledge holders and potential recipients:* The degree to which knowledge holders and potential recipients have close inter-personal relationships can affect the extent to which knowledge is shared between them (Marsden, 1990). This is especially so for tacit knowledge because sharing it requires more frequent and intimate interactions, including discussions and learning by doing (Nonaka, 1994; Szulanski, 1996). By implication, physical proximity can affect both the opportunities for, and the effectiveness of knowledge sharing (Von Krogh et al., 2000; Cross & Cummings, 2004). Related to this, if senders and receivers have a common knowledge background, then the former are more likely to express the knowledge in a way that fits the latter's cognitive capacity (Marr & Schiuma, 2001). In a similar vein, the trust that knowledge holders and recipients have for each other can affect the extent of sharing (Perloff, 1993). Some employees may lack sufficient trust in others who work outside of their work units or groups, or resent knowledge that had originated from an external source (the "not invented here" syndrome) (Katz & Allen, 1982; Hayes & Clark, 1985). If the knowledge holder is not viewed as being credible, then his/her knowledge is more likely to be challenged or discounted, in turn discouraging the holder from revealing what he/she knows (Szulanski, 1996). This is because the knowledge holder may be concerned that his/her knowledge will be used inappropriately or misevaluated (Riege, 2003). *Organizational characteristics:* The extent to which decision making authority is centralized or decentralized can have a significant impact on the extent of knowledge sharing (Tsai, 2002; Ives et al., 2000; Kwan & Cheung, 2006). In organizations with more centralized structures, knowledge flows tend to be uni-directional (downward from the top) (Ives et al. 2000). Since managers below the top level have relatively limited decision making authority, they also have less incentive to share knowledge horizontally because the recipients would have limited ability to act on them.

The firm's performance evaluation and reward system also can affect knowledge sharing via affecting the costs and benefits of doing so. In particular, the use of team-based (as compared to individual-based) performance evaluation could increase the incentives to share knowledge, as doing so could help to improve the performance of the collective (Pfeffer, 1998; Bartol & Srivastava, 2002).

However, the effects of the performance evaluation scheme also may depend on the tightness of the performance standard. In general, performance measures cannot cover all relevant aspects of employees' work effort or contributions (Van der Stede et al., 2006). As such, an overly tight performance standard, or one that is too narrowly focused, may motivate employees to maximize those aspects of their job that are measured, at the expense of non-measured aspects—such as the extent of their knowledge sharing, especially in the case of implicit knowledge—which nevertheless may be beneficial to the firm (Husted & Michailova, 2002). This result may arise, for example, if employees feel a high level of time or workload pressure (Grant, 1996; Gold et al., 2001). Recognition of this effect has led some large corporations (e.g., IBM, Lotus Development) to create bonus pools explicitly tied to knowledge sharing by employees (Davenport, 2002).[iii]

But even if employees are willing to share their knowledge, their ability to do so could be affected by the degree to which the organization is structured, processes are formalized, and communication channels are available (McDermott & O'Dell, 2001; Zhou & Fink, 2003). The more formally functional areas are demarcated, and the more processes are subject to rules and regulations, the more numerous are the barriers that need to be breached for knowledge to be shared. This is especially so for tacit knowledge, since its effective sharing requires frequent interactions and direct observation (Nonaka, 1994; Brown & Duguid, 2000). More generally, the firm's structure, systems and processes can affect employees' identification with, and commitment to the firm (Nonaka, 1994; Nonaka & Takeuchi, 1995; Glisby & Holden, 2003). Unless employees identify with and feel a commitment to the firm's objectives and values, top management's effort to encourage knowledge sharing may not bear fruit.

- *Characteristics of the environment:* Among the many attributes of a firm's operating environment, the extent of competition is likely to be particularly relevant to employees' knowledge sharing propensity. When a firm operates in a highly competitive market, or when its members perceive that they are operating under competitive market conditions, they are more likely to accept the need to subordinate their personal interests to that of the firm. In a highly competitive industry such as computers and consumer electronics, for example, "the value and uniqueness of knowledge-intensive resources can be swiftly lost to competitors" (Balkin et al., 2000, p. 1118). As such, competition can increase employees' willingness to make their knowledge available to others within the firm. This quote about computers and consumer electronics also suggests the potential importance of industry. In industries with shorter product life cycles and rapid technological advances, a firm's ability to fully and quickly deploy employees' collective knowledge is key to competitive advantage (Grant, 1996).

It should be obvious from the preceding discussion that extant Western literature has considered a wide range of factors and knowledge sharing contexts. A further implication of the extant literature is that different factors may interact. For example, Bartol and Locke (2000) maintain that individual employees' work-related motivation is not merely affected by the firm's compensation structure, but also by their personal desire for self actualization. Indeed, Deci et al. (1999a, b) have suggested that excessive extrinsic rewards from the organization may lower employees' intrinsic motivation at work.

3. POTENTIAL DETERMINANTS OF KNOWLEDGE SHARING IN CHINESE FIRMS

While many of the impediments in the developed Western economies probably exist in Chinese firms as well, yet others may exist that are relatively unique to the Chinese setting. This section discusses some of these potential impediments and reviews several studies that have examined knowledge sharing in the Chinese context. The objective is to show the need for, and potential insights from further studies in the Chinese setting.

First consider factors relating to the societal context in which Chinese firms operate. In addition to Chinese cultural values—discussed further below—Chinese firms face an institutional environment that differs from those of firms in the more developed Western countries (Chow et al., 2007; Tsui et al., 2006). Up to the end of the 1970s, the People's Republic of China (PRC) had a centrally planned economy in which business enterprises were merely units for implementing government plans with very little autonomy (Expert Group, 1995). Even though a move towards privatization was initiated in 1979, the more sweeping changes were delayed till the 1990s (e.g., establishment of the Shanghai and Shenzhen stock exchanges, termination of financial support for most state-owned-enterprises) (Chow et al., 2007). Since the beginning of the new millennium, the shift towards privatization and open markets has maintained a strong pace, if not accelerated. For example, China's entry into the World Trade Organization in 2001 has brought requirements for increased market openness, reduced government interference, and increased management autonomy. Mutual funds also have become increasingly important participants in the Chinese stock market since then.[iv] Thus, within a relatively short time period, Chinese firms have had to evolve from being highly protected to being faced with competition from both other domestic enterprises and foreign competitors. Yet in responding to these challenges, they are handicapped by a relative lack of trained and/or experienced managerial personnel (Wang & Zhang, 2000). This shortfall suggests that as compared to companies from the more developed economies, Chinese firms have relatively few employees with the expertise to make effective managerial decisions. As such, the extent to which available knowledge within the organization is fully channeled to these personnel can have a significant impact on the firm's efficiency and effectiveness. But at the same time that this consideration may prompt Chinese firms to place particular emphasis on knowledge sharing, they also face many potential impediments. It is reasonable to expect some overlap with factors found in Western settings, such as the nature of the knowledge (explicit vs. implicit) and the proximity between sharer and receiver. Other impediments, however, may be relatively unique to the Chinese context. For example, because of their lack of training/experience, Chinese firms' employees may be more likely to feel uncertain about the value of their private knowledge. In conjunction with evaluation apprehension, this uncertainty could reduce their willingness to share private knowledge with co-workers and/or superiors, and result in a lower level of knowledge sharing in Chinese firms as compared to their Western counterparts.

Yet another possible hurdle is the entitlement mentality inherited from China's central planning and public ownership era. During this recent period, workers were assured of life time employment and social welfare ("the iron rice bowl", see Kornai, 1980). Furthermore, people often were appointed to managerial positions for reasons other than ability (e.g., political ties, seniority) (Hassard et al., 1999). Appointees of this type may resist practices—such as those aimed at increased knowledge sharing—that may threaten their position or authority (Xu & Wang, 1999; Yang et al., 2001). There also was no separation of responsibilities between the government and the firm, or between the government as the owner

and the government as the manager. Managers had little discretion, and firms did not have to worry about over-spending and loss making because both losses and profits were borne by the state (Xiang, 1999). Under this system, there was little room or incentive for personal initiative. Even though China has moved towards a responsibility system and greater managerial autonomy, there still may exist a large cadre of employees with little concern for how well their firms perform, in turn reducing their emphasis on or efforts toward knowledge sharing.

National culture is another society level factor that may influence people's actions. It does this either by supplying the values toward which the actions are oriented, or by shaping a repertoire of action strategies in which certain patterns of action are facilitated while others are discouraged (Erez & Earley, 1993; Hodgetts & Luthans, 2003). Across multiple taxonomies that have been proposed for operationalizing the national culture construct (e.g., Hofstede, 1980, 1991; Ronen & Shenkar, 1985; Schwartz, 1994; Smith et al., 1996; Trompenaars, 1994), individualism/collectivism and power distance have consistently been identified as being basic, or core, values that distinguish members of different cultural groups from one another (e.g., Lachman et al., 1994; Earley & Gibson, 1998; Smith et al., 2002). Individualism and its opposite, collectivism, relate to the relative emphasis that members of a society place on their self-interests versus those of the group (Earley, 1993; Triandis, 1995), while power distance has been defined as the degree to which people accept interpersonal inequality in power and the organizational institutionalization of such inequality (Hofstede, 1991). Observers of Chinese culture have consistently placed it among the highest in collectivism and power distance, while members of the Anglo-American cluster are generally seen as being low on these dimensions (Hofstede, 1980, 1991, 2001; Humborstad et al., 2008). Chinese nationals' higher level of collectivism suggests that as compared to their Western counterparts, they would be more inclined to share their knowledge with others within their organizations, whereas their higher level of power distance may have the opposite effect because sharing knowledge may be seen as challenging superiors' expertise or authority (Chow et al., 1999).[v] Also potentially relevant is Chinese culture's emphasis on the "Middle Way," "face," and interpersonal relations ("guanxi"). What this entails is according special importance to maintaining peace and harmony, and avoiding extremes in one's actions (Chinese Cultural Connection, 1987; Zhang et al., 2001). In an organizational setting, adherence to the "Middle Way" implies a reluctance to stand out in the crowd ("birds that stick their heads out are more likely to be shot"), while the emphasis on "face" suggests avoiding actions that could damage one's own as well as others' standing or welfare, such as by asking questions or expressing contrary opinions (Chow et al., 2000; Shen, 2005). Emphasis on "guanxi" may have the opposite effect because interpersonal networks can be an important facilitator of knowledge sharing (Weir & Hutchings, 2005; Huang et al., 2008).

Thus on the whole, different attributes of Chinese culture may have offsetting effects on people's propensity to share knowledge. Several studies have supported the importance of Chinese culture on knowledge sharing, though they fall short of determining the net effect of multiple cultural dimensions. Chow et al. (2000) used an experiment to compare the knowledge sharing propensities of 142 executive MBA students from the U.S. and PRC. They focused on two contextual factors—the nature of the knowledge, and the relationship with the potential recipient—and found the openness of sharing to be affected by the interaction between these factors and aspects of Chinese culture (e.g., collectivism and concern with "face"). PRC and U.S. nationals were equally willing to share knowledge that does not involve a conflict between self and collective interests (a cost estimation error made by an anonymous friend). But when the knowledge does involve

such a tradeoff (a cost estimation error made by oneself), PRC nationals expressed a greater willingness to share than did their U.S. counterparts. However, this willingness to share was not without qualification, as the PRC nationals are significantly less inclined than their U.S. counterparts to share knowledge with other employees who are not considered to be part of their "ingroup." The participants' open-ended responses further identified the company's culture as another major determinant of behavior, with this factor receiving relatively more emphasis from the U.S. nationals.

More recently, Voelpel and Han (2005) conducted interviews with 35 managers, supplemented by secondary data such as internal documents and project manuals. They found that "concern for face" negatively influences Chinese employees' knowledge sharing, and that there is less willingness to share knowledge with "outgroup" (as compared to "ingroup") members. Complexity of the knowledge sharing system also was noted as a barrier. Yao et al. (2007) obtained survey responses from 42 officers of Hong Kong Special Administrative Region (HKSAR) government departments. Seventy percent of the respondents indicated that the Chinese-dominated culture of the HKSAR negatively affected knowledge sharing. Finally, Huang et al. (2008) surveyed 159 Chinese MBA students and found that the concern about saving "face" significantly reduced their intention to share knowledge. On the other hand, the potential to gain "face" and the subjects' "guanxi" orientation significantly increased their knowledge sharing propensity. These findings as a whole support the contention that Chinese culture affects people's propensity to share knowledge. However, they are subject to the limitation of being based on only a few studies of specific populations and relatively limited scope.

Beyond these society level factors, the Chinese business environment has other attributes that may differentially affect knowledge sharing in firms with different characteristics. Some of these factors may overlap ones found to be operational in developed/Western settings. An example is the industry to which a firm belongs. Firms in different industries tend to face different demands, constraints and opportunities, in turn affecting their design of internal systems and processes (Fisher, 1995, 1998; Chapman, 1997; Williams & Seaman, 2001). For example, firms in high tech industries, such as electronics and telecommunications, face greater demands for innovativeness and being responsive to changing customer demands (Balkin et al., 2000). Thus, it stands to reason that the focus of systems/processes, including the emphasis on knowledge sharing, also could differ across firms from different industries. Firm size also may affect knowledge sharing because as firm size increases, problems of measurement, communication and control also increase (Libby & Waterhouse, 1996; Hoque & James, 2000; Chenhall, 2003).

Other factors may be relatively unique to the Chinese setting. In particular, the Chinese government still plays an active, if decreasing, role in regulating business and the economy, including maintaining dominant ownership in some firms (Chow et al., 2007; Li et al., 2008). State-owned-enterprises tend to get special protection and support; furthermore, governmental shareholders do not reap personal benefits from share ownership, and tend to have objectives that deviate from profitability, such as maintaining social order and effecting wealth redistribution (Liu, 2006; Tang et al., 2006). As such, whether a firm is state- vs. privately-owned can affect its emphasis on performance enhancing initiatives, including ones aimed at increasing knowledge sharing. Whether a firm is domestically vs. foreign owned also may have an effect, as foreign owners tend to demand greater transparency while facilitating the adoption of performance enhancing practices (Firth, 1996).

While there is room for speculating about yet other determinants of knowledge sharing in China—such as firms' internal characteristics and individuals' attributes—two points are clear from the preceding discussion. First is that many factors are likely to have an impact, including both ones that have been found in other settings and ones that are relatively unique to the Chinese context. Second, only limited research has delved into the knowledge sharing aspect of Chinese firms' operations. Considering the current state of knowledge on the topic, we considered it more useful to gain a better understanding of the overall picture than to test hypotheses about a small number of variables. Below, we explain how we undertook such an inquiry.

4. DATA COLLECTION METHOD

Instrument

We used a survey to collect data because most of the variables needed for analysis are not available in formal internal and external reports (e.g., openness of knowledge sharing, employee commitment). In addition to demographic questions about the respondents, we also sought information on several firm characteristics (e.g., firm size, industry, public vs. private ownership, and domestic vs. foreign ownership).[vi] The instrument was developed and administered in Chinese. We first sought feedback from two experienced controllers, and then conducted a pre-test with another two experienced accounting professionals. Only a few minor changes were suggested by their feedback.

Sample

Since interpersonal relationships are crucial to obtaining responses to surveys in China (O'Connor et al., 2004), we distributed the instrument through the accounting, MBA, and EMBA student and alumni network of the Chinese university where the first two authors are based.[vii] Each contact was sent a copy of the survey, and asked to direct it to a middle or high level manager of his/her firm. Complete anonymity was guaranteed for both individual respondents and their firms, and the completed surveys were mailed directly back to the China-based members of the research team.

In total, we sent surveys to 805 randomly selected members of the alumni base, and followed up with phone calls or emails one month after the initial mailing. This process yielded a total of 257 completed surveys. Eliminating surveys with large numbers of unanswered questions (66 firms) and those from 27 very small firms (fewer than 100 employees or below Renmenbi 100,000,000 in annual sales) yielded a final sample of 164 firms. The range of industries included construction, forestry, mining, food products, textiles, petrochemicals, transportation, trading, electronics, pharmaceuticals, telecommunications, finance, real estate, and other services. Geographically, the sample firms were dispersed across numerous provinces. Comparing the deleted and retained firms on number of employees, annual sales, respondent position and years of work experience revealed no significant differences (p=0.362, 0.970, 0.995, and 0.844, respectively).[viii]

The respondents' current positions were distributed as follows: high-level financial manager (n=35, or 21.34% of the sample), high-level non-financial manager (n=26, 15.85%), middle-level financial manager (n=64, 39.2%), and other (n=39, 23.78%). Their years of work experience in their current positions were: less than two years (10.4%), two to four years (23.1%), five to nine years (24%), ten to nineteen years (26.7%), twenty years or more (11.3%) and missing (4.5%), with the average being 8.8 years. These characteristics suggest that on the whole, the respondents would be sufficiently knowledgeable about their firms to provide informed answers.[ix]

5. RESULTS

Extent of Knowledge Sharing

The question used to gauge the extent of knowledge sharing was phrased as follows:

Individuals often know things that others within the company do not know, such as the real productive capacity of a machine, how given procedures can be improved, mistakes to avoid, and even information about customers, suppliers and competitors. People also may know about things that may be hurting their companies' performance, such as co-workers slacking off on the job or taking actions to "game" the system. What we want to focus on here is the knowledge that people with authority in the company can use to improve the company's performance.

Assume that the total amount of this potentially useful knowledge within your company is equal to 100. Compared to that, what is the amount that is typically shared by the people within your company? Please put down a number in the range 0 to 100. 0 means that none of the knowledge is shared, and 100 means that all of this knowledge is shared.[x]

Our 0-100 response scale was patterned after Chow et al. (2008). As compared to the Likert scale used by some prior related research, this scale has the advantage of greater comparability across responses because with the Likert scale, there is more room for respondents to ascribe different meanings to the same scale anchor (e.g., "very little," "a lot"). The respondents' answers ranged from a minimum of zero to a maximum of 95%, with a median of 60% and a mean of 57.28%. The plot of these responses (Figure 1) shows that about 5 percent each of the respondents saw their firms' extent of knowledge sharing as being below 10% and 20%, respectively and that in total, about 40 percent of the responses were below 60%.

Because the respondents had come from different hierarchical levels and functional areas, we investigated whether their ratings of knowledge sharing differed systematically due to these characteristics. Both t-tests and the non-parametric Wilcoxon tests revealed no significant difference between high and low level managers, high level financial and non-financial managers, high and middle level financial managers, financial and

Figure 1. Extent of knowledge sharing in Chinese firms

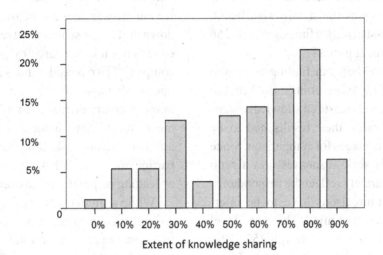

non-financial managers, and between high level non-financial managers and other employees (all ps ≥0.33). We also used analysis of variance (ANOVA) to compare respondents with less than two years in their current positions, two to nine years, and ten years and above, and found no significant difference among them (F=1.071, p=0.345). Based on these results, we aggregated all 164 respondents into one sample.

Table 1 shows the reported extents of knowledge sharing for the entire sample as well as across different firm sizes, industries (high-tech vs. non-high-tech), state vs. private ownership, and domestic vs. foreign ownership.[xi] ANOVA

Table 1. Extent of knowledge sharing in Chinese firms

	Mean	**Median**	**Min.**	**Max.**	**Std.Dev.**
Panel A					
All firms	57.28	60	0	95	25.23
Panel B					
Small	57.64	60	5	95	25.97
Medium-sized	58.73	60	0	95	24.56
Large	55.27	70	20	90	25.86
Panel C			0		
Foreign-owned	61.23	60	0	85	25.70
Domestically-owned	55.88	60	0	95	25.70
Panel D					
High-tech	58.88	70	10	90	26.28
Non high-tech	56.60	60	0	95	26.28
Panel E					
State-owned	55.68	60	10	90	25.86
Privately owned	57.65	60	0	95	25.86

revealed that none of the differences across these firm characteristics was statistically significant. For example, the F-statistic for firm size was 0.166 and only significant at p=0.847.

We also explored how our finding compared with those from other Asian settings. But because these other studies had measured knowledge sharing with Likert scales, their results had to be converted into percentages for comparison. Since converting ordinal scale responses into a ratio scale may not accurately reflect the respondents' true intent, the comparisons have to be interpreted with this caveat in mind. The mean level of knowledge sharing for our sample (57.28%) was somewhat lower than the 61.86% (=4.33÷7) that Kim and Lee (2006) had found from a survey of 322 employees from five public sector and five private sector South Korean organizations. It also was below the 63.32% (=4.43÷7) and 70% (=4.9÷7), respectively, that Chen et al. (2009) and Yang (2008) had found for Taiwan where the former was a survey study of 396 MBA and senior college students, and the latter was a survey of 499 employees of nine international tourist hotels. Our sample mean was even further below the 78.7% (=5.51÷7) that Srivastava et al. (2006) had found from a study of 389 managers in a chain of medium-sized hotels in the U.S. Considering the caveat about scale conversion and that the studies had sampled from different populations (e.g., students vs. managers, hotels vs. manufacturing entities), these comparisons are inadequate for evaluating claims like that of Yao et al. (2007) that on the whole, Chinese culture impedes knowledge sharing. Nevertheless, they do indicate that like their foreign counterparts, Chinese firms are not free of impediments to knowledge sharing. This finding, in turn, provides impetus to an investigation of the specific impediments that Chinese firms face.

Impediments to Knowledge Sharing

Our question for eliciting the impediments was as follows: "There are many reasons why people may not share all the knowledge that they have. If your answer above is below 100, please write down the two most important reasons why knowledge is not totally shared by people within your company." Two considerations underlie use of this open-ended approach. First, asking respondents to rate a comprehensive list of potential impediments would have made answering the survey a rather onerous task, thus potentially deterring participation. Second, the format avoided biasing or leading respondents' answers.

While a small number of respondents did not answer this question, many wrote in more than the two items requested. In total, 477 impediments were reported for an average of 2.9 per participant. We take this as an indication that on the whole, the participants had taken the survey seriously.

As might be expected, there was considerable overlap across the written responses. To reduce subjective biases in interpreting these materials, two members of the research team jointly developed a list of summary phrases for capturing commonalities in the responses. Then, each independently classified the responses using this schema. Comparison of the two sets of classifications revealed almost no divergence between them. The few instances where the two raters differed were resolved through consultation.

Table 2 shows the impediments identified by the respondents, together with the frequency with which each was mentioned. The picture that emerges is that attributes of the organization dominate the other factors. Across the entire set of impediments, by far the most often mentioned is an organizational level factor: ineffective organizational culture and leadership, mentioned by 103, or 62.8 percent of the sample. Examples of how respondents described this impediment include the lack of an emphasis on knowledge sharing, lack of cultivating a sense of common purpose among the employees, lack of a sense among employees that the company was concerned about their welfare, and the drain of facing a complex web of inter-personal relationships.

Table 2. Factors identified as being key impediments to knowledge sharing

Impediment Type	Examples of Respondents' Answers	Number of times mentioned	Proportion of sample mentioning this factor
Attributes of the knowledge holder Lack of commitment to or identification with the company	Employees lack a sense of loyalty or belonging to the company; lack of satisfaction with the company; lack of a sense of ownership.	58	35.3%
Emphasis on protecting self-interest	Concern about hurting unity of the group/department, or hurting one's own interests or those of the group/department.	44	26.8%
Feeling of uncertainty about the usefulness of the knowledge one possesses	Concern that the knowledge may have no value.	21	12.8%
Lack of a sense that oneself is valued or trusted by the organization	Feeling useless and/or that one's suggestions may not be valued.	20	12.2%
Lack of quality/qualification	Low self confidence; low cooperative spirit; low ability to judge value of knowledge; low ability to communicate; low aspirations.	14	8.5%
Lack of sense of responsibility	Unwillingness to bear responsibility; low sense of professionalism.	11	6.7%
Attributes of potential knowledge recipient Lack of motivation	Low sense of motivation.	49	29.9%
Lack of judgment	Insufficient attention to received knowledge.	14	8.5%
Lack of ability	Low ability to seek or make use of knowledge.	11	6.7%
Organizational factors Ineffective organizational culture and leadership	Lack of emphasis on knowledge sharing; lack of concern for employees' welfare; lack of sense of common purpose; complex inter-personal relationships.	103	62.8%
Obstructed/inadequate communication channels	Lack of communication channels; obstructed communication channels; rigid modes of communication.	47	28.7%
Insufficient incentives	Imbalance between the responsibility and benefits of knowledge sharing; insufficient or lack of concrete rewards for knowledge sharing; divergence between individual and company interests.	46	28%
Cultural factors Emphasis on following the "Middle Way"	Emphasis on not rocking the boat, not offending others, and not challenging the authority of others. Avoiding conflict and trouble.	39	23.8%

The second most often mentioned impediment is a general lack of employee commitment to, or identification with the company ("employees lack a sense of loyalty or belonging to the company," "lack of a sense of ownership"), mentioned by 58 (35.3%) of the participants. Closely behind is the lack of motivation among potential knowledge recipients, mentioned by 49 participants, or about 30% of the sample. Both of these impediments, especially the latter, seem likely to relate to an-

other oft-mentioned organizational factor: the lack of rewards or incentives for knowledge sharing (mentioned by 46 respondents, or 28% of the sample). The lack of communication channels, knowledge holders' emphasis on protecting their self interests, and employees' emphasis on following the "Middle Way" of not offending others and not challenging the authority of others, also are frequently mentioned obstacles to knowledge sharing.

We also tested whether the distribution of reported impediments differed across firm size, industry and ownership type. Chi-square tests revealed only one significant difference for firm size: "Lack of a sense that oneself is valued or trusted by the organization" was mentioned much more frequently in large firms than in small and medium-sized firms (χ^2=6.804, p=0.048). At a more marginal significance level, this impediment also was mentioned more frequently in domestic vs. foreign-owned firms (χ^2=3.098, p=0.078), as was "Obstructed/inadequate communication channels" (χ^2=2.881, p=0.090). No significant differences were found between high-tech and non-high-tech firms, and between state-owned and non-state-owned firms.

While the preceding descriptive statistics are informative, they do not reveal which impediments are more frequently associated with restricted knowledge sharing. To gain insight into this issue, we divided the sample into three subgroups: high knowledge sharing (80 percent or higher, n=46), medium knowledge sharing (50-79 percent, n=71) and low knowledge sharing (below 50 percent, n=47). Then we counted the number of times each impediment was mentioned by the firms in each group. Table 3 presents the results.

Table 3. Impediments' frequencies of mention across knowledge sharing categories

Impediments	High sharing (n=47)		Medium sharing (n=71)		Low sharing (n=46)		Chi-square Test	
	Number of Mentions	%	Number of Mentions	%	Number of Mentions	%	Chi-square	Sig.
Attributes of the knowledge holder								
Lack of commitment to or identification with the company	20	42.6	24	33.8	14	30.4	1.63	0.44
Emphasis on protecting self-interest	10	21.3	21	29.6	13	28.3	1.06	0.59
Feeling of uncertainty about the usefulness of the knowledge one possesses	7	14.9	7	9.9	7	15.2	0.98	0.61
Lack of a sense that oneself is valued or trusted by the organization	6	12.8	8	11.3	6	13.0	0.10	0.95
Lack of quality/qualification	8	17.0	3	4.2	3	6.5	6.26**	0.04
Lack of sense of responsibility	4	8.5	5	7.0	2	4.4	0.67	0.72
Attributes of potential knowledge recipient								
Lack of motivation	8	17.0	24	33.8	17	37.0	5.33*	0.07
Lack of judgment	3	6.4	5	7.0	6	13.0	1.68	0.43
Lack of ability	4	8.5	3	4.2	4	8.7	1.23	0.54
Organizational factors								
Ineffective organizational culture and leadership	29	61.7	46	64.8	28	60.9	0.44	0.80
Obstructed/inadequate communication channels	11	23.4	25	35.2	11	23.9	5.43*	0.07
Insufficient incentives	8	17.0	24	33.8	14	30.4	4.13	0.13
Cultural factors								
Emphasis on following the "Middle Way"	10	21.3	19	26.8	10	21.7	0.62	0.74

*=significant at p=.10; **=significant at p=.05.

Two aspects of Table 3 are particularly worthy of note. First, some impediments are mentioned by similarly low proportions in all three subgroups. These include "Feeling of uncertainty about the usefulness of the knowledge," "Lack of quality/ qualification," "Lack of a sense that oneself is valued or trusted by the organization," and "Lack of a sense of responsibility." All four of these relate to the knowledge holder. Lack of judgment and lack of ability on the part of potential knowledge recipients also have relatively low frequencies of mention.

In contrast, all three organizational level impediments are mentioned frequently by all subgroups. Of these, "Ineffective organizational culture and leadership" stands out with over 60 percent of all three subgroups noting its obstructing effect. Another highly cited impediment is knowledge holders' lack of commitment to or identification with the company which may, at least in part, relate to the three organizational impediments.

The other notable feature of Table 3 is that three of the impediments have significantly different frequencies of mention across the knowledge sharing subgroups, as indicated by the significant Chi-square statistics. These impediments are knowledge holders' "lack of quality/qualification," knowledge recipients' "lack of motivation," and the organization's "obstructed/inadequate communication channels." Interestingly, greater frequencies of mention are not necessarily associated with lower levels of knowledge sharing. For example, knowledge holders' lack of quality/qualification is mentioned most frequently by members of the high knowledge sharing subgroup.[xii]

It also is of interest to place our findings in the context of prior China-focused studies. As we had reported earlier, Chow et al. (2000) had found Chinese national culture to interact with the nature of the knowledge and the relationship between knowledge holder and the potential recipient. They also identified organizational culture as being important. Voelpel and Han (2005), Yao et al. (2007) and Huang et al. (2008) also had found

effects for Chinese culture. In addition, Voelpel and Han (2005) had found complexity of the knowledge sharing system to be a barrier. Our findings confirm the importance of all of these factors, and bring into the picture a number of other firm attributes as well as individual characteristics.

6. SUMMARY AND DISCUSSION

This study has used a survey of experienced Chinese managers to explore the extent of, and impediments to knowledge sharing within Chinese firms. We find that knowledge sharing in these firms is far from complete and open, and that a wide range of factors impede sharing. The participants' open-ended responses identified one aspect of Chinese culture—emphasis on following the "Middle Way" of not offending others and not challenging the authority of others—as being a deterrent to knowledge sharing. More so than this factor, however, characteristics of the organization, in particular the presence of an ineffective organizational culture and leadership, and the absence of rewards or incentives are seen as major obstacles. These factors, in turn, could be underlying causes for another frequently mentioned impediment: employees' lack of commitment to or identification with the company. The participants also pointed to the lack of communication channels, employees' lack of qualifications/expertise, and knowledge holders' emphasis on protecting their self interests as obstacles. Almost without exception, these impediments were seen as equally applicable across firms of different sizes, ownership types (state vs. private; foreign vs. domestic) and industry (high-tech vs. non-high-tech).

Since most of the impediments identified can be influenced by firm managers, our findings have potential to guide Chinese firms' improvement efforts. The apparent linkages among impediments suggest that such efforts should be based on a holistic approach rather than treating each factor as an independent entity. For example, top managers can adopt a leadership style that makes knowledge sharing a highly visible organizational priority.[xiii] In conjunction with changes like increasing the rewards and channels for knowledge sharing, and initiatives for increasing employees' qualification and expertise, organization members' identification with and commitment to the firm can be increased, in turn increasing their motivation and ability to share knowledge with other members of the firm. Admittedly, many of these initiatives have long been recommended for improving employee morale, satisfaction, and performance. But our finding that they also affect knowledge sharing should increase the motivation for their adoption.

From a research perspective, our study has contributed evidence that factors at multiple levels—ranging from national culture to individual employees' attributes—affect the openness of knowledge sharing in Chinese firms. At the same time that these findings validate prior China-based studies' focus on Chinese culture, they also indicate the need to adopt a much broader scope of inquiry. Many fruitful directions are available for such future research. First, it is desirable to obtain a much larger sample. While the sample size of this study is reasonably large and comparable to those of many related works (e.g., Chow et al., 2000; Huang et al., 2008), other China-focused studies have managed to obtain substantially larger samples for greater statistical power (e.g., Firth, 1996). Increasing the number of firms in the sample also can make it feasible to examine an expanded mix and range of firm characteristics. For example, this study has assumed that firms in the high-tech sector would face more intensive competitive pressures than their non-high-tech counterparts, in turn increasing their emphasis on knowledge sharing. But even firms in the same industry may respond to the same external pressures differently. For example, some may focus on attaining growth by improving market share and competitive position at the expense of short term performance, while others may choose to maximize short-term profit and cash flow at the expense of growth and market share (Fisher & Govindarajan, 1993). Adding measures of the sample firms' strategic foci will allow a finer distinction among firms in the sample. Along the same vein, the sample for this study was comprised totally of Chinese firms operating in the Chinese environment. While this limitation had not prevented Chinese culture from being identified as a relevant factor, effective tests of society level factors like national culture will require comparisons with samples from other nations.

Another desirable improvement is to go beyond our study's use of only one informant per firm. Even though our tests indicated no systematic difference in responses between financial and non-financial managers or between high and low level executives, one person's experience is unlikely to capture the full richness of the interactions that take place in a firm. Increasing the number of informants in each firm can improve data reliability by allowing tests of consensus across respondents. And by obtaining multiple respondents from different functional areas and hierarchical levels, the analysis can be focused on more homogeneous units to reduce the noise from extraneous factors. In similar fashion, additional insights may result from focusing on particular industries.

Yet another limitation of our study is the lack of distinction between implicit and explicit knowledge. Because the two types of knowledge have different attributes, the conditions conducive to their sharing also could differ. For example, it has been observed that the sharing of implicit knowledge requires more frequent and intimate contact between the knowledge holder and recipient. In turn, this difference between implicit and explicit knowledge could affect the relevance of other factors (e.g., employee attributes and their relationships) in presenting challenges to management. Along the same vein, the types of knowledge-sharing situations may differ across functional areas. There is room for future research to delve into these additional layers of intricacy.

Instead of relying on managers' perceptions about knowledge sharing, more direct observation methods may be used to improve data reliability (Birnberg et al., 1990). Another benefit of using other methods, such as in-depth field studies, is the ability to examine processes and to delve into "how" and "why" questions (Yin, 2003). Finally, a maintained hypothesis of this study is that greater knowledge sharing is beneficial to the firm. Whether this is the case, especially for Chinese firms with their limited supply of trained/ experienced personnel, deserves scrutiny.

ACKNOWLEDGMENT

The authors are indebted to Professors Yang Xiong Sheng, Zhang Chaomi and Jia liang Ding of Nanjing University for their assistance and guidance, and the Nanjing University students who assisted us with data coding and analysis. We also thank the respondents for their time and effort in completing the survey, and the Editor and two anonymous reviewers for many insightful and helpful comments.

REFERENCES

Alavi, M., & Leidner, D. (2001). Review: Knowledge management and knowledge management systems: Conceptual foundations and research issues. *Management Information Systems Quarterly*, *25*(1), 107–132. doi:10.2307/3250961

Ambrosini, V., & Bowman, C. (2001). Tacit knowledge: Some suggestions for operationalization. *Journal of Management Studies*, *38*(6), 811–829. doi:10.1111/1467-6486.00260

Ancori, B., Bureth, A., & Cohendet, P. (2000). The economics of knowledge: The debate about codification and tacit knowledge. *Industrial and Corporate Change*, *9*(2), 255–287. doi:10.1093/icc/9.2.255

Ardichvili, A. (2008). Learning and knowledge sharing in virtual communities of practice: Motivators, barriers and enablers. *Advances in Developing Human Resources*, *10*(4), 541–554. doi:10.1177/1523422308319536

Argote, L. (1999). *Organizational Learning: Creating, Retaining, and Transferring Knowledge*. Norwell, MA: Kluwer.

Baiman, S. (1990). Agency research in managerial accounting: A second look. *Accounting, Organizations and Society*, *15*, 341–371. doi:10.1016/0361-3682(90)90023-N

Balkin, D. B., Markman, G. D., & Gomez-Mejia, L. R. (2000). Is CEO pay in high-technology firms related to innovation? *Academy of Management Journal*, *43*(6), 1118–1129. doi:10.2307/1556340

Banker, R., Chang, H., & Kao, Y.-C. (2002). Impact of information technology on public accounting firm productivity. *Journal of Information Systems*, *16*(2), 209–222. doi:10.2308/jis.2002.16.2.209

Bartol, K., & Locke, E. (2000). Incentives and motivation. In Rynes, S., & Gerhart, B. (Eds.), *Compensation in Organizations: Progress* (pp. 104–147). San Francisco: Jossey-Bass.

Bartol, K., & Srivastava, A. (2002). Encouraging knowledge sharing: The role of organizational reward systems. *Journal of Leadership & Organizational Studies*, *9*(1), 64–76. doi:10.1177/107179190200900105

Birnberg, J., Shields, M., & Young, M. (1990). The case for multiple methods in empirical management accounting research (With an illustration from budget setting). *Journal of Management Accounting Research*, *2*, 33–66.

Bonner, S., Hastie, R., Sprinkle, G., & Young, S. M. (2000). A review of the effects of financial incentives on performance in laboratory tasks: Implications for management accounting. *Journal of Management Accounting Research*, *12*(1), 19–64. doi:10.2308/jmar.2000.12.1.19

Brazel, J., Agoglia, C., & Hatfield, R. (2004). Electronic versus face-to-face review: The effects of alternative forms of review on auditors' performance. *Accounting Review, 79*(4), 949–966. doi:10.2308/accr.2004.79.4.949

Brown, J., & Duguid, P. (2000). Balancing act: How to capture knowledge without killing it. *Harvard Business Review, 78*(5), 3–7.

Chapman, C. S. (1997). Reflections on a contingent view of accounting. *Accounting, Organizations and Society, 22*, 189–205. doi:10.1016/S0361-3682(97)00001-9

Chen, I. Y. L., & Chen, N. S., & Kinshuk. (2009). Examining the factors influencing participants' knowledge sharing behavior in virtual learning communities. *Journal of Educational Technology & Society, 12*(1), 134–148.

Chenhall, R. H. (2003). Management control system design within its organizational context: Findings from contingency-based research and directions for the future. *Accounting, Organizations and Society, 28*(2/3), 127–168. doi:10.1016/S0361-3682(01)00027-7

China Economic Times. (2002, August 20). *The development of securities investment funds in China.*

Chinese Cultural Connection. (1987). Chinese values and the search for culture-free dimensions of culture. *Journal of Cross-Cultural Psychology, 18*(2), 143–164. doi:10.1177/0022002187018002002

Chow, C., Cooper, J., & Waller, W. (1988). Participative budgeting: Effects of a truth-inducing pay scheme and information asymmetry on slack and performance. *Accounting Review, 63*(1), 111–122.

Chow, C., Duh, R. R., & Xiao, J. (2007). Current management accounting practice in the People's Republic of China. In Chapman, C. S., Hopwood, A. G., & Shields, M. D. (Eds.), *Handbook of Management Accounting Research* (*Vol. 2*, pp. 941–986). Oxford, UK: Elsevier.

Chow, C., Harrison, G., McKinnon, J., & Wu, A. (1999). Cultural influences on information sharing in Chinese and Anglo-American organizations: An exploratory study. *Accounting, Organizations and Society, 24*(7), 561–582. doi:10.1016/S0361-3682(99)00022-7

Chow, C., Ho, J., & Vera-Munoz, S. (2008). Exploring the extent and determinants of knowledge sharing in audit engagements. *Asia-Pacific Journal of Accounting & Economics, 15*(2), 141–160.

Chow, C. W., Deng, J., & Ho, J. (2000). The openness of knowledge sharing within organizations: A comparative study of the United States and the People's Republic of China. *Journal of Management Accounting Research, 12*(1), 65–95. doi:10.2308/jmar.2000.12.1.65

Collins, C. J., & Smith, K. G. (2006). Knowledge exchange and combination: The role of human resource practices in the performance of high-technology firms. *Academy of Management Journal, 49*(3), 544–560.

Connelly, C. E., & Kelloway, E. K. (2003). Predictors of employees' perceptions of knowledge-sharing culture. *Leadership and Organization Development Journal, 24*(5/6), 294–305. doi:10.1108/01437730310485815

Cross, R., & Cummings, J. H. (2004). Tie and network correlates of individual performance in knowledge intensive work. *Academy of Management Journal, 47*(6), 928–937. doi:10.2307/20159632

Davenport, T. (2002). *Some principles of knowledge management.* Retrieved from http://www.bus.utexas.edu/ Kman/kmprin.htm

Davenport, T., & Prusak, L. (1998). *Working Knowledge: How Organizations Manage What They Know.* Boston: Harvard Business School Press.

Deci, E., Koestner, R., & Ryan, R. (1999a). A meta-analytic review of experiments examining the effects of extrinsic rewards on intrinsic motivation. *Psychological Bulletin, 125*(6), 627–668. doi:10.1037/0033-2909.125.6.627

Deci, E., Koestner, R., & Ryan, R. (1999b). The undermining effect is a reality after all—extrinsic rewards, task interest, and self-determination: Reply to Eisenberger, Pierce, and Cameron. *Psychological Bulletin, 125*(6), 692–700. doi:10.1037/0033-2909.125.6.692

DeLong, D., & Fahey, L. (2000). Diagnosing cultural barriers to knowledge management. *The Academy of Management Executive, 14*(4), 113–127.

DeZoort, F., & Lord, A. (1997). A review and synthesis of pressure effects research in accounting. *Journal of Accounting Literature, 16*, 28–85.

Earley, C. (1993). East meets West meets Mideast: Further explorations of collectivistic and individualistic work groups. *Academy of Management Journal, 36*(2), 319–348. doi:10.2307/256525

Earley, C., & Gibson, C. B. (1998). Taking stock in our progress on Individualism-collectivism: 100 years of solidarity and community. *Journal of Management, 24*(3), 265–304. doi:10.1016/S0149-2063(99)80063-4

Epple, D., Argote, L., & Devadas, R. (1991). Organizational learning curves: A method for investigating intra-plant transfer of knowledge acquired through learning by doing. *Organization Science, 2*(1), 58–70. doi:10.1287/orsc.2.1.58

Erez, M., & Earley, C. (1993). *Culture, Self-identity, and Work.* New York: Oxford University Press.

Expert Group. (1995). *Report on Reform and Development in China - The Chinese Road.* Beijing, China: Chinese Finance and Economic Press.

Firth, M. (1996). The diffusion of managerial accounting procedures in the People's Republic of China and the influence of foreign partnered joint ventures. *Accounting, Organizations and Society, 21*(7/8), 629–654. doi:10.1016/0361-3682(95)00039-9

Fisher, J. (1995). Contingency-based research on management control systems: Categorization by level of complexity. *Journal of Accounting Literature, 14*, 24–53.

Fisher, J. (1998). Contingency theory, management control systems and firm outcomes: Past results and future directions. *Behavioral Research in Accounting, 10*, 47–64.

Fisher, J., & Govindarajan, V. (1993). Incentive compensation design, strategic business unit mission, and competitive strategy. *Journal of Management Accounting Research, 5*, 129–144.

Frappaolo, C., & Wilson-Todd, L. (2000). *After the Gold Rush: Harvesting Corporate Knowledge Resources.* Retrieved from http://www.inteligentkm.com/ feature/ feat1.shtml#Case1

Garfield, S. (2006). Ten reasons why people don't share their knowledge. *Knowledge Management Review, 9*(2), 10–11.

Ghosh, D. (1997). De-escalation strategies: Some experimental evidence. *Behavioral Research in Accounting, 9*, 88–112.

Glisby, M., & Holden, N. (2003). Contextual constraints in knowledge management theory: The cultural embeddedness of Nonaka's knowledge-creating company. *Knowledge and Process Management, 10*(1), 29–36. doi:10.1002/kpm.158

Gold, A. H., Malhotra, A., & Segars, A. (2001). Knowledge management: An organizational capabilities perspective. *Journal of Management Information Systems, 18*, 185–214.

Grant, R. (1996). Toward a knowledge-based theory of the firm. *Strategic Management Journal, 17*, 109–122.

Harrison, P. D., & Harrell, A. (1993). Impact of adverse selection on managers' project evaluation decisions. *Academy of Management Journal, 36*(3), 635–643. doi:10.2307/256596

Hassard, J., Sheehan, J., & Morris, J. (1999). Enterprise reform in post-Deng China. *International Studies of Management & Organization, 29*(3), 54–83.

Hayes, R. H., & Clark, K. B. (1985). Exploring the sources of productivity differences at the factory level. In Clark, K., (Eds.), *The Uneasy Alliance: Managing the Productivity Technology Dilemma* (pp. 151–188). Boston: Harvard Business School Press.

Hedlund, G. (1994). A model of knowledge management and the N-form corporation. *Strategic Management Journal, 15*(5), 73–90.

Hinds, P. J., & Pfeffer, J. (2003). Why organizations don't "know what they know": Cognitive and motivational factors affecting the transfer of expertise. In *Sharing Expertise: Beyond Knowledge Management* (pp. 3–26). Cambridge: MIT Press.

Hodgetts, R., & Luthans, F. (2003). *International Management: Culture, Strategy and Behavior.* New York: McGraw-Hill Irwin.

Hofstede, G. H. (1980). *Culture's Consequences: International Differences in Work-Related Values.* Beverly Hills, CA: Sage.

Hofstede, G. H. (1991). *Cultures and Organizations: Software of the Mind.* Berkshire, UK: McGraw-Hill.

Hofstede, G. H. (2001). *Culture's Consequences: Comparing Values, Behaviors, Institutions, and Organizations across Nations.* Thousand Oaks, CA: Sage.

Hoque, Z., & J. W. (2000). Linking balanced scorecard measures to size and market factors: Impact on organizational performance. *Journal of Management Accounting Research, 12*(1), 1–17. doi:10.2308/jmar.2000.12.1.1

Huang, Q., Davison, R., & Gu, J. (2008). Impact of personal and cultural factors on knowledge sharing in China. *Asia Pacific Journal of Management, 25*(3), 451–471. doi:10.1007/s10490-008-9095-2

Huber, G. (1991). Organizational learning: The contributing processes and the literatures. *Organization Science, 2*(1), 88–115. doi:10.1287/orsc.2.1.88

Humborstad, S. I. W., Humborstad, B., Whitfield, R., & Perry, C. (2008). Implementation of empowerment in Chinese high power-distance Organizations. *International Journal of Human Resource Management, 19*(7), 1349–1364. doi:10.1080/09585190802110224

Husted, K., & Michailova, S. (2002). Knowledge sharing in Russian companies with Western participation. *Management International, 6*(2), 17–28.

Ipe, M. (2003). Knowledge sharing in organizations: A conceptual framework. *Human Resource Development Review, 2*(4), 337–359. doi:10.1177/1534484303257985

Irmer, B., Bordia, P., & Abusah, D. (2002). Evaluation apprehension and perceived benefit in interpersonal and database knowledge sharing. In *Academy of Management Proceedings* (pp. B1–B6). OCIS.

Ives, W., Torrey, B., & Gordon, C. (2000). Knowledge sharing is a human behavior. In Morey, D., (Eds.), *Knowledge Management* (pp. 99–129). Cambridge, MA: MIT Press.

Jung, D., Chow, C., & Wu, A. (2008). Towards understanding the direct and indirect effects of transformational leadership on firm innovation. *The Leadership Quarterly, 19*, 582–594. doi:10.1016/j.leaqua.2008.07.007

Katz, R., & Allen, T. J. (1982). Investigating the NOT Invented Here (NIH) syndrome: A look at the performance, tenure, and communication patterns of 50 R&D project groups. *R & D Management*, *12*(1), 7–19. doi:10.1111/j.1467-9310.1982. tb00478.x

Kim, S., & Lee, H. (2006). The impact of organizational context and information technology on employee knowledge-sharing capabilities. *Public Administration Review*, *66*(3), 370–385. doi:10.1111/j.1540-6210.2006.00595.x

Kornai, J. (1980). *Economic of Shortage: Volumes A and B*. New York: North-Holland.

Kraiger, K., Ford, J. K., & Salas, E. (1993). Application of cognitive, skill-based, and affective theories of learning outcomes to new methods of training evaluation. *The Journal of Applied Psychology*, *78*(2), 311–328. doi:10.1037/0021-9010.78.2.311

Kwan, M. M., & Cheung, P. (2006). The knowledge transfer process: From field studies to technology development. *Journal of Database Management*, *17*(1), 16–32.

Lachman, R., Nedd, A., & Hinings, B. (1994). Analyzing cross-national management and organizations: A theoretical framework. *Management Science*, *40*(1), 40–55. doi:10.1287/mnsc.40.1.40

Lev, B. (2001). What, why, and who? In *Intangibles—Management, Measurement, and Reporting* (pp. 5–20). Washington, DC: The Brookings Institution.

Li, J. J., Poppo, L., & Zhou, K. Z. (2008). Do managerial ties in China always produce value? Competition, uncertainty, and domestic vs. foreign firms. *Strategic Management Journal*, *29*(4), 383–400. doi:10.1002/smj.665

Libby, T., & Waterhouse, J. H. (1996). Predicting change in management accounting systems. *Journal of Management Accounting Research*, *8*(1), 137–150.

Liu, Q. (2006). Corporate governance in China: Current practices, economic effects and institutional determinants. *CEIsfo Economic Studies*, *52*(2), 415–453. doi:10.1093/cesifo/ifl001

Long, D., & Fahey, L. (2000). Diagnosing cultural barriers to knowledge management. *The Academy of Management Executive*, *14*(4), 113–127.

Lu, L., Leung, K., & Koch, P. T. (2006). Managerial knowledge sharing: The role of individual, interpersonal and organizational factors. *Management and Organization Review*, *2*(1), 15–41. doi:10.1111/j.1740-8784.2006.00029.x

Marsden, P. V. (1990). Network data and measurement. *Annual Review of Sociology*, *16*(1), 435–463. doi:10.1146/annurev.so.16.080190.002251

McDermott, R., & O'Dell, C. (2001). Overcoming culture barriers to sharing knowledge. *Journal of Knowledge Management*, *5*(1), 76–85. doi:10.1108/13673270110384428

Merchant, K. (1990). The effects of financial controls on data manipulation and management myopia. *Accounting, Organizations and Society*, *15*, 297–313. doi:10.1016/0361-3682(90)90021-L

Nonaka, I. (1991). The knowledge-creating company. *Harvard Business Review*, *69*(6), 96–104.

Nonaka, I. (1994). A dynamic theory of organizational knowledge creation. *Organization Science*, *5*(1), 14–37. doi:10.1287/orsc.5.1.14

Nonaka, I., & Takeuchi, H. (1995). *The Knowledge-Creating Company*. New York: Oxford University Press.

O'Connor, N. G., Chow, C., & Wu, A. (2004). The adoption of "Western" management accounting/ controls in China's state-owned enterprises during economic transition. *Accounting, Organizations and Society*, *29*(3/4), 349–375. doi:10.1016/ S0361-3682(02)00103-4

Organization for Economic Cooperation and Development (OECD). (2005). *Economic Survey of China 2005*. Retrieved from http://www.oecd.org/ eco/surveys/china

Perloff, R. M. (1993). *The Dynamics of Persuasion*. Hillsdale, NJ: Erlbaum.

Pfeffer, J. (1998). *New Directions for Organization Theory*. New York: Oxford University Press.

Polanyi, M. (1976). Tacit knowledge. In Marx, M., & Goodson, F. (Eds.), *Theories in Contemporary Psychology* (2nd ed., pp. 330–344). New York: Macmillan.

Putti, J., Aryee, S., & Phua, J. (1990). Communication relationship satisfaction and organizational commitment. *Group and Organization Studies*, *15*(1), 44–52. doi:10.1177/105960119001500104

Richter, F., & Vettel, K. (1995). Successful joint ventures in Japan: Transferring knowledge through organizational learning. *Long Range Planning*, *28*(3), 37–45. doi:10.1016/0024-6301(95)00019-F

Riege, A. (2003). Validity and reliability tests in case study research: A literature review with "hands-on" applications for each research phase. *Qualitative Market Research*, *6*, 75–86. doi:10.1108/13522750310470055

Riege, A. (2005). Three-dozen knowledge-sharing barriers managers must consider. *Journal of Knowledge Management*, *9*(3), 18–35. doi:10.1108/13673270510602746

Roberts, D., & Engardis, P. (2006, November 27). Secrets, lies and sweatshops. *Business Week*, 50-58.

Robinson, H. S., Anumba, C. J., Carrillo, P. M., & Al-Ghassani, A. M. (2006). STEPS: A knowledge management maturity roadmap for corporate sustainability. *Harvard Business Review*, *12*(6), 793–808.

Ronen, S., & Shenkar, O. (1985). Clustering countries on attitudinal dimensions: A review and synthesis. *Academy of Management Review*, *10*(3), 435–454. doi:10.2307/258126

Schwartz, S. (1994). Cultural dimensions of values: Toward an understanding of national differences. In Kim, U., Triandis, H., Kagitcibasi, C., Choi, S., & Yoon, G. (Eds.), *Individualism and Collectivism: Theory, Method, and Application* (pp. 85–119). Thousand Oaks, CA: Sage.

Securities Daily. (2005, January). *The History of Investment Funds in China*.

Sharp, D. (2003). Knowledge management today: Challenges and opportunities. *Information Systems Management*, *20*(2), 32–37. doi:10.1201/1078/43204.20.2.20030301/41468.6

Shen, Y. (2005). Renyuan-orientation: Interpersonal practice of zhongyong- Reconsidering Chinese social action orientation. *Journal of Nanjing University (Philosophy, Humanities and Social Science)*, *5*, 130-137.

Smith, P., Dugan, S., & Trompenaars, F. (1996). National culture and the values of organizational employees: A dimensional analysis across 43 nations. *Journal of Cross-Cultural Psychology*, *27*(2), 231–264. doi:10.1177/0022022196272006

Smith, P. B., Peterson, M. F., & Schwartz, S. H. (2002). Cultural values, sources of guidance, and their relevance to managerial behavior. *Journal of Cross-Cultural Psychology*, *33*(2), 188–208. doi:10.1177/0022022102033002005

Sobol, M., & Lei, D. (1994). Environment, manufacturing technology and embedded knowledge. *The International Journal of Human Factors in Manufacturing*, *4*(2), 167–189. doi:10.1002/hfm.4530040205

Srivastava, A., Bartol, K. M., & Locke, E. A. (2006). Empowering leadership in management teams: Effects on knowledge sharing, efficacy, and performance. *Academy of Management Journal, 49*(6), 1239–1251.

Stenmark, D. (2000). Leveraging tacit organizational knowledge. *Journal of Management Information Systems, 17*(3), 9–24.

Sternberg, R. (1994). Tacit knowledge and job success. In Anderson, N., & Herriot, P. (Eds.), *Assessment and Selection in Organizations: Methods and Practice for Recruitment and Appraisal* (pp. 27–39). London: John Wiley.

Stevens, L. (2000). Incentives for sharing. *Knowledge Management, 3*(10), 54–60.

Stimpson, J. (1999). In the know. *Practical Accountant,* 34-39.

Szulanski, G. (1994). *Intra-firm Transfer of Best Practice Project: Executive Summary of the Findings.* Houston, TX: American Productivity and Quality Center.

Szulanski, G. (1996). Exploring internal stickiness: Impediments to the transfer of best practice within the firm. *Strategic Management Journal, 17,* 27–43.

Szulanski, G. (2000). The process of knowledge transfer: A diachronic analysis of stickiness. *Organizational Behavior and Human Decision Processes, 82*(1), 9–27. doi:10.1006/obhd.2000.2884

Szulanski, G. (2003). *Sticky Knowledge: Barriers to Knowing in the Firm.* Thousand Oaks, CA: Sage.

Tang, F. F., Xi, Y., Chen, G., & Wang, R. (2006). Ownership, corporate governance, and management in the state-owned hotels in the People's Republic of China. *The Cornell Hotel and Restaurant Administration Quarterly, 47*(2), 182–191. doi:10.1177/0010880405284845

Tapscott, D., Lowy, A., & Ticoll, D. (1998). *Blueprint to the Digital Economy: Creating Wealth in the Era of e-business.* New York: McGraw-Hill Professional Publishing.

Triandis, H. (1995). *Individualism and Collectivism.* Boulder, CO: Westview Press.

Trompenaars, F. (1994). *Riding the Waves of Culture.* New York: Irwin.

Tsai, W. (2002). Social structure of "Coopetition" within a multiunit organization: Coordination, competition, and intraorganizational knowledge sharing. *Organization Science, 13*(2), 179–191. doi:10.1287/orsc.13.2.179.536

Tsui, A. S., Wang, H., & Xin, K. R. (2006). Organizational culture in China: An analysis of culture dimensions and culture types. *Management and Organization Review, 2*(3), 345–376. doi:10.1111/j.1740-8784.2006.00050.x

Van der Stede, W., Chow, C., & Lin, T. (2006). Strategy, choice of performance measures, and performance. *Behavioral Research in Accounting, 18*(1), 185–205. doi:10.2308/bria.2006.18.1.185

Vera-Munoz, S., Ho, J., & Chow, C. (2006). Enhancing knowledge sharing in public accounting firms. *Accounting Horizons, 20*(2), 133–155. doi:10.2308/acch.2006.20.2.133

Voelpel, S. C., & Han, Z. (2005). Managing knowledge sharing in China: The case of Siemens ShareNet. *Journal of Knowledge Management, 9*(3), 51–63. doi:10.1108/13673270510602764

Volberda, H. (2005). Knowledge and competitive advantage: The coevolution of firms, technology, and national institutions. *Academy of Management Review, 30*(2), 446–448.

Von Hippel, E. (1994). "Sticky information" and the locus of problem solving: Implications for innovation. *Management Science, 40*(4), 429–439. doi:10.1287/mnsc.40.4.429

Von Krogh, G., Ichijo, K., & Nonaka, I. (2000). *Enabling Knowledge Creation: How to Unlock the Mystery of Tacit Knowledge and Release the Power of Innovation*. Oxford, UK: Oxford University Press.

Wang, L. Y., & Zhang, R. (2000). The management value of accounting information - Past, present and future of management accounting. *Finance and Accounting, 2*, 20–23.

Wasko, M. M., & Faraj, S. (2000). It is what one does: Why people participate and help others in electronic communities of practice. *The Journal of Strategic Information Systems, 9*(2/3), 55–173.

Weick, K. (2005). Managing the future: Foresight in the knowledge economy. *Academy of Management Review, 30*(4), 871–873.

Weir, D., & Hutchings, K. (2005). Cultural embeddedness and contextual constraints: Knowledge sharing in Chinese and Arab cultures. *Knowledge and Process Management, 12*(2), 89–98. doi:10.1002/kpm.222

Williams, J. J., & Seaman, A. E. (2001). Predicting change in management accounting systems: National culture and industry effects. *Accounting, Organizations and Society, 26*, 443–460. doi:10.1016/S0361-3682(01)00002-2

Xiang, H. C. (Ed.). (1999). *Accounting in the 50 Years of New China*. Beijing, China: China Finance and Economic Press.

Xu, X., & Wang, Y. (1999). Ownership structure and corporate governance in Chinese stock companies. *China Economic Review, 10*, 75–89. doi:10.1016/S1043-951X(99)00006-1

Yang, J. T. (2008). Individual attitudes and organizational knowledge sharing. *Tourism Management, 29*(2), 345–353. doi:10.1016/j.tourman.2007.03.001

Yang, X. S., Chen, L. H., Su, W. B., Liu, Y., & Liu, J. (2001). Application and effectiveness of management accounting in China—views from enterprise accountants. *China Accounting and Finance Review, 2*, 73–138.

Yao, L. J., Kam, T. H. Y., & Chan, S. H. (2007). Knowledge sharing in Asian public administration sector: The case of Hong Kong. *Journal of Enterprise Information Management, 20*(1), 51–69. doi:10.1108/17410390710717138

Yin, R. K. (2003). *Case Study Research: Design and Methods* (3rd ed.). Beverly Hills, CA: Sage.

Young, S. M., & Lewis, B. (1995). Experimental incentive contracting research in management accounting. In Ashton, R., & Ashton, A. (Eds.), *Judgment and Decision Making Research in Accounting and Auditing* (pp. 55–75). Cambridge, UK: Cambridge University Press. doi:10.1017/CBO9780511720420.005

Zhang, D. S., Jin, Y. J., Chen, H. W., Chen, J. M., Yang, Z. F., & Zhao, Z. Y. (2001). Zhongyong rationality: Beyond instrumental rationality, value rationality and communicative rationality. *Sociological Research, 2*, 33–48.

Zhou, A. Z., & Fink, D. (2003). Knowledge management and intellectual capital: An empirical examination of current practice in Australia. *Knowledge Management Research & Practice, 1*(2), 86–94. doi:10.1057/palgrave.kmrp.8500009

ENDNOTES

[i] A survey study carried out by the Delphi Group asked more than 700 U.S. companies this question: "What is the primary repository for knowledge within the organization?" The responses received suggested that on average, 42 percent of corporate knowledge is housed exclusively in the brains of employees (Frappaolo & Wilson-Todd, 2000).

Another study reports that 80 percent of the information that companies need to know about their competitors is already known to their own employees, suppliers, or customers (Tapscott et al., 1998).

ii Technically, a wide range of heavily-studied topics in accounting and allied disciplines can be considered to be related to knowledge sharing. These studies have examined actions ranging from data manipulation (e.g., Merchant 1990), biasing communications to create budgetary slack (e.g., Chow et al., 1988), to escalating resource commitment to losing courses of action (e.g., Harrison and Harrell 1993). Studies also have examined the effects of management controls (e.g., audits and performance evaluation/reward systems) on such behavior (see Baiman, 1990; Young & Lewis, 1995; Ghosh, 1997 for reviews.) For purposes of our exploratory study, we subsume all of these topics under the general label "knowledge sharing," rather than delve into finer distinctions among them.

iii Stevens (2000) reports that in a large accounting firm, employees who are judged as not having shared knowledge cannot attain a performance rating above 3 on a 2-5 rating scale.

iv The first open-end mutual fund was introduced to China in September of 2001 (*China Economic Times* 2002). By the end of 2003, 54 closed-end and 41 open-end mutual funds had been established. By the end of 2004, the net assets of mutual funds had grown to nearly 25 percent, and they held 13 percent of the total tradable share market capitalization in China's two domestic stock exchanges (*Securities Daily* 2005).

v Indeed, a common saying among the Chinese people is that "if you have a low position, what you say will carry little weight."

vi For each firm characteristic, respondents were given several descriptions and asked to check the one that best described their firm. For example, the following choices were available for ownership: (1) Sino-foreign joint venture; (2) Foreign-owned company; (3) Wholly state-owned enterprise; (4) Subsidiary of a domestic Chinese company; (5) Private Chinese owned company; and (6) Other. The instrument is not reproduced here to reduce redundancy with our discussion of it in the text. However, a copy is available from the first author on request.

vii This university is among the key universities in China and also one of the largest. Its graduates are employed throughout the country.

viii Detailed statistics for all tests not tabulated are available from the first author on request.

ix Because of logistical reasons, the surveys were sent out over a period of several months rather than simultaneously. In conjunction with the anonymous nature of the survey, this precluded identifying responses as being "early" or "late" for conducting the popular test for non-response bias.

x We did not distinguish between implicit and explicit knowledge because this would require respondents to classify different types of knowledge. Such a task may not be part of their normal routine and has a high potential of introducing noise or errors into their responses. We discuss the implications of differentiating knowledge types in the final section of the paper.

xi Since annual sales and number of employees reflect different aspects of a firm's scale, we used both measures to place the firms into different size classes. First, we converted each firm's annual sales and number of employees into natural logarithms. The two statistics were then summed and rounded to the next lower integer, and the sample firms were placed into small, medium, and large categories based on whether their sum was below 9, from 9 to 11, or above 11.

This approach placed 88, 55, and 22 firms, respectively, into the three size classes. For industry, we considered telecommunications, electronics, petro-chemicals, and pharmaceuticals to be in the high-tech sector (n=33), and placed the other industries (e.g., construction, forestry, mining, food products, textiles, and transportation) into the non-high-tech sector (n=131).

[xii] For completeness, we also ran a multiple regression using each firm's reported extent of knowledge sharing as the dependent variable. The independent variables were 0/1 dummy variables representing whether each

of the factors in Table 1 had been mentioned as an impediment. There also were control variables to capture potentially relevant aspects of the firm and its context (e.g., industry, size, ownership). The coefficients for only two impediments were statistically significant: lack of incentives/motivation and ineffective/inadequate communication channels. Detailed results are available from the first author on request.

[xiii] Jung et al. (2008) provide an overview of how top managers' leadership style can affect subordinates' motivation and effort.

This work was previously published in International Journal of Knowledge Management, Volume 6, Issue 4, edited by Murray E. Jennex, pp. 24-46, copyright 2010 by IGI Publishing (an imprint of IGI Global).

Chapter 15
Situated Learning and Activity Theory–Based Approach to Designing Integrated Knowledge and Learning Management Systems

Seung Won Yoon
Western Illinois University, USA

Alexandre Ardichvili
University of Minnesota, USA

ABSTRACT

Current Knowledge Management (KM) design approaches recognize the importance of integrating codification, personalization, and collaboration strategies. Incorporating various database systems, search functions, managerial support, performance appraisal, personalized widgets, and case summaries into seamless functions are exemplary efforts. However, KM is rarely integrated with organizational learning and development systems. In this article, the authors use concepts from the situated learning literature, Vygotskian cultural-historical theory of cognition, and a holistic learning and performance architecture to signify the integration of KM and organizational learning systems.

INTRODUCTION

Today's organizations operate in global and innovation-pressured environments, and face the challenge of coordinating responsive information and management systems (Prahalad & Krishnan, 2008). In such environments, competitive ad-

DOI: 10.4018/978-1-4666-0035-5.ch015

vantage is only sustainable when the organization's strategy, financial management, customer interaction, and work processes are coordinated and integrated with organizational learning and development (Kaplan & Norton, 1996). Knowledge Management (KM), as a process of creating, accumulating, organizing, and disseminating information, expertise, and insight within and across people is at the core of supporting and improving organizations' learning and development functions (Davenport, DeLong, & Beers, 1998; Rosenberg, 2006).

Scholars have identified various organizational and personal KM success factors beyond technologies, such as *knowledge strategy*, *motivation/ commitment*, *organizational culture*, *leadership support*, *work design*, and *strong measurements* (Jennex & Olfman, 2005). Studies also reported the importance of user-driven sharing of knowledge through communities of practice and personal networks for successful KM adoption (Kimble & Bourdon, 2008; Jasimuddin, 2008). However, few studies attempted to explicitly align KM with organizational learning. We believe that theories of learning and knowledge as mediated processes should be recognized as key drivers of integrating both. Relevant concepts embrace: the role of user participation in knowledge creation/ sharing (Wenger, McDermott, & Snyder, 2002), promotion of converting tacit knowledge into explicit knowledge assets (Nonaka & Konno, 1998), and codification of reciprocal feedback, resulting from social interactions (Lin, Lin, & Huang, 2008). KM as organizational memory system (Cross & Baird, 2000) can be effectively built when knowledge is conceptualized as a social and evolving artifact (Collison & Parcell, 2005; Prusak & Matson, 2006).

In this article we utilize ideas and concepts from the situated learning literature (Brown & Duguid, 1991; Lave & Wenger, 1991), Vygotskian cultural-historical theory of cognition and the activity theory (Barab et al., 2004; Engeström, 2001, 2007; Kaptelinin & Nardi, 2005), and a holistic and integrative learning and performance architecture (Rosenberg, 2006) as theoretical foundations for designing integrated learning and KM systems. In the remainder of the article we review theoretical perspectives on organizational learning and knowledge management as applied to integrated learning and knowledge management systems design, propose learning- and activity-based design principles to be applied in

KM design work, and summarize our conclusions and implications for KM users.

UNDERSTANDING ORGANIZATIONAL KNOWLEDGE AND LEARNING: TWO THEORETICAL PERSPECTIVES

In an analysis of theoretical and applied models of organizational learning and knowledge creation, Antonacopoulou and Chiva (2007) argued that all existing models are based on either the individual or the social view of learning and knowledge. As illustrated in the tradition of behaviorism, information processing theory, and nativisitic developmental perspectives, the individual view considers learning as an internal process of obtaining knowledge, and knowledge is viewed as objective realities to be mastered. On the other hand, the social view sees learning as a mediated process and knowledge is always continually defined as justified truth by members of the society (Nonaka, 1994).

The individual view is best summarized by Simon's (1991) often-quoted statement: "All learning takes place inside individual human heads" (p. 125). However, as Tsoukas and Mylonopoulos (2004) pointed out, this view is subject to the "apple tree" fallacy: knowledge used by individuals in their organizational work is assumed to be readily available to be picked from the organizational tree of knowledge (a.k.a. organizational digital databases). Tsoukas and Mylonopoulos (2004) explained that the main problem with this view is that it "tends to ignore... the *constructed* [emphasis in the original] nature of knowledge: whatever knowledge is, the form as well as the content it takes depends on what questions are asked..." (p. S3). In presenting this argument, they drew on Foucault's (1972) work to suggest that knowledge is "the outcome of particular social practices" (S3).

The social perspective emphasizes that knowledge can be regarded as a form of "social expertise"

(Yanow, 2004), and makes a distinction between *knowing* (verb) and *knowledge* (noun) (Cook & Brown, 1999). Central to the social perspective is the notion that knowledge is a product of collective action and practice, situated in specific localized cultural contexts (Gherardi, 2001; Nicolini, Gherardi, & Yanow, 2003). Such localized knowledge is situated in communities of practice and groups of front-line employees, is often tacit rather than explicit, and is not easily quantifiable and recordable in databases (Yanow, 2004).

The individual view of knowledge is at core of information management systems, aimed at codification of knowledge in digital databases. This is clearly visible in the KM Value Chain model (Lee & Yang, 2000) and the KM Effectiveness model (Lindsey, 2002). On the other hand, the social view emphasizes a shift from codification to knowledge sharing approaches, which are built on the ideas from the situated learning and communities of practice perspectives (Brown & Duguid, 1991; Lave & Wenger, 1991). The codification approach is the foundation of linear design models that focus on capturing and managing transactions. For designing information repositories and performance support systems (to support well-defined work procedures), this is an effective approach. However, linear models do not take into full consideration two fundamentally important qualities of complex human systems: the fact that knowledge in such systems is never static and is constantly being created and modified by user interactions (Prahalad & Krishnan, 2008; Rosenberg, 2006); and the fact that system rules and changes are frequently driven by cognitive conflicts and tensions, and not by planned goals (Engeström, 2001).

LEARNING THEORIES, INFORMING THE SOCIAL VIEW OF KM AND LEARNING SYSTEMS DESIGN

Despite the rigidity of the codification approach, one could argue that at least this approach has some

systematic design models to rely upon. Linear-design models, such as ADDIE (Analyze, Design, Develop, Implement, and Evaluate) definitely ensure clarity in decision making on the part of the system designers. An additional strength of such approaches is consistency across design products. By comparison, the social view- based KM design is at a significant disadvantage, since it does not seem to have a variety of well-articulated models and procedures to follow other than concepts to be utilized. We believe that a number of existing theories and frameworks, grounded in the social view of learning, can be used to advance the current literature on designing integrative KM and learning systems, enabling knowledge creation through collaborative inquiry, joint task completion, and collaborative problem solving. In the remainder of this section we will discuss these theories and frameworks. Models attempting to align work and learning with KM have been proposed, such as a 'living system design model' by Pluss and Salisbury (2002) and the KnowledgeScope by Kwan and Balasubramanian (2003), and we review the KnowledgeScope model later in this article to illustrate how concepts we highlight can be applied to KM designing.

Vygotskian Constructivist Interactional Theory of Cognitive Development

Lev Vygotsky (1978) was one of the pioneers of constructivist interactional psychology of learning. This branch of psychology is based on the assumption that knowledge is constructed by learners in social interactions as they attempt to make sense of their experiences. As a result of his field research and theorizing, Vygotsky introduced an original explanation of individual learning as a product of socially-situated and goal-oriented activities. The following elements of the Vygotskyan theory are of special importance to our discussion: learning as a mediated action; cognition and knowledge resulting from dynamic interaction between subjects of learning, artifacts, and social others; and the idea of the Zone of Proximal Development (ZPD).

Vygotsky argued that all knowledge originates in social interaction, is developed by human beings engaged in productive activities, and is mediated by tools. This view is also the foundation of the organizational knowledge conversion theory (Nonaka, 1994; Nonaka & Konno, 1998). Tools can be tangible, intangible, and psychological to include various artifacts, such as computers, books, documents, production equipment, transportation, mental models, procedures, routines, and informal rules of behavior. Use of tools affects the accomplishment of system goals, and is socially constructed. Therefore, they must be examined in the longitudinal context of the past and the present. This perspective somewhat contrasts with that of the KM Effectiveness model (Lindsey, 2002), where technologies are conceptualized as a 'fixed' connector between knowledge sources and users.

Another important Vygotskian concept for aligning KM with learning is the Zone of Proximal Development (ZPD). A ZPD is a cognitive distance between the current cognitive level of an individual and the level one can reach if interacting with knowledgeable others (Vygotsky, 1978). Before Vygotsky, previous learning theories and instructional strategies stopped at a point of identifying learners' current and past capabilities in an effort to bring *unknown* into existing capacity. Vygotsky was unique in that he was also interested in what will yet develop and how this development would differ with different arrangements, such as demonstration, questioning, or scaffolding. Such a concept can be utilized as a guiding principle of introducing multiple communication and interaction channels for system users and evaluating the effectiveness of the system based on proactive experimentation.

Situated Learning Theory

The situated learning theory is a further development and elaboration of Vygotskyan ideas. One of its main contributions is the notion that knowledge is an integral part of practice and, therefore, cannot have an abstract existence outside work or learning practices (Brown, Collins, & Duguid, 1989; Lave & Wenger, 1991; Wenger et al., 2002). In his investigation of learning processes, Wenger (1998) focused his attention on learners' situated identities and modes of belonging rather than on individual mental processes. In this perspective, learning is viewed as a reciprocal process of transformation of both knowledge and learners in action and through actions (activities). Thus, "the knowledge, the subjects and the objects of knowledge may be understood as being produced together within a situated practice" (Gherardi, 2001, p. 132). A view like this challenges the notion of *learning then transfer* seen in the training approach that separates learning from knowledge. Situated learning theory also highlights the importance of guiding novices through sequential phases of interacting with coaches, collaborating with model performers, reflecting and articulating experiences, and making generalizations to become effective problem solvers (Brown et al., 1989).

Activity Theory of Learning and Cognition

The basic Vygotskian triangle of subject-object-tools was further expanded by post-Vygotskian sociocultural theorists in an effort to clarify how the divide between the organism (individuals) and its environment is overcome. Vygotsky's disciple, Leont'ev (1974) believed that although activities are observable, goals and means that comprise the middle link are open to subjective interpretations, thus he proposed a three level scheme of analysis, which examined the relationship between observable human behaviors (activity-action-operation) and non-observable human terms of motive-goal-instrumental conditions.

Engeström (1987, 1999) expanded the basic Vygotskian triangle to include the interaction of these three elements with the community, division of labor, and rules of interaction. Explaining the elements of the activity model, Yamagata-Lynch (2003) defined *rules* as "any formal or informal regulations that in varying degree can constrain or liberate the activity and provide guidance to the subject on what are correct procedures and acceptable interactions to take with other community members" (p. 102), *community* as a group with which the subject of activity identifies herself while engaging in the activity, and *the division of labor* as the way of distributing tasks among community members. Cole and Engeström (1993) pointed out that once individuals' goal oriented activities are institutionalized, they become a robust and enduring tool within the culture shaping the rules of the community, thus human organizations are not viewed as static collections of bounded components, but as complex dynamic systems of interlocking activities (Engeström & Miettinen, 1999). These concepts inform the KM designers of the need for capturing users' goals, participation, and interaction for future directions.

Integrative Models of Learning and Performance Architecture

The final theoretical foundation of our proposed integrative learning and KM systems design approach is provided by models that integrate learning and performance architecture (Rosenberg, 2006; Yoon & Lim, 2007). Rosenberg (2006) pointed out that most learning takes place on the job, employees never stops learning (by asking questions, watching others, accessing information, mentoring, and trials and errors), and organizations must leverage technologies for learning as they have done for workforce productivity. Rosenberg (2006) defined an integrative learning and performance architecture as "a systematic integration of electronic and non-electronic approaches that facilitates both formal and informal workplace learning and support and, ultimately, improved human performance." (p. 70), and defined KM "the creation, archiving, and sharing of valued information, expertise, and insight within and

across communities of people and organizations with similar interests and needs, the goal of which is to build competitive advantage" (pp. 73-74). Furthermore, strategic blending (of onsite and technology-based solutions) is needed for a purposeful integration of learning and performance solutions, which should be guided by the goals and needs of the business (Yoon & Lim, 2007). When strategic blending is implemented, technologies are selectively and purposefully implemented to best support the business-driven learning and performance solutions.

SITUATED LEARNING AND ACTIVITY THEORY BASED DESIGN PRINCIPLES

The theoretical foundations, discussed above, are providing a solid analytical lens for planning and analyzing the system design requirements by focusing on socially mediated activities and their constituent elements. In this section, we will first present several key design considerations based on social views of learning. Instead of taking a prescriptive stance, we would be better served by a strategy of applying these principles selectively and evaluating their effectiveness. Then we will propose steps grounded in activity theory to apply in the design process, which integrates KM with learning from AT perspectives. Speaking about most important *design considerations*, we suggest that KM and learning system design, based on the principles of AT and situated learning and cognition, should:

- Integrate in one seamless, transactional system both the codification and knowledge sharing tools and processes. Specifically, the system should include codification/ storage/retrieval tools; knowledge sharing systems; and blended formal and informal learning solutions (Rosenberg, 2006)

- Allow for flexible changes in the composition of constituents of the activity (subjects, tools, and the community) (Engeström, 2001, 2007)
- Provide structure and means for defining and re-defining rules of interaction (Yamagata-Lynch, 2003)
- Incorporate an ability to constantly monitor the evolution of the system, and to make needed changes in real time (Cole & Engeström, 1993)
- Allow boundary crossing and communication between multiple internal and external communities (Lave & Wenger, 1991; Wenger, 1998)
- Utilize the idea of a special zone of transaction and proximal development, where learning and knowledge creation will occur (Vygotsky, 1978)
- Account for essential tensions in the system, and make sure that the tensions are acting as productive, not destructive elements of the system (Engeström, 2001, 2007; Yamagata-Lynch, 2003)

The first of these principles helps to close the gap between individual (codification) and social (participation) approaches to KM. By conceptualizing learning and KM as one seamless system, it also helps eliminate the separation of managing learning and work support functions. Here, the concept of blended learning goes beyond the traditional notion of mixing classroom instruction with e-learning. Rather, it refers to the strategic selection and positioning of learning and performance solutions and implementing technologies selectively and purposefully. Since social interaction is conceptualized as the key to knowledge creation, the importance of creating various avenues for such interaction becomes paramount. Therefore, a Web-enabled KM and learning system, based on the proposed principles, will need to include seamless interaction between online learning, virtual community collaboration, online and face-to-face meetings of community

members, virtual and face-to-face access to experts, and mentoring and coaching. To ensure that technology-based solutions, such as e-learning or KM systems are effective, they should be simple, stable, sustainable, scalable, and sociable (Vaccare & Sherman, 2001).

Social interaction by itself will not produce innovative solutions if the actors will not have access to well-organized databases and easy-to-use interfaces, allowing just-in-time access to a variety of information (recall Ashby's (1956) law of requisite variety). "It is only when tacit knowledge is linked to the explicit knowledge in the system, and the system's external knowledge base, that innovations appear." (Johannessen et al., 2001, p. 12).

Two approaches can be particularly useful for enhancing the speed and quality of knowledge processing. First, technologies, such as AJAX (Asynchronous JavaScript and XML) allows any form-field data entries to constantly communicate with remote servers without having to type up the finished word, thus this feature enables one to look up and retrieve targeted or related search words faster. Second, in organizing and sharing information repositories, more metadata (data about data) related to artifacts will be useful. Robson (2007) claimed that for learning objects to be reused, designers must include at least the following: (a) descriptions of the contents and their creators, (b) contexts (e.g., audience, difficulty, objectives, content types, content relations, etc.), (c) rights (e.g., copyright, terms of use), and technicalities (e.g., format, software version, platform requirements, and conversion rules, etc.). This task does not have to be either cumbersome, or information-overload generating. Here designers of corporate KM systems could learn from user-friendly designs utilized in popular applications, like Facebook or Myspace. Adding textual meta-tags to pictures on Facebook is easy, and tags are made visible (through rolling the mouse over the relevant parts of the picture) only when the user decides to access them.

Next three principles further support the idea that the distinction between learning and work is unnecessary and that co-configuration of the system with the users in real time is essential for KM success. Activity theory posits that work can improve and be meaningful only if reflective, collaborative, and supportive exchanges happen over an extended timeframe to enhance the system (Engeström, 2000). Initial and iconic specifications may be entered by KM system designers, but with more users contributing information, connecting with others and sharing post-usage experiences through KM systems, more focus can be directed to accommodating participation and identifying patterns, rules, tensions, directions, and possibilities, etc. End user tools that allow approvals or disapprovals of entered information can play a gatekeeper and quality-check role (e.g., rating system) and this is frequently found in judging the quality and usefulness of knowledge-in-context (Sage & Rouse, 1999). Analytical frameworks are also available to examine the strength and concentration of network resources and communications (Gourlay, 2001).

Next, the idea of a zone of co-creation and proximal development is not unique to the AT literature (c.f. concept of "ba," introduced by Nonaka & Konno, 1998). However, Vygotskian thought provides the clearest and most practical explanation of why the creation of these zones is necessary. Such zones fulfill several functions. First, they create a bounded framework, a space for interaction and exchange among the subjects of the activity. Second, they allow for proximal development of new and less experienced subjects of activity though interactions with more experienced peers. Finally, they can be viewed as special spaces where designers and users not only collaborate, but also learn from each other. This last point is based on the "participatory design" principle, which emphasizes the need for "incorporating end users' local knowledge of work practices relevant to the technology in question" (Yanow, 2004, p. S17), and overcomes

the designer-user duality (Barab et al., 2004, p. 42), by collapsing the distinction between design experts and end users. The zones could be conceptualized and designed as physical or virtual spaces. Thus, Barab et al. (2004) suggested the creation of virtual workrooms, where participants (both designers and end users) can collaboratively build knowledge objects, discuss lessons learned, etc. (p. 37). Such collaboration will result in the evolution of the system through field testing and co-design with users (Barab et al., p. 26). An illustrative case can be found from the blogging space of Adobe Systems. In several blogging spaces, customers, application developers, and business managers frequently exchange product information, user experiences, and business plans to make rapid adjustments. There are numerous examples of cases where the features of future program releases have been altered in the course of designer and end-user discourse.

In addition to general principles of design, discussed above, we can provide specific practical steps in applying principles of activity theory as follows:

1. Identify the main subjects of activity, tools, object, rules and community.
2. Conduct the analysis of the structure and process of the users' main work activities.
3. Identify the division of labor among subjects.
4. Identify main tensions in the system.
5. Incorporate the analysis of the extent to which technology facilitates or constrains the achievement of goals of these activities.
6. Produce at least two different representations of the system (one from the point of view of the user, and another from the point of view of the designer), and then merge them into one integrated representation (see Barab et al., 2004).
7. Construct a model of the system, including subjects, objects, rules, tools, community, interactions, and tensions.

8. Design individual elements of the system using the rapid prototyping and ongoing modification approach that facilitate changes in the composition and functionality of system's elements.

Suggested principles and steps do not necessarily conflict with, nor denounce the ADDIE-based linear approaches to KM design. Rather, they can be applied at the same time (this would be preferred) or after the more familiar linear approach is applied to the designing of individual components of the system. Steps above can be followed in the suggested order or in an iterative manner. The ultimate goal is to deploy virtual workspace where information, expertise, and insights are more effectively and efficiently created, accumulated, organized, and disseminated to develop seamless learning and performance systems. KM designers should articulate how design specifications, tools, and user activities impact targeted performance goals (e.g., growth in revenues, more customers, cost reduction, time to reach market, innovation, etc.).

In identifying main areas that need to be covered by KM systems, Rosenberg (2006) pointed out that most organizations should leverage relationships between employees, partners, suppliers, and customers. Likewise, in the proposed design approach, users of KM systems (subjects) may be conceptualized from the viewpoint of various relationships these groups can form. CoPs may be also created based on considerations of learning and performance targets (e.g., customers, developers, and managers) or desired tensions, such as between mentors and mentees, trainers and trainees, supervisors and supervisees, and business organization and its clients. Desired user activities usually start at more explicitly goal-driven actions, such as posting troubleshooting inquiries or posting service records, or additional resources, but gradually need to move to higher levels, involving managing expertise and expert insights.

Activity theory posits that activities in organizations are hierarchical, horizontal, and interlocked. To participate, subjects will use various tangible (e.g., computers) or intangible (e.g., informal or formal procedures and processes), and psychological (e.g., power relationships) tools. Shared activities will emerge from social exchanges. For KM designers, this indicates the importance of accommodating various onsite and online CoPs, identifying appropriate ways of belonging to CoPs, determining who are the active members, enabling members to quickly retrieve the information from and contribute to CoPs, and capturing the history and evolution of CoPs. Rules (e.g., *what* to post – documents or audio records, or *who*, *when*, *where*, and *how* can post) may be initially introduced or suggested by system designers working together with leadership, but will need to be modified and improved in the course of desired shared activities with end users.

In analyzing the structure and process of user activities, it is necessary to capture user credentials, participation in communities (e.g., tagging, numbers of posts or solutions, and ratings received on posts), and the history and evolution of knowledge creating and shaping (e.g., solution initiation and acceptance). The above information can help to understand what to do when issues arise from tensions and division of labor. If most of the core subjects, tools, communities, and rules are identified and they interact with each other, the volume of data increases rapidly, and locating value-adding knowledge becomes a daunting task. Determining which user-contributed information to accept and utilize is one example of potential tensions between designers and end users. Rosenberg (2006) pointed out that, when knowledge is not *firmed up* yet or is changing fast and the nature of work is related to new or untested ideas, experts can be most valuable by (a) validating ideas, (b) providing sound judgment, (c) locating what is important, and (d) pointing people to additional, reliable knowledge sources. Technologies can save time and cost in achieving this task by locating experts based on credentials, filtering active community contributors, or retrieving and comparing communication threads by subjects or objects.

Cole and Engeström (1993) emphasized that activity systems are hardly stable and tensions among system elements drive the evolution of any system. System capacity that traces contributions, exchanges, and acceptance can be very useful in dealing with issues related to tensions and division of labor. If distributions of tasks and contributions of the members show discrepancy in regards to members' profiles, responsibilities, and rewards, new rules (e.g., work arrangements, recognition, or monetary incentives) will have to be introduced. Indeed, extra time needed for the experts to answer questions and for end users to update the repository are real concerns that inhibit knowledge sharing (Bartol & Srivastava, 2002). In identifying main tensions of the system and the division of labor, we believe that lagging performance results, dissatisfaction with tools, the lack of emergence of new rules, or lack of support for proposed rules can be a sign of detrimental tensions and poor division of labor.

Once the step of identifying system elements and examining their interaction patterns (i.e., tensions, division of labor, and their impact on performance goals) is completed, subsequent steps require on-going analyses and improvements of tools with a goal of improving community learning, in which all of the system elements and their interactions should continuously evolve. Community learning is different from learning communities where members learn from or with others, but the learning process stops once learning tasks are finished. In community learning, the primary task is to transfer the knowledge of the learning community to new communities. Boundary spanning individuals and objects may fulfill this role of connecting different communities.

The KnowledgeScope Model

Suggested principles and steps above await validation through empirical research. In the mean while, a design model (KnowledgeScope), proposed by Kwan and Balasubramanian (2003) illustrates how a system, integrating codification and sharing approaches can be implemented. The authors argued that existing KM models, such as *knowledge repository, process memory systems*, and *organizational memory information systems* are insufficient for aligning KM use with organizational workflow processes (Cross & Baird, 2000). They stated that explicit categorization (i.e., information repository), prescriptive inclusion of subjects and actions (e.g., projects, users, events, meetings, documentation, and process archives in process memory systems), and integration of activity experiences with resource systems, such as intelligence or expert-help systems (in organizational memory information systems) are insufficient for capturing contextual information manifested in different perspectives of different roles in most work processes.

Aligning the use of social KM systems with their daily work routines calls for constructing a knowledge-in-context model, which needs to synthesize multiple-perspectives of KM systems (i.e., *functional* – task processes, *informational* – about what and whom, *organizational* – organizational structure and configuration, and *behavioral* – sequence, control flow, and conditions governing the *functional* perspectives) (Kwan & Balasubramanian, 2003). The KnowledgeScope model consists of multiple databases (process archives, process instance-case archives, documents, and discussions), workflow-support services (workflow templates, workflow client application, and process modeling tool) and knowledge applications (exception handling and document/discussion search) in which system elements interact with each other in the process of *process planning, work in progress, process completion*, and *process evaluation*. Although this model needs to be empirically verified in a variety of settings, we find that its emphasis on capturing knowledge based on work processes is reverberated by many studies (Asimakou, 2009; Ferrari & de Toledo, 2004). Similar to this model, we believe that an effective KM system should be an integrative system that connects multiple databases, learning and work applications, and performance support tools that help users perform work more effectively and efficiently. System components and applications need to be continuously added or modified by all KM stakeholders: system users, business managers, and designers. Ideally, these constant improvements will be happening without the users' awareness of abrupt changes.

For example, search engine used to be a tool that simply searches through databases and web pages to retrieve results conforming to what the user provided. Over time, it has evolved into an interface that collects, analyzes, and contributes the user experiences to the system to enable it become smarter and capable of retrieving accurate results even when users do not use accurate Boolean operators. With growing XML implementation, contents in remote databases and applications can be searched and shared more rapidly and openly enabling collective wisdom and artifacts being produced even in massive virtual worlds. Social tagging on popular Web services and a site like Wikipedia are examples that leverage collaboration and social exchanges for effective knowledge management without burdening the users. In such spaces, end users by their choice keep defining the rules of the community by tagging user-defined keywords and descriptions, whose aggregated tabulations define what is culturally accepted, dominant, and trivial. Industry standards, such as XML and SCORM (Sharable Content Object Reference Model) enable contents and tools to be shared across different communities faster: user creates contents on one Web service only and this content can be immediately available on multiple other sites by simple button-clicking. These virtual communities have an ever-expanding

potential to develop shared cognition or collective understanding of complex problems and solutions (Stahl, 2006). Organizations wanting to leverage Web tools for knowledge management should promote the culture of openness, freedom, and empowerment for employees, who are familiar with policies of power and control (Schnecken-berg, 2009).

CONCLUSIONS AND IMPLICATIONS FOR KM SYSTEM DESIGNERS AND MANAGERS

In this article we argued that to achieve sustainable competitive advantage, business organizations need to ensure that their strategy, financial management, customer interaction, and work processes are closely integrated with social and network-based learning solutions, and that Knowledge Management (KM) is integrated with organizations' learning systems. To incorporate social views of learning into KM systems, our proposal integrates such Vygotskian ideas as the conceptualization of learning as a mediated action, cognition and knowledge creation as a result of dynamic interaction between subjects of learning, artifacts, and social others, and the idea of the Zone of Proximal Development (ZPD); and the notion of creative tensions and their role in the KM system design.

The situated learning and AT perspectives provide a strong support for the idea of integrating formal learning (training and e-learning) and work (activity/work process design) with informal learning and KM solutions (e.g., knowledge management and EPSS, Rosenberg, 2006). If learning is conceptualized as situated knowing and the creation of new knowledge though participating in practice, then it does not make much sense to create and maintain two separate systems: one for learning management, and another for knowledge management. In addition to clarifying specific design considerations, our suggestions help to demonstrate that collaborations among information technology and learning professionals are essential in designing KM systems that enable collaborative knowledge creation environments and adaptive systems (Ardichvili, 2001). Existing models for designing KM systems utilize a number of theories, notably economic values (e.g., Lee and Yang's (2000) KM Value Chain, and Lindsey's (2002) KM Effectiveness model) and organizational knowledge creation (Malhotra, 2000), but few models explicitly emphasize design principles drawn from social views of learning and human interactions. Situated learning and activity theory will provide a useful mechanism for continuous development of the constituents of the activity (subjects, tools, and the community); creation of a special transactional zone, where learning and knowledge creation will occur; enabling of boundary crossing and communication between multiple internal and external communities; monitoring of essential tensions in the system, making sure that the tensions are acting as productive elements of the system; and constantly refining evolving working rules.

REFERENCES

Antonacopoulou, E., & Chiva, R. (2007). The social complexity of organizational learning: The dynamics of learning and organizing. *Management Learning, 38*(3), 277–295. doi:10.1177/1350507607079029

Ardichvili, A. (2001). The role of human resource development in transitioning from technology-focused to people-centered knowledge management. In Sleezer, C., Wentling, T., & Cude, R. (Eds.), *Human resource development and information technology: Making global connections* (pp. 89–104). Boston, MA: Kluwer Academic Publishers.

Ashby, W. R. (1956). *Introduction to Cybernetics*. London: Wiley.

Asimakou, T. (2009). The knowledge dimension of innovation management. *Knowledge Management. Research & Practice, 7,* 82–90.

Barab, S., Schatz, S., & Scheckler, R. (2004). Using activity theory to conceptualize online community and using online community to conceptualize activity theory. *Mind, Culture, and Activity, 11*(10), 25–47. doi:10.1207/s15327884mca1101_3

Bartol, K. M., & Srivastava, A. (2002). Encouraging knowledge sharing: The role of organizational reward systems. *Journal of Leadership & Organizational Studies, 9*(1), 64–76. doi:10.1177/107179190200900105

Brown, J. S., Collins, A., & Duguid, P. (1989). Situated cognition and the culture of learning. *Educational Research, 18*(1), 32–42.

Brown, J. S., & Duguid, P. (1991). Organizational learning and communities of practice. *Organization Science, 2*(1), 40–47. doi:10.1287/orsc.2.1.40

Cole, M., & Engeström, Y. (1993). A cultural-historical approach to distributed cognition. In Solomon, G. (Ed.), *Distributed cognitions: Psychological and educational considerations.* Cambridge, UK: Cambridge University Press.

Collison, C., & Parcell, G. (2005). *Learning to fly: Practical knowledge management from leading and learning organizations.* New York: Capstone.

Cook, S., & Brown, J. S. (1999). Bridging epistemologies: The generative dance between organizational knowledge and organizational knowing. *Organization Science, 10*(4), 381–400. doi:10.1287/orsc.10.4.381

Cross, R., & Baird, L. (2000). Technology is not enough: Improving performance by building organizational memory. *Sloan Management Review, 41*(3), 41–54.

Davenport, T. H., DeLong, D. W., & Beers, M. C. (1998). Successful knowledge management projects. *Sloan Management Review, 39*(2), 43–57.

Engeström, Y. (1987). *Learning by expanding: An activity-theoretical approach to developmental research*. Helsinki, Finland: Orienta-Konsultit Oy.

Engeström, Y. (1999). Activity theory and individual and social transformation. In Engestrom, Y., Miettinen, R., & Punamaki, R. (Eds.), *Perspectives on activity theory* (pp. 19–38). New York: Cambridge University Press.

Engeström, Y. (2000). Activity theory as a framework for analyzing and redesigning work. *Ergonomics*, *43*(7), 960–974. doi:10.1080/001401300409143

Engeström, Y. (2001). Expansive learning at work: Toward an activity theoretical reconceptualization. *Journal of Education and Work*, *14*(1), 133–156.

Engeström, Y. (2007). Enriching the theory of expansive learning: Lessons from journeys toward coconfiguration. *Mind, Culture, and Activity*, *14*(1-2), 23–39.

Engeström, Y., & Miettinen, R. (1999). Introduction. In Engeström, Y., Miettinen, R., & Punamaki, R.-L. (Eds.), *Perspectives on activity theory* (pp. 1–16). New York: Cambridge University Press.

Ferrari, F. M., & de Toledo, J. C. (2004). Analyzing the knowledge management through the product development process. *Journal of Knowledge Management*, *8*(1), 117–129. doi:10.1108/13673270410523952

Foucault, M. (1972). *The archeology of knowledge*. London: Routledge.

Gherardi, S. (2001). From organizational learning to practice-based knowing. *Human Relations*, *54*(1), 131–139. doi:10.1177/0018726701541016

Gourlay, S. (2001). Knowledge management and HRD. *Human Resource Development International*, *4*(1), 27–46. doi:10.1080/13678860121778

Jasimuddin, S. (2008). A holistic view of knowledge management strategy. *Journal of Knowledge Management*, *12*(2), 57–66. doi:10.1108/13673270810859514

Jennex, M. E., & Olfman, L. (2005). Assessing Knowledge Management success/effectiveness models. *International Journal of Knowledge Management*, *1*(2), 33–49.

Johannessen, J.-A., Olaisen, J., & Olsen, B. (2001). Mismanagement of tacit knowledge: The importance of tacit knowledge, the danger of information technology, and what to do about it. *International Journal of Information Management*, *21*, 3–20. doi:10.1016/S0268-4012(00)00047-5

Kaptelinin, V., & Nardi, B. (2005). *Acting with technology: Activity theory and interaction design*. Cambridge, MA: MIT Press.

Kimble, C., & Bourdon, I. (2008). Some success factors for the communal management of knowledge. *International Journal of Information Management*, *28*(6), 461–467. doi:10.1016/j.ijinfomgt.2008.08.007

Kwan, M. M., & Balasubramanian, P. (2003). KnowledgeScope: Managing knowledge in context. *Decision Support Systems*, *35*, 467–486. doi:10.1016/S0167-9236(02)00126-4

Lave, J., & Wenger, E. (1991). *Situated Learning: Legitimate peripheral participation*. New York: Cambridge University Press.

Lee, C. C., & Yang, J. (2000). Knowledge value chain. *Journal of Management Development*, *19*(9), 783–794. doi:10.1108/02621710010378228

Leont'ev, A. N. (1974). The problem of activity in psychology. *Social Psychology*, *13*(2), 4–33.

Lin, F., Lin, S., & Huang, T. (2008). Knowledge sharing and creation in a teachers' professional virtual community. *Computers & Education*, *50*(3), 742–756. doi:10.1016/j.compedu.2006.07.009

Lindsey, K. (2002). Measuring knowledge management effectiveness: A task-contingent organizational capabilities perspective. In *Proceedings of the Eighth Americas Conference on Information Systems* (pp. 2085-2090).

Malhotra, Y. (2000). From information management to knowledge management: Beyond the 'Hi-Tech Hidebound' systems. In Srikantaiah, K., & Koenig, M. E. D. (Eds.), *Knowledge Management for the Information Professional* (pp. 37–61). Medford, NJ: Information Today Inc.

Nicolini, D., Gherardi, S., & Yanow, D. (2003). *Knowing in organizations.* Armonk, NY: M. E. Sharpe.

Nonaka, I. (1994). A dynamic theory of organizational knowledge creation. *Organization Science, 5*(1), 14–37. doi:10.1287/orsc.5.1.14

Nonaka, I., & Konno, N. (1998). The concept of "ba": Building a foundation for knowledge creation. *California Management Review, 40*(3), 40–54.

Pluss, J., & Salisbury, M. (2002). A living-systems design model for web-based knowledge management systems. *Educational Technology Research and Development, 50*(1), 35–56. doi:10.1007/BF02504960

Prahalad, C. K., & Krishnan, M. S. (2008). *The new age of innovation: Driving co-created value through global networks.* Columbus, OH: McGraw-Hill.

Prusak, L., & Matson, E. (2006). *Knowledge management and organizational learning: A reader.* Oxford, UK: Oxford University Press.

Robson, R. (2007). Reusability and reusable design. In Reiser, R. A., & Dempsey, J. V. (Eds.), *Trends and issues in instructional design and technology* (pp. 301–310). Upper Saddle River, NJ: Merrill/Prentice Hall.

Rosenberg, M. (2006). *Beyond E-Learning: Approaches and technologies to enhance organizational knowledge, learning, and performance.* New York: Pfeiffer.

Sage, A. P., & Rouse, W. B. (1999). Information systems frontiers in Knowledge Management. *Information Systems Frontiers, 1*(3), 205–219. doi:10.1023/A:1010046210832

Schneckenberg, D. (2009). Web 2.0 and the empowerment of knowledge worker. *Journal of Knowledge Management, 13*(6), 509–520. doi:10.1108/13673270910997150

Simon, H. (1991). Bounded rationality and organizational learning. *Organization Science, 2*(1), 125–134. doi:10.1287/orsc.2.1.125

Stahl, G. (2006). *Group cognition: Computer support for building collaborative knowledge.* Cambridge, MA: MIT Press.

Tsoukas, H., & Mylonopoulos, N. (2004). Introduction: Knowledge construction and creation in organizations. *British Journal of Management, 15*, S1–S8. doi:10.1111/j.1467-8551.2004.t01-2-00402.x

Vaccare, C., & Sherman, G. (2001). A pragmatic model for instructional technology selection. In Branch, R. M., & Fitzgerald, A. (Eds.), *Educational Media and Technology Yearbook* (*Vol. 27*). Englewood, CO: Libraries Unlimited.

Vygotsky, L. S. (1978). *Mind in Society: The development of higher psychological processes.* Cambridge, MA: Harvard University Press.

Wenger, E. (1998). *Communities of practice: Learning, meaning, and identity.* New York: Cambridge University Press.

Wenger, E., McDermott, R., & Snyder, W. (2002). *Cultivating communities of practice: A Guide to managing knowledge.* Boston: Harvard Business School Press.

Yamagata-Lynch, L. (2003). Using Activity theory as an analytic lens for examining technology professional development in schools. *Mind, Culture, and Activity, 10*(2), 100–119. doi:10.1207/S1532-7884MCA1002_2

Yanow, D. (2004). Translating local knowledge at organizational peripheries. *British Journal of Management, 15*, S9–S25. doi:10.1111/j.1467-8551.2004.t01-1-00403.x

Yoon, S. W., & Lim, D. H. (2007). Strategic blending: A conceptual framework to improve learning and performance. *International Journal on E-Learning, 6*(3), 475–489.

This work was previously published in International Journal of Knowledge Management, Volume 6, Issue 4, edited by Murray E. Jennex, pp. 47-59, copyright 2010 by IGI Publishing (an imprint of IGI Global).

Chapter 16
Culture and Knowledge Transfer Capacity:
A Cross-National Study

Omar Khalil
Kuwait University, Kuwait

Ahmed A. S. Seleim
Alexandria University, Egypt

ABSTRACT

Increasing interest exists in understanding the factors that explain knowledge transfer capacity (KTC) at the societal level. In this paper, the authors posit that national culture may explain the differences among countries in their knowledge transfer capacities. The authors adopt House and colleagues' (2004) national culture taxonomy as the theoretical framework to derive and test eighteen hypotheses relating national culture values and practices to societal KTC. KTC correlates positively with gender egalitarianism values, uncertainty avoidance practices, and future orientation practices. KTC also correlates negatively with uncertainty avoidance values, future orientation values, institutional collectivism values, in-group collectivism values, humane orientation practices, in-group collectivism values and practices, and power distance practices. Further analysis using gross domestic product (GDP) as a control variable revealed that only humane orientation practices influence KTC. The research findings are discussed, research limitations are identified, and implications are drawn.

INTRODUCTION

Knowledge management (KM) poses a major challenge for the societies that aim at developing and sustaining knowledge-based economies. People's skills, knowledge and creativity have become increasingly important in the creation of economic value (Stewart, 1997, p. 49). It's almost impossible for a society to achieve sustainable growth without constantly creating and transferring knowledge. Societies, however, may vary in their capabilities to create and transfer knowledge. Differences in national culture

DOI: 10.4018/978-1-4666-0035-5.ch016

may create barriers to effective knowledge transfer (Banerjee & Richter, 2001, p. 13).

Culture is a collective programming of the mind that discerns the members of one group of people from another (Hofstede, 1991, p. 5) and shapes values, beliefs, assumptions, expectations, perceptions, and behaviors. Societies differ significantly in their cultural profiles (e.g. House, 2004; Hofstede, 2001; Nicholson & Stepina, 1998). Research indicates that differences in societal cultures influence a wide variety of social phenomena (House et al., 2002; Hofstede, 1983).

Culture has been recognized as a major barrier to leveraging knowledge at the organizational level (e.g., Abou-Zeid, 2002; Gupta & Covindarajan, 2000; De Long & Fahey, 2000). Culture may also influence KM, e.g., knowledge creation, transfer, and application, behavior through shaping assumptions regarding identifying the knowledge that is important to manage, determining how knowledge is distributed and utilized in an organization, creating the context for social interaction that determines how knowledge is used in particular situations, and forming the processes by which new knowledge is applied (De Long & Fahey, 2000; Chaminade & Johanson, 2003).

The effectiveness of knowledge transfer within and among entities, such as countries, is believed to be affected by the degree of cultural heterogeneity among the entities involved (Abou-Zeid, 2002). Most of KM research, however, has focused mainly on the influence of culture on intra-organizational and inter-organizational knowledge transfer. Spicer (1997) posits that knowledge can and should be examined at the level of a country's culture. Although organizational cultures are believed to reflect societal cultures (House et al., 2004, p. xvi), the question that has yet to be answered in the cross-national KM literature is whether national culture influences knowledge transfer-related factors such as knowledge transfer capacity (KTC).

KTC, i.e., the capability of people and institutions in a society to exchange knowledge with each other and with others in other societies, can pose significant challenges to effective knowledge transfer (Parent et al., 2007). Managing such challenges requires an understanding of knowledge transfer capacities at the societal level as well as the factors that may affect these capacities. This research explores the influence that national culture may have on societal KTC. The underlying assumption is that national cultures are malleable rather than stable, and government policies and actions are in fact an important source of influence on cultural change (Li & Karakowsky, 2002).

The remainder of this paper is organized accordingly. The research background is described next, followed by the research model and hypotheses, research methodology, research results, discussion of the findings, research limitations and future research, and the paper ends with conclusions and implications.

RESEARCH BACKGROUND

National Culture

Culture is viewed as a set of beliefs and shared values (Javidan & House, 2001). Beliefs are people's perceptions of how things are done in their countries (House et al., 2002). Cultural values are people's aspirations about the way things should be done. They are also their reported preferred practices (House et al., 2002). These basic values and beliefs are acquired early in life through socialization and education, and make people of a society share certain beliefs and assumptions and prefer certain matters and issues (Hofstede, 1980, p. 25; Shore & Venkatachalam, 1995).

The present study adopts the culture taxonomy of House et al. (2004) as its theoretical foundation. Derived and tested in the Global Leadership and Organizational Behavior Effectiveness (GLOBE) project, this taxonomy includes nine dimensions: uncertainty avoidance, future orientation, institutional collectivism, humane orientation, performance orientation, in-group collectivism, power distance, gender egalitarianism, and assertiveness. House et al. (2004) published a data set that includes two scores for each dimension: values and practices.

While values illustrate the way things should be done in a culture, practices describe the acts or the way things are done in such a culture (House, 2004). Contrary to the conventional wisdom in the national culture literature, House et al. (2004, p. xvii) found that practices and values were often negatively correlated. Particularly, the correlations between cultural values and practices were found to be positive for gender egalitarianism, positive but insignificant for in-group collectivism, and negative for the other seven dimensions (Javidan et al., 2004, 2006).

Significant differences do exist in the cultural values and practices structure across societies and regions (House, 2004; Hofstede, 2001; Nicholson & Stepina, 1998). In addition, researchers from different disciplines have explored and reported relationships between national culture and a number of social and economic phenomena including leadership (e.g., House et al., 2004), organizational culture and conflict (Spicer, 1997), information technology (IT) adoption (Hasan & Ditsa, 1999; Straub, 1994; Straub et al., 1997, 2001; Bagchi et al., 2003; Erumban & de Jong, 2006; Martinsons & Davison, 2003, 2007), information generation, presentation, transfer and use (Menou, 1983), availability and dissemination of information (Pook & Fustos, 1999), openness in sharing private knowledge (Chow et al., 2000), R&D activities (Varsakelis, 2001; Couto & Vieira, 2004), foreign investment in R&D (Jones & Teegen, 2001; Head & Sorensen, 2005), continuous improvement practices (Robert et al., 2000), societal information dissemination capacity (Khalil & Seleim, 2009), and standardization versus adaptation of knowledge management (Ang & Massingham, 2007). However, the influence that national culture may have on societal KTC has yet to be investigated.

National Culture and KM

The theoretical roots for the research on national culture's influence on KM, in general, and knowledge transfer, in particular, can be found in the literature on the relationship between national culture and innovation (e.g., Shane 1992, 1993; Herbig & Dunphy, 1998; Herbig & Miller 1992; Kedia, Keller, & Julian, 1992; Nakata & Sivakumar, 1996). Such literature suggests that culture has a profound influence on the innovative capacity of a society, which is believed to be strongly related to the society's knowledge creation and transfer capacity. A national culture that values creativity will have a greater number of innovations, innovative activities, and supportive practices for innovation.

Herbig and Dunphy (1998) speculate that individualist societies value freedom more than collectivist societies, and freedom is necessary for creativity. Individualist societies that are characterized by independence and achievement were found to encourage innovation (Shane, 1992). Hofstede (1984) indicates that individualist societies have a greater tendency to innovative. In addition, Herbig and Dunphy (1998) argue that low power distance cultures prefer decentralized hierarchical structure, which promotes innovation. Moreover, openness to new information is important for innovative capacity in a society (Herbig & Dunphy, 1998).

Furthermore, the deployment of IT capabilities is believed to enhance the opportunity for sharing information and knowledge worldwide (Seetharaman, Lo, & Saravanan, 2004). However, the adoption of IT without an appropriate consideration of culture will likely generate unacceptable results (Gajendran & Brewer, 2007). Bagchi et al. (2003) found IT adoption to correlate with national value systems. Also, in an investigation of the impact of culture on telephone, e-mail and fax use in the U.S and Japan, Straub (1994) found telephone use to be the same in the two countries while fax and e-mail use varies significantly. In addition, Straub et al. (2001) found Arab cultural beliefs to be a strong predictor of resistance to IT adoption; and Hasan and Ditsa (1999) found national culture to be an important factor that affected IT adoption in West Africa, the Middle East and Australia.

With regard to the relationship of national culture to R&D, Varsakelis (2001) found national culture to correlate with R&D investment. Jones and Teegen (2001) reported national culture (e.g., power distance, uncertainty avoidance, individualism) to associate with foreign R&D investment. In addition, Head and Sorensen (2005) concluded that acquisition based investments will prefer a low uncertainty avoidance, low power distance, individualist, and masculine cultural set. However, Robert et al. (2000) found no differences among the United States, Mexico, Poland, and India in their continuous improvement practices.

As to information and knowledge transfer, Pook and Fustos (1999) found national culture values to influence information availability and the amount of information exchanged in a cross-cultural investigation. In addition, Menou (1983) argues various ways in which objective and subjective cultural traits affect the generation, presentation, transfer and use of information in different societies. Also, Chow, Deng, and Ho (2000) examined how knowledge nature and the knowledge owner's relationship to the potential recipient interact with national culture to affect people's openness in sharing their private knowledge.

Furthermore, in an investigation of the relationship of societal information dissemination capacity and national culture dimensions, Khalil and Seleim (2009) found information dissemination capacity to correlate negatively with uncertainty avoidance values, future orientation values, and institutional collectivism values. They also found information dissemination capacity to correlate positively with gender egalitarianism values.

While the aforementioned research investigated national culture's influence on socioeconomic phenomena that are relevant to KM, only a few studies directly addressed national culture's possible influence on KM related factors. Phillips and Vollmer (2000) posit that culture is recognized as the most difficult component of KM. Chaminade and Johanson (2003) argue that culture might affect the assumptions of knowledge and the adoption of new knowledge. Wang (2004, p. 45) adds that national culture should be treated as the main issue in KM. Furthermore, Barkema et al. (1996) believe that national culture plays an important role in the learning curve and international experience of organizations, and those management capabilities are built on core cultural values that can hinder or enhance knowledge accumulation (Tsang, 1999).

Empirically, Wang (2004) explored the effect of national culture on KM factors, expectations and practices in a cross-cultural setting. He found that, compared to individualist cultures (e.g., United States), collectivist organizations (e.g., in Taiwan) have a higher readiness for KM (p. 215), knowledge workers to share more ideas (p. 217), the philosophy of sharing knowledge to be part of the mindset (p. 218), and the beliefs about the critical success factors of KM and expectations regarding the benefits of KM investments to be significantly different (p. 164, 167).

Nevertheless, achieving the expected benefits of KM investment in a society appears to depend not only on the society's capacity to generate knowledge but also on its capacity to transfer knowledge internally and internationally. In their dynamic knowledge transfer capacity (DKTC) model, Parent et al. (2007) identify two pre-existing conditions and four capacities that are essential for social systems, such as societies, to generate, disseminate and use new knowledge to meet their needs. The two pre-existing conditions include the knowledge that the system needs and the level of existing related knowledge that the system possesses. The four capacities that the system needs to acquire in order to be able to transfer knowledge successfully include generative capacity, dissemination capacity, absorptive capacity, and adaptive & responsive capacity).

Among the four capacities of the DKTC model, only knowledge transfer (or dissemination) capacity is of interest in this investigation. Knowledge dissemination capacity is defined in the model as the ability to contextualize, format, adapt, translate and diffuse knowledge through social and/or technological networks and build commitment from stakeholders. Such ability depends on the existence of social networks (i.e., social capital), brokers and other intermediaries, including technological and social infrastructure of communications (Parent et al., 2007).

This investigation operationalizes societal KTC by identifying and measuring a number of items representing the social and technological infrastructure of communications that support intra and inter-societal knowledge transfer. Although the literature often makes a distinction between tacit and explicit knowledge, different types of knowledge are not completely distinct. When knowledge is transferred, the process gen-

erally involves both tacit and explicit knowledge (Nonaka & Takeuchi, 1995). Nevertheless, this research focuses primarily on a society's capacity to transfer explicit knowledge.

RESEARCH MODEL AND HYPOTHESES

Figure 1 depicts the research model used in this investigation, including the research variables and the hypothesized relationships. This research design explores the possible influence of the nine national cultural values and practices of House et al. (2004) on societal KTC. The model is drawn based on the findings of the prior research that investigated the cultural impact on KM as well as other relevant socioeconomic perspectives which were reviewed in the above section.

1. *Uncertainty avoidance and KTC:* Uncertainty avoidance is the extent to which individuals in a society rely on social norms, rules, and

Figure 1. Research model

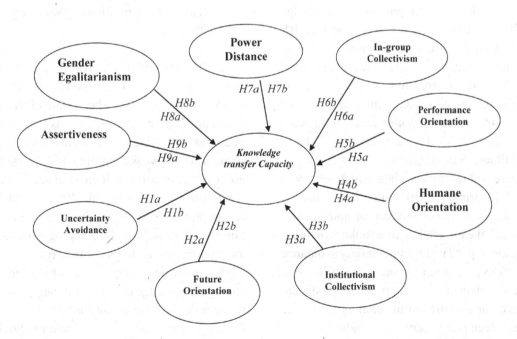

procedures to alleviate the unpredictability of future events (House et al., 2004, p. 30). In societies with high uncertainty avoidance, detailed controls are favored, and people are more likely to structure activities carefully and provide detailed instructions to subordinates (Heals et al., 2004). Francis (1997) indicates that codification or diffusion of information is complementary to Hofstede's dimension of uncertainty avoidance. Low uncertainty avoidance corresponds to information diffusion whereas high uncertainty avoidance corresponds to codification.

In societies that are high in uncertainty avoidance, organizations would be less likely to choose risky options (Heals et al., 2004). Jones and Teegen (2001) argue that low uncertainty avoiding cultures are associated with innovative efforts while higher uncertainty avoiding cultures are expected to be associated more with adaptive efforts. In addition, Shane (1993) found that low scores of uncertainty avoidance were associated with innovation. Bureaucratic cultures suffer from a lack of trust and failure to reward and promote cooperation and collaboration (Liebowitz, 1999, pp. 1-13), which are prerequisites for knowledge transfer. In addition, the results of the GLOBE project suggest that countries that are higher in uncertainty avoidance practices are more prosperous, enjoy more government support for economic development, are more competitive in the global market, and tend to be more successful in basic science research (De Luque & Javidan, 2004).

Khalil and Seleim (2009) found uncertainty avoidance values to correlate negatively with societal information dissemination capacity. Nevertheless, knowledge creation and transfer help reduce the uncertainty of an unknown future (Wang, 2004, p. 62); a high uncertainty avoidance culture is expected to promote more efforts that build and sustain effective knowledge transfer capacities compared to a low uncertainty avoidance culture. Given that uncertainty avoidance values

and practices are negatively correlated (Javidan et al., 2004; 2006), this expectation is formulated in the following two hypotheses:

H1a: KTC is lower in nations with higher uncertainty avoidance values.
H1b: KTC is greater in nations with higher uncertainty avoidance practice.

2. *Future orientation and KTC:* Future orientation refers to people's consideration of the future. In a long-term orientation culture, people tend to persevere methodically toward results and save for the future. People in a short-term orientation culture, however, tend to expect and emphasize quick results (Hasan, Ditsa, 1999). Societies with high future orientation culture have a propensity to achieve economic success, have organizations with a longer strategic orientation, have flexible and adoptive organizations and managers, place a higher priority on long term success, have a strong capability and willingness to imagine future contingences, formulate future goals, and seek to achieve goals and develop strategies for meeting their future aspirations (Ashkanasy et al., 2004).

The findings of the GLOBE project show that success in basic science is positively related to future orientation practice but negatively related to future orientation value (Ashkanasy et al., 2004). Societies may value future orientation in order to transform their weak capabilities in basic science, not just to transform their societal and economic conditions (Ashkanasy et al., 2004). In addition, Khalil and Seleim (2009) found future orientation values to negatively correlate with societal information dissemination capacity.

A future orientation culture is believed to encourage knowledge creation and transfer in order to meet the knowledge and information needed for long-term planning and execution. Societies with future orientation cultures are expected to encourage investment in means and channels to facilitate knowledge sharing among people and institutions. Given that future orientation values and practices are negatively correlated (Javidan et al., 2004, 2006), this expectation is formulated in the following two hypotheses:

H2a: KTC is lower in nations with higher future orientation value.

H2b: KTC is greater in nations with higher future orientation practice.

3. *Institutional collectivism and KTC:* Institutional collectivism is the degree to which organizational and societal institutional practices encourage and reward collective distribution of resources and collective action (House et al., 2004, p. 30). In institutional collectivist societies, people prefer working together in collective styles, where cooperation and synergy are more prominent (Hofstede & Bond, 1988; House et al., 2001). In addition, people of collectivist cultures have a greater tendency to cooperate (Cox et al., 1991; Wagner, 1995), therefore, they are expected to share their knowledge more fully (Chow, Deng, & Ho, 2000).

On the other hand, Jones and Teegen (2001) argue that the characteristics of a collectivist culture are detrimental to innovation and would be more conducive to adaptive efforts. Societal institutional collectivism values were negatively correlated with economic prosperity, public sector support for economic prosperity, and competitiveness index indicators (Gelfand et al., 2004). Also, the GLOBE project findings indicate that institutional collectivism practices are positively correlated to success in basic science, whereas institutional collectivism values are negatively correlated to success in basic science (Gelfand et al., 2004). In addition, Khalil and Seleim (2009) found institu-

tional collectivism values to negatively correlate with societal information dissemination capacity.

Knowledge transfer is more likely to rely on collective activities. Wang (2004, pp. 175-176) argues that collectivist cultures are strong enablers of knowledge sharing while individualist cultures create barriers to effective communication and shared understanding of knowledge. Therefore, institutional collectivist cultures are more likely to provide an environment that is conducive to building and sustaining effective knowledge transfer capacities. Given that institution collectivism values and practices are negatively correlated (Javidan et al., 2004, 2006), this expectation is formulated in the following two hypotheses:

H3a: KTC is lower in nations with higher institutional collectivism value.

H3b: KTC is greater in nations with higher institutional collectivism practice.

4. *Humane orientation and KTC:* Humane orientation refers to the degree to which a collective encourages and rewards individuals for being fair, altruistic, generous, caring, and kind to others (House et al., 2004, p. 30; Ralston et al., 1992). Societies with high humane orientation cultures are likely to have projects that allow people to be tolerant of mistakes (Heals et al., 2004), and are friendly and sensitive, and value harmony (Javidan & House, 2001).

Low humane orientation culture, on the other hand, involves self-interest promotion and lack of human consideration. Low humane orientation is observed in societies that are economically developed, modern, and urbanized (Kabasakal & Bodur, 2004). Furthermore, in a low humane orientation culture, it is difficult to successfully adopt participative management, which support the adoption of means and channels that facilitate knowledge and information sharing (e.g., Seliem et al., 2003; Torkzadeh, & Doll, 1994; Gyampah

& White, 1993). Moreover, Khalil and Seleim (2009) found no relationship between humane orientation values and societal information dissemination capacity.

Nevertheless, in a humane oriented culture, trust is considered a valuable asset that forms the nature of knowledge exchange among people and institutions. In high humane orientation societies, people are likely to be more tolerant, have the opportunity to get more involved in a variety of activities and share more knowledge and information. Therefore, humane oriented societies are expected to develop and adopt more means to enable knowledge transfer. Given that humane orientation values and practices are negatively correlated (Javidan et al., 2004, 2006), this expectation is formulated in the following two hypotheses:

H4a: KTC is lower in nations with higher humane orientation value.

H4b: KTC is greater in nations with higher humane orientation practice.

5. *Performance orientation and KTC:* Performance orientation refers to the extent to which a collective encourages and rewards group members for performance improvement and excellence (House et al., 2004, p. 30). Societies that score high on performance orientation tend to believe that schooling and education are critical for success, value training and development, emphasize results more than people, value competitiveness, value taking initiative, believe that anyone can succeed if he or she tries hard enough, value what a person does more than what he or she is, and have a monochronic approach to time (Javidan, 2004, p. 245).

The GLOBE project found that performance oriented societies are more economically prosperous and exhibit higher national competitiveness (Javidan, 2004). In societies that foster performance orientation, people prefer projects

that allow them to perform well (Heals et al., 2004). Therefore, compared to less performance oriented societies, more performance oriented societies are expected to value knowledge and commit more resources that enable individuals and groups to share and use such knowledge to enhance performance.

Higher performance oriented societies are expected to have higher knowledge transfer capacities than do less performance oriented societies. Given that performance orientation values and practices are negatively correlated (Javidan et al., 2004, 2006), this expectation is formulated in the following two hypotheses:

H5a: KTC is lower in nations with higher performance orientation value.

H5b: KTC is greater in nations with higher performance orientation practice.

6. *In-group collectivism and KTC:* In-group collectivism culture reflects the tendency of people to look after their own self-interest and their immediate family and friends and neglect the needs of a society. Individuals in such a culture cannot split themselves from their ties and groups. Therefore, they are more influenced by the norms of these groups, which protect the interests of their members. These characteristics are more likely to influence knowledge transfer among people and groups.

In-group collectivism increases dependence and trust among individuals, which in turn increase knowledge transfer. Trust facilitates a culture of openness that allows knowledge and information exchange (Eppler & Sukowski, 2000). Moreover, social capital is more likely to be dominant in in-group collectivism culture, which fosters knowledge transfer. Chow, Deng, and Ho (2000) found that Chinese vs. U.S. nationals' openness of knowledge sharing was related to their different degrees of collectivism. Compared to U.S.

nationals, Chinese nationals were found to share knowledge significantly less with a potential recipient who was not a member of their "in-group."

On the other hand, in individualist societies, individual goals take precedence over group goals, people emphasize rationality, individuals are likely to engage in activities alone, and individuals make fewer distinctions between in-group and out-groups (Gelfand et al., 2004). In addition, the GLOBE project findings indicate that in-group collectivism values and practices are negatively and significantly correlated with success in basic science (Gelfand et al., 2004).

Nevertheless, collectivist cultures are expected to promote trust and social capital, which, in turn, enable knowledge transfer and facilitate the building of knowledge sharing infrastructure. Given that the positive correlation between in-group collectivism values and practices is insignificant (Javidan et al., 2004, 2006), this expectation is formulated in the following two hypotheses:

H6a: KTC is greater in nations with higher in-group collectivism value.

H6b: KTC is greater in nations with higher in-group collectivism practices.

7. *Power distance and KTC:* Power distance refers to the extent to which the members of a society expect power to be distributed equally (House et al., 2004, p. 30). Compared to a lower power distance culture, a high power distance culture supports more formal hierarchy of authority and control, greater centralization of knowledge and responsibility, more excessive rules, and more restricted flow and exchange of knowledge (Heals et al., 2004). In high power distance culture, only few people have access to resources, and mass use of technology, which supports general power distance reduction (Carl et al., 2004). Lower power distance societies, on the other hand, tend to be more innovative (Hofstede, 1980).

The findings of the GLOBE project show that societal power distance practices are associated with lower economic prosperity, less supportive public and social polices, lower national competitiveness, and less success in basic science (Carl et al., 2004). Shane (1992) found that low power distance culture is more inventive. Societies that have lower score of power distance are characterized by less hierarchy, fewer rules, and greater decentralization of knowledge and free flow of information (Jones & Teegen, 2001). Moreover, the level of trust among people of high power distance is low, which reduces knowledge transfer and does not encourage investing in the development and enhancement of knowledge exchange means.

Societies that are characterized by low power distance culture are expected to commit appropriate resources to establish and grow their KTC. Given that power distance values and practices are negatively correlated (Javidan et al., 2004, 2006), this expectation is formulated in the following two hypotheses:

H7a: KTC is greater in nations with higher power distance values.

H7b: KTC is lower in nations with higher power distance practice.

8. *Gender Egalitarianism and KTC.* Gender egalitarianism refers to societies that seek to minimize differences between the roles of females and males at homes, organizations, and communities (Emrich et al., 2004). Some societies are more gender egalitarian and seek to minimize gender role differences whereas other societies are less gender egalitarian and seek to maximize such differences (House et al., 2004). Societies that score higher on gender egalitarianism tend to have more women in position of authority, accord women a higher status in society, afford women a greater role in community decision making, have a higher percentage

313

of women participating in the labor force, have higher female literacy rates, and have similar levels of education of females and males (Emrich et al., 2004).

In the GLOBE project, gender egalitarianism practices were found to have no correlation with any of the three indicators of economic health (economic prosperity, economic productivity, and GNP). In contrast, gender egalitarianism values were found to positively correlate with the three indicators (Emrich et al., 2004). Heals et al. (2004) found women to be more network oriented and cooperative, but men were found to be more individualistic. On the other hand, Herbig and Miller (1992) point out that high masculinity cultures are characterized by lower innovative activities. In addition, Jones and Teegen (2001) indicate that masculine societies are usually associated with innovation. Shane (1992), however, found masculinity to have no relationship with innovation.

Khalil and Seleim (2009) found gender egalitarianism values to positively correlate with societal information dissemination capacity. People in societies that minimize gender role differences are likely to be more tolerant and cooperative, which fosters knowledge transfer. Therefore, higher gender egalitarian societies are expected to invest more resources to expand their knowledge transfer capacities. Given that gender egalitarianism values and practices are positively correlated (Javidan et al., 2004, 2006), this expectation is formulated in the following two hypotheses:

H8a: KTC is greater in nations with higher gender egalitarianism value.

H8b: KTC is greater in nations with higher gender egalitarianism practice.

9. *Assertiveness and KTC:* As a cultural dimension, assertiveness refers to the nature of the relationship of individuals, groups, and societies with the outside world (Den Hartog, 2004). It is an internally consistent set of practices and values regarding the way in which people are seen, and ought, to behave in social relationships in a community (Den Hartog, 2004). Societies that score higher on assertiveness tend to value assertiveness, dominance, tough behavior, try to have control over the environment, and act and think of others as opportunistic (Den Hartog, 2004).

Societies with high assertiveness culture do well in global competitiveness, but exhibit low levels of psychological health (House et al., 2004, p. xvi). In the GLOBE project, assertiveness values were found to positively correlate with success in science and technology (House, 2004, p. 432; Den Hartog, 2004). Societies with high assertiveness tend to be more focused on accomplishment and success. Such societies are expected to value knowledge creation and sharing.

A culture that values assertiveness, performance, success, and competition is likely to encourage and reward the adoption and use of means that facilitate knowledge sharing. Societies that are high in assertiveness are expected to appropriate sufficient resources that facilitate knowledge creation and transfer in order to support performance and success. Given that assertiveness values and practices are negatively correlated (Javidan et al., 2004, 2006), this expectation is formulated in the following two hypotheses:

H9a: KTC is lower in nations with higher assertiveness value.

H9b: KTC is greater in nations with higher assertiveness practice.

METHODOLOGY

Research Variables

1. *The independent variables:* The independent variables include the nine cultural

dimensions of House et al. (2004), namely, power distance, uncertainty avoidance, future orientation, institutional collectivism, in-group collectivism, humane orientation, performance orientation, gender differentiation, and assertiveness.

2. *The dependent variable:* KTC is defined as the capability of people and institutions in a society to exchange knowledge with each other and with others in other societies. Since societal knowledge transfer commonly occurs in a technological, social, and economical context, a measure of societal KTC should include elements representing that context.

Due to the unavailability of direct measures, this investigation adopts a surrogate measure to operationalize societal KTC. Six items from the World Bank's (2004) World Development Indicators and Human Development Indicators are used to represent the social and technological infrastructure of communications in a society that support intra and inter societal knowledge transfer were identified. These indicators include imports, exports, foreign direct investments, telephone main lines, cellular subscribers, and internet users. The number of Internet users was adopted from Khalil and Seleim (2009) who used this indicator as part of their measure of societal information dissemination capacity.

Foreign direct investments may take different forms such as direct acquisition of foreign firms, construction of facilities in foreign countries, investment in joint ventures, strategic alliances with foreign firms with attendant input of technology, and licensing of intellectual property. Foreign direct investments provide opportunities for knowledge as well as technology transfer.

While the six indicators generally enable intra and inter societal knowledge transfer, imports, exports, and direct foreign investments are particularly instrumental to inter-societal transfer of explicit and implicit knowledge. Explicit knowledge transfer includes all encoded knowledge and information (e.g., ingredients and contents, production methods, usage and maintenance directions, transactions and contracts, licensing of intellectual properties, etc.) that are usually transferred with the exchanged products and services. Implicit knowledge transfer, however, usually occurs through formal and informal contacts among the trading partners as well as any embedded knowledge that facilitates the transfer and use of products, services, and investments.

Sample and Data Sources

This research relies on the data published by House and colleagues (House et al., 2004), which measure the nine national cultural variables in sixty-two societies (sixty-one countries). The data set includes both culture values and culture practices that were collected using a sample of 18,000 managers representing telecommunications, food, and banking industries. The sample covers all major geographic regions of the world and all different types of economic, political, and business institutional systems across the nine cultural dimensions. Appendix A displays the countries that are included in this study.

Table 1 includes the minimum, maximum, mean, and standard deviation values for the nine national culture variables (values and practices). The reliability of the nine national culture scores are documented in House et al. (2004, p. xv, 725). The GLOBE researchers did pilot tests, used double translations, and checked the psychometric characteristics of their instruments. They checked the reliability and construct validity of the instrument using multitrait, multimethod approaches, and the survey data yielded reliable and valid estimates of the cultural-level constructs (Javidan et al., 2004).

On the other hand, the six indicators that are drawn from the World Bank's World Development Indicators and Human Development report include telephone main lines, cellular subscribers, internet

Table 1. Descriptive statistics for national culture values and practices

Cultural Dimensions	N	Min	Max	Mean	Std. Dev.
Uncertainty avoidance values (UA-V)	61	3.16	5.61	4.5938	.6105
Uncertainty avoidance practices (UA-P)	61	2.88	5.37	4.1748	.6020
Future orientation values (FO-V)	61	2.95	6.20	5.4377	.5166
Future orientation practices (FO-P)	61	2.88	5.07	3.8446	.4629
Institutional collectivism values (INSC-V)	61	3.83	5.65	4.6997	.4907
Institutional collectivism practices (INSC-P)	61	3.25	5.22	4.2434	.4294
Human orientation values (HO-V)	61	3.39	6.09	5.3864	.3614
Human orientation practices (HO-P)	61	3.18	5.23	4.0851	.4668
Performance orientation values (PO-V)	61	2.35	6.58	5.8782	.5683
Performance orientation practices (PO-P)	61	3.20	4.94	4.0902	.4040
In-group collectivism values (INGC-V)	61	4.06	6.52	5.6330	.4083
In-group collectivism practices (INGC-P)	61	3.18	6.36	5.0833	.7620
Power distance values (PD-V)	61	2.04	4.35	2.7715	.4048
Power distance practices (PD-P)	61	3.59	5.80	5.1387	.4537
Gender egalitarian values (GE-V)	61	3.18	5.17	4.5080	.4804
Gender egalitarian practices (GE-P)	61	2.50	4.08	3.3828	.3690
Assertiveness values (AS-V)	61	2.66	5.56	3.8093	.6297
Assertiveness practices (AS-P)	61	3.38	4.89	4.1318	.3760

users, imports, exports, and foreign direct investments. While telephone main lines, cellular subscribers, and Internet subscribers' data are measured as numbers per 1000 capita, exports, imports, and foreign direct investment data are measured as percentages of the gross domestic products (GDPs) for the countries in the sample. Year 2004 indicators are chosen in order to minimize the time gap between the national culture data set and the World Development Indicators.

Table 2 depicts the minimum, maximum, mean, and standard deviation values for the six indicators of societal KTC. It should be noted that the maximum imports and exports figures that are greater than 100% indicate that the imports and exports in some countries for year 2004 exceeded their GDPs. In addition, the negative percentage of minimum foreign direct investment indicates that year 2004 outflows of foreign direct invest-

ments for some countries exceeded their inflows of foreign direct investments.

Factor analysis was applied to the six indicators (items) representing KTC in order to remove redundancy in the data and reveal the underlying pattern that existed between the items, reduce the number of factors, and measure their reliability coefficients. The extraction method used is the principle component analysis, one or higher eigenvalue, and the Varimax rotation method. The results of the factor analysis are displayed in Table 3.

The produced statistics suggest the appropriateness of the factor analysis. The Bartlett test of sphericity, a test for the presence of correlations among the variables, is significant ($p = .000$); and the measure of sampling adequacy (MSA), a measure of the intercorrelations among the variables, is 0.717, which is well beyond the 0.70 threshold of adequacy (Hair et al., 1998, p. 99).

Table 2. Descriptive statistics for the KTC indicators

Indicators	N	Minimum	Maximum	Mean	Std. Deviation
Telephone main lines	60	5.00	739.00	328.4167	238.78118
Cellular subscribers	60	3.00	907.00	402.2167	307.87198
Internet users	60	1.00	521.10	186.5717	176.67280
Imports	59	10.00	152.00	41.1864	26.07514
Exports	59	10.00	174.00	41.6102	29.66539
Foreign direct investment	31	-.10	15.20	1.7516	2.90641

Table 3. Factors analysis results for knowledge transfer capacity measures

Factor and Indicators	Factor Loading	Extracted Variance
KTC- Index		65.881%
Land-line telephones	.747	
Cellular subscribers	.785	
Internet users	.867	
Imports	.876	
Exports	.859	
Foreign direct investment	.722	

As depicted in Table 3, the six measures of KTC are loaded on one factor, Knowledge Transfer Capacity-Index (KTC-Index), with approximately 66% extracted variance. The factor scores were captured and used to represent an overall surrogate measure of KTC. KTC-Index was computed for each country by weighing the original scores of the six indicators with their factor loadings, and dividing the result by the factor loadings total. The KTC-Index has a mean of 31.1475 (Std. Deviation = 23.00997), a maximum of 69.79 and a minimum of 2.20.

The overall reliability--the internal consistency of the 6-indicator scale-- of the KTC-Index was measured using Cronbach's alpha coefficient, which was found to be 0 .758. This coefficient is greater than 0.60, the acceptable lower level recommended by Hair et al. (1998, p. 118) for an exploratory research such as this one.

RESULTS

Pearson correlations for the nine national culture dimensions and KTC were calculated. Table 4 and Table 5 depict the significant correlations among the cultural dimensions (values and practices) scores and knowledge transfer index.

The results appear in Tables 4 and 5 may suggest the existence of multicollinearity in the data set since there are a number of significant correlations existing among the national culture dimensions (values and practices). This means that the effects of some of the cultural variables (dimensions) can be predicted or accounted for by the other variables in the model (Hair et al., 1998, p. 24).

In order to minimize the possible effect of multicollinearity and unmask any other possible relationships that the other national culture dimensions may have with the knowledge transfer index (KTC-Index), the scores were standardized. However, the recalculated correlation matrix, using the standardized scores, shows significant correlations between the national culture dimensions and KTC-Index that are similar to those reported in Tables 4 and 5.

In addition, the results of two common measures of multicollinearity (tolerance and variance inflation factor (VIF) were computed, and the results suggest an insignificant effect of multicollinearity on the relationships between the national culture dimensions and KTC.

Table 4. Pearson correlations for the national culture values and KTC-index

	UA-V	FO-V	INSC-V	HO-V	PO-V	INGC-V	PD-V	GE-V	AS-V
KTC-Index	-.800**	-.501**	-.385**	.113	-.146	-.313*	-.067	.417**	-.109
UA-V		.638**	.427**	.010	.245	.349**	.038	-.475**	.154
FO-V			.495**	.378**	.691**	.656**	-.360**	-.142	.008
INSC-V				.053	.432**	.353**	-.382**	.046	-.282*
HO-V					.604**	.265*	-.618**	.303*	-.143
PO-V						.698**	-.610**	.296(*)	-.074
INGC-V							-.423**	.228	-.040
PD-V								-.521**	.292(*)
GE-V									-.252

** Correlation is significant at the 0.01 level (2-tailed).
* Correlation is significant at the 0.05 level (2-tailed).

Table 5. Pearson correlations for the national culture practices and KTC-index

	UA-P	FO-P	INSC-P	HO-P	PO-P	INGC-P	PD-P	GE-P	AS-P
KTC-Index	.587**	.474**	.163	-.379**	.243	-.715**	-.360**	.082	-.011
UA-P		.756**	.374**	.008	.604**	-.581**	-.472**	-.069	-.087
FO-P			.460**	.069	.639**	-.397**	-.437**	-.070	.072
INSC-P				.423**	.445**	-.096	-.291*	-.052	-.383**
HO-P					.249	.271*	-.152	-.140	-.417**
PO-P						-.136	-.340**	-.290*	.059
INGC-P							.603**	-.214	.135
PD-P								-.319*	.217
GE-P									-.101

** Correlation is significant at the 0.01 level (2-tailed).
* Correlation is significant at the 0.05 level (2-tailed).

The correlation results of Table 4 are used to test the first set of hypotheses (H1a-H9a) describing the predicted relationships between the nine cultural dimensions values, on one hand, and KTC-Index, on the other hand. KTC-Index) associates positively with gender egalitarianism values (r = .417, p < .01). In addition, KTC-Index associates negatively with uncertainty avoidance values (r = -.800, p < .01), future orientation value (r = -.501, p < .01), institutional collectivism values (r = -.385, p < .01), and in-group collectivism values (r = -.313, p < .05). KTC-Index, however, doesn't associate with human orientation values, performance orientation values, power distance values, and assertiveness values.

The results of Table 4 suggest the acceptance of hypotheses H1a, H2a, H3a, and H8a. It should also be noted that the significant negative relationship of in-group collectivism values to KTC-Index is contrary to what was predicted. Therefore, the results suggest the rejection of H4a, H5a, H6a, H7a, and H9a.

The correlations results of Table 5 are used to test the second set of hypotheses (H1b-H9b) describing the predicted relationships between the nine cultural dimensions practices, on one hand, and the KTC-Index, on the other hand. KTC associates positively with uncertainty avoidance practices (r = .587, p < .01) and future orientation practices (r = .474, p < .01). Also, KTC associates negatively with human orientation practices (r = -.379, p < 01), in-group collectivism practices (r = -.715, p < .01), and power distance practices (r = -.360, p < .01). KTC, however, does not correlate with institutional collectivism practices, performance orientation practices, gender egalitarianism practices, and assertiveness practices.

The results of Table 5 suggest the acceptance of hypotheses H1b, H2b, and H7b. The significant negative relationships of KTC-Index to humane orientation practices and in-group collectivism practices are contrary to what was predicted. These results suggest the rejection of H3b, H4b, H5b, H6b, H8b, and H9b.

For further analysis, gross domestic product GDP--the total market values of goods and services produced by people and capital in country--was used as a statistical control variable. Ccorrelation analyses of the data set including the GDP indexes for the participating countries showed GDP to correlate positively with KTC-Index (r = .945, p <.01). GDP was also found to correlate positively with gender egalitarianism values (r = .443, p < .01) and negatively with uncertainty avoidance values (r = -.801, p < .01), future orientation values (r = -.483, p < .01), institutional collectivism values (r = -.342, p < .01), and in-group collectivism values (r = -.282, p < .05). Also, GDP was found to correlate positively with uncertainty avoidance practices (r = .549, p < .01) and future orientation practices (r = .449, p < .01); and correlate negatively with humane orientation practices (r = -.322, p < .01), in-group collectivism practices (r = -.715, p < .01), and power distance practice (r = -.388).

Given the correlations that GDP has with KTC-Index, cultural values, and cultural practices, regression analysis was performed in order to spot the variance in KTC that may be explained by only national culture values and practices. The analysis was performed using the nine cultural dimensions and KTC-Index before and after controlling for GDP effect.

Table 6 displays the regression models of national culture values and KTC-Index without and with the inclusion of GDP. Without controlling for the GDP effect, the regression model (Model 1) includes only uncertainty avoidance values as the independent (exogenous) variable (*beta* = -.730, p < .001) which explains approximately 61% (adjusted R^2 = .607) of the variance in KTC-Index. Adding GDP to the regression analysis, however, produced a model (Model 2) that includes none of the national culture values. GDP in Model 2 explains approximately 89% (beta = .855, p < .001; adjusted R square = .885) of the variance in KTC-Index.

On the other hand, the regression analysis in Table 7 depicts the regression models for cul-

Table 6. KTC as a function of cultural values and GDP (standardized coefficients)

Variables	Model 1 (without GDP)	Model 2 (with GDP)
GDP		.855**
UA-V	-.730***	-.77
FO-V	.034	.020
INSC-V	-.078	-.085
HO-V	.101	-.033
PO-V	.056	-.010
INGC-V	-.120	-.044
PD-V	.009	-.088
GE-V	.080	-.203
AS-V	.029	-.007
F	11.142***	46.574***
R^2	.667	.905
Adjusted R^2	.607	.885
Tolerance Range	.228-.769	.220-.765
VIF	1.301-4.394	1.307-4.538
Durbin-Watson	1.835	2.088

* $p < 0.05$; ** $p < 0.01$; *** $p < 0.001$

tural practices and KTC-Index without and with the inclusion of GDP. Without controlling for GDP effect, the regression model (Model 1) includes humane orientation practices (beta = -.317, p < .05) and in-group collectivism practices (beta = -. 519, p < .01) as independent (exogenous) variables that explain approximately 58% (adjusted R square = .675) of the variance in KTC-Index. Adding GDP to the regression analysis, however, produced a model (Model 2) that includes GDP (beta = .817, p < .01) and humane orientation practices (beta = -.141, p < .05). Model 2 explains approximately 90% (adjusted R^2 = .899) of the variance in KTC-Index.

DISCUSSION

Understanding the influence that national culture values and practices may have on KTC is essen-tial to the effective management of knowledge transfer at the societal level. This investigation was designed to explore the influence that national culture values and practice may have on KTC at the societal level. Eighteen hypotheses were formulated and tested to explore such relationships. Table 8 summarizes the hypotheses testing results.

The findings of this research suggest that countries that have high knowledge transfer capacities have a pattern of low uncertainty avoidance values, low future orientation values, low institutional collectivism values, low in-group collectivism values, and high gender egalitarianism values. In addition, countries that have high knowledge transfer capacities have a pattern of high uncertainty avoidance practices, high future orientation practices, low human orientation practices, low in-group collectivism practices, and low power distance practices.

Table 7. KTC as a function of cultural practices and GDP (standardized coefficients)

Variables	Model 1 (without GDP)	Model 2 (with GDP)
GDP		.817**
UA-P	.153	-.097
FO-P	.131	-.039
INSC-P	.112	.048
HO-P	-.317*	-.141*
PO-P	.053	-.016
INGC-P	-.519**	-.034
PD-P	.095	.037
GE-P	-.006	.001
AS-P	-.049	-.047
F	9.880***	53.322***
R^2	.640	.916
Adjusted R^2	.575	.899
Tolerance Range	.277-.702	.268-.702
VIF	1.766-3.606	1.425-3.618
Durbin-Watson	1.959	2.334

* $p < 0.05$; ** $p < 0.01$; *** $p < 0.001$

These findings are generally consistent with the prior research findings of relationships between national culture values and practices and socioeconomic phenomena such as economic health, national competitiveness, societal health, life expectancy, and human development (House et al., 2004; Javidan et al., 2006). They also lend support to the earlier IT research that emphasizes the social context as an important determinant of IT adoption and use.

KTC was found to associate positively with uncertainty avoidance practice and negatively with uncertainty avoidance values. This finding was expected, since the value and practice scores of uncertainty avoidance are negatively correlated (Javidan et al., 2004, 2006). Societies that have lower uncertainty avoidance values have also higher uncertainty avoidance practices, which,

in turn, affect positively their KTC. This finding is also consistent with the finding of a negative correlation between uncertainty avoidance values and societal information dissemination capacity (Khalil & Seleim, 2009).

Societies with high uncertainty avoidance practice may experience greater KTC, compared to societies with low uncertainty avoidance practice. This finding supports the view that people and institutions in high uncertainty avoidance exhibit stronger desire to establish rules allowing predictability of behaviors (de Luque & Javidan, 2004) and attempt to avoid vague situations and a less predictable future by providing norms, values, and beliefs in the form of rules, laws, and regulations (Armstrong, 1996).

Knowledge transfer capacities reflect the existence of means such as telephones, computer networks, the Internet, fax machines, imports, exports, and foreign direct investment that can reduce uncertainties in a society. In addition, compared to societies with low uncertainty avoidance practice, societies with high uncertainty avoidance practice are more economically prosperous (de Luque & Javidan, 2004), more information intensive, and are expected to prefer a higher degree of systemization and accuracy in their actions and decisions. They are expected to develop and maintain sophisticated communication infrastructures, e.g., telephone networks, computer networks, Internet access, and knowledge transfer, in order to support a growing need for knowledge and information through risk- avoiding behaviors.

KTC was also found to positively correlate with future orientation practice and negatively with future orientation values. This finding was expected, since the value and practice scores of future orientation are negatively correlated (Javidan et al., 2004, 2006). Societies that have lower future orientation values have also higher future orientation practices, which, in turn, affect positively its KTC. This finding is in agreement with the finding of a negative correlation between

Table 8. Summary of the hypotheses testing results

National Culture Dimensions	Hypothesized Relationship with KTC-Index	Detected Relationship with KTC-Index	Acceptance/ Rejection Decision
Uncertainty avoidance			
H1a	-	-	Accept
H1b	+	+	Accept
Future orientation			
H2a	-	-	Accept
H2b	+	+	Accept
Institutional collectivism			
H3a	-	-	Accept
H3b	+	NS*	Reject
Humane orientation			
H4a	-	NS	Reject
H4b	+	-	Reject
Performance orientation			
H5a	-	NS	Reject
H5b	+	NS	Reject
In-group collectivism			
H6a	+	-	Reject
H6b	+	-	Reject
Power distance			
H7a	+	NS	Reject
H7b	-	-	Accept
Gender egalitarianism			
H8a	+	+	Accept
H8b	+	NS	Reject
Assertiveness			
H9a	-	NS	Reject
H9b	+	NS	Reject

*NS = Not Significant

future orientation values and societal information dissemination capacity (Khalil & Seleim, 2009).

Societies with stronger future orientation practices are more inclined to possess higher knowledge transfer capacities than do societies with low future orientation practices. They tend to show better economic and societal health, more scientific advancement, more democratic political ideals, more empowered gender status, and greater domestic savings than do societies with lower future orientation practices (Ashkanasy et al., 2004).

In addition, societies with high future orientation practices are likely to make decisions and allocate sufficient resources in order to enhance and strengthen their knowledge transfer capacities through enhancing their IT capabilities (Heals et al., 2004). People and institutions in such societies must have access to the knowledge they need in order to effectively participate in vibrant social and economic activities. Therefore, plans to develop knowledge transfer infrastructures (e.g., adoption of IT tools and means, technology transfer via exports and foreign investments) in these societies must complement their long term social and economic transformation plans.

Since it was found to correlate positively with gender egalitarianism values, KTC tends to be greater in societies with higher gender egalitarian values. This finding is consistent with the finding of a positive correlation between gender egalitarianism values and societal information dissemination capacity (Khalil & Seleim, 2009). It is also consistent with those reported by Heals et al. (2004) and Bagchi et al. (2004) regarding the adoption of IT applications for information production and dissemination.

Women in high gender egalitarian societies tend to have a greater role in community decision making, have a higher participation in the labor force, have higher literacy rates, and have similar levels of education to men (Emrich et al., 2004). In addition, people and institutions in such societies tend to be more aware of the importance of and need for knowledge transfer than do people and institutions in low gender egalitarianism societies. Since women play a significant role in social and economic developments, more knowledge will be needed, and more tools and means for knowledge access are expected to be adopted and used.

On the other hand, KTC was found to negatively correlate with institutional collectivism values, humane orientation practices, in-group collectivism values and practices, and power distance practices. As to institutional collectivism, the value and practice scores are negatively correlated (Javidan et al., 2004, 2006). Therefore, lower institutional collectivism values in a society are expected to reflect higher institutional collectivism practice. Societies with lower institutional collectivism values (or higher instructional collectivism practices) are expected to have higher knowledge transfer capacities than do societies with higher institutional collectivism values (or lower institutional collectivism practices). Societies with high institutional collectivism practices seem to support an environment that encourages people to work cooperatively, which, in turn, raises a need for providing effective means such as telephone lines, Internet access, exports, imports, and foreign direct investment that facilitate intra and inter knowledge exchange at the societal level.

This finding supports the ones that are reported in House et al. (2004, pp. 482-483) and suggest

economic prosperity, competitiveness and success in basic science to have negative relationships with institutional collectivism values and positive relationships with institutional collectivism practices. People and institutions in societies that are economically developed and are advanced in basic science are expected to have access to more knowledge transfer channels than do their counterparts in societies that are less economically developed and less advanced in basic science.

In addition, KTC was found to negatively correlate with humane orientation practices. Compared to societies with lower humane orientation practices, societies with higher humane orientation practices have less knowledge transfer capacities. A lower humane orientation practice seems to support an environment that encourages using more tools and means that facilitate KTC. This finding supports Jones and Teegen's (2001) assertion that societies that emphasize relationships are believed to be less supportive of innovation, which stimulates knowledge creation and transfer. It is also consistent with the GLOBE's results indicating that less humane orientation is observed in societies that are economically developed, modern, and urbanized (House et al., 2004, pp. 595-596).

In addition, although informational support that involves supplying the necessary information and skills to cope with problems is considered a basic source of social support (House et al., 2004, p. 569), societies that are more humanely oriented appear to have less knowledge transfer capacities than do societies that are less humanely oriented. One interpretation for this finding is that less economically and socially developed societies may not have sufficient resources (e.g., information technology infrastructure, technology transfer, direct foreign investment) to build and expand their knowledge transfer mechanisms.

Contrary to expectation, however, KTC was found to correlate negatively with both in-group collectivism values and practices. Societies that are low in in-group collectivism values and practices (e.g., individualistic societies) tend to have higher knowledge transfer capacities (e.g., telephone lines, Internet subscriptions, imports and exports) than do societies with high in-group collectivism values and practice (e.g., collectivistic societies). In such societies, people and institutions appear to be more task-oriented and rational in actions and decisions (Hofstede, 1980; Gelfand et al., 2004), and, therefore, are expected to have higher demand for, and access to, knowledge.

This finding is in agreement with those of Shane (1992, 1993) who found individualistic cultures to be more inventive and innovative than collectivistic cultures. People in individualistic cultures demand extensive knowledge transfer and produce new knowledge that will be eventually exchanged. In addition, in-group collectivism practice correlates negatively with economic prosperity, the world competitiveness index, and success in basic science research (Gelfand et al., 2004). Therefore, individualistic societies appear to be prosperous, have vibrant economies, and have high needs for knowledge transfer.

As to power distance, power distance practice was found to correlate negatively with KTC. The lower the power distance practice, the higher the society's KTC. In societies with high power distance practice, information and knowledge are controlled, and only few people have access to resources and mass use of technology (Carl et al., 2004). Therefore, compared to their counterparts in low power distance practice societies, governments and institutions in high power distance practice societies are less likely to adopt means and tools that allow public access and knowledge transfer in order to maintain the existing power distance structure.

This finding supports the notion that people and institutions in societies with low power distance practice are better prepared and more willing to adopt means and tools that facilitate knowledge and information production and distribution than their counterparts in societies with high power distance practice (Bandura, 1986; Shane, 1992; Compeau & Higgins, 1995; Hasan & Ditsa, 1999;

Gelfand et al., 2004). Consequently, societal KTC is expected to expand in order to provide the knowledge and informational support that is needed for teams and network structures to emerge.

Given the spotted relationships of KTC to the above-mentioned cultural values and practices and the possible confounding effect of GDP, it was essential to identify the cultural values and practices that influence KTCs and subsequently explain the variance in KTCs across societies.

The results of the cultural values models (Table 6) show that GDP alone explains approximately 89% of KTC variance; and the results of the cultural practices models (Table 7) show that GDP and humane orientation practices explain approximately 90% of KTC variance. Therefore, when GDP is taken into consideration, national cultural practices, especially humane orientation practices, provide a better interpretation for KTC variance than do national cultural values. Societies with higher GDPs (i.e., more prosperous societies) and lower humane orientation practices tend to develop and maintain higher KTCs than do societies with lower GDPs (i.e., less prosperous societies) and higher humane orientation practices.

However, when GDP is not controlled for, cultural values (e.g., uncertainty avoidance values) were found to explain approximately 67% of KTC variance, and cultural practices (e.g., humane orientation practices and in-group collectivism practices) were found to explain approximately 58% of KTC variance. Therefore, national culture values, especially uncertainty avoidance values, provide a better culturally-based interpretation for KTC variance across societies than do culture practices. Societies with low uncertainty avoidance values (or high uncertainty avoidance practices) have a propensity to develop and maintain greater KTC than do societies with high uncertainty avoidance values (or low uncertainty avoidance practice). This culturally-based interpretation for KTC can be used as a foundation for formulating policies aiming at enhancing the capacities for knowledge transfer at the societal level.

RESEARCH LIMITATIONS AND FUTURE RESEARCH

Since this research pioneers providing a cultural interpretation of societal KTC, its findings should be viewed as preliminary and should be carefully interpreted. A surrogate measure was adopted for KTC because of the lack of direct, objective measures. Only six indicators were selected to operationalize the KTC construct. Therefore, the findings of this research may interpret only a portion of what may be considered the 'real' KTC of a society. Future research designs should provide a more precise definition for the 'societal KTC' construct and adopt more direct, objective measures to accurately operationalize the construct in order to measure a society's capacity to transfer both explicit and tacit societal knowledge.

In addition, although GDP was expected to partially confine the relationships that culture values and practices may have with KTC, the correlation between GDP and KTC ($r = .945$, $p < .01$) is noticeably high. One reason for this high correlation between GDP and KTC is that three of the six KTC elements (exports, imports, and direct foreign investment) are actually calculated and presented as percentages of the national GDP index. Consequently, the regression models in this investigation didn't accurately detect the relationships that culture values and practices could have had with the residual of knowledge transfer capacity after removing GDP effect. Future research models should adopt other KTC measures that do not highly correlate with GDP as a measure of economic prosperity.

In addition, although GDP influence on KTC was accounted for in this investigation, there are other possible determinants of KTC at the societal level, such as literacy and other human development indicators that merit exploration in future research designs. Finally, future research designs may expand this investigation and explore the relationships of cultural values and practices on other KM related phenomena such as societal knowledge creation capacity, knowledge documentation capacity, and knowledge application capacity.

CONCLUSION AND IMPLICATIONS

This research explored the impact that national culture may have on KTC at the societal level. Eighteen hypotheses describing the relationships of KTC to national culture values and practices were tested. The results support the acceptance of seven hypotheses correlating KTC positively to uncertainty avoidance practices, future orientation practices, and gender egalitarianism values; and negatively to uncertainty avoidance values, future orientation values, institutional collectivism values, and power distance practices.

Overall, these research findings suggest that countries that have high knowledge transfer capacities have a pattern of low uncertainty avoidance values, low future orientation values, low institutional collectivism values, low in-group collectivism values, and high gender egalitarianism values. In addition, countries that have high knowledge transfer capacities have a pattern of high uncertainty avoidance practices, high future orientation practices, low humane orientation practices, low in-group collectivism practices, and low power distance practices. However, only uncertainty avoidance values and humane orientation practices appear to influence KTC.

In spite of its exploratory nature and limitations, this research introduces a new cultural perspective that explains KTC differences among societies. Its finding puts forward culturally-based implications for policies and decisions pertinent to improving societal KTC.

Policies should be made in order to leverage the KTC enabling factors that normally exist in the cultures that are conducive to the development of knowledge transfer channels such as those investigated in this research, e.g., main telephone lines, cellular phone lines, Internet subscriptions, exports, imports, and foreign direct investment. In particular, government policies should take advantage of national cultures that are characterized by being low in uncertainty avoidance values and low in humane orientation practices, which are considered favorable cultures for expanding a society's KTC.

In additions, policies should be formulated in order to reduce the adverse impact of the factors that may well exist in national cultures and thwart the adoption of means that advance KTC. In formulating these policies, national cultures should be viewed as supple and can be changed (Li & Karakowsky, 2002; Myers & Tan, 2002; Ralston et al., 1993; McGrath et al., 1992). Policies that enable rapid development of communication technology, greater interaction among societies, and economic developments may cause cultural changes (e.g., Bohannan, 1959). Governments should adopt policies and programs that facilitate changing national cultures in favor of building and enhancing KTCs. More specifically, policies should be formulated in order to weaken and leverage uncertainty avoidance values and human orientation practices. Such policies, however, must be comprehensive, and cover the economic, social, political, educational, and culture aspects of a country in order to accomplish the long-term desired cultural changes.

REFERENCES

Abou-Zeid, E. S. (2002). A knowledge management reference model. *Journal of Knowledge Management*, 6(5), 486–499. doi:10.1108/13673270210450432

Ang, Z., & Massingham, P. (2007). National Culture and standardization versus adaptation of knowledge management. *Journal of Knowledge Management*, 11(2), 5–21. doi:10.1108/13673270710738889

Armstrong, R. W. (1996). The relationship between culture and perception of ethical problems in international Marketing. *Journal of Business Ethics*, 15(11), 1199–1208. doi:10.1007/BF00412818

Ashkanasy, N., Gupta, V., Mayfield, M. S., & Trevor-Roberts, E. (2004). Future orientation. In House, R. J., Hanges, P. J., Javidan, M., Dorfman, P. W., & Gupta, V. (Eds.), *Culture, leadership, and organizations: The GLOBE study of 62 societies* (pp. 282–343). Thousand Oaks, CA: Sage.

Bagchi, K., Cerveny, R., Hart, P., & Peterson, M. (2003). The influence of national culture on information technology product adoption. In *Proceedings of the 9th American Conference on Information Systems (AMCIS)* (pp. 112-131).

Bagchi, K., Hart, P., & Peterson, M. (2004). National culture and information technology product adoption. *Journal of Global Information Technology Management*, 7(4), 29–46.

Bandura, A. (1986). *Social foundations of thought and action: A social cognitive theory*. Englewood Cliffs, NJ: Prentice-Hall.

Banerjee, P., & Richter, F. J. (2001). *Intangibles in competition and cooperation: Euro-Asian perspectives*. New York: Palgrave.

Barkema, H. G., Bell, H. J., & Pennings, J. M. (1996). Foreign entry, cultural barriers, and learning. *Strategic Management Journal*, 17, 151–166. doi:10.1002/(SICI)1097-0266(199602)17:2<151::AID-SMJ799>3.0.CO;2-Z

Bohannan, P. (1959). The impact of money on an African subsistence economy. *The Journal of Economic History*, 19, 491–503.

Carl, D., Gupta, V., & Javidan, M. (2004). Power distance. In House, R. J., Hanges, P. J., Javidan, M., Dorfman, P. W., & Gupta, V. (Eds.), *Culture, leadership, and organizations: The GLOBE study of 62 societies* (pp. 513–563). Thousand Oaks, CA: Sage.

Chaminade, C., & Johanson, U. (2003). Can guidelines for intellectual capital management and reporting be considered without addressing cultural differences? *Journal of Intellectual Capital, 4*(4), 528–542. doi:10.1108/14691930310504545

Chow, C. W., Deng, J., & Ho, J. (2000). The Openness of Knowledge Sharing within Organizations: A Comparative Study of the United States and the People's Republic of China. *Journal of Management Accounting Research, 12*(1), 65–95. doi:10.2308/jmar.2000.12.1.65

Compeau, D., & Higgins, C. (1995). Computer self-efficacy: Development of a measure and initial test. *Management Information Systems Quarterly, 19*(2), 189–211. doi:10.2307/249688

Couto, J. P., & Vieira, J. C. (2004). National culture and research and development activities. *The Multinational Business Review, 12*(10), 19–35.

Cox, T. H., Lobel, S. A., & McLeod, P. L. (1991). Effects of ethnic group cultural differences on cooperative and competitive behavior on a group task. *Academy of Management Journal, 34,* 827–847. doi:10.2307/256391

De Long, D. W., & Fahey, L. (2000). Diagnosing Cultural Barriers to Knowledge Management. *The Academy of Management Executive, 14*(4), 113–127.

De Luque, M. S., & Javidan, M. (2004). Uncertainty avoidance. In House, R. J., Hanges, P. J., Javidan, M., Dorfman, P. W., & Gupta, V. (Eds.), *Culture, leadership, and organizations: The GLOBE study of 62 societies* (pp. 602–653). Thousand Oaks, CA: Sage.

Den Hartog, D. N. (2004). Assertiveness. In House, R. J., Hanges, P. J., Javidan, M., Dorfman, P. W., & Gupta, V. (Eds.), *Culture, leadership, and organizations: The GLOBE study of 62 societies* (pp. 395–436). Thousand Oaks, CA: Sage.

Emrich, C. G., Denmark, F. L., & den Hartog, D. (2004). Cross-cultural differences in gender egalitarianism. In House, R. J., Hanges, P. J., Javidan, M., Dorfman, P. W., & Gupta, V. (Eds.), *Culture, leadership, and organizations: The GLOBE study of 62 societies* (pp. 343–394). Thousand Oaks, CA: Sage.

Eppler, M. J., & Sukowski, O. (2000). Managing team knowledge: Core processes, tools and enabling factors. *European Management Journal, 18*(3), 334–341. doi:10.1016/S0263-2373(00)00015-3

Erumban, A., & de Jong, S. B. (2006). Cross-country differences in ICT adoption: A consequence of Culture? *Journal of World Business, 41*(4), 302. doi:10.1016/j.jwb.2006.08.005

Francis, H. (1997). National cultural differences in theory and practice Evaluating Hofstede's national cultural framework. *Information Technology & People, 10*(2), 132–146. doi:10.1108/09593849710174986

Gajendran, T., & Brewer, G. J. (2007). Integration of information and communication technology: Influence of the cultural environment. *Engineering, Construction, and Architectural Management, 14,* 532–549. doi:10.1108/09699980710829003

Gelfand, M. J., Bhawuk, D. P. S., Nishii, L. H., & Bechtold, D. J. (2004). Individualism and collectivism. In House, R. J., Hanges, P. J., Javidan, M., Dorfman, P. W., & Gupta, V. (Eds.), *Culture, leadership, and organizations: The GLOBE study of 62 societies* (pp. 438–512). Thousand Oaks, CA: Sage.

Gupta, A. K., & Govindarajan, V. (2000). Knowledge Management's Social Dimension: Lessons From Nucor Steel. *Sloan Management Review, 42*(1), 71–81.

Gyampah, K., & White, K. (1993). User involvement and user satisfaction: An exploratory contingency model. *Information & Management, 25,* 1–10. doi:10.1016/0378-7206(93)90021-K

Hair, J. F., Anderson, R. E., Tatham, R. L., & Blac, W. C. (1998). *Multivariate data analysis* (5th ed.). Englewood Cliffs, NJ: Prentice-Hall.

Hasan, H., & Ditsa, G. (1999). The impact of culture on the adoption of IT: An interpretive study. *Journal of Global Information Management, 7*(1), 5–15.

Head, T., & Sorensen, P. F., (2005). Attracting foreign direct investment: The potential role of national culture. *The Journal of American Academy of Business,* 205-209.

Heals, J., Cockcroft, S., & Raduescu, C. (2004). The Influence of National Culture on the Level and Outcome of IS Development Decisions. *Journal of Global Information Technology, 7*(4), 3–28.

Herbig, P., & Dunphy, S. (1998). Culture and innovation. *Cross Cultural Management, 5*(4), 13–21. doi:10.1108/13527609810796844

Herbig, P., & Miller, J. (1992). Culture and technology: does the traffic move in both directions? *Journal of Global Marketing, 6*(3), 75–104. doi:10.1300/J042v06n03_05

Hofstede, G. (1980). *Culture's Consequences: International Differences in Related Values.* Beverly Hills, CA: Sage.

Hofstede, G. (1983). National culture in four dimensions. *International Studies of Management and Organization, 13*(2), 46–74.

Hofstede, G. (1984). *Culture's consequences: International differences in work-related values.* London: Sage.

Hofstede, G. (1991). *Cultures and organizations: Software of the mind.* New York: McGraw-Hill.

Hofstede, G. (2001). *Culture's Consequences* (2nd ed.). Thousand Oaks, CA: Sage.

Hofstede, G., & Bond, M. H. (1988). The Confucius connection: from cultural roots to economic growth. *Organizational Dynamics, 16,* 4–21. doi:10.1016/0090-2616(88)90009-5

House, R. J. (2004). Foreword. In House, R. J., Hanges, P. J., Javidan, M., Dorfman, P. W., & Gupta, V. (Eds.), *Culture, leadership, and organizations: The GLOBE study of 62 societies* (pp. xv–xix). Thousand Oaks, CA: Sage.

House, R. J., Javidan, M., & Dorfman, P. (2001). Project GLOBE: An introduction. *Applied Psychology: An International Review, 50*(4), 489–505. doi:10.1111/1464-0597.00070

House, R. J., Javidan, M., Hanges, P., & Dorfman, P. (2002). Understanding cultures and implicit leadership theories across the globe: an introduction to project GLOBE. *Journal of World Business, 37*(1), 3–10. doi:10.1016/S1090-9516(01)00069-4

Javidan, M. (2004). Performance orientation. In House, R. J., Hanges, P. J., Javidan, M., Dorfman, P. W., & Gupta, V. (Eds.), *Culture, leadership, and organizations: The GLOBE study of 62 societies* (pp. 239–281). Thousand Oaks, CA: Sage.

Javidan, M., & House, R. J. (2001). Cultural acumen for the global manager: Lessons from Project GLOBE. *Organizational Dynamics, 29*(4), 289–305. doi:10.1016/S0090-2616(01)00034-1

Javidan, M., House, R. J., Dorfman, P. W., Hanges, P. J., & de Luque, M. S. (2006). Conceptualizing and measuring cultures and their consequences: A comparative review of GLOBE's and Hofstede's approaches. *Journal of International Business Studies*, *37*(6), 897–914. doi:10.1057/palgrave. jibs.8400234

Javidan, M., House, R. J., Dorfman, W. P., Gupta, V., Hanges, P. J., & de Luque, M. S. (2004). Conclusion. In House, R. J., Hanges, P. J., Javidan, M., Dorfman, P. W., & Gupta, V. (Eds.), *Culture, leadership, and organizations: The GLOBE study of 62 societies* (pp. 721–732). Thousand Oaks, CA: Sage.

Jones, G. K., & Teegen, H, J. (2001). Global R & D activity of U.S. MNCS: does national culture affect investment decisions? *Multinational Business Review*, *9*(2), 1–7.

Kabasakal, H., & Bodur, M. (2004). Human orientation in societies, organizations, and leader attitudes. In House, R. J., Hanges, P. J., Javidan, M., Dorfman, P. W., & Gupta, V. (Eds.), *Culture, leadership, and organizations: The GLOBE study of 62 societies* (pp. 564–601). Thousand Oaks, CA: Sage.

Kedia, B. L., Keller, R. T., & Julian, S. D. (1992). Dimensions of national culture and the productivity of R&D units. *The Journal of High Technology Management Research*, *3*, 1–18. doi:10.1016/1047-8310(92)90002-J

Khalil, O., & Seleim, A. (2009). A cultural values interpretation for societal information dissemination capacity: An exploratory study. *Arab Journal of Administrative Sciences*, *16*(3), 455–488.

Li, J., & Karakowsky, L. (2002). Cultural malleability in an East Asian Context: An illustration of the relationship between government policy, national culture, and firm behavior. *Administration & Society*, *34*(2), 176–201. doi:10.1177/0095399702034002003

Liebowitz, J. (Ed.). (1999). *Knowledge management Handbook*. CRC.

Martinsons, M., & Davison, R. (2003). Cultural Issues and IT Management. *IEEE Transactions on Engineering Management*, *50*(1), 113–117. doi:10.1109/TEM.2003.808299

Martinsons, M., & Davison, R. (2007). Culture's consequences for IT application and business process change: a research agenda. *International Journal of Internet and Enterprise Management*, *5*(2), 158. doi:10.1504/IJIEM.2007.014087

McGrath, R. G., Macmillan, I. C., Yang, E. A., & Tsai, W. (1992). Does culture endure, or is it malleable? Issues for entrepreneurial economic development. *Journal of Business Venturing*, *7*, 441–458. doi:10.1016/0883-9026(92)90019-N

Menou, M. J. (1983). Cultural barriers to the international transfer of information. *Information Processing & Management*, *19*(3), 121–129. doi:10.1016/0306-4573(83)90065-1

Myers, M. D., & Tan, F. D. (2002). Beyond models of national culture in information systems research. *Journal of Global Information Management*, *10*(1), 24–32.

Nakata, C., & Sivakumar, K. (1996). National Culture and New Product Development: An Integrative Review. *Journal of Marketing*, *60*, 61–72. doi:10.2307/1251888

Nicholson, J. D., & Stepina, L. P. (1998). Cultural values: A cross-national study. *Cross Cultural Management -. International Journal (Toronto, Ont.)*, *5*(1), 34–49.

Nonaka, I., & Takeuchi, H. (1995). *The Knowledge-Creating Company*. New York: Oxford Press.

Parent, R., Roy, M., & St-Jacques, D. (2007). A systems-based dynamic knowledge transfer capacity model. *Journal of Knowledge Management*, *11*(6), 81–93. doi:10.1108/13673270710832181

Phillips, T., & Vollmer, M. (2000). Knowledge management in the current marketplace. *Oil & Gas Journal*, 4–5.

Pook, L. A., & Fustos, J. (1999). Information sharing by management: some cross-cultural results. *Human Systems Management*, *18*(1), 9–22.

Ralston, D. A., Gustafson, D. J., Cheung, F. M., & Terpstra, R. H. (1993). Differences in managerial values: A study of U.S., Hong Kong, and PRC managers. *Journal of International Business Studies*, *24*(2), 249–275. doi:10.1057/palgrave.jibs.8490232

Ralston, D. A., Gustafson, D. J., Elsass, P. M., Cheung, F., & Terpstra, R. H. (1992). Eastern Values: A Comparison of Managers in the United States, Hong Kong, and the People's Republic of China. *The Journal of Applied Psychology*, *77*(5), 664–671. doi:10.1037/0021-9010.77.5.664

Robert, C., Probst, T. M., Martocchio, J. J., Drasgow, F., & Lawler, J. J. (2000). Empowerment and continuous improvement in the United States, Mexico, Poland, and India: Predicting fit on the basis of the dimensions of power distance and individualism. *The Journal of Applied Psychology*, *85*, 643–658. doi:10.1037/0021-9010.85.5.643

Seetharaman, A., Lo, K., & Saravanan, A. S. (2004). Comparative justification on intellectual capital. *Journal of Intellectual Capital*, *5*(4), 522–539. doi:10.1108/14691930410566997

Seliem, A., Ashour, A., Khalil, O., & Miller, S. (2003). The relationship of some organizational factors to information system effectiveness: Egyptian data and contingent analysis. *Journal of Global Information Management*, *11*(1), 40–71.

Shane, S. (1992). Why do some societies invent more than others? *Journal of Business Venturing*, *7*, 29–46. doi:10.1016/0883-9026(92)90033-N

Shane, S. (1993). Cultural influences on national rates of innovation. *Journal of Business Venturing*, *8*, 59–73. doi:10.1016/0883-9026(93)90011-S

Shore, B., & Venkatachalam, A. R. (1995). The role of national culture in systems analysis and design. *Journal of Global Information Management*, *3*(3), 5–14.

Spicer, A. (1997). Cultural and knowledge transfer: Conflict in Russian Multi-National Settings. In *Proceedings of the Academy of Management Conference* (pp.194-198).

Stewart, T. A. (1997). *Intellectual capital-the new wealth of organizations*. New York: Doubleday/Currency.

Straub, D. W. (1994). The effect of culture on IT diffusion: E-mail and Fax in Japan and the U.S. *Information Systems Research*, *5*(1), 23–47. doi:10.1287/isre.5.1.23

Straub, D. W., Keil, M., & Brenner, W. (1997). Testing the technology acceptance model across cultures: A three country study. *Information & Management*, *33*(1), 1–11. doi:10.1016/S0378-7206(97)00026-8

Straub, D. W., Loch, K., & Hill, C. (2001). Transfer of information technology to the Arab World: A test of cultural influence modeling. *Journal of Global Information Management*, *9*(4), 6–27.

Torkzadeh, G., & Doll, W. (1994). The test-retest reliability of user involvement instruments. *Information & Management*, *26*, 21–31. doi:10.1016/0378-7206(94)90004-3

Tsang, D. (1999). National culture and national competitiveness: a study of the microcomputer component industry. *Advances in Competitiveness Research*, *7*(1), 1–34.

Varsakelis, N. C. (2001). The impact of patent protection, economy openness and national culture on R&D investment: a cross-country empirical investigation. *Research Policy, 30*(7), 1059–1068. doi:10.1016/S0048-7333(00)00130-X

Wagner, J. A. (1995). Studies of individualism-collectivism: Effects on cooperation. *Academy of Management Journal, 38*, 152–167. doi:10.2307/256731

Wang, P. (2004). *An exploratory study of the effect of national culture on knowledge management factors, expectations and practices: A cross-cultural analysis of Taiwanese and U.S. perceptions.* Unpublished PhD dissertation, George Washington University.

World Bank. (2004). *World Development Indicators.* Washington, DC: Author.

APPENDIX A

Table A1. The countries included in the data set (N = 61)

1	Albania	32	Japan
2	Argentina	33	Kazakhstan
3	Australia	34	Kuwait
4	Austria	35	Malaysia
5	Bolivia	36	Mexico
6	Brazil	37	Morocco
7	Canada	38	Namibia
8	China	39	Netherlands
9	Colombia	40	New Zealand
10	Costa Rica	41	Nigeria
11	Czech Republic	42	Philippines
12	Denmark	43	Poland
13	Ecuador	44	Portugal
14	Egypt	45	Qatar
15	El Salvador	46	Russia
16	England	47	Singapore
17	Finland	48	Slovenia
18	France	49	South Africa Black sample
19	Switzerland	50	South Africa White sample
20	Georgia	51	South Korea
21	Germany West	52	Spain
22	Germany East	53	Sweden
23	Greece	54	Switzerland
24	Guatemala	55	Taiwan
25	Hong Kong	56	Thailand
26	Hungary	57	Turkey
27	India	58	USA
28	Indonesia	59	Venezuela
29	Ireland	60	Zambia
30	Israel	61	Zimbabwe
31	Italy		

Chapter 17
Taking Charities Seriously:
A Call for Focused Knowledge Management Research

Kathleen E. Greenaway
Ryerson University, Canada

David C. H. Vuong
Dundas Data Visualization Inc., Canada

ABSTRACT

The voluntary service not-for-profit sector (VSNFP), also called the charitable sector, is a neglected setting for knowledge management research. It is also an area with distinctive characteristics that preclude direct importation of knowledge management approaches developed for the for-profit sector. In this paper, the authors adapt a model for examining knowledge management research issues to the charitable sector and examine what is known about knowledge management in this important sector of society. Research and practitioner suggestions are provided.

INTRODUCTION

Charities, also called voluntary-service not-for-profit organizations (VSNFP), play a vital role in modern societies by addressing needs and providing services that benefit the public. These services frequently are available from neither markets nor governments. Many charitable organizations have been created to deliver or have expanded their range or scope of services as the result of governments "devolving" or transferring services

to the non-profit sector (Gunn, 2004). Therefore, it is unsurprising that charities have a significant impact economically and socially. For example, volunteer work in Argentina, the United Kingdom, Japan, and the United States is valued at 2.7, 21, 23, and 109 billion (US) dollars respectively (Johns Hopkins University, 2005). Volunteering translates into significant resources for non-profit organizations. For example, Statistics Canada estimates that work equivalent to 1 million fulltime jobs in Canada was provided through volunteer labor in 2004 (Statistics Canada, 2006). While charities are part of the non-profit sector, research

DOI: 10.4018/978-1-4666-0035-5.ch017

demonstrates that charitable organizations differ from for-profit organizations in terms of their human capital management, management practices, and strategies (Bontis & Serenko, 2009). Failing to account for such differences may adversely affect theory (Orlikowski & Barley, 2001) and practice (Kilbourne & Marshall, 2005).

Research is beginning to provide a picture of the increasing use of information and communication technologies (ICTs) by the non-profit and voluntary sector. Examples include Burt and Taylor's (2003) case studies of the challenges of ICT adoption by highly autonomous voluntary organizations in the U.K., Cukier and Middleton's (2003) evaluation of web sites for Canadian charities, Denison and Johanson's (2007) survey of the use of ICTs by community groups in Australia, Canada, the U.K. and the United States, and Finn, Maher and Forster's (2007) archival study of the evolution of ICT adoption by non-profit organizations. These studies are beginning to round out the portrait of the voluntary sector as ICT user but there remains many blank spots. Our key question is: *What is the extent of our understanding of the role of knowledge management, both as process and system, in charitable organizations?* We discuss this question by adapting the knowledge management (KM) research framework originally developed for examining KM in knowledge-based enterprises (Staples, Greenaway, & McKeen, 2001). Non-profits are "knowledge-intensive" organizations (Lettieri et al., 2004, p. 17). Therefore, this research model should be applicable broadly to non-profit organizations including charities.

Charities are distinguished from other types of not-for-profit organizations by their staffing (more volunteers than paid workers) and their sources of revenue (more donation than fee-based) (Kilbourne & Marshall, 2005). Hence, they have a unique set of challenges. They are particularly vulnerable to economic ups and downs. Their missions typically are counter-cyclical. That is, in "bad times" the demand for their services rise at the same time as the sources for revenues shrink (The Center for Philanthropy at Indiana University, 2008). Human resource management challenges include declining numbers of volunteers, fewer volunteers contributing more hours, and the need to constantly replenish the volunteer base (Brock, 2003). As well, there is the need to manage administrative, professional/clinical or similar expert service delivery personal as well as the variety of volunteers. Assessing organizational performance is another challenge. The "bottom line" for VSPNs is outcomes- focused (including knowledge) and not financially-focused (Hatry, 2007). Finally, charities may be limited in their ability to invest in or to make information technology a priority because they lack IT skills and financial depth (Corder, 2001). At the same time, Saidel and Cour (2003) reported that not-for-profits are frequently forced into adopting technologies to satisfy outside administrative requirements such as for government reporting and accountability.

Complicating this picture is the way "volunteering," defined as "any activity in which time is given freely to benefit another person, group or organization" (Wilson 2000, p. 215) is changing. Handy and Brudney (2007) identify four types of "volunteer labor resources" that engage with non-profits: service learning (e.g., students earning credits for hours served with charities); episodic (e.g., assisting with a fundraising event or providing expert service); virtual (e.g., providing service electronically such as web design); and long term traditional (e.g., analogous to unpaid work). Volunteer turnover and the changing nature of volunteerism create organizational memory loss which may cause charities to repeat mistakes (Walsh & Ungson, 1991). Knowledge management (KM) initiatives provide a means for stemming this loss through increasing the retention of knowledge, facilitating the creation and acquisition of new knowledge, improving the connections among paid staff, volunteers and beneficiaries of services, and reducing the need for and associated costs of re-training volunteers.

Figure 1. Research Model (adapted from Staples, Greenaway & McKeen 2001, p. 5. © 2001. International Journal of Management Reviews. Used with permission.)

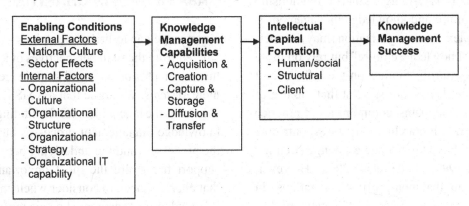

KNOWLEDGE MANAGEMENT IN CHARITABLE ORGANIZATIONS

Staples et al. (2001) proposed a research framework for investigating knowledge management in knowledge-based enterprises. We adapt this model to the VSNFP context as illustrated in Figure 1. Note that we attend to the Enabling Conditions, Capabilities and Success aspects of the model. Intellectual Capital Formation is not addressed.

Enabling Conditions for Knowledge Management in Charities

External enabling conditions include national culture and sector effects. These conditions are those to which voluntary organizations must respond but over which they have little say. These conditions affect the general operation of a voluntary sector organization and will exert greater or lesser bearing on the organization's knowledge management deployment. *National culture* influences knowledge management processes in organizations (Ang & Massingham, 2007; Bock et al., 2005; Michailova & Hutchings, 2006). As well, it influences levels of volunteerism (Erlinghagen & Hank, 2006).

However, the influence of national culture on knowledge management in VSNFPs has not been researched. *Sector effects* should also be

considered (Kim & Lee, 2006). For example, in the "for profit" sector, institutional influences such as isomorphism, lead to imitation among competing organizations in a variety of ways including the adoption of KM systems (Rizzi, Ponte, & Bonifacio 2009). Non-profits typically have less invested in IT per employee than their commercial/industrial peers (Finn, Maher, & Forster, 2006). Therefore, we do not understand the combined influence of sectoral "peer pressure," lower rates of IT investment, and organizational size on the rates of KM adoption in the voluntary subsector. Finally, the charitable sector, as a sub-sector of NFP, is heterogeneous in its makeup (Lettieri et al., 2004, p. 17). Charities provide a variety of types of services (e.g., healthcare, housing, arts, advocacy) through a variety of types of organizations (e.g., different sizes, missions, structures). Hence, this complex context may require different models for KM deployment.

Internal enabling conditions include organizational culture, structure, strategy and IT capability. *Organizational culture and institutions* characterized by trust, communication, reward systems (Constant et al., 1994), tolerance for failure and pro-social norms (Leonard & Sensiper, 1998) as well as formal and informal KM leadership and championship processes (Nonaka, von Krogh, & Voelpel, 2006) have been shown to promote effective knowledge management organizations. However, King (2007) argues that the relationship between culture and knowledge management is more complex. Some organizations may not operate with a "knowledge culture" but rely on more traditional controls. Studies on the influence of *organizational structure* suggest that the use of cross-functional teams, communities of practice and similar non-hierarchical structures contribute to more effective knowledge exchange (Bennett & Gabriel, 1999; Rhodes et al., 2008). However, to the extent that non-profit organizations, in general, are characterized as "bureaucratic ... risk averse, conservative and non-innovative" (Bontis & Serenko, 2009, p. 11) we can argue that more research is needed to specify the influence of structural contingencies in charities on KM initiatives. *Organizational strategy* refers to what the organization wants to achieve with its knowledge. For-profit organizations pursue competitive advantage while non-profit organizations pursue a self-defined mission, such as pursuing a goal that eliminates the need for the charity's existence. This fundamental difference in strategy suggests that the knowledge requirements of the organization may differ. For example, charities may be more interested in managing their volunteers' "miscellaneous or non-characteristic knowledge" (Lettieri et al., 2004, p. 25) while for-profit firms are more interested in managing declarative, procedural or causal knowledge (Zack, 1999). Lastly, *organizational IT capability* speaks to a charity's capacity to manage the IT function in order to be able to take advantage of ICTs (Sowa, Seldon, & Sandfort, 2004), in general, and knowledge management systems, in particular. Nevo and Chan (2007a) in a Delphi study of KM systems in 21 organizations, determined that adaptability (ability to integrate across systems), security (decision and access rights), ease of use, and cost efficiency were the most desired KM system capabilities even though these are not KMS specific.

KNOWLEDGE MANAGEMENT CAPABILITIES IN CHARITIES

Knowledge capabilities in charities can be considered from the twin perspectives of knowledge management *processes* and knowledge management *systems*. We argue that a KMS is best considered as the mechanism for facilitating efficient knowledge management processes but that that the processes (and the underlying behaviors that support them) are the most important aspects that charities need to consider when engaging in knowledge management. For example, Iverson and Burkart (2007) studied the use of "content management systems" a type of KMS. Among their conclusions was the importance of studying work processes "before reifying workflows" and not "losing connection to mission through overly reifying and commodifying organizational work" (p. 416). Of particular concern would be the loss of contact with clients and increased difficulty in coordination among staff and volunteers. However, given the paucity of research on KM or KMS per se in charities we do not systematically separate processes from systems in our discussion. Therefore, we consider knowledge capabilities from a classic perspective that begins with knowledge acquisition and creation, moves to knowledge capture and storage, and concludes with knowledge diffusion and transfer.

Knowledge Acquisition and Creation

Knowledge acquisition means getting existing knowledge from external sources while knowledge creation means developing knowledge within the organization. Nonaka (1994) distinguished among four modes of knowledge conversion: socialization, combination, externalization and internalization. These modes explain the different manners in which tacit and explicit knowledge combine to create new understanding and capability within organizations. Becerra-Fernandez and Sabherwal (2001) refined this approach with a contingency perspective to distinguish among broad versus focused and process versus content knowledge. These theories has been tested in various for-profit settings but our understanding of their applicability to non-profits, particularly charitable organizations, is lacking.

The types of knowledge (process or content, broad or narrow) acquired or created may be influenced by the kind of workers and volunteers available to the organizations. Lettieri et al. (2004) mapped the knowledge domains of four Italian social service nonprofits and found differences within the six main categories. They argued that, paradoxically, high rates of volunteer turnover may have a positive effect by constantly introducing new knowledge into the affected organizations. However, organizational memory loss may be accelerated by turnover thus creating a constant need to reacquire/recreate lost knowledge. The influence of the changing composition of the "volunteer labor force" also needs consideration. von Krogh (1998) argues the importance of informal relationships in enterprises to the success of knowledge conversion. The extent to which socialization might dominate as a knowledge creation mode (given that charities depend on "social" assets more than "system" assets) is unknown.

Most knowledge creation and acquisition models assume that competitive advantage is the ultimate goal and, thus, seek barriers to preserve the value of knowledge through protections such as patents (Chakravarthy et al., 2005). In contrast, non-profit organizations operate in environments in which much knowledge is publicly available and readily shared through community level externalization (Lettieri et al., 2004). The influence of the VSNFP's mission orientation as a catalyst for internalization could also be argued. Thus, the actual goals being pursued by charities deploying KM/KMS need to be better understood in order that appropriate knowledge acquisition and creation processes are implemented.

Knowledge Capture and Storage in Charities

Knowledge capture represents another poorly understood aspect of knowledge management in charitable organizations. Knowledge capture involves the technology, processes and strategies to identify and classify, store, and retrieve the knowledge the organization wants to make available to its members. Hansen et al. (1999) propose two main approaches to managing knowledge capture based on whether the organization primarily emphasizes a technological (codification) or social approach (personalization). Codification works best with explicit knowledge and presumes an organizational capacity to effectively classify, store and manage retrieval from electronic repositories using highly structured tools. Personalization works best with tacit knowledge and presumes close working relationships among peers such that informal (e.g., asking questions, storytelling, mentoring) and formal (e.g., seminars, communities of practice) mechanisms can be used as appropriate for knowledge transfer. In this manner, the people are the knowledge repositories and access is less structured and more situational. Research has demonstrated the effectiveness of both strategies in different profit-oriented contexts. Hurley and Green (2005) argue for the applicability of the approaches to non-governmental organizations. The challenges of managing large scale knowledge repositories may be beyond the financial and organizational capacity of charities. Further, the selection of the capture and storage processes may have significant implications for the way in which work is accomplished and may undermine existing successful "ways of doing things." These are areas requiring more research.

Knowledge Diffusion and Transfer in Charities

Once knowledge has been created or acquired, it is essential for it to be shared in order to maximize its usefulness to the organization. Knowledge sharing is the act of communicating knowledge to another individual and is arguably the most important of the KM processes. At the same time, it is the process most likely to fail due to numerous factors (Hutzschenreuter & Listner, 2007). Effective knowledge sharing strategies in charities are believed to differ versus those in for-profit corporations and public entities (Bontis & Serenko, 2009). However, there are few studies that explicitly examine what those differences may be (Riege, 2005).

Volunteers at the operational level may experience greater levels of disengagement in the organization since they are often tasked with menial/mindless duties and may not be involved in any decision making or decision support functions. Disengagement adversely impacts turnover and knowledge sharing (Ford, 2008). Thus, charities with a sizable volunteer complement may be more predisposed to experience a greater proportion of disengagement than for-profits that carry no volunteers. However, this may not be the case for employees of charitable organizations. Bontis and Serenko (2009) found different patterns of knowledge sharing between for-profit and non-profit workers that suggested non-profit workers were more intrinsically motivated and continued to share knowledge even in situations where models would have predicted otherwise (such as reduced financial rewards and counter-productive behaviors like knowledge hoarding by some co-workers).

Self-perceived expertise is believed to create positive attitudes towards knowledge sharing as a result of self-consistency theory (Korman, 1970). This theory posits that one behaves in a way that is consistent with the positive praise of one's peers. Hence, if one is perceived to be an expert then one would likely value behaviors aligned with this trait such as sharing more knowledge. However, it appears that volunteers in a charity may be sharing what they know regardless of whether they believe themselves to be an expert.

This is believed to be due to the fact that volunteers are more likely to possess higher social capital which in turn promotes pro-social behaviors such as knowledge sharing (Vuong & Staples, 2008).

For charities, delivering effective programs in a professional manner requires paid staff who often bring specialized training and experience (Eisinger, 2002). Factors such as altruism payoff and interpersonal relationships may impact how paid staff in charities are motivated (Parsons & Broadbridge, 2006). Areas where tasks are interchangeable between paid and volunteer staff may be good targets/areas for knowledge transfer in order to minimize adverse impacts should a volunteer be required to substitute for paid worker (Handy et al., 2008).

EVALUATING THE SUCCESS OF KM IN CHARITIES

Evaluating the success of knowledge-based organizational initiatives has been a preoccupation of a stream of researchers (Nevo & Chan, 2007a; Jennex & Olfman, 2004, 2005; Massey et al., 2002 Turban & Aaronson, 2001; Wu & Wang, 2006). To begin with is the question of what the KM/KMS is supposed to accomplish. KMS are typically described as serving one of three purposes − transferring best practices, creating a directory of internal experts, and/or facilitating networking and communication among individuals (Alavi & Leidner, 2001). Any of these approaches would be useful to charities seeking ways to manage knowledge. For example, Gilmour and Stancliffe (2004) documented a case where an international charity was able to use a content management system to improve its effectiveness by cultivating best practices and avoiding duplication of effort. Nevo and Chan (2007b) discussed the nature of the "expectations" and "desires" of managers implementing KMS. Expectations were tied to the tangible attributes of systems usually based on past experiences while desires were based on the business needs and perceptions of how the KMS would benefit the organizations (p. 305). While the wording is not the same, the concepts underlying expectations and desires map well to the models of KMS success that appear in the literature. However, the applicability to not-for-profits and charities is less apparent.

Turban and Aronson (2001) argue that KMS success should be measured in order to assess organizational value, guide management decisions, and justify knowledge management investments. DeLone and McLean (1992) model information systems success as the individual and organizational impact that originates from the quality of the system (e.g., usability, reliability, response time) and information (e.g., easy to understand, comprehensive, relevant). This model was adapted for use in a KMS context by Jennex and Olfman (2004) and Maier (2002). Both models propose the inclusion of management support (service quality) as a contributing factor. Additionally, Jennex and Olfman (2004) suggest including feedback effects from the dependent construct. This is supported by DeLone and McLean (2003) who update their 1992 model to incorporate findings from the previous ten years. However, whereas the net benefits discussed by DeLone and McLean (2003) include metrics such as increased sales and cost savings, the net benefits for a KMS have to do with improved individual and organizational performance. In a non-profit setting, these net benefits should be measured in terms of outcomes related to the achievement of their mission such as reduced time to addiction recovery or delivering service within a larger catchment area.

Jennex and Olfman (2005) survey the literature on KMS success and find four key success factors of KMS: 1) an integrated technical infrastructure, 2) a comprehensive knowledge strategy, 3) an easily understood, communal, and organization-wide knowledge structure, and 4) the motivation and commitment of the end users. Out of the five KMS models they examined, only two had these key success factors modeled: Massey et al. (2002)

and Jennex and Olfman (2004). The failures of knowledge management initiatives are less well documented. Nevo and Chan (2007a) found three primary reasons for KMS failure according to senior managers in for-profit settings – lack of use, ineffectiveness, and technical issues including slowness and difficulty in implementation. These "failure" factors mirror the generally accepted systems "success" factors and should be noted by managers and researchers alike. The charitable organizational setting would appear to provide a new opportunity to consider success/failure factors.

Fundamental to models of KM success is the issue of the quality of the knowledge being provided by the system. While this has been well documented in for-profit organizations (Devo & Chan, 2007a), there is limited understanding of the knowledge quality construct in other sectors. Taylor and Wright (2004) found that the quality of the information provided by an information system supports knowledge sharing in governmental organizations. An important research issue is to consider whether Intellectual Capital Formation (originally modeled by Staples et al as antecedent to KM success) should remain independent or be subsumed into the KM success construct. Although beyond the scope of this paper, we raise the question of how to appropriately model information/knowledge accumulation as part of KMS success or an end unto itself.

Charities should consider the potential benefits of knowledge management systems on the effectiveness of their organizations. Successful KMS do not need to capture everything that every member knows, only what is relevant. With management support, an easily accessible KMS might help charities make a more profound impact than they could without it. Charities typically have limited finances which constrains their ability to invest in KMS. This underscores the need for the system to be thoughtfully implemented with a clear view of what constitutes success.

CONCLUSION

Charities will continue to be challenged by tight budgets, the changing composition of their volunteer ranks as well as the ageing of their workforce. Knowledge management offers a means to ensure that service delivery can continue but charities must address several key issues in order to lay the groundwork for success. The limited research into knowledge management in charities leads us to suggest that VSNFP managers should consider how best to:

- Engage their volunteers as well as their administrative and professional staff in developing and implementing KM initiatives. The shift from traditional long-term volunteers to shorter-term relationships reflects our changing society. Engaging short-term volunteers, especially those with digital skills, may offer more meaningful and hence more valuable "work" that can include contributing to KM initiatives.
- Address process issues before knowledge issues. Good processes are the basis for any successful system. To ensure that limited resources are well used, managers should work with staff and volunteers to ensure that critical processes are identified and refined prior to "reifying" them within a KMS.
- Focus on key knowledge requirements. The issue for charities may be to use KM as a means to reduce the level of their staff's involvement in non-essential activities by providing a KM based support to volunteers. At the same time, managers should strive to link KM activities to the outcomes that are most meaningful to the charity's mission and be willing to trade off some efficiency to maintain key positive attributes of the organization's culture.
- Accelerate knowledge sharing within the sector. Focusing on learning about and

adopting the best practices and proven techniques from other charitable organizations rather than trying to retrofit models designed for other purposes is a positive approach. Organizations within the VSNFP sector compete for resources and volunteers but have also shown remarkable abilities to learn from others. This talent should be harnessed in the service of greater long term sector capacity.

Charities, like other non-profit and for-profit organizations, need effective knowledge management processes and systems to succeed. However, charities face challenges distinct from those in for-profit corporations: organizational strategies and missions are different, the nature of the cash flow is different, and the nature of the labor is different. Acknowledging such differences when executing a knowledge management initiative could mean the difference between success and failure. The research questions posed in this article can form the basis for future research into the many subtle and not so subtle differences between charities and for-profit organizations. As the non-profit sector continues to increase in its importance in service delivery to many groups, researchers need to pay more attention to ensure that appropriate models and practices are developed and conveyed to the busy managers who lead and the professional and administrative staff and volunteers who deliver the services that underlie their important missions. The charitable sector would benefit from further KMS investigations.

ACKNOWLEDGMENT

We acknowledge that this title is a play on Chiasson & Davidson's 2005 paper Taking industry seriously in information systems research. *MIS Quarterly, 29*(4), 599-606.

REFERENCES

Alavi, M., & Leidner, D. (2001). Knowledge Management and Knowledge Management Systems: Conceptual Foundations and Research Issues. *Management Information Systems Quarterly, 5*(1), 107–156. doi:10.2307/3250961

Ang, Z., & Massingham, P. (2007). National culture and the standardization versus adaptation of knowledge management. *Journal of Knowledge Management, 11*(2), 5–21. doi:10.1108/13673270710738889

Becerra-Fernandez, I., & Sabherwal, R. (2001). Organizational Knowledge Management: A Contingency Perspective. *Journal of Management Information Systems, 18*(1), 23–55.

Bennett, R., & Gabriel, H. (1999). Organisational factors and knowledge management within large marketing departments: an empirical study. *Journal of Knowledge Management, 3*(3), 212–225. doi:10.1108/13673279910288707

Bock, G. W., Zmud, R. W., Kim, Y., & Lee, J. (2005). Behavioral Intention Formation in Knowledge Sharing: Examining the Roles of Extrinsic Motivators, Social-Psychological Forces, and Organizational Climate. *Management Information Systems Quarterly, 29*(1), 87–111.

Bontis, N., & Serenko, A. (2009). A causal model of human capital antecedents and consequents in the financial services industry. *Journal of Intellectual Capital, 10*(1), 53–69. doi:10.1108/14691930910922897

Brock, K. L. (2003). Introduction. In Brock, K. L., & Banting, K. G. (Eds.), *The Nonprofit Sector in Interesting Times*. Kingston, ON, Canada: McGill-Queen's University Press.

Burt, W., & Taylor, J. (2003). New Technologies, Embedded Values and Strategic Change: Evidence From the U.K. Voluntary Sector. *Nonprofit and Voluntary Sector Quarterly, 32*(1), 115–127. doi:10.1177/0899764002250009

Chakravarthy, B., McEvily, S., Doz, Y., & Rau, D. (2005). Knowledge Management and Competitive Advantage. In Easterby-Smith, M., & Lyles, M. A. (Eds.), *Handbook of Organizational Learning and Knowledge Management* (pp. 305–323). Oxford, UK: Blackwell.

Constant, D., Keisler, S., & Sproull, L. (1994). What's mine is ours, or is it? A study of attitudes about information sharing. *Information Systems Research, 5*, 400–421. doi:10.1287/isre.5.4.400

Corder, K. (2001). Acquiring New Technology: Comparing Nonprofit and Public Sector Agencies. *Administration & Society, 33*(2), 193–219. doi:10.1177/00953990122019730

Cukier, W., & Middleton, C. (2003). Evaluating the Web Presence of Voluntary Sector Organizations: An Assessment of Canadian Web Sites. *IT & Society, 1*(3), 102–130.

DeLone, W. H., & McLean, E. R. (1992). Information systems success: The quest for the dependent variable. *Information Systems Research, 3*(1), 60–95. doi:10.1287/isre.3.1.60

DeLone, W. H., & McLean, E. R. (2003). The DeLone and MacLean Model of Information Systems Success: A Ten-Year Update. *Journal of Management Information Systems, 19*(4), 9–30.

Denison, T., & Johanson, G. (2007). Surveys of the use of information and communications technologies by community-based organizations. *Journal of Community Informatics, 3*(2). Retrieved from http://ci-journal.net/index.php/ ciej/article/ view/316.

Eisinger, P. (2002). Organizational capacity and organizational effectiveness among street-level food assistance programs. *Nonprofit and Voluntary Sector Quarterly, 31*(1), 115–130. doi:. doi:10.1177/0899764002311005

Erlinghagen, M., & Hank, K. (2006). The participation of older Europeans in volunteer work. *Ageing and Society, 26*, 567–584. doi:10.1017/ S0144686X06004818

Finn, S., Maher, J. K., & Forster, J. (2006). Indicators of Information and Communication Technology Adoption in the Nonprofit Sector: Changes Between 2000 and 2004. *Nonprofit Management & Leadership, 16*(3), 277–295. doi:10.1002/nml.107

Ford, D. P. (2008). *Disengagement from Knowledge Sharing: The Alternative Explanation for Why People Are Not Sharing.* Paper presented at the Administrative Sciences Association of Canada, Halifax, NS, Canada.

Gilmour, J., & Stancliffe, M. (2004). Managing knowledge in an international organisation: the work of voluntary services overseas (VSO). *Records Management Journal, 14*(3), 124–128. doi:.doi:10.1108/09565690410566783

Gunn, C. (2004). *Third-sector development: making up for the market.* Ithaca, NY: Cornell University Press.

Handy, F., & Brudney, J. L. (2007). When to Use Volunteer Labor Resources? An Organizational Analysis for Nonprofit Management. *Vrijwillige Inzet Onderzoch, 4*, 91–100.

Handy, F., Mook, L., & Quarter, J. (2008). The Interchangeability of Paid Staff and Volunteers in Nonprofit Organizations. *Nonprofit and Voluntary Sector Quarterly, 37*(1), 76–92. doi:10.1177/0899764007303528

Hansen, M. T., Nohria, N., & Tierney, T. (1999). What's your strategy for managing knowledge? *Harvard Business Review, 77*(2), 106–116.

Hatry, H. P. (2007). *Performance Measurement: Getting Results* (2nd ed.). Washington, DC: Urban Institute.

Hurley, T. A., & Green, C. W. (2005). Knowledge Management and the Non-Profit Industry: A Within and Between Approach. *Journal of Knowledge Management Practice, 6*. Retrieved July 29, 2008, from http://www.tlainc.com/ articl79.htm

Hutzschenreuter, T., & Listner, F. (2007). A contingency view on knowledge transfer: empirical evidence from the software industry. *Knowledge Management Research & Practice, 5*(2), 136–151. doi:10.1057/palgrave.kmrp.8500136

Iverson, J., & Burkart, P. (2007). Managing Electronic Documents and Work Flows: Enterprise Content Management at Work in Nonprofit Organizations. *Nonprofit Management & Leadership, 17*(4), 403–419. doi:10.1002/nml.160

Jennex, M. E., & Olfman, L. (2004). *Modeling Knowledge Management Success.* Paper presented at the Conference on Information Science and Technology Management, CISTM.

Jennex, M. E., & Olfman, L. (2005). Assessing Knowledge Management Success. *International Journal of Knowledge Management, 1*(2), 33–49.

Johns Hopkins University. (2005). *Comparative Non-Profit Sector Project – Comparative Data Tables (Table 2: Volunteering in 36 countries).* Retrieved July 29, 2008, from http://www.jhu.edu/ ~cnp/pdf/table201.pdf

Kilbourne, W. E., & Marshall, K. P. (2005). The transfer of for profit marketing technology to the non-for-profit domain: from the theory of technology. *Journal of Marketing Theory and Practice, 13*(1), 14–25.

Kim, S., & Lee, H. (2006). The Impact of Organizational Context and Information Technology on Employee Knowledge-Sharing Capabilities. *Public Administration Review, 66*(3), 370–385. doi:10.1111/j.1540-6210.2006.00595.x

King, W. R. (2007). Keynote paper: Knowledge management: a systems perspective. *International Journal of Business Systems and Research, 1*(1), 5–28.

Korman, A. K. (1970). Toward a Hypothesis of Work Behavior. *The Journal of Applied Psychology, 54*(1), 31–41. doi:10.1037/h0028656

Leonard, D., & Sensiper, S. (1998). The role of tacit knowledge in group innovation. *California Management Review, 40*(3), 112–132.

Lettieri, E., Borga, F., & Savoldelli, A. (2004). Knowledge management in non-profit organizations. *Journal of Knowledge Management, 8*(6), 16–30. doi:10.1108/13673270410567602

Maier, R. (2002). *Knowledge Management Systems: Information and Communication Technologies for Knowledge Management*. Berlin: Springer-Verlag.

Massey, A. P., Montoya-Weiss, M. M., & O'Driscoll, T. M. (2002). Knowledge Management in Pursuit of Performance: Insights from Nortel Networks. *Management Information Systems Quarterly, 26*(3), 269–289. doi:10.2307/4132333

Michailova, S., & Hutchings, K. (2006). National Cultural Influences on Knowledge Sharing: A Comparison of China and Russia. *Journal of Management Studies, 43*(3), 383–405. doi:10.1111/j.1467-6486.2006.00595.x

Nevo, D., & Chan, Y. E. (2007a). A Delphi study of knowledge management systems: Scope and requirements. *Information & Management, 44*, 583–597. doi:10.1016/j.im.2007.06.001

Nevo, D., & Chan, Y. E. (2007b). A temporal approach to expectations and desires from knowledge management systems. *Decision Support Systems, 44*, 298–312. doi:10.1016/j.dss.2007.04.003

Nonaka, I. (1994). A Dynamic theory of Organizational Knowledge Creation. *Organization Science, 5*(1), 14–37. doi:10.1287/orsc.5.1.14

Nonaka, I., von Krogh, G., & Voelpel, S. (2006). Organizational Knowledge Creation Theory: Evolutionary Paths and Future Advances. *Organization Studies, 27*(8), 1179–1208. doi:10.1177/0170840606066312

Orlikowski, W. J., & Barley, S. R. (2001). Technology and Institutions: What Can Research on Information Technology and Research on Organizations Learn from Each Other? *Management Information Systems Quarterly, 25*(2), 145–165. doi:10.2307/3250927

Parsons, E., & Broadbridge, A. (2006). Job motivation and satisfaction: Unpacking the key factors for charity shop managers. *Journal of Retailing and Consumer Services, 13*(2), 121–131. doi:10.1016/j.jretconser.2005.08.013

Rhodes, J., Hung, R., Lok, P., Lien, B., & Wu, C. (2008). Factors influencing organizational knowledge transfer: implications for corporate performance. *Journal of Knowledge Management, 12*(3), 84–100. doi:10.1108/13673270810875886

Riege, A. (2005). Three-dozen knowledge-sharing barriers managers must consider. *Journal of Knowledge Management, 9*(3), 18–35. doi:10.1108/13673270510602746

Rizzi, C., Ponte, D., & Bonifacio, M. (2009). A new institutional reading of knowledge management technology adoption. *Journal of Knowledge Management, 13*(4), 75–85. doi:10.1108/13673270910971842

Saidal, J. R., & Cour, S. (2003). Information Technology and the Voluntary Sector Workplace. *Nonprofit and Voluntary Sector Quarterly, 32*(1), 5–24. doi:10.1177/0899764002250004

Sowa, J. E., Selden, S. C., & Sandfort, J. R. (2004). No Longer Unmeasurable? A Multidimensional Integrated Model of Nonprofit Organizational Effectiveness. *Nonprofit and Voluntary Sector Quarterly, 33*(4), 711–728. doi:10.1177/0899764004269146

Staples, D. S., Greenaway, K., & McKeen, J. D. (2001). Opportunities for research about managing the knowledge-based enterprise. *International Journal of Management Reviews, 3*(19), 1–20. doi:10.1111/1468-2370.00051

Statistics Canada. (2006). *Canada Survey of Giving, Volunteering and Participating 2004.* Retrieved July 29, 2008, from http://www.statcan.ca/Daily/ Emglish/060605/d060605a.htm

Taylor, W. A., & Wright, G. H. (2004). Organizational Readiness for Successful Knowledge Sharing: Challenges for Public Sector Managers. *Information Resources Management Journal,* *17*(2), 22–37.

The Center for Philanthropy at Indiana University. (2008). *Briefing on the Economy and Giving.* Retrieved September 29, 2009, from http://www.philanthropy.iupui.edu/ Research/docs/ December2008_BriefingOnTheEconomyAndGiving.pdf

Turban, E., & Aronson, J. E. (2001). *Decision Support Systems and Intelligent Systems* (6th ed.). Upper Saddle River, NJ: Prentice Hall.

Von Krogh, G. (1998). Care in knowledge creation. *California Management Review, 40*(3), 133–153.

Vuong, D., & Staples, D. S. (2008). *Sharing Knowledge in Voluntary Not-For-Profit Organizations.* Paper presented at the Administrative Sciences Association of Canada Conference, Halifax, NS, Canada.

Walsh, J. P., & Ungson, G. R. (1991). Organizational Memory. *Academy of Management Review, 16*(1), 57–91. doi:10.2307/258607

Wilson, J. (2000). Volunteering. *Annual Review of Sociology, 26,* 215–240. doi:10.1146/annurev.soc.26.1.215

Wu, J. H., & Wang, Y. M. (2006). Measuring KMS success: A respecification of the DeLone and MacLean model. *Information & Management, 43*(6), 728–739. doi:10.1016/j.im.2006.05.002

Zack, M. (1999). Managing Codified Knowledge. *Sloan Management Review, 40*(4), 45–48.

This work was previously published in International Journal of Knowledge Management, Volume 6, Issue 4, edited by Murray E. Jennex, pp. 87-97, copyright 2010 by IGI Publishing (an imprint of IGI Global).

Compilation of References

Abou-Zeid, E. S. (2002). A knowledge management reference model. *Journal of Knowledge Management, 6*(5), 486–499. doi:10.1108/13673270210450432

Achrol, R. S., & Kotler, P. (1999). Marketing in the network economy. *Journal of Marketing, 63*, 146–163. doi:10.2307/1252108

Afiouni. (2007). Human resource management and knowledge management: A road map toward improving organizational performance. *Journal of American Academy of Business, 11*(2), 124-130.

Agarwal, R., & Tanniru, M. R. (1990). Knowledge acquisition using structured interviewing: An empirical investigation. *Journal of Management Information Systems, 7*(11), 123–140.

Aggestam, L. (2006a, September 4-8). Towards a maturity model for learning organizations – the role of Knowledge Management. In *Proceedings of the 7th International Workshop on Theory and Applications of Knowledge Management (TAKMA 2006), 17th International Conference on Database and Expert Systems Applications (DEXA 2006),* Krakow, Poland (pp. 141-145).

Aggestam, L. (2006b, May 21-24). Wanted: A framework for IT-supported KM. In *Proceedings of the 17th Information Resources Management Association (IRMA) Conference,* Washington, DC (pp. 46-49).

Aggestam, L., & Backlund, P. (2007). *Strategic knowledge management issues when designing knowledge repositories.* Paper presented at the 15th European Conference on Information Systems (ECIS).

Ahlgren, R., & Markkula, J. (2005, June 13-15). *Design Patterns and Organisational Memory in Mobile Application Development.* Paper presented at the Sixth International Conference on Product Focused Software Process Improvement (PROFES 2005), Oulu, Finland. Alexander, C. (1979). *The Timeless Way of Building.* New York: Oxford University Press.

Ajzen, I. (1991). The theory of planned behavior. *Organizational Behavior and Human Decision Processes, 50*, 179–211. doi:10.1016/0749-5978(91)90020-T

Ajzen, I., & Fishbein, M. (1977). Attitude-behavior relations: A theoretical analysis and review of empirical research. *Psychological Bulletin, 84*, 888–918. doi:10.1037/0033-2909.84.5.888

Akhavan, P., Jafari, M., & Fathian, M. (2006). Critical success factors of knowledge management systems: A multi-case analysis. *European Business Review, 18*(2), 97–113. doi:10.1108/09555340610651820

Alavi, M., & Leidner, D. (1999). Knowledge Management Systems: Issues, Challenges, and Benefits. *Communication of the AIS, 1*(7), 2–37.

Alavi, M., & Leidner, D. (2001). Knowledge Management and Knowledge Management Systems: Conceptual Foundations and Research Issues. *Management Information Systems Quarterly, 5*(1), 107–156. doi:10.2307/3250961

Alavi, M., & Leidner, D. (2001). Review: Knowledge management and knowledge management system: Conceptual foundations and research issues. *MIS Quarterly, 25*(1), 107–136. doi:10.2307/3250961

Al-Busaidi, K. A. (2005). *A Socio-Technical Investigation of the Determinants of Knowledge Management Systems Usage*. Unpublished doctoral dissertation, Claremont Graduate University, Claremont, CA.

Al-Busaidi, K. A. (2009). Strengths and Weaknesses of Corporate Portal. In K. Soliman (Ed.), *Proceedings of the 13th International Business Information Management Association Conference: Knowledge Management and Innovation in Advancing Economies* (pp. 875-882). International Business Information Management Association (IBIMA).

Al-Busaidi, K., & Olfman, L. (2005). An Investigation of the Determinants of Knowledge Management Systems Success in Omani Organizations. *Journal of Global Information Technology Management, 8*(3), 6–27.

Alexander, C., Ishikawa, S., & Silverstein, M. (1977). *A Pattern Language: Towns, Buildings, Construction*. New York: Oxford University Press.

AlKhaldi, F., Karadsheh, L., & Alhawari, S. (2006). *Knowledge management life cycle: An investigative methodology toward a conceptual framework*. Paper presented at the Sixth Annual international Conference for Business Ethics and Knowledge Society, Al-Zaytoonah Private University of Jordan.

Allee, V. (1997). *The knowledge evolution: Expanding organizational intelligence*. Boston: Butterworth-Heinemann.

Alryalat, H., & Alhawari, S. (2008, January 4-6). A review of theoretical framework: How to make process about, for, from knowledge work. In *Proceedings of the 9th International Business Information Management Association Conference (IBIMA) in the Information Management in Modern Organization*, Marrakech, Morocco (pp. 37-50). ISBN: 0-9753393-8-9.

Alryalat, H., Alhawari, S., & Al-Omoush, K. (2007, June 20-22). An integrated model for knowledge management and customer relationship management. In *Proceedings of the 8th International Business Information Management Association Conference (IBIMA) in the Networked Economy*, Dublin, Ireland (pp. 446- 453). ISBN: 0-9753393-7-0.

Althoff, K.-D., Decker, B., Hartkopf, S., Jedlitschka, A., Nick, M., & Rech, J. (2001, July 24-25). *Experience Management: The Fraunhofer Institute for Experimental Software Engineering (IESE) Experience Factory*. Paper presented at the Industrial Conference Data Mining: Data Mining, Data Warehouse and Knowledge Management, Leipzig, Germany.

Ambler, S. (2002). *Agile Modeling: Effective Practices for eXtreme Programming and the Unified Process*. John Wiley & Sons, Inc.

Ambrosini, V., & Bowman, C. (2001). Tacit knowledge: Some suggestions for operationalization. *Journal of Management Studies, 38*(6), 811–829. doi:10.1111/1467-6486.00260

American Productivity and Quality Center. Arthur Andersen. (2005). *The Knowledge Management Assessment Tool (KMAT)*. Retrieved July 17, 2009, from http://kwork.org/White_Papers/KMAT_BOK_DOC.pdf

Amin, A., & Roberts, J. (2008). Knowing in action, beyond communities of practice. *Research Policy, 37*, 353–369. doi:10.1016/j.respol.2007.11.003

Ancori, B., Bureth, A., & Cohendet, P. (2000). The economics of knowledge: The debate about codification and tacit knowledge. *Industrial and Corporate Change, 9*(2), 255–287. doi:10.1093/icc/9.2.255

Aneja, A., Rowan, C., & Brooksby, B. (2000). Corporate portal framework for transforming content chaos on Intranets. *Intel Technology Journal, Q1*, 1-7.

Ang, Z., & Massingham, P. (2007). National Culture and standardization versus adaptation of knowledge management. *Journal of Knowledge Management, 11*(2), 5–21. doi:10.1108/13673270710738889

Antonacopoulou, E., & Chiva, R. (2007). The social complexity of organizational learning: The dynamics of learning and organizing. *Management Learning, 38*(3), 277–295. doi:10.1177/1350507607079029

Appleton, B. A. (1997). Patterns and Software: Essential Concepts and Terminology. *Object Magazine Online, 3*(5), 20–25.

Arbuckle, J. (2007). *Amos 7.0 User's Guide. Spring House*. PA: Amos Development Corporation.

Ardichvili, A. (2001). The role of human resource development in transitioning from technology-focused to people-centered knowledge management . In Sleezer, C., Wentling, T., & Cude, R. (Eds.), *Human resource development and information technology: Making global connections* (pp. 89–104). Boston, MA: Kluwer Academic Publishers.

Ardichvili, A. (2008). Learning and knowledge sharing in virtual communities of practice: Motivators, barriers and enablers. *Advances in Developing Human Resources*, *10*(4), 541–554. doi:10.1177/1523422308319536

Ardichvili, A., Maurer, M., Li, W., Wentling, T., & Stuedemann, R. (2006). Cultural influences on knowledge sharing through online communities of practice. *Journal of Knowledge Management*, *10*(1), 94–107. doi:10.1108/13673270610650139

Argote, L. (1999). *Organizational Learning: Creating, Retaining, and Transferring Knowledge*. Norwell, MA: Kluwer.

Argyris, C., & Schön, D. (1978). *Organizational learning: A theory of action perspective*. Reading, MA: Addison Wesley.

Armario, J. M., Ruiz, D. M., & Armario, E. M. (2008). Market Orientation and Internationalization in Small and Medium-Sized Enterprises. *Journal of Small Business Management*, *46*(4), 485–511. doi:10.1111/j.1540-627X.2008.00253.x

Armstrong, R. W. (1996). The relationship between culture and perception of ethical problems in international Marketing. *Journal of Business Ethics*, *15*(11), 1199–1208. doi:10.1007/BF00412818

Ashby, W. R. (1956). *Introduction to Cybernetics*. London: Wiley.

Ashkanasy, N., Gupta, V., Mayfield, M. S., & Trevor-Roberts, E. (2004). Future orientation . In House, R. J., Hanges, P. J., Javidan, M., Dorfman, P. W., & Gupta, V. (Eds.), *Culture, leadership, and organizations: The GLOBE study of 62 societies* (pp. 282–343). Thousand Oaks, CA: Sage.

Asian Economic News. (2005). Chinese economy to surpass Japan by 2020: World bank. Retrieved February 11, 2009, from http://findarticles.com/p/ articles/ mi_m0WDP/is_/ ai_n15801767

Asimakou, T. (2009). The knowledge dimension of innovation management. *Knowledge Management . Research & Practice*, *7*, 82–90.

Assimakopoulos, D., & Yan, J. (2006). Sources of knowledge acquisition for Chinese software engineers. *R & D Management*, *36*(1), 97–106. doi:10.1111/j.1467-9310.2005.00418.x

Avison, D. E., & Fitzgerald, G. (1998). *Information systems development: Methodologies, techniques and tools* (2nd ed.). New York: McGraw Hill

Baark, E. (2007). Knowledge and innovation in China: Historical legacies and emerging institutions. *Asia Pacific Business Review*, *13*(3), 337–356. doi:10.1080/13602380701291917

Bagchi, K., Cerveny, R., Hart, P., & Peterson, M. (2003). The influence of national culture on information technology product adoption. In *Proceedings of the 9th American Conference on Information Systems (AMCIS)* (pp. 112-131).

Bagchi, K., Hart, P., & Peterson, M. (2004). National culture and information technology product adoption. *Journal of Global Information Technology Management*, *7*(4), 29–46.

Baggetun, R., Rusman, E., & Poggi, C. (2004, June 21-26). Paper presented at the 2004 World Conference on Educational Multimedia, Hypermedia and Telecommunications (ED-MEDIA 2004), Lugano, Switzerland.

Baiman, S. (1990). Agency research in managerial accounting: A second look. *Accounting, Organizations and Society*, *15*, 341–371. doi:10.1016/0361-3682(90)90023-N

Balkin, D. B., Markman, G. D., & Gomez-Mejia, L. R. (2000). Is CEO pay in high-technology firms related to innovation? *Academy of Management Journal*, *43*(6), 1118–1129. doi:10.2307/1556340

Ballou, D. P., & Pazer, H. L. (1985). Modeling data and process quality in multi-input, multi-output information systems. *Management Science, 31*(2), 150–162. doi:10.1287/mnsc.31.2.150

Bandura, A. (1996). *Social foundations of thought and action: a social cognitive theory.* Englewood Cliffs, NJ: Prentice-Hall.

Banerjee, P., & Richter, F. J. (2001). *Intangibles in competition and cooperation: Euro-Asian perspectives.* New York: Palgrave.

Banker, R., Chang, H., & Kao, Y.-C. (2002). Impact of information technology on public accounting firm productivity. *Journal of Information Systems, 16*(2), 209–222. doi:10.2308/jis.2002.16.2.209

Bao, Y., & Zhao, S. (2004). MICRO contracting for tacit knowledge – a study of contractual arrangements in international technology transfer. *Problems and Perspectives in Management, 2,* 279–303.

Barab, S., Schatz, S., & Scheckler, R. (2004). Using activity theory to conceptualize online community and using online community to conceptualize activity theory. *Mind, Culture, and Activity, 11*(10), 25–47. doi:10.1207/s15327884mca1101_3

Barkema, H. G., Bell, H. J., & Pennings, J. M. (1996). Foreign entry, cultural barriers, and learning. *Strategic Management Journal, 17,* 151–166. doi:10.1002/(SICI)1097-0266(199602)17:2<151::AID-SMJ799>3.0.CO;2-Z

Barney, J. (1991). Firm resources and sustained competitive advantage. *Journal of Management, 17*(1), 99–120. doi:10.1177/014920639101700108

Baron, R. M., & Kenny, D. A. (1986). The moderator-mediator variable distinction in social psychological research: Conceptual, strategic, and statistical considerations. *Journal of Personality and Social Psychology, 51*(6), 1173–1182. doi:10.1037/0022-3514.51.6.1173

Barry, B., & Richard, T. (2003). Using Risk to Balance Agile and Plan-Driven Methods. *Computer, 36*(6), 57–66. doi:10.1109/MC.2003.1204376

Barsky, N., & Marchant, G. (2000). The most valuable resource: measuring and managing intellectual capital. *Strategic Finance Magazine, 81*(8), 58–62.

Bartol, K. M., & Srivastava, A. (2002). Encouraging knowledge sharing: The role of organizational reward systems. *Journal of Leadership & Organizational Studies, 9*(1), 64–76. doi:10.1177/107179190200900105

Bartol, K., & Locke, E. (2000). Incentives and motivation. In Rynes, S., & Gerhart, B. (Eds.), *Compensation in Organizations: Progress* (pp. 104–147). San Francisco: Jossey-Bass.

Bartol, K., & Srivastava, A. (2002). Encouraging knowledge sharing: The role of organizational reward systems. *Journal of Leadership & Organizational Studies, 9*(1), 64–76. doi:10.1177/107179190200900105

Basili, V. R., Lindvall, M., & Costa, P. (2001, June 13-15). *Implementing the Experience Factory concepts as a set of Experience Bases.* Paper presented at the 13th Int. Conf. on Software Engineering & Knowledge Engineering, Buenos Aires, Argentina.

Basili, V. R., Caldiera, G., & Rombach, H. D. (1994). Experience Factory. In Marciniak, J. J. (Ed.), *Encyclopedia of Software Engineering* (Vol. 1, pp. 469–476). New York: John Wiley & Sons.

Bass, B. (1985). *Leadership and performance beyond expectations.* New York: The Free Press.

Bassi, L., & Van Buren, M. (1999). Valuing investments in intellectual capital. *International Journal of Technology Management, 18*(5), 414–432. doi:10.1504/IJTM.1999.002779

Bastøe, K., & Dahl, P. (1996). *Organisationsutveckling i offentlig verksamhet.* Lund, Sweden: Utbildningshuset Studentlitteratur.

Bate, P. (1994). *Strategic for culture change.* Oxford, UK: Butterworth-Heinemann.

Becerra-Fernandez, I., Gonzalez, A., & Sabherwal, R. (2004). *Knowledge management: Challenges, solutions and technologies* (1st ed.). Upper Saddle River, NJ: Pearson Education Inc.

Becerra-Fernandez, I., & Sabherwal, R. (2001). Organizational Knowledge Management: A Contingency Perspective. *Journal of Management Information Systems, 18*(1), 23–55.

Beck, K. (1999b). *eXtreme Programming eXplained: Embrace Change*. Reading, MA: Addison-Wesley.

Becker, S., & Whisler, T. (1967). The innovative organization: A selective review of current theory and research. *The Journal of Business, 40*, 462–469. doi:10.1086/295011

Beckhard, R., & Pritchard, P. (1992). *Changing the essence: the art of creating and leading fundamental change in organizations*. San Francisco: Jossey-Bass.

Beck, K. (1999a). *Extreme programming explained: embrace change*. Harlow, UK: Addison-Wesley.

Beck, K., & Fowler, M. (1999). Bad Smells in Code . In Booch, G., Jacobson, I., & Rumbaugh, J. (Eds.), *Refactoring: Improving the Design of Existing Code* (1st ed., pp. 75–88). Reading, MA: Addison-Wesley.

Begel, A., & Nagappan, N. (2008). *Pair programming: what's in it for me?* Kaiserslautern, Germany: ACM.

Belardo, S., Ballou, D. P., & Pazer, H. L. (2004). Analysis and design of information systems: A knowledge quality perspective . In Anderson, K. V., & Vendelo, M. T. (Eds.), *The Past and Future of Information Systems* (pp. 43–59). New York: Elsevier.

Belardo, S., & Pazer, H. L. (1985). Scope/Complexity: A framework for the classification and analysis of information-decision systems. *Journal of Management Information Systems, 2*(2), 55–72.

Belbaly, N., Benbya, H., & Meissonier, R. (2007). An empirical investigation of the customer knowledge creation impact on NPD performance. In *Proceedings of the 40th Hawaii International Conference on System Sciences* (pp. 193a). Washington, DC: IEEE Computer Society.

Benbya, H., Passiante, G., & Belbaly, N. (2004). Corporate portal: a tool for knowledge management synchronization. *International Journal of Information Management, 24*, 201–220. doi:10.1016/j.ijinfomgt.2003.12.012

Bennett, R., & Gabriel, H. (1999). Organisational factors and knowledge management within large marketing departments: an empirical study. *Journal of Knowledge Management, 3*(3), 212–225. doi:10.1108/13673279910288707

Bergeron, F., Raymond, L., & Rivard, S. (2004). Ideal patterns of strategic alignment and business performance. *Information & Management, 41*(8), 1003–1020. doi:10.1016/j.im.2003.10.004

Bergman, J.-P. (2005). *Supporting Knowledge Creation and Sharing in the Early Phases of the Strategic Innovation Process (Tech. Rep.)*. Lappeenranta, Finland: Lappeenranta University of Technology.

Bernard, R. (1988). *Research methods in cultural anthropology*. Newbury Park, CA: Sage.

Berrell, M., Wrathall, J., & Wright, P. (2001). A model for Chinese management education: Adapting the case study method to transfer management knowledge. *Cross Cultural Management, 8*(1), 28–44. doi:10.1108/13527600110797182

Bersin., & Associates. (2006). *New study looks at US corporate learning market. Institute for Competitive Intelligence*. Retrieved from http://www.trainingreference.co.uk/ news/gn060329a.htm

Beveren, J. V. (2003). Does health care for knowledge management? *Journal of Knowledge Management, 7*(1), 90–95. doi:10.1108/13673270310463644

Bhaskar, R., & Zhang, Y. (2005). CRM systems used for targeting market: A case at Cisco Systems. In *Proceedings of the International Conference on e-Business Engineering* (pp. 183-186). Washington, DC: IEEE Computer Society.

Bhatt, G. D. (2001). Knowledge management in organizations: Examining the interaction between technologies, techniques, and people. *Journal of Knowledge Management, 5*(1), 68–75. doi:10.1108/13673270110384419

Bhatt, G. D., & Zaveri, J. (2002). The enabling role of decision support systems in organizational learning. *Decision Support Systems, 32*, 297–309. doi:10.1016/S0167-9236(01)00120-8

Bierly, P., & Chakrabarti, A. (1999). Generic knowledge strategies in the U.S. pharmaceutical industry. In M. H. Zack (Ed.), *Knowledge and strategy*. Boston: Butterworth-Heinemann.

Binney, D. (2001). The knowledge management spectrum – understanding the KM landscape. *Journal of Knowledge Management, 5*(1), 33–42. doi:10.1108/13673270110384383

Birk, A., Dingsøyr, T., & Stålhane, T. (2002). Postmortem: Never Leave a Project without It. *IEEE Software*, *19*(3), 43–45. doi:10.1109/MS.2002.1003452

Birkinshaw, J., & Hood, N. (1998). Multinational subsidiary evolution: Capability and charter change in foreign-owned subsidiary companies. *Academy of Management Review*, *23*(4), 773–795. doi:10.2307/259062

Birkinshaw, J., Hood, N., & Jonsson, S. (1998). Building firm-specific advantages in multinational corporations: the role of subsidiary initiative. *Strategic Management Journal*, *19*(3), 221–242. doi:10.1002/(SICI)1097-0266(199803)19:3<221::AID-SMJ948>3.0.CO;2-P

Birnberg, J., Shields, M., & Young, M. (1990). The case for multiple methods in empirical management accounting research (With an illustration from budget setting). *Journal of Management Accounting Research*, *2*, 33–66.

Bjørnson, F. O., & Dingsøyr, T. (2008). Knowledge Management in Software Engineering: A Systematic Review of Studied Concepts, Findings and Research Methods Used. *Information and Software Technology*, *50*(11), 1055–1068. doi:10.1016/j.infsof.2008.03.006

Blanning, R. W., & Reinig, B. A. (2005). A Framework for Conducting Political Event Analysis Using Group Support Systems. *Decision Support Systems*, *38*, 511–527. doi:10.1016/j.dss.2003.09.006

Blodgood, J. M., & Salisbury, W. D. (2001). Understanding the influence of organizational change strategies on information technology and knowledge management strategies. *Decision Support Systems*, *31*, 55–69. doi:10.1016/S0167-9236(00)00119-6

Bloom, B. S. (1956). *Taxonomy of Educational Objectives*. New York: David McKay Co.

Bock, G. W., Zmud, R. W., Kim, Y., & Lee, J. (2005). Behavioral Intention Formation in Knowledge Sharing: Examining the Roles of Extrinsic Motivators, Social-Psychological Forces, and Organizational Climate. *Management Information Systems Quarterly*, *29*(1), 87–111.

Bohannan, P. (1959). The impact of money on an African subsistence economy. *The Journal of Economic History*, *19*, 491–503.

Bohn, R. E. (1994). Measuring and managing technological knowledge. *Sloan Management Review*, 61–73.

Bolman, L. G., & Deal, T. E. (1997). *Nya perspektiv på organisation och ledarskap*. Lund, Sweden: Andra upplagan, Studentlitteratur.

Bonner, S., Hastie, R., Sprinkle, G., & Young, S. M. (2000). A review of the effects of financial incentives on performance in laboratory tasks: Implications for management accounting. *Journal of Management Accounting Research*, *12*(1), 19–64. doi:10.2308/jmar.2000.12.1.19

Bontis, N., & Serenko, A. (2009). A causal model of human capital antecedents and consequents in the financial services industry. *Journal of Intellectual Capital*, *10*(1), 53–69. doi:10.1108/14691930910922897

Boonmatthaya, R., Benjathum, C., Pomdong, P., Witaporn, S., Jimmee, S., & Paireenart, S. (2005). *Synthesizing the local body of knowledge concerning knowledge management for Joyful Communities in Northeast Thailand: A case study of Indra Paeng Network, Isan Folk Sages and Si Sa Asok community*. Bangkok, Thailand: Office of Research Supporting Fund.

Bostrom, R. P. (1989). Successful application of communication techniques to improve the systems development process. *Information & Management*, *16*(5), 279–295. doi:10.1016/0378-7206(89)90005-0

Bouthillier, F., & Shearer, K. (2002). Understanding knowledge management and information management: the need for an empirical perspective. *Information Research Journal*, *8*(1), 1–39.

Bradfield, R., Wright, G., Burt, G., Cairns, G., & van der Heijden, K. (2005). The origins and evolution of scenario techniques in long range business planning. *Futures*, *37*, 795–812. doi:10.1016/j.futures.2005.01.003

Bradshaw, D., & Brash, C. (2001). Management customer relationships in the e business world: how to personalise computer relationships for increased profitability. *International Journal of Retail & Distribution Management*, *29*(12), 520–530. doi:10.1108/09590550110696969

Braga, R., Ré, R., & Masiero, P. C. (2007, May 27-30). *A Process to Create Analysis Pattern Languages for Specific Domains*. Paper presented at the Sixth Latin American Conference on Pattern Languages of Programming (SugarLoafPLoP 2007), Porto de Galinhas, Brazil.

Branine, M. (1996). Observations on training and management development in the People's Republic of China. *Management Development in China, 25*(1), 25–39.

Brazel, J., Agoglia, C., & Hatfield, R. (2004). Electronic versus face-to-face review: The effects of alternative forms of review on auditors' performance. *Accounting Review, 79*(4), 949–966. doi:10.2308/accr.2004.79.4.949

Broadbent, M. (1998). The phenomenon of knowledge management: What does it mean to the information profession? *Information Outlook, 2*(5), 23–33.

Brock, K. L. (2003). Introduction . In Brock, K. L., & Banting, K. G. (Eds.), *The Nonprofit Sector in Interesting Times*. Kingston, ON, Canada: McGill-Queen's University Press.

Brown, J. S., & Duguid, P. (2000). *The social life of information*. Boston: Harvard Business School Press.

Browne, G. J., & Rogich, M. B. (2001). An empirical investigation of user requirements elicitation: Comparing the effectiveness of prompting techniques. *Journal of Management Information Systems, 17*(4), 223–249.

Brown, J. S., Collins, A., & Duguid, P. (1989). Situated cognition and the culture of learning. *Educational Research, 18*(1), 32–42.

Brown, J. S., & Duguid, P. (1991). Organizational learning and communities of practice. *Organization Science, 2*(1), 40–47. doi:10.1287/orsc.2.1.40

Brown, J. S., & Duguid, P. (1991). Organizational learning and communities of practice: Toward a unified view of working, learning, and innovation. *Organization Science, 2*(1), 40–57. doi:10.1287/orsc.2.1.40

Brown, J. S., & Duguid, P. (1996). Organizational Learning and Communities-of-Practice: Toward a Unified View of Working, Learning, and Innovation . In Cohen, M. D., & Sproull, L. S. (Eds.), *Organizational Learning* (pp. 58–82). Thousand Oaks, CA: Sage.

Brown, J. S., & Duguid, P. (2001a). Knowledge and organization: A social-practice perspective. *Organization Science, 12*(2), 198–213. doi:10.1287/orsc.12.2.198.10116

Brown, J. S., & Duguid, P. (2001b). Structure and Spontaneity: Knowledge and Organization . In Nonaka, I., & Teece, D. (Eds.), *Managing Industrial Knowledge* (pp. 44–67). London: Sage.

Brown, J., & Duguid, P. (2000). Balancing act: How to capture knowledge without killing it. *Harvard Business Review, 78*(5), 3–7.

Broy, M., & Rombach, H. D. (2002). Software Engineering. Wurzeln, Stand und Perspektiven. *Informatik-Spektrum, 25*(6), 438–451. doi:10.1007/s002870200266

Bruton, G. D., Dess, G. G., & Janney, J. J. (2007). Knowledge management in technology-focused firms in emerging economics: Caveats on capabilities, networks, and real options. *Asia Pacific Journal of Management, 24*(2), 115–130. doi:10.1007/s10490-006-9023-2

Bryson, J. M., & Alston, F. K. (1996). *Creating and implementing your strategic plan: A workbook for public and nonprofit organizations*. San Francisco, CA: Josssey-Bass.

Bubenko, J. A., Jr., Persson, A., & Stirna, J. (2001). *User guide of the knowledge management approach using enterprise knowledge patterns* (Deliverable D3, IST Project No. IST-2000-28401). Stockholm, Sweden: Department of Computer and Systems Sciences, Royal Institute of Technology.

Buckley, P. J., Clegg, J., & Tan, H. (2004). Knowledge transfer to China: Policy lesions from foreign affiliates. *Transnational Corporations, 13*(1), 31–72.

Buckman, R. (1999). Collaborative knowledge. *Human Resource Planning, 22*(1), 22–23.

Bueren, A., Schierholz, R., Kolbe, L., & Brenner, W. (2004). Customer knowledge management improving performance of customer relationship management with knowledge management. In *Proceedings of the 37th Hawaii International Conference on System Sciences* (pp. 70172b). Washington, DC: IEEE Computer Society.

Bueren, A., Schierholz, R., Kolbe, L., & Brenner, W. (2005). Improving performance of customer processes with knowledge management. *Business Process Management Journal, 11*(5), 573–588. doi:10.1108/14637150510619894

Bukowitz, W. R., & Williams, R. L. (1999). *The knowledge management field book*. Upper Saddle River, NJ: Prentice-Hall.

Bukowitz, W., & Petrash, G. (1997). Visualizing, measuring and managing knowledge. *Research Technology Management, 40*(4), 24–31.

Burrows, G. R., Drummond, D. L., & Martinsons, M. G. (2005). To understand KM in China. *Communications of the ACM, 48*(4), 73–76. doi:10.1145/1053291.1053322

Burt, W., & Taylor, J. (2003). New Technologies, Embedded Values and Strategic Change: Evidence From the U.K. Voluntary Sector. *Nonprofit and Voluntary Sector Quarterly, 32*(1), 115–127. doi:10.1177/0899764002250009

Buschmann, F., Henney, K., & Schmidt, D. C. (2007). Pattern-Oriented Software Architecture: *Vol. 5. On Patterns and Pattern Languages*. New York: John Wiley and Sons Inc.

Bush, V. (1945). As We May Think. *The Atlantic Online, 176*, 101–108.

Buttle, F. (2004). *Customer relationship management*. Oxford, UK: Elsevier Butterworth- Heinemann.

Byrd, T. A., Cossick, K. L., & Zmud, R. W. (1992). A synthesis of research on requirements determination and knowledge acquisition techniques. *Management Information Systems Quarterly, 16*(1), 117–138. doi:10.2307/249704

Cai, J., Gao, J., Wang, H. Y., & Bai, C. L. (2006). Factorings effecting core competency of knowledge organization in China. [Science and Technology]. *Journal of Tsinghua University, 46*(s1), 970–974.

Cao, Y., & Gruca, T. S. (2005). Reducing adverse selection through customer relationship management. *Journal of Marketing, 69*, 219–229. doi:10.1509/jmkg.2005.69.4.219

Carl, D., Gupta, V., & Javidan, M. (2004). Power distance. In House, R. J., Hanges, P. J., Javidan, M., Dorfman, P. W., & Gupta, V. (Eds.), *Culture, leadership, and organizations: The GLOBE study of 62 societies* (pp. 513–563). Thousand Oaks, CA: Sage.

Carlile, P., & Rebentisch, E. S. (2003). Into the Black Box: The Knowledge Transformation Cycle. *Management Science, 49*(9), 1180–1195. doi:10.1287/mnsc.49.9.1180.16564

Carlsson, S. A. (2001, June 27-29). *Knowledge management in network context*. Paper presented at the Ninth Conference on Information Systems, Bled, Slovenia.

Carnall, C. (1997). *Strategic change*. Boston: Butterworth-Heinmann.

Carroll, J. (1967). A note on departmental autonomy conflict. *Administrative Science Quarterly, 14*, 507–522.

Carroll, S., Beyerlein, S., Ford, M., & Apple, D. (1996). The Learning Assessment Journal as a tool for structured reflection in process education. In [Washington, DC: IEEE.]. *Proceedings of Frontiers in Education, 96*, 310–313.

Cascella, V. (2002). Effective strategic planning. *Quality Progress, 35*(11), 62–67.

Chakravarthy, B. S. (1987). On tailoring a strategic planning system to its context: some empirical evidence. *Strategic Management Journal, 8*(6), 517–534.

Chakravarthy, B., McEvily, S., Doz, Y., & Rau, D. (2005). Knowledge Management and Competitive Advantage. In Easterby-Smith, M., & Lyles, M. A. (Eds.), *Handbook of Organizational Learning and Knowledge Management* (pp. 305–323). Oxford, UK: Blackwell.

Chaminade, C., & Johanson, U. (2003). Can guidelines for intellectual capital management and reporting be considered without addressing cultural differences? *Journal of Intellectual Capital, 4*(4), 528–542. doi:10.1108/14691930310504545

Chan, I., & Chau, P. Y. K. (2005). Why knowledge management fails – lessons from a case study. In M. Jennex (Ed.), *Case studies in knowledge management*. Hershey, PA: Idea Group Publishing.

Chang, S.-C., & Lee, M.-S. (2007). The effects of organizational culture and knowledge management mechanisms on organizational innovation: an empirical study in Taiwan. *Business Review (Federal Reserve Bank of Philadelphia), 7*(1), 295–301.

Chang, S., & Lee, M. (2007). The Effects of Organizational Culture and Knowledge Management Mechanisms on Organizational Innovation: An empirical study in Taiwan. *The Business Review-Cambridge, 7*(1), 295–301.

Chang, W.-C., & Li, S.-T. (2007). Fostering knowledge management deployment in R&D workspaces: a five-stage approach. *R & D Management, 37*(5), 479–493. doi:10.1111/j.1467-9310.2007.00484.x

Chan, I., & Chao, C. (2008). Knowledge management in small and medium-sized enterprises. *Communications of the ACM, 51*(4), 83–88. doi:10.1145/1330311.1330328

Chantarasombat, C. (2004). *Constructing and developing networks for self-reliant communities*. Maha Sarakham, Thailand: Network Center for Learning and Creating Community and Grassroot Economy, Faculty of Education, Mahasarakham University.

Chapman, C. S. (1997). Reflections on a contingent view of accounting. *Accounting, Organizations and Society, 22*, 189–205. doi:10.1016/S0361-3682(97)00001-9

Chau, T., Maurer, F., & Melnik, G. (2003). *Knowledge Sharing: Agile Methods vs. Tayloristic Methods*. Washington, DC: IEEE Press.

Chen, F. (2005). Salesforce incentives, market information, and production/inventory planning. *Management Science, 51*(1), 60–75. doi:10.1287/mnsc.1040.0217

Chenhall, R. H. (2003). Management control system design within its organizational context: Findings from contingency-based research and directions for the future. *Accounting, Organizations and Society, 28*(2/3), 127–168. doi:10.1016/S0361-3682(01)00027-7

Chen, I. J., & Popovich, K. (2003). Understanding Customer Relationship Management (CRM) people, process and technology. *Business Process Management Journal, 9*(5), 672–688. doi:10.1108/14637150310496758

Chen, I. Y. L., & Chen, N. S., & Kinshuk. (2009). Examining the factors influencing participants' knowledge sharing behavior in virtual learning communities. *Journal of Educational Technology & Society, 12*(1), 134–148.

Chen, J., Tong, L., & Ngai, E. W. T. (2007). Inter-organizational knowledge management in complex products and systems: challenges and an exploratory framework. *Journal of Technology Management in China, 2*(2), 134–144. doi:10.1108/17468770710756077

Chen, P., & Forman, C. (2006). Can vendors influence switching costs and compatibility in an environment with open standards? *Management Information Systems Quarterly, 30*, 541–562.

Chen, Q., & Chen, H. (2004). Exploring the success factors of eCRM strategies in practice. *Database Marketing & Customer Strategy Management, 11*(4), 333–343. doi:10.1057/palgrave.dbm.3240232

Chen, S. C., Yang, C. C., Lin, W. T., Yeh, T. M., & Lin, Y. S. (2007). Construction of key model for knowledge management system using AHP-QFD for semiconductor industry in Taiwan. *Journal of Manufacturing Technology Management, 18*(5), 576–598. doi:10.1108/17410380710752671

Child, J., & Tse, D. (2001). China's transition and its implications for international business. *Journal of International Business Studies, 32*, 5–21. doi:10.1057/palgrave.jibs.8490935

China Economic Times. (2002, August 20). *The development of securities investment funds in China*.

Chinese Cultural Connection. (1987). Chinese values and the search for culture-free dimensions of culture. *Journal of Cross-Cultural Psychology, 18*(2), 143–164. doi:10.1177/0022002187018002002

Chin, W. (1998). The partial least square approach to structural equation modelling. In Marcoulides, G. A. (Ed.), *Modern Methods for Business Research* (pp. 295–336). London: Lawrence Erlbaum Associates.

Cho, J. (2008). Issues and Challenges of Agile Software Development with Scrum. *Issues in Information Systems, 9*(2), 188–195.

Chong, S. (2006). KM critical success factors: A comparison of perceived importance versus implementation in Malaysian ICT companies. *The Learning Organization, 13*(3), 230–256. doi:10.1108/09696470610661108

Choo, C. W. (2006). *The knowing organization: how organizations use information to construct meaning, create knowledge, and make decisions*. New York: Oxford University Press.

Chow, C. W., Deng, J., & Ho, J. (2000). The openness of knowledge sharing within organizations: A comparative study of the United States and the People's Republic of China. *Journal of Management Accounting Research, 12*(1), 65–95. doi:10.2308/jmar.2000.12.1.65

Chow, C., Cooper, J., & Waller, W. (1988). Participative budgeting: Effects of a truth-inducing pay scheme and information asymmetry on slack and performance. *Accounting Review, 63*(1), 111–122.

Chow, C., Duh, R. R., & Xiao, J. (2007). Current management accounting practice in the People's Republic of China . In Chapman, C. S., Hopwood, A. G., & Shields, M. D. (Eds.), *Handbook of Management Accounting Research* (*Vol. 2*, pp. 941–986). Oxford, UK: Elsevier.

Chow, C., Harrison, G., McKinnon, J., & Wu, A. (1999). Cultural influences on information sharing in Chinese and Anglo-American organizations: An exploratory study. *Accounting, Organizations and Society, 24*(7), 561–582. doi:10.1016/S0361-3682(99)00022-7

Chow, C., Ho, J., & Vera-Munoz, S. (2008). Exploring the extent and determinants of knowledge sharing in audit engagements. *Asia-Pacific Journal of Accounting & Economics, 15*(2), 141–160.

Chua, A., & Lam, W. (2005). Why KM projects fail: A multi-case analysis. *Journal of Knowledge Management, 9*(3), 6–17. doi:10.1108/13673270510602737

Churchman, C. W. (1979). *The systems approach*. New York: Dell Publishing.

Churchman, C. W., & Schainblatt, A. H. (1965). The researcher and the manager: A Dialectic of Implementation. *Management Science, 11*(4), B69–B87. doi:10.1287/mnsc.11.4.B69

Cinneide, M. O., Kushmerick, N., & Veale, T. (2004, July). Automated Support for Agile Software Reuse. *ERCIM News*.

Clarke, T. (2001). The knowledge economy. *Education + Training, 43*(4/5), 189–196. doi:10.1108/00400910110399184

Cockburn, A. (2006). *Agile Software Development: The Cooperative Game* (2nd ed.). Reading, MA: Addison-Wesley.

Cockburn, A., & Jones, S. (2000). Which way now? Analysing and easing inadequacies in WWW navigation. *International Journal of Human-Computer Studies, 45*, 105–129. doi:10.1006/ijhc.1996.0044

Cody, W. F., Kreulen, J. T., Krishna, V., & Spangler, W. S. (2002). The integration of business intelligence and knowledge management. *IBM Systems Journal, 41*(4), 697–713. doi:10.1147/sj.414.0697

Cohen, W. M., & Levinthal, D. A. (1990). Absorptive Capacity: A new Perspective on Learning and Innovation. *Administrative Science Quarterly, 35*, 128–152. doi:10.2307/2393553

Cole, M., & Engeström, Y. (1993). A cultural-historical approach to distributed cognition . In Solomon, G. (Ed.), *Distributed cognitions: Psychological and educational considerations*. Cambridge, UK: Cambridge University Press.

Collins, C. J., & Smith, K. G. (2006). Knowledge exchange and combination: The role of human resource practices in the performance of high-technology firms. *Academy of Management Journal, 49*(3), 544–560.

Collison, C., & Parcell, G. (2005). *Learning to fly: Practical knowledge management from leading and learning organizations*. New York: Capstone.

Compeau, D., & Higgins, C. (1995). Computer self-efficacy: Development of a measure and initial test. *Management Information Systems Quarterly, 19*(2), 189–211. doi:10.2307/249688

Conant, J. S., & White, J. C. (1999). Marketing program planning, process benefits, and store performance: An initial study among small retail firms. *Journal of Retailing, 75*(4), 525–541. doi:10.1016/S0022-4359(99)00017-2

Connelly, C. E., & Kelloway, E. K. (2003). Predictors of employees' perceptions of knowledge-sharing culture. *Leadership and Organization Development Journal, 24*(5/6), 294–305. doi:10.1108/01437730310485815

Constant, D., Keisler, S., & Sproull, L. (1994). What's mine is ours, or is it? A study of attitudes about information sharing. *Information Systems Research, 5*, 400–421. doi:10.1287/isre.5.4.400

Contractor, F., & Lorange, P. (1988). *Cooperative strategies in international business.* Lexington, MA: Lexington Books.

Cook, S. D. N., & Brown, J. S. (1999). Bridging Epistemologies: The Generative Dance Between Organizational Knowledge and Organizational Knowing. *Organization Science, 10*(4), 381–400. doi:10.1287/orsc.10.4.381

Cook, S., & Brown, J. S. (1999). Bridging epistemologies: The generative dance between organizational knowledge and organizational knowing. *Organization Science, 10*(4), 381–400. doi:10.1287/orsc.10.4.381

Cooper, R. B., & Swanson, E. B. (1979). Management information requirements assessment: The state of the art. *Database, 10*, 5–16.

Coplien, J. O. (1996). *Software Patterns.* SIGS Books.

Coplien, J. O. (2000). A Pattern Language for Writers' Workshops . In Harrison, N. B., Foote, B., & Rohnert, H. (Eds.), *Pattern Languages of Program Design 4.* Reading, MA: Addison-Wesley.

Corder, K. (2001). Acquiring New Technology: Comparing Nonprofit and Public Sector Agencies. *Administration & Society, 33*(2), 193–219. doi:10.1177/00953990122019730

Corral, K., Griffin, J., & Jennex, M. E. (2005). BI experts' perspective: The potential of knowledge management in data warehousing. *Business Intelligence Journal, 10*(1), 36–40.

Coughlan, J. M., Lycett, M., & Macredie, R. D. (2003). Communication issues in requirements elicitation: A content analysis of stakeholder experiences. *Information and Software Technology, 45*(8), 525–537.

Couto, J. P., & Vieira, J. C. (2004). National culture and research and development activities. *The Multinational Business Review, 12*(10), 19–35.

Cox, T. H., Lobel, S. A., & McLeod, P. L. (1991). Effects of ethnic group cultural differences on cooperative and competitive behavior on a group task. *Academy of Management Journal, 34*, 827–847. doi:10.2307/256391

Cram, D., Fuchs, B., Prié, Y., & Mille, A. (2008, June 8-12). *An approach to User-Centric Context-Aware Assistance based on Interaction Traces.* Paper presented at the Fifth International Workshop Modeling and Reasoning in Context (MRC 2008), Delft, The Netherlands.

Cronbach, L. J. (1951). Coefficient alpha and the internal structure of tests. *Psychometrika, 16*, 297–333. doi:10.1007/BF02310555

Cross, R., & Baird, L. (2000). Technology is not enough: Improving performance by building organizational memory. *Sloan Management Review, 41*(3), 41–54.

Cross, R., & Cummings, J. H. (2004). Tie and network correlates of individual performance in knowledge intensive work. *Academy of Management Journal, 47*(6), 928–937. doi:10.2307/20159632

Cukier, W., & Middleton, C. (2003). Evaluating the Web Presence of Voluntary Sector Organizations: An Assessment of Canadian Web Sites. *IT & Society, 1*(3), 102–130.

Daniel, E., & Ward, J. (2006). Integrated service delivery: Exploratory case studies of enterprise portal adoption in UK local government. *Business Process Management Journal, 12*(1), 113–123. doi:10.1108/14637150610643805

DATech .(2004). DATech-Prüfungshandbuch. Usability-Engineering-Prozess. Leitfaden für die Evaluierung des Usability-Engineering-Prozesses bei der Herstellung und Pflege von interaktiven Systemen auf der Grundlage von DIN EN ISO 13407. Frankfurt a. M.: Deutsche Akkreditierungsstelle Technik e.V.

Davenport, T. (2002). *Some principles of knowledge management.* Retrieved from http://www.bus.utexas.edu/Kman/kmprin.htm

Davenport, T. H., & Prusak, L. (1998). *Working knowledge.* Cambridge, MA: Harvard Business School Press.

Davenport, T. H. (1998). Enterprise systems. *Harvard Business Review*, (July-August): 121.

Davenport, T. H., De Long, D. W., & Beers, M. C. (1998). Successful knowledge management projects. *Sloan Management Review, 39*(2), 10–18.

Davenport, T. H., Harris, J. G., De Long, D. W., & Jacobson, A. L. (2001). Data to knowledge to results: Building an analytical capability. *California Management Review*, *43*(2), 117–138.

Davenport, T. H., Jarvenpaa, S. L., & Beers, M. C. (1996). Improving knowledge work processes. *Sloan Management Review*, *39*(2), 43–57.

Davenport, T. H., & Prusak, L. (1998). *Working knowledge*. Boston: Harvard Business School Press.

Davenport, T. H., & Prusak, L. (1998). *Working Knowledge*. Cambridge, MA: Harvard Business Press.

Davenport, T. H., & Prusak, L. (1998). *Working knowledge: How organizations manage what they know*. Boston: Harvard Business School Press.

Davenport, T., Delong, D., & Beers, M. (1998). Successful knowledge management programs. *Sloan Management Review*, *39*, 43–57.

Davenport, T., & Prusak, L. (1998). *Working Knowledge: How Organizations Manage What They Know*. Boston: Harvard Business School Press.

David Skyrme Associates. (2005). *Know-all 10: A quick KM assessment*. Retrieved July 17, 2009, from http://www.skyrme.com/ tools/know10.htm

Davis, A. M. (1988). A comparison of techniques for specification of external systems behavior. *Communications of the ACM*, *31*(9), 1098–1115. doi:10.1145/48529.48534

Davis, F. D. (1989). Perceived usefulness, perceived ease of use, and user acceptance of information technology. *Management Information Systems Quarterly*, *13*(3), 319–340. doi:10.2307/249008

De Carvalho, R. B., Ferreira, M. A., Choo, C. W., & Da Silva, R. V. (2007). The Effects of Enterprise Portals on Knowledge Management Projects . In Tatnall, A. (Ed.), *Encyclopedia of Portal Technologies and Applications* (pp. 296–303). Hershey, PA: IGI Global.

De Long, D. (1997). *Building the knowledge-based organization: How culture drives knowledge behavior. Working paper for the center for business innovation.* London: Ernst & Young LLP.

De Long, D. W., & Fahey, L. (2000). Diagnosing Cultural Barriers to Knowledge Management. *The Academy of Management Executive*, *14*(4), 113–127.

De Luque, M. S., & Javidan, M. (2004). Uncertainty avoidance . In House, R. J., Hanges, P. J., Javidan, M., Dorfman, P. W., & Gupta, V. (Eds.), *Culture, leadership, and organizations: The GLOBE study of 62 societies* (pp. 602–653). Thousand Oaks, CA: Sage.

Deci, E., Koestner, R., & Ryan, R. (1999a). A meta-analytic review of experiments examining the effects of extrinsic rewards on intrinsic motivation. *Psychological Bulletin*, *125*(6), 627–668. doi:10.1037/0033-2909.125.6.627

Deci, E., Koestner, R., & Ryan, R. (1999b). The undermining effect is a reality after all—extrinsic rewards, task interest, and self-determination: Reply to Eisenberger, Pierce, and Cameron. *Psychological Bulletin*, *125*(6), 692–700. doi:10.1037/0033-2909.125.6.692

Decker, B., Ras, E., Rech, J., Klein, B., Reuschling, C., Höcht, C., et al. (2005). *A Framework for Agile Reuse in Software Engineering using Wiki Technology*. Paper presented at the Conference Professional Knowledge Management - Experiences and Visions, Kaiserslautern, Germany.

DeLone, W. H., & McLean, E. R. (1992). Information systems success: The quest for the dependent variable. *Information Systems Research*, *3*(1), 60–95. doi:10.1287/isre.3.1.60

DeLone, W. H., & McLean, E. R. (2003). The DeLone and MacLean Model of Information Systems Success: A Ten-Year Update. *Journal of Management Information Systems*, *19*(4), 9–30.

DeLone, W., & McLean, E. (1992). Information Systems Success: The quest for the dependent variable. *Information Systems Research*, *3*, 60–95. doi:10.1287/isre.3.1.60

DeLone, W., & McLean, E. R. (2003). The DeLone and McLean model of information systems success: A ten-year update. *Journal of Management Information Systems*, *19*(4), 9–30.

DeLong, D., & Fahey, L. (2000). Diagnosing cultural barriers to knowledge management. *The Academy of Management Executive*, *14*(4), 113–127.

Den Hartog, D. N. (2004). Assertiveness . In House, R. J., Hanges, P. J., Javidan, M., Dorfman, P. W., & Gupta, V. (Eds.), *Culture, leadership, and organizations: The GLOBE study of 62 societies* (pp. 395–436). Thousand Oaks, CA: Sage.

Deng, Q., & Yu, D. (2006). An approach to integrating knowledge management into the product development process. *Journal of Knowledge Management Practice, 7*(2).

Deng, S., & Dart, J. (1994). Measuring market orientation: A multi-factor multi-item approach. *Journal of Marketing Management, 10*(8), 725–742. doi:10.1080/026725 7X.1994.9964318

Denison, T., & Johanson, G. (2007). Surveys of the use of information and communications technologies by community-based organizations. *Journal of Community Informatics, 3*(2). Retrieved from http://ci-journal.net/index.php/ ciej/article/view/316.

Derntl, M., & Botturi, L. (2006). Essential Use Cases for Pedagogical Patterns. *Computer Science Education, 16*(2), 137–156. doi:10.1080/08993400600768182

Després, C. (2001). *Modélisation et Conception d'un Environnement de Suivi Pédagogique Synchrone d'Activités d'Apprentissage à Distance*. Thèse de Doctorat, Université du Maine, Le Mans.

Dess, G., & Picken, J. (2000). Changing roles, leadership in the 21st century. *Organizational Dynamics, 28*(3), 18–34. doi:10.1016/S0090-2616(00)88447-8

Detlor, B. (2000). The corporate portal as information infrastructure: towards a framework for portal design. *International Journal of Information Management, 20*, 91–101. doi:10.1016/S0268-4012(99)00058-4

Devedžic, V. (2002). Understanding Ontological Engineering. *Communications of the ACM, 45*(4), 136–144. doi:10.1145/505248.506002

DeZoort, F., & Lord, A. (1997). A review and synthesis of pressure effects research in accounting. *Journal of Accounting Literature, 16*, 28–85.

Diamantopoulos, A., & Hart, S. (1993). Linking market orientation and company performance: Preliminary evidence on Kohli and Jaworski's framework. *Journal of Strategic Marketing, 1*, 93–121. doi:10.1080/09652549300000007

Dias, C. (2001). Corporate portals: a literature review of a new concept in Information Management. *International Journal of Information Management, 21*, 269–287. doi:10.1016/S0268-4012(01)00021-4

Dillenbourg, P. (1999). What do you mean by collaborative learning? In Dillenbourg, P. (Ed.), *Collaborative learning: Cognitive and Computational Approaches* (pp. 1–19). Oxford, UK: Elsevier.

Dillman, D. (2000). *Mail and Internet surveys: The tailored design method*. New York: John Wiley & Sons.

Ding, Z., Ng, F., & Cai, Q. (2007). Personal constructs affecting interpersonal trust and willingness to share knowledge between architects in project design teams. *Construction Management and Economics, 25*, 937–950. doi:10.1080/01446190701468828

Dixon, N. M. (2000). *Common Knowledge: How Companies Thrive by Sharing What They Know*. Boston: Harvard Business School Press.

Doemel, P. (1994). WebMap - A Graphical Hypertext Navigation Tool. In *Proceedings of 2nd International Conference on the World Wide Web*, Chicago, IL (pp. 785-789).

Dourish, P. (2003). The Appropriation of Interactive Technologies: Some Lessons from Placeless Documents. *Computer-Supported Cooperative Work: Special Issue on Evolving Use of Groupware, 12*, 465–490. doi:10.1023/A:1026149119426

Dous, M., Salomann, H., Kolbe, L., & Brenner, W. (2005). Knowledge management capabilities in CRM: Making knowledge For, from and about customers work. In *Proceedings of the Eleventh Americas Conference on Information Systems*, Omaha, NE (pp. 167-178).

Dromey, R. G. (2003). Software Quality - Prevention Versus Cure? *Software Quality Journal, 11*(3), 197–210. doi:10.1023/A:1025162610079

Drucker, P. F. (1995). *Managing in time of great change*. New York: Truman Talley Books.

Drucker, P. F. (1993). *Post-capitalist Society*. New York: Butterworth Heineman.

Dubois, J.-M., Dao-Duy, J.-M., & Eldika, S. (2000). L'analyse des traces informatiques des usages: un outil pour valider la conception d'un site web. In *Proceedings of Dans Actes des rencontres jeunes chercheurs en Interaction Homme-Machine* (pp. 85-89).

Duguid, P. (2006). Limits of self–organization: Peer produc-tion and 'laws of quality'. *First Monday, 11*(10). ePyDoc. (2005). *Epydoc website.* Retrieved 5 October, 2005 from http://epydoc.sourceforge.net/

Dumas, M., van der Aalst, W. M., & ter Hofstede, A. H. (2006). *Process-Aware Information Systems: Bridging People and Software through Process Technology.* New York: John Wiley and Sons Inc.

Dyer, J. H., & Singh, H. (1998). The relational view: Cooperative strategy and sources of interorganizational competitive advantage. *Academy of Management Review, 23*, 660–679. doi:10.2307/259056

Earley, C. (1993). East meets West meets Mideast: Further explorations of collectivistic and individualistic work groups. *Academy of Management Journal, 36*(2), 319–348. doi:10.2307/256525

Earley, C., & Gibson, C. B. (1998). Taking stock in our progress on Individualism-collectivism: 100 years of solidarity and community. *Journal of Management, 24*(3), 265–304. doi:10.1016/S0149-2063(99)80063-4

Earl, M. J., & Scott, I. A. (1999). What is a chief knowl-edge officer? *Sloan Management Review, 40*(2), 29–38.

Eisinger, P. (2002). Organizational capacity and organi-zational effectiveness among street-level food assistance programs. *Nonprofit and Voluntary Sector Quarterly, 31*(1), 115–130. doi:.doi:10.1177/0899764002311005

ELEKTRA Consortium. (1999). *Newton: Validated ESI knowledge base* (ELEKTRA Project Deliverable Docu-ment, ESPRIT Project No. 22927). Cologne, Germany: ELEKTRA Project.

Emrich, C. G., Denmark, F. L., & den Hartog, D. (2004). Cross-cultural differences in gender egalitarianism . In House, R. J., Hanges, P. J., Javidan, M., Dorfman, P. W., & Gupta, V. (Eds.), *Culture, leadership, and organiza-tions: The GLOBE study of 62 societies* (pp. 343–394). Thousand Oaks, CA: Sage.

Engestrom, Y. (1987). *Learning by expanding: An activity-theoretical approach to developmental research.* Helsinki, Finland: Orienta-Konsultit Oy.

Engeström, Y. (1999). Activity theory and individual and social transformation . In Engestrom, Y., Miettinen, R., & Punamaki, R. (Eds.), *Perspectives on activity theory* (pp. 19–38). New York: Cambridge University Press.

Engeström, Y. (2000). Activity theory as a framework for analyzing and redesigning work. *Ergonomics, 43*(7), 960–974. doi:10.1080/001401300409143

Engeström, Y. (2001). Expansive learning at work: Toward an activity theoretical reconceptualization. *Journal of Education and Work, 14*(1), 133–156.

Engeström, Y. (2007). Enriching the theory of expansive learning: Lessons from journeys toward coconfiguration. *Mind, Culture, and Activity, 14*(1-2), 23–39.

Engeström, Y., & Miettinen, R. (1999). Introduction . In Engeström, Y., Miettinen, R., & Punamaki, R.-L. (Eds.), *Perspectives on activity theory* (pp. 1–16). New York: Cambridge University Press.

Epple, D., Argote, L., & Devadas, R. (1991). Organiza-tional learning curves: A method for investigating intra-plant transfer of knowledge acquired through learning by doing. *Organization Science, 2*(1), 58–70. doi:10.1287/orsc.2.1.58

Eppler, M. J., & Sukowski, O. (2000). Managing team knowledge: Core processes, tools and enabling fac-tors. *European Management Journal, 18*(3), 334–341. doi:10.1016/S0263-2373(00)00015-3

Epstein, L. D. (2000). *Sharing knowledge in organization: How people use media to communication.* Unpublished Doctoral Dissertation, University of California, Berkeley.

Erez, M., & Earley, C. (1993). *Culture, Self-identity, and Work.* New York: Oxford University Press.

Erlinghagen, M., & Hank, K. (2006). The participation of older Europeans in volunteer work. *Ageing and Society, 26*, 567–584. doi:10.1017/S0144686X06004818

Erumban, A., & de Jong, S. B. (2006). Cross-country differences in ICT adoption: A consequence of Culture? *Journal of World Business, 41*(4), 302. doi:10.1016/j.jwb.2006.08.005

Everard, J. (2001). We are Plato's children. *Library Management*, 22(6/7), 297–302. doi:10.1108/EUM0000000005594

Ewusi-Mensah, K. (1997). Critical issues in abandoned information systems projects. *Communications of the ACM*, 40(9), 74–80. doi:10.1145/260750.260775

Expert Group. (1995). *Report on Reform and Development in China - The Chinese Road*. Beijing, China: Chinese Finance and Economic Press.

Felton, S. M. (2002). Knowledge is capital, the rest is just money. *Strategy and Leadership*, 30(3), 41–42.

Fenwick, T. (2003). Innovation: examining workplace learning in new enterprises. *Journal of Workplace Learning*, 15(3), 123–132. doi:10.1108/13665620310468469

Ferrari, F. M., & de Toledo, J. C. (2004). Analyzing the knowledge management through the product development process. *Journal of Knowledge Management*, 8(1), 117–129. doi:10.1108/13673270410523952

Feurstein, M., Natter, M., Mild, A., & Taudes, A. (2001, January 3-6). Incentives to share knowledge. In *Proceedings of Hawaii International Conference on System Sciences* (p. 8). Los Alamitos, CA, USA: IEEE Computer Society.

Finn, S., Maher, J. K., & Forster, J. (2006). Indicators of Information and Communication Technology Adoption in the Nonprofit Sector: Changes Between 2000 and 2004. *Nonprofit Management & Leadership*, 16(3), 277–295. doi:10.1002/nml.107

Firestone, J. M., & McElroy, M. W. (2005). Doing knowledge management. *The Learning Organization Journal*, 12, 1–29.

Firth, M. (1996). The diffusion of managerial accounting procedures in the People's Republic of China and the influence of foreign partnered joint ventures. *Accounting, Organizations and Society*, 21(7/8), 629–654. doi:10.1016/0361-3682(95)00039-9

Fisher, J. (1995). Contingency-based research on management control systems: Categorization by level of complexity. *Journal of Accounting Literature*, 14, 24–53.

Fisher, J. (1998). Contingency theory, management control systems and firm outcomes: Past results and future directions. *Behavioral Research in Accounting*, 10, 47–64.

Fisher, J., & Govindarajan, V. (1993). Incentive compensation design, strategic business unit mission, and competitive strategy. *Journal of Management Accounting Research*, 5, 129–144.

Fjermestad, J., & Romano, N. C. (2003). Electronic customer relationship management revisiting the general theories of usability and resistance: An integrative implementation framework. *Business Process Management Journal*, 9(5), 572–591. doi:10.1108/14637150310496695

Folcher, V., & Rabardel, P. (2004). Hommes, artefacts, activités: perspective instrumentale . In Falzon, P. (Ed.), *Ergonomie*. Paris: PUF.

Fong, P. S.-W., Hills, M. J., & Hayles, C. S. (2007). Dynamic knowledge creation through value management teams. *Journal of Management Engineering*, 23(1), 40–49. doi:10.1061/(ASCE)0742-597X(2007)23:1(40)

Foray, D. (2006). Optimizing the Use of Knowledge . In Kahin, B., & Foray, D. (Eds.), *Advancing Knowledge and the Knowledge Economy* (pp. 9–16). Cambridge, MA: MIT Press.

Ford, D. P. (2008). *Disengagement from Knowledge Sharing: The Alternative Explanation for Why People Are Not Sharing*. Paper presented at the Administrative Sciences Association of Canada, Halifax, NS, Canada.

Fornell, C., & Bookstein. (1982). Two structural equation models: LISREL and PLS applied to consumer exit-voice theory. *JMR, Journal of Marketing Research*, 19(4), 440–452. doi:10.2307/3151718

Fornell, C., & Larcker, D. (1981). Evaluating structural equation models with unobservable variables and measurement error. *JMR, Journal of Marketing Research*, 18, 39–50. doi:10.2307/3151312

Foucault, M. (1972). *The archeology of knowledge*. London: Routledge.

Francis, H. (1997). National cultural differences in theory and practice Evaluating Hofstede's national cultural framework. *Information Technology & People*, 10(2), 132–146. doi:10.1108/09593849710174986

Frappaolo, C., & Wilson-Todd, L. (2000). *After the Gold Rush: Harvesting Corporate Knowledge Resources.* Retrieved from http://www.inteligentkm.com/ feature/ feat1.shtml#Case1

Friedman, T. L. (2007). *The World Is Flat: A brief history of the twenty-first century.* New York: Farrar, Straus and Giroux.

Fukuyama, F. (1995). *Trust: The Social Virtues and the Creation of Prosperity.* New York: The Free Press.

Fukuyama, F. (2004). *State-Building: Governance and World Order in the 21ˢᵗ Century.* New York: Cornell University Press.

Fu, P. P., Tsui, A. S., & Dess, G. G. (2006). The dynamics of Guanxi in Chinese high-tech firms: Implications for knowledge management and decision making. *Management International Review, 46*(3), 277–305. doi:10.1007/s11575-006-0048-z

Gabriel, R. P. (1996). *Patterns of Software: Tales from the Software Community.* New York: Oxford University Press.

Gajendran, T., & Brewer, G. J. (2007). Integration of information and communication technology: Influence of the cultural environment. *Engineering, Construction, and Architectural Management, 14,* 532–549. doi:10.1108/09699980710829003

Galunic, D. C., & Rodan, S. A. (1998). Resource recombinations in the firm: Knowledge structures and the potential for Schumpeterian innovation. *Strategic Management Journal, 19*(12), 1193–1201. doi:10.1002/(SICI)1097-0266(1998120)19:12<1193::AID-SMJ5>3.0.CO;2-F

Gama, C. (2003*). Towards a model of Metacognition Instruction in Interactive Learning Environments.* Unpublished doctoral dissertation, University of Sussex, England.

Gamma, E., Helm, R., Johnson, R., & Vlissides, J. (1995). *Design Patterns: Elements of Reusable Object-Oriented Software.* Reading, MA: Addison-Wesley.

Gammelgaard, J., & Ritter, T. (2008). Virtual Communities of Practice: A Mechanism for Efficient Knowledge Retrieval in MNCs. *International Journal of Knowledge Management, 4*(2), 46–51.

Garfield, S. (2006). Ten reasons why people don't share their knowledge. *Knowledge Management Review, 9*(2), 10–11.

Garzás, J., & Piattini, M. (2005). An Ontology for Micro-architectural Design Knowledge. *IEEE Software, 22*(2), 28–33. doi:10.1109/MS.2005.26

Gašević, D., Djuric, D., & Devedžic, V. (2006). *Model Driven Architecture and Ontology Development.* New York: Springer Verlag.

Gebert, H., Geib, M., Kolbe, L., & Riempp, G. (2002). Towards customer knowledge management: Integrating customer relationship management and knowledge management concepts. In *Proceedings of the 2nd International Conference on Electronic Business,* Taipei, Taiwan.

Gelfand, M. J., Bhawuk, D. P. S., Nishii, L. H., & Bechtold, D. J. (2004). Individualism and collectivism . In House, R. J., Hanges, P. J., Javidan, M., Dorfman, P. W., & Gupta, V. (Eds.), *Culture, leadership, and organizations: The GLOBE study of 62 societies* (pp. 438–512). Thousand Oaks, CA: Sage.

Gendron, E., Carron, T., & Marty, J.-C. (2008, October 16-17). *Collaborative Indicators in Learning Games: an immersive factor.* Paper presented at the 2nd European Conference on Games Based Learning, Barcelona, Spain.

Geng, Q., Townley, C., Huang, K., & Zhang, J. (2005). Comparative knowledge management: a pilot study of Chinese and American universities. *Journal of the American Society for Information Science and Technology, 56*(10), 1031–1044. doi:10.1002/asi.20194

Georgeon, O., Mille, A., & Bellet, T. (2006). Analyzing behavioral data for refining cognitive models of operator. In *Proceedings of the Philosophies and Methodologies for Knowledge Discovery,* Krakow, Poland. Washington, DC: IEEE.

Germain, R., Droge, C., & Christensen, W. (2001). The mediating role of operations knowledge in the relationship of context with performance. *Journal of Operations Management, 19,* 453–469. doi:10.1016/S0272-6963(00)00067-X

Getzels, J. W., & Guba, E. G. (1957). Social behavior and the administrative process. *The School Review, 65,* 423–444. doi:10.1086/442411

Gherardi, S. (2001). From organizational learning to practice-based knowing. *Human Relations*, *54*(1), 131–139. doi:10.1177/0018726701541016

Ghoshal, S., & Bartlett, C. (1990). The multinational corporation as an interorganizational network. *Academy of Management Review*, *15*(4), 603–625. doi:10.2307/258684

Ghosh, D. (1997). De-escalation strategies: Some experimental evidence. *Behavioral Research in Accounting*, *9*, 88–112.

Gibbert, M., Leibold, M., & Probst, G. (2002). Five styles of customer knowledge management and how smart companies use them to create value. *European Management Journal*, *20*(5), 459–546. doi:10.1016/S0263-2373(02)00101-9

Gilmour, J., & Stancliffe, M. (2004). Managing knowledge in an international organisation: the work of voluntary services overseas (VSO). *Records Management Journal*, *14*(3), 124–128. doi:.doi:10.1108/09565690410566783

Glazer, R. (1991). Marketing in an information-intensive environment: Strategic implications of knowledge as an asset. *Journal of Marketing*, *55*, 1–19. doi:10.2307/1251953

Glisby, M., & Holden, N. (2003). Contextual constraints in knowledge management theory: The cultural embeddedness of Nonaka's knowledge-creating company. *Knowledge and Process Management*, *10*(1), 29–36. doi:10.1002/kpm.158

Goguen, J. A. (1997). Toward a social, ethical theory of information . In Bowker, G. C., Star, S., Turner, W., & Gasser, L. (Eds.), *Social Science, Technical Systems and Cooperative Work: Beyond the Great Divide* (pp. 27–56). Mahwah, NJ: Lawrence Erlbaum Associates.

Goh, A. L S. (2005). Adoption of Customer Relationship Management (CRM) solutions as an Effective Knowledge Management (KM) tool: A systems Value Diagnostic. *Journal of Knowledge Management Practice, 6*. Retrieved from http://www.tlainc.com/jkmpv6.htm. ISSN 1705-9232.

Goh, D., Chua, A., Luyt, B., & Lee, C. (2008). Knowledge access, creation and transfer in e-government portals. *Online Information Review*, *32*(3), 348–369. doi:10.1108/14684520810889664

Goh, S. (1998). Towards a learning organization: The strategic building blocks. *Advanced Management Journal*, *63*(2), 15–18.

Goh, S. C. (2002). Managing effective knowledge transfer: an integrative framework and some practice implications. *Journal of Knowledge Management*, *6*(1), 23–30. doi:10.1108/13673270210417664

Gold, A. H., Malhorta, A., & Segars, A. H. (2001). Knowledge management: An organizational capabilities perspective. *Journal of Management Information Systems*, *18*(1), 185–214.

Gore, C., & Gore, E. (1999). Knowledge management: The way forward. *Total Quality Management, 10*(4,5), 554-560.

Gosh, B., & Scott, J. E. (2007). Effective knowledge management systems for a clinical nursing setting. *Information Systems Management*, *24*(1), 73–84. doi:10.1080/10580530601038188

Gourlay, S. (2003, September 18-19). *The SECI Model of Knowledge Creation: Some Empirical Shortcomings*. Paper presented at the Fourth European Conference on Knowledge Management (ECKM 2003), Oxford, England.

Gourlay, S. (2001). Knowledge management and HRD. *Human Resource Development International*, *4*(1), 27–46. doi:10.1080/13678860121778

Granlund, Å., Lafrenière, D., & Carr, D. A. (2001, August 5-10). *A Pattern-Supported Approach to the User Interface Design Process*. Paper presented at the Ninth International Conference on Human-Computer Interaction (HCI International 2001), New Orleans, Louisiana, USA.

Grant, R. (1996). Toward a knowledge-based theory of the firm. *Strategic Management Journal*, *17*, 109–122.

Grant, R. M. (1991). The resource-based theory of competitive advantage: Implication for strategy formulation. *California Management Review*, *33*(3), 114–135.

Grant, R. M. (1996). Toward a knowledge-based theory of the firm. *Strategic Management Journal*, *17*, 109–122.

Grant, R. M., & Baden-Fuller, C. (1995). A knowledge-based theory of inter-firm collaboration. *Academy of Management Journal*, 17–21.

Gray, B., Matear, S., Boshoff, C., & Matheson, P. (1998). Developing a better measure of market orientation. *European Journal of Marketing*, *32*, 884–903. doi:10.1108/03090569810232327

Greenberg, S., & Cockburn, A. (1999, June 3). Getting Back to Back: Alternate Behaviors for a Web Browser's Back Button. In *Proceedings of the 5th Annual Human Factors and the Web Conference*, Gaithersburg, MD.

Greenberg, S., & Witten, I. H. (1988, June 15-19). How Users Repeat Their Actions on Computers: Principles for Design of History Mechanisms. In E. Soloway, D. Frye, & S. B. Sheppard (Eds.), *Proceedings of the ACM CHI 88 Human Factors in Computing Systems Conference* (pp. 171-178). Washington, DC: IEEE.

Greenley, G. E. (1995). Market orientation and company performance: Empirical evidence from UK companies. *British Journal of Management*, *6*, 1–13. doi:10.1111/j.1467-8551.1995.tb00082.x

Grover, V., & Davenport, T. H. (2001). General perspectives on knowledge management: Fostering a research agenda. *Journal of Management Information Systems*, *18*(1), 5–21.

Gruber, H. G. (2000). *Does organizational culture affect the sharing of knowledge? The case of a department in a high-technology company*. Unpublished master's thesis, Carleton University.

Gruber, T. R. (1995). Toward principles for the design of ontologies used for knowledge sharing. *International Journal of Human-Computer Studies*, *43*(Nov), 907. doi:10.1006/ijhc.1995.1081

Gummesson, E. (2001). Are current research approaches in marketing leading us astray? *Marketing Theory*, *1*(1), 27–48. doi:10.1177/147059310100100102

Gunn, C. (2004). *Third-sector development: making up for the market*. Ithaca, NY: Cornell University Press.

Gupta, A. K., & Govindarajan, V. (2000). Knowledge flows within multinational corporations. *Strategic Management Journal*, *21*, 473–496. doi:10.1002/(SICI)1097-0266(200004)21:4<473::AID-SMJ84>3.0.CO;2-I

Gupta, A. K., & Govindarajan, V. (2000). Knowledge Management's Social Dimension: Lessons From Nucor Steel. *Sloan Management Review*, *42*(1), 71–81.

Gurugé, A. (2002). Living and Breathing Portals. *Corporate Portals Empowered with XML and Web Services*, 273-284.

Guthrie, D. (1998). The declining significance of guanxi in China's economic transition. *The China Quarterly*, *3*, 254–282. doi:10.1017/S0305741000002034

Guzdial, M., Kolodner, J., Hmelo, C., Narayanan, H., Carlso, D., & Rappin, N. (1996). The collaboratory notebook. *Communications of the ACM*, *39*(4), 32–33. doi:10.1145/227210.227218

Gyampah, K., & White, K. (1993). User involvement and user satisfaction: An exploratory contingency model. *Information & Management*, *25*, 1–10. doi:10.1016/0378-7206(93)90021-K

Hagedoorn, J. (1993). Understanding the rationale of strategic technology partnering: Interorganizational modes of cooperation and sectoral differences. *Strategic Management Journal*, *14*, 371–385. doi:10.1002/smj.4250140505

Hair, J. F., Anderson, R. E., Tatham, R. L., & Blac, W. C. (1998). *Multivariate data analysis* (5th ed.). Englewood Cliffs, NJ: Prentice-Hall.

Hall, E. T. (1976). *Beyond culture*. NY: Anchor Press.

Handy, F., & Brudney, J. L. (2007). When to Use Volunteer Labor Resources? An Organizational Analysis for Nonprofit Management. *Vrijwillige Inzet Onderzoch*, *4*, 91–100.

Handy, F., Mook, L., & Quarter, J. (2008). The Interchangeability of Paid Staff and Volunteers in Nonprofit Organizations. *Nonprofit and Voluntary Sector Quarterly*, *37*(1), 76–92. doi:10.1177/0899764007303528

Hanphanit, B. (2003). *Developing a knowledge management model at Thai higher educational institutes*. Unpublished doctoral dissertation, Chulalongkorn University, Bangkok, Thailand.

Hansen, M. T., Nohria, N., & Tierney, T. (1999). What's your strategy for managing knowledge? *Harvard Business Review*, *77*(2), 106–116.

Han, W., & Ji, S. (2006). Empirical study on the effect of knowledge creation at the individual and group levels. [Science and Technology]. *Journal of Tsinghua University*, *46*(s1), 942–948.

Hari, S., Egbu, C., & Kumar, B. (2005). A knowledge capture awareness tool An empirical study on small and medium enterprises in the construction industry. *Engineering, Construction, and Architectural Management, 12*(6), 533–567. doi:10.1108/09699980510634128

Harrigan, K. R. (1988). Strategic alliances and partner asymmetries. *Management International Review, 28,* 53–72.

Harrison, N. B. (2003, June 25-29). *Advanced Pattern Writing*. Paper presented at the Eighth European Conference on Pattern Languages of Programs (EuroPLoP 2003), Irsee, Germany.

Harrison, N. B. (2000). The Language of Shepherding: A Pattern Language for Shepherds and Sheep . In Harrison, N. B., Foote, B., & Rohnert, H. (Eds.), *Pattern Languages of Program Design 4*. Reading, MA: Addison-Wesley.

Harrison, P. D., & Harrell, A. (1993). Impact of adverse selection on managers' project evaluation decisions. *Academy of Management Journal, 36*(3), 635–643. doi:10.2307/256596

Hasan, H., & Ditsa, G. (1999). The impact of culture on the adoption of IT: An interpretive study. *Journal of Global Information Management, 7*(1), 5–15.

Hassard, J., Sheehan, J., & Morris, J. (1999). Enterprise reform in post-Deng China. *International Studies of Management & Organization, 29*(3), 54–83.

Hatry, H. P. (2007). *Performance Measurement: Getting Results* (2nd ed.). Washington, DC: Urban Institute.

Hayes, R. H., & Clark, K. B. (1985). Exploring the sources of productivity differences at the factory level . In Clark, K., (Eds.), *The Uneasy Alliance: Managing the Productivity Technology Dilemma* (pp. 151–188). Boston: Harvard Business School Press.

Head, T., & Sorensen, P.F., (2005). Attracting foreign direct investment: The potential role of national culture. *The Journal of American Academy of Business,* 205-209.

Heals, J., Cockcroft, S., & Raduescu, C. (2004). The Influence of National Culture on the Level and Outcome of IS Development Decisions. *Journal of Global Information Technology, 7*(4), 3–28.

Hedlund, G. (1994). A model of knowledge management and the N-form corporation. *Strategic Management Journal, 15*(5), 73–90.

Heili, J., & Ollagnier-Beldame, M. (2008). *Analyse de l'activité et complexité des interactions homme-machine: Pour une revalorisation des études de cas*. Actes 13eme conférence AIM 2008, Paris.

Heili, J., Ollagnier-Beldame, M., & Héraud, J.-M. (2008). Traces d'utilisation, utilisation de traces: Application à l'adaptation des IHM. In *Proceedings of the 13ème Conférence AIM 2008*, Paris.

Heisig, P. (2009). Harmonisation of Knowledge Management – Comparing 160 KM Frameworks around the Globe. *Journal of Knowledge Management, 13*(4), 4–31. doi:10.1108/13673270910971798

Henderson, J. C., & Venkatraman, N. (1999). Strategic alignment: Leveraging information technology for transforming organizations. *IBM Systems Journal, 38*(2-3), 472–484. doi:10.1147/SJ.1999.5387096

Hendler, J., Lassila, O., & Berners-Lee, T. (2001). The Semantic Web. *Scientific American, 284*(5), 34–43. doi:10.1038/scientificamerican0501-34

Hendriks, P. (1999). Why share knowledge? The influence of ICT on the motivation for knowledge sharing. *Knowledge and Process Management, 6*(2), 91–100. doi:10.1002/(SICI)1099-1441(199906)6:2<91::AID-KPM54>3.0.CO;2-M

Herbig, P., & Dunphy, S. (1998). Culture and innovation. *Cross Cultural Management, 5*(4), 13–21. doi:10.1108/13527609810796844

Herbig, P., & Miller, J. (1992). Culture and technology: does the traffic move in both directions? *Journal of Global Marketing, 6*(3), 75–104. doi:10.1300/J042v06n03_05

Herschel, R. T., & Jones, N. E. (2005). Knowledge management and business intelligence: The importance of integration. *Journal of Knowledge Management, 9*(4), 45–55. doi:10.1108/13673270510610323

Hess, C., & Ostrom, E. (2007). *Understanding Knowledge as a Commons: From Theory to Practice*. Cambridge, MA: MIT Press.

Highsmith, J. A. III. (2000). *Adaptive software development: a collaborative approach to managing complex systems*. New York: Dorset House Publishing Co., Inc.

Hightower, R., Ring, L., Helfman, J., Bederson, B., & Hollan, J. (1998). Graphical multiscale web histories: A study of PadPrints. In . *Proceedings of Hypertext, 98*, 58–65.

Hill, W. C., & Hollan, J. D. (1993). History-enriched digital objects. In *Proceedings of Third ACM Conference on Computers, Freedom and Privacy*, San Francisco, CA (pp. 917-920). New York: ACM.

Hinds, P. J., & Pfeffer, J. (2003). Why organizations don't "know what they know": Cognitive and motivational factors affecting the transfer of expertise . In *Sharing Expertise: Beyond Knowledge Management* (pp. 3–26). Cambridge: MIT Press.

Höcht, C., & Rech, J. (2006). Human-centered Design of a Semantically Enabled Knowledge Management System for Agile Software Engineering . In Lytras, M. D., & Naeve, A. (Eds.), *Open Source for Knowledge and Learning Management: Strategies beyond Tools*. Hershey, PA: IGI Global.

Hodgetts, R., & Luthans, F. (2003). *International Management: Culture, Strategy and Behavior*. New York: McGraw-Hill Irwin.

Hofstede, G. (1994). *Cultures and organizations: Software of the mind-intercultural cooperation and its importance for survival*. London: Harper-Collins.

Hofstede, G. (1980). *Culture's Consequences: International Differences in Related Values*. Beverly Hills, CA: Sage.

Hofstede, G. (1983). National culture in four dimensions. *International Studies of Management and Organization, 13*(2), 46–74.

Hofstede, G. (1984). *Culture's consequences: International differences in work-related values*. London: Sage.

Hofstede, G. (1991). *Cultures and organizations: Software of the mind*. New York: McGraw-Hill.

Hofstede, G. (2001). *Culture's Consequences* (2nd ed.). Thousand Oaks, CA: Sage.

Hofstede, G. H. (1980). *Culture's Consequences: International Differences in Work-Related Values*. Beverly Hills, CA: Sage.

Hofstede, G. H. (1991). *Cultures and Organizations: Software of the Mind*. Berkshire, UK: McGraw-Hill.

Hofstede, G. H. (2001). *Culture's Consequences: Comparing Values, Behaviors, Institutions, and Organizations across Nations*. Thousand Oaks, CA: Sage.

Hofstede, G., & Bond, M. H. (1988). The Confucius connection: from cultural roots to economic growth. *Organizational Dynamics, 16*, 4–21. doi:10.1016/0090-2616(88)90009-5

Ho, L. (2008). What affects organizational performance? The linking of learning and knowledge management. *Industrial Management & Data Systems, 108*(9), 1234–1254. doi:10.1108/02635570810914919

Holsapple, C. W., & Joshi, K. D. (2002). Knowledge management: A threefold framework. *The Information Society, 18*, 47–64. doi:10.1080/01972240252818225

Holsapple, C. W., & Joshi, K. D. (2002). Knowledge Manipulation Activities: Results of a Delphi study. *Information & Management, 39*, 477–490. doi:10.1016/S0378-7206(01)00109-4

Holsapple, C. W., & Joshi, K. D. (2004). A formal knowledge management ontology: Conduct, activities, resources, and influences. *Journal of the American Society for Information Science and Technology, 55*(7), 593–612. doi:10.1002/asi.20007

Holsapple, C., & Joshi, K. D. (2000). An investigation of factors that influence the management of knowledge in organizations. *The Journal of Strategic Information Systems, 9*, 235–261. doi:10.1016/S0963-8687(00)00046-9

Holtzblatt, K., & Beyer, H. R. (1995). Requirements gathering: The human factor. *Communications of the ACM, 38*(5), 31–32. doi:10.1145/203356.203361

Hong, J. F. L., Easterby-Smith, M., & Snell, R. S. (2006). Transferring organizational learning systems to Japanese subsidiaries in China. *Journal of Management Studies, 43*(5), 1027–1058. doi:10.1111/j.1467-6486.2006.00628.x

Hoque, Z., & J. W. (2000). Linking balanced scorecard measures to size and market factors: Impact on organizational performance. *Journal of Management Accounting Research, 12*(1), 1–17. doi:10.2308/jmar.2000.12.1.1

Horibe, F. (1999). *Managing knowledge workers: New skills and attitudes to unlock the intellectual capital in your organization.* New York: John Wiley.

House, R. J. (2004). Foreword . In House, R. J., Hanges, P. J., Javidan, M., Dorfman, P. W., & Gupta, V. (Eds.), *Culture, leadership, and organizations: The GLOBE study of 62 societies* (pp. xv–xix). Thousand Oaks, CA: Sage.

House, R. J., Javidan, M., & Dorfman, P. (2001). Project GLOBE: An introduction. *Applied Psychology: An International Review, 50*(4), 489–505. doi:10.1111/1464-0597.00070

House, R. J., Javidan, M., Hanges, P., & Dorfman, P. (2002). Understanding cultures and implicit leadership theories across the globe: an introduction to project GLOBE. *Journal of World Business, 37*(1), 3–10. doi:10.1016/S1090-9516(01)00069-4

http://www.wissensmanagement.net/ download/ muenchener_modell.pdf

Huang, W. (2006). Acquiring Innovative Knowledge via Effective Process Management. In *Proceedings of IEEE International Conference on Management of Innovation and Technology* (pp. 384-388).

Huang, Q., Davison, R., & Gu, J. (2008). Impact of personal and cultural factors on knowledge sharing in China. *Asia Pacific Journal of Management, 25*(3), 451–471. doi:10.1007/s10490-008-9095-2

Huang, W. W., Wei, K.-K., Watson, R. T., & Tan, B. C. Y. (2002). Supporting virtual team-building with a GSS: an empirical investigation. *Decision Support Systems, 34*, 359–367. doi:10.1016/S0167-9236(02)00009-X

Huang, Y. (2009). Private Ownership: The real source of China's economic miracle. *The McKinsey Quarterly,* (1): 148–155.

Huber, G. (1991). Organizational learning: The contributing processes and the literatures. *Organization Science, 2*(1), 88–115. doi:10.1287/orsc.2.1.88

Hult, G. T. M. (2003). An integration of thoughts on knowledge management. *Decision Sciences, 34*, 189. doi:10.1111/1540-5915.02264

Humborstad, S. I. W., Humborstad, B., Whitfield, R., & Perry, C. (2008). Implementation of empowerment in Chinese high power-distance Organizations. *International Journal of Human Resource Management, 19*(7), 1349–1364. doi:10.1080/09585190802110224

Hung, Y. C., Huang, S. M., Lin, Q. P., & Tsai, M. L. (2005) Critical factors in adopting a knowledge management system for the pharmaceutical industry. *Industrial Management + Data Systems, 105*(1/2), 164-183.

Hung, Y., Huang, S., Lin, Q., & Tsai, M. (2005). Critical factors in adopting a knowledge management system for the pharmaceutical industry. *Industrial Management & Data Systems, 105*(2), 164–183. doi:10.1108/02635570510583307

Hurley, T. A., & Green, C. W. (2005). Knowledge Management and the Non-Profit Industry: A Within and Between Approach. *Journal of Knowledge Management Practice, 6.* Retrieved July 29, 2008, from http://www.tlainc.com/articl79.htm

Husted, K., & Michailova, S. (2002). Knowledge sharing in Russian companies with Western participation. *Management International, 6*(2), 17–28.

Hutchings, K. (2005). Examining the impacts of institutional change on knowledge sharing and management learning in the PRC. *Thunderbird International Business Review, 47*(4), 447–468. doi:10.1002/tie.20062

Hutchings, K., & Michailova, S. (2004). Facilitating knowledge sharing in Russian and Chinese subsidiaries: The role of personal networks and group membership. *Journal of Knowledge Management, 8*(2), 84–94. doi:10.1108/13673270410529136

Hutzschenreuter, T., & Listner, F. (2007). A contingency view on knowledge transfer: empirical evidence from the software industry. *Knowledge Management Research & Practice, 5*(2), 136–151. doi:10.1057/palgrave.kmrp.8500136

Iba, T. (2007, December 3). *Creation toward Quality Without a Name - Sociological Analysis of Pattern Language*. Paper presented at the First International Workshop on Software Patterns and Quality (SPAQu 2007), Nagoya, Japan.

Inkpen, A. C., & Pien, W. (2006). An examination of collaboration and knowledge transfer: China-Singapore Suzhou industrial park. *Journal of Management Studies, 43*(4), 779–811. doi:10.1111/j.1467-6486.2006.00611.x

Ipe, M. (2003). Knowledge sharing in organizations: A conceptual framework. *Human Resource Development Review, 2*(4), 337–359. doi:10.1177/1534484303257985

Irmer, B., Bordia, P., & Abusah, D. (2002). Evaluation apprehension and perceived benefit in interpersonal and database knowledge sharing. In *Academy of Management Proceedings* (pp. B1–B6). OCIS.

ISO-13407. (1999). *Human-centred design processes for interactive systems (Standard ISO).ISO*. International Organization for Standardization.

ISO-9241-11. (1998). *Ergonomic requirements for office work with visual display terminals (VDTs) -- Part 11: Guidance on usability* (Standard No. ISO 9241-11:1998(E), ISO TC 159/SC 4/WG 5). ISO (the International Organization for Standardization).

Issa, A., Odeh, M., & Coward, D. (2006). Using Use Case Patterns to Estimate Reusability in Software Systems. *Information and Software Technology, 48*(9), 836–845. doi:10.1016/j.infsof.2005.10.005

Iverson, J., & Burkart, P. (2007). Managing Electronic Documents and Work Flows: Enterprise Content Management at Work in Nonprofit Organizations. *Nonprofit Management & Leadership, 17*(4), 403–419. doi:10.1002/nml.160

Ives, W., Torrey, B., & Gordon, C. (2000). Knowledge sharing is a human behavior. In Morey, D., (Eds.), *Knowledge Management* (pp. 99–129). Cambridge, MA: MIT Press.

Jagetia, L. C., & Patel, D. M. (1981). Developing an end-use intelligence system. *Industrial Marketing Management, 10*(2), 101–107. doi:10.1016/0019-8501(81)90003-1

Janz, B. D., & Prasarnphanich, P. (2003). Understanding the antecedents of effective knowledge management: The importance of a knowledge-centered culture. *Decision Sciences, 34*(2), 351–384. doi:10.1111/1540-5915.02328

Jasimuddin, S. (2008). A holistic view of knowledge management strategy. *Journal of Knowledge Management, 12*(2), 57–66. doi:10.1108/13673270810859514

Javidan, M. (2004). Performance orientation . In House, R. J., Hanges, P. J., Javidan, M., Dorfman, P. W., & Gupta, V. (Eds.), *Culture, leadership, and organizations: The GLOBE study of 62 societies* (pp. 239–281). Thousand Oaks, CA: Sage.

Javidan, M., & House, R. J. (2001). Cultural acumen for the global manager: Lessons from Project GLOBE. *Organizational Dynamics, 29*(4), 289–305. doi:10.1016/S0090-2616(01)00034-1

Javidan, M., House, R. J., Dorfman, P. W., Hanges, P. J., & de Luque, M. S. (2006). Conceptualizing and measuring cultures and their consequences: A comparative review of GLOBE's and Hofstede's approaches. *Journal of International Business Studies, 37*(6), 897–914. doi:10.1057/palgrave.jibs.8400234

Javidan, M., House, R. J., Dorfman, W. P., Gupta, V., Hanges, P. J., & de Luque, M. S. (2004). Conclusion . In House, R. J., Hanges, P. J., Javidan, M., Dorfman, P. W., & Gupta, V. (Eds.), *Culture, leadership, and organizations: The GLOBE study of 62 societies* (pp. 721–732). Thousand Oaks, CA: Sage.

Jaworski, B., & Kohli, A. (1993). Market orientation: Antecedents and consequences. *Journal of Marketing, 57*, 53–70. doi:10.2307/1251854

Jennex, E. M., Smolnik, S., & Croasdell, D. (2007). Towards defining knowledge management success. In *Proceedings of the 40th Hawaii International Conference on Systems Science* (pp. 193c).

Jennex, M. E., & Olfman, L. (2004). *Modeling Knowledge Management Success*. Paper presented at the Conference on Information Science and Technology Management, CISTM.

Jennex, M. (2008a). Impacts From Using Knowledge: A longitudinal study from a nuclear power plant. *International Journal of Knowledge Management, 4*(1), 51–64.

Jennex, M. (2008b). Exploring System Use as a Measure of Knowledge Management Success. *Journal of Organizational and End User Computing, 20*(1), 50–63.

Jennex, M. E. (2005). What is knowledge management? *International Journal of Knowledge Management, 1*(4), i–iv.

Jennex, M. E., & Adelakun, O. (2003). Successfactors for offshore information system development. *Journal of Information Technology Cases and Applications, 5*(3), 12–31.

Jennex, M. E., Amoroso, D., & Adelakun, O. (2004). E-commerce infrastructure success factors for small companies in developing economies. *Electronic Commerce Research, 4*(3), 263–286. doi:10.1023/B:ELEC.0000027983.36409.d4

Jennex, M. E., & Olfman, L. (2005). Assessing knowledge management success. *International Journal of Knowledge Management, 1*(2), 33–49.

Jennex, M. E., & Olfman, L. (2006). A model of knowledge management success. *International Journal of Knowledge Management, 2*(3), 51–68.

Jennex, M., & Olfman, L. (2006). A Model of Knowledge Management Success. *International Journal of Knowledge Management, 2*(3), 51–68.

Jensen, P. E. (2005). A contextual theory of learning and the learning organization. *Knowledge and Process Management, 12*(1), 53–64. doi:10.1002/kpm.217

Jermann, P. R., Soller, A., & Mühlenbrock, M. (2001). From mirroring to guiding: A review of state of the art technology for supporting collaborative learning. In *Proceedings of European Perspectives on Computer-Supported Collaborative Learning*, Bergen, Norway (pp. 324-331).

Jessop, A. (2004). Pattern Language: A Framework for Learning. *European Journal of Operational Research, 153*(2), 457–465. doi:10.1016/S0377-2217(03)00165-6

Jiang, X., & Lia, Y. (2008). An empirical investigation of knowledge management and innovative performance: The case of alliances. *Research Policy, 38*(2), 358–368. doi:10.1016/j.respol.2008.11.002

Jin, Z. (1999). Organizational innovation and virtual institutes. *Journal of Knowledge Management, 3*(1), 75–83. doi:10.1108/13673279910259420

Johannessen, J.-A., Olaisen, J., & Olsen, B. (2001). Mismanagement of tacit knowledge: The importance of tacit knowledge, the danger of information technology, and what to do about it. *International Journal of Information Management, 21*, 3–20. doi:10.1016/S0268-4012(00)00047-5

Johns Hopkins University. (2005). *Comparative Non-Profit Sector Project – Comparative Data Tables (Table 2: Volunteering in 36 countries).* Retrieved July 29, 2008, from http://www.jhu.edu/~cnp/pdf/table201.pdf

Jones, G. K., & Teegen, H, J. (2001). Global R & D activity of U.S. MNCS: does national culture affect investment decisions? *Multinational Business Review, 9*(2), 1–7.

Jordan, A., Carlile, O., & Stack, A. (2008). *Approaches to Learning: A Guide for Teachers.* New York: McGraw-Hill.

Jung, D., Chow, C., & Wu, A. (2008). Towards understanding the direct and indirect effects of transformational leadership on firm innovation. *The Leadership Quarterly, 19*, 582–594. doi:10.1016/j.leaqua.2008.07.007

Ju, T. L., Li, C.-Y., & Lee, T.-S. (2006). A contingency model for knowledge management capability and innovation. *Industrial Management & Data Systems, 106*(6), 855–877. doi:10.1108/02635570610671524

Kabasakal, H., & Bodur, M. (2004). Human orientation in societies, organizations, and leader attitudes. In House, R. J., Hanges, P. J., Javidan, M., Dorfman, P. W., & Gupta, V. (Eds.), *Culture, leadership, and organizations: The GLOBE study of 62 societies* (pp. 564–601). Thousand Oaks, CA: Sage.

Kahin, B. (2006). Prospects for knowledge policy. In Kahin, B., & Foray, D. (Eds.), *Advancing Knowledge and the Knowledge Economy* (pp. 1–8). Cambridge, MA: MIT Press.

Kahn, H., & Wiener, A. J. (1967). *The Year 2000: A Framework for Speculation on the Next Thirty-Three Years.* London: Collier-Macmillan Limited.

Kaiser, K. M., & King, W. R. (1982). The manager analyst interface in systems development. *Management Information Systems Quarterly, 6*(1), 49–59. doi:10.2307/248754

Kamakura, W., Mela, C., Ansari, A., Bodapati, A., Fader, P., & Iyengar, R. (2005). Choice models and customer relationship management. *Marketing Letters*, *16*(3), 279–291. doi:10.1007/s11002-005-5892-2

Kamthan, P. (2009b, October 25). *On the Symbiosis between Quality and Patterns*. Paper presented at the Third International Workshop on Software Patterns and Quality (SPAQu 2009), Orlando, FL, USA.

Kamthan, P. (2006). A Critique of Pattern Language Markup Language . *Interfaces*, *68*, 14–15.

Kamthan, P. (2008). A Situational Methodology for Addressing the Pragmatic Quality of Web Applications by Integration of Patterns. *Journal of Web Engineering*, *7*(1), 70–92.

Kamthan, P. (2009a). A Framework for Integrating the Social Web Environment in Pattern Engineering. *International Journal of Technology and Human Interaction*, *5*(2), 36–62.

Kamthan, P., & Pai, H.-I. (2006a). Knowledge Representation in Pattern Management . In Schwartz, D. (Ed.), *Encyclopedia of Knowledge Management*. Hershey, PA: IGI Global.

Kamthan, P., & Pai, H.-I. (2006b). Representation of Web Application Patterns in OWL . In Taniar, D., & Rahayu, J. W. (Eds.), *Web Semantics and Ontology*. Hershey, PA: IGI Global.

Kankanhalli, A., Tan, B. C. Y., & Wei, K.-K. (2005). Contributing knowledge to electronic knowledge repositories: an empirical investigation. *MIS Quarterly*, *29*(1), 113–143.

Kao, H., Kao, P. H., & Mazzuchi, T. A. (2006). Taiwanese executive practice knowledge management in mainland China and Southeast Asia (Malaysia). *The Journal of Information and Knowledge Management Systems*, *36*(3), 341–352.

Kaptelinin, V., & Nardi, B. (2005). *Acting with technology: Activity theory and interaction design*. Cambridge, MA: MIT Press.

Kates, R., Parris, T., & Leiserowitz, A. (2005). What is Sustainable Development? *Environment*, *47*(3), 8–21.

Katz, R., & Allen, T. J. (1982). Investigating the NOT Invented Here (NIH) syndrome: A look at the performance, tenure, and communication patterns of 50 R&D project groups. *R & D Management*, *12*(1), 7–19. doi:10.1111/j.1467-9310.1982.tb00478.x

Katz, S., Lesgold, A., Eggan, G., & Gordin, M. (1992). Modelling the student in Sherlock II. *Artificial Intelligence in Education*, *3*(4), 495–518.

Kedia, B. L., Keller, R. T., & Julian, S. D. (1992). Dimensions of national culture and the productivity of R&D units. *The Journal of High Technology Management Research*, *3*, 1–18. doi:10.1016/1047-8310(92)90002-J

Kelly, D., & Amburgey, T. (1991). Organizational inertia and momentum: A dynamic model of strategic change. *Academy of Management Journal*, *34*(3), 591–612. doi:10.2307/256407

Khalil, O., & Seleim, A. (2009). A cultural values interpretation for societal information dissemination capacity: An exploratory study. *Arab Journal of Administrative Sciences*, *16*(3), 455–488.

Kilbourne, W. E., & Marshall, K. P. (2005). The transfer of for profit marketing technology to the non-for-profit domain: from the theory of technology. *Journal of Marketing Theory and Practice*, *13*(1), 14–25.

Kimble, C., & Bourdon, I. (2008). Some success factors for the communal management of knowledge. *International Journal of Information Management*, *28*(6), 461–467. doi:10.1016/j.ijinfomgt.2008.08.007

Kimble, C., Hildred, P., & Wright, P. (2001). Communities of Practice: Going Virtual . In Malhotra, Y. (Ed.), *Knowledge Management and Business Model Innovation* (pp. 220–234). Hershey, PA: IGI Global.

Kim, C. W., & Mauborgne, R. (1997). Fair process: managing in the knowledge economy. *Harvard Business Review*, (July-August): 65–75.

Kim, S. S., & Malhotra, N. K. (2005). A longitudinal model of continued IS use: An integrative view of four mechanisms underlying post-adoption phenomena. *Management Science*, *51*(5), 741–755. doi:10.1287/mnsc.1040.0326

Kim, S., & Lee, H. (2006). The impact of organizational context and information technology on employee knowledge-sharing capabilities. *Public Administration Review*, *66*(3), 370–385. doi:10.1111/j.1540-6210.2006.00595.x

King, W. R. (2007). Keynote paper: Knowledge management: a systems perspective. *International Journal of Business Systems and Research*, *1*(1), 5–28.

Kivijärvi, H. (2008). Aligning Knowledge and Business Strategies within an Artificial Ba . In Abou-Zeid, E.-S. (Ed.), *Knowledge Management and Business Strategies: Theoretical Frameworks and Empirical Research*. Hershey, PA: IGI Global.

Kivijärvi, H., Piirainen, K., Tuominen, M., Elfvengren, K., & Kortelainen, S. (2008). A Support System for the Strategic Scenario Process . In Adam, F., & Humphreys, P. (Eds.), *Encyclopedia of Decision Making and Decision Support Technologies*. Hershey, PA: IGI Global.

Kjaegaard, A., & Kautz, K. (2008). A process model of establishing knowledge management: Insights from a longitudinal field study. *Omega*, *36*, 282–297. doi:10.1016/j.omega.2006.06.009

Klein, H. K., & Myers, M. D. (1999). A set of principles for conducting and evaluating interpretive field studies in information systems. *MIS Quarterly*, *23*(1), 67–94. doi:10.2307/249410

Kogut, B. (1988). Joint ventures: Theoretical and empirical perspectives. *Strategic Management Journal*, *9*, 319–332. doi:10.1002/smj.4250090403

Kogut, B., & Zander, U. (1992). Knowledge of the firm, combinative capabilities and the replication of technology. *Organization Science*, *3*(3), 383–397. doi:10.1287/orsc.3.3.383

Kohli, A., & Jaworski, B. (1990). Market orientation: The construct, research propositions, and managerial implications. *Journal of Marketing*, *54*, 1–18. doi:10.2307/1251866

Kohli, A., Jaworski, B. K., & Kumar, A. (1993). MARKOR: A Measure of Market Orientation. *JMR, Journal of Marketing Research*, *30*(4), 467–477. doi:10.2307/3172691

Kohls, C., & Scheiter, K. (2008, October 18-20). *The Psychology of Patterns*. Paper presented at the Fifteenth Conference on Pattern Languages of Programs (PLoP 2008), Nashville, TN, USA.

Korman, A. K. (1970). Toward a Hypothesis of Work Behavior. *The Journal of Applied Psychology*, *54*(1), 31–41. doi:10.1037/h0028656

Kornai, J. (1980). *Economic of Shortage: Volumes A and B*. New York: North-Holland.

Kotler, P., Jatusripitak, S., & Maesincee, S. (1997). *The Marketing of Nations: A Strategic Approach to Building National Wealth*. New York: The Free Press.

Koulopoulos, T. M., & Frappaolo, C. (1999). *Smart things to know about knowledge management*. New York: John Wiley.

KPMG. (2003). *Insights from KPMG's European Knowledge Management Survey 2002/2003*. KPMG Knowledge Advisory Services.

Kraiger, K., Ford, J. K., & Salas, E. (1993). Application of cognitive, skill-based, and affective theories of learning outcomes to new methods of training evaluation. *The Journal of Applied Psychology*, *78*(2), 311–328. doi:10.1037/0021-9010.78.2.311

Kruchten, P. (2004, December 2-3). *An Ontology of Architectural Design Decisions in Software-Intensive Systems*. Paper presented at the Second Gröningen Workshop on Software Variability Management: Software Product Families and Populations, Gröningen, The Netherlands.

Kulkarni, U., Ravindran, S., & Freeze, R. (2006). A knowledge management success model: Theoretical development and empirical validation. *Journal of Management Information Systems*, *23*(3), 309–347. doi:10.2753/MIS0742-1222230311

Kunert, T. (2009). *User-Centered Interaction Design Patterns for Interactive Digital Television Applications*. New York: Springer-Verlag.

Kuofie, M. H. S. (2005). E-management: E-knowledge management for optimizing rural medical services. *The International Journal of Management and Technologies*, *1*(1), 37–50.

Kusunoki, K., Nonaka, I., & Nagata, A. (1998). Organizational capabilities in product development of Japanese firms: A conceptual framework and empirical findings. *Organization Science*, 9(6), 699–718. doi:10.1287/orsc.9.6.699

Kwan, M. M., & Balasubramanian, P. (2003). KnowledgeScope: Managing knowledge in context. *Decision Support Systems*, 35, 467–486. doi:10.1016/S0167-9236(02)00126-4

Kwan, M. M., & Cheung, P. (2006). The knowledge transfer process: From field studies to technology development. *Journal of Database Management*, 17(1), 16–32.

Kwok, R. C. W., & Khalifa, M. (1998). Effect of GSS on Knowledge Acquisition. *Information & Management*, 34, 307–315. doi:10.1016/S0378-7206(98)00062-7

Kydd, C. T. (1989). Understanding the information content in MIS management tools. *Management Information Systems Quarterly*, 13(3), 277–290. doi:10.2307/249002

Lachman, R., Nedd, A., & Hinings, B. (1994). Analyzing cross-national management and organizations: A theoretical framework. *Management Science*, 40(1), 40–55. doi:10.1287/mnsc.40.1.40

Laframboise, K., Croteau, A., Beaudry, A., & Manovas, M. (2007). Interdepartmental knowledge transfer success during information technology projects. *International Journal of Knowledge Management*, 3(2), 47–67.

Lai, H., & Chu, T. H. (2000). Knowledge management: A review of theoretical frameworks and industrial cases. In *Proceedings of the 33rd Hawaii International Conference on System Sciences* (pp. 3022). Washington, DC: IEEE Computer Society.

Lai, I. L. A. (2005). Knowledge management for Chinese medicines: A conceptual model. *Information Management & Computer Security*, 13(3), 244–255. doi:10.1108/09685220510602059

Lai, L. (2007). A knowledge engineering approach to knowledge management. *Information Sciences*, 177, 4072–4094. doi:10.1016/j.ins.2007.02.028

Lai, M.-F., & Lee, G.-G. (2007). Relationships of organizational culture toward knowledge activities. *Business Process Management Journal*, 13(2), 306–322. doi:10.1108/14637150710740518

Lam, W., & Chua, A. (2005). Knowledge management project abandonment: An exploratory examination of root causes. *Communications of the Association for Information Systems*, 16, 723–743.

Lang, J. C. (2001). Managerial concerns in knowledge management. *Journal of Knowledge Management*, 5(1), 43–57. doi:10.1108/13673270110384392

Lariviere, B., & Poel, D. V. D. (2004). investigating the role of product features in preventing customer churn, by using survival analysis and choice modeling: The case of financial services. *Expert Systems with Applications*, 27, 277–285. doi:10.1016/j.eswa.2004.02.002

Lau, C.-M., Lu, Y., Makino, S., Chen, X., & Yeh, R.-S. (2002). Knowledge management of high-tech firms. In A. S. Tsui & C. M. Lau (Eds.), *Management of enterprises in People's Republic of China* (pp. 183-210). Boston: Kluwer Academic Publishers.

Lave, J., & Wenger, E. (1991). *Situated Learning: Legitimate peripheral participation*. New York: Cambridge University Press.

Law, K. S., Wong, C., & Mobley, W. H. (1998). Toward a taxonomy of multidimensional constructs. *Academy of Management Review*, 23(4), 741–753. doi:10.2307/259060

Leacock, M., Malone, E., & Wheeler, C. (2005, March 3-7). *Implementing a Pattern Library in the Real World: A Yahoo! Case Study*. The 2005 American Society for Information Science and Technology Information Architecture Summit (ASIS&T IA 2005), Montreal, Canada.

Lea, D. (1994). Christopher Alexander: An Introduction for Object-Oriented Designers. *ACM*, 19(1), 39–46.

Lee, C. C., & Yang, J. (2000). Knowledge value chain. *Journal of Management Development*, 19(9), 783–794. doi:10.1108/02621710010378228

Lee, H., & Choi, B. (2003). Knowledge management enablers, process, and organizational performance: an integrative view and empirical examination. *Journal of Management Information Systems*, 20(1), 179–228.

Lee, H., & Suh, Y. (2003). Knowledge conversion with information technology of Korean companies. *Business Process Management Journal*, 9(3), 317–336. doi:10.1108/14637150310477911

Lee, M. K. O., Cheung, C. M. K., Lim, K. H., & Sia, C. L. (2006). Understanding customer knowledge sharing in web-based discussion boards: An exploratory study. *Internet Research*, *16*(3), 289–303. doi:10.1108/10662240610673709

Lemaire, B., & Moore, J. (1994). An improved interface for tutorial dialogues: browsing a visual dialogue history. In *Proceedings of the Conference on Human Factors in Computing Systems* (pp. 16-22).

Leonard, D., & Sensiper, S. (1998). The role of tacit knowledge in group innovation. *California Management Review*, *40*(3), 112–132.

Leont'ev, A. N. (1974). The problem of activity in psychology. *Social Psychology*, *13*(2), 4–33.

Lesgold, A., Lajoie, S., Bunzo, M., & Eggan, G. (1992). Sherlock A Coached Practice Environment for an Electronics Troubleshooting Job . In Larkin, J., & Chabay, R. (Eds.), *Computer Assisted Instruction and Intelligent Tutoring Systems: Shared Goals and Complementary Approaches*. Hillsdale, NJ: Lawrence Erlbaum Associates.

Lesser, E., & Everest, K. (2001). *Using Communities of Practice to manage Intellectual Capital'. Ivey Business Journal*. March/April.

Lettieri, E., Borga, F., & Savoldelli, A. (2004). Knowledge management in non-profit organizations. *Journal of Knowledge Management*, *8*(6), 16–30. doi:10.1108/13673270410567602

Leuf, B., & Cunningham, W. (2001). *The Wiki Way: Quick Collaboration on the Web*. Reading, MA: Addison-Wesley.

Lev, B. (2001). What, why, and who? In *Intangibles—Management, Measurement, and Reporting* (pp. 5–20). Washington, DC: The Brookings Institution.

Levine, S. (2000). The rise of CRM. *America's Network*, *104*(6), 34.

Levinson, N. S., & Asahi, M. (1995). Cross-national alliances and interorganizational learning. *Organizational Dynamics*, *24*, 50–63. doi:10.1016/0090-2616(95)90071-3

Levitt, B., & March, J. G. (1988). Organizational learning. *Annual Review of Sociology*, *14*, 319–340. doi:10.1146/annurev.so.14.080188.001535

Lewis, B. R., Snyder, C. A., & Rainer, K. R. (1995). An empirical assessment of the information resource management construct. *Journal of Management Information Systems*, *12*(1), 199–210.

Lewis, W., Agarwal, R., & Sambamurthy, V. (2003). Sources of influence on beliefs about information technology use: An empirical study of knowledge workers. *Management Information Systems Quarterly*, *27*(4), 657–678.

Libby, T., & Waterhouse, J. H. (1996). Predicting change in management accounting systems. *Journal of Management Accounting Research*, *8*(1), 137–150.

Lieberman, H. (2001). Interfaces that Give and Take Advice . In Carroll, J. (Ed.), *Human-Computer Interaction for the New Millenium* (pp. 475–485). New York: ACM Press.

Liebowitz, J. (2000). *Building organizational intelligence: A knowledge management primer*. Boca Raton, FL: CRC Press.

Liebowitz, J., & Beckman, T. (1998). *Knowledge organizations: What every manager should know*. Boca Raton, FL: St. Luice Press.

Liebowitz, J. (1999). Key ingredients to the success of an organization's knowledge management strategy. *Knowledge and Process Management*, *6*(1), 37–40. doi:10.1002/(SICI)1099-1441(199903)6:1<37::AID-KPM40>3.0.CO;2-M

Liebowitz, J. (Ed.). (1999). *Knowledge management Handbook*. CRC.

Lien, B. Y. H., Hung, R. Y., & McLean, G. N. (2007). Organizational learning as an organization development intervention in six high-technology firms in Taiwan: An exploratory case study. *Human Resource Development Quarterly*, *18*(2), 211–228. doi:10.1002/hrdq.1200

Li, J. (2003). U.S. and Chinese cultural beliefs about learning. *Journal of Education & Psychology*, *95*(2), 258–267. doi:10.1037/0022-0663.95.2.258

Li, J. J., Poppo, L., & Zhou, K. Z. (2008). Do managerial ties in China always produce value? Competition, uncertainty, and domestic vs. foreign firms. *Strategic Management Journal*, *29*(4), 383–400. doi:10.1002/smj.665

Li, J., & Karakowsky, L. (2002). Cultural malleability in an East Asian Context: An illustration of the relationship between government policy, national culture, and firm behavior. *Administration & Society, 34*(2), 176–201. doi:10.1177/0095399702034002003

Li, L., Barner-Rasmussen, W., & Björkman, I. (2007). What difference does the location make? A social capital perspective on transfer of knowledge from multinational corporation subsidiaries located in China and Finland. *Asia Pacific Business Review, 13*(2), 233–249. doi:10.1080/13602380601133185

Lin, C., & Tseng, S. M. (2005). The implementation gaps for the knowledge management system. *Industrial Management + Data Systems, 105*(1/2), 208-222.

Lin, C., Tan, B., & Chang, S. (2002). The critical factors for technology absorptive capacity. *Industrial Management + Data Systems, 102*(5/6), 300-308.

Lin, C., Chang, S., & Chang, C. S. (2004). The impact of technology absorptive capacity on technology transfer performance. *International Journal of Technology Transfer & Commercialisation, 3*(4), 384–409. doi:10.1504/IJTTC.2004.005610

Lin, C.-P. (2007). To share or not to share, modeling tacit knowledge sharing, its mediators and antecedents. *Journal of Business Ethics, 70*, 411–428. doi:10.1007/s10551-006-9119-0

Lincoln, Y. S., & Guba, E. G. (1985). *Naturalistic inquiry.* Newbury Park, CA: SAGE Publications.

Lindqvist, A., Piirainen, K., & Tuominen, M. (2008). Utilising group innovation to enhance business foresight for capital-intensive manufacturing industries. In *Proceedings of the 1st ISPIM Innovation Symposium.* Singapore.

Lindsey, K. (2002). Measuring knowledge management effectiveness: A task-contingent organizational capabilities perspective. *Eighth Americas Conference on Information Systems*, 2085-2090.

Lindsey, K. (2002). Measuring knowledge management effectiveness: A task-contingent organizational capabilities perspective. In *Proceedings of the Eighth Americas Conference on Information Systems* (pp. 2085-2090).

Lin, F., Lin, S., & Huang, T. (2008). Knowledge sharing and creation in a teachers' professional virtual community. *Computers & Education, 50*(3), 742–756. doi:10.1016/j.compedu.2006.07.009

Lin, H.-F., & Lee, G.-G. (2006). Effects of socio-technical factors on organizational intention to encourage knowledge sharing. *Management Decision, 44*(1), 74–88. doi:10.1108/00251740610641472

Lin, L., & Kwok, L. (2006). Challenges to KM at Hewlett Packard China. *Knowledge Management Review, 9*(1), 20–23.

Lin, Y., Su, H.-Y., & Shihen, C. (2006). A knowledge enabled procedure for customer relationship management. *Industrial Marketing Management, 35*, 446–456. doi:10.1016/j.indmarman.2005.04.002

Li, S., & Scullion, H. (2006). Bridging the distance: Managing cross-border knowledge holders. *Asia Pacific Journal of Management, 23*, 71–92. doi:10.1007/s10490-006-6116-x

Li, S., & Wood, W. (2005). Portals In The Academic World: Are They Meeting Expectations? *Journal of Computer Information Systems, 45*(4), 50–55.

Li, T., & Calantone, R. J. (1998). The impact of market knowledge competence on new product advantage: Conceptualization and empirical examination. *Journal of Marketing, 62*(4), 13–29. doi:10.2307/1252284

Li, T., & Cavusgil, S. T. (1999). Measuring the dimensions of market knowledge competence in new product development. *European Journal of Innovation Management, 2*(3), 129–146. doi:10.1108/14601069910289068

Liu, S. (2003). *A study of factors that facilitate use of knowledge management systems and the impact of use on individual learning.* Unpublished doctoral dissertation, Claremont Graduate University, Claremont, CA.

Liu, C.-C. (2006). Modeling the transfer of technology to Taiwan from China. *International Research Journal of Finance and Economics, 7*, 48–66.

Liu, P. L., Chen, W. C., & Tsai, C. H. (2005). An empirical study on the correlation between the knowledge management method & new product development strategy on product performance in Taiwan's industries. *Technovation, 25*(7), 637–644.

Liu, P., & Tsai, C. (2007). Effect of Knowledge Management Systems on Operating Performance: An Empirical study of hi-tech companies sing the balanced scorecard approach. *International Journal of Management, 24*(4), 734–744.

Liu, Q. (2006). Corporate governance in China: Current practices, economic effects and institutional determinants. *CEIsfo Economic Studies, 52*(2), 415–453. doi:10.1093/cesifo/ifl001

Liu, Y. W., Pucel, D. J., & Bartlett, K. R. (2006). Knowledge transfer practices in multinational corporations in China's information technology industry. *Human Resource Development International, 9*(4), 529–552. doi:10.1080/13678860601032635

Li, W., Ardichvili, A., Maurer, M., Wentling, T., & Stuedemann, R. (2007). Impact of Chinese culture values on knowledge sharing through online communities of practice. *International Journal of Knowledge Management, 3*(3), 46–59.

Li, Y., Liu, Y., Li, M. F., & Wu, H. B. (2007). Transformational offshore outsourcing: empirical evidence from alliances in China. *Journal of Operations Management.* doi:.doi:10.1016/j.jom.2007.02.011

Lo, C., & Wang, J. (2007). The relationship between defender and prospector business strategies and organizational performance in two different industries. *International Journal of Management, 24*(1), 174–183.

Loermans, J. (2002). Synergizing the learning organization. *Journal of Knowledge Management, 6*(3), 285–294. doi:10.1108/13673270210434386

Long, D., & Fahey, L. (2000). Diagnosing cultural barriers to knowledge management. *The Academy of Management Executive, 14*(4), 113–127.

Louridas, P. (2006). Using Wikis in Software Development. *IEEE Software, 23*(2), 88–91. doi:10.1109/MS.2006.62

Lucier, C. E., & Torsilieri, J. D. (1997). Why knowledge programs fail: A C.E.O.'s guide to managing learning. *Strategy & Business, 9*(4), 14–28.

Luecke, R., & Katz, R. (2003). *Managing Creativity and Innovation.* Boston, MA: Harvard Business School Press.

Lu, L., Leung, K., & Koch, P. T. (2006). Managerial knowledge sharing: The role of individual, interpersonal and organizational factors. *Management and Organization Review, 2*(1), 15–41. doi:10.1111/j.1740-8784.2006.00029.x

Lundberg, C. C. (1996). Managing in a culture that values learning. In S. A. Cavaleri & D. S. Fearson (Eds.), *Managing in organizations that learn.* Cambridge, MA: Blackwell.

Luo, Y. (1999). Dimensions of knowledge: comparing Asian and Western MNEs in China. *Asia Pacific Journal of Management, 16*(1), 75–93. doi:10.1023/A:1015410219287

Maier, R. (2002). *Knowledge Management Systems: Information and Communication Technologies for Knowledge Management.* Berlin: Springer-Verlag.

Maier, R., & Remus, U. (2002). Defining process-oriented knowledge management strategies. *Knowledge and Process Management, 9*(2), 103–118. doi:10.1002/kpm.136

Majchrzak, A., Beath, C. M., Lim, R. A., & Chin, W. W. (2005). Managing Client Dialogues During Information Systems Design to Facilitate Client Learning. *Management Information Systems Quarterly, 29*(4), 653–672.

Malhotra, Y. (2000). From information management to knowledge management: Beyond the 'Hi-Tech Hidebound' systems . In Srikantaiah, K., & Koenig, M. E. D. (Eds.), *Knowledge Management for the Information Professional* (pp. 37–61). Medford, NJ: Information Today Inc.

Manolescu, D., Kozaczynski, W., Miller, A., & Hogg, J. (2007). The Growing Divide in the Patterns World. *IEEE Software, 24*(4), 61–67. doi:10.1109/MS.2007.120

Marakas, G. M., & Elam, J. J. (1998). Semantic structuring in analyst acquisition and representation of facts in requirements analysis. *Information Systems Research, 9*(1), 37–63. doi:10.1287/isre.9.1.37

March, J. G. (1991). Exploration and exploitation in organization learning. *Organization Science, 2*, 71–87. doi:10.1287/orsc.2.1.71

Marinova, D. (2004). Actualizing innovation effort: The impact of market knowledge diffusion in a dynamic system of competition. *Journal of Marketing, 68*(3), 1–20. doi:10.1509/jmkg.68.3.1.34768

Markus, L. M. (2001). Toward a theory of knowledge reuse: Types of knowledge reuse situations and factors in reuse success. *Journal of Management Information Systems, 18*(1), 57–93.

Marquardt, J. (1996). *Building the learning organization.* New York: McGraw Hill.

Marsden, P. V. (1990). Network data and measurement. *Annual Review of Sociology, 16*(1), 435–463. doi:10.1146/annurev.so.16.080190.002251

Martinsons, M. G., & Martinsons, A. B. (1996). Conquering cultural constraints to cultivate Chinese management creativity and innovation. *Journal of Management Development, 15*(9), 18–35. doi:10.1108/02621719610146239

Martinsons, M., & Davison, R. (2003). Cultural Issues and IT Management. *IEEE Transactions on Engineering Management, 50*(1), 113–117. doi:10.1109/TEM.2003.808299

Martinsons, M., & Davison, R. (2007). Culture's consequences for IT application and business process change: a research agenda. *International Journal of Internet and Enterprise Management, 5*(2), 158. doi:10.1504/IJIEM.2007.014087

Masrek, M. (2007). Measuring campus portal effectiveness and the contributing factors. *Campus-Wide Information Systems, 24*(5), 342–354. doi:10.1108/10650740710835760

Massey, A. P., Montoya-Weiss, M. M., & O'Driscoll, T. M. (2002). Knowledge management in pursuit of performance: Insights from Nortel Networks. *Management Information Systems Quarterly, 26*(3), 269–289. doi:10.2307/4132333

Massey, A. P., Montoya-Weiss, M., & Holcom, K. (2001). Re-engineering the customer relationship: Leveraging knowledge assets at IBM. *Decision Support Systems, 32*(2), 155–170. doi:10.1016/S0167-9236(01)00108-7

Mata, F. J., Fuerst, W. L., & Barney, J. B. (1995). Information technology and sustained competitive advantage: A resource-based analysis. *Management Information Systems Quarterly, 19*(4), 487–505. doi:10.2307/249630

Mathiassen, L., & Pourkomeylian, P. (2003). Managing knowledge in a software organization. *Journal of Knowledge Management, 7*(2), 63–80. doi:10.1108/13673270310477298

Matsumoto, I. T., Stapleton, J., Glass, J., & Thorpe, T. (2005). A knowledge capture report for multidisciplinary design environments. *Journal of Knowledge Management, 9*(3), 83–92. doi:10.1108/13673270510602782

May, D., & Taylor, P. (2003). Knowledge Management with Patterns. *Communications of the ACM, 46*(7), 94–99. doi:10.1145/792704.792705

McAfee, A. P. (2006). Enterprise 2.0: The Dawn of Emergent Collaboration. *MIT Sloan Management Review, 47*(3), 21–28.

McDermott, R., & O'Dell, C. (2001). Overcoming culture barriers to sharing knowledge. *Journal of Knowledge Management, 5*(1), 76–85. doi:10.1108/13673270110384428

McEvily, B., & Zaheer, A. (1999). Bridging ties: A source of firm heterogeneity in competitive capabilities. *Strategic Management Journal, 20*, 1133–1156. doi:10.1002/(SICI)1097-0266(199912)20:12<1133::AID-SMJ74>3.0.CO;2-7

McFarlan, F. W. (1984). Information technology changes the way you compete. *Harvard Business Review, 62*(3), 98–103.

McGrath, R. G., Macmillan, I. C., Yang, E. A., & Tsai, W. (1992). Does culture endure, or is it malleable? Issues for entrepreneurial economic development. *Journal of Business Venturing, 7*, 441–458. doi:10.1016/0883-9026(92)90019-N

Mead, R. (1994). *International management.* Oxford, UK: Blackwell.

Mei, S., & Nie, M. (2007). Relationship between knowledge sharing, knowledge characteristics, absorptive capacity and innovation: An empirical study of Wuhan optoelectronic cluster. *Business Review (Federal Reserve Bank of Philadelphia), 7*(2), 154–160.

Menou, M. J. (1983). Cultural barriers to the international transfer of information. *Information Processing & Management, 19*(3), 121–129. doi:10.1016/0306-4573(83)90065-1

Merchant, K. (1990). The effects of financial controls on data manipulation and management myopia. *Accounting, Organizations and Society, 15*, 297–313. doi:10.1016/0361-3682(90)90021-L

Meszaros, G., & Doble, J. (1998). A Pattern Language for Pattern Writing . In Martin, R. C., Riehle, D., & Buschmann, F. (Eds.), *Pattern Languages of Program Design 3* (pp. 529–574). Reading, MA: Addison-Wesley.

Michailova, S., & Hutchings, K. (2006). National cultural influences on knowledge sharing: a comparison of China and Russia. *Journal of Management Studies, 43*(3), 383–405. doi:10.1111/j.1467-6486.2006.00595.x

Miesing, P., Kriger, M. P., & Slough, N. (2007). Towards a model of effective knowledge transfer within transnationals: The case of Chinese foreign invested enterprises. *The Journal of Technology Transfer, 32*, 109–122. doi:10.1007/s10961-006-9006-y

Millerand, F., Giroux, L., & Proulx, S. (2001). La culture technique dans l'appropriation cognitive des TIC. Une étude des usages du courrier électronique, Dans *Actes du colloque international ICUST 2001*, Paris (pp. 400-410).

Miltiadis, D. L., Pouloudi, A., & Poulymenakou, A. (2002). Knowledge management convergence expanding learning frontiers. *Journal of Knowledge Management, 6*(1), 40–51. doi:10.1108/13673270210417682

Miner, A. S., & Mezias, S. J. (1996). Ugly duckling no more: Pasts and futures of organizational learning research. *Organization Science, 7*(1), 88–99. doi:10.1287/orsc.7.1.88

Mitra, D., & Golder, P. N. (2002). Whose culture matters? Near-market knowledge and its impact on foreign market entry timing. *JMR, Journal of Marketing Research, 39*(3), 350–365. doi:10.1509/jmkr.39.3.350.19112

Monk, A., Wright, P., Haber, J., & Davenport, L. (1993). *Improving your human-computer interface*. New York: Prentice Hall.

Montequin, V. R., Fernandez, F. O., Cabal, V. A., & Gutierrez, N. R. (2006). An integrated framework for intellectual capital measurement and knowledge management implementation in small and medium-sized enterprises. *Journal of Information Science, 32*(6), 525–538. doi:10.1177/0165551506067127

Moorman, C. (1995). Organizational marketing information processes: Cultural antecedents and new product outcomes. *JMR, Journal of Marketing Research, 32*, 318–335. doi:10.2307/3151984

Morgan, N. A., Zou, S., Vorhies, D. W., & Katsikeas, C. S. (2003). Experiential and informational knowledge, architectural marketing capabilities, and the adaptive performance of export ventures: a cross-national study. *Decision Sciences, 34*(2), 287–321. doi:10.1111/1540-5915.02375

Morgan, R. E., & Turnell, C. R. (2003). Market-based organizational learning and market performance gains. *British Journal of Management, 14*, 255–274. doi:10.1111/1467-8551.00378

Moyer, M. S. (1972). Market intelligence for modern merchants. *California Management Review, 14*(4), 3–69.

Mullen, T. P., & Lyles, M. A. (1993). Toward improving management development's contribution to organizational learning. *Human Resource Planning, 16*(2), 35–49.

Murray, P. (2002). Knowledge management as a sustained competitive advantage. *Ivey Business Journal, 66*(4), 71–76.

Myers, M. D., & Tan, F. D. (2002). Beyond models of national culture in information systems research. *Journal of Global Information Management, 10*(1), 24–32.

Nadler, D., & Nadler, M. (1996). *Champions of change*. San Francisco: Jossey-Bass.

Nadler, D., & Tushman, M. (1997). *Competing by design*. New York: Oxford University Press.

Nahapiet, J., & Ghoshal, S. (1998). Social capital, intellectual capital, and the organizational advantage. *Academy of Management Review, 23*, 242–266. doi:10.2307/259373

Nakata, C., & Sivakumar, K. (1996). National Culture and New Product Development: An Integrative Review. *Journal of Marketing, 60*, 61–72. doi:10.2307/1251888

Narver, J. C., & Slater, S. F. (1990). The effect of a market orientation on business profitability. *Journal of Marketing, 54*, 20–35. doi:10.2307/1251757

Neal, A. S., & Simons, R. M. (1983). Playback: A method for evaluating the usability of software and its documentation. In *Proceedings of CHI '83* (pp. 78-82).

Nelson, H. J., & Monarchi, D. E. (2007). Ensuring the Quality of Conceptual Representations. *Software Quality Journal, 15*(2), 213–233. doi:10.1007/s11219-006-9011-2

Nelson, K., & Cooprider, J. (1996). The contribution of shared knowledge to IS group performance. *MIS Quarterly*, *20*(4), 409–429. doi:10.2307/249562

Nevo, D., & Chan, Y. E. (2007). A Delphi study of knowledge management systems: Scope and requirements. *Information & Management*, *44*, 583–597. doi:10.1016/j.im.2007.06.001

Nevo, D., & Chan, Y. E. (2007b). A temporal approach to expectations and desires from knowledge management systems. *Decision Support Systems*, *44*, 298–312. doi:10.1016/j.dss.2007.04.003

Newell, F. (2000). *Loyalty.com: Customer relationship management in the new era of internet marketing*. New York: McGraw-Hill, New York.

Newell, S. (1999). The transfer of management knowledge to China: Building learning communities rather than translating Western textbooks? *Education + Training*, *41*(6/7), 286-293.

Newell, S., Huang, J., Galliers, R., & Pan, S. (2003). implementing enterprise resource planning and knowledge management systems in tandem: fostering efficiency and innovation complementarily. *Information and Organization*, *13*, 25–52. doi:10.1016/S1471-7727(02)00007-6

Nicholson, J. D., & Stepina, L. P. (1998). Cultural values: A cross-national study. *Cross Cultural Management - . International Journal (Toronto, Ont.)*, *5*(1), 34–49.

Nickols, F. W. (2000). The Knowledge in Knowledge Management . In Cortada, J. W., & Woods, J. A. (Eds.), *The Knowledge Management Yearbook 2000-2001* (pp. 12–21). Woburn, MA: Butterworth-Heinemann.

Nicolini, D., Gherardi, S., & Yanow, D. (2003). *Knowing in organizations*. Armonk, NY: M. E. Sharpe.

Niehoff, B. P., & Whitney-Bammerlin, D. L. (1995). Don't let your training process derail your journey to total quality management. *S.A.M. Advanced Management Journal*, *60*(1), 39–45.

Noble, J., & Biddle, R. (2002, June 10-14). *Patterns as Signs*. Paper presented at the Sixteenth European Conference on Object-Oriented Programming (ECOOP 2002), Malaga, Spain.

Nonaka, I., & Takeuchi, H. (1995). *The knowledge-creating company: How Japanese companies create the dynamics of innovation*. New York: Oxford University Press.

Nonaka, I. (1991). The knowledge creating company. *Harvard Business Review*, *69*(6), 96–104.

Nonaka, I. (1994). A dynamic theory of organizational knowledge creation. *Organization Science*, *5*(1), 14–37. doi:10.1287/orsc.5.1.14

Nonaka, I., & Konno, N. (1998). The concept of "ba": Building a foundation for knowledge creation. *California Management Review*, *40*(3), 40–54.

Nonaka, I., Konno, N., & Toyama, R. (2001). The Emergence of "Ba": A Conceptual Framework for the Continuous and Self-transcending Process of Knowledge Creation . In Nonaka, I., & Nishiguchi, T. (Eds.), *Knowledge Emergence, Social, Technical, and Evolutionary Dimensions of Knowledge Creation* (pp. 13–29). Oxford, NY: University Press.

Nonaka, I., Reinmoeller, P., & Senoo, D. (1998). The 'ART' of knowledge: Systems to capitalize on market knowledge. *European Management Journal*, *16*(6), 673–684. doi:10.1016/S0263-2373(98)00044-9

Nonaka, I., & Takeuchi, H. (1995). *The Knowledge-Creating Company*. New York: Oxford University Press.

Nonaka, I., & Takeuchi, H. (1995). *The Knowledge-creating Company: How Japanese Companies Create the Dynamics of Innovation*. New York: Oxford University Press.

Nonaka, I., Toyama, R., & Konno, N. (2000). SECI, *Ba* and Leadership: A unified model of dynamic knowledge creation. *Long Range Planning*, *33*, 5–34. doi:10.1016/S0024-6301(99)00115-6

Nonaka, I., von Krogh, G., & Voelpel, S. (2006). Organizational Knowledge Creation Theory: Evolutionary Paths and Future Advances. *Organization Studies*, *27*(8), 1179–1208. doi:10.1177/0170840606066312

Norman, P. (2002). Protecting knowledge in strategic alliances: Resource and relational characteristics. *The Journal of High Technology Management Research*, *13*, 177–202. doi:10.1016/S1047-8310(02)00050-0

Nunnally, J. C. (1978). *Psychometric theory* (2nd ed.). New York: McGraw-Hill.

O'Connor, N. G., Chow, C., & Wu, A. (2004). The adoption of "Western" management accounting/controls in China's state-owned enterprises during economic transition. *Accounting, Organizations and Society, 29*(3/4), 349–375. doi:10.1016/S0361-3682(02)00103-4

O'Reilly, T. (2005, September 30). *What Is Web 2.0: Design Patterns and Business Models for the Next Generation of Software*. O'Reilly Network.

Ocker, R. J., & Mudambi, S. (2002). Assessing the readiness of firms for CRM: A literature review and research model. In *Proceedings of the 36th Hawaii International Conference on System Sciences* (pp. 10). Washington, DC: IEEE Computer Society.

OECD. (1996). *The Knowledge Based Economy*. Paris: OECD.

OECD. (2004). *The Economic Impact of ICT: Measurement, Evidence and Implications*. Paris: OECD.

Office of Special Committee for Coordination in Projects from H.M. the King's Considerations. (n.d.). *The Working Principles of H.M. the King*. Bangkok, Thailand: King Chulalongkorn's Cadet School.

Ollagnier-Beldame, M. (2006). *Traces d'interactions et processus cognitifs en activité conjointe: Le cas d'une co-rédaction médiée par un artefact numérique*. Thèse de Doctorat, Université Lumière Lyon2, France.

Oltra, V. (2005). Knowledge management effectiveness factors: The role of HRM. *Journal of Knowledge Management, 9*(4), 70–86. doi:10.1108/13673270510610341

Organization for Economic Cooperation and Development (OECD). (2005). *Economic Survey of China 2005*. Retrieved from http://www.oecd.org/ eco/surveys/china

Orlikowski, W. J., & Barley, S. R. (2001). Technology and Institutions: What Can Research on Information Technology and Research on Organizations Learn from Each Other? *Management Information Systems Quarterly, 25*(2), 145–165. doi:10.2307/3250927

Orlokowski, W. J. (1993). CASE tools as organizational vhange investigating incremental and radical changes in systems development. *MIS Quarterly, 17*(3).

Orzano, A. J., Tallia, A. F., McInerney, C. R., McDaniel, R. R. Jr, & Crabtree, B. F. (2007). Strategies for developing a knowledge-driven culture in your practice. *Family Practice Management, 14*(4), 32–34.

Osborn, R. N., & Hagedoorn, J. (1997). The institutionalization and evolutionary dynamics of interorganizational alliances and networks. *Academy of Management Journal, 40*, 261–278. doi:10.2307/256883

Paap, J., & Katz, R. (2004). Anticipating Disruptive Innovation: Predicting the "unpredictable". *Research & Technology Management*, (Sept.-Oct.), 13-22.

Pablos, P. O. D. (2002). Knowledge management and organizational learning: typologies of knowledge strategies in the Spanish manufacturing industry from 1995 to 1999. *Journal of Knowledge Management, 6*(1), 52–62. doi:10.1108/13673270210417691

Paisittanand, A., Digman, L. A., & Lee, S. M. (2007). Managing Knowledge capabilities for strategy implementation effectiveness. *International Journal of Knowledge Management, 3*(4), 84–110.

Panich, V. (2005). *Knowledge management, a practitioner's version*. Bangkok, Thailand: Institute of Knowledge Management Promotion for the Society (IKMPS).

Papoutsakis, H., & Vallès, R. S. (2006). Linking knowledge management and information technology to business performance: A literature review and a proposed model. *Journal of Knowledge Management Practice, 7*(1).

Parent, R., Roy, M., & St-Jacques, D. (2007). A systems-based dynamic knowledge transfer capacity model. *Journal of Knowledge Management, 11*(6), 81–93. doi:10.1108/13673270710832181

Parsons, E., & Broadbridge, A. (2006). Job motivation and satisfaction: Unpacking the key factors for charity shop managers. *Journal of Retailing and Consumer Services, 13*(2), 121–131. doi:10.1016/j.jretconser.2005.08.013

Patthamasiriwat, D. (2004). Public policy for good quality of life by decentralization to the local and people participation. *The Good Public Policy, 4*(8).

Patton, M. Q. (2002). *Qualitative research & evaluation methods* (3rd ed.). Thousands Oaks, CA: Sage Publications. ISBN: 0-7619-1971-6.

Paulson, D. S. (2002). *Competitive business, caring business: An integral business perspective for the 21st century.* New York: Paraview Press.

Pavlou, P. A., & Fygenson, M. (2006). Understanding and predicting electronic commerce adoption: An extension of the theory of planned behavior. *Management Information Systems Quarterly, 30*(1), 115–143.

Payne, A., Christopher, M., Clark, M., & Peck, H. (1999). *Relationship marketing for competitive advantage* (2nd ed.). Oxford, UK: Butterworth Heinemann.

Pearson, T. (1999). Measurements and the knoweldge revolution. *Quality Progress, 32*(9), 31–37.

Peng, J., Li-Hua, R., & Moffett, S. (2007). Trend of knowledge management in China: Challenges and opportunities. *Journal of Technology Management in China, 2*(3), 198–211. doi:10.1108/17468770710825142

Peng, M. W. (2003). Institutional transitions and strategic choices. *Academy of Management Review, 28*(2), 275–296.

Perloff, R. M. (1993). *The Dynamics of Persuasion.* Hillsdale, NJ: Erlbaum.

Persson, A. (2001). *Enterprise Modelling in Practice: Situational Factors and their Influence on Adopting a Participative Approach,* Ph.D. Thesis, Department of Computer and System Sciences, Stockholm University, ISSN 1101-8526

Persson, A., & Stirna, J. (2002). Creating an organisational memory through integration of enterprise modelling, patterns and hypermedia: The HyperKnowledge approach. In M. Kirikova et al. (Eds.), *Information systems development – advances in methodologies, components and management* (pp. pp. 181-192). New York: Kluwer Academic.

Persson, A., Stirna, J., Dulle, H., Hatzenbichler, G., & Strutz, G. (2003). Introducing a pattern based knowledge management approach - the Verbundplan Case. In *Proceedings of the 4ᵗʰ International Workshop on Theory and Applications of Knowledge Management (TAKMA'03), 14ᵗʰ International Workshop on Database and Expert Systems Applications (DEXA'03),* (pp. 1529-4188/03). Washington, DC: IEEE Computer Society.

Persson, A., Stirna, J., & Aggestam, L. (2008). How to disseminate professional knowledge in health care – the case of Skaraborg hospital. *Journal of Cases on Information Technology, 10*(4), 41–64.

Peterson, R. (2000). A meta-analysis of variance accounted for and factor loadings in exploratory factor analysis. *Marketing Letters, 11,* 261–275. doi:10.1023/A:1008191211004

Pfeffer, J. (1998). *New Directions for Organization Theory.* New York: Oxford University Press.

Phillips, T., & Vollmer, M. (2000). Knowledge management in the current marketplace. *Oil & Gas Journal,* 4–5.

Phongphit, S., Wichit, N., & Jumnong, R. (2001). *Community enterprises, master plan, concepts, model guidelines.* Bangkok, Thailand: Tai Wisdom.

Piaget, J. (1952). *The Origins of Intelligence in Children.* Madison, CT: International University Press. doi:10.1037/11494-000

Piirainen K., Kortelainen S., Elfvengren K., & Tuominen, M. (in press). A scenario approach for assessing new business concepts, *Management Research News, 32*(7).

Pinto, M., & Doucet, A. (2007). An educational resource for information literacy in higher education: Functional and users analyses of the e-COMS academic portal. *Scientometrics, 72*(2), 225–252. doi:10.1007/s11192-007-1725-9

Plainoi, N. (2007). An analysis of learning process in transcribing lessons: Using after-action review instruments. In *Supplement to training* (pp. 2-5).

Plaisant, C., Rose, A., Rubloff, G., Salter, R., & Shneiderman, B. (1999). The Design of History Mechanism and Their Use in Collaborative Educational Simulations. In *Proceedings of the Computer Support for Collaborative Learning,* Palo Alto, CA (pp. 348-359).

Plessis, M. D. (2007). Knowledge management: What makes complex implementations successful? *Journal of Knowledge Management, 11*(2), 91–101. doi:10.1108/13673270710738942

Pluss, J., & Salisbury, M. (2002). A living-systems design model for web-based knowledge management systems. *Educational Technology Research and Development*, *50*(1), 35–56. doi:10.1007/BF02504960

Polanyi, M. (1983). *The tacit dimension.* Glouster, MA: Peter Smith Publisher. ISBN: 0-8446-5999-1.

Polanyi, M. (1966). *The Tacit Dimension.* Gloucester, MA: Peter Smith.

Polanyi, M. (1976). Tacit knowledge . In Marx, M., & Goodson, F. (Eds.), *Theories in Contemporary Psychology* (2nd ed., pp. 330–344). New York: Macmillan.

Polanyi, M. (1983). *The Tacit Dimension.* Gloucester, MA: Peter Smith.

Pólya, G. (1945). *How to Solve It: A New Aspect of Mathematical Method.* Princeton, NJ: Princeton University Press.

Pook, L. A., & Fustos, J. (1999). Information sharing by management: some cross-cultural results. *Human Systems Management*, *18*(1), 9–22.

Poon, P., & Wagner, C. (2001). Critical success factors revisited: success and failure cases of information systems for seniior executives. *Decision Support Systems*, *30*, 393–418. doi:10.1016/S0167-9236(00)00069-5

Porter-Libskind, J. (1996). Knowledge, strategy, and the theory of the firm. *Strategic Management Journal*, *17*, 93–107.

Porter, M. E. (1998). Clusters and the New Economics of Competition. *Harvard Business Review*, 77–90.

Porter, M. E., & Millar, V. E. (1985). How information gives you competitive advantage. *Harvard Business Review*, *63*(4), 149–160.

Prahalad, C. K. (2005). *The Fortune at the Bottom of the Pyramid: Eradicating Poverty Through Profits.* Philadelphia: Wharton School Publishing.

Prahalad, C. K., & Krishnan, M. S. (2008). *The new age of innovation: Driving co-created value through global networks.* Columbus, OH: McGraw-Hill.

Prusak, L., & Matson, E. (2006). *Knowledge management and organizational learning: A reader.* Oxford, UK: Oxford University Press.

Putnam, R. D. (2001). *Bowling alone: the collapse and revival of American community.* New York: Simon & Schuster.

Putti, J., Aryee, S., & Phua, J. (1990). Communication relationship satisfaction and organizational commitment. *Group and Organization Studies*, *15*(1), 44–52. doi:10.1177/105960119001500104

Rabardel, P., & Samurçay, R. (2001, March 21-23). From Artifact to Instrument-Mediated Learning. In *Proceedings of International symposium on New challenges to research on Learning*, Helsinki, Finland.

Ralston, D. A., Gustafson, D. J., Cheung, F. M., & Terpstra, R. H. (1993). Differences in managerial values: A study of U.S., Hong Kong, and PRC managers. *Journal of International Business Studies*, *24*(2), 249–275. doi:10.1057/palgrave.jibs.8490232

Ralston, D. A., Gustafson, D. J., Elsass, P. M., Cheung, F., & Terpstra, R. H. (1992). Eastern Values: A Comparison of Managers in the United States, Hong Kong, and the People's Republic of China. *The Journal of Applied Psychology*, *77*(5), 664–671. doi:10.1037/0021-9010.77.5.664

Ramasamy, B., Goh, K. W., & Yeung, M. C. H. (2006). Is Guanxi (relationship) a bridge to knowledge transfer? *Journal of Business Research*, *59*, 130–139. doi:10.1016/j.jbusres.2005.04.001

Rech, J. (2007). Handling of Software Quality Defects in Agile Software Development . In Stamelos, I., & Sfetsos, P. (Eds.), *Agile Software Development Quality Assurance*. Hershey, PA: IGI Global.

Rech, J., Decker, B., Ras, E., Jedlitschka, A., & Feldmann, R. L. (2007). The Quality of Knowledge: Knowledge Patterns and Knowledge Refactorings. *International Journal of Knowledge Management*, *3*(3), 74–103.

Rech, J., Ras, E., & Decker, B. (2007b). RIKI: A System for Knowledge Transfer and Reuse in Software Engineering Projects . In Lytras, M. D., & Naeve, A. (Eds.), *Open Source for Knowledge and Learning Management*. Hershey, PA: IGI Global.

Reed, R., & DeFillippi, R. J. (1990). Causal Ambiguity, barriers to imitation, and sustainable competitive advantage. *Academy of Management Review*, 15(1), 88–102. doi:10.2307/258107

Reichheld, F. (1996). *The loyalty effect*. Cambridge, MA: Harvard Business School Press.

Reinartz, W., Krafft, M., & Hoyer, W. (2004). The customer relationship management process: Its measurement and impact on performance. *JMR, Journal of Marketing Research*, 61(1), 293–305. doi:10.1509/jmkr.41.3.293.35991

Reinmann-Rothmeier, G. (2000). *Wissen managen: Das Münchener Modell*. Retrieved from.

Remus, U., & Schub, S. (2003). A blueprint for the implementation of process-oriented knowledge management. *Knowledge and Process Management*, 10(4), 237–253. doi:10.1002/kpm.182

Renié, D. (2000). Apport d'une trace informatique dans l'analyse du processus d'apprentissage d'une langue seconde ou étrangère . In Duquette, L., & Laurier, M. (Eds.), *Apprendre une langue dans un environnement multimédia* (pp. 281–301). Outremont, Canada: Les Éditions Logiques.

Retalis, S., Georgiakakis, P., & Dimitriadis, Y. (2006). Eliciting Design Patterns for E-Learning Systems. *Computer Science Education*, 16(2), 105–118. doi:10.1080/08993400600773323

Rhodes, J., Hung, R., Lok, P., Lien, B., & Wu, C. (2008). Factors influencing organizational knowledge transfer: implications for corporate performance. *Journal of Knowledge Management*, 12(3), 84–100. doi:10.1108/13673270810875886

Rich, C., & Sidner, C. L. (1997). Segmented Interaction History in a Collaborative Interface Agent. In *Proceedings of International Conference on Intelligent User Interfaces*, Orlando, FL (pp. 23-30).

Richter, F., & Vettel, K. (1995). Successful joint ventures in Japan: Transferring knowledge through organizational learning. *Long Range Planning*, 28(3), 37–45. doi:10.1016/0024-6301(95)00019-F

Riege, A. (2003). Validity and reliability tests in case study research: A literature review with "hands-on" applications for each research phase. *Qualitative Market Research*, 6, 75–86. doi:10.1108/13522750310470055

Riege, A. (2005). Three-dozen knowledge-sharing barriers managers must consider. *Journal of Knowledge Management*, 9(3), 18–35. doi:10.1108/13673270510602746

Rigby, D., Reichheld, F., & Schefter, P. (2002). Avoid the four perils of CRM. *Harvard Business Review*, 80(2), 101.

Ringland, G. (2008). Innovation: scenarios of alternative futures can discover new opportunities for creativity. *Strategy and Leadership*, 36(5), 22–27. doi:10.1108/10878570810902086

Rising, L. (2000). *The Pattern Almanac 2000*. Reading, MA: Addison-Wesley.

Rizzi, C., Ponte, D., & Bonifacio, M. (2009). A new institutional reading of knowledge management technology adoption. *Journal of Knowledge Management*, 13(4), 75–85. doi:10.1108/13673270910971842

Robert, C., Probst, T. M., Martocchio, J. J., Drasgow, F., & Lawler, J. J. (2000). Empowerment and continuous improvement in the United States, Mexico, Poland, and India: Predicting fit on the basis of the dimensions of power distance and individualism. *The Journal of Applied Psychology*, 85, 643–658. doi:10.1037/0021-9010.85.5.643

Roberts, D., & Engardis, P. (2006, November 27). Secrets, lies and sweatshops. *Business Week*, 50-58.

Roberts, J. (2000). From know-how to show how? Questioning the role of information and communication technologies in knowledge transfer. *Technology Analysis and Strategic Management*, 12, 429–443. doi:10.1080/713698499

Robinson, H. S., Anumba, C. J., Carrillo, P. M., & Al-Ghassani, A. M. (2006). STEPS: A knowledge management maturity roadmap for corporate sustainability. *Harvard Business Review*, 12(6), 793–808.

Robson, R. (2007). Reusability and reusable design . In Reiser, R. A., & Dempsey, J. V. (Eds.), *Trends and issues in instructional design and technology* (pp. 301–310). Upper Saddle River, NJ: Merrill/Prentice Hall.

Rodan, S., & Galunic, C. (2004). More than network structure: How knowledge heterogeneity influences managerial performance and innovativeness. *Strategic Management Journal, 25,* 541–562. doi:10.1002/smj.398

Rolland, C., Stirna, J., Prekas, N., Loucopoulos, P., Grosz, G., & Persson, A. (2000). Evaluating a pattern approach as an aid for the development of organisational knowledge: An empirical study. In In *Proceedings of the 12th International Conference on Advanced Information System Engineering (CAiSE)* (LNCS 1789, pp. 176-191). ISBN 3-540-67630-9.

Rollins, M., & Halinen, A. (2005). Customer knowledge management competence: Towards a theoretical framework. In *Proceedings of the 38th Hawaii International Conference on System Sciences*. Washington, DC: IEEE. DOI: 0-7695-2268-8/05. Retrieved from www.hicss.hawaii.edu

Ronen, S., & Shenkar, O. (1985). Clustering countries on attitudinal dimensions: A review and synthesis . *Academy of Management Review, 10*(3), 435–454. doi:10.2307/258126

Rosenberg, M. (2006). *Beyond E-Learning: Approaches and technologies to enhance organizational knowledge, learning, and performance*. New York: Pfeiffer.

Rowley, J. (2004). Partnering paradigms? Knowledge management and relationship marketing. *Industrial Management & Data Systems, 104*(2), 149–157. doi:10.1108/02635570410522125

Ruggles, R. (1998). The state of the notion: Knowledge management in practice. *California Management Review, 40*(3), 80–89.

Ryals, L., & Knox, S. (2001). Cross functional issues in the implementation of relationship marketing through customer relationship management. *European Management Journal, 19*(5), 534. doi:10.1016/S0263-2373(01)00067-6

Sabherwal, R., & Chan, Y. E. (2001). Alignment between business and IS strategies: A study of prospectors, analyzers, and defenders. *Information Systems Research, 12*(1), 11–33. doi:10.1287/isre.12.1.11.9714

Sage, A. P., & Rouse, W. B. (1999). Information systems frontiers in Knowledge Management. *Information Systems Frontiers, 1*(3), 205–219. doi:10.1023/A:1010046210832

Saidal, J. R., & Cour, S. (2003). Information Technology and the Voluntary Sector Workplace. *Nonprofit and Voluntary Sector Quarterly, 32*(1), 5–24. doi:10.1177/0899764002250004

Saint-Onge, H. (1999). *Developing an effective knowledge strategy*. Paper presented at Chief Learning Officer Conference, Boston.

Salomann, H., Dous, M., Kolbe, L., & Brenner, W. (2005). Rejuvenating customer management: How to make knowledge for, from and about customers work. *European Management Journal, 23*(4), 392–403. doi:10.1016/j.emj.2005.06.009

Sanchez, R., & Mahoney, J. T. (1996). Modularity, flexibility, and knowledge management in product and organization design. *Strategic Management Journal, 17,* 63–76.

Satyadas, A., Harigopal, U., & Cassaigne, N. P. (2001). Knowledge management tutorial: An editorial overview. *IEEE Transactions on Systems, Man and Cybernetics. Part C, Applications and Reviews, 31*(4), 429–437. doi:10.1109/5326.983926

Saunders, M., Lewis, P., & Thornhill, A. (2007). *Research methods for business students* (4th ed.). Upper Saddle River, NJ: Prentice Hhall.

Scarbrough, H. (2003). Knowledge management, HRM and the innovation process. *International Journal of Manpower, 24*(5), 501–516. doi:10.1108/01437720310491053

Schein, E. H. (1985). *Organizational culture and leadership: A dynamic view*. San Francisco: Jossey-Bass.

Schick, S. (2002). Bleak future painted for KM projects. *Computing Canada, 28*(9), 1–4.

Schneckenberg, D. (2009). Web 2.0 and the empowerment of knowledge worker. *Journal of Knowledge Management, 13*(6), 509–520. doi:10.1108/13673270910997150

Schneider, M., Bauer, M., & Kröner, A. (2005). Building a personal memory for situated user support. In *Proceedings of the First International Workshop on Exploiting Context Histories in Smart Environments (ECHISE 2005)* at Pervasive 2005, Munich.

Schon, D. A. (1983). *The Reflective Practitioner: How Professionals Think in Action*. New York: Basic Books.

Schreiber, G., Akkermans, H., Anjewierden, A., de Hoog, R., Shadbolt, N., Van de Velde, W., et al. (2000). *Knowledge engineering and management the CommonKADS Methodology.* Cambridge, MA: MIT Press. ISBN: 0-262-19300-0

Schwaber, K., & Beedle, M. (2001). *Agile Software Development with Scrum.* Upper Saddle River, NJ: Prentice Hall.

Schwartz, P. (1996). *The Art of the Long View: Planning for the Future in an Uncertain World.* New York: Doubleday Dell Publishing Inc.

Schwartz, S. (1994). Cultural dimensions of values: Toward an understanding of national differences . In Kim, U., Triandis, H., Kagitcibasi, C., Choi, S., & Yoon, G. (Eds.), *Individualism and Collectivism: Theory, Method, and Application* (pp. 85–119). Thousand Oaks, CA: Sage.

Securities Daily. (2005, January). *The History of Investment Funds in China.*

Seetharaman, A., Lo, K., & Saravanan, A. S. (2004). Comparative justification on intellectual capital. *Journal of Intellectual Capital, 5*(4), 522–539. doi:10.1108/14691930410566997

Seliem, A., Ashour, A., Khalil, O., & Miller, S. (2003). The relationship of some organizational factors to information system effectiveness: Egyptian data and contingent analysis. *Journal of Global Information Management, 11*(1), 40–71.

Seruca, I., & Loucopoulos, P. (2003). Towards a Systematic Approach to the Capture of Patterns within a Business Domain. *Journal of Systems and Software, 67*(1), 1–18. doi:10.1016/S0164-1212(02)00083-3

Shane, S. (1992). Why do some societies invent more than others? *Journal of Business Venturing, 7*, 29–46. doi:10.1016/0883-9026(92)90033-N

Shane, S. (1993). Cultural influences on national rates of innovation. *Journal of Business Venturing, 8*, 59–73. doi:10.1016/0883-9026(93)90011-S

Shanks, G. (1999, September 29). *Semiotic Approach to Understanding Representation in Information Systems.* Information Systems Foundations Workshop, Sydney, Australia.

Sharma, S., & Bock, G.-W. (2005). Factor's influencing individual's knowledge seeking behaviour in electronic knowledge repository. In D. Bartmann, F. Rajola, J. Kallinikos, D. Avison, R. Winter, P. Ein-Dor, et al. (Eds.), *Proceedings of the Thirteenth European Conference on Information Systems,* Regensburg, Germany (pp. 390-403). ISBN 3-937195-09-2.

Sharma, R. S., Ekundayo, M. S., & Ng, E. W. (2009). Beyond the digital divide: policy analysis for knowledge societies. *Journal of Knowledge Management, 13*(5), 373–386. doi:10.1108/13673270910988178

Sharma, R., & Mokhtar, I. (2006). Bridging the Digital Divide in Asia. *The International Journal of Technology . Knowledge and Society, 1*(3), 15–30.

Sharma, R., Ng, E. W. J., Dharmawirya, M., & Lee, C. K. (2008). Beyond the Digital Divide: A Conceptual Framework for Analyzing Knowledge Societies. *Journal of Knowledge Management, 12*(5), 151–164. doi:10.1108/13673270810903000

Sharp, D. (2003). Knowledge management today: Challenges and opportunities. *Information Systems Management, 20*(2), 32–37. doi:10.1201/1078/43204.20.2.2003 0301/41468.6

Shen, Y. (2005). Renyuan-orientation: Interpersonal practice of zhongyong- Reconsidering Chinese social action orientation. *Journal of Nanjing University (Philosophy, Humanities and Social Science), 5,* 130-137.

Sher, P. J., & Lee, V. C. (2004). Information technology as a facilitator for enhancing dynamic capabilities through knowledge management. *Information & Management, 41*(8), 933–945. doi:10.1016/j.im.2003.06.004

Sheth, N. J. (2002). The future of relationship marketing. *Journal of Services Marketing, 16*(7), 590–593. doi:10.1108/08876040210447324

Shore, B., & Venkatachalam, A. R. (1995). The role of national culture in systems analysis and design. *Journal of Global Information Management, 3*(3), 5–14.

Simard, C., & Rice, R. E. (2007). The practice gap: Barriers to the diffusion of best practices . In McInerney, C. R., & Day, R. E. (Eds.), *Re-thinking knowledge management: From knowledge objects to knowledge processes* (pp. 87–124). Dordrecht, The Netherlands: Springer-Verlag.

Simon, H. (1991). Bounded rationality and organizational learning. *Organization Science, 2*(1), 125–134. doi:10.1287/orsc.2.1.125

Simon, H. A. (1960). *The New Science of Management Decision*. New York: Harper and Row.

Sinkula, J. M. (1994). Market information processing and organizational learning. *Journal of Marketing, 58,* 35–45. doi:10.2307/1252249

Sinlarat, P. (1998). *Principle and general higher education.* Bangkok, Thailand: Chulalongkorn University.

Si, S., & Bruton, G. (1999). Knowledge transfer in international joint ventures in transitional economies: The China experience. *The Academy of Management Executive, 13*(1), 83–90.

Sivaramakrishnan, S., Delbaere, M., & Bruning, E. (2004). The role of knowledge management in the market orientation–business performance linkage. *International Journal of Knowledge, Culture, and Change Management, 4,* 775–783.

Slater, S., & Narver, J. (1994). Does competitive environment moderate the market orientation-performance relationship? *Journal of Marketing, 58,* 46–55. doi:10.2307/1252250

Smith, H. A., & McKeen, J. D. (2005). Customer knowledge management: Adding value for our customers. *Communications of the Association for Information Systems, 16,* 744–755.

Smith, J. M., & Webster, L. (2000). The knowledge economy and SMEs: a survey of skills requirements. *Business Information Review, 17*(3), 138–146. doi:10.1177/0266382004237656

Smith, P. B., Peterson, M. F., & Schwartz, S. H. (2002). Cultural values, sources of guidance, and their relevance to managerial behavior. *Journal of Cross-Cultural Psychology, 33*(2), 188–208. doi:10.1177/0022022102033002005

Smith, P., Dugan, S., & Trompenaars, F. (1996). National culture and the values of organizational employees: A dimensional analysis across 43 nations. *Journal of Cross-Cultural Psychology, 27*(2), 231–264. doi:10.1177/0022022196272006

Sobol, M. G., & Lei, D. (1994). Environment, manufacturing technology, and embedded knowledge. *The International Journal of Human Factors in Manufacturing, 4*(2), 167–189. doi:10.1002/hfm.4530040205

Sowa, J. E., Selden, S. C., & Sandfort, J. R. (2004). No Longer Unmeasurable? A Multidimensional Integrated Model of Nonprofit Organizational Effectiveness. *Nonprofit and Voluntary Sector Quarterly, 33*(4), 711–728. doi:10.1177/0899764004269146

Spence, M. (2008). *The Growth Report – Strategies for Suatainable Growth and Inclusive Development*. Washington, DC: The World Bank.

Spicer, A. (1997). Cultural and knowledge transfer: Conflict in Russian Multi-National Settings. In *Proceedings of the Academy of Management Conference* (pp.194-198).

Srivastava, A., Bartol, K. M., & Locke, E. A. (2006). Empowering leadership in management teams: Effects on knowledge sharing, efficacy, and performance. *Academy of Management Journal, 49*(6), 1239–1251.

Srivastava, R. K., Shervani, T. A., & Fahey, L. (1998). Market-based assets and shareholder value: A framework for analysis. *Journal of Marketing, 62,* 2–18. doi:10.2307/1251799

Stahl, G. (2006). *Group cognition: Computer support for building collaborative knowledge*. Cambridge, MA: MIT Press.

Standfield, K. (2002). *Intangible management: tools for solving the accounting and management crisis*. Boston: Academic Press.

Staples, D. S., Greenaway, K., & McKeen, J. D. (2001). Opportunities for research about managing the knowledge-based enterprise. *International Journal of Management Reviews, 3*(19), 1–20. doi:10.1111/1468-2370.00051

Stapleton, J. (1999). *DSDM: Dynamic Systems Development Method*. Washington, DC: IEEE.

Statistics Canada. (2006). *Canada Survey of Giving, Volunteering and Participating 2004*. Retrieved July 29, 2008, from http://www.statcan.ca/Daily/Emglish/060605/d060605a.htm

Stefanou, J., Sarmaniotis, C., & Stafyla, A. (2003). A CRM and customer-centric knowledge management: An empirical research. *Business Process Management Journal, 9*(5), 617–634. doi:10.1108/14637150310496721

Stein, E. W., & Zwass, V. (1995). Actualizing Organizational Memory with Information Systems. *Information Systems Research, 6*(2), 85–117. doi:10.1287/isre.6.2.85

Stenmark, D. (2000). Leveraging tacit organizational knowledge. *Journal of Management Information Systems, 17*(3), 9–24.

Sternberg, R. (1994). Tacit knowledge and job success . In Anderson, N., & Herriot, P. (Eds.), *Assessment and Selection in Organizations: Methods and Practice for Recruitment and Appraisal* (pp. 27–39). London: John Wiley.

Stevens, L. (2000). Incentives for sharing. *Knowledge Management, 3*(10), 54–60.

Stewart, T. A. (1997). *Intellectual capital-the new wealth of organizations*. New York: Doubleday/Currency.

Stimpson, J. (1999). In the know. *Practical Accountant*, 34-39.

Stirna, J., Persson, A., & Aggestam, L. (2006, June 12-14). Building knowledge repositories with enterprise modelling and patterns – from theory to practice. In *Proceedings of the 14th European Conference on Information Systems (ECIS)*, Gothenburg, Sweden (No. 239).

Stirna, J., Persson, A., & Kaindl, H. (2002). *Evaluation of the trial applications* (Deliverable D7, IST Project no. IST-2000-28401). Stockholm, Sweden: Department of Computer and Systems Sciences, Royal Institute of Technology.

Storey, J., & Barnett, E. (2000). Knowledge management initiatives: Learning from failures. *Journal of Knowledge Management, 4*(2), 145–156. doi:10.1108/13673270010372279

Straub, D. W. (1994). The effect of culture on IT diffusion: E-mail and Fax in Japan and the U.S. *Information Systems Research, 5*(1), 23–47. doi:10.1287/isre.5.1.23

Straub, D. W., Keil, M., & Brenner, W. (1997). Testing the technology acceptance model across cultures: A three country study. *Information & Management, 33*(1), 1–11. doi:10.1016/S0378-7206(97)00026-8

Straub, D. W., Loch, K., & Hill, C. (2001). Transfer of information technology to the Arab World: A test of cultural influence modeling. *Journal of Global Information Management, 9*(4), 6–27.

Sullivan, P. H. (2000). *Value-driven intellectual capital: how to convert intangible corporate assets into market value*. New York: Wiley.

Sun, Z. (2004). A waterfall model for knowledge management and experience management. In *Proceedings of the 4th International Conference on Hybrid Intelligent Systems*, Kitakyushu, Japan, (pp. 472-475). Washington, DC: IEEE Computer Society.

Sun, Z., & Gang, G. (2006). HSM: A Hierarchical Spiral Model for knowledge management. In *Proceedings the 2nd International Conference on Information Management and Business*, Sydney, Australia (pp. 542-551).

Sunassee, N. N., & Sewry, D. A. (2002). A theoretical framework for knowledge management implementation. In *Proceedings of the Annual Research Conference of the South African Institute of Computer Scientists and Information Technologists (SAICSIT) on Enablement through Technology* (pp. 235-245).

Svensson, M. (2000). *Defining and designing social navigation*. Unpublished doctoral dissertation, Stockholm University, Department of computer and system sciences.

Swan, J., Scarborough, H., & Robertson, M. (2002). The Construction of `Communities of Practice' in the Management of Innovation. *Management Learning, 33*(4), 477–496. doi:10.1177/1350507602334005

Szilas, N., & Kavakli, M. (2006, January 29-February 1). PastMaster@Strorytelling: A Controlled Interface for Interactive Drama. In *Proceedings of IUI 2006: International Conference on Intelligent user Interfaces*, Sydney, Australia (pp. 288-290).

Szulanski, G. (1994). *Intra-firm Transfer of Best Practice Project: Executive Summary of the Findings*. Houston, TX: American Productivity and Quality Center.

Szulanski, G. (1996). Exploring internal stickiness: Impediments to the transfer of best practice within the firm. *Strategic Management Journal, 17*, 27–43.

Szulanski, G. (2000). The process of knowledge transfer: A diachronic analysis of stickiness. *Organizational Behavior and Human Decision Processes*, 82(1), 9–27. doi:10.1006/obhd.2000.2884

Szulanski, G. (2003). *Sticky Knowledge: Barriers to Knowing in the Firm*. Thousand Oaks, CA: Sage.

Taibi, T., & Ngo, C. L. (2002, July 14-18). *A Pattern for Evaluating Design Patterns*. Paper presented at the Sixth World Multiconference on Systemics, Cybernetics and Informatics (SCI 2002), Orlando, FL, USA.

Tang, F. F., Xi, Y., Chen, G., & Wang, R. (2006). Ownership, corporate governance, and management in the state-owned hotels in the People's Republic of China. *The Cornell Hotel and Restaurant Administration Quarterly*, 47(2), 182–191. doi:10.1177/0010880405284845

Tapscott, D., Lowy, A., & Ticoll, D. (1998). *Blueprint to the Digital Economy: Creating Wealth in the Era of e-business*. New York: McGraw-Hill Professional Publishing.

Tauscher, L., & Greenberg, S. (1997). How People Revisit Web Pages: Empirical Findings and Implications for the Design of History Systems. *International Journal of Human-Computer Studies*, 47(1), 97–138. doi:10.1006/ijhc.1997.0125

Taylor, W. A., & Wright, G. H. (2004). Organizational Readiness for Successful Knowledge Sharing: Challenges for Public Sector Managers. *Information Resources Management Journal*, 17(2), 22–37.

Tchounikine, P. (2002). Pour une ingénierie des Environnements Informatiques pour l'Apprentissage Humain. *Revue I3 information – interaction – intelligence, 2*(1). Retrieved from www.revue-i3.org

Teece, D. (1998). Capturing Value from Knowledge Assets: the new economy, markets for Know-How and Intangible Assets. *California Management Review, 40*(3), 55–79.

Teevan, J., Alvarado, C., Ackerman, M. S., & Karger, D. R. (2004). *The perfect search engine is not enough: a study of orienteering behavior in directed search*. Vienna, Austria: ACM.

Teo, T., & Men, B. (2008). Knowledge portals in Chinese consulting firms: A task–technology fit perspective. *European Journal of Information*, 17, 557–574. doi:10.1057/ejis.2008.41

Terveen, L. G., McMackin, J., Amento, B., & Hill, W. (2002, April). Specifying Preferences Based On User History. In *Proceedings of CHI'2002*, Minneapolis MN (pp. 315-322). New York: ACM Press.

The Center for Philanthropy at Indiana University. (2008). *Briefing on the Economy and Giving*. Retrieved September 29, 2009, from http://www.philanthropy.iupui.edu/Research/docs/ December2008_BriefingOnTheEconomyAndGiving.pdf

The Economist Group. (2008a). *Economist Intelligence Unit Index of Democracy 2008*. London: Author.

The Economist Group. (2008b). *E-readiness rankings 2008: Maintaining momentum*. London: The Economist Group.

Therin, F. (2002). Organizational learning and innovation in high-tech small firms. In *Proceedings of the 36th Hawaii International Conference on System Sciences,* Hawaii.

Thinnalak, Y. (2006). *Riddles of local wisdom*. Bangkok, Thailand: Withithat Institute.

Thompson, J. L., & Martin, F. (2005). *Strategic Management: Awareness & Change*. London: South-Western Cengage Learning.

Thong, J., Yap, C., & Raman, K. (1996). Top management support, external expertise and information systems implementation in small business. *Information Systems Research*, 7(2), 248–267. doi:10.1287/isre.7.2.248

Tikhomirova, N., Gritsenko, A., & Pechenkin, A. (2008). University Approach to Knowledge Management. VINE. *The journal of information and knowledge management systems, 38*(1), 16-21.

Tiwana, A. (2004). An empirical study of the effect of knowledge integration on software development performance. *Information and Software Technology, 46*(13), 899–906. doi:10.1016/j.infsof.2004.03.006

Toften, K., & Olsen, S. O. (2003). Export market information use, organizational knowledge, and firm performance: A conceptual framework. *International Marketing Review, 20*(1), 95–110. doi:10.1108/02651330310462284

Torkzadeh, G., & Doll, W. (1994). The test-retest reliability of user involvement instruments. *Information & Management, 26*, 21–31. doi:10.1016/0378-7206(94)90004-3

Triandis, H. (1995). *Individualism and Collectivism.* Boulder, CO: Westview Press.

Trompenaars, F. (1994). *Riding the Waves of Culture.* New York: Irwin.

Trussler, S. (1998). The rules of the game. *The Journal of Business Strategy, 19*, 16–19. doi:10.1108/eb039904

Tsai, C. H., & Chen, H. Y. (2007). Assessing knowledge management system success: An empirical study in Taiwan's high-tech industry. *Journal of American Academy of Business, 10*(2), 257–262.

Tsai, W. (2002). Social structure of "Coopetition" within a multiunit organization: Coordination, competition, and intraorganizational knowledge sharing. *Organization Science, 13*(2), 179–191. doi:10.1287/orsc.13.2.179.536

Tsang, D. (1999). National culture and national competitiveness: a study of the microcomputer component industry. *Advances in Competitiveness Research, 7*(1), 1–34.

Tsang, E. W. K. (2002). Acquisition knowledge by foreign partners for international joint ventures in a transition economy: Learning-by-doing and learning myopia. *Strategic Management Journal, 23*(9), 835–854. doi:10.1002/smj.251

Tsoukas, H., & Mylonopoulos, N. (2004). Introduction: Knowledge construction and creation in organizations. *British Journal of Management, 15*, S1–S8. doi:10.1111/j.1467-8551.2004.t01-2-00402.x

Tsoukas, H., & Vladimirou, E. (2001). What is Organizational Knowledge? *Journal of Management Studies, 38*(7), 973–993. doi:10.1111/1467-6486.00268

Tsui, A. S., & Farh, J. L. (1997). Where guanxi matters. *Work and Occupations, 24*, 56–79. doi:10.1177/0730888497024001005

Tsui, A. S., Wang, H., & Xin, K. R. (2006). Organizational culture in China: An analysis of culture dimensions and culture types. *Management and Organization Review, 2*(3), 345–376. doi:10.1111/j.1740-8784.2006.00050.x

Turban, E., Aronson, J., & Liang, T.-P. (2005). *Decision Support Systems and Intelligent Systems* (7th ed.). A Simon & Schuster Company.

Turban, E., & Aronson, J. E. (2001). *Decision support systems and intelligent systems* (6th ed.). Upper Saddle River, NJ: Prentice Hall.

Turban, E., & Aronson, J. E. (2001). *Decision Support Systems and Intelligent Systems* (6th ed.). Upper Saddle River, NJ: Prentice Hall.

Turban, E., Leidner, D., McLean, E., & Wetherbe, J. (2008). *Information Technology for Management: Transforming organizations in the digital economy.* New York: Wiley & Sons, Inc.

Tyre, M. J., & Von Hippel, E. (1997). The situated nature of adaptive learning in organizations. *Organization Science, 8*, 71–83. doi:10.1287/orsc.8.1.71

Tzokas, N., & Saren, M. (2004). Competitive advantage, knowledge and relationship marketing: where, what and how? *Journal of Business and Industrial Marketing, 19*(2), 125–135. doi:10.1108/08858620410524007

Udompaichitkul, T. (2005). *Sustainable economy based on the king's permanent ideas.* Bangkok, Thailand: Srinakharinwirot University.

Ulrich, D., & Wiersema, M. (1989). Gaining strategic and organizational capability in a turbulent business environment. *The Academy of Management Executive, 3*(2), 115–122.

UNDP. (2007). *Human Development Report 2007 / 2008.* Retrieved January 12, 2008, from http://hdr.undp.org/en/media/ HDR_20072008_EN_Complete.pdf

United Nations. (2008). *UN E-Government Survey 2008.* Retrieved March 13, 2009, from http://unpan1.un.org/intradoc/ groups/public/documents/ UN/UNPAN028607.pdf

Uzzi, B. (1999). Embeddedness in the making of financial capital: How social relations and networks benefit firms seeking financing. *American Sociological Review, 64,* 481–505. doi:10.2307/2657252

Vaccare, C., & Sherman, G. (2001). A pragmatic model for instructional technology selection . In Branch, R. M., & Fitzgerald, A. (Eds.), *Educational Media and Technology Yearbook (Vol. 27).* Englewood, CO: Libraries Unlimited.

Van de Ven, A. H., Polley, D., Garud, R., & Venkatraman, S. (1999). *The innovation journey.* New York: Oxford University Press.

Van der Meij, H. (1990). Question Asking: To know that you do not know is not enough. *Journal of Educational Psychology, 82*(3), 505–512. doi:10.1037/0022-0663.82.3.505

Van der Stede, W., Chow, C., & Lin, T. (2006). Strategy, choice of performance measures, and performance. *Behavioral Research in Accounting, 18*(1), 185–205. doi:10.2308/bria.2006.18.1.185

Van Maanen, J. (1988). Tales of the field: On writing ethnography. Chicago: *University of Chicago Press.*

Van Welie, M., & Van der Veer, G. C. (2003, September 1-5). *Pattern Languages in Interaction Design: Structure and Organization.* Paper presented at the Ninth IFIP TC13 International Conference on Human-Computer Interaction (INTERACT 2003), Zürich, Switzerland.

Varsakelis, N. C. (2001). The impact of patent protection, economy openness and national culture on R&D investment: a cross-country empirical investigation. *Research Policy, 30*(7), 1059–1068. doi:10.1016/S0048-7333(00)00130-X

Vera-Munoz, S., Ho, J., & Chow, C. (2006). Enhancing knowledge sharing in public accounting firms. *Accounting Horizons, 20*(2), 133–155. doi:10.2308/acch.2006.20.2.133

Vessey, I., & Conger, S. (1994). Requirements specification: learning object, process, and data methodologies. *Communications of the ACM, 37*(5), 102–113. doi:10.1145/175290.175305

Voelpel, S. C., & Han, Z. (2005). Managing knowledge sharing in China: The case of Siemens ShareNet. *Journal of Knowledge Management, 9*(3), 51–63. doi:10.1108/13673270510602764

Volberda, H. (2005). Knowledge and competitive advantage: The coevolution of firms, technology, and national institutions. *Academy of Management Review, 30*(2), 446–448.

Von Hippel, E. (1994). "Sticky information" and the locus of problem solving: Implications for innovation. *Management Science, 40*(4), 429–439. doi:10.1287/mnsc.40.4.429

Von Krogh, G. (1998). Care in knowledge creation. *California Management Review, 40*(3), 133–153.

Von Krogh, G., Ichijo, K., & Nonaka, I. (2000). *Enabling Knowledge Creation: How to Unlock the Mystery of Tacit Knowledge and Release the Power of Innovation.* Oxford, UK: Oxford University Press.

Vuong, D., & Staples, D. S. (2008). *Sharing Knowledge in Voluntary Not-For-Profit Organizations.* Paper presented at the Administrative Sciences Association of Canada Conference, Halifax, NS, Canada.

Vygotsky, L. S. (1978). *Mind in Society: The Development of Higher Psychological Processes* (Cole, M., John-Steiner, V., Scribner, S., & Souberman, E., Eds.). Boston, MA: Harvard University Press.

Wade, M., & Hulland, J. (2004). Review: The resource-based view and information systems research: Review, extension, and suggestions for future research. *Management Information Systems Quarterly, 28*(1), 107–142.

Wagner, J. A. (1995). Studies of individualism-collectivism: Effects on cooperation. *Academy of Management Journal, 38,* 152–167. doi:10.2307/256731

Walsh, J. P., & Ungson, G. R. (1991). Organizational Memory. *Academy of Management Review, 16*(1), 57–91. doi:10.2307/258607

Wand, Y., & Weber, R. (2002). Research Commentary: Information systems and conceptual modeling--A research agenda. *Information Systems Research, 13*(4), 363–376. doi:10.1287/isre.13.4.363.69

Wang, P. (2004). *An exploratory study of the effect of national culture on knowledge management factors, expectations and practices: A cross-cultural analysis of Taiwanese and U.S. perceptions.* Unpublished PhD dissertation, George Washington University.

Wang, L. Y., & Zhang, R. (2000). The management value of accounting information - Past, present and future of management accounting. *Finance and Accounting, 2,* 20–23.

Wang, P., Wong, T. W., & Koh, C. P. (2004). An integrated model of knowledge transfer from MNC parent to China subsidiary. *Journal of World Business, 39,* 168–182. doi:10.1016/j.jwb.2003.08.009

Wang, R. Y., & Strong, D. (1996). Beyond Accuracy: What data quality means to data consumers. *Journal of Management Information Systems, 12*(4), 5–34.

Wang, X. F., & Lihua, R. (2006). Examining knowledge management factors in the creation of new city. *Journal of Technology Management in China, 1*(3), 243–261. doi:10.1108/17468770610704921

Wang, Y., & Nicholas, S. (2005). Knowledge transfer, knowledge replication, and learning in non-equity alliances: Operating contractual joint ventures in China. *Management International Review, 45*(1), 99–118.

Warner, M. (1993). Human resource management with Chinese characteristics. *International Journal of Human Resource Management, 4,* 45–65.

Wasi, P. (2002). *Knowledge management.* Bangkok, Thailand: The Knowledge Management Institute.

Wasko, M. M., & Faraj, S. (2000). It is what one does: Why people participate and help others in electronic communities of practice. *The Journal of Strategic Information Systems, 9*(2/3), 55–173.

Watthanasiritham, P. (2003). *Social administration: Science of the century for Thai society and global society.* Bangkok, Thailand: Institute for Community Organization Development (Public Organization).

Webster, J., & Watson, R. T. (2002). Analyzing the past to prepare for the future: Writing a literature review. *MIS Quarterly, 26*(2), xiii–xxiii.

Weerawardena, J., O'Cass, A., & Julian, C. (2006). Does industry matter? Examining the role of industry structure and organizational learning in innovation and brand performance. *Journal of Business Research, 59*(1), 37–45. doi:10.1016/j.jbusres.2005.02.004

Wei, C. C., Choy, C. S., & Yeow, P. H. P. (2006). KM implementation in Malaysian telecommunication industry: An empirical analysis. *Industrial Management + Data Systems, 106*(8), 1112-1132.

Weick, K. (2005). Managing the future: Foresight in the knowledge economy. *Academy of Management Review, 30*(4), 871–873.

Weir, D., & Hutchings, K. (2005). Cultural embeddedness and contextual constraints: knowledge sharing in Chinese and Arab cultures. *Knowledge and Process Management, 12*(2), 89–98. doi:10.1002/kpm.222

Wendorff, P., & Apshvalka, D. (2005). *The Knowledge Management Strategy of Agile Software Development.*

Wenger, E. (1998). *Communities of practice: Learning, meaning, and identity.* New York: Cambridge University Press.

Wenger, E., McDermott, R., & Snyder, W. (2002). *Cultivating communities of practice: A Guide to managing knowledge.* Boston: Harvard Business School Press.

Wertsch, J. (1998). *Mind as Action.* Oxford, UK: Oxford University Press.

Wesson, J., & Cowley, L. (2003, September 1-2). *Designing with Patterns: Possibilities and Pitfalls.* Paper presented at the Second Workshop on Software and Usability Cross-Pollination, Zürich, Switzerland.

Wexelblat, A., & Maes, P. (1999). Footprints: History-rich tools for information foraging. In *Proceedings of ACM CHI 99 Conference on Human Factors in Computing Systems* (pp. 270-277).

Wichianpanya, C. (2005). *Document in supplement to workshop meeting on librarians/information scientists and knowledge management.* Changwat Nonthaburi, Thailand: Mental Health Department.

Wiggins, R. F., & Ruefli, T. W. (2005). Schumpeter's Ghost: Is Hypercompetition Making the Best of Times Shorter? *Strategic Management Journal, 26*, 887–911. doi:10.1002/smj.492

Wiig, K. (1993). *Knowledge management foundations.* Arlington, TX: Schema Press.

Wiig, K. M. (1993). *Knowledge management foundations – thinking about thinking – how people and organizations create, represent, and use knowledge.* Arlington, TX: Schema Press LTD.

Wiig, K. M. (1994). *Knowledge management the central management focus for intelligent-acting organizations.* Arlington, TX: Schema Press LTD.

Wiig, K. M. (1995). *Knowledge management methods. Practical approaches to managing knowledge.* Arlington, TX: Schema Press.

Wiig, K. M. (1997). Knowledge management: Where did it come from and where will it go? *Expert Systems with Applications, 13*(1), 1–14. doi:10.1016/S0957-4174(97)00018-3

Wiig, K. M. (1999). What future knowledge management users may expect. *Journal of Knowledge Management, 3*(2), 155–166. doi:10.1108/13673279910275611

Wiig, K. M., de Hoog, R., & van der Spek, R. (1997). Supporting knowledge management: A selection of methods and techniques. *Expert Systems with Applications, 13*(1), 15–27. doi:10.1016/S0957-4174(97)00019-5

Williams, J. J., & Seaman, A. E. (2001). Predicting change in management accounting systems: National culture and industry effects. *Accounting, Organizations and Society, 26*, 443–460. doi:10.1016/S0361-3682(01)00002-2

Williamson, K., Bow, A., Burstein, F., Darke, P., Harvey, R., Johanson, G., et al. (2002). *Research methods for students, academics and professionals.* Wagga Wagg, New South Wales, Australia: Quick Print. ISBN: 1 876 938 42 0.

Wilson, J. (2000). Volunteering. *Annual Review of Sociology, 26*, 215–240. doi:10.1146/annurev.soc.26.1.215

Winters, N., & Mor, Y. (2008). IDR: A Participatory Methodology for Interdisciplinary Design in Technology Enhanced Learning. *Computers & Education, 50*(2), 579–600. doi:10.1016/j.compedu.2007.09.015

Wong, K. Y., & Aspinwall, E. (2004). Knowledge management implementation frameworks: A review. *Knowledge and Process Management, 11*(2), 93–104. doi:10.1002/kpm.193

Wong, Y. K. (2006). Issues of software quality and management in practice: An empirical investigation of use of explicit documents in software review. *International Journal of Internet and Enterprise Management, 4*(1), 37–53. doi:10.1504/IJIEM.2006.008864

Wong, Y.-Y., Maher, T. E., & Luk, S. T. K. (2002). The hesitant transfer of strategic management knowledge to international joint ventures in China: Greater willingness seems likely in the future. *Management Research News, 25*(1), 1–15. doi:10.1108/01409170210782981

World Bank. (1998). *World Development Report 1998/99: Knowledge for Development.* Retrieved from http://www.worldbank.org/wsr/wsr98/contents.htm.

World Bank. (2004). *World Development Indicators.* Washington, DC: Author.

World Bank. (2007). *Building Knowledge Economies: Advanced Strategy for Development.* Retrieved October 14, 2008, from http://siteresources.worldbank.org/ KFDLP/ Resources/4611971199907090464/ BuildingKEbook.pdf

World Bank. (2008a). *World Bank Knowledge Assessment Methodology.* Retrieved February 1, 2009, from http://web.worldbank.org/WBSITE/EXTERNAL/ WBI/ WBIPROGRAMS/KFDLP/EXTUNIKAM/ 0,menuPK: 1414738~pagePK:64168427~ piPK:64168435~theSite PK:1414721,00.html

World Bank. (2008b). *Migration and Remittances Factbook 2008.* Retrieved January 30, 2009, from http:// econ.worldbank.org/WBSITE/ EXTERNAL/EXTDEC/ EXTDECPROSPECTS/ 0,contentMDK:21352016~me nuPK:3145470~ pagePK:64165401~piPK:64165026~ theSitePK:476883~isCURL:Y,00.html

World Bank. (2009). *World Development Report 2009.* Retrieved March 1, 2009, from http://econ.worldbank. org/WBSITE/EXTERNAL/EXTDEC/EXTRESEARCH/ EXTWDRS/EXTWDR2009/ 0,menuPK:4231145~page PK:64167702~ piPK:64167676~theSitePK:4231059,00. html

World Economic Forum. (2008). *The Global Competitiveness Report 2008-2009.* Retrieved February 3, 2009, from http://www.weforum.org/ en/initiatives

Wu, J. H., & Wang, Y. M. (2006). Measuring KMS success: A respecification of the DeLone and MacLean model. *Information & Management, 43*(6), 728–739. doi:10.1016/j.im.2006.05.002

Wu, X. B., Liu, X. F., & Du, J. (2007). Local firm's knowledge acquisition in the global manufacturing network: Evidence from Chinese samples. *International Journal of Innovation and Technology Management, 4*(3), 267–281. doi:10.1142/S0219877007001119

Xiang, H. C. (Ed.). (1999). *Accounting in the 50 Years of New China.* Beijing, China: China Finance and Economic Press.

Xing, W. (2006). Knowledge capitalism put into practice as an operational mechanism. *Journal of Knowledge Management, 10*(1), 119–130. doi:10.1108/13673270610650157

Xu, M., & Walton, J. (2005). Gaining customer knowledge through analytical CRM. *Industrial Management & Data Systems, 105*(7), 955–971. doi:10.1108/02635570510616139

Xu, X., & Wang, Y. (1999). Ownership structure and corporate governance in Chinese stock companies. *China Economic Review, 10,* 75–89. doi:10.1016/S1043-951X(99)00006-1

Yadin, A. (2007). *Implementation of Bloom's Taxonomy on Systems Analysis Workshops.* Paper presented at the AIS SIG-ED IAIM 2007 Conference.

Yamagata-Lynch, L. (2003). Using Activity theory as an analytic lens for examining technology professional development in schools. *Mind, Culture, and Activity, 10*(2), 100–119. doi:10.1207/S1532-7884MCA1002_2

Yang, J. (2005). Knowledge integration and innovation: Securing new product advantage in high technology industry. *The Journal of High Technology Management Research, 16,* 121–135. doi:10.1016/j.hitech.2005.06.007

Yang, J. T. (2008). Individual attitudes and organizational knowledge sharing. *Tourism Management, 29*(2), 345–353. doi:10.1016/j.tourman.2007.03.001

Yang, X. S., Chen, L. H., Su, W. B., Liu, Y., & Liu, J. (2001). Application and effectiveness of management accounting in China—views from enterprise accountants. *China Accounting and Finance Review, 2,* 73–138.

Yang, Z., Cai, S., Zhouc, Z., & Zhou, N. (2005). Development and validation of an instrument to measure user perceived service quality of information presenting Web portals. *Information & Management, 42,* 575–589. doi:10.1016/S0378-7206(04)00073-4

Yanow, D. (2004). Translating local knowledge at organizational peripheries. *British Journal of Management, 15,* S9–S25. doi:10.1111/j.1467-8551.2004.t01-1-00403.x

Yan, Y., & Zhang, J. A. (2003). Performance of high-tech firms' resource and capability-based development: Knowledge acquisition, organizational utilization and management involvement. *International Journal of Business Studies, 11*(1), 45–67.

Yao, L. J., Kam, T. H. Y., & Chan, S. H. (2007). Knowledge sharing in Asian public administration sector: The case of Hong Kong. *Journal of Enterprise Information Management, 20*(1), 51–69. doi:10.1108/17410390710717138

Yeh, Y. J., Lai, S. Q., & Ho, C. T. (2006). Knowledge management enablers: a case study. *Industrial Management & Data Systems, 106*(6), 793–810. doi:10.1108/02635570610671489

Yin, R. K. (1994). *Case study research: Design and methods* (2nd ed.). Thousand Oaks, CA: Sage.

Yin, E., & Bao, Y. (2006). The acquisition of tacit knowledge in China: an empirical analysis of the 'supplier-side individual level' and 'recipient-side' factors. *Management International Review, 46*(3), 327–348. doi:10.1007/s11575-006-0050-5

Yin, R. K. (2003). *Case Study Research, Design and Methods.* Thounsand Oaks, CA: Sage.

Yoon, S. W., & Lim, D. H. (2007). Strategic blending: A conceptual framework to improve learning and performance. *International Journal on E-Learning, 6*(3), 475–489.

Young, S. M., & Lewis, B. (1995). Experimental incentive contracting research in management accounting . In Ashton, R., & Ashton, A. (Eds.), *Judgment and Decision Making Research in Accounting and Auditing* (pp. 55–75). Cambridge, UK: Cambridge University Press. doi:10.1017/CBO9780511720420.005

Zack, M. (1999). Managing Codified Knowledge. *Sloan Management Review*, *40*(4), 45–48.

Zack, M. H. (1999). Developing a knowledge strategy. *California Management Review*, *41*(3), 125–145.

Zander, U., & Kogut, B. (1995). Knowledge and the speed of transfer and imitation of organizational capabilities: an empirical test. *Organization Science*, *6*, 76–92. doi:10.1287/orsc.6.1.76

Zeleny, M. (2005). *Human Systems Management: Integrating Knowledge, Management and Systems*. World Scientific Publishing.

Zhang, L., Tian, Y., & Li, P. (2005). Organizational knowledge sharing based on the ERP implementation of Yongxin Paper Co., Ltd. In M. Jennex (Ed.), *Case studies in knowledge management*. Hershey, PA: Idea Group Publishing.

Zhang, D. S., Jin, Y. J., Chen, H. W., Chen, J. M., Yang, Z. F., & Zhao, Z. Y. (2001). Zhongyong rationality: Beyond instrumental rationality, value rationality and communicative rationality. *Sociological Research*, *2*, 33–48.

Zhang, L., Tian, Y., & Qi, Z. (2006). Impact of organizational memory on organizational performance: an empirical study. *Business Review (Federal Reserve Bank of Philadelphia)*, *5*(1), 227–232.

Zhang, Q. P., Chintakovid, T., & Sun, X. N. (2007). Saving face or sharing personal information? A cross-cultural study on knowledge sharing. *Journal of Information & Knowledge Management*, *5*(1), 73–79. doi:10.1142/S0219649206001335

Zhang, Q., Lim, J. S., & Cao, M. (2004). Innovation-driven learning in new product development: A conceptual model. *Industrial Management & Data Systems*, *104*(3), 252–261. doi:10.1108/02635570410525799

Zhou, A. Z., & Fink, D. (2003). Knowledge management and intellectual capital: An empirical examination of current practice in Australia. *Knowledge Management Research & Practice*, *1*(2), 86–94. doi:10.1057/palgrave.kmrp.8500009

Zhu, K., Kraemer, K. L., Gurbaxani, V., & Xu, S. X. (2006). Migration to open-standard interorganizational systems: Network effects, switching costs and path dependency. *Management Information Systems Quarterly*, *30*, 515–539.

Ziman, J. M. (1968). *Public knowledge*. Cambridge, UK: Cambridge University Press.

Zmud, R. W. (1978). An empirical investigation of the dimensionality of the concept of information. *Decision Sciences*, *9*, 187–195. doi:10.1111/j.1540-5915.1978.tb01378.x

Zmud, R. W., Anthony, W. P., & Stair, R. M. (1993). The use of mental imagery to facilitate information identification in requirements analysis. *Journal of Management Information Systems*, *9*(4), 175–191.

About the Contributors

Murray E. Jennex is an associate professor at San Diego State University, editor in chief of the *International Journal of Knowledge Management*, co-editor in chief of the *International Journal of Information Systems for Crisis Response and Management*, and president of the Foundation for Knowledge Management (LLC). Dr. Jennex specializes in knowledge management, system analysis and design, IS security, e-commerce, and organizational effectiveness. Dr. Jennex serves as the Knowledge Management Systems Track co-chair at the Hawaii International Conference on System Sciences. He is the author of over 100 journal articles, book chapters, and conference proceedings on knowledge management, end user computing, international information systems, organizational memory systems, ecommerce, cyber security, and software outsourcing. Jennex conducts research for the National Center for Border Security Issues on risk management and technology integration. Jennex is a former US Navy Nuclear Power Propulsion officer and holds a BA in chemistry and physics from William Jewell College, an MBA and an MS in software engineering from National University, an MS in telecommunications management and a PhD in information systems from the Claremont Graduate University. Jennex is also a registered professional mechanical engineer in the state of California and a Certified Information Systems Security Professional (CISSP) and a Certified Secure Software Lifecycle Professional (CSSLP).

* * *

Lena Aggestam is a researcher and a teacher at the University of Skövde. She received a degree of Doctor of Philosophy in computer and systems sciences from Stockholm University, Sweden (2008). Her research interest is development and use of organizational information systems with a specific focus on how these systems can support and enable Knowledge Management (KM) and organizational learning. More specifically her research interests include success factors in KM work and the relationship between Learning Organizations and KM.

Kamla Ali Al-Busaidi is an assistant professor of information systems at Sultan Qaboos University in Oman. She received her PhD in management information systems from Claremont Graduate University in California in 2005, MSc in information systems management from Duquesne University in Pennsylvania in 1999, and BSc in information systems from Sultan Qaboos University in Oman in 1997. Her research interests include knowledge management systems, decision support systems, learning management systems, e-government and the deployment of information and communication technologies in Arab countries. She has published several conference proceedings and journal papers, and served as a reviewer for several conference proceedings.

Samer Alhawari has a PhD in management Information Systems from the Arab Academy for Banking and Financial Sciences, Amman-Jordan. He is an assistant professor in the Department of Management Information System at the Applied Science Private University, Jordan. His research interest includes knowledge management, customer relationship management, customer knowledge management, risk management, strategic management, information systems, data mining, and text categorization. Dr. Alhawari has published 20 articles in refereed journal as well as national and international conference proceedings.

Haroun Alryalat is a general manager of Center for Banking and Financial Consultancy and assistant professor in the Department of Management Information System at the Arab Academy for Banking and Financial Sciences. He received a PhD in information systems from Brunel University, U.K. He received a BSc in politics and economics from the University of Jordan. He obtained his high diploma in commercial banking and his MSc in financial market from the Arab Academy for Banking and Financial Sciences. Haroun's research interests are in information systems, methods of automating the process of trading in financial markets, customer relationship management, and meta-analysis in information systems. He has written more than 29 papers for academic journals and international conferences on these topics. He taught 24 different modules in finance and information systems in various universities.

Alexandre Ardichvili is professor at the University of Minnesota. He holds a PhD in human resource development and MBA from the University of Minnesota and a PhD in management from the University of Moscow. Alexandre has published an edited book and more than 50 peer-reviewed articles and book chapters in the areas of human resource development, entrepreneurship, and knowledge management. He has done applied research and consulting on knowledge management and communities of practice with Caterpillar, ADM, and a number of health care organizations and professional services firms.

Per Backlund is a researcher and a teacher at the University of Skövde. He is also managing the InGaMe Lab research group (www.his.se/ingame). Per Backlund has a background in the fields of teaching, cognitive science and information systems development. He holds a BSc in cognitive science and an MSc in computer science from University of Skövde and a PhD in information systems from Stockholm University in 2004. His research interests are in serious games, in particular how games and game technology can be used for training and dissemination of information. This includes analyzing the needs of clients to see how game technology and game design can contribute to achieve their goals.

Donal P. Ballou is a Professor Emeritus in the Management Science and Information Systems unit of the School of Business at SUNY-Albany. His PhD was in applied mathematics and his research has involved mathematical modeling in several disciplines, especially in the area of data and information quality. His pioneering work in this area in the 1980s with his colleague Harold Pazer was recognized at the 1996 Conference on Information Quality held at MIT. He has published in various journals including Communications of the ACM, MIS Quarterly, and Management Science. He has been co-guest editor of special sections on information quality appearing in *Communications of the ACM* and *Journal of Management Information Systems*.

Salvatore Belardo is Professor Emeritus in the Management Science and Information Systems unit of the School of Business at SUNY-Albany. His PhD was in Management of Information Systems. Professor Belardo has been a visiting professor at the Copenhagen School of Business, the University of Passau in Germany, the University of Del Salvador in Argentina, and the Graduate School of Business Administration in Zurich Switzerland. He has written and edited several books and has published widely in a number of top journals including *Management Science, Decision Sciences, IEEE Transactions on Systems Man and Cybernetics*, and the *Journal of Management Information Systems*. He has been recognized as one of the most prolific authors of decision support systems related research.

Christian Bogner graduated in educational sciences, psychology and sociology and is a research assistant at the Department of Educational Sciences and Professional Development at the Technical University of Kaiserslautern, Germany. He leads a regional group of usability professionals within the German Chapter of the Usability Professionals' Association (GC-UPA). He is also an active member of a national technical committee within the German Institute for Standardization (DIN) and thus involved in the international standardization process related to ergonomic guidelines for interactive systems. In his research he focuses on professional support for software engineers which have to comply with user requirements. His aim is to establish methods and techniques to assist developers in that way. Contact him at christian.bogner@sowi.uni-kl.de

Ed Bruning is Professor of Marketing at the I. H. Asper School of Business, University of Manitoba, Canada. He received his Ph.D. from the University of Alabama. Ed's research interests have focused on the economic analysis of marketing channel relationships, national loyalty as an influence on consumption choice, the role of commitment and trust as antecedents to firm-level market orientation, the role of knowledge management as a mediating factor between market orientation and business performance, and feedback effects upon individual brands once an alliance brand is created. Ed has won numerous research and teaching awards and grants in both Canada and the United States.

Ganesh Chandrasekar is a Knowledge Management Professional working as a Business Analyst with Cognizant Technology Solutions. He graduated with a Masters of Science in Knowledge Management from Nanyang Technological University, Singapore. A keen student of developmental economics and knowledge societies, Ganesh, lives in Chennai, India.

Chalard Chantarsobat is an assistant professor at Mahasarakham University and head of research unit of Strength Community and Knowledge Managament (RUSCKM). Chalard specialized is Nonformal Education, research community and development, knowledge management in community, network organization, and group process effectiveness. Dr.Chalard serves as the knowledge management systems track conference co-chair at the 1st International Conference Education Reform 2007, Sofitel Raja Orchild Hotel, Thailand, and the 2 nd International Conference Education Reform 2009, themes "Cultural Diversity and Sustainable Education in a Changing World",Charoensri Grand Royal Hotel, Thailand. He is the author of over 30 journal articles, book chapters, and conference proceeding on knowledge management, community organization, network community and enterprise. He hold B.Ed in Geography from Srinakharinwirot Mahasarakhm University, and an MEd in Adult Education from Srinakharinwirot Prasanmit University, an a EdD in Educational Administration and Development from Mahasarakham University.

Chee W. Chow is Professor of Accounting Emeritus at San Diego State University. His research spans many areas of accounting, including auditing, financial accounting, accounting education, taxation, and management accounting and controls. Winner of numerous awards for his writing, Professor Chow has published well over one hundred articles in leading academic and practitioner journals. Professor Chow has served as President of the American Accounting Association's (AAA) Management Accounting Section as well as Editor of its *Journal of Management Accounting Research*. He also has received the Outstanding International Accounting Educator Award from the AAA's International Accounting Section, and the Lifetime Contribution to Management Accounting Award from the AAA's Management Accounting Section.

Kimiz Dalkir is currently an associate professor in the McGill School of Information Studies, where she developed and now coordinates the Knowledge Management stream. Her book, *Knowledge Management in Theory and Practice*, has been widely adopted by both the academic and practitioner communities. In 2006, she received the Faculty of Education Excellence in Teaching Prize. Her most recent research grant is to investigate how knowledge management can be applied to universities. Prior to joining McGill University, Dr. Dalkir was director of Global KM Services at DMR Consulting where she was actively involved in knowledge transfer to clients around the world.

Marjorie Delbaere is Associate Professor of Marketing at the Edwards School of Business, University of Saskatchewan, Canada. She received her Ph.D. from the University of Manitoba. Marjorie's research focuses on knowledge utilization and management at both the macro- and micro-levels. At the macro-level, her research explores the relationship between the market orientation of firms and the effectiveness of their knowledge management activities. At the micro-level, she explores the interplay between the persuasive use of language and images (specifically rhetorical figures such as metaphors and analogies), consumer knowledge utilization, and the marketing of controversial products to consumers, such as genetically engineered food and prescription drugs.

Paul Dion received his Ph.D. in Management Studies from the University of Toronto in 1986. He has taught at the University of Minnesota, Bryant University in Rhode Island and presently at Susquehanna University in Selinsgrove PA. His research interests include sales and marketing performance, service quality, and marketing logistics and he has published approximately forty articles in refereed publications such as: The Journal of Business Research, the Journal of Academy of Marketing Science, the International Journal of Purchasing and Materials Management and Industrial Marketing Management. He has taught a number of courses at the doctoral level, mainly in market research and advanced statistics and has developed a Ph.D. program in management for the University of the West Indies in St. Augustine Trinidad and Tobago. He is also a consultant and instructor in a number of doctoral programs in Thailand.

Kathleen E. Greenaway is an Assistant Professor at the Ted Rogers School of Information Technology Management at Ryerson University in Toronto, Canada. She earned her PhD in Management at Queen's University, Kingston, Canada. Among her research interests are knowledge management, information privacy, ICTs as tools for democratic enablement, and business ethics. Dr. Greenaway's work has been published in the Journal of the AIS, Communications of the AIS and the International Journal of Management Reviews. Her research has been presented at various conferences including the Academy of

Management, the Americas Conference on Information Systems, the Information Resource Management Association, and the Administrative Sciences Association of Canada. Prior to joining academia, she had twenty years experience as a manager and consultant in the private, public and non-profit sectors.

Pankaj Kamthan has been teaching in academia and industry for several years. He has also been a technical editor, participated in standards development, and served on program committees of international conferences and on the editorial board of international journals. His teaching and research interests include Knowledge Representation, Web Engineering, and Software Quality.

Omar Khalil is currently a Professor of Information Systems at the Quantitative Methods & Information Systems (QMIS) Department, College of Business Administration, Kuwait University. Has a PhD in Information Systems from the University of North Texas. His publications have appeared in journals such as the Journal of Global Information Management, Journal of Organizational and End-User Computing, Information Resources management Journal, International Journal of Production and Economics, International Journal of Man-Machine Studies, Journal of Business Ethics, Journal of Informing Science, Arab Journal of Administrative Sciences, International Journal of Enterprise Information Systems, Journal of Information and Knowledge Management, and International Journal of Knowledge Management. His research interest includes information systems effectiveness, global information systems, information quality, and knowledge management.

Hannu Kivijärvi is a professor in Information Systems Science at Aalto University School of Economics. He received his PhD in management science. His research interests include knowledge management, decision support systems in financial, production and marketing planning, IT Governance, and investments in information systems. His publications have appeared in a number of journals, including *European Journal of Information Systems, European Journal of Operational Research, Journal of Decision Systems, Decision Support Systems, Managerial and Decision Economics, International Journal of Production Economics*, and *Interfaces*.

Matthew Kuofie holds a PhD in Systems Engineering from Oakland University USA, an MBA in Business Administration from Northern Illinois University, USA, an MS in Computer Science from Old Dominion University, USA, and a BS in Statistics and Mathematics from the University of Ghana. Professor Kuofie teaches business management and information technology courses at the Central Michigan University, University of Michigan and Lawrence Technology University. His research interests include knowledge management, business management strategies and information technology. He has published numerous journal and conference papers. He serves as editor-in-chief and associate editor-in-chief of a number of journals including the *International Journal of Global Business* and the *Journal of Electronic Commerce in Organizations*. He has served on a number of doctoral dissertation committees. He has served as distinguished keynote speaker at a number of conferences. He worked for Electronic Data Systems/General Motors in Michigan.

Xin Li teaches in the Arts Department of Jinling College at Nanjing University. She received her bachelor and master degrees in the School of Business of Nanjing University, and worked as a tax and audit professional in Deloitte China before returning to academe. Xin Li has published papers in two academic journals and attended, as a key member, a program of the National Natural Science Foundation of China. Her current research interests include work boundary, work-life balance, justice and motivation.

Yang Lin is currently a PhD candidate at McGill's School of Information Studies, and expects to finish his program in 2010. His thesis topic addresses strategic decision-making, knowledge management, and information science. In specific, his doctoral study is to investigate the perceptions of Chinese business managers in the process of deciding whether and how to use KM strategies for their organizations from environmental, informational, and decision-specific perspectives. Over the past five years he was the project manager of two KM projects which aimed at helping both commercial and non-commercial organizations to better retain and transfer their critical knowledge and know-how. He was also the Canadian representative for a Chinese venture capital investment company between 2007 and 2008.

Annette M Mills is a Senior Lecturer at the University of Canterbury (New Zealand). Annette holds a PhD in Information Systems from the University of Waikato (New Zealand). Annette has published a number of refereed articles in edited books and in journals including Information and Management, and Computers and Education. She currently serves on the editorial boards for the Journal of Cases on Information Technology as an Associate Editor, the Journal of Global Information Management, and the International Journal of e-Collaboration. Her research interests include social computing, technology adoption and diffusion, service expectations, and user sophistication.

Amine Nehari –Talet is an associate professor, MIS KFUPM, teaching undergraduate and postgraduate courses, 21 years teaching experience IIc has authored many articles in information systems, e-learning, knowledge management and customer relationship management. He is member International Association for Computer Information Systems (IACIS) editorial for many journals, and IBIMA Conference Advisory Committee. He is reviewer for Pearson education and Oxford University. He has been awarded a certificate on Online teaching from University Illinois October 2005 and Oracle certificate from oracle university.2009.

Magali Ollagnier-Beldame holds a Ph.D. in cognitive science from the University Louis Lumière in Lyon. Since 1999, she is a researcher at LIRIS laboratory in Lyon, a computer science research lab. She joined the SILEX team in 2001. She developed multidisciplinary works on tracing systems and learning processes. Her researches are based on qualitative experiments and activity analysis. They lead to fundamental knowledge on ICT-mediated human activities and the role of activity inscriptions (such as traces) in these activities. They also conduct to functional specifications for the development of tracing systems.

Harold L Pazer, works for the Information Systems unit of the School of Business at SUNY-Albany. He played a major role in the design of both the graduate and undergraduate specializations in MIS. His major teaching interest was the design and implementation of Decision Support Systems. His research has involved the analysis of quality in both production and information systems. In addition to co-authoring three text books, he has published in various journals including *Management Science, Decision Sciences, International Journal of Production Research* and *Information Systems Research.* In conjunction with Professor Ballou he was recognized at the MITs Conference on Information Quality for his pioneering contributions to the field.

Anne Persson is a professor in informatics at the University of Skövde, Sweden. She received a degree of Doctor of Philosophy in Computer and Systems Sciences from Stockholm University, Sweden (2001). Her main research interest is development and use of organizational information systems. More specifically her research interests include enterprise modeling methods and tools, requirements engineering as well as knowledge management and organizational patterns. Anne Persson is an author or co-author of some 50 research reports and publications and has participated in several EU financed research projects. She has co-developed the EKP - Enterprise Knowledge Patterns and the EKD – Enterprise Knowledge Development approaches.

Kalle Piirainen is a Research Assistant in the Laboratory of Innovation Management in the department of Industrial Management at Lappeenranta University of Technology. His main areas of expertise are technology foresight, theory of the firm and competitive advantage and decision support systems in industrial management. His other interests include design science and collaborative design as methodologies to enhance the performance of industrial companies and to raise the relevance of scientific research.

Joerg Rech is an Entrepreneur in the area of enterprise 2.0 and the Semantic Web and founder of the company Semantic Technologies. Previously he was a senior scientist and project manager at the Fraunhofer Institute for Experimental Software Engineering (IESE) in Kaiserslautern, Germany. His research mainly concerns semantic technologies in software organizations, context-sensitive diagnosis of quality-defects, experience and knowledge management, knowledge patterns, and software engineering, with a focus on model-driven software engineering. Joerg Rech authored over 40 international journal articles, book chapters, and refereed conference papers, mainly on software engineering and knowledge management, edited several books in the domain of software engineering and knowledge management, was the speaker of the GI working group on architectural and design patterns, and is a member of the German Computer Society (Gesellschaft für Informatik, GI). Contact him at joerg.rech@ semantictechnologies.de.

Ahmed A. S. Seleim is an Assistant Professor in the Business Administration Department, College of Commerce, Alexandria University, Egypt. He holds B. com., MBA, and PhD degrees from Alexandria University, Egypt. His research has been published in journals such as Journal of Global Information Management, International Journal of Knowledge Management, Journal of Intellectual Capital, Management Decision, The Learning Organization, and Arab Journal of Administration Sciences. His research interest includes management information systems, knowledge management, intellectual capital, Corruption, and Culture.

Ravi S. Sharma is Associate Professor at the Wee Kim Wee School of Communication and Information at the Nanyang Technological University since January 2004. Ravi had spent the previous 10 years in industry as Asean Communications Industry Principal at IBM Global Services and Director of the Multimedia Competency Centre of Deutsche Telekom Asia. Ravi's teaching, consulting and research interests are in multimedia applications, services and strategies. Ravi received his PhD in engineering from the University of Waterloo, Canada.

Subramanian Sivaramakrishnan (Subbu) is Associate Professor of Marketing at the I. H. Asper School of Business, University of Manitoba, Canada. He received his Ph.D. from Penn State University. Subbu's research concerns the use of information in decision-making by organizations and by consumers. In the organizational context, he has examined aspects such as information overload among managers and knowledge management by firms. In the consumer behavior context, he has studied a variety of topics such as the effects of performing multiple tasks on the ability to use information, consumer's reaction to health risk warnings, stigma consciousness, and consumers' perception of virtual salespeople in retail websites.

Trevor Smith, DBA, is the head of the units of Marketing, International Business, Entrepreneurship and Strategy in the Department of Management Studies at the University of the West Indies, Mona. He lectures in Marketing and Research Methods at both undergraduate and graduate Levels. His research interests include consumer marketing, tourism & hospitality management and business strategy. Another area of interest is knowledge management and its impact on firms' performance. He is also a consultant in field of marketing research and strategy.

Boonchom Srisa-ard is an associate professor at Mahasarakham University, chair of doctoral degree program in educational research and evaluation, Mahasarakham University. Dr.Boonchom specialized in educational measurement and evaluation, educational research, statistical methods for research. He is the author of over 60 journal articles, book chapters, and conference proceedings on educational measurement, educational research, curriculum research and development, teaching and learning development, knowledge management, etc. He holds a BEd. in secondary education from The College of Education Prasarnmit, a M.Ed. in test and measurement, and a EdD in Curriculum Research and Development from Srinakharinwirot University.

Wen Bing Su is an associate professor of accountancy at Nanjing University, where he has taught since 1997. His primary teaching interests are in cost and management accounting. On the research front, his activities have spanned many areas of accounting, including management accounting, financial accounting and auditing. Professor Su has published more than 30 academic papers and won second prize for Excellent Works of Jiangsu Province Social Science Research.

Markku Tuominen is a professor in Industrial Management and dean of the Faculty of Technology Management at Lappeenranta University of Technology (Finland). He is also adjunct professor at Portland State University (USA), and Nihon University (Japan). He has been a board member of Science and Technology at Finnish Academy. His research interests are in innovation and technology management, and decision support in industrial management. He has published over 100 refereed journal articles.

Bharathkumar Vaitheeswaran holds a Masters Degree in Knowledge Management from Nanyang Technological University, Singapore. He currently works with the Singapore Sports Council, in support of various KM initiatives including Content Management and Community of Practice. Prior to this, he was involved with Information Technology projects for Fortune 500 clients specializing in Business Process Reengineering & Organizational Learning. Bharath holds a Bachelor Degree in Computer Science & Engineering from India and is an avid exponent of Cricket and Table Tennis.

David C. H. Vuong is a Master of Science in Management graduate of Queen's University, Kingston, Canada. He currently works in the Business Intelligence industry for a company that develops digital dashboard software. In his spare time, he volunteers his IT expertise to various non-profit organizations.

Seung Won Yoon is associate professor of Instructional Design and Technology at Western Illinois University. His PhD is in Human Resource Development from the University of Illinois. His research focuses on applying theories of learning, instruction, and information design to e-learning, blended learning, and human performance technology solutions and measuring impacts using mixed methods. He has several years of work experiences as a Web/e-learning developer, database manager, and IT project manager.

Index